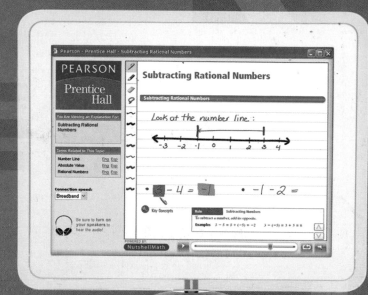

PRENTICE HALL

MATHEMATICS
COURSE 3

Randall I. Charles
Mark Illingworth
Bonnie McNemar
Darwin Mills
Alma Ramirez
Andy Reeves

PEARSON

Prentice
Hall

Boston, Massachusetts
Upper Saddle River, New Jersey

Acknowledgments appear on p. 744, which constitutes an extension of this copyright page.

DK Dorling Kindersley (DK) is an international publishing company that specializes in the creation of high-quality, illustrated information books for children and adults. Dorling Kindersley's unique graphic presentation style is used in this program to motivate students in learning about real-world applications of mathematics. DK is part of the Pearson family of companies.

Pearson Prentice Hall™ is a trademark of Pearson Education, Inc.
Pearson® is a registered trademark of Pearson plc.
Prentice Hall® is a registered trademark of Pearson Education, Inc.

ISBN 0-13-133993-1
3 4 5 6 7 8 9 10   10 09 08

Authors

Series Author

Randall I. Charles, Ph.D., is Professor Emeritus in the Department of Mathematics and Computer Science at San Jose State University, San Jose, California. He began his career as a high school mathematics teacher, and he was a mathematics supervisor for five years. Dr. Charles has been a member of several NCTM committees and is the former Vice President of the National Council of Supervisors of Mathematics. Much of his writing and research has been in the area of problem solving. He has authored more than 75 mathematics textbooks for kindergarten through college. *Scott Foresman-Prentice Hall Mathematics Series Author Kindergarten through Algebra 2*

Program Authors

Mark Illingworth has taught in both elementary and high school math programs for more than twenty years. During this time, he received the Christa McAuliffe sabbatical to develop problem-solving materials and projects for middle grades math students, and he was granted the Presidential Award for Excellence in Mathematics Teaching. Mr. Illingworth's specialty is in teaching mathematics through applications and problem solving. He has written two books on these subjects and has contributed to math and science textbooks at Prentice Hall.

Bonnie McNemar is a mathematics educator with more than 30 years' experience in Texas schools as a teacher, administrator, and consultant. She began her career as a middle school mathematics teacher and served as a supervisor at the district, county, and state levels. Ms. McNemar was the director of the Texas Mathematics Staff Development Program, now known as TEXTEAMS, for five years, and she was the first director of the Teachers Teaching with Technology (T³) Program. She remains active in both of these organizations as well as in several local, state, and national mathematics organizations, including NCTM.

Darwin Mills, an administrator for the public school system in Newport News, Virginia, has been involved in secondary level mathematics education for more than fourteen years. Mr. Mills has served as a high school teacher, a community college adjunct professor, a department chair, and a district level mathematics supervisor. He has received numerous teaching awards, including teacher of the year for 1999–2000 and an Excellence in Teaching award from the College of Wooster, Ohio, in 2002. He is frequent presenter at workshops and conferences. He believes that all students can learn mathematics if given the proper instruction.

Alma Ramirez is co-director of the Mathematics Case Project at WestEd, a nonprofit educational institute in Oakland, California. A former bilingual elementary and middle school teacher, Ms. Ramirez has considerable expertise in mathematics teaching and learning, second language acquisition, and professional development. She has served as a consultant on a variety of projects and has extensive experience as an author for elementary and middle grades texts. In addition, her work has appeared in the 2004 NCTM Yearbook. Ms. Ramirez is a frequent presenter at professional meetings and conferences.

Andy Reeves, Ph.D., teaches at the University of South Florida in St. Petersburg. His career in education spans 30 years and includes seven years as a middle grades teacher. He subsequently served as Florida's K–12 mathematics supervisor, and more recently he supervised the publication of The Mathematics Teacher, Mathematics Teaching in the Middle School, and Teaching Children Mathematics for NCTM. Prior to entering education, he worked as an engineer for Douglas Aircraft.

Contributing Author

Denisse R. Thompson, Ph.D., is a Professor of Mathematics Education at the University of South Florida. She has particular interests in the connections between literature and mathematics and in the teaching and learning of mathematics in the middle grades. Dr. Thompson contributed to the Guided Problem Solving features.

iii

Reviewers

Course 3 Reviewers

Linda E. Addington
Andrew Lewis Middle School
Salem, Virginia

Jeanne Arnold
Mead Junior High School
Schaumburg, Illinois

Sheila S. Brookshire
A. C. Reynolds Middle School
Asheville, North Carolina

Jennifer Clark
Mayfield Middle School
Putnam City Public Schools
Oklahoma City, Oklahoma

Nicole Dial
Chase Middle School
Topeka, Kansas

Christine Ferrell
Lorin Andrews Middle School
Massillon, Ohio

Virginia G. Harrell
Education Consultant
Hillsborough County, Florida

Jonita P. Howard
Mathematics Curriculum Specialist
Lauderdale Lakes Middle School
Lauderdale Lakes, Florida

Patricia Lemons
Rio Rancho Middle School
Rio Rancho, New Mexico

Susan Noce
Robert Frost Junior High School
Schaumburg, Illinois

Carla A. Siler
South Bend Community School Corp.
South Bend, Indiana

Kathryn E. Smith-Lance
West Genesee Middle School
Camillus, New York

Kathleen D. Tuffy
South Middle School
Braintree, Massachusetts

Patricia R. Wilson
Central Middle School
Murfreesboro, Tennessee

Patricia Young
Northwood Middle School
Pulaski County Special School District
North Little Rock, Arkansas

Content Consultants

Ann Bell
Mathematics
Prentice Hall Consultant
Franklin, Tennessee

Blanche Brownley
Mathematics
Prentice Hall Consultant
Olney, Maryland

Joe Brumfield
Mathematics
Prentice Hall Consultant
Altadena, California

Linda Buckhalt
Mathematics
Prentice Hall Consultant
Derwood, Maryland

Andrea Gordon
Mathematics
Prentice Hall Consultant
Atlanta, Georgia

Eleanor Lopes
Mathematics
Prentice Hall Consultant
New Castle, Delaware

Sally Marsh
Mathematics
Prentice Hall Consultant
Baltimore, Maryland

Bob Pacyga
Mathematics
Prentice Hall Consultant
Darien, Illinois

Judy Porter
Mathematics
Prentice Hall Consultant
Fuquay Varena, North Carolina

Rose Primiani
Mathematics
Prentice Hall Consultant
Harbor City, New Jersey

Jayne Radu
Mathematics
Prentice Hall Consultant
Scottsdale, Arizona

Pam Revels
Mathematics
Prentice Hall Consultant
Sarasota, Florida

Barbara Rogers
Mathematics
Prentice Hall Consultant
Raleigh, North Carolina

Michael Seals
Mathematics
Prentice Hall Consultant
Edmond, Oklahoma

Margaret Thomas
Mathematics
Prentice Hall Consultant
Indianapolis, Indiana

Dear Student,

We have designed this unique mathematics program with you in mind. We hope that Prentice Hall Mathematics will help you make sense of the mathematics you learn. We want to enable you to tap into the power of mathematics.

Examples in each lesson are broken into steps to help you understand how and why math works. Work the examples so that you understand the concepts and the methods presented. Then do your homework. Ask yourself how new concepts relate to old ones. Make connections! As you practice the concepts presented in this text, they will become part of your mathematical power.

The many real-world applications will let you see how you can use math in your daily life and give you the foundation for the math you will need in the future. The applications you will find in every lesson will help you see why it is important to learn mathematics. In addition, the Dorling Kindersley Real-World Snapshots will bring the world to your classroom.

This text will help you be successful on the tests you take in class and on high-stakes tests required by your state. The practice in each lesson will prepare you for the format as well as for the content of these tests.

Ask your teacher questions! Someone else in your class has the same question in mind and will be grateful that you decided to ask it.

We wish you the best as you use this text. The mathematics you learn this year will prepare you for your future as a student and your future in our technological society.

Sincerely,

Randy Charles.

Andy Reeves

Darwin E. Mills

Mark Illingworth

Bonnie McNemar

Alma Beatriz Ramirez

Contents in Brief

Integers and Algebraic Expressions

CHAPTER 2

Rational Numbers

Student Support

Vocabulary

Vocabulary Review 52, 57, 62, 66, 72, 81, 86, 92

New Vocabulary 52, 57, 62, 72, 81, 86, 92

Vocabulary Builder 77

Vocabulary Tip 58, 81, 86

Exercises 54, 59, 64, 74, 83, 88, 94

GO Online

Video Tutor Help 73

Active Math 63, 82

Homework Video Tutor 56, 60, 65, 68, 75, 84, 89, 95

Lesson Quiz 55, 59, 65, 69, 75, 83, 89, 95

Vocabulary Quiz 98

Chapter Test 100

GPS Guided Problem Solving

Exercises 55, 59, 64, 68, 75, 83, 88, 94

Practice Solving Problems 78

DK Applications: Applying Real Numbers, 102–103

Assessment and Test Prep

CHAPTER 3

Real Numbers and the Coordinate Plane

CHAPTER 4

Applications of Proportions

Student Support

Vocabulary

Vocabulary Review 160, 166, 174, 181, 187, 192, 197
New Vocabulary 160, 166, 174, 181, 187, 192, 197
Vocabulary Tip 175, 183, 187
Exercises 162, 169, 176, 183, 189, 193, 198

GO Online

Video Tutor Help 161, 197
Active Math 160, 188
Homework Video Tutor 162, 170, 177, 184, 190, 195, 200
Lesson Quiz 163, 169, 177, 183, 189, 195, 199
Vocabulary Quiz 202
Chapter Test 204
Math at Work 171

GPS Guided Problem Solving

Exercises 162, 169, 177, 183, 189, 194, 199
Using Rates and Proportions 179
DK Applications: Applying Proportions, 206–207

Assessment and Test Prep

CHAPTER 5

Applications of Percent

Student Support

Vocabulary 🔊

Vocabulary Review 210, 214, 218, 224, 230, 234, 242, 246
New Vocabulary 210, 230, 234, 242, 246
Vocabulary Builder 228
Vocabulary Tip 214, 243
Exercises 212, 232, 237, 243, 248

GO Online

Video Tutor Help 210, 219
Active Math 211, 220
Homework Video Tutor 213, 216, 221, 226, 233, 237, 244, 249
Lesson Quiz 213, 217, 221, 227, 233, 237, 243, 249
Vocabulary Quiz 252
Chapter Test 254

GPS Guided Problem Solving

Exercises 213, 216, 221, 226, 233, 237, 244, 249
Practice Solving Problems 240
DK Applications: Applying Percents, 256–257

Assessment and Test Prep

CHAPTER 6

Equations and Inequalities

Assessment and Test Prep

CHAPTER 7

Geometry

Student Support

Vocabulary 🔊

GO Online

GPS Guided Problem Solving

Assessment and Test Prep

CHAPTER 8

Measurement

Assessment and Test Prep

Using Graphs to Analyze Data

Student Support

Vocabulary 🔊

GO Online

GPS Guided Problem Solving

Assessment and Test Prep

CHAPTER 10

Probability

Student Support

Vocabulary

Vocabulary Review 470, 475, 480, 486, 491, 496
New Vocabulary 470, 480, 486, 491, 496
Vocabulary Builder 500
Vocabulary Tip 493, 496
Exercises 472, 482, 488, 493, 498

GO Online

Video Tutor Help 471, 497
Active Math 486
Homework Video Tutor 473, 478, 482, 489, 494, 498
Lesson Quiz 473, 477, 483, 489, 495, 499
Vocabulary Quiz 504
Chapter Test 506

GPS Guided Problem Solving

Exercises 472, 477, 482, 488, 494, 498
Permutations, Combinations, and Probability 501
DK Applications: Applying Probability, 508–509

Assessment and Test Prep

CHAPTER 11

Functions

Student Support

Vocabulary 🔊

GO Online

GPS Guided Problem Solving

Assessment and Test Prep

Polynomials and Properties of Exponents

Algebra

Assessment and Test Prep

Connect Your Learning
through problem solving, activities, and the Web

Applications: Real-World Applications

Activity Labs: Data Analysis

Activity Labs: Data Collection

Activity Labs: Algebra Thinking

Activities: Chapter Projects

Problem Solving Strategies

Guided Problem Solving features

Go Online

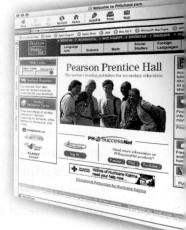

Throughout this book you will find links to the Prentice Hall Web site. Use the Web Codes provided with each link to gain direct access to online material. Here's how to *Go Online*:

1. Go to PHSchool.com
2. Enter the Web Code
3. Click Go!

Lesson Web Codes

Lesson Quiz Web Codes: There is an online quiz for every lesson. Access these quizzes with Web Codes asa-0101 through asa-1205 for Lesson 1-1 through Lesson 12-5. See page 7.

Homework Video Tutor Web Codes: For every lesson, there is additional support online to help students complete their homework. Access the Homework Video Tutors with Web Codes ase-0101 through ase-1205 for Lesson 1-1 through Lesson 12-5. See page 8.

Lesson Quizzes
Web Code format: asa-0204 02 = Chapter 2   04 = Lesson 4

Homework Video Tutor
Web Code format: ase-0605 06 = Chapter 6   05 = Lesson 5

Chapter Web Codes

Chapter	Vocabulary Quizzes	Chapter Tests	Chapter Projects
1	asj-0151	asa-0152	asd-0161
2	asj-0251	asa-0252	asd-0261
3	asj-0351	asa-0352	asd-0361
4	asj-0451	asa-0452	asd-0461
5	asj-0551	asa-0552	asd-0561
6	asj-0651	asa-0652	asd-0661
7	asj-0751	asa-0752	asd-0761
8	asj-0851	asa-0852	asd-0861
9	asj-0951	asa-0952	asd-0961
10	asj-1051	asa-1052	asd-1061
11	asj-1151	asa-1152	asd-1161
12	asj-1251	asa-1252	asd-1261
End-of-Course		asa-1254	

Additional Web Codes

Video Tutor Help:
Use Web Code ase-0775 to access engaging online instructional videos to help bring math concepts to life. See page 17.

Data Updates:
Use Web Code asg-9041 to get up-to-date government data for use in examples and exercises. See page 11.

Math at Work:
For information about each Math at Work feature, use Web Code asb-2031. See page 123.

Using Your Book for Success

Welcome to *Prentice Hall Course 3*. There are many features built into the daily lessons of this text that will help you learn the important skills and concepts you will need to be successful in this course. Look through the following pages for some study tips that you will find useful as you complete each lesson.

Getting Ready to Learn

Check Your Readiness

Complete the *Check Your Readiness* exercises to see what topics you may need to review before you begin the chapter.

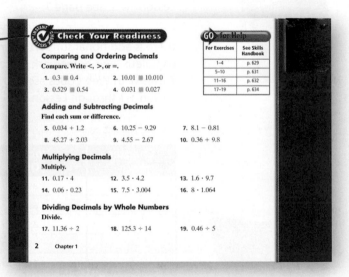

Check Skills You'll Need

Complete the *Check Skills You'll Need* exercises to make sure you have the skills needed to successfully learn the concepts in the lesson.

New Vocabulary

New Vocabulary is listed for each lesson, so you can pre-read the text. As each term is introduced, it is highlighted in yellow.

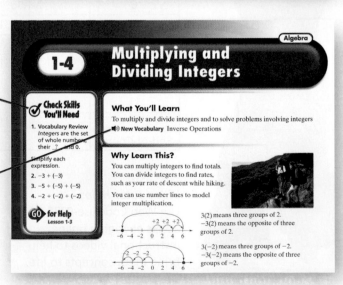

Built-In Help

Go for Help

Look for the green labels throughout your book that tell you where to "Go" for help. You'll see this built-in help in the lessons and in the homework exercises.

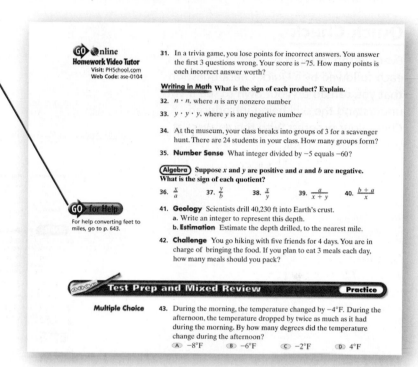

Video Tutor Help

Go online to see engaging videos to help you better understand important math concepts.

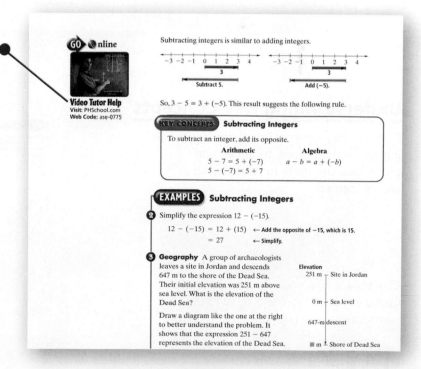

Understanding the Mathematics

Quick Check

Every lesson includes numerous examples, each followed by a *Quick Check* question that you can do on your own to see if you understand the skill being introduced. Check your progress with the answers at the back of the book.

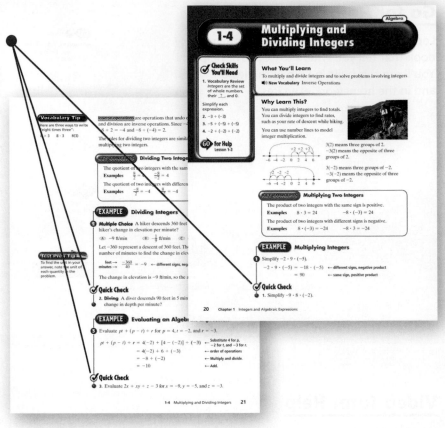

Understanding Key Concepts

Frequent *Key Concept* boxes summarize important definitions, formulas, and properties. Use these to review what you've learned.

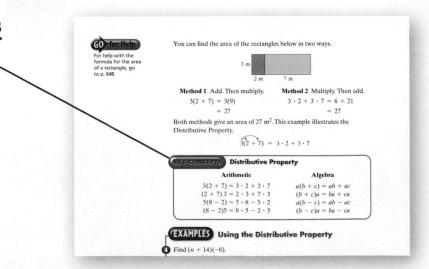

Online Active Math

Make math come alive with these online activities. Review and practice important math concepts with these engaging online tutorials.

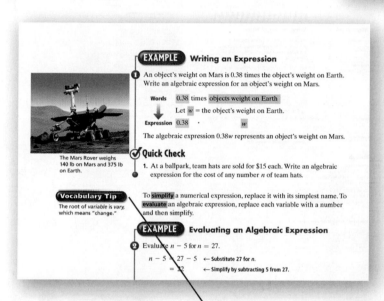

GO for Help
Lesson 1-3

An equation is like a balance scale. If you do something to one side of an equation, you must do the same to the other side to keep it balanced.

$x + 2 = 5$

Two weights were taken from each side of the upper balance scale at the right. The result, shown on the lower balance scale, illustrates a property of equality.

$x = 3$

KEY CONCEPTS **Properties of Equality**

Addition Property of Equality

If you add the same number to each side of an equation, the two sides remain equal.

Arithmetic	Algebra
$10 = 5(2)$, so $10 + 3 = 5(2) + 3$	If $a = b$, then $a + c = b + c$.

Subtraction Property of Equality

If you subtract the same number from each side of an equation, the two sides remain equal.

Arithmetic	Algebra
$10 = 5(2)$, so $10 - 3 = 5(2) - 3$	If $a = b$, then $a - c = b - c$.

1-6 Solving Equations by Adding and Subtracting   **33**

EXAMPLE **Writing an Expression**

An object's weight on Mars is 0.38 times the object's weight on Earth. Write an algebraic expression for an object's weight on Mars.

Words   0.38 times objects weight on Earth

Let w = the object's weight on Earth.

Expression   0.38 · w

The algebraic expression $0.38w$ represents an object's weight on Mars.

✓**Quick Check**

1. At a ballpark, team hats are sold for $15 each. Write an algebraic expression for the cost of any number n of team hats.

The Mars Rover weighs 140 lb on Mars and 375 lb on Earth.

Vocabulary Tip

The root of *variable* is *vary*, which means "change."

To **simplify** a numerical expression, replace it with its simplest name. To **evaluate** an algebraic expression, replace each variable with a number and then simplify.

EXAMPLE **Evaluating an Algebraic Expression**

Evaluate $n - 5$ for $n = 27$.

$n - 5 = 27 - 5$ ← Substitute 27 for n.

$= 22$ ← Simplify by subtracting 5 from 27.

Vocabulary Support

Understanding mathematical vocabulary is an important part of studying mathematics. *Vocabulary Tips* and *Vocabulary Builders* throughout the book help focus on the language of math.

Vocabulary Builder

High-Use Academic Words

High-frequency academic words are words that you will see often in textbooks and on tests. These words are not math vocabulary terms, but knowing them will help you to succeed in mathematics.

Direction Words

Some words tell what to do in a problem. I need to understand what these words are asking so that I give the correct answer.

Word	Meaning
Find	To get after searching or making an effort
Compare	To show how two or more things are alike or different
Order	To put in a specific arrangement

Exercises

1. Find the shortest path to the pencil sharpener in your classroom.

Understanding the Mathematics

Guided Problem Solving

These features throughout your Student Edition provide practice in problem solving. Solved from a student's point of view, this feature focuses on the thinking and reasoning that goes into solving a problem.

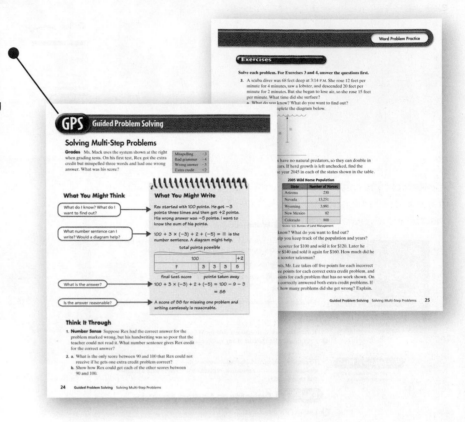

Activity Labs

Activity Labs throughout the book give you an opportunity to explore a concept. Apply the skills you've learned in these engaging activities.

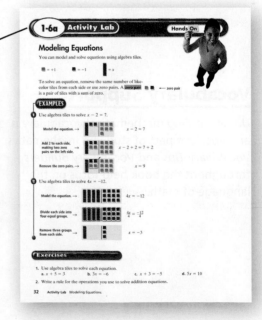

Practice What You've Learned

There are numerous exercises in each lesson that give you the practice you need to master the concepts in the lesson. The following exercises are included in each lesson.

Check Your Understanding

These exercises help you prepare for the Homework Exercises.

Practice by example

These exercises refer you back to the Examples in the lesson, in case you need help with completing these exercises.

Apply your skills

These exercises combine skills from earlier lessons to offer you richer skill exercises and multi-step application problems.

Homework Video Tutor

These interactive tutorials provide you with homework help for *every lesson*.

Challenge

This exercise gives you an opportunity to extend and stretch your thinking.

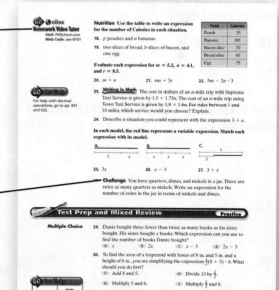

Beginning-of-Course Diagnostic Test

For Exercises 1–2, write the value of the underlined digit.

1. 842,9<u>7</u>6

2. 761.03<u>2</u>5

3. Write seven and ninety-six thousandths as a decimal.

4. Write 9.204 in words.

5. Write 0.000073 in words.

For Exercises 6–7, use <, >, or = to compare the decimals.

6. 0.008 _?_ 0.06

7. 0.000307 _?_ 0.003007

For Exercises 8–11, write the decimals in order from least to greatest.

8. 7.21 0.712 72.1 0.721

9. 0.01010 0.10101 0.01001 0.00101

10. Round 15,763 to the nearest thousand.

11. Round 96.853 to the nearest tenth.

For Exercises 12–13, round to the place of the underlined digit.

12. 123.9<u>8</u>47

13. 14<u>7</u>.48

For Exercises 14–17, find each sum or difference.

14. $\begin{array}{r} 76.87 \\ -\ 45.91 \\ \hline \end{array}$

15. $\begin{array}{r} 21.283 \\ +\ 9.72 \\ \hline \end{array}$

16. $9 - 3.245$

17. $1.309 + 2.46 + 2.6$

For Exercises 18–24, multiply or divide.

18. $\begin{array}{r} 38.6 \\ \times\ 0.4 \\ \hline \end{array}$

19. $0.0027 \cdot 0.04$

20. $16.8 \div 4$

21. $7,354 \div 0.01$

22. $5.697 \times 10,000$

23. $3.813 \div 4.1$

24. $0.002847 \div 0.73$

For Exercises 25–26, write each improper fraction as a mixed number.

25. $\frac{11}{3}$

26. $\frac{48}{11}$

For Exercises 27–28, write each mixed number as an improper fraction.

27. $6\frac{4}{7}$

28. $9\frac{1}{8}$

For Exercises 29–32, add or subtract. Write each answer in simplest form.

29. $\frac{9}{12} + \frac{5}{12}$

30. $\frac{7}{14} - \frac{5}{14}$

31. $6\frac{3}{8} + 8\frac{5}{8}$

32. $9\frac{8}{10} - 7\frac{3}{10}$

For Exercises 33–34, measure each angle. Classify it as *acute, right, obtuse,* or *straight*.

33.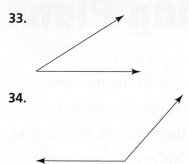

34.

For Exercises 35–36, draw an angle with the given measure.

35. 75°

36. 130°

37. Draw a bar graph for the data below.

Number of Movies Rented Per Month

Number of Movies	0	1	2	3	more than 3
Number of Rentals	2	3	7	5	8

38. Draw a double bar graph for the data below.

Favorite Vegetable in Ms. Green's Class

	Corn	Cabbage	Green Beans	Peas
Boys	8	5	6	1
Girls	5	7	6	3

39. Draw a line graph for the data below.

Forest Service Expenditures for Emergency Fire Suppression

Year	Cost Per Acre Burned
1	$388.40
2	$740.65
3	$545.45
4	$818.71
5	$487.56
6	$623.08
7	$575.87
8	$932.54
9	$376.12
10	$640.03
11	$716.67
12	$976.86

40. Draw a double line graph for the data below.

Average Temperatures

Month	Avg. High (°F)	Avg. Low (°F)
January	61	43
February	64	45
March	70	52
April	76	58
May	83	66
June	89	72
July	91	75
August	90	74
September	87	70
October	79	60
November	70	51
December	63	45

Problem Solving Handbook

USING THE Problem Solving Plan

One of the most important skills you can have is the ability to solve problems. An integral part of learning mathematics is how adept you become at unraveling problems and looking back to see how you found the solution. Maybe you don't realize it, but you solve problems every day—some problems are easy to solve, and others are challenging and require a good plan of action. In this Problem Solving Handbook you will learn how to work through mathematical problems using a simple four-step plan:

THE 4-STEP PLAN

1. Understand **Understand the problem.**
Read the problem. Ask yourself, "What information is given? What is missing? What am I being asked to find or to do?"

2. Plan **Make a plan to solve the problem.**
Choose a strategy. As you use problem solving strategies throughout this book, you will decide which one is best for the problem you are trying to solve.

3. Carry Out **Carry out the plan.**
Solve the problem using your plan. Organize your work.

4. Check **Check the answer to be sure it is reasonable.**
Look back at your work and compare it against the information and question(s) in the problem. Ask yourself, "Is my answer reasonable? Did I check my work?"

Problem Solving Strategies

Creating a good plan to solve a problem means that you will need to choose a strategy. What is the best way to solve that challenging problem? Perhaps drawing a diagram or making a table will lead to a solution. A problem might seem to have too many steps. Maybe working a simpler problem is the key. There are a number of strategies to choose from. You will decide which strategy is most effective.

As you work through this book, you will encounter many opportunities to improve your problem solving and reasoning skills. Working through mathematical problems using this four-step process will help you to organize your thoughts, develop your reasoning skills, and explain how you arrived at a particular solution.

Putting this problem solving plan to use will allow you to work through mathematical problems with confidence. Getting in the habit of planning and strategizing for problem solving will result in success in future math courses and high scores on those really important tests!

Good Luck!

THE STRATEGIES

Here are some examples of problem solving strategies. Which one will work best for the problem you are trying to solve?

- **Draw a Picture**
- **Look for a Pattern**
- **Systematic Guess and Check**
- **Act It Out**
- **Make a Table**
- **Work a Simpler Problem**
- **Work Backward**
- **Write an Equation**

Draw a Picture

When to Use This Strategy Some word problems are hard to solve mentally. In such cases, you can *Draw a Picture* of the problem.

The tail of a kite steadies the kite in the air. One of the longest kites is a Chinese dragon kite. The length of one dragon kite, including its tail, is 21 ft. If the tail is 15 ft longer than the kite body, how long is the body of the kite?

Understand The combined length of the kite tail and body is 21 ft. The tail is 15 ft longer than the kite body. The goal is to find the length of the kite body.

Plan *Draw a Picture* to show that the kite with its tail is 21 ft long and the tail is 15 ft longer than the body.

Carry Out The diagram shows that the total length of 21 ft is equal to 15 ft plus two body lengths.

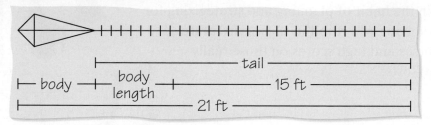

Subtracting 15 ft from 21 ft results in 6 ft, which is twice the body length. The kite's body length is 3 ft.

Check If the body is 3 ft, then the length of the tail is 3 ft + 15 ft = 18 ft. The length of the kite is then 3 ft + 18 ft = 21 ft. The answer checks.

● Practice

1. Your aunt is building a garden in her backyard. She has 90 ft of fencing to surround it. If she wants the length to be 15 feet longer than the width, what should the dimensions of her garden be?

2. You bike 32 mi in two days. On the second day, you bike 9 mi more than on the first day. How many miles do you bike each day?

3. If you have 20 yards of ribbon and need to cut it into 2-yard lengths, how many cuts do you have to make?

Look for a Pattern

When to Use This Strategy Sometimes you are given a few parts of a sequence and you are asked to predict how the sequence will continue. In such a problem, you can *Look for a Pattern* to help make your prediction.

A group in Spain built a human pyramid with ten levels. How many people were in the pyramid?

Understand A human pyramid has ten levels. The top level will have just one person. The bottom level will have ten people. The goal is to find the total number of people needed to form the pyramid.

Plan *Look for a Pattern* in pyramids with fewer levels and then extend the pattern to ten levels.

Carry Out Use a dot to represent each person. Draw one-, two-, three-, and four-level pyramids.

Number of People   1   1 + 2 = 3   1 + 2 + 3 = 6   1 + 2 + 3 + 4 = 10

The total number increases from 1, to 1 + 2 = 3 to 1 + 2 + 3 = 6, and to 1 + 2 + 3 + 4 = 10. The total number for n-levels is the sum of the numbers from 1 to n. The sum of 1 + 2 + . . . + 9 + 10 is 55. So there were 55 people in the pyramid.

Check Draw a diagram of a ten-level pyramid. It has 55 dots.

● Practice

1. In a tournament, each person plays one game against each of the other players. There are 20 players. How many games are played?

2. Starting with 1, multiply by 2. Then multiply the result by 3. Then continue to alternate multiplying by 2 and by 3. What is the ones digit after the twelfth multiplication?

3. A baby hamster weighs 4 g when it is born. It weighs 28 g at 4 weeks and 52 g at 8 weeks. Assume a constant rate of increase. How much will the hamster weigh at 14 weeks?

Systematic Guess and Check

When to Use This Strategy Use *Systematic Guess and Check* in situations where you can make a guess and then, based on the result, make a better guess.

Money Your friend used equal numbers of quarters and nickels in a vending machine to buy a drink for $1.20. How many quarters and how many nickels did your friend use?

Understand The drink cost $1.20. He paid with equal numbers of quarters and nickels. You need to find how many of each it will take to add up to $1.20.

Plan Use *Systematic Guess and Check* to find the answer. Make a table to record your guesses.

Carry Out Start the table with a guess. Suppose you use one quarter and one nickel. From the table, you can see how the result of each guess helps you make a better guess.

GUESS Number (n)	CHECK $n \times \$.25 + n \times \$.05 =$	RESULT Compare to $1.20
1	$1 \times \$.25 + 1 \times \$.05 = \$.30$	too low
2	$2 \times \$.25 + 2 \times \$.05 = \$.60$	too low
5	$5 \times \$.25 + 5 \times \$.05 = \$1.50$	too high
4	$4 \times \$.25 + 4 \times \$.05 = \$1.20$	correct

You friend used four quarters and four nickels to make $1.20.

Check Another way to think about this problem is to consider that one quarter and one nickel are worth $.30. How many times does 30 go into 120? The answer is 4 times, so you need four of each coin.

● Practice

1. A groomer clips the claws of 40 dogs and birds. There are 110 feet among them. How many dogs and how many birds are there?

2. You can buy balloons in packs of 25 or packs of 75. Suppose you buy 8 packs and have 450 balloons in all. How many packs of each size do you buy?

Act It Out

When to Use This Strategy For problems involving probability, you can *Act It Out* by conducting an experiment.

What is the probability of guessing all the answers correctly on a three-question true-or-false quiz?

Understand Your goal is to find the probability of guessing the answers to three questions correctly. The probability of guessing correctly for one question is $\frac{1}{2}$.

Plan Since the probability of guessing correctly for one question is $\frac{1}{2}$, you can *Act It Out* by tossing a coin. Let heads represent a correct guess and tails represent an incorrect guess. Three tosses represent the quiz. Simulate 30 quizzes by tossing a coin 90 times.

90 Tosses

HHT TTH HTH
(HHH) TTH THT
THH HTH TTT
HHT HTT (HHH)
TTT THH THT
HTT HHT THH
TTH (HHH) HTT
HTT TTH THT
THH (HHH) TTH
HTH TTT HTH

Carry Out The data at the left show the results from acting out 30 quizzes. Circle each instance of three heads. In 30 quiz simulations HHH occurs 4 times.

$$P(3 \text{ correct guesses}) = \frac{\text{number of times HHH occurs}}{\text{total number of quizzes}}$$

$$= \frac{4}{30}, \text{ or about } 13\%$$

Check Compute the theoretical probability.

$$P(3 \text{ correct}) = P(1 \text{ correct}) \cdot P(1 \text{ correct}) \cdot P(1 \text{ correct}).$$

$$= \frac{1}{2} \cdot \frac{1}{2} \cdot \frac{1}{2} = \frac{1}{8}, \text{ or } 12.5\%$$

The theoretical probability is close to the result of acting it out.

● Practice

1. Suppose a license plate contains four digits. The probability of a plate number having an even or an odd digit is the same. What is the probability of having a license plate with all even digits?

2. A true-or-false test has five questions. What is the probability of guessing exactly four out of the five answers correctly?

3. Your cat is expecting a litter of kittens. Suppose the probability of a male kitten is $\frac{1}{2}$. What is the probability that a litter of five kittens contains all male kittens?

Make a Table

When to Use This Strategy You can *Make a Table* to help you keep track of possible solutions to a problem. A table can help you organize your data and compare solutions.

A company makes boxes without tops by cutting square corners out of the corners of rectangular sheets of cardboard. Each rectangular sheet is 7 in. by 10 in. Using whole-inch lengths only, find the dimensions of the box with the greatest possible volume.

Understand The goal is to find the dimensions of a box that will result in the greatest volume. The piece of cardboard used to make the box is 7 in. by 10 in.

Plan *Make a Table* to organize the information in the problem. Start with square cuts 1 in. on each side. Then increase the size 1 in. at a time.

Carry Out Let x represent the size of the squares. The length of the box is represented by $10 - 2x$. The width of the box is represented by $7 - 2x$. The expression $x(10 - 2x)(7 - 2x)$ represents volume.

Height (Size of Cut) x	Length $10 - 2x$	Width $7 - 2x$	Volume $x(10 - 2x)(7 - 2x)$
1 in.	8 in.	5 in.	40 in.^{3}
2 in.	6 in.	3 in.	36 in.^{3}
3 in.	4 in.	1 in.	12 in.^{3}

As the size of the square cut increases, the volume decreases. Square cuts of 1 in. result in the maximum volume of 40 in.^{3}.

Check A value of 4 for x makes the expression $(7 - 2x)$ negative, which is an impossible value for length. The possible lengths are 1, 2, and 3 in.

● Practice

1. A dog owner has 200 ft of fencing and wants to enclose the greatest possible rectangular area for her dog. What dimensions should she use?

2. A customer gives a cashier a $100 bill for a $64 shirt. The customer will accept no more than six $1 bills. In what ways can the cashier give change using bills only? Assume that the cashier has no $2 bills.

Work a Simpler Problem

When to Use This Strategy A problem may have too many steps. When you *Work a Simpler Problem,* you can gain insight that can help with the more difficult problem.

A standard checkerboard has 8 squares on each side. How many squares of different sizes are there on a standard 8-by-8 board?

Understand The goal is to find the total number of squares on a checkerboard. Squares can be 1×1, 2×2, ... 8×8.

Plan You can *Work a Simpler Problem* by examining boards that are 1×1, 2×2, and 3×3. Make a conjecture about the solution.

Carry Out Consider the simpler boards. Then organize your data.

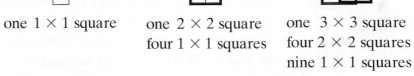

one 1×1 square

one 2×2 square
four 1×1 squares

one 3×3 square
four 2×2 squares
nine 1×1 squares

Size of checkerboard 1×1 2×2 3×3
Number of squares $1^2 = 1$ $1^2 + 2^2 = 5$ $1^2 + 2^2 + 3^2 = 14$

On an $n \times n$ checkerboard, the total number of squares is the sum of the squares of the positive integers from 1 to n ($1^2 + 2^2 + \ldots + n^2$). An 8×8 board has $1 + 4 + 9 + 16 + 25 + 36 + 49 + 64$, or 204 squares.

Check Test your conjecture by drawing a diagram of a 4×4 board.

● Practice

Geometry Use the figure at the left.

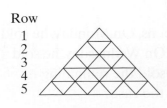

Row
1
2
3
4
5

1. Find the number of small triangles.

2. How many small triangles will there be in the complete figure if you extend the figure to 10 rows? What about n rows?

3. The houses on one side of Hall Avenue are numbered with even numbers. Of the even house numbers from 140 to 224, how many have at least one 6?

Work Backward

When to Use This Strategy Use the *Work Backward* strategy to solve problems that give only a final result and ask you to find an initial value.

At the start of a mission, international spy Rex King withdrew half of the money in his bank account in Paris. Later, he withdrew $5,000 in Cairo. In Istanbul, he withdrew half of the remaining money. He had $7,500 left. What amount did he have at the start of the mission?

Understand   The goal is to find the initial amount. Rex withdrew half the initial amount in Paris, $5,000 in Cairo, and half the remaining amount in Istanbul. He had $7,500 left.

Plan   *Work Backward* by starting with what you know.

Carry Out   Start with $7,500 and work backward.
- The final amount, $7,500, is half the amount in the bank before Rex went to Istanbul. So he had $15,000 when he arrived in Istanbul.
- He withdrew $5,000 in Cairo. So he left Paris with $20,000.
- At the start, he withdrew half of the amount he had. So at the start he had $40,000 in the bank account.

Check   Start with $40,000 and work forward.

Paris	Cairo	Istanbul
$\frac{1}{2}$ of $40,000 = $20,000	$20,000 − $5,000 = $15,000	$\frac{1}{2}$ of $15,000 = $7,500 ✔

● Practice

1. You returned home from mowing lawns at 3:00 P.M. on Saturday. It took $1\frac{1}{2}$ hours to mow the first lawn. It took twice as long to mow the next lawn. After a half-hour lunch break, it took $1\frac{1}{4}$ hours to mow one more lawn. At what time did you start?

2. **Business** A salesperson bought a case of pens. On Monday, he sold $\frac{1}{2}$ of the pens. On Tuesday, he sold 30 more. On Wednesday, he sold $\frac{1}{3}$ of the pens that were left. On Thursday, he sold the remaining 40 pens. How many pens were originally in the case?

Write an Equation

When to Use This Strategy You can *Write an Equation* when a real-world situation involves two related variables.

You plan a party at a restaurant. A buffet dinner costs $15 per person. For dessert, you plan to buy a birthday cake for $30. You have $275 to spend. How much will you have left if there are 16 people at the party?

Understand Your goal is to find out how much money you will have left out of $275. You must spend $15 for each person plus an additional $30 for the cake.

Plan *Write an Equation* to represent the total cost of the party. Subtract the total cost from $275 to see how much money you will have left.

Carry Out Write an equation to represent the total cost.

Words total cost is cost per person times number of people plus cost of cake

Let t = the total cost.

Let p = the number of people.

Equation t = 15 · p + 30

$$t = 15p + 30$$

Substitute 16 for p. This gives $t = 15 \cdot 16 + 30 = 240 + 30 = 270$. Now subtract the total cost from $275. This gives $275 - $270 = 5.

Check Estimate. The cost for 20 people would be $300 + $30 = $330, which is more than $270. Similarly, the cost for 10 people would be $150 + $30 = $180, which is less than $270. A cost of $270 is reasonable.

● Practice

1. You buy a belt for $10 and some socks. Each pair of socks costs $3. The total shipping cost is $3. What is the total cost if you buy 11 pairs of socks?

2. You mix 8 oz of concentrate with 64 oz of water to make orange juice. If you need a total of 288 oz of juice, how much concentrate should you buy?

CHAPTER 1

Integers and Algebraic Expressions

What You've Learned

- In a previous course, you learned to compare and order decimals.

- You used addition, subtraction, multiplication, and division to solve problems involving decimals.

- You simplified numerical expressions involving order of operations.

 **Check Your Readiness**

Comparing and Ordering Decimals

Compare. Write <, >, or =.

1. 0.3 ■ 0.4 **2.** 10.01 ■ 10.010

3. 0.529 ■ 0.54 **4.** 0.031 ■ 0.027

GO for Help	
For Exercises	**See Skills Handbook**
1–4	p. 629
5–10	p. 631
11–16	p. 632
17–19	p. 634

Adding and Subtracting Decimals

Find each sum or difference.

5. 0.034 + 1.2 **6.** 10.25 − 9.29 **7.** 8.1 − 0.81

8. 45.27 + 2.03 **9.** 4.55 − 2.67 **10.** 0.36 + 9.8

Multiplying Decimals

Multiply.

11. 0.17 · 4 **12.** 3.5 · 4.2 **13.** 1.6 · 9.7

14. 0.06 · 0.23 **15.** 7.5 · 3.004 **16.** 8 · 1.064

Dividing Decimals by Whole Numbers

Divide.

17. 11.36 ÷ 2 **18.** 125.3 ÷ 14 **19.** 0.46 ÷ 5

What You'll Learn Next

- In this chapter, you will learn to compare and order integers.
- You will use appropriate operations to solve problems involving integers.
- You will learn and use the properties of numbers.
- You will find solutions to application problems using equations.

 Problem Solving Application On pages 48 and 49, you will work an extended activity involving lakes.

🔊 Key Vocabulary

- absolute value (p. 10)
- additive inverses (p. 16)
- algebraic expression (p. 4)
- associative properties (p. 26)
- commutative properties (p. 26)
- Distributive Property (p. 28)
- evaluate (p. 5)
- identity properties (p. 26)
- integers (p. 10)
- inverse operations (p. 21)
- isolate (p. 34)
- opposites (p. 10)
- order of operations (p. 5)
- simplify (p. 5)
- solution (p. 34)
- variable (p. 4)

1-1 Algebraic Expressions and the Order of Operations

Check Skills You'll Need

1. **Vocabulary Review** Which expression does not use multiplication: $3 \cdot 4$, $\frac{3}{4}$, 3×4, or $3(4)$?

Multiply.

2. $12 \cdot 8$ 3. $2.5 \cdot 4$

4. $7.4 \cdot 6$ 5. $0.6 \cdot 5$

 **for Help**

Skills Handbook
p. 632

What You'll Learn

To write algebraic expressions and evaluate them using the order of operations

◀)) **New Vocabulary** variable, algebraic expression, simplify, evaluate, order of operations

Why Learn This?

Values such as an astronaut's weight on the moon and on Earth follow a pattern or relationship. You can use tables and symbols to show relationships between numbers.

The table below shows the relationship between an astronaut's weight on the moon and the astronaut's weight on Earth.

Weight on Earth (lb)	Weight on Moon (lb)
100	$0.16 \cdot 100$
120	$0.16 \cdot 120$
140	$0.16 \cdot 140$
160	$0.16 \cdot 160$
w	$0.16 \cdot w$

The second column gives a numerical expression for each weight on the moon.

variable representing weight on Earth ⟶ w

$0.16 \cdot w$ ⟵ algebraic expression for weight on the moon

A **variable** is a symbol that stands for one or more numbers. An **algebraic expression** is a mathematical phrase that uses numbers, variables, and operation symbols.

You can translate word phrases into algebraic expressions.

Word Phrase	Algebraic Expression
3 more than a number a number increased by 3	$x + 3$
the quotient of a number and 8	$k \div 8$ or $\frac{k}{8}$
6 times a number the product of 6 and a number	$6 \cdot y$ or $6y$
15 less than a number 15 subtracted from a number	$z - 15$

The Mars Rover weighs
140 lb on Mars and 375 lb
on Earth.

EXAMPLE Writing an Expression

1 An object's weight on Mars is 0.38 times the object's weight on Earth. Write an algebraic expression for an object's weight on Mars.

Words 0.38 times object's weight on Earth

Let w = the object's weight on Earth.

Expression 0.38 · w

The algebraic expression $0.38w$ represents an object's weight on Mars.

✓ Quick Check

1. At a ballpark, team hats are sold for $15 each. Write an algebraic expression for the cost of any number n of team hats.

To simplify a numerical expression, replace it with its simplest name. To evaluate an algebraic expression, replace each variable with a number and then simplify.

EXAMPLE Evaluating an Algebraic Expression

2 Evaluate $n - 5$ for $n = 27$.

$n - 5 = 27 - 5$ ← Substitute 27 for n.

$= 22$ ← Simplify by subtracting 5 from 27.

✓ Quick Check

2. Evaluate $7 - m$ for $m = 2$.

Here is an expression simplified in two ways, with different results.

$$16 - 4 \cdot 3 \qquad 16 - 4 \cdot 3$$
$$12 \cdot 3 \qquad\quad 16 - 12$$
$$36 \ ✗ \qquad\qquad 4 \ ✔$$

To avoid confusion when simplifying an expression, mathematicians have established a standard order of operations.

KEY CONCEPTS Order of Operations

Work inside grouping symbols.

1. Multiply and divide in order from left to right.

2. Add and subtract in order from left to right.

The symbols ( ) and [ ] are grouping symbols. A fraction bar is also a grouping symbol. So $\frac{5+4}{3+6} = (5+4) \div (3+6)$.

EXAMPLE **Using the Order of Operations**

③ Evaluate $n + (13 - n) \div 5$ for $n = 3$.

$$\begin{aligned} n + (13 - n) \div 5 &= 3 + (13 - 3) \div 5 &&\leftarrow \textbf{Substitute 3 for } n. \\ &= 3 + 10 \div 5 &&\leftarrow \textbf{Work inside parentheses.} \\ &= 3 + 2 &&\leftarrow \textbf{Divide.} \\ &= 5 &&\leftarrow \textbf{Add.} \end{aligned}$$

✓ Quick Check

3. Evaluate $3x + x \div 3$ for $x = 12$.

The value of an algebraic expression can vary, or change, depending upon the value you give the variable.

EXAMPLE **Application: Fitness**

④ A fitness club charges $100 to join and $33 for each month. Write an expression for the total cost. Find the cost for 6 months of membership.

Make a Table to show the pattern of costs by month.

Use *m* to represent any number of months. →

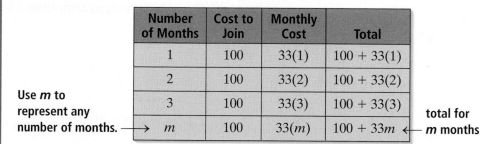

Number of Months	Cost to Join	Monthly Cost	Total
1	100	33(1)	100 + 33(1)
2	100	33(2)	100 + 33(2)
3	100	33(3)	100 + 33(3)
m	100	33(*m*)	100 + 33*m*

total for *m* months

The expression $100 + 33m$ models the total cost.

$$\begin{aligned} 100 + 33m &= 100 + 33(6) &&\leftarrow \textbf{Substitute 6 for } m \textbf{ to evaluate for 6 months.} \\ &= 100 + 198 &&\leftarrow \textbf{Multiply.} \\ &= 298 &&\leftarrow \textbf{Add.} \end{aligned}$$

The total cost for 6 months is $298.

✓ Quick Check

4. The monthly cost increases to $35. Write an expression to model the total cost. Find the cost for 12 months of membership.

1. **Vocabulary** What is the difference between an algebraic expression and a numerical expression?

2. **Mental Math** Evaluate the expression $4x$ for $x = 12$.

Match each word phrase with an expression.

3. There are two fewer guests.

4. There are half as many cars.

5. There are two more books.

A. $m + 2$
B. $n \div 2$
C. $p - 2$

Homework Exercises

For more exercises, see Extra Skills and Word Problems.

GO for Help

For Exercises	See Examples
6–8	1
9–11	2
12–14	3
15	4

Write an algebraic expression for each word phrase.

6. 13 less than a number q

7. number of days in w weeks

8. A florist divides 60 roses into equal bunches of f flowers. Write an expression for the number of bunches the florist can make.

Find the value of each expression for the given values of the variable.

9.

a	$a - 17$
20	▪
22	▪
25	▪

10.

m	$9m$
7	▪
9	▪
11	▪

11.

d	$4d + 7$
0	▪
2	▪
4	▪

Evaluate each expression for $n = 3$.

12. $2n + 5 - n$

13. $\dfrac{3n + 18}{3n}$

14. $\dfrac{24}{4 - n} \cdot n$

15. A hiking club charges \$60 to join and \$12 for each hiking trip. Write an expression to model the total cost. Find the cost of six hikes.

GPS 16. **Guided Problem Solving** A hot-air balloon is at a height of 2,250 feet. It descends 150 feet each minute. Find its height after 6, 8, and 10 minutes.
   - Make a table to show the pattern of heights.
   - Write an expression for the balloon's height at m minutes.

17. a. **Amusement Park** An amusement park charges \$5 for admission and \$2 for each ride. Write an expression for the total cost of admission and r rides.
   b. **Number Sense** How many rides can you go on if you have \$16?

Nutrition Use the table to write an expression for the number of Calories in each situation.

Food	Calories
Peach	35
Banana	105
Bacon slice	37
Bread slice	65
Egg	75

18. p peaches and n bananas

19. two slices of bread, b slices of bacon, and one egg

Evaluate each expression for $m = 5.2$, $n = 4.1$, and $r = 8.5$.

20. $m + n$

21. $mn + 3r$

22. $5m - 2n \cdot 3$

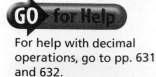

For help with decimal operations, go to pp. 631 and 632.

23. **Writing in Math** The cost in dollars of an n-mile trip with Supreme Taxi Service is given by $1.5 + 1.75n$. The cost of an n-mile trip using Town Taxi Service is given by $1.9 + 1.6n$. For rides between 1 and 10 miles, which service would you choose? Explain.

24. Describe a situation you could represent with the expression $3 + a$.

In each model, the red line represents a variable expression. Match each expression with its model.

A.

```
|-------+-------|
   3       x
```

B.

```
|-----+-----+-----|
   x     x     x
```

C.

```
          x
|---+-------------|
  3
```

25. $3x$

26. $x - 3$

27. $3 + x$

28. **Challenge** You have quarters, dimes, and nickels in a jar. There are twice as many quarters as nickels. Write an expression for the number of coins in the jar in terms of nickels and dimes.

Test Prep and Mixed Review

Practice

Multiple Choice

29. Dante bought three fewer than twice as many books as his sister bought. His sister bought x books. Which expression can you use to find the number of books Dante bought?

Ⓐ x Ⓑ $2x$ Ⓒ $x - 3$ Ⓓ $2x - 3$

30. To find the area of a trapezoid with bases of 8 in. and 5 in. and a height of 6 in., you are simplifying the expression $\frac{1}{2}(8 + 5) \cdot 6$. What should you do first?

Ⓕ Add 8 and 5.   Ⓗ Divide 13 by $\frac{1}{2}$.

Ⓖ Multiply 5 and 6.   Ⓙ Multiply $\frac{1}{2}$ and 6.

For Exercises	Skills Handbook
31–33	p. 631

Find each sum or difference.

31. $12.5 + 6.39$

32. $4.7 - 0.85$

33. $2.111 + 5.99$

Vocabulary Builder

High-Use Academic Words

High-frequency academic words are words that you will see often in textbooks and on tests. These words are not math vocabulary terms, but knowing them will help you to succeed in mathematics.

Direction Words

Some words tell what to do in a problem. I need to understand what these words are asking so that I give the correct answer.

Word	Meaning
Find	To get after searching or making an effort
Compare	To show how two or more things are alike or different
Order	To put in a specific arrangement

Exercises

1. Find the shortest path to the pencil sharpener in your classroom.

2. Compare the path you take to the pencil sharpener to the path your friend takes.

3. Order your five favorite foods from the food you like most to the food you like least.

4. Decorated notepads cost $1.25 each. Find the number of notepads you can buy if you have $5.25.

5. Three printed T-shirts cost $21.60. Five plain T-shirts cost $25. Compare the cost of a printed T-shirt to the cost of a plain T-shirt.

6. Order the following numbers from least to greatest: 1.71, 1.17, 7.11, 1.7, 7.1.

7. **Word Knowledge** Think about the word *represent*.
   a. Choose the letter for how well you know the word.
      A. I know its meaning.
      B. I've seen it, but I don't know its meaning.
      C. I don't know it.
   b. **Research** Look up and write the definition of *represent*.
   c. Use the word in a sentence involving mathematics.

1-2 Integers and Absolute Value

✓ Check Skills You'll Need

1. **Vocabulary Review** What is an *algebraic expression*?

Evaluate each expression for $x = 4$.

2. $2x + 3$

3. $5(x - 1)$

4. $7x - 4x$

GO for Help
Lesson 1-1

What You'll Learn

To find absolute values of integers and to use absolute value to compare integers

◀)) **New Vocabulary** opposites, integers, absolute value

Why Learn This?

You probably have heard some temperatures described as "below zero." You can use integers to describe and compare numbers that are less than zero.

Numbers that are the same distance from zero on a number line but in opposite directions are **opposites.**

4 units from 0   4 units from 0

−4 and 4 are opposites.

Recall that $0, 1, 2, 3, \ldots$ are whole numbers. **Integers** are the set of whole numbers and their opposites. Zero is its own opposite.

Integers: $\ldots -5, -4, -3, -2, -1, 0, 1, 2, 3, 4, 5, \ldots$

negative integers   zero   positive integers

Vocabulary Tip

Ellipses (. . .) indicate that the list continues. You read . . . as "and so on."

A number's distance from zero on the number line is its **absolute value.** You write "the absolute value of negative 6" as $|-6|$.

EXAMPLE   Finding Absolute Value

1 Find $|-6|$.

6 units

−6 −5 −4 −3 −2 −1 0 1

On the number line, −6 is 6 units from 0. So $|-6| = 6$.

✓ Quick Check

1. Find $|7|$ and $|-7|$.

You can use a number line to compare and order integers. Numbers increase from left to right on a number line. You can also order negative integers by finding their absolute values. The negative integer with the greatest absolute value is the least integer.

EXAMPLES Comparing and Ordering Integers

❷ Order −2, 3, and −6 from least to greatest.

Put the integers ← on the same number line.

The numbers from left to right are −6, −2, and 3.

❸ **Multiple Choice** Which continent has the lowest recorded temperature?

  Ⓐ Africa   Ⓒ Antarctica
  Ⓑ Asia   Ⓓ South America

Lowest Recorded Temperatures	
Continent	**°F**
Africa	−11
Antarctica	−129
Asia	−90
South America	−27

Source: National Climatic Data Center. Go to **www.PHSchool.com** for a data update. Web Code: asg-9041

Find the negative integer with the greatest absolute value.

$$|-11| = 11$$
$$|-129| = 129$$
$$|-90| = 90$$
$$|-27| = 27$$

The greatest absolute value is $|-129|$.

The correct answer is Antarctica, choice C.

Not all penguins live in Antarctica. Some types are found in South Africa and South America.

✓ Quick Check

2. Order 0, −5, and 4 from least to greatest.

3. Which has the lower recorded temperature: Asia or South America?

Like parentheses, absolute value symbols are grouping symbols.

EXAMPLE Absolute Value in Algebraic Expressions

Test Prep Tip

Write out each step to be sure that you are using the correct order of operations.

❹ Evaluate $|2b| - 6$ for $b = 4$.

$$|2b| - 6 = |2(4)| - 6$$ ← Substitute 4 for b.
$$= |8| - 6$$ ← Work within grouping symbols first. Multiply.
$$= 8 - 6$$ ← Find the absolute value.
$$= 2$$ ← Subtract.

✓ Quick Check

4. Evaluate $3|s|$ for $s = -5$.

1. **Vocabulary** How are whole numbers different from integers?

Write the letter for the point on the number line that describes each temperature.

Temperature (°F)

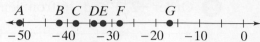

2. Coventry, Connecticut
   January 22, 1961: −32°F

3. Vanderbilt, Michigan
   February 9, 1934: −51°F

4. Mt. Mitchell, North Carolina
   January 21, 1985: −34°F

5. Smethport, Pennsylvania
   January 5, 1904: −42°F

Homework Exercises

For more exercises, see Extra Skills and Word Problems.

GO for Help

For Exercises	See Examples
6–9	1
10–14	2–3
15–18	4

Find each absolute value. You may find a number line helpful.

6. $|-52|$

7. $|26|$

8. $|0|$

9. $|-200|$

Order the integers in each set from least to greatest.

10. −9, 5, 2, −8, 0, 10, −12

11. −13, −16, 11, −6, 7, 2, −4

12. −9, −2, −12, −6, −15, −1

13. −33, 33, −19, 19, 27, −27

14. Order the elements in the table at the right from least to greatest boiling point.

Boiling Point (at sea level)

Element	°F
Chlorine	−29
Helium	−452
Iodine	364
Neon	−411
Nitrogen	−320
Oxygen	−297
Radon	−79

Evaluate each expression for the given value.

15. $8|w|$ for $w = -6$

16. $5 + |t|$ for $t = -8$

17. $10|a|$ for $a = -7$

18. $|3z|$ for $z = 62$

19. **Guided Problem Solving** Mount Kilimanjaro has an altitude of 19,340 ft. The lowest point in the Dead Sea has an altitude of −1,312 ft. Which altitude is farther from sea level?
    - The integer ■ represents sea level.
    - To compare the distances from sea level, use their ___?___.

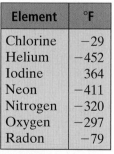

20. **Golf** In golf, the lowest score wins. One golfer finishes a course at −9. A second golfer finishes at −12.
    a. Which golfer wins?
    b. By how much does the winner beat the other golfer?

Visit: PHSchool.com
Web Code: ase-0102

21. **Number Sense** Which is greater, $-5|x|$ or $5|-x|$?

Data Analysis Use the graph at the right.

22. Which state had the lower temperature?

23. The lowest temperature ever recorded in Illinois was $-38°C$. Was it ever that cold in Kansas? Explain.

Compare. Write <, >, or =.

24. $|-12| \blacksquare |12|$ 25. $|3| \blacksquare |-4|$

26. $|-19| \blacksquare |-7|$ 27. $|6| \blacksquare |-9|$

28. **Open-Ended** Write an integer that is greater than 10 and less than $|-15|$.

29. **Writing in Math** Suppose a and b are integers, and $|a| > |b|$. Must a be greater than b? Use examples to support your answer.

30. **Reasoning** Do decimals have opposites? Explain.

31. **Challenge** For what values of x does $|x| = -x$?

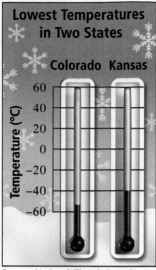

Lowest Temperatures in Two States

SOURCE: National Climatic Data Center. Go to **PHSchool.com** for a data update. Web Code: asg-9041

Test Prep and Mixed Review   Practice

Multiple Choice

32. Which integer is greater than -6 and less than -3?
    - Ⓐ 4   Ⓑ -2 Ⓒ -5 Ⓓ -7

33. Kyle's family drove 40.8 miles east to visit his grandmother, and then 5.2 miles farther east to a restaurant. His family then drove west to return home. How many miles did his family travel in all?
    - Ⓕ 46   Ⓖ 81.6   Ⓗ 86.8   Ⓙ 92

34. Refer to the table. Which expression represents the cost of t tickets?
    - Ⓐ $21.00 - 5.25t$
    - Ⓑ $5.25t$
    - Ⓒ $\dfrac{5.25}{t}$
    - Ⓓ $5.25 + t$

Tickets	Cost ($)
1	5.25
2	10.50
3	15.75
4	21.00

35. **Cable Service** A cable company charges a $25 setup fee and $34.95 each month for basic service. Write an expression to model these charges. Find the costs for 1, 3, and 6 months.

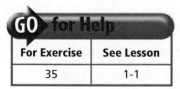

For Exercise	See Lesson
35	1-1

Online lesson quiz, PHSchool.com, Web Code: asa-0102   **1-2** Integers and Absolute Value   **13**

Integers and Differences

In finance, negative values represent debts or losses. The graph shows the month-to-month account of one business. The year begins with a negative value because Chantal borrowed money to pay startup costs.

ACTIVITY

Chantal's Web-Site Business

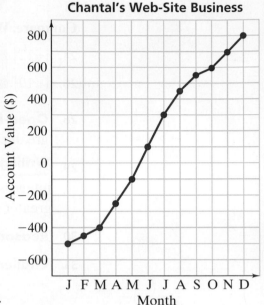

1. Write an expression to calculate the amount of money Chantal made from August to October.

2. Simplify the expression. Explain why you chose to use a particular operation.

3. Write a subtraction expression to find how much money Chantal made during the year.

4. Explain how to simplify the expression by applying absolute value to one of the numbers.

5. Describe a procedure for simplifying $225 - (-315)$.

✓ Checkpoint Quiz 1

Lessons 1-1 through 1-2

Write an algebraic expression for each phrase.

1. the product of -3 and a number s

2. a number v divided by 12

3. the quotient of a number m and 10

4. the sum of 4 and a number f

Simplify each expression.

5. $|-304|$

6. $|15|$

7. $2 \cdot |8|$

8. $6 - |-3|$

Evaluate each expression for the given values.

9. $3|c|$ for $c = -3.5$

10. $|f \cdot g|$ for $f = 4$ and $g = 7$

11. $|x| + y$ for $x = -4.2$ and $y = 3$

12. A mechanic charges $168 for parts and $35 per hour for labor. Write an expression for the total charge. Evaluate the expression to find the total charge for 3 hours of labor.

1-3a Activity Lab

Adding Integers

You can use number lines to add integers. Start at 0.
Move right on the number line to add positive integers
and left to add negative integers.

EXAMPLE **Using Number Lines**

1 Use a number line to find the sum $-5 + 7$.

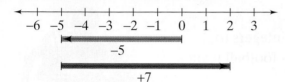

← Start at 0.

← Move 5 units left.

← Then move 7 units right.

After moving 7 units right, you are at 2. The number line shows that
$-5 + 7 = 2$.

Exercises

1. Find the sum modeled by each number line.

a. 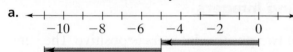 b.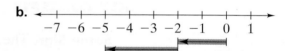

2. A *conjecture* is a prediction that suggests what can be expected to
happen. Make a conjecture about the sign of the sum of two
negative integers. Use a number line to support your conjecture.

3. Write an addition expression modeled by each number line. Then
find the sum.

a. 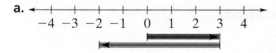 b.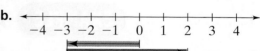

4. Use a number line to find each sum.
a. $-4 + 5$ b. $8 + (-4)$ c. $2 + (-6)$ d. $-9 + 2$

5. When is the sum of a positive integer and a negative integer
positive? Use a number line to support your answer.

6. When is the sum of a positive integer and a negative integer
negative? Use a number line to support your answer.

1-3 Adding and Subtracting Integers

✓ Check Skills You'll Need

1. **Vocabulary Review** How is *simplifying* an expression different from *evaluating* an expression?

Evaluate each expression for $x = 7$.

2. $x + 12$ 3. $x - 5$

4. $7x - 11$ 5. $\dfrac{12 + 9}{x}$

GO for Help
Lesson 1-1

What You'll Learn

To add and subtract integers and to solve problems involving integers

🔊 **New Vocabulary** additive inverses

Why Learn This?

You can add and subtract integers to describe changes, such as a football team's movement on the field.

If a team loses 9 yards and then gains 9 yards, it is back where it started: $-9 + 9 = 0$. Two numbers whose sum is 0 are **additive inverses.**

The following rules explain how to add two integers.

> **KEY CONCEPTS** **Adding Integers**
>
> **Same Sign** The sum of two positive integers is positive. The sum of two negative integers is negative.
>
> **Different Signs** Find the absolute value of each integer. Subtract the lesser absolute value from the greater. The sum has the sign of the integer with the greater absolute value.

Online active math

For: Integers Activity
Use: Interactive Textbook, 1-3

EXAMPLE Adding Integers

1 Simplify $6 + (-15)$.

$|6| = 6$ and $|-15| = 15$ ← Find the absolute value of each integer.

$15 - 6 = 9$ ← Subtract 6 from 15 because $|6| < |-15|$.

$6 + (-15) = -9$ ← The sum has the same sign as -15.

✓ Quick Check

1. Simplify each expression.
   a. $-12 + 30$ b. $-12 + (-3)$

Subtracting integers is similar to adding integers.

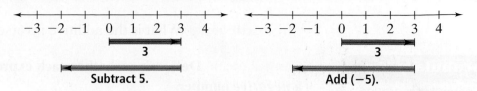

Subtract 5.   Add (−5).

So, $3 - 5 = 3 + (-5)$. This result suggests the following rule.

> **KEY CONCEPTS**   **Subtracting Integers**
>
> To subtract an integer, add its opposite.
>
> | Arithmetic | Algebra |
> |---|---|
> | $5 - 7 = 5 + (-7)$ | $a - b = a + (-b)$ |
> | $5 - (-7) = 5 + 7$ | $a - (-b) = a + b$ |

EXAMPLES   **Subtracting Integers**

2 Simplify the expression $12 - (-15)$.

$12 - (-15) = 12 + (15)$ ← **Add the opposite of −15, which is 15.**

$\qquad\qquad\quad = 27$ ← **Simplify.**

3 **Geography** A group of archaeologists leaves a site in Jordan and descends 647 m to the shore of the Dead Sea. Their initial elevation was 251 m above sea level. What is the elevation of the Dead Sea?

Draw a diagram like the one at the right to better understand the problem. It shows that the expression $251 - 647$ represents the elevation of the Dead Sea.

Elevation

251 m ┬ Site in Jordan

0 m ┼ Sea level

647-m descent

■ m ┴ Shore of Dead Sea

$251 - 647 = 251 + (-647)$ ← **Add the opposite of 647, which is −647.**

$\qquad\qquad\quad = -396$ ← **Use the rule for adding integers with different signs.**

The elevation of the Dead Sea is −396 m, or 396 m below sea level.

✓ Quick Check

2. Simplify each expression.
   a. $8 - (-4)$ **b.** $-23 - (-11)$ **c.** $-140 - 60$

3. **Diving** A scuba diver goes 94 ft below the surface of the ocean, and then descends 87 ft farther. What is the diver's depth?

✓ Check Your Understanding

1. **Vocabulary** What is the additive inverse of 0? Explain.

Vocabulary Tip

The parentheses around negative numbers help avoid confusion with subtraction signs.

Mental Math Determine whether each expression equals a *positive* or a *negative* number.

2. $2 + (-6)$ 3. $-1 + (-4)$ 4. $-5 + 9$

Simplify each expression.

5. $6 + 2$ 6. $-8 + 3$

7. $-7 + 5$ 8. $4 - 1$

9. $4 + (-3)$ 10. $-4 - 4$

Homework Exercises

For more exercises, see Extra Skills and Word Problems.

Simplify each expression. You may find a number line helpful.

For Exercises	See Examples
11–19	1
20–26	2 and 3

11. $-3 + (-5)$ 12. $49 + (-13)$ 13. $-15 + 14$

14. $3 + (-12)$ 15. $-25 + (-7)$ 16. $-17 + 18$

17. $-23 + 35$ 18. $215 + (-117)$ 19. $-508 + 507$

20. $-5 - 8$ 21. $-3 - (-7)$ 22. $6 - 18$

23. $21 - (-15)$ 24. $-38 - 38$ 25. $-23 - (-23)$

26. **Temperature** The temperature was 2°F. By midnight, the temperature had dropped 7°F. What was the temperature at midnight?

27. **Guided Problem Solving**
The graph shows temperatures at various altitudes. How much colder is it at 6,000 m than at 4,000 m?
- What is the temperature at 4,000 m?
- What is the temperature at 6,000 m?
- What is the difference in temperature?

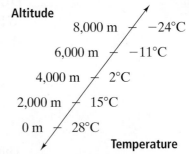

Altitude

8,000 m   −24°C
6,000 m   −11°C
4,000 m   2°C
2,000 m   15°C
0 m   28°C

Temperature

28. **Golf** In a golf tournament, a player scores −8 on the first day and +5 on the second day. What is the player's overall score?

29. **Money** On Monday, you had $151 in your checking account. On Tuesday, you wrote a check for $248. How much money should you deposit to prevent your account balance from going below $0?

Reasoning Is each statement *sometimes, always,* or *never* true? Explain.

30. The sum of a number and its opposite is negative.

31. The difference of a number and its opposite is negative.

Math in the Media Use the cartoon below for Exercises 32 and 33.

32. What would you add to 8 to get the sum 7?

33. **Writing in Math** Is the statement Calvin's father makes in the last frame always true? Explain.

34. Evaluate $x + y - z$ for $x = 2$, $y = -2$, and $z = -3$.

35. **Challenge** For what integer values of x is $|x + 1| - 2$ positive?

Test Prep and Mixed Review

Practice

Multiple Choice

36. A stock price was $43 on Monday morning. That week, the value of the stock gained $3, lost $5, lost $1, gained $2, and gained $4. What was the stock price at the end of the day on Friday?
  Ⓐ $28   Ⓑ $37   Ⓒ $46   Ⓓ $58

37. In a trivia game, you earn 15 points for a correct answer and lose 10 points for an incorrect answer. With −45 points, you answer the next question wrong. Which expression describes your new score?
  Ⓕ −45 + 15   Ⓗ −45 − 10
  Ⓖ −45 − 15   Ⓙ 10 − 45

38. At a library, copies cost $0.15 each. You made 8 copies and paid $1.25 for overdue books. Which expression can you use to find the amount you spent at the library?
  Ⓐ 0.15 + 1.25   Ⓒ 1.25 − 0.15(8)
  Ⓑ 0.15(8) + 1.25   Ⓓ 0.15 + 1.25(8)

GO for Help

For Exercises	See Lesson
39–41	1-2

Compare. Write <, >, or =.

39. −14 ▣ 12   **40.** −3 ▣ −4   **41.** −6 ▣ −10

1-4 Multiplying and Dividing Integers

What You'll Learn

To multiply and divide integers and to solve problems involving integers

🔊 **New Vocabulary** inverse operations

Why Learn This?

You can multiply integers to find totals. You can divide integers to find rates, such as your rate of descent while hiking.

You can use number lines to model integer multiplication.

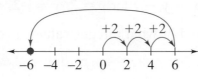

3(2) means three groups of 2.
−3(2) means the opposite of three groups of 2.

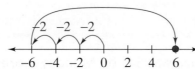

3(−2) means three groups of −2.
−3(−2) means the opposite of three groups of −2.

KEY CONCEPTS **Multiplying Two Integers**

The product of two integers with the same sign is positive.

Examples $8 \cdot 3 = 24$ $\qquad$ $-8 \cdot (-3) = 24$

The product of two integers with different signs is negative.

Examples $8 \cdot (-3) = -24$ $\qquad$ $-8 \cdot 3 = -24$

EXAMPLE Multiplying Integers

1 Simplify $-2 \cdot 9 \cdot (-5)$.

$-2 \cdot 9 \cdot (-5) = -18 \cdot (-5)$ ← different signs, negative product

$= 90$ ← same sign, positive product

✓ Quick Check

1. Simplify $-9 \cdot 8 \cdot (-2)$.

Inverse operations are operations that undo each other. Multiplication and division are inverse operations. Since $-4 \cdot 2 = -8$, it follows that $-8 \div 2 = -4$ and $-8 \div (-4) = 2$.

The rules for dividing two integers are similar to the rules for multiplying two integers.

KEY CONCEPTS **Dividing Two Integers**

The quotient of two integers with the same sign is positive.

Examples $\frac{8}{2} = 4$ $\frac{-8}{-2} = 4$

The quotient of two integers with different signs is negative.

Examples $\frac{-8}{2} = -4$ $\frac{8}{-2} = -4$

EXAMPLE **Dividing Integers**

2 **Multiple Choice** A hiker descends 360 feet in 40 minutes. What is the hiker's change in elevation per minute?

   Ⓐ -9 ft/min   Ⓑ $-\frac{1}{9}$ ft/min   Ⓒ $\frac{1}{9}$ ft/min   Ⓓ 9 ft/min

Let -360 represent a descent of 360 feet. Then divide the descent by the number of minutes to find the change in elevation per minute.

$$\begin{array}{l}\text{feet} \rightarrow \\ \text{minutes} \rightarrow\end{array} \quad \frac{-360}{40} = -9 \quad \leftarrow \textbf{different signs, negative quotient}$$

The change in elevation is -9 ft/min, so the answer is A.

Test Prep Tip ⒶⒷⒸⒹ

To find the unit in your answer, note the unit of each quantity in the problem.

✓ **Quick Check**

2. **Diving** A diver descends 90 feet in 5 minutes. What is the diver's change in depth per minute?

EXAMPLE **Evaluating an Algebraic Expression**

3 Evaluate $pt + (p - t) \div r$ for $p = 4$, $t = -2$, and $r = -3$.

$$\begin{aligned}
pt + (p - t) \div r &= 4(-2) + [4 - (-2)] \div (-3) &&\leftarrow \begin{array}{l}\textbf{Substitute 4 for } p, \\ \textbf{-2 for } t, \textbf{ and -3 for } r.\end{array} \\
&= 4(-2) + 6 \div (-3) &&\leftarrow \textbf{order of operations} \\
&= -8 + (-2) &&\leftarrow \textbf{Multiply and divide.} \\
&= -10 &&\leftarrow \textbf{Add.}
\end{aligned}$$

✓ **Quick Check**

3. Evaluate $2x + xy \div z - 3$ for $x = -9$, $y = -5$, and $z = -3$.

1. **Vocabulary** $-5(3)$ means the opposite of five groups of ■.

2. **Number Sense** Which product is greater, a negative number multiplied by a negative number or a negative number multiplied by a positive number? Explain.

Mental Math Compare. Write <, >, or =.

3. $-3 \cdot 6$ ■ $9 \cdot 5$ 4. $6(-7)$ ■ $-2(-8)$ 5. $12 \cdot 4$ ■ $8(-11)$

Simplify each expression.

6. $8 \cdot 3$ 7. $7(-5)$ 8. $\dfrac{24}{6}$ 9. $\dfrac{-12}{-3}$

Homework Exercises

For more exercises, see **Extra Skills and Word Problems.**

Simplify each expression.

For Exercises	See Examples
10–15	1
16–22	2
23–28	3

GO for Help

10. $3 \cdot (-15) \cdot 2$ 11. $-8 \cdot (-5) \cdot 4$ 12. $-7(-2)(-1)$

13. $-1 \cdot 3 \cdot 2 \cdot (-6)$ 14. $-3(-1)(-4)(-7)$ 15. $2(-4)(-8)(-6)$

16. $\dfrac{-45}{9}$ 17. $\dfrac{50}{5}$ 18. $-64 \div 8$

19. $\dfrac{35}{-7}$ 20. $-72 \div 9$ 21. $\dfrac{-48}{-6}$

22. **Elevators** An elevator descends 1,000 feet in 8 seconds. What is the change in height per second?

Evaluate each expression for $c = -2$ and $d = 5$.

23. $cd - 5d$ 24. $dc + (c - d)$

25. $d + 3c \div 2$ 26. $(2d - c) \div [4(d + c)]$

27. $\dfrac{d - c + 8}{5}$ 28. $\dfrac{12d}{c - 4}$

GPS 29. **Guided Problem Solving** You withdraw $260 from your bank account in 5 trips to the ATM. What is the average change in your account balance for each trip?
- What integer represents the amount of money you withdraw?
- What integer represents the number of trips made to the ATM?
- Do you need to multiply or divide?

30. **Measurement** A submarine descends 60 ft/min. What depth below the water's surface will the submarine reach in 4 min after leaving the surface?

31. In a trivia game, you lose points for incorrect answers. You answer the first 3 questions wrong. Your score is −75. How many points is each incorrect answer worth?

Writing in Math What is the sign of each product? Explain.

32. $n \cdot n$, where n is any nonzero number

33. $y \cdot y \cdot y$, where y is any negative number

34. At the museum, your class breaks into groups of 3 for a scavenger hunt. There are 24 students in your class. How many groups form?

35. **Number Sense** What integer divided by −5 equals −60?

Algebra Suppose x and y are positive and a and b are negative. What is the sign of each quotient?

36. $\dfrac{x}{a}$ **37.** $\dfrac{y}{b}$ **38.** $\dfrac{x}{y}$ **39.** $\dfrac{a}{x+y}$ **40.** $\dfrac{b+a}{x}$

41. **Geology** Scientists drill 40,230 ft into Earth's crust.
a. Write an integer to represent this depth.
b. **Estimation** Estimate the depth drilled, to the nearest mile.

42. **Challenge** You go hiking with five friends for 4 days. You are in charge of bringing the food. If you plan to eat 3 meals each day, how many meals should you pack?

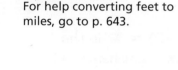
for Help

For help converting feet to miles, go to p. 643.

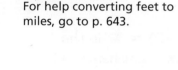
Test Prep and Mixed Review **Practice**

Multiple Choice

43. During the morning, the temperature changed by −4°F. During the afternoon, the temperature dropped by twice as much as it had during the morning. By how many degrees did the temperature change during the afternoon?
Ⓐ −8°F Ⓑ −6°F Ⓒ −2°F Ⓓ 4°F

44. Which set of integers is in order from least to greatest?
Ⓕ 8, 5, 3, −1, −6, −9 Ⓗ −13, −7, −2, −1, 1, 4
Ⓖ −1, 2, 5, −6, 8, −9 Ⓙ −3, −10, −12, 0, 4, 18

45. A 165-foot ship was sunk off an island in Hawaii to make an artificial reef. It is located 90 feet below the ocean's surface. If the elevation at the ocean's surface is 0, which integer best represents the elevation of the ship?
Ⓐ −165 Ⓑ −90 Ⓒ 90 Ⓓ 165

For Exercises	See Lesson
46–49	1-3

Simplify each expression.

46. $8 + (−5)$ **47.** $−13 + 7$ **48.** $−10 − 3$ **49.** $2 − (−6)$

Solving Multi-Step Problems

Grades Ms. Mack uses the system shown at the right when grading tests. On his first test, Rex got the extra credit but misspelled three words and had one wrong answer. What was his score?

Misspelling	−3
Bad grammar	−4
Wrong answer	−5
Extra credit	+2

What You Might Think

What do I know? What do I want to find out?

What number sentence can I write? Would a diagram help?

What is the answer?

Is the answer reasonable?

What You Might Write

Rex started with 100 points. He got −3 points three times and then got +2 points. His wrong answer was −5 points. I want to know the sum of his points.

$100 + 3 \times (−3) + 2 + (−5) = \blacksquare$ is the number sentence. A diagram might help.

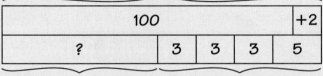

total points possible

100				+2
?	3	3	3	5

final test score   points taken away

$100 + 3 \times (−3) + 2 + (−5) = 100 − 9 − 3$
$= 88$

A score of 88 for missing one problem and writing carelessly is reasonable.

Think It Through

1. **Number Sense** Suppose Rex had the correct answer for the problem marked wrong, but his handwriting was so poor that the teacher could not read it. What number sentence gives Rex credit for the correct answer?

2. **a.** What is the only score from 90 to 100 that Rex could not receive if he gets one extra credit problem correct?
   b. Show how Rex could get each of the other scores between 90 and 100.

Exercises

Solve each problem. For Exercises 3 and 4, answer the questions first.

3. A scuba diver was 68 feet deep at 3:14 P.M. She rose 12 feet per minute for 4 minutes, saw a lobster, and descended 20 feet per minute for 2 minutes. But she began to lose air, so she rose 15 feet per minute. What time did she surface?
   a. What do you know? What do you want to find out?
   b. Copy and complete the diagram below.

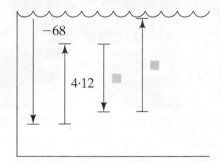

4. Wild horse herds have no natural predators, so they can double in size every five years. If herd growth is left unchecked, find the population by the year 2045 in each of the states shown in the table.

2005 Wild Horse Population

State	Number of Horses
Arizona	230
Nevada	13,251
Wyoming	3,991
New Mexico	82
Colorado	800

SOURCE: U.S. Bureau of Land Management

   a. What do you know? What do you want to find out?
   b. Will a table help you keep track of the population and years?

5. A man bought a scooter for $100 and sold it for $120. Later he bought it back for $140 and sold it again for $160. How much did he make or lose as a scooter salesman?

6. When grading tests, Mr. Lee takes off five points for each incorrect answer, adds three points for each correct extra credit problem, and takes off three points for each problem that has no work shown. On the last test, Sara correctly answered both extra credit problems. If her score was 90, how many problems did she get wrong? Explain.

What You'll Learn

To identify the properties of numbers and use the properties to solve problems

🔊 **New Vocabulary** commutative properties, associative properties, identity properties, Distributive Property

Why Learn This?

When you go shopping, you might find the cost mentally to be sure you have enough money. Understanding operations with numbers can help you make calculations easily and quickly.

You can add or multiply two numbers in any order and get the same result. For example, $7 + 2 = 2 + 7$ and $7 \cdot 2 = 2 \cdot 7$. You can also change the grouping of numbers before you add or multiply them.

KEY CONCEPTS Properties of Operations

Commutative Properties of Addition and Multiplication

Arithmetic	**Algebra**
$7 + 12 = 12 + 7$	$a + b = b + a$
$7 \cdot 12 = 12 \cdot 7$	$a \cdot b = b \cdot a$

Associative Properties of Addition and Multiplication

Arithmetic	**Algebra**
$(4 + 7) + 3 = 4 + (7 + 3)$	$(a + b) + c = a + (b + c)$
$(4 \cdot 7) \cdot 3 = 4 \cdot (7 \cdot 3)$	$(a \cdot b) \cdot c = a \cdot (b \cdot c)$

Adding 0 and multiplying by 1 do not change the value of a number.

KEY CONCEPTS Identity Properties

Arithmetic	**Algebra**
$6 + 0 = 0 + 6 = 6$	$a + 0 = 0 + a = a$
$6 \cdot 1 = 1 \cdot 6 = 6$	$a \cdot 1 = 1 \cdot a = a$

You can use mental math and the properties of numbers to simplify expressions.

EXAMPLES Using Mental Math

1 Mental Math Use mental math to simplify $2.5 + 5.3 + 7.5$.

What you think

I should look for numbers that are easy to add: $2.5 + 7.5 = 10$. Then I can add 5.3: $10 + 5.3 = 15.3$.

Why it works

$$2.5 + 5.3 + 7.5 = 2.5 + 7.5 + 5.3 \quad \leftarrow \text{Commutative Property of Addition}$$
$$= 10 + 5.3 \quad \leftarrow \text{order of operations}$$
$$= 15.3 \quad \leftarrow \text{Simplify.}$$

Test Prep Tip

You can use mental math as a quick way to check an answer.

2 Mental Math Use mental math to simplify $58 - 73$.

What you think

I can make the problem easier by splitting 58 into 5 and 53. First, I should find $53 - 73$, which equals -20. Then, I can add the rest of 58: $5 + (-20) = -15$.

Why it works

$$58 - 73 = (5 + 53) - 73 \quad \leftarrow \text{Write 58 as } 5 + 53.$$
$$= 5 + (53 - 73) \quad \leftarrow \text{Associative Property of Addition}$$
$$= 5 + (-20) \quad \leftarrow \text{order of operations}$$
$$= -15 \quad \leftarrow \text{Simplify.}$$

3 Mental Math Use mental math to simplify $-5 \cdot 7 \cdot 8$.

What you think

It is easy to multiply with multiples of 10. I should multiply -5 by 8 to get -40. Then I can multiply by 7: $-40 \cdot 7 = -280$.

Why it works

$$-5 \cdot 7 \cdot 8 = -5 \cdot 8 \cdot 7 \quad \leftarrow \text{Commutative Property of Addition}$$
$$= -40 \cdot 7 \quad \leftarrow \text{order of operations}$$
$$= -280 \quad \leftarrow \text{Simplify.}$$

✓ Quick Check

Use mental math to simplify each expression.

1. $26 + (-12) + 34$ **2.** $46 - 92$ **3.** $-4 \cdot 121 \cdot (-5)$

For help with the
formula for the area
of a rectangle, go
to p. 648.

You can find the area of the rectangles below in two ways.

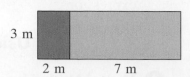

3 m

2 m   7 m

Method 1 Add. Then multiply.

$3(2 + 7) = 3(9)$
$= 27$

Method 2 Multiply. Then add.

$3 \cdot 2 + 3 \cdot 7 = 6 + 21$
$= 27$

Both methods give an area of 27 m². This example illustrates the Distributive Property.

$$3(2 + 7) = 3 \cdot 2 + 3 \cdot 7$$

KEY CONCEPTS   **Distributive Property**

Arithmetic	**Algebra**
$3(2 + 7) = 3 \cdot 2 + 3 \cdot 7$	$a(b + c) = ab + ac$
$(2 + 7)\,3 = 2 \cdot 3 + 7 \cdot 3$	$(b + c)a = ba + ca$
$5(8 - 2) = 5 \cdot 8 - 5 \cdot 2$	$a(b - c) = ab - ac$
$(8 - 2)5 = 8 \cdot 5 - 2 \cdot 5$	$(b - c)a = ba - ca$

EXAMPLES   **Using the Distributive Property**

4 Find $(n + 14)(-8)$.

$(n + 14)(-8) = n(-8) + 14(-8)$ ← **Distributive Property**

$= -8n + (-112)$ ← **Simplify.**

$= -8n - 112$ ← **Rewrite as a subtraction expression.**

5 **Art Supplies** A teacher orders supply kits for a class of 20 students. Each kit costs $5.90. What is the total cost?

$20(5.9) = 20(6 - 0.1)$ ← **Replace 5.9 with 6 − 0.1.**

$= 20(6) - 20(0.1)$ ← **Distributive Property**

$= 120 - 2$ ← **Multiply.**

$= 118$ ← **Subtract.**

The total cost is $118.

✓ Quick Check

4. Find $6(m + 3)$.

5. A large supply kit costs $8.10. What is the cost of 20 large kits?

1. **Vocabulary** By the Identity Property of Multiplication, multiplying a number by ■ does not change the number's value.

Identify each property.

2. $-19.1 + 0 = -19.1$

3. $6(-8) = (-8)6$

4. $(9 + 10) + 20 = 9 + (10 + 20)$

5. $-6.2 + 7.9 = 7.9 + (-6.2)$

6. $4(wx) = (4w)x$

7. $m \cdot 1 = m$

Use mental math to simplify each expression.

8. $3.5 + 9 + 6.5$

9. $14 - 31$

10. $-4 \cdot 6 \cdot (-25)$

11. Use the Distributive Property to rewrite $27 \cdot 2 + 73 \cdot 2$.

Homework Exercises

For more exercises, see Extra Skills and Word Problems.

Mental Math Use mental math to simplify each expression.

GO for Help	
For Exercises	**See Examples**
12–20	1–3
21–26	4
27–30	5

12. $67 + 63 + 25$

13. $87 + 32 + 13$

14. $178 + 288 + 22$

15. $13 - 67$

16. $38 - 59$

17. $24 - 46$

18. $5 \cdot 245 \cdot 20$

19. $-2(43)(-5)$

20. $20(34)(-5)$

Find each product.

21. $5(a + 6)$

22. $7(b - 9)$

23. $-4(t + 3)$

24. $(v - 2)9$

25. $(8 + r)4$

26. $(-11 + w)(-2)$

27. $6(2.5)$

28. $5(0.9)$

29. $4(1.98)$

30. **School Supplies** At the school store, notebooks cost $3.49. How much will you pay for 4 notebooks?

31. **Guided Problem Solving** At the bakery, you want to buy 3 loaves of bread for $1.99 each and 2 muffins for $.89 each. You have $7 to spend. Do you have enough money?
    • To find the cost of the bread, replace 1.99 with ■ − ■.
    • Multiply by 3 using the __?__ Property.

32. **Tickets** Four students sell 38 tickets each to a school play. The school auditorium can seat 150 people. Are there enough seats?

33. Find the total cost of buying 4 pairs of candles for $2.97 per pair, 3 cards for $1.99 each, and 5 colored markers for $.99 each.

34. You have $3 to spend on lunch. You want to buy a sandwich for $1.95, a carton of milk for $.40, and a banana for $.60.
   a. Do you have enough money for lunch?
   b. If so, how much change do you get? If not, how much more money do you need?

35. **Choose a Method** Four picture frames cost $5.98 each. Which would you use to find the total cost—mental math or paper and pencil? Explain your choice.

Use mental math to simplify each expression.

36. $-50 + 2 + 108 + (-450)$ 37. $(40)(-2)(29)(-10)$

38. **Track** In a women's 4×100 m relay race, a team's times for the legs of the race are 11.92 seconds, 12.20 seconds, 12.08 seconds, and 11.86 seconds. What is the difference between the team's total time and the world record time of 41.37 seconds?

39. **Writing in Math** Explain how to use the properties of numbers to simplify $(-68) + 6(-99) + (-32)$.

40. **Error Analysis** A student claims that $7 \cdot 6 + 4 = 7 \cdot 4 + 6$ by the Commutative Property of Addition. Explain the student's error.

41. **Challenge** A volunteer at a food bank is packing boxes with cans of fruit. Each box must weigh 20 lb or less. Can the volunteer put two dozen 15-oz cans in the box? Explain. (*Hint:* 1 lb = 16 oz)

Test Prep and Mixed Review

Practice

Multiple Choice

42. Scarlet bought 1 box of markers for $3.49, 1 package of lined paper for $1.19, and 2 packages of folders for $0.79 each. To make sure she had enough money, Scarlet estimated the total cost. Which is a reasonable estimate for this situation?
   Ⓐ $5.50   Ⓑ $5.75   Ⓒ $6.30   Ⓓ $7.00

43. On a 100-point exam, you got 4 questions wrong. Each question was worth 5 points. What would you do to find your score?
   Ⓕ Multiply and add.   Ⓗ Divide and subtract.
   Ⓖ Multiply and subtract.   Ⓙ Add and subtract.

44. Which group of numbers is in order from least to greatest?
   Ⓐ 7, 3, −15, −7, −1, 1   Ⓒ −1, −7, −15, 1, 3, 7
   Ⓑ −1, 1, 3, −7, 7, −15   Ⓓ −15, −7, −1, 1, 3, 7

For Exercises	See Lesson
45–47	1-4

Simplify each expression.

45. $-6 \cdot (-2) \cdot 3$ 46. $3(-4) \cdot 2$ 47. $-2 \cdot 5 \cdot (-1) \cdot 6$

Simplify each expression.

1. $-79 + 15$

2. $23 - (-14)$

3. $-32 - 11$

4. $-4 \div (-1)$

5. $-30 \div (-3 \cdot 2)$

6. $7 - (-9) \cdot 2$

Mental Math **Use mental math to simplify each expression.**

7. $70 + 19 + 30$

8. $540 + 160 - 280 - 10$

9. An animal shelter purchases dog food for $15.98 per bag. Use the Distributive Property to find how much the shelter will pay for 4 bags of dog food.

10. **Fishing** A fishing boat sets its net 37 ft below the ocean's surface. Then it lowers the net an additional 16.5 ft. Write an expression to represent the new depth of the net.

MATH GAMES

Integer Flip

What You'll Need
- 25 index cards numbered from 1 to 25
- 25 index cards numbered from −1 to −25

How To Play
- Shuffle the two piles of index cards together. Deal the same number of cards face down to each player.
- Each player keeps his or her pile face down. All players turn over two cards at a time.
- The player whose cards have the largest sum wins all of the cards that are face up.
- The winner of the game is the player who wins all of the cards.

Modeling Equations

You can model and solve equations using algebra tiles.

 = +1   ■ = −1   ▮ = x

To solve an equation, remove the same number of like-color tiles from each side or use zero pairs. A **zero pair** is a pair of tiles with a sum of zero. ■ ■ ← zero pair

EXAMPLES

1 Use algebra tiles to solve $x - 2 = 7$.

Model the equation. →  $x - 2 = 7$

Add 2 to each side, making two zero pairs on the left side. →  $x - 2 + 2 = 7 + 2$

Remove the zero pairs. →  $x = 9$

2 Use algebra tiles to solve $4x = -12$.

Model the equation. → 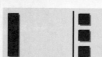 $4x = -12$

Divide each side into four equal groups. →  $\dfrac{4x}{4} = \dfrac{-12}{4}$

Remove three groups from each side. →  $x = -3$

Exercises

1. Use algebra tiles to solve each equation.
   a. $x + 5 = 3$ **b.** $3x = -6$ **c.** $x + 3 = -5$ **d.** $5x = 10$

2. Write a rule for the operations you use to solve addition equations.

1-6 Solving Equations by Adding and Subtracting

✓ Check Skills You'll Need

1. **Vocabulary Review**
   4 and −4 are
   additive __?__ .

Simplify each
expression.

2. −4 + (−7)

3. 12 + (−12)

4. 3 − 10

5. −5 − 1

for Help
Lesson 1-3

What You'll Learn

To write and solve equations using addition and subtraction

🔊 **New Vocabulary** equation, Addition Property of Equality, Subtraction Property of Equality, solution, isolate

Why Learn This?

You have probably used the library to find information for a project. In math, you often solve equations to find unknown information, such as account balances or altitudes.

An **equation** is a mathematical sentence with an equal sign.

An equation is like a balance scale. If you do something to one side of an equation, you must do the same to the other side to keep it balanced.

$x + 2 = 5$

Two weights were taken from each side of the upper balance scale at the right. The result, shown on the lower balance scale, illustrates a property of equality.

$x = 3$

Online
active math

For: Equations Activity
Use: Interactive
Textbook, 1-6

KEY CONCEPTS Properties of Equality

Addition Property of Equality
If you add the same number to each side of an equation, the two sides remain equal.

Arithmetic	**Algebra**
$10 = 5(2)$, so $10 + 3 = 5(2) + 3$	If $a = b$, then $a + c = b + c$.

Subtraction Property of Equality
If you subtract the same number from each side of an equation, the two sides remain equal.

Arithmetic	**Algebra**
$10 = 5(2)$, so $10 - 3 = 5(2) - 3$	If $a = b$, then $a - c = b - c$.

A solution to an equation is any value that makes the equation true. To find a solution, isolate the variable, or get it alone on one side. Use inverse operations, which are operations that undo each other.

Addition Undoes Subtraction		Subtraction Undoes Addition
$2 - 8 + 8 = 2$	← arithmetic →	$5 + 7 - 7 = 5$
$n - 6 + 6 = n$	← algebra →	$n + 9 - 9 = n$

After you solve an equation, check your solution by substituting it for the variable in the original equation.

EXAMPLES Solving Equations

1 Solve $-2 = k - 14$.

$$-2 = k - 14$$
$$-2 + 14 = k - 14 + 14 \quad \leftarrow \text{Isolate the variable. Use the Addition Property of Equality.}$$
$$12 = k \quad \leftarrow \text{Simplify.}$$

Check $\quad -2 = k - 14 \quad \leftarrow$ Check the solution in the original equation.
$$-2 \stackrel{?}{=} 12 - 14 \quad \leftarrow \text{Substitute 12 for } k.$$
$$-2 = -2 \ ✔ \quad \leftarrow \text{Subtract.}$$

2 **Altitude** An airplane climbs 7,900 ft during a flight. The airplane's altitude is then 13,220 ft. What was the airplane's original altitude?

Words   original altitude   plus   climb   =   new altitude

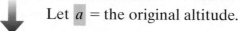

Let a = the original altitude.

Equation a +   7,900   =   13,220

$$a + 7,900 = 13,220$$
$$a + 7,900 - 7,900 = 13,220 - 7,900 \quad \leftarrow \text{Isolate the variable. Use the Subtraction Property of Equality.}$$
$$a = 5,320 \quad \leftarrow \text{Simplify.}$$

Before climbing, the airplane was 5,320 feet above the ground.

Check for Reasonableness Round 7,900 to 8,000 and 5,320 to 5,000. Since $8,000 + 5,000 = 13,000$, and 13,000 is close to 13,220, the answer is reasonable.

Careers An air-traffic controller monitors both the direction and altitude of a plane.

✓ Quick Check

1. Solve $x - 7 = -10$.

2. Yesterday an official mailed some notices for a meeting. Today she mailed 8 more notices. She mailed 52 notices in all. Write and solve an equation to find the number of notices mailed yesterday.

✓ Check Your Understanding

1. **Vocabulary** How is an expression different from an equation?

2. **Mental Math** What is the solution to $m - 9 = 8$?

3. Your friend made y bracelets. After she gave four away, she had eight bracelets left. Write an equation to model the situation.

Mental Math For each equation, determine whether -3 is a solution.

4. $a + 4 = 7$	**5.** $w - 7 = -10$	**6.** $-1 + c = 4$
7. $z - 3 = 0$	**8.** $7 + p = 4$	**9.** $r + 3 = 0$

Homework Exercises

For more exercises, see **Extra Skills and Word Problems.**

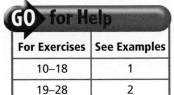

For Exercises	See Examples
10–18	1
19–28	2

Solve each equation. Check the solution.

10. $p - 1 = -12$	**11.** $a - 9 = 45$
12. $-37 = y - 2$	**13.** $b - 2 = -2$
14. $-36 = t - 14$	**15.** $m - 45 = 1$
16. $23 = q - 12$	**17.** $d - 15 = -31$
18. $w - 32 = -5$	**19.** $a + 15 = 10$
20. $x + 1 = 22$	**21.** $v + 9 = -2$
22. $r + 27 = -52$	**23.** $b + 61 = 27$
24. $-10 = 3 + c$	**25.** $19 + g = 32$
26. $f + 47 = 100$	**27.** $h + 21 = -50$

28. **Money** You deposit $450 into a bank account. The new balance is $512. Write and solve an equation to find the original balance.

29. **Guided Problem Solving** Between 1950 and 2000, the population of Kansas increased by 783,000. Use the graph to find the population of Kansas in 1950.
    - What operation should you use to show the change in population from 1950 to 2000?
    - What equation models the situation?
    - How can you check your answer for reasonableness?

    Population (thousands)
    2,688
    p
    Topeka
    1950   2000
    Kansas

30. The temperature at 6:00 P.M. was 12°F. At 6:00 A.M., it was 15 degrees cooler. What was the temperature at 6:00 A.M.?

Number Sense Choose from −3, −2, −1, 0, 1, 2, and 3. Find *all* the numbers that are solutions of each equation.

31. $-|n| = -3$ **32.** $|n| + 1 = 2$ **33.** $|n + 1| = 2$

34. A collector sold a baseball card for $9.30. This was $3.75 more than the price he paid. How much did the collector pay for the card?

35. **Recycling** In one weekend, a student collected p lb of cans to take to the recycling center. After delivering 5.2 lb of cans, the student still had 7.8 lb of cans. How many pounds of cans did the student collect?

36. **Writing in Math** Describe a problem that could be solved using the equation $a + 8.40 = 11.55$.

Solve each equation.

37. $w - 2.45 = 3.1$ **38.** $h - (-7) = 4.3$ **39.** $-12 = -6.4 + m$

40. **Challenge** For what values of x is $x + 15 = x + 6 + 9$ true? Explain.

Test Prep and Mixed Review   **Practice**

Multiple Choice

41. Which problem situation matches the equation $x + 96 = 102$?
  - (A) Nathan rented two movies with run times of 96 minutes and 102 minutes. What is x, the time it took to watch both movies?
  - (B) A class sells 96 concert tickets. They earn $102. What is x, the price of each ticket?
  - (C) On her last two math exams, Kathy got scores of 96 and 102. What is x, her average score?
  - (D) Together, Joey and his cat weigh 102 pounds. Alone, Joey weighs 96 pounds. What is x, the weight of Joey's cat?

42. Three friends agreed to split a dinner bill equally. The dinner cost $81, and tax was an additional $4.05. They left a $15 tip. Which expression can be used to find how much each person paid?
  - (F) $\dfrac{81 + 4.05 + 15}{3}$ (H) $3(81 + 4.05 + 15)$
  - (G) $3 \div (81 + 4.05 + 15)$ (J) $\dfrac{8 + 15}{3 + 4.05}$

43. A basketball team has 18 points. The team then scores six 2-point baskets and two 3-point baskets. What is the team's score?
  - (A) 23   (B) 26   (C) 31   (D) 36

Simplify each expression.

44. $3 + (-12)$ **45.** $-15 + (-6)$ **46.** $-21 - 37$ **47.** $-24 - (-9)$

Number Squares

A number square is a square table with the same number of rows as columns. Each row, column, and main diagonal in the square has the same sum. Each entry in the square is a different number. At the right is a 3-by-3 number square. The sum of each row, column, and main diagonal is 15.

8	3	4
1	5	9
6	7	2

EXAMPLE

Write and solve an equation to find each missing value in the square at the right.

-4	-6	b
6	-2	-10
a	2	0

Step 1 Use a row, column, or diagonal without variables to find the sum.
$$6 + (-2) + (-10) = -6$$

Step 2 Write and solve two equations.

First column:
$$-4 + 6 + a = -6$$
$$a + 2 = -6$$
$$a + 2 - 2 = -6 - 2$$
$$a = -8$$

First row:
$$-4 + (-6) + b = -6$$
$$b - 10 = -6$$
$$b - 10 + 10 = -6 + 10$$
$$b = 4$$

Exercises

Write and solve an equation to find the value of each variable.

1.

2	b	-2
a	-1	c
0	1	-4

2.

17	x	7
12	22	z
w	y	27

3.

-6	4	5	-9
2	m	-1	-3
-5	1	n	0
p	-7	-8	z

4. Use the number square at the top of the page. Add -5 to each number. Is the result still a number square? Explain.

5. **Writing in Math** In a 3-by-3 square, what is the least number of values you must know before you can write equations to complete the square? Explain.

Solving Equations by Multiplying and Dividing

1. Vocabulary Review *Inverse operations* are operations that __?__ each other.

Simplify each expression.

2. $6 \cdot 4$ **3.** $-7 \cdot 3$

4. $\dfrac{10}{-5}$ **5.** $\dfrac{-27}{-9}$

GO for Help
Lesson 1-4

What You'll Learn

To write and solve equations using multiplication and division

◀)) **New Vocabulary** Multiplication Property of Equality, Division Property of Equality

Why Learn This?

Some equations model the relationships between sizes of groups. When you can solve multiplication and division equations, you can find unknown values such as the number of people in an audience or school.

KEY CONCEPTS Properties of Equality

Multiplication Property of Equality If you multiply each side of an equation by the same number, the two sides remain equal.

Arithmetic	**Algebra**
$20 = \dfrac{40}{2}$, so $2(20) = 2\left(\dfrac{40}{2}\right)$	If $a = b$, then $ac = bc$.

Division Property of Equality If you divide each side of an equation by the same nonzero number, the two sides remain equal.

Arithmetic	**Algebra**
$30 = 3(10)$, so $\dfrac{30}{6} = \dfrac{3(10)}{6}$	If $a = b$ and $c \neq 0$, then $\dfrac{a}{c} = \dfrac{b}{c}$.

Vocabulary Tip

The symbol $\neq$ means "does not equal."

EXAMPLE Solving by Multiplying

1 Solve $\dfrac{x}{-7} = 15$.

$$-7 \cdot \left(\dfrac{x}{-7}\right) = -7 \cdot 15 \quad \leftarrow \text{Isolate the variable. Use the Multiplication Property of Equality.}$$

$$x = -105 \quad \leftarrow \text{Simplify.}$$

✓ Quick Check

1. Solve $\dfrac{t}{8} = -5$.

For help multiplying and dividing integers, go to Lesson 1-4, Examples 1 and 2.

EXAMPLE Solving by Dividing

2 Solve $816 = 8c$.

$$\frac{816}{8} = \frac{8c}{8}$$ ← Isolate the variable. Use the Division Property of Equality.

$102 = c$ ← Simplify.

Check $816 \overset{?}{=} 8(102)$ ← Check the solution in the original equation. Substitute 102 for c.

$816 = 816$ ✔ ← Multiply.

✓ Quick Check

2. Solve $3y = -12$.

● More Than One Way

One out of every five people attending a town rock concert came to support the local high school rock band. The band had 112 supporters. How many people were in the audience?

Daryl's Method

I see that 112 supporters equal one out of five audience members. I know there are five groups of 112 people in the audience.

| 112 | 112 | 112 | 112 | 112 |

So, there are 5 · 112, or 560 audience members.

Tina's Method

I can represent the number of people in the audience as p. The number of supporters is p divided by 5. I can write the equation as $\frac{p}{5} = 112$ and solve for p.

$$\frac{p}{5} = 112$$

$$5\left(\frac{p}{5}\right) = 5(112)$$

$$p = 560$$

There are 560 people in the audience.

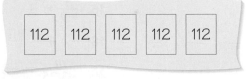

Choose a Method

One out of three students at a school likes gym. If 120 students like gym, how many students go to the school? Explain your method.

Check Your Understanding

1. **Vocabulary** When is a value a solution to an equation?

Which property of equality does each equation illustrate?

2. $\frac{24}{4} = \frac{8(3)}{4}$

3. $36 + (-10) = 4(9) + (-10)$

4. $8(-7) = \left(\frac{-56}{-7}\right)(-7)$

5. $-5(6) - 13 = -30 - 13$

Mental Math For each equation, find whether −5 is a solution.

6. $25v = -5$

7. $\frac{15}{m} = -3$

8. $10 = -2t$

9. $-5p = 25$

10. $7 = \frac{35}{w}$

11. $\frac{-45}{z} = -9$

Homework Exercises

For more exercises, see Extra Skills and Word Problems.

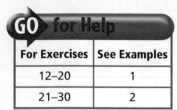

For Exercises	See Examples
12–20	1
21–30	2

Solve each equation. Check the solution.

12. $\frac{d}{10} = 34$

13. $\frac{x}{5} = -1$

14. $-17 = \frac{w}{9}$

15. $-52 = \frac{a}{-11}$

16. $\frac{h}{-9} = 3$

17. $\frac{k}{-7} = 5$

18. $-1.4 = \frac{g}{7}$

19. $2.5 = \frac{c}{24}$

20. $\frac{m}{-3.25} = -8$

21. $-6y = -30$

22. $4t = 432$

23. $3w = -99$

24. $-2p = 1$

25. $-24k = 144$

26. $20b = -460$

27. $-16 = -8d$

28. $112h = 336$

29. $-85 = 17j$

30. **Surveys** In a survey, 124 students reported they do community service. This is four times as many as those who reported they are in the band. How many of the students surveyed are in the band?

31. **Guided Problem Solving** A bicycle has 44 teeth on the front gear. This is four times the number of teeth on the rear gear. Write and solve an equation to find the number of teeth on the rear gear.
    - Translate the words into an equation.
       Words: four times __?__ equals __?__
       Equation: $4 \cdot \blacksquare = \blacksquare$

32. **Animals** A zoo has six adult tigers. Their caretaker orders a total of 40.8 kilograms of meat for them each day. Each tiger receives the same amount. How much meat does a single tiger eat in a week?

40 Chapter 1 Integers and Algebraic Expressions

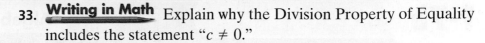

GO Online
Homework Video Tutor
For:PHSchool.com
Web Code: ase-0107

33. <u>Writing in Math</u> Explain why the Division Property of Equality includes the statement "$c \neq 0$."

34. a. Open-Ended Write an equation that you can solve using the Multiplication Property of Equality.
   b. Describe a real-world situation that you can solve using the equation you wrote in part (a).

Savings Use the picture at the left for Exercises 35 and 36.

$48.00

35. You plan to buy the bodyboard nine weeks from now. How much money must you save per week?

36. Your friend saves $12 per week. How many weeks will it take your friend to save enough to buy the bodyboard?

Solve each equation.

37. $-1 = \frac{-b}{7}$ **38.** $-p = 29.16$ **39.** $0.4f = 300$ **40.** $-8.1 = \frac{r}{-5.2}$

41. Choose a Method Your class sold raffle tickets. Out of every 15 tickets, 14 tickets did not win. There were 24 winners. How many tickets were sold? Explain why you chose the method you used.

42. Challenge Twice as many students go to the park than to the theater. Five more students go to the theater than to the museum. If 16 students go to the park, how many students go to the museum?

Test Prep and Mixed Review   **Practice**

Multiple Choice

43. A woodcarver made a model of a chair. The equation $0.08h = 3$ can be used to find the actual height h of the chair in inches. What was the actual height of the chair?
   Ⓐ 0.24 in.   Ⓑ 3.75 in.   Ⓒ 24 in.   Ⓓ 37.5 in.

44. Holly is simplifying the expression $-39 + 1.5(-24)$ to estimate the wind chill when the air temperature is $-24°F$ and the wind speed is 20 miles per hour. What should she do first?
   Ⓕ Add -39 and 1.5.   Ⓗ Add -39 and -24.
   Ⓖ Subtract -24 from 1.5.   Ⓙ Multiply 1.5 and -24.

45. Brian has four fewer than twice as many sports cards as Miles, who has c cards. Write an expression for the number of Brian's cards.
   Ⓐ $2c - 4$ Ⓑ $4c + 2$ Ⓒ $-4 - 2c$ Ⓓ $4 - 2c$

GO for Help

For Exercises	See Lesson
46–48	1-5

Use mental math to simplify each expression.

46. $5(0.98)$ **47.** $7(1.2)$ **48.** $3.1(9)$

The Cover-Up Method

You can use the cover-up method to solve some equations. Number sense is involved.

EXAMPLES

1 Solve $6x = -48$.

$6\blacksquare = -48$ ← **Cover up x. Ask, "What number times 6 is −48?"**

$\blacksquare = -8$ ← **6 × 8 is 48, so 6 × (−8) = −48.**

The answer is −8.

2 Solve $y - 4\frac{1}{2} = 20\frac{1}{2}$.

$\blacksquare - 4\frac{1}{2} = 20\frac{1}{2}$ ← **Cover up y. Ask, "What number, less $4\frac{1}{2}$, is $20\frac{1}{2}$?"**

$\blacksquare = 25$ ← **Use mental math. $25 - 4\frac{1}{2} = 20\frac{1}{2}$.**

The answer is 25.

Exercises

Solve each equation using the cover-up method or paper and pencil. Explain why you chose the method you used.

1. $\frac{x}{3} = 40$

2. $x + 11 = 71$

3. $y - 45 = 110$

4. $25x = 175$

5. $\frac{y}{2} = 62$

6. $y - 17\frac{1}{2} = 33\frac{1}{2}$

7. $x + 29\frac{1}{2} = 89\frac{1}{2}$

8. $y - 1.7 = 1.3$

9. $0.5x = 3.5$

10. $15x = 225$

11. Error Analysis Aimee says that the solution to the equation $x + 43 = 103$ is 146. Ivan says that the solution is 60. Explain how you know who is correct without solving the equation.

12. A homeowner enlarged the fenced-in area of a yard to be a square 10 ft by 10 ft. The length of the new fenced-in area is twice that of the original square. Write and solve an equation to find the area of the original fenced-in area.

Writing Gridded Responses

Some test questions have answers with gridded responses. To answer these questions, first find a numerical answer. Then write your answer at the top of the grid. Fill in the corresponding bubbles.

EXAMPLE

Chad walks his dog the same distance every week. If he walks his dog a total of 42 miles in 8 weeks, how many miles does he walk each week? Record your answer and fill in the bubbles. Be sure to use the correct place value.

The answer is $\frac{42}{8}$. You can grid this as $\frac{42}{8}$, $\frac{21}{4}$ or 5.25.

Exercises

Find each answer. If you have a grid, record your answer and fill in the bubbles. Be sure to use the correct place value.

1. A play is 90 minutes long. There is a 15-minute intermission. How many hours should you plan to be at the theater?

2. Megan rides her bike to work. She bikes 3.2 miles to work, 1.3 miles to a coffee shop, 2.7 miles to the library, and then 3.6 miles home. How many miles does Megan bike?

3. At a movie theater, tickets cost $9 each and parking costs $4. The expression $9t + 4$ models the cost of going to the movies, where t represents the number of movie tickets. In dollars, how much would it cost you and three friends to go to the movies in one car?

4. You have $11.27. You want to buy a book that costs $14.95. In dollars, how much money do you need to save before you can buy the book?

Vocabulary Review

🔊 absolute value (p. 10)
Addition Property of Equality (p. 33)
additive inverses (p. 16)
algebraic expression (p. 4)
Associative Property of Addition (p. 26)
Associative Property of Multiplication (p. 26)
Commutative Property of Addition (p. 26)

Commutative Property of Multiplication (p. 26)
Distributive Property (p. 28)
Division Property of Equality (p. 38)
equation (p. 33)
evaluate (p. 5)
Identity Property of Addition (p. 26)
Identity Property of Multiplication (p. 26)
integers (p. 10)

inverse operations (p. 21)
isolate (p. 34)
Multiplication Property of Equality (p. 38)
opposites (p. 10)
order of operations (p. 5)
simplify (p. 5)
solution (p. 34)
Subtraction Property of Equality (p. 33)
variable (p. 4)

Go Online
PHSchool.com
For: Online Vocabulary Quiz
Web Code: asj-0151

Choose the correct term to complete each sentence.

1. You ___?___ $4 + 4 \cdot 2$ as 12.

2. The ___?___ of a number is its distance from zero on a number line.

3. The statement $5(a + 6) = 5a + 30$ shows the ___?___.

4. A value that makes an equation true is a(n) ___?___.

5. Use ___?___ to isolate a variable in an equation.

6. A(n) ___?___ is a symbol that stands for one or more numbers.

7. The set of whole numbers and their opposites are ___?___.

8. A mathematical sentence with an equal sign is a(n) ___?___.

Skills and Concepts

Lesson 1-1

• To write algebraic expressions and evaluate them using the order of operations

To **simplify** a numerical expression, use the **order of operations.** To **evaluate** an **algebraic expression,** replace each variable with a number and then simplify.

Evaluate each expression for $x = 2$.

9. $6(x - 1)$ 10. $-42 \div x + 5.5$ 11. $-42 \div (x + 5.5)$

Write an algebraic expression for each word phrase.

12. the sum of 27 and a number g

13. the quotient of a number y and 4

14. the number of pages in r reams of paper if each ream has 500 pages

Lesson 1-2

- To find the absolute values of integers and to use absolute value to compare integers

Integers are the set of whole numbers, their **opposites,** and zero. The **absolute value** of a number is its distance from zero on the number line.

Compare. Write $<$, $>$, or $=$.

15. -18 ▉ -11 **16.** -37 ▉ 2 **17.** $|-34|$ ▉ 21 **18.** $|-4|$ ▉ $|4|$

19. The lowest recorded temperature in Australia was $-9°$F. The lowest recorded temperature in North America was $-81°$F. Which continent has the lower recorded temperature?

Lessons 1-3, 1-4

- To add and subtract integers and to solve problems involving integers
- To multiply and divide integers and to solve problems involving integers

Two numbers are **additive inverses** if their sum is zero. The sum of two positive numbers is positive. The sum of two negative integers is negative.

The product or quotient of two integers with the same sign is positive. The product or quotient of two integers with different signs is negative.

Simplify each expression.

20. $-9 + (-3)$ **21.** $-11 - (-5)$ **22.** $-34 \div (-2)$

23. $4(-10)$ **24.** $-5 - 2$ **25.** $39 \div (-3)$

26. Kai has \$315 in her bank account. She withdraws \$65 for a new jacket and another \$13 for lunch with her friends. She deposits \$26. What is the balance in Kai's account?

Lesson 1-5

- To identify the properties of numbers and use the properties to solve problems

You can use the commutative, associative, identity, and distributive properties to simplify an expression.

Mental Math Use mental math to simplify each expression.

27. $(-5)(168)(20)$ **28.** $125 + 394 + 575$ **29.** $4(-18)(25)$

Find each product.

30. $3(p - 7)$ **31.** $(m + 4)8$ **32.** $-5(-2 - k)$

Lessons 1-6, 1-7

- To write and solve equations using addition and subtraction
- To write and solve equations using multiplication and division

A value of the variable that makes an **equation** true is a **solution.** You can solve an equation using **inverse operations** and the properties of equality to **isolate** the variable.

Solve each equation. Check the solution.

33. $d - 7 = 23$ **34.** $6 = r + 3$ **35.** $8 = -3 + a$

36. $7p = 49$ **37.** $\frac{h}{-4} = -12$ **38.** $\frac{z}{5} = 0.4$

Write an algebraic expression for each word phrase.

1. the sum of a number v and 18

2. the number of miles a motorcycle gets per gallon if you use g gallons to travel 462 miles

3. the number of years equal to d days

4. the number of seconds equal to m minutes

Simplify each expression.

5. $6 + 3 \cdot 5$

6. $18 \div (3 \cdot 2) + 3$

7. $(10 + 14) \div 4 \cdot 2$

8. $5 - (8 + 6 \div 2)$

9. $9 - 5 + 2 \cdot 4$

10. $5 \div (1 + 4) \cdot 6$

11. Find the value of each expression for the given values of b in the table at the right.

b	$b + 7$
8	■
12	■
20	■

Evaluate each expression for the given value.

12. $|c|$ for $c = -15$

13. $5 + |h|$ for $h = 8$

14. $-|3v|$ for $v = -7$

15. $6 - |-t|$ for $t = 9$

16. $4|y|$ for $y = -3$

17. $|5f|$ for $f = 16$

Simplify each expression.

18. $-14 + 60$

19. $7 - 24$

20. $\dfrac{-15}{5}$

21. $-4 \cdot 3$

22. $-9(-8)$

23. $(-2)(-2)(-2)$

24. **Football** A football team gained 6 yd on a play. On the next play, the team lost 9 yd. What is the net yardage for the team?

Order the integers in each set from least to greatest.

25. $-2, 0, 3, -4, -9$

26. $-17, -14, 8, -13$

27. $4, -3, -10, -7, -1$

28. $-21, 22, -17, 5, 2$

Evaluate each expression for $m = -4$ and $p = 2$.

29. $mp - 5p$

30. $(4p - m) \div 4$

31. $\dfrac{p - m + 3}{5}$

32. $m + p \cdot (-7)$

33. **Writing in Math** Explain how positive and negative integers can be used to describe changes in depth.

Identify each property.

34. $3(ck) = (3c)k$

35. $j = j \cdot 1$

36. $-7 + 5 = 5 + (-7)$

37. $(x + 5)2 = x \cdot 2 + 5 \cdot 2$

Mental Math Use mental math to simplify each expression.

38. $30(12)$

39. $6 \cdot 32$

40. $4(8.8)$

Solve each equation.

41. $m - 45 = 10$

42. $\dfrac{a}{-2} = 2.5$

43. $3h = -18$

44. $x + 4 = -1.2$

45. $w + 7 = 18$

46. $2 + y = -7$

47. **Hiking** A hiker begins a hike in Death Valley National Park at the park's lowest point. She climbs 11,331 feet to the park's highest point, 11,049 feet above sea level. Find the elevation of Death Valley's lowest point.

48. A store sells bicycles for $250 each. In one week the store had $1,250 in bicycle sales. How many bicycles did the store sell?

49. Write an addition expression modeled by the number line below.

Reading Comprehension

Read each passage and answer the questions that follow.

Moore Power Computers keep getting more and more powerful; not long after you buy one, there is likely to be a more powerful model available for the same price. A "law" called Moore's Law was created to express this trend. It says the amount of computer power you can buy for a fixed price will double about every 18 months. This law has been remarkably accurate for more than 35 years, and most computer experts think it will continue to hold for several decades more.

1. Suppose you have $750 to spend on a computer. According to Moore's Law, about how much more powerful a computer will you be able to buy for the amount if you wait $1\frac{1}{2}$ years to make your purchase?
   - (A) 1.5 times
   - (B) 2 times
   - (C) 3 times
   - (D) 18 times

2. About how much more powerful are computers that sell for $1,000 today than those that sold for $1,000 only 3 years ago?
   - (F) 2 times
   - (G) 3 times
   - (H) 4 times
   - (J) 6 times

3. If Moore's Law continues to hold, about how much more powerful will computers be in around $4\frac{1}{2}$ years?
   - (A) 4 times
   - (B) 6 times
   - (C) 8 times
   - (D) 16 times

4. According to Moore's Law, how long will it take before computers are 128 times as powerful as they are today?
   - (F) 7 years
   - (G) 10.5 years
   - (H) 12 years
   - (J) 25 years

Perfect 10 The Pythagorean Greeks were fascinated by properties of numbers. They discovered that some numbers were equal to the sum of their lesser whole-number divisors. They called these numbers "perfect." For example, 6 is a perfect number because its divisors less than 6 are 1, 2, and 3, which add up to 6. The number 8 is "deficient" because the sum of its lesser divisors (1 + 2 + 4) is less than the number itself. The number 12 is "abundant" because the sum of its lesser divisors (1 + 2 + 3 + 4 + 6) is greater than it is.

5. According to the article, which number is a deficient number?
   - (A) 15
   - (B) 20
   - (C) 36
   - (D) 48

6. According to the article, the number 18 is
   - (F) abundant.
   - (G) deficient.
   - (H) divisible.
   - (J) perfect.

7. What is the sum of the divisors of 28?
   - (A) 24
   - (B) 27
   - (C) 28
   - (D) 32

8. According to the article, which number is an abundant number?
   - (F) 9
   - (G) 16
   - (H) 32
   - (J) 40

Applying Integers

Treasure Hunt For centuries, explorers used a compass and a sextant to plot expeditions. Today, global positioning system (GPS) satellites find locations accurately, even when the sun or stars are not visible. On Earth's surface, two coordinates define a position. In the air or the oceans, a third coordinate, elevation above or below Earth's surface, joins the first two.

What's Up There?

Space near Earth contains meteoroids and man-made debris traveling at speeds of about 17,000 mi/h. At that speed, even tiny particles can cause damage.

Global Positions

GPS satellites orbit 12,660 mi above Earth. Coordinating signals from three satellites can tell your position on or above Earth to within about 300 ft.

Half Rocket, Half Airplane

At lift-off, the space shuttle weighs about 4.5 million lb. When it lands, it weighs only about 230,000 lb.

Go Online
PHSchool.com
For: Information about navigation
Web Code: ase-0153

NAUTILE

Submersible Vehicles

Although the ocean is about 36,000 ft deep at its deepest point, a submersible designed to operate at 20,000 ft can reach 98% of the ocean floor.

Sound Detection

Submarines determine the depth of the ocean beneath them by bouncing sound waves off the ocean floor and analyzing the echoes.

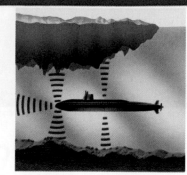

Put It All Together

Materials graph paper

Suppose you are navigating a treasure-hunting submarine. The sub starts on the ocean surface outside a cave (point *A*). Plot a course through the cave to the treasure, marked with an *X*.

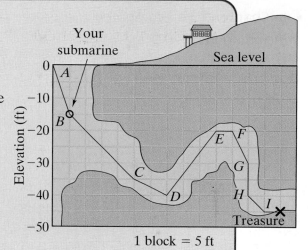

1 block = 5 ft

1. The Navigation Instruction Sheet shows how to get from point *A* to point *B*.

   a. Why are the entries for the initial horizontal and vertical positions each 0?

   b. Why is the horizontal change a positive number while the vertical change is a negative number?

2. Use the map. Follow the style of the Navigation Instruction Sheet to write instructions to reach the treasure.

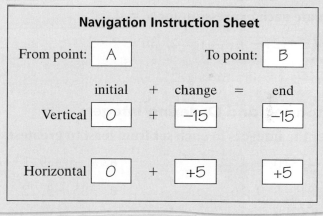

Navigation Instruction Sheet				
From point:	A		To point:	B
	initial	+ change	=	end
Vertical	0	+ −15		−15
Horizontal	0	+ +5		+5

3. a. **Open-Ended** Draw an underwater cave on a piece of graph paper and put a treasure somewhere inside it. Make sure that a sub can reach the treasure in eight moves or less.

   b. Draw a course that the sub could follow to reach the treasure. Write a set of instructions for the course.

   c. **Writing in Math** Exchange instructions with a classmate. Follow your classmate's instructions on a blank grid. When you finish, check your work with your classmate. Did you find the treasure? Explain.

What You've Learned

- In a previous course, you solved problems involving fractions.
- In Chapter 1, you compared and ordered rational numbers, including integers.
- You used addition, subtraction, multiplication, and division to solve problems involving integers.

Check Your Readiness

GO for Help	
For Exercises	**See Lessons**
1–4	1-1
5–8	1-2
9–12	1-3
13–16	1-4

Evaluating Algebraic Expressions

Evaluate each expression for $n = 4$.

1. $3(n + 2) - n$ **2.** $3n + 2 \cdot 5$

3. $\dfrac{3}{n + 2} \cdot n$ **4.** $\dfrac{3 + 5}{n}$

Comparing and Ordering Integers

Order the integers in each set from least to greatest.

5. $-4, 3, 0, -11$ **6.** $8, -6, -9, 13$

7. $-21, -8, 9, 16$ **8.** $-35, -3, 22, -17$

Adding and Subtracting Integers

Simplify each expression.

9. $-5 + 8$ **10.** $16 - 29$ **11.** $-23 + (-14)$ **12.** $-36 - (-11)$

Multiplying and Dividing Integers

Simplify each expression.

13. $4 \cdot (-12)$ **14.** $\dfrac{-54}{9}$ **15.** $-7 \cdot 2 \cdot (-3)$ **16.** $\dfrac{-108}{-12}$

What You'll Learn Next

- In this chapter, you will compare and order rational numbers, including positive and negative fractions and decimals.

- You will use addition, subtraction, multiplication, and division to solve problems involving rational numbers.

- You will write and use numbers with exponents, including numbers in scientific notation.

 Problem Solving Application On pages 102 and 103, you will work an extended activity on frequency.

◀)) Key Vocabulary

- base (p. 86)
- composite number (p. 52)
- divisible (p. 52)
- exponent (p. 86)
- factor (p. 52)
- formula (p. 81)
- greatest common factor (p. 53)
- least common denominator (p. 62)
- least common multiple (p. 62)
- multiplicative inverse (p. 73)
- power (p. 86)
- prime factorization (p. 53)
- prime number (p. 52)
- rational number (p. 57)
- reciprocals (p. 73)
- relatively prime (p. 57)
- scientific notation (p. 92)

Check Skills You'll Need

1. **Vocabulary Review**
   When you multiply two numbers, the result is called the __?__.

Simplify each expression.

2. −10(10)   3. −8(−7)

4. 5(−4)(−2)

5. −1 · 1 · 0

 **for Help**
Lesson 1-4

What You'll Learn

To identify prime and composite numbers and to find the greatest common factor

🔊 **New Vocabulary** divisible, factor, prime number, composite number, prime factorization, greatest common factor (GCF)

Why Learn This?

Sometimes you want to arrange items or people in groups. You can use factors to help you find the size of each group.

A number is **divisible** by a second number if the number can be divided by the second number with a remainder of 0. You can use divisibility tests to see if one number is divisible by another.

Divisible by	Divisibility Test
2	The ones digit is 0, 2, 4, 6, or 8.
3	The sum of the digits is divisible by 3.
4	The last two digits are divisible by 4.
5	The ones digit is 0 or 5.
9	The sum of the digits is divisible by 9.
10	The ones digit is 0.

An integer that divides another integer with a remainder of 0 is a **factor.** A **prime number** is a whole number greater than 1 with exactly two factors, 1 and the number itself. A **composite number** is a whole number greater than 1 with more than two factors. The number 1 is neither prime nor composite.

EXAMPLE   Prime and Composite Numbers

1 Identify 2,727 as prime or composite. Explain.

The sum of the digits is 18, which is divisible by 3. Since 2,727 is divisible by 3, it is composite.

✓ Quick Check

1. Identify 15,482 as *prime* or *composite.* Explain.

A composite number written as a product of prime numbers is the **prime factorization** of the number. There is only one prime factorization for a number, regardless of the order of the factors. For example, the prime factorization 2 · 3 is the same as 3 · 2.

You can use divisibility tests and a factor tree to find the prime factorization of a number.

EXAMPLE Finding Prime Factorization

2 Use a factor tree to find the prime factorization of 54.

The number 54 is divisible by 2 because it is an even number. Begin the factor tree with 2 · 27.

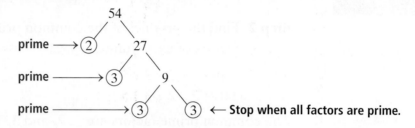

The prime factorization of 54 is 2 · 3 · 3 · 3.

✓ Quick Check

2. Use a factor tree to find the prime factorization of each number.
   a. 96 **b.** 240

The **greatest common factor (GCF)** of two or more numbers is the greatest number that is a factor of all of the numbers. You can list factors to find the GCF of two numbers.

EXAMPLE Finding the GCF by Listing

3 Find the GCF of 42 and 36.

Begin by finding the factors of 42 and 36.

42: 1, 2, 3, 6, 7, 14, 21, 42

36: 1, 2, 3, 4, 6, 9, 12, 18, 36

The factors 1, 2, 3, and 6 are common to both numbers. So the GCF of 42 and 36 is 6.

✓ Quick Check

3. Find the GCF of each pair of numbers by listing their factors.
   a. 54, 63 **b.** 18, 42

You can also use prime factorization to find the GCF of two numbers.

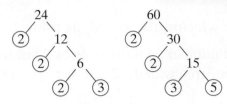

EXAMPLE **Finding the GCF with Prime Factorization**

4 **Gridded Response** A parade director wants two bands to have the same number of people in every row. One band has 24 members. The other has 60. What is the greatest possible number of people in a row?

Step 1 Find the prime factorization of each number.

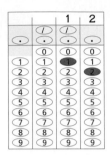

Step 2 Find the product of the common prime factors of each number.

$$24 = 2 \cdot 2 \cdot 2 \cdot 3$$
$$60 = 2 \cdot 2 \cdot 3 \cdot 5$$

The common prime factors are 2, 2, and 3. The GCF of 24 and 60 is $2 \cdot 2 \cdot 3 = 12$.

Test Prep Tip

Remember, whole numbers go to the left of the decimal point when writing your answer in the grid.

✓ **Quick Check**

4. Two pipes have lengths 63 ft and 84 ft. You cut them into pieces of equal length with nothing left over. What is the greatest possible length of the pieces?

✓ **Check Your Understanding**

1. **Vocabulary** The greatest number that is a factor of two or more numbers is the __?__ of the numbers.

2. Find the factors of 54.

Is the first number divisible by the second? Explain.

3. 105; 2   4. 91; 5   5. 123; 3

6. **Error Analysis** Whose work is correct? Explain.

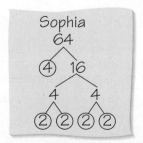

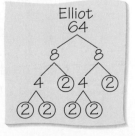

For more exercises, see Extra Skills and Word Problems.

GO for Help	
For Exercises	**See Examples**
7–14	1
15–22	2
23–30	3
31–39	4

Identify each number as *prime* or *composite*. Explain.

7. 48 **8.** 25 **9.** 73 **10.** 79

11. 99 **12.** 250 **13.** 101 **14.** 1011

Use a factor tree to find the prime factorization of each number.

15. 20 **16.** 12 **17.** 16 **18.** 400

19. 27 **20.** 26 **21.** 56 **22.** 39

Find the GCF of each pair of numbers by listing their factors.

23. 6, 18 **24.** 15, 54 **25.** 42, 72 **26.** 21, 63

27. 52, 78 **28.** 38, 82 **29.** 44, 68 **30.** 30, 50

Use prime factorization to find the GCF of each pair of numbers.

31. 14, 35 **32.** 27, 36 **33.** 30, 45 **34.** 32, 48

35. 44, 66 **36.** 62, 93 **37.** 86, 94 **38.** 57, 76

39. Students are cleaning a local park in groups. There are 50 boys and 75 girls. Each group has the same number of boys and the same number of girls. What is the greatest possible number of groups?

GPS **40. Guided Problem Solving** You are dividing a community garden 35 m long by 15 m wide into equal-sized square gardens. Find the greatest possible dimensions of each square.
- **Make a Plan** Draw a picture to help you visualize the problem. Then find the GCF.
- **Carry Out the Plan** The GCF is ■. The largest possible dimensions of each square are ■ m by ■ m.

41. The cafeteria has 144 bananas, 36 pears, and 72 apples. Each student gets the same number of pieces of each fruit. What is the greatest number of students who can receive fruit?

42. Reasoning Use factor trees starting with 6 · 16 and 8 · 12 to find the prime factorization of 96. Explain why the prime factorization of 96 is the same for both factor trees.

43. Performances The 48 members of a chorus will sit in rows in front of the 300 members of the audience. All the rows have the same number of chairs. What is the greatest possible number of chairs in each row?

Find the GCF.

44. 22, 33, 44   **45.** 27, 45, −81   **46.** 12, −24, 36

47. In 1742, the mathematician Christian Goldbach made a conjecture that every even number greater than 2 can be expressed as the sum of two prime numbers. Write the number 60 as the sum of two prime numbers.

48. **Art** The art teacher hands out her entire inventory of art supplies, listed at the right. Each class gets the same number of each item.
 a. How many classes receive supplies?
 b. How many of each item does each class get?

paintbrushes	120
boxes of markers	78
packs of paper	24
sets of watercolors	54

49. **Reasoning** If w is divisible by 2, what can you conclude about the factors of $w + 2$?

50. **Writing in Math** What is the GCF of any two prime numbers? Explain.

51. ⟨**Algebra**⟩ Show that the expression $-x^2 + 7x + 7$ is a prime number when $x = 0$, $x = 2$, and $x = 3$.

52. **Challenge** What is the least number that has exactly five factors? List the factors.

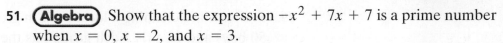

Test Prep and Mixed Review
Practice

Gridded Response

53. Max bought $2\frac{1}{2}$ ft of ribbon. He used 18 in. to wrap a gift. How many feet of ribbon did he have left?

54. The amount c Jeff spends on juice and muffins during the week can be found using the equation $c = 5(1.25) + x(1.45)$, where x represents the number of muffins Jeff ate during the week. Find the total cost, in dollars, for a week in which Jeff ate 3 muffins.

55. On Rita's science test, the first 10 questions were worth 3 points each, the next 6 questions were worth 4 points each, and the last 4 questions were worth 5 points each. If Rita answered each question correctly, how many points did she score on the test?

For Exercises	See Lesson
56–58	1-5

Choose a Method Use paper and pencil, number lines, or mental math to simplify each expression.

56. 3.4 + 5.6 + 8.3   **57.** 6 · −7 · 5   **58.** 12(8.1)

2-2 Equivalent Forms of Rational Numbers

Check Skills You'll Need

1. **Vocabulary Review** Write the *prime factorization* of 100.

Find the GCF of each pair of numbers.

2. 6, 12   3. 8, 12

4. 25, 50   5. 36, 40

GO for Help
Lesson 2-1

What You'll Learn

To write equivalent fractions and decimals

🔊 **New Vocabulary** rational number, relatively prime, terminating decimal, repeating decimal

Why Learn This?

The baseball standings at the right use both decimals and fractions. Decimals and fractions are rational numbers.

A **rational number** is a number that can be written in the form $\frac{a}{b}$, where a is an integer and b is any nonzero integer. Two integers a and b are **relatively prime** if 1 is their only common factor. A fraction $\frac{a}{b}$ is in simplest form when a and b are relatively prime.

Team Standings			
	W	**L**	**PCT**	**GB**
Houston	24	14	.632	—
St. Louis	19	19	.500	5
Milwaukee	17	20	.459	$6\frac{1}{2}$
Chicago	17	20	.459	$6\frac{1}{2}$
Pittsburgh	15	23	.395	9
Cincinnati	14	25	.359	$10\frac{1}{2}$

EXAMPLES Simplifying a Fraction

1 Write $\frac{36}{40}$ in simplest form using the GCF.

The GCF of 36 and 40 is 4.

$$\frac{36}{40} = \frac{36 \div 4}{40 \div 4} \quad \leftarrow \text{Divide the numerator and denominator by the GCF.}$$

$$= \frac{9}{10} \quad \leftarrow \text{Simplify.}$$

2 Write $\frac{54}{60}$ in simplest form using prime factorization.

$$\frac{54}{60} = \frac{2 \cdot 3 \cdot 3 \cdot 3}{2 \cdot 2 \cdot 3 \cdot 5} \quad \leftarrow \begin{array}{l}\text{Write the prime factorizations of the}\\\text{numerator and denominator.}\end{array}$$

$$= \frac{\overset{1}{\cancel{2}} \cdot 3 \cdot \overset{1}{\cancel{3}} \cdot 3}{\underset{1}{\cancel{2}} \cdot 2 \cdot \underset{1}{\cancel{3}} \cdot 5} \quad \leftarrow \text{Divide the common factors.}$$

$$= \frac{9}{10} \quad \leftarrow \text{Simplify.}$$

✓ Quick Check

1. Write $\frac{12}{20}$ in simplest form using the GCF.

2. Write $\frac{27}{45}$ in simplest form using prime factorization.

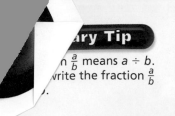
You can represent a rational number as a fraction. You can write a fraction as a decimal by dividing the numerator by the denominator.

If the division results in a decimal that stops, the decimal is called a <mark>terminating decimal.</mark> If the division results in a decimal that repeats the same digit or group of digits forever, the decimal is a <mark>repeating decimal.</mark> A bar indicates the repeating digits. So $0.\overline{3} = 0.3333\ldots$

EXAMPLE Writing an Equivalent Decimal

③ Baseball In baseball, a player's batting average is $\frac{\text{number of hits}}{\text{number of times at bat}}$. A batting average is rounded to three decimal places and is written without the leading 0.

a. Find the batting average of a hitter with 36 hits in 125 times at bat.

$\dfrac{36}{125}$ ← Write the batting average as a fraction.

0.288 ← Divide. This is a terminating decimal.

The player's batting average is .288.

b. Find the batting average of a hitter with 27 hits in 99 times at bat.

$\dfrac{27}{99}$ ← Write the batting average as a fraction.

$0.27272727\ldots = 0.\overline{27}$ ← Divide. This is a repeating decimal.

The player's batting average is about .273.

✓ Quick Check

3. Find the batting average of a hitter with 39 hits in 85 times at bat.

You can write a terminating decimal as a fraction by multiplying both the numerator and the denominator by the same power of 10.

EXAMPLE Writing an Equivalent Fraction

④ Write 1.345 as a mixed number in simplest form.

$1.345 = \dfrac{1.345}{1}$ ← Write as a fraction with the denominator 1.

$= \dfrac{1,345}{1,000}$ ← Since there are 3 digits to the right of the decimal, multiply the numerator and the denominator by 1,000.

$= \dfrac{1,345 \div 5}{1,000 \div 5}$ ← Divide the numerator and the denominator by the GCF, 5.

$= \dfrac{269}{200} = 1\dfrac{69}{200}$ ← Simplify. Write as a mixed number.

✓ Quick Check

4. Write 1.42 as a mixed number in simplest form.

1. **Vocabulary** Since 123 is a rational number, it can be written in the form $\frac{123}{\blacksquare}$.

2. **Number Sense** A player has 15 hits in 34 times at bat and then gets another hit. Did the batting average increase? Explain.

Match each fraction with its equivalent decimal.

3. $\frac{1}{4}$

4. $\frac{3}{10}$

5. $\frac{1}{2}$

6. $\frac{2}{5}$

A. 0.5
B. 0.4
C. 0.3
D. 0.25

Homework Exercises

For more exercises, see Extra Skills and Word Problems.

GO for Help

For Exercises	See Examples
7–14	1 and 2
15–23	3
24–31	4

Write each fraction in simplest form.

7. $\frac{15}{20}$

8. $\frac{48}{64}$

9. $-\frac{40}{60}$

10. $-\frac{12}{54}$

11. $\frac{20}{100}$

12. $\frac{18}{81}$

13. $-\frac{4}{14}$

14. $\frac{12}{60}$

Write each fraction as a decimal. Round to three decimal places.

15. $\frac{2}{3}$

16. $\frac{8}{25}$

17. $\frac{17}{16}$

18. $\frac{16}{17}$

19. $-\frac{13}{7}$

20. $\frac{9}{45}$

21. $\frac{5}{13}$

22. $-\frac{28}{35}$

23. **Sports** A baseball player has 34 hits in 102 times at bat. Another baseball player has 24 hits in 96 times at bat. Write each player's batting average.

Write each decimal as a mixed number or fraction in simplest form.

24. 1.4

25. 0.33

26. 0.24

27. 4.44

28. 2.8

29. 0.05

30. 0.005

31. 7.32

32. **Guided Problem Solving** At a chili festival over the past few years, Restaurant A won 56 out of 98 contests. Restaurant B won 84 out of 147 contests. Which restaurant has the better record?
   • What fraction represents the wins for Restaurant A?
   • What fraction represents the wins for Restaurant B?

33. **Population** In 2003, 0.219 of the people in the United States were younger than 15 years old. Write the decimal as a fraction.

34. The circle graph at the right shows the sizes of American households. Write a decimal for the fraction of households in each category.

35. **(Algebra)** Evaluate $\frac{1+a}{2b}$ for $a = 3$ and $b = -5$. Write your answer in simplest form.

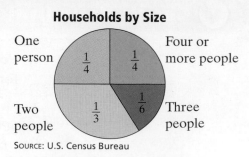

Households by Size

One person — $\frac{1}{4}$

Four or more people — $\frac{1}{4}$

Two people — $\frac{1}{3}$

Three people — $\frac{1}{6}$

SOURCE: U.S. Census Bureau

Math in the Media Refer to the cartoon below.

36. If Leroy Lockhorn missed one of Loretta Lockhorn's birthdays in 25 years, what would his "batting average" be?

37. **Writing in Math** Explain why, in 25 years of marriage, Leroy Lockhorn could never have a "batting average" of .980.

THE LOCKHORNS

"SO I MISSED ONE OF YOUR BIRTHDAYS IN 25 YEARS OF MARRIAGE. WHAT'S WRONG WITH A .980 BATTING AVERAGE?"

38. **Challenge** The number 77 is what fractional part of 7,777?

Test Prep and Mixed Review

Practice

Multiple Choice

39. Tyler reads for 3 hours each day. There are 24 hours in a day. What fraction of each day does he spend reading?

- Ⓐ $\frac{1}{8}$
- Ⓑ $\frac{1}{21}$
- Ⓒ $\frac{1}{27}$
- Ⓓ $\frac{1}{72}$

40. Which list shows the numbers in order from least to greatest?

- Ⓕ $1, 5, -11, -3$
- Ⓗ $-3, -11, 1, 5$
- Ⓖ $1, -3, 5, -11$
- Ⓙ $-11, -3, 1, 5$

41. Brandon simplified an expression as shown below.

$$4 + 16 \div 4 \times 2 - 6 \times 2 - 1$$

Step 1: $4 + 16 \div 8 - 6 \times 2 - 1$
Step 2: $4 + 16 \div 8 - 6 \times 1$
Step 3: $4 + 16 \div 8 - 6$
Step 4: $4 + 2 - 6$
Step 5: 0

In which step did Brandon make his first mistake?

- Ⓐ Step 1
- Ⓑ Step 2
- Ⓒ Step 3
- Ⓓ Step 4

GO for Help

For Exercises	See Lesson
42–45	1-3

Simplify each expression.

42. $-19 + (-6)$ **43.** $-11 + 20$ **44.** $-25 - 25$ **45.** $19 - (-15)$

Repeating Decimals

In Lesson 2-2, you learned how to write a terminating decimal as a fraction. You use algebra to write a repeating decimal as a fraction.

EXAMPLE Writing a Repeating Decimal as a Fraction

In a recent survey, $0.\overline{45}$ of those asked chose blue as their favorite color. Write $0.\overline{45}$ as a fraction in simplest form.

Step 1 Represent the given decimal with a variable.

$$n = 0.\overline{45}$$

Step 2 Multiply by 10^n, where $n =$ the number of digits that repeat. In this case, multiply by 10^2, or 100, because the repeating part of the decimal is 45.

$$100n = 45.\overline{45}$$

Step 3 Subtract to eliminate the repeating part.

$$
\begin{aligned}
100n &= 45.454545\ldots \\
-n &= -0.454545\ldots \quad \leftarrow \text{Use the Subtraction Property of Equality.} \\
99n &= 45.000000\ldots \quad \leftarrow \text{Simplify.} \\
99n &= 45
\end{aligned}
$$

Step 4 Solve the new equation.

$$\frac{99n}{99} = \frac{45}{99} \quad \leftarrow \text{Divide each side by 99.}$$

$$n = \frac{45}{99} = \frac{5}{11} \quad \leftarrow \text{Simplify using the GCF, 9.}$$

The repeating decimal $0.\overline{45}$ equals $\frac{5}{11}$.

Exercises

Write each repeating decimal as a fraction in simplest form.

1. $0.\overline{5}$
2. $0.\overline{7}$
3. $0.\overline{24}$
4. $0.\overline{15}$
5. $0.\overline{135}$
6. $0.\overline{282}$

7. **Writing in Math** Explain why a repeating decimal is a rational number. Justify your answer with an example.

Comparing and Ordering Rational Numbers

✓ Check Skills You'll Need

1. **Vocabulary Review** Explain what the *numerator* of a fraction represents.

Use the GCF to write each fraction in simplest form.

2. $\frac{12}{20}$ 3. $\frac{15}{55}$

4. $\frac{16}{64}$ 5. $\frac{50}{550}$

 **for Help**
Lesson 2-2

What You'll Learn

To use least common denominators, decimals, and number lines to compare and order rational numbers

🔊 **New Vocabulary** least common multiple (LCM), least common denominator (LCD)

Why Learn This?

When you conduct a survey or do research, you often want to analyze and compare your results. The data you collect will be in the form of rational numbers.

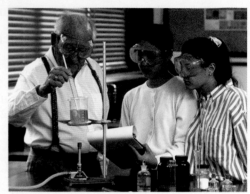

You can compare rational numbers by finding a common denominator and then comparing the numerators. A common denominator is any common multiple of two denominators.

The least common multiple (LCM) of two or more numbers is the least multiple that is common to all of the numbers. The LCM of the denominators is called the least common denominator (LCD).

EXAMPLE Comparing Using the LCD

① Which is greater, $\frac{4}{9}$ or $\frac{5}{12}$?

List multiples of each denominator to find their LCD.

Multiples of 9: 9, 18, 27, 36
Multiples of 12: 12, 24, 36

The LCM of 9 and 12 is 36. So the LCD of the fractions is 36.

$\frac{4}{9} = \frac{4 \cdot 4}{9 \cdot 4}$ ← Multiply the numerator and denominator by 4. $\frac{5}{12} = \frac{5 \cdot 3}{12 \cdot 3}$ ← Multiply the numerator and denominator by 3.

$= \frac{16}{36}$ ← Simplify. $= \frac{15}{36}$ ← Simplify.

Since $\frac{16}{36} > \frac{15}{36}$, $\frac{4}{9} > \frac{5}{12}$.

✓ Quick Check

1. Rewrite $\frac{1}{6}$ and $\frac{1}{9}$ using their LCD. Which fraction is greater?

When it is not easy to find a common denominator, you can write equivalent decimals.

EXAMPLE **Comparing Using Decimals**

Students Who Prefer Adventure Movies

School A
37 out of 58

School B
45 out of 71

② **Surveys** A random group of middle-school students from two schools was asked which types of movies they preferred. Which school had the greater fraction of students who preferred adventure movies?

Change each fraction to a decimal. Compare the decimals.

$$\left. \begin{array}{l} \text{School A: } \dfrac{37}{58} \approx 0.6379310 \\[1em] \text{School B: } \dfrac{45}{71} \approx 0.6338028 \end{array} \right\} \text{Divide. Use a calculator.}$$

Since $0.637 > 0.633$, School A had the greater fraction of students who preferred adventure movies.

✓ Quick Check

2. At the local pet store, 7 out of 10 cats are male, and 12 out of 17 dogs are male. Which animal has the greater fraction of males?

To order a set of rational numbers, write each number as a decimal.

EXAMPLE **Ordering Rational Numbers**

Online active math*

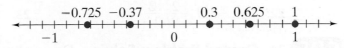

For: Rational Numbers Activity
Use: Interactive Textbook, 2-3

③ Order $\dfrac{5}{8}$, -0.37, 1, $-\dfrac{29}{40}$ and 0.3 from least to greatest.

Write each fraction as a decimal.

$$\frac{5}{8} = 0.625$$

$$-\frac{29}{40} = -0.725$$

Then graph each decimal on a number line.

The order of the points from left to right gives the order of the numbers from least to greatest.

$$-0.725 < -0.37 < 0.3 < 0.625 < 1$$

So $-\dfrac{29}{40} < -0.37 < 0.3 < \dfrac{5}{8} < 1$.

✓ Quick Check

3. Order $\dfrac{8}{5}$, $1\dfrac{1}{2}$, -0.625, $-\dfrac{7}{8}$, and 1.61 from least to greatest.

1. **Vocabulary** What is the difference between a multiple of two numbers and the LCM of two numbers?

2. Is $\frac{15}{28}$ greater or less than $\frac{1}{2}$? Justify your answer.

Determine which rational number is greater by rewriting each pair of fractions with a common denominator.

3. $\frac{2}{9}, \frac{1}{7}$

4. $\frac{5}{7}, \frac{2}{3}$

5. $\frac{3}{4}, \frac{4}{5}$

6. Which rational number is the greatest: $-\frac{5}{12}, -0.4, -\frac{1}{2}$, or $-\frac{4}{9}$?

Homework Exercises

For more exercises, see Extra Skills and Word Problems.

Determine which rational number is greater by rewriting each pair of fractions using their LCD.

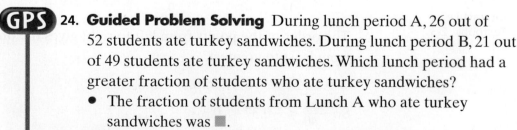

For Exercises	See Examples
7–14	1
15–19	2
20–23	3

7. $\frac{2}{15}, \frac{4}{25}$

8. $\frac{2}{5}, \frac{4}{11}$

9. $-\frac{10}{21}, -\frac{5}{14}$

10. $\frac{7}{8}, \frac{6}{7}$

11. $\frac{3}{8}, \frac{5}{12}$

12. $-\frac{6}{26}, -\frac{9}{39}$

13. $-\frac{13}{22}, -\frac{14}{33}$

14. $-\frac{9}{20}, -\frac{7}{15}$

15. **Surveys** A survey found that 13 out of 108 men and 23 out of 233 women were left-handed. Which group had the greater fraction of left-handed people?

🖩 **Calculator** Which fraction is greater?

16. $\frac{9}{13}, \frac{19}{28}$

17. $\frac{29}{17}, \frac{19}{11}$

18. $-\frac{11}{8}, -\frac{41}{30}$

19. $-\frac{12}{19}, -\frac{17}{27}$

Order each set of numbers from least to greatest.

20. $\frac{10}{13}, \frac{15}{19}, 0.8, -3.13$

21. $\frac{1}{3}, \frac{3}{10}, 0.03, 0.33$

22. $-4, -3.9, -\frac{2}{9}, \frac{2}{11}$

23. $\frac{5}{7}, \frac{5}{3}, \frac{5}{6}, \frac{5}{2}$

24. **Guided Problem Solving** During lunch period A, 26 out of 52 students ate turkey sandwiches. During lunch period B, 21 out of 49 students ate turkey sandwiches. Which lunch period had a greater fraction of students who ate turkey sandwiches?
   - The fraction of students from Lunch A who ate turkey sandwiches was ■.
   - The fraction of students from Lunch B who ate turkey sandwiches was ■.

25. **Number Sense** If 1 is added to the numerator and denominator of $\frac{5}{12}$, is the new number greater than or less than $\frac{5}{12}$? Explain.

Compare. Write <, >, or =.

26. $\frac{1}{8}$ ▣ $\frac{5}{7}$

27. $-\frac{3}{8}$ ▣ -0.375

28. $\frac{1}{4}$ ▣ 0.025

29. -1 ▣ $-\frac{9}{11}$

30. **Writing in Math** Explain how you can tell if a fraction is greater or less than $\frac{1}{2}$.

31. **Video Games** In a video game, you successfully completed 30 out of 55 levels. Your friend completed all but 7 out of 46 levels of another game. Who completed a greater fraction of a game?

32. **Reasoning** Order $\frac{5}{3}, \frac{5}{8}, \frac{5}{4}$, and $\frac{5}{7}$ from least to greatest. Explain how you would order fractions with the same numerator *without* writing them as decimals or finding the LCD.

33. Erika worked from 4:55 P.M. to 5:30 P.M. Maria worked $\frac{2}{3}$ of an hour. Who worked longer?

34. **Challenge** In the repeating decimal $0.\overline{365} = 0.365365365\ldots$, which digit is 100 places to the right of the decimal point?

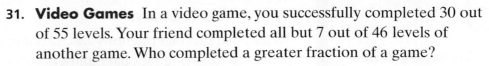

Test Prep and Mixed Review   **Practice**

Multiple Choice

35. The table shows the number of eighth-graders taught by four teachers, and the number of eighth-graders in each teacher's school. Which teacher taught the greatest fraction of his or her school's eighth-graders?

Teacher	Mr. Alpert	Ms. Bee	Mr. Coe	Ms. Drew
Students Taught	7	20	12	37
Students in School	42	80	36	74

Ⓐ Mr. Alpert   Ⓑ Ms. Bee   Ⓒ Mr. Coe   Ⓓ Ms. Drew

36. Adrianna spent 3 of the 7 dollars she had. Paul spent 4 of his 9 dollars. Jennifer spent 2 of her 4 dollars. Brian spent 5 of his 11 dollars. Who spent the third-greatest fraction of their money?

Ⓕ Adrianna   Ⓖ Brian   Ⓗ Jennifer   Ⓙ Paul

37. In the morning, the temperature was 58°F. By noon, the temperature had risen 14°F. After an afternoon rain, the temperature dropped 4°F, and then rose 2°F. The temperature rose 1°F just before sunset. What was the temperature at sunset?

Ⓐ 63°F   Ⓑ 67°F   Ⓒ 71°F   Ⓓ 79°F

For Exercises	See Lesson
38–40	1-5

Find each product.

38. $9(r - 7)$

39. $-8(-6 + b)$

40. $(t - 4)10$

Adding and Subtracting Rational Numbers

✓ Check Skills You'll Need

1. **Vocabulary Review**
   Which numbers are *integers*: 2, 4.5, 0, −6, $\frac{1}{3}$?

Simplify each expression.

2. −9 − 1

3. 10 − 100

4. 12 + (−2)

GO for Help
Lesson 1-3

What You'll Learn

To add and subtract fractions and mixed numbers and to solve problems involving rational numbers

Why Learn This?

Understanding how to add and subtract fractions allows you to make more accurate measurements. Carpenters, electricians, plumbers, and tailors all use fractions in their work.

To add or subtract fractions, rewrite them with a common denominator. You can use the LCD to make calculations easier.

EXAMPLES Adding and Subtracting Fractions

1 A cake recipe calls for $\frac{5}{8}$ cup of walnuts and $\frac{1}{2}$ cup of pecans. How many cups of nuts do you need?

$$\frac{5}{8} + \frac{1}{2} = \frac{5}{8} + \frac{1 \cdot 4}{2 \cdot 4} \quad \leftarrow \text{Write equivalent fractions with the same denominator.}$$

$$= \frac{5}{8} + \frac{4}{8} \quad \leftarrow \text{Simplify.}$$

$$= \frac{9}{8} \quad \leftarrow \text{Add the numerators.}$$

You need $\frac{9}{8}$, or $1\frac{1}{8}$, cups of nuts.

2 Find $\frac{1}{6} - \frac{4}{9}$.

The LCM of 6 and 9 is 18, so the LCD of $\frac{1}{6}$ and $\frac{4}{9}$ is 18.

$$\frac{1}{6} - \frac{4}{9} = \frac{3}{18} - \frac{8}{18} \quad \leftarrow \text{Write equivalent fractions using the LCD.}$$

$$= \frac{3 - 8}{18} = -\frac{5}{18} \quad \leftarrow \text{Subtract the numerators.}$$

✓ Quick Check

1. Find $\frac{2}{15} + \frac{1}{10}$ by using $15 \cdot 10 = 150$ as the common denominator.

2. Find $\frac{1}{10} - \frac{1}{4}$.

You can add or subtract mixed numbers by writing improper fractions. You can also add or subtract the integers and fractions separately.

EXAMPLE **Adding Mixed Numbers**

③ Find $3\frac{2}{3} + 5\frac{1}{2}$.

Estimate $3\frac{2}{3} + 5\frac{1}{2} \approx 4 + 6 = 10$

See Skills Handbook p. 638 for writing mixed numbers as improper fractions.

$$3\frac{2}{3} + 5\frac{1}{2} = \frac{11}{3} + \frac{11}{2} \quad \leftarrow \text{Write each mixed number as an improper fraction.}$$

$$= \frac{22}{6} + \frac{33}{6} \quad \leftarrow \text{Write equivalent fractions using the LCD, 6.}$$

$$= \frac{55}{6} \quad \leftarrow \text{Add the numerators.}$$

$$= 9\frac{1}{6} \quad \leftarrow \text{Change the improper fraction to a mixed number.}$$

Check for Reasonableness Since $9\frac{1}{6} \approx 10$, the answer is reasonable.

✓ Quick Check

3. Find $4\frac{1}{5} + 2\frac{3}{4}$.

EXAMPLE **Subtracting Mixed Numbers**

④ **Multiple Choice** A spool holds 60 ft of TV cable. Installation for a house uses 23 ft 5 in. of cable. Which equation can be used to find the amount t of cable left?

Ⓐ $t = 60 + 23\frac{5}{12}$ Ⓒ $t = 60 - 23\frac{5}{12}$

Ⓑ $t = 23\frac{5}{12} + 60$ Ⓓ $t = 23\frac{5}{12} - 60$

To find the amount left, you *subtract* the amount used from the original amount. Since 5 in. $= \frac{5}{12}$ ft, the amount left is $60 - 23\frac{5}{12}$ ft.

The answer is C. You can find the amount left on the roll by subtracting.

$$60 - 23\frac{5}{12} = 59\frac{12}{12} - 23\frac{5}{12} \quad \leftarrow \text{Rewrite 60 as } 59 + \frac{12}{12}, \text{ or 1.}$$

$$= 36\frac{7}{12} \quad \leftarrow \begin{array}{l} \text{Subtract the integers: } 59 - 23. \\ \text{Then subtract the fractions: } \frac{12}{12} - \frac{5}{12}. \end{array}$$

The amount of cable left is $36\frac{7}{12}$ ft.

Use estimation to check that your answer is reasonable.

✓ Quick Check

4. Weather In 2000, a single storm dropped $20\frac{3}{10}$ in. of snow in North Carolina. The previous record was $17\frac{4}{5}$ in. in 1927. Write and solve an equation to find how much more snow fell in 2000 than in 1927.

Find the LCD for each pair of fractions.

1. $\frac{1}{2}, \frac{1}{10}$

2. $\frac{1}{3}, \frac{1}{5}$

3. $\frac{1}{4}, \frac{1}{14}$

Find each sum or difference. Write your answer in simplest form.

4. $\frac{5}{8} + \left(-\frac{7}{8}\right)$

5. $\frac{5}{6} - \frac{2}{6}$

6. $3\frac{1}{3} + 2\frac{4}{5}$

7. **Reasoning** Without simplifying the expression, determine whether $\frac{1}{50} - \frac{1}{51}$ is a positive or a negative number. Explain.

Homework Exercises

For more exercises, see Extra Skills and Word Problems.

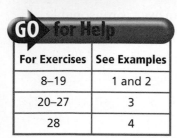

For Exercises	See Examples
8–19	1 and 2
20–27	3
28	4

Use common denominators to find each sum or difference.

8. $\frac{1}{7} + \frac{2}{3}$

9. $\frac{7}{8} + \frac{1}{5}$

10. $-\frac{2}{7} + \left(-\frac{2}{5}\right)$

11. $\frac{2}{5} + \frac{2}{3}$

12. $\frac{1}{10} + \frac{1}{9}$

13. $-\frac{1}{9} + \left(-\frac{5}{6}\right)$

14. $\frac{5}{12} + \frac{1}{9}$

15. $\frac{2}{3} - \frac{2}{9}$

16. $\frac{2}{7} - \frac{2}{21}$

17. $\frac{9}{10} - \frac{4}{5}$

18. $\frac{2}{15} - \frac{1}{10}$

19. $\frac{3}{10} - \frac{11}{15}$

Find each sum or difference. Write your answer in simplest form.

20. $3\frac{5}{6} - \left(-\frac{2}{3}\right)$

21. $\frac{3}{4} - \left(-2\frac{5}{12}\right)$

22. $1\frac{1}{15} - \left(-\frac{5}{60}\right)$

23. $-2\frac{1}{8} - 4\frac{1}{4}$

24. $-4\frac{2}{3} - 6\frac{1}{4}$

25. $-5\frac{1}{2} + 8\frac{2}{3}$

26. $-7\frac{2}{5} + \left(-\frac{3}{4}\right)$

27. $7\frac{4}{5} + 11\frac{1}{3}$

28. **Weather** It snowed $6\frac{3}{5}$ in. during the first three months of the year. It didn't snow again until December. The total snowfall for the year was $7\frac{1}{2}$ in. Find the December snowfall.

GPS 29. **Guided Problem Solving** A group of students was asked which computer activity occupied the most time: e-mailing, playing games, or burning CDs. One half of the students chose e-mailing, and $\frac{1}{10}$ of the students chose burning CDs. What fraction of the students chose playing games?

- **Understand the Problem** Read the problem again. What information is given? What information is missing?
- **Check Your Answer** Look at your work and compare it against the information in the problem. Is your answer reasonable?

GO **Online**
Homework Video Tutor
Visit: PHSchool.com
Web Code: ase-0204

30. **Carpentry** The piece of wood that a carpenter calls a "2-by-4" is actually $1\frac{1}{2}$ in. thick by $3\frac{1}{2}$ in. wide. If two 2-by-4 pieces are joined with their $3\frac{1}{2}$-in. surfaces touching, what is the thickness of the new piece?

(**Algebra**) **Solve each equation for x when $a = \frac{1}{2}$, $b = \frac{1}{3}$, and $c = \frac{1}{4}$. Write each answer in simplest form.**

31. $a + x = 3$ **32.** $2\frac{1}{6} + x = -b$ **33.** $c + x = \frac{1}{8}$

34. $x - a = c$ **35.** $-5\frac{1}{2} + x = 2 + a$ **36.** $x - 1\frac{1}{2} = b$

37. Student Council The student council needs $\frac{2}{3}$ of its members to vote favorably for a motion in order for it to pass. Currently, $\frac{2}{7}$ of the members are in favor of a certain motion. What additional fraction of the council needs to be in favor of the motion in order for it to pass?

38. Golf The diameter of a golf ball is $1\frac{2}{3}$ in., and the diameter of a hole is $4\frac{1}{4}$ in. Find the difference between the two diameters.

39. Error Analysis A student adds $\frac{1}{a} + \frac{1}{b}$ and says the answer is $\frac{1}{a+b}$. Give an example that shows the student is incorrect.

40. Writing in Math Explain why you do *not* have to change mixed numbers to improper fractions before you find the LCD.

41. Challenge If $b = a + \frac{1}{3}$, what is the value of $b - 1$ in terms of a?

Test Prep and Mixed Review   **Practice**

Multiple Choice

42. Miguel recorded the distance he ran each day last week. What is the total number of miles he ran last week?

Day	Distance (mi)
Monday	$1\frac{1}{2}$
Tuesday	$2\frac{1}{10}$
Wednesday	$\frac{3}{4}$
Thursday	$3\frac{1}{5}$
Friday	$1\frac{4}{5}$

    Ⓐ $9\frac{1}{4}$ Ⓒ $9\frac{7}{20}$

    Ⓑ $9\frac{3}{10}$ Ⓓ $9\frac{2}{5}$

43. How many integers are greater than $\frac{9}{37}$ and less than $\frac{37}{9}$?

    Ⓕ 2   Ⓗ 4

    Ⓖ 3   Ⓙ 5

44. Emilio is marking a flagpole using colored tape. The red tape is halfway up the pole. The blue tape is $\frac{7}{11}$ of the way up the pole. The white tape is $\frac{5}{9}$ of the way up the pole. The green tape is $\frac{4}{5}$ of the way up the pole. What color tape is highest on the flagpole?

    Ⓐ Blue   Ⓑ Green   Ⓒ Red   Ⓓ White

Order each set of numbers from least to greatest.

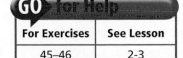

For Exercises	See Lesson
45–46	2-3

45. $0.8, \frac{1}{125}, 0.808, \frac{22}{25}$ **46.** $-2\frac{33}{50}, -2\frac{3}{50}, -2.006, -2.6$

1. Find the prime factorization of 504.

2. What is the GCF of 99 and 132?

3. **Baseball** Find the batting average of a hitter with 8 hits in 27 times at bat.

4. Write 0.56 as a fraction in simplest form.

5. Order the following numbers from least to greatest:
$\frac{8}{25}, -\frac{15}{7}, 0.35, 2, -2.6$

Simplify each expression.

6. $\frac{2}{3} + \frac{1}{9}$

7. $5 - \frac{2}{5}$

8. $-2\frac{1}{6} + \frac{5}{24}$

9. $2\frac{4}{5} - 5\frac{1}{4}$

10. **Cooking** A cook needs $1\frac{1}{2}$ cups of sugar. The cook has $\frac{3}{8}$ cup. How many more cups of sugar does the cook need?

MATH GAMES

Force Out!

What You'll Need

Three or more players

How To Play

- The first player says a composite number.
- The next player chooses a factor of the previous player's number that is less than the number.
- The second player subtracts the factor from the number and says the result.
- The game continues with each player subtracting a factor from the previous player's number.
- The game ends when a player says "one." That player wins.

Player Thinks	Player Says
18	"eighteen"
$18 = 6 \cdot 3$ $18 - 6 = 12$	"twelve"
$12 = 4 \cdot 3$ $12 - 3 = 9$	"nine"

Modeling Fraction Multiplication

You can shade grids to model fraction multiplication. Use one color to represent the first fraction. Use another color to represent the second fraction. The overlap represents the product.

EXAMPLE **Multiplying Rational Numbers**

Use models to multiply $\frac{3}{4}$ by $\frac{9}{10}$.

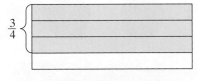

← Shade 3 out of 4 rows red to model $\frac{3}{4}$.

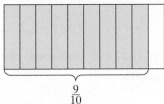

← Shade 9 out of 10 columns blue to model $\frac{9}{10}$.

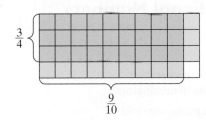

← To find the product, model both fractions in one rectangle. 27 out of 40 squares are purple.

So $\frac{3}{4} \cdot \frac{9}{10} = \frac{27}{40}$.

Exercises

Use models to find each product.

1. $\frac{1}{2} \cdot \frac{5}{6}$

2. $\frac{3}{4} \cdot \frac{1}{5}$

3. $\frac{2}{3} \cdot \frac{3}{8}$

4. $\frac{3}{10} \cdot \frac{4}{9}$

5. $\frac{1}{4} \cdot \frac{1}{4}$

6. Write a numeric equation to represent the model at the right.

7. Write a multiplication expression for the numerator of the product of $\frac{3}{4}$ and $\frac{9}{10}$.

8. Write a multiplication expression for the denominator of the product of $\frac{3}{4}$ and $\frac{9}{10}$.

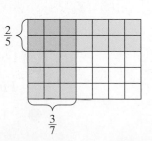

Multiplying and Dividing Rational Numbers

Check Skills You'll Need

1. **Vocabulary Review**
   A *rational number*
   can be written in
   the form ■, where
   $b \neq 0$.

Write each fraction in
simplest form.

2. $\frac{7}{21}$ 3. $\frac{12}{20}$

4. $\frac{9}{81}$ 5. $\frac{36}{66}$

GO for Help
Lesson 2-2

What You'll Learn

To multiply and divide fractions and mixed numbers and to solve
problems involving rational numbers

🔊 **New Vocabulary** reciprocals, multiplicative inverse

Why Learn This?

Sometimes objects need to be divided
into smaller pieces. For example,
when you divide 3 apples into four
sections each, you get 12 smaller
pieces. Dividing 3 by $\frac{1}{4}$ is the same as
multiplying 3 by 4.

To find the product of rational numbers that are fractions, multiply the
numerators and multiply the denominators.

EXAMPLES Multiplying Rational Numbers

① Find $-\frac{5}{8} \cdot \frac{7}{15}$.

$$-\frac{5}{8} \cdot \frac{7}{15} = -\frac{5 \cdot 7}{8 \cdot 15} \quad \leftarrow \text{Multiply the numerators.} \\ \text{Multiply the denominators.}$$

$$= -\frac{\overset{1}{5} \cdot 7}{8 \cdot \underset{3}{15}} \quad \leftarrow \text{Divide the numerator and} \\ \text{denominator by their GCF, 5.}$$

$$= -\frac{7}{24} \quad \leftarrow \text{Simplify.}$$

② Find the product $-2\frac{1}{4} \cdot \left(-3\frac{3}{5}\right)$.

$$-2\frac{1}{4} \cdot \left(-3\frac{3}{5}\right) = -\frac{9}{4} \cdot \left(-\frac{18}{5}\right) \quad \leftarrow \text{Write as improper fractions.}$$

$$= \frac{9 \cdot \overset{9}{18}}{\underset{2}{4} \cdot 5} \quad \leftarrow \text{Divide the numerator and denominator} \\ \text{by their GCF, 2.}$$

$$= \frac{81}{10} = 8\frac{1}{10} \quad \leftarrow \text{Simplify. Write as a mixed number.}$$

✓ Quick Check

Find each product. Write the answer in simplest form.

1. $-\frac{4}{5} \cdot \left(-\frac{3}{8}\right)$

2. $2\frac{1}{10} \cdot \left(-1\frac{2}{5}\right)$

Two numbers with a product of 1 are called **reciprocals.** The reciprocal of $\frac{a}{b}$ is $\frac{b}{a}$, where $a \neq 0$ and $b \neq 0$. The reciprocal of a number is also called its **multiplicative inverse.** Remember that dividing by a fraction is the same as multiplying by the reciprocal of the fraction.

GO **O**nline

Video Tutor Help
Visit: PHSchool.com
Web Code: ase-0775

EXAMPLE **Dividing Rational Numbers**

3 **Fashion Design** A handbag designer has $15\frac{1}{2}$ yards of fabric. Each bag uses $\frac{7}{8}$ yard of fabric. How many bags can the designer make?

You need to find how many $\frac{7}{8}$-yard pieces there are in $15\frac{1}{2}$ yards. Divide $15\frac{1}{2}$ by $\frac{7}{8}$.

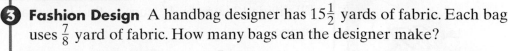

$$15\frac{1}{2} \div \frac{7}{8} = \frac{31}{2} \div \frac{7}{8} \quad \leftarrow \text{Write the mixed number as an improper fraction.}$$

$$= \frac{31}{2} \cdot \frac{8}{7} \quad \leftarrow \text{Multiply by the reciprocal of } \frac{7}{8}.$$

$$= \frac{248}{14} \quad \leftarrow \text{Multiply.}$$

$$= 17\frac{5}{7} \quad \leftarrow \text{Write as a mixed number.}$$

Since no one can make $\frac{5}{7}$ of a bag, the designer can make only 17 bags.

Check for Reasonableness Round $15\frac{1}{2}$ to 16 and $\frac{7}{8}$ to 1. Then $16 \div 1 = 16$, which is close to 17. The answer is reasonable.

✓ Quick Check

3. Sewing You have $13\frac{3}{4}$ yards of material to cut into $2\frac{1}{2}$-yard lengths. How many lengths can you cut from the material?

You can use reciprocals to solve equations involving multiplication.

EXAMPLE **Solving Equations by Multiplying**

4 Solve $\frac{4}{5}x = -\frac{9}{10}$.

$$\frac{4}{5}x = -\frac{9}{10}$$

$$\frac{1\cancel{5}}{1\cancel{4}} \cdot \frac{\cancel{4}1}{\cancel{5}1}x = \frac{1\cancel{5}}{4} \cdot \left(-\frac{9}{\cancel{10}2}\right) \quad \leftarrow \text{Multiply each side by the reciprocal of } \frac{4}{5}.$$

$$1x = -\frac{1 \cdot 9}{4 \cdot 2} \quad \leftarrow \text{Multiply the numerators and the denominators.}$$

$$x = -\frac{9}{8} = -1\frac{1}{8} \quad \leftarrow \text{Simplify. Write the fraction as a mixed number.}$$

✓ Quick Check

4. Solve the equation $\frac{3}{7}p = 3\frac{1}{2}$.

More Than One Way

A pancake recipe calls for $1\frac{2}{3}$ cups of flour to make about 20 pancakes. You have 13 cups of flour. Do you have enough for 100 pancakes?

Eric's Method

I'll divide 13 cups by $1\frac{2}{3}$ cups to find how many times I can make the recipe.

$$13 \div 1\frac{2}{3} = 13 \div \frac{5}{3} \quad \leftarrow \text{Write the mixed number as an improper fraction.}$$

$$= 13 \cdot \frac{3}{5} \quad \leftarrow \text{Multiply the reciprocal of } \frac{5}{3}.$$

$$= \frac{39}{5} = 7\frac{4}{5} \quad \leftarrow \text{Multiply. Write as a mixed number.}$$

I can make the recipe 7 times. Since $7 \cdot 20 = 140$, I have enough flour to make 100 pancakes.

Nicole's Method

For 100 pancakes, I need 5 times the amount of flour for one recipe.

$$5 \cdot 1\frac{2}{3} = 5 \cdot \frac{5}{3} \quad \leftarrow \text{Change the mixed number to an improper fraction.}$$

$$= \frac{25}{3} = 8\frac{1}{3} \quad \leftarrow \text{Multiply. Write as a mixed number.}$$

I need $8\frac{1}{3}$ cups, so I have plenty of flour.

Choose a Method

Your dog eats $1\frac{1}{2}$ cups of food per day. You have 50 cups of food. Do you have enough for 40 days? Explain why you chose the method you used.

✓ Check Your Understanding

1. **Vocabulary** The reciprocal of a number is also called its __?__.

2. **Estimation** Estimate the solution of $\frac{6}{7}x = 2\frac{4}{5}$.

Copy and complete each equation.

3. $\frac{3}{5} \cdot \frac{5}{3} = $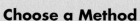

4. $-\frac{7}{2} \cdot \blacksquare = 1$

5. $\blacksquare \cdot \left(-\frac{1}{5}\right) = 1$

For more exercises, see Extra Skills and Word Problems.

GO for Help

For Exercises	See Examples
6–14	1 and 2
15–25	3
26–31	4

Find each product. Write the answer in simplest form.

6. $-\frac{4}{5} \cdot \left(-\frac{1}{2}\right)$

7. $\frac{9}{10} \cdot \left(-\frac{2}{3}\right)$

8. $-\frac{34}{35} \cdot \left(-\frac{7}{2}\right)$

9. $-\frac{5}{6} \cdot \frac{1}{4}$

10. $-\frac{1}{2} \cdot \frac{2}{3}$

11. $\frac{8}{9} \cdot \left(-\frac{3}{4}\right)$

12. $-1\frac{1}{2} \cdot \left(-4\frac{1}{2}\right)$

13. $3\frac{3}{4} \cdot 2\frac{1}{3}$

14. $\left(-2\frac{3}{4}\right) \cdot 4$

Find each quotient. Write the answer in simplest form.

15. $\frac{1}{2} \div \left(-\frac{3}{4}\right)$

16. $-\frac{8}{9} \div \frac{1}{6}$

17. $8 \div \frac{8}{17}$

18. $-\frac{7}{9} \div \left(-\frac{9}{7}\right)$

19. $\frac{100}{101} \div 100$

20. $-3\frac{3}{10} \div \frac{1}{10}$

21. $\frac{1}{4} \div \left(-\frac{1}{3}\right)$

22. $3\frac{3}{5} \div (-9)$

23. $\frac{2}{7} \div 1\frac{2}{7}$

24. Running A jogger is running around a $\frac{1}{4}$-mile track. How many laps does the jogger have to run in order to go $5\frac{1}{2}$ miles?

25. Trail Mix You have $6\frac{2}{3}$ lb of raisins to divide evenly among 5 bags of trail mix. How many pounds of the raisins will go in each bag?

Solve each equation.

26. $\frac{1}{2}j = 12\frac{1}{2}$

27. $\frac{2}{3}y = \frac{2}{5}$

28. $\frac{1}{2}m = 1\frac{1}{3}$

29. $-\frac{2}{7}b = 1\frac{1}{14}$

30. $1\frac{1}{3}p = -4\frac{1}{3}$

31. $-\frac{1}{3}u = 6\frac{1}{3}$

32. Guided Problem Solving Justin needs to make cardboard signs. He has $50\frac{4}{5}$ ft of cardboard, and each sign uses $3\frac{1}{10}$ ft of board. Write and solve an equation to find how many signs he can make. Use estimation to check your answer.
- **Understand the Problem** To find how many signs he can make, should you multiply or divide?
- **Check Your Answer** To check your answer, what values can you substitute in the problem?

33. Recycling A family uses $14\frac{1}{2}$ pounds of paper in a week and recycles about $\frac{3}{4}$ of its waste. How many pounds of paper does the family recycle?

GO Online
Homework Video Tutor
Visit: PHSchool.com
Web Code: ase-0205

34. Choose a Method A hiking trail is $43\frac{5}{9}$ mi long. There is a cabin every $4\frac{1}{2}$ mi. How many cabins are along the trail? Explain why you chose the method you used.

Algebra Evaluate each expression for $x = 1$, $y = 2$, and $z = 3$.

35. $\left(x + \dfrac{x}{5}\right) \div \dfrac{1}{5}$ **36.** $\dfrac{x}{y}\left(\dfrac{y}{z} - x\right)$ **37.** $3 \div \left(\dfrac{y}{z} - \dfrac{x}{yz}\right)$

38. Baking You are making apple pies for a school fundraiser. You have 4 baskets of apples, and each basket contains 11 apples. Each pie requires $3\frac{1}{5}$ cups of apples. One apple fills about $\frac{1}{2}$ cup.
  a. How many cups of apples do you have?
  b. How many pies can you make?

39. Reasoning When you divide a positive number by a fraction that is between 0 and 1, the answer is always greater than the positive number. Explain why.

40. Writing in Math Explain the difference between dividing 10 by 4 and dividing 10 by $\frac{1}{4}$. Use diagrams to support your answer.

41. The school band uses $1\frac{3}{4}$ yd of blue fabric and $\frac{3}{8}$ yd of gold fabric to make one banner. How many yards of fabric does the band need to make 5 banners?

42. Challenge Your uncle has 36 coins in nickels and quarters. The value of his nickels is $\frac{1}{15}$ of the value of his quarters. Find the number of nickels.

 Test Prep and Mixed Review **Practice**

Multiple Choice

43. Ali is tiling a bathroom that is $10\frac{1}{3}$ ft by $10\frac{1}{3}$ ft. How many tiles like the one at the right will fit along one side of the bathroom?

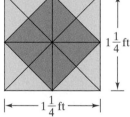
$1\frac{1}{4}$ ft
$1\frac{1}{4}$ ft

Ⓐ $7\frac{1}{2}$ Ⓒ $8\frac{4}{15}$

Ⓑ $8\frac{1}{3}$ Ⓓ $12\frac{11}{12}$

44. Shelly keeps track of the time she spends on her cell phone. Today she made three calls that lasted 3.2 minutes, $12\frac{1}{2}$ minutes, and 20 minutes 15 seconds. How many minutes did Shelly spend on the phone today?
  Ⓕ 35.55 min   Ⓖ 35.75 min   Ⓗ 35.85 min   Ⓙ 35.95 min

45. Scott is twice as old as Ben. Donna is 6 years older than Ben. The sum of their ages is 34. Which expression can you use to represent the sum of ages?
  Ⓐ $x + 2x - 6x$ Ⓒ $x + 2x + (x - 6)$
  Ⓑ $x + 2x + 6x$ Ⓓ $x + 2x + (x + 6)$

GO for Help

For Exercises	See Lesson
46–48	1-6

Solve each equation.

46. $a + 12 = -31$ **47.** $-9 = b - 16$ **48.** $-36 = c - 36$

Vocabulary Builder

Learning Vocabulary

Your textbook has vocabulary terms that may be new.
Make your own mathematics dictionary in a notebook.
Use the following ideas to write your definitions.

- Write the vocabulary term and its definition. Include any symbols.
- If possible, draw a diagram.
- Give one or more examples of the term.
- Give one or more nonexamples and explain how they are different.
- Include details, using other related terms you know.

Here is a possible entry for your dictionary.

Two numbers are reciprocals if their product is 1.

10 and $\frac{1}{10}$ are reciprocals, because their product is 1.

2 and −2 are not reciprocals, because their product is −4.

reciprocals
2, $\frac{1}{2}$
−1, −1

not reciprocals
2, 0.2
3, −$\frac{1}{3}$

EXAMPLE   **A Dictionary Entry**

a. What term is being defined? *reciprocal*

b. Why do 10 and $\frac{1}{10}$ satisfy the definition? *Their product is 1.*

c. Why do 2 and −2 not satisfy the definition? *Their product is not 1.*

d. What does the diagram show? *It shows examples of reciprocals and nonreciprocals.*

Exercises

1. Write a dictionary entry for *multiplicative inverse.*

2. Error Analysis A student wrote the definition for *prime factorization* at the right. Which parts are incorrect? Explain.

When a number is written in prime factorization, it is written as the product of two factors.

The prime factorization of 14 is 1 · 2 · 7 because 1, 2, and 7 are prime numbers.

The prime factorization of 20 is not 4 · 5, because 4 is not a prime number.

Practice Solving Problems

Collections An art collector sold $\frac{1}{3}$ of his collection to a friend. The collector then donated $\frac{1}{2}$ of what was left to a museum. What part of the original collection did the collector have left?

What You Might Think

What do I know? What do I want to find out?

How do I show the main idea?

How do I calculate an answer?

Is the answer reasonable?

What You Might Write

The collector sold $\frac{1}{3}$, so he had $\frac{2}{3}$ left. He gave away $\frac{1}{2}$ of that. How much was left?

I can draw a diagram.

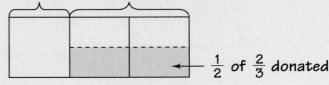

$\frac{1}{3}$ sold $\frac{2}{3}$ left after selling

$\frac{1}{2}$ of $\frac{2}{3}$ donated

$1 - \frac{1}{3} = \frac{2}{3}$. That's what he had left after selling part of the collection.

$$\frac{1}{2} \cdot \frac{2}{3} = \frac{2}{6}$$
$$= \frac{1}{3}$$

He had $\frac{1}{3}$ of the original collection left.

Yes; the answer matches the diagram.

Think It Through

1. How does the diagram show $\frac{1}{2} \cdot \frac{2}{3} = \frac{2}{6}$? Explain.

2. **Reasoning** If the collector had donated $\frac{1}{2}$ of $\frac{2}{3}$ of the collection, is the amount he had left the same as the amount he donated? Use the diagram to explain how you know the answer without calculating.

3. You can find $\frac{1}{2}$ of $\frac{2}{3}$ using a similar diagram, but without dividing the rectangle horizontally into halves. Draw another diagram you can use to find the answer. Which method do you prefer?

Exercises

Solve each problem. For Exercises 4 and 5, answer parts (a) and (b) first.

4. Julio feeds his dog $1\frac{1}{3}$ cans of dog food each day Monday through Saturday. On Sunday, he feeds his dog half as much. How many cans of dog food does Julio feed his dog in a week?

   a. What do you know, and what do you want to find out?

   b. Use the diagram at the right. Make a similar diagram to show six times $1\frac{1}{3}$ cans of dog food plus half of $1\frac{1}{3}$. Calculate $6 \cdot 1\frac{1}{3} + \frac{1}{2} \cdot 1\frac{1}{3}$. Do your answers match?

5. Kendra ordered pizzas for a party. After the party, she had $2\frac{3}{4}$ pizzas left. She estimates that $\frac{1}{2}$ of a pizza is one meal. How many meals does she have left?

   a. What do you know, and what do you want to find out?

   b. Copy and complete the diagram below. Explain how the drawing matches the number sentence for the problem.

6. Max has published a book. He earns $5.50 as a royalty for each copy of the book that is sold. The royalties for the first five months of the year are shown in the graph below. He expects similar royalties for the rest of year. How much should Max expect to earn in royalties during the year?

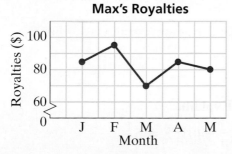

7. Melita had some hardboiled eggs. She gave away $\frac{1}{2}$ of the eggs, plus $\frac{1}{2}$ an egg, to Sam. She then gave away $\frac{1}{2}$ of what she had left, plus $\frac{1}{2}$ an egg, to Alonzo. After she gave $\frac{1}{2}$ of what she had left, plus $\frac{1}{2}$ an egg, to Jacquelyn, she had no eggs left. How many eggs did Melita have before giving any away?

Estimating Solutions

Estimating solutions helps you solve equations. You can round the numbers in an equation or formula to estimate the solution. Then you can compare your solution of the original equation to the estimated solution and decide whether your answer is reasonable.

EXAMPLE Estimating a Solution

1 Your friend says the solution of the equation $x + 31\frac{2}{3} = 727\frac{5}{8}$ is $x = 596\frac{3}{4}$. Is the solution reasonable?

$$x + 30 \approx 730 \quad \leftarrow \text{Round } 31\tfrac{2}{3} \text{ to 30 and } 727\tfrac{5}{8} \text{ to 730.}$$

$$x \approx 700 \quad \leftarrow \text{Use mental math: } 700 + 30 = 730.$$

The value of x is about 700. Your friend's solution is not reasonable.

EXAMPLE Estimating With a Formula

2 The formula to convert from Fahrenheit to Celsius is $C = \frac{5}{9}(F - 32)$. Estimate the Celsius temperature for 0°F.

$$C \approx \frac{1}{2}(F - 30) \quad \leftarrow \text{Round } \tfrac{5}{9} \text{ to } \tfrac{1}{2} \text{ and } -32 \text{ to 30.}$$

$$\approx \frac{1}{2}(0 - 30) \quad \leftarrow \text{Substitute 0 for } F.$$

$$\approx \frac{1}{2}(-30) = -15 \quad \leftarrow \text{Subtract. Multiply.}$$

The Celsius temperature for 0°F is about −15°C.

Exercises

Decide whether the solution to each equation is reasonable. Explain.

1. $y + 19\frac{1}{4} = 102\frac{3}{5}; \ y = 83\frac{7}{20}$

2. $-39\frac{5}{6}z = -401; \ z = 5\frac{1}{6}$

3. $\frac{t}{48} = 2\frac{9}{10}; \ t = 139\frac{2}{10}$

4. $m - 34\frac{7}{8} = -21\frac{1}{3}; \ m = -56\frac{5}{24}$

5. Estimate the maximum heart rate for a $13\frac{10}{12}$-year-old male using the formula $M = \frac{4}{5}(220 - A)$, where A represents his age.

6. Estimate the maximum heart rate for a $13\frac{10}{12}$-year-old female using the formula $F = \frac{4}{5}(226 - A)$, where A represents her age.

2-6 Formulas

✓ Check Skills You'll Need

1. **Vocabulary Review** According to the *order of operations,* you multiply and divide before you __?__ and __?__ .

Evaluate each expression for $w = 2$ and $t = -3$.

2. $4w + t$

3. $4(w + t)$

4. $4w + 4t$

5. $-4t - w$

 **for Help**
Lesson 1-1

What You'll Learn

To use formulas to solve problems and to solve a formula for a variable

🔊 **New Vocabulary** formula

Why Learn This?

Understanding formulas allows you to find quantities such as area, distance, rate, and time. You can use these formulas in aviation and sports.

A **formula** is a rule that shows a relationship between two or more quantities. The variables represent the quantities.

Recall that the perimeter of a figure is the distance around it. The area of a figure is the amount of space that it encloses. The diagram at the right shows the relationship between the area of a rectangle and its two dimensions. You use the formula $A = \ell w$ to find the area.

$A = \ell w$

EXAMPLE   Using Formulas to Solve Problems

1 Find the area of the trapezoid at the right.

$b_1 = 4.3$ cm
$h = 4$ cm
$b_2 = 9.1$ cm

$A = \frac{1}{2}h(b_1 + b_2)$ ← **Use the formula for the area of a trapezoid.**

$= \frac{1}{2}(4)(4.3 + 9.1)$ ← **Substitute.**

$= \frac{1}{2}(4)(13.4)$ ← **Add within the parentheses.**

$= 2(13.4)$ ← **Multiply from left to right.**

$= 26.8$ ← **Simplify.**

The area of the trapezoid is 26.8 cm².

Vocabulary Tip

The variables b_1 and b_2 stand for "base 1" and "base 2." The lowered numbers 1 and 2 are called subscripts.

✓ Quick Check

1. Find the area of each figure.
   a. trapezoid: $h = 4.2$ cm, $b_1 = 1.4$ cm, $b_2 = 4.6$ cm
   b. rectangle: $\ell = \frac{2}{3}$ yd, $w = 3$ yd

You can use formulas to solve some real-world problems.

EXAMPLE **Application: Sports**

2 The Iditarod is a 1,159-mile dog-sled race from Anchorage, Alaska, to Nome, Alaska. Susan Butcher won the race four times. Her time for one race was 11 days. Find the average distance she went each day.

Use the distance formula $d = rt$, where d is the distance traveled, r is the rate of travel, and t is the time spent traveling.

$$d = rt \quad \leftarrow \text{Use the distance formula.}$$

$$1{,}159 = r \cdot 11 \quad \leftarrow \text{Substitute 1,159 for } d \text{ and 11 for } t.$$

$$\frac{1{,}159}{11} = \frac{r \cdot 11}{11} \quad \leftarrow \text{Divide each side by 11 to isolate } r \text{ on the right.}$$

$$\frac{1{,}159}{11} = r \quad \leftarrow \text{Simplify.}$$

$$1{,}159 \;\boxed{\div}\; 11 \;\boxed{=}\; \mathit{105.36364} \quad \leftarrow \text{Use a calculator.}$$

Susan Butcher traveled about 105 miles per day.

Check for Reasonableness Round 1,159 to 1,000 and 11 to 10. $1{,}000 \approx r \cdot 10$, so $r \approx 100$. The answer is reasonable.

nline
active math

For: Formulas Activity
Use: Interactive
Textbook, 2-6

✓ **Quick Check**

2. In 1900, Johann Hurlinger walked 870 miles on his hands. He did this in 55 ten-hour shifts, or 550 hours. Find his rate in miles per hour.

You can use the properties of equality to isolate a variable in a formula.

EXAMPLE **Isolating a Variable**

3 **Multiple Choice** Which formula can be used to find the side length s of a square, given the perimeter P?

  Ⓐ $P = \frac{s}{4}$ Ⓑ $s = 4P$ Ⓒ $s = \frac{P}{4}$ Ⓓ $s = \frac{4}{P}$

$$P = 4s \quad \leftarrow \text{Use the perimeter formula for a square.}$$

$$\frac{P}{4} = \frac{4s}{4} \quad \leftarrow \text{Divide each side by 4 to isolate the variable } s.$$

$$\frac{P}{4} = s \quad \leftarrow \text{Simplify.}$$

The formula for the side of a square is $s = \frac{P}{4}$, so the answer is C.

Test Prep Tip

Circle the variable you are isolating so that you don't solve for the wrong variable by mistake.

✓ **Quick Check**

3. Solve $A = w - 5$ for w.

1. **Vocabulary** In the formulas $A = \ell w$ and $P = 2\ell + 2w$, what do the variables ℓ and w represent?

2. **Reasoning** Suppose you know a friend's distance and time for a race. How would you find your friend's rate of travel?

Use the formula $A = \ell w$ to find the area of each rectangle.

3. $\ell = 1.75$ cm, $w = 0.5$ cm

4. $\ell = 2\frac{1}{3}$ ft, $w = 1\frac{1}{4}$ in.

Name each formula and identify its variables.

5. $A = \frac{1}{2}h(b_1 + b_2)$

6. $d = rt$

7. $P = 4s$

Homework Exercises

For more exercises, see Extra Skills and Word Problems.

GO for Help

For Exercises	See Examples
8–12	1
13	2
14–19	3

Find the area of each figure.

8.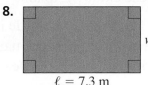
$w = 4.1$ m
$\ell = 7.3$ m

9.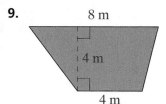
8 m
4 m
4 m

10.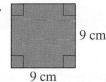
9 cm
9 cm

11.
5 in.
$2\frac{1}{2}$ in.

12.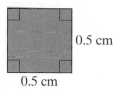
0.5 cm
0.5 cm

13. Charles Lindbergh flew nonstop across the Atlantic Ocean in 1927. He flew 3,610 miles in 33.5 hours. Find his rate of travel.

(Algebra) Solve each formula for the variable indicated in red.

14. $V = \ell wh$

15. $d = rt$

16. $C = 2\pi r$

17. $K = C + 273$

18. $V = \frac{1}{3}Bh$

19. $W = g - 25$

20. **Guided Problem Solving** A black mamba travels 20 mi/h for $\frac{1}{4}$ mile. How many seconds does it take the snake to travel $\frac{1}{4}$ mile?
   - Solve the distance formula for time. For which variables in the formula should you substitute 20 and $\frac{1}{4}$?
   - How many seconds are in an hour?

Use the formula $d = rt$ to find each of the following.

21. r for $d = 12$ mi and $t = 0.5$ h

22. t for $d = 120$ km and $r = 45$ km/h

23. (**Algebra**) Find the height h of a cone with a radius of 3 ft and a volume of 27 ft^3. Use the formula $V = \frac{1}{3}\pi r^2 h$.

24. **Writing in Math** How is transforming a formula similar to solving an equation with just one variable? How is it different?

25. **Clouds** Cumulus clouds have flat bases and lumpy tops. The tops are usually about 1 mile above sea level. To find the height in feet of the base of a cumulus cloud, you can use the formula
height = 222(air temperature − dew-point temperature).
The air and dew-point temperatures are in degrees Fahrenheit.
  a. Find the height of the base of a cumulus cloud when the air temperature is 80°F and the dew-point temperature is 70°F.
  b. **Number Sense** Suppose the dew point drops and the air temperature remains constant. What happens to the height of the base of the cloud? Explain.

26. **Challenge** The length of a rectangle is 5 cm. The area of the rectangle is the same as that of a square whose side measures 4 cm. Find the width of the rectangle.

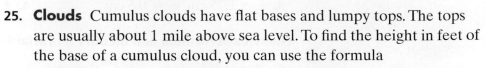

Test Prep and Mixed Review   **Practice**

Multiple Choice

27. The circumference C of a circle can be found using the formula $C = 2\pi r$, where r represents the radius of the circle. What should Olivia do to write a formula to find the radius of a circle?
  Ⓐ Subtract 2π from C and $2\pi r$.   Ⓒ Divide C and $2\pi r$ by 2π.
  Ⓑ Multiply C and $2\pi r$ by r.   Ⓓ Divide C and $2\pi r$ by r.

28. Jose is sharing half of a pizza with two friends. Which expression can be used to find the fraction of a whole pizza each person will get, if they split what they have evenly?
  Ⓕ $\frac{1}{2} \cdot 3$ Ⓖ $\frac{1}{2} \cdot \frac{1}{3}$ Ⓗ $2 \cdot 3$ Ⓙ $2 \cdot \frac{1}{3}$

29. Your school is having three speakers on career day. One fifth of the students are going to hear Speaker A, and $\frac{2}{3}$ are going to hear Speaker B. What fraction of students are going to hear Speaker C?
  Ⓐ $\frac{1}{15}$ Ⓑ $\frac{2}{15}$ Ⓒ $\frac{1}{5}$ Ⓓ $\frac{4}{15}$

For Exercises	See Lesson
30–32	2-1

GO for Help

Use prime factorization to find the GCF of each pair of numbers.

30. 32, 48   **31.** 51, 68   **32.** 84, 90

Using Formulas

Use the LIST key on a graphing calculator to evaluate a formula.

EXAMPLE

Evaluate the formula $P = 2\ell + 2w$ for $\ell = 3$ and for whole-number values of w from 8 to 11.

Step 1 Press **STAT** 1 to open the stat list editor window. If columns are not clear, use the arrow keys to go to the top of each column. Press **CLEAR** **ENTER**.

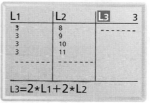

Step 2 In the column labeled L1, enter the four values of ℓ. In this example, each value of ℓ is 3. In the column labeled L2, enter the four values of w from 8 to 11.

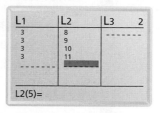

Step 3 Go to the top of the column marked L3 and highlight L3. To enter the formula $P = 2\ell + 2w$, think L3 = 2 · L1 + 2 · L2. Use these keystrokes.

2 **X** **2nd** **STAT** 1 **+** 2 **X** **2nd** **STAT** 2

Press **ENTER**. The calculator automatically calculates the value of the perimeters.

Hint: Before starting a new exercise, clear the columns.

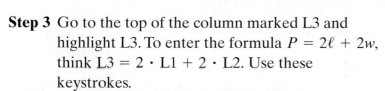

Exercises

Suppose the values of a and b are listed in L1 and L2 of a graphing calculator. Write the keystrokes you would use to enter each formula in L3.

1. $P = a + b$ **2.** $X = 3a + 5b$ **3.** $A = 0.5ab$ **4.** $T = a^2$

5. Calculator Evaluate the formula $A = \frac{1}{2}bh$ for the given values.
   a. $b = 8$; $h = 10, 11, 12, 13, 14, 15$ **b.** $b = 8, 9, 10, 11, 12$; $h = 10$

6. Patterns Enter the numbers 1 through 7 in L1. Enter the formula L2 = $\frac{L1}{9}$. What number pattern do you see in L2?

7. Enter the numbers 1 through 7 in L1. Enter L2 = L1^2 − L1 + 41. Are all the numbers in L2 prime?

What You'll Learn

To write, simplify, and evaluate expressions involving exponents

🔊 **New Vocabulary** exponent, base, power

Why Learn This?

Designing a bridge or other large structure involves many calculations and measurements. You can use exponents to represent some of these numbers.

An **exponent** tells how many times a number, or **base,** is used as a factor. An expression using a base and an exponent is a **power.**

$$\text{power} \longrightarrow \underset{\text{base}}{\overset{\text{exponent}}{2^5}} = \underbrace{2 \cdot 2 \cdot 2 \cdot 2 \cdot 2}_{\text{5 factors of 2}} = 32 \longleftarrow \text{value of the expression}$$

A power with an exponent of 1 means that the base is used as a factor only once. For example, $3^1 = 3$.

EXAMPLE Writing With Exponents

1 Write $3 \cdot 3 \cdot 5 \cdot 5 \cdot 5$ using exponents.

$3^2 \cdot 5^3$ ← **3 is a factor 2 times, and 5 is a factor 3 times.**

✓ Quick Check

1. Write $6 \cdot 6 \cdot 7 \cdot 7 \cdot 7 \cdot 7 \cdot 7 \cdot 7$ using exponents.

Vocabulary Tip

You read 3^2 as "3 to the second power" or "3 squared." You read 5^3 as "5 to the third power" or "5 cubed."

You can extend the order of operations to include powers.

KEY CONCEPTS Order of Operations

1. Work inside grouping symbols.

2. Simplify the powers.

3. Multiply and divide from left to right.

4. Add and subtract from left to right.

The expression $(-5)^4$ means the fourth power of -5. The expression -5^4 means the opposite of the fourth power of 5.

EXAMPLES Simplifying Expressions

Calculator Tip

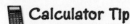

You can use the exponent key ⚲ on your calculator to find the value of any power. To evaluate $(-5)^4$, press ((-) 5) ⚲ 4 ▦.

2 Simplify $(-5)^4$.

$(-5)^4 = (-5)(-5)(-5)(-5)$ ← The base is -5.

$= 625$ ← Multiply.

3 Simplify -5^4.

$-5^4 = -(5 \cdot 5 \cdot 5 \cdot 5)$ ← The base is 5.

$= -625$ ← Multiply.

4 Simplify $26 - (2 \cdot 5)^2$.

$26 - (2 \cdot 5)^2 = 26 - (10)^2$ ← Work inside the grouping symbols.

$= 26 - 100$ ← Simplify the power.

$= -74$ ← Subtract.

✓ Quick Check

Simplify each expression.

2. $(-7)^3$ **3.** -7^3 **4.** $-4 + 6 \cdot 3^2$

You can evaluate algebraic expressions using the order of operations.

EXAMPLE Evaluating Expressions

5 **Architecture** You can find the radius of the arch in a doorway with the expression $\frac{s^2 + h^2}{2h}$. Find the radius r of a doorway with dimensions $s = 4$ ft and $h = 2$ ft.

$\frac{s^2 + h^2}{2h} = \frac{4^2 + 2^2}{2 \cdot 2}$ ← Substitute 4 for s and 2 for h.

$= \frac{16 + 4}{2 \cdot 2}$ ← Simplify the powers in the numerator.

$= \frac{20}{4} = 5$ ← Simplify. Then divide.

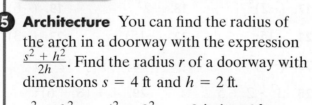

The radius of the arch is 5 ft.

Careers Architects design a wide variety of buildings and complexes.

✓ Quick Check

5. Find the radius r of a doorway with dimensions $s = 5$ m and $h = 3$ m.

Vocabulary Match the variable(s) with the correct term.

1. 3^x

2. m^5

3. y^z

   A. base
   B. power
   C. exponent

4. Reasoning Is $x^2 \cdot x^3$ the same as x^5? Explain.

Write using exponents.

5. $9 \cdot 9 \cdot 9 \cdot x$ **6.** $4 \cdot 4 \cdot 4 \cdot 4 \cdot 4$ **7.** $z \cdot z \cdot z \cdot z \cdot z \cdot z$

Simplify each expression.

8. -8^2 **9.** $(-8)^2$ **10.** $(-1)^2 - 2 \cdot 4$

Homework Exercises

For more exercises, see Extra Skills and Word Problems.

Write using exponents.

For Exercises	See Examples
11–16	1
17–24	2 and 3
25–30	4
31	5

GO for Help

11. $4 \cdot 4 \cdot 8 \cdot 8 \cdot 8 \cdot 8$ **12.** $6 \cdot 6 \cdot 6 \cdot 11$

13. $5 \cdot 5 \cdot x \cdot x \cdot x \cdot y$ **14.** $9 \cdot a \cdot a \cdot b \cdot c \cdot c \cdot c$

15. $m \cdot p \cdot m \cdot p \cdot p$ **16.** $7 \cdot w \cdot t \cdot 7 \cdot t$

Simplify each expression.

17. $(-2)^5$ **18.** -2^5 **19.** $(-6)^3$ **20.** -6^3

21. -15^2 **22.** $(-15)^2$ **23.** $(-3)^4$ **24.** -3^4

25. $(-3)^2 + 12 \cdot 4$ **26.** $-3^2 + 12 \cdot 5$ **27.** $(3 \cdot 2)^2 + 5$

28. $3^2 \cdot 2 + 5$ **29.** $4 + (8 - 6)^2$ **30.** $4 + 8 - 6^2$

31. Geometry The formula for the volume of a cylinder is $V = \pi r^2 h$, where r is the radius of the base, and h is the height of the cylinder. Find the volume of the cylinder with a radius of 6 cm and a height of 30 cm. Use $\pi = 3.14$.

GPS

32. Guided Problem Solving The formula for the area of a square is $A = s^2$. The formula for the area of a circle is $A = \pi r^2$. What is the difference in the areas of the figures if the square has a side length of 10 units and the circle has a radius length of 10 units? Use $\pi \approx 3.14$.
- What is the area of the square?
- What is the area of the circle?

Evaluate each expression for $n = -3$.

33. $5n^2 - 5(2n - 3)^2$

34. $(4n)^2 + 48 \div (-4n)$

35. $\dfrac{n^2 + 9}{n^2}$

36. $5(2n - 3)^2$

37. Skydiving The formula $d = 16t^2$ describes the number of feet d a skydiver falls in t seconds of free fall assuming there is no air resistance. How far does a skydiver fall between the third and fourth seconds?

38. Model Rockets You can use the formula $h = 160t - 16t^2$ to estimate the number of feet a model rocket rises in t seconds. How high is a rocket 2 seconds after takeoff?

39. Writing in Math Can the square of a number be negative? Explain.

40. The formula for the volume of a cone is $V = \frac{1}{3}\pi r^2 h$, where r is the radius, and h is the height. The formula for the volume of a sphere is $V = \frac{4}{3}\pi r^3$, where $r =$ the radius. How many fewer cubic units of space does a sphere with a radius of 3 units occupy than a cone with a radius of 6 units and a height of 9 units? Use $\pi \approx 3.14$.

41. Reasoning Does $(ab)^2 = ab^2$ for any values of a and b? Explain.

42. Challenge Write an expression for 100 using five 5's.

Test Prep and Mixed Review
Practice

Multiple Choice

43. The number of square feet that represent the area of a square is twice the number of feet that represents the perimeter of the square. Which of the following could be the area of the square?

    Ⓐ 4 ft^2 Ⓑ 16 ft^2 Ⓒ 36 ft^2 Ⓓ 64 ft^2

44. In science class, Julian learned that he can use the formula $C = \frac{5}{9}(F - 32)$ to convert between degrees Celsius C and degrees Fahrenheit F. If the temperature outside is 95°F, what is the temperature in degrees Celsius?

    Ⓕ 35°C   Ⓖ 63°C   Ⓗ 113°C   Ⓙ 203°C

45. In Amanda's CD collection, $\frac{1}{3}$ of the CDs are pop and $\frac{1}{5}$ are rock. Of her rock CDs, $\frac{1}{2}$ of the artists are bands and $\frac{1}{4}$ are solo female singers. The rest of her CDs are movie soundtracks. What fraction of Amanda's CDs are soundtracks?

    Ⓐ $\frac{1}{15}$ Ⓑ $\frac{1}{8}$ Ⓒ $\frac{7}{15}$ Ⓓ $\frac{8}{15}$

GO for Help

For Exercises	See Lesson
46–49	2-2

Write each decimal as a fraction in simplest form.

46. 0.3   **47.** 6.36   **48.** 0.003   **49.** 0.45

Evaluating Expressions

You can use a graphing calculator to evaluate any expression. Note that on a graphing calculator, $-$ means subtract, while $(-)$ means the opposite of a number.

EXAMPLE Evaluating for One Value

1 Use a graphing calculator to evaluate $-3x^2 - x + 14$ for $x = -7$.

Keystrokes

$(-)$ 7 STO▶ x ENTER ← Store the value -7 to the variable x.
Use the negative key $(-)$.

$(-)$ 3 x x^2 $-$ x $+$ 14 ENTER ← Evaluate the expression.

The value of the expression when $x = -7$ is -126.

Screen

```
-7→X            -7
-3X2-X+14     -126
```

EXAMPLE Evaluating for Many Values

2 Evaluate the expression in Example 1 for integer values of x from 1 to 7.

Step 1 Press Y= . Next to Y1, enter the expression $-3x^2 - x + 14$.

```
Plot 1  Plot 2  Plot 3
\Y1=-3X2-X+14
\Y2=
\Y3=
\Y4=
```

Step 2 Press 2nd WINDOW and set TblStart = 1 and △Tbl = 1.

```
TABLE SETUP
 TblStart=1
 △Tbl=1
Indpnt: Auto Ask
Depend: Auto Ask
```

Step 3 Press 2nd GRAPH to view the table.

```
 X   | Y1
 1   | 10
 2   | 0
 3   | -16
 4   | -38
 5   | -66
 6   | -100
 7   | -140
X=1
```

Exercises

Use a graphing calculator to evaluate each expression for the given value.

1. $x^2 - 2x + 5$ for $x = -10$ **2.** $\frac{5}{9}(x - 32)$ for $x = 98.6$ **3.** $-4x^2 + 34x - 6$ for $x = 25$

4. Use a graphing calculator to evaluate the expression $4x^2 - 7x + 19$ for integer values of x from 1 to 7.

Find each product or quotient. Write the answer in simplest form.

1. $\frac{2}{5} \cdot (-7)$ 2. $1\frac{1}{3} \cdot 1\frac{1}{3}$ 3. $1\frac{2}{3} \div 3\frac{4}{7}$ 4. $-\frac{1}{6} \div 4\frac{3}{4}$

Simplify each expression.

5. $10 - 2^4 \cdot 3$ 6. $(-5)^2 - 6 \cdot 4^2$ 7. $(3^2 + 1)^2$ 8. $(3 + 2)^3 - 8 \cdot 4$

9. Solve the formula $T = \frac{1}{3}ab$ for b.

10. The formula for the area of a trapezoid is $A = \frac{1}{2}h(b_1 + b_2)$. Find A for a trapezoid with height $2\frac{1}{3}$ cm and bases $4\frac{3}{4}$ cm and $3\frac{5}{6}$ cm.

11. The formula for the volume of a cone is $V = \frac{1}{3}\pi r^2 h$, where r is the radius, and h is the height. Find the height h of a cone with a radius of 6 cm and a volume of 48 cm^3.

2-8a   Activity Lab

Multiplying by Powers of 10

ACTIVITY

1. Copy and complete the table.

$6.71 \times 10^6 = 6.71 \times 1,000,000$	$=$ ▢
$6.71 \times 10^5 = 6.71 \times 100,000$	$=$ ▢
$6.71 \times 10^4 = 6.71 \times 10,000$	$=$ ▢
$6.71 \times 10^3 = 6.71 \times$ ▢	$=$ ▢
$6.71 \times 10^2 = 6.71 \times 100$	$=$ ▢
$6.71 \times 10^1 = 6.71 \times$ ▢	$=$ ▢

2. **Patterns** What relationship do you see between the exponent of 10 and the number being multiplied by 6.71?

3. Explain what happens in your table as the exponent of 10 increases.

4. **Writing in Math** Write a rule for multiplying by powers of 10.

2-8 Scientific Notation

Check Skills You'll Need

1. **Vocabulary Review**
   An expression using a base and an exponent is a __?__.

Multiply.

2. 2×10

3. 4.51×100

4. $1.5 \times 1,000$

5. $1.803 \times 10,000$

6. $2.39 \times 1,000,000$

GO for Help
Skills Handbook
p. 635

What You'll Learn

To write numbers in both standard form and scientific notation

◀) **New Vocabulary** scientific notation

Why Learn This?

When you are dealing with very large or very small numbers in science, it is helpful to be able to write them in a shorter form.

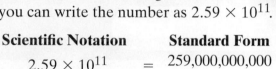

Written in standard form, or standard notation, the volume of Earth is about 259,000,000,000 cubic miles. Using scientific notation, you can write the number as 2.59×10^{11}.

Scientific Notation		Standard Form
2.59×10^{11}	=	$259,000,000,000$

KEY CONCEPTS Scientific Notation

A number is in **scientific notation** if the first factor is greater than or equal to 1 and less than 10 and the second factor is a power of 10.

Examples $\quad 1 \times 10^8 \qquad 1.54 \times 10^7 \qquad 9.99 \times 10^4$

Multiplying a number by 10^n, when n is positive, moves the decimal point n places to the right.

EXAMPLE Writing in Standard Form

1 **Science** The temperature at the sun's core is about 1.55×10^6 degrees Celsius. Write the temperature in standard form.

$$1.55 \times 10^6 = 1.550000. \leftarrow \text{Move the decimal point 6 places to the right. Insert zeros as necessary.}$$
$$= 1,550,000$$

The temperature at the sun's core is $1,550,000°C$.

Calculator Tip

1.55E6 on a calculator means 1.55×10^6.

✓ Quick Check

1. Write $7.66 \times 10^6 \text{ km}^2$, the area of Australia, in standard form.

To write a number in scientific notation, determine the first factor. Then write the second factor as a power of 10.

EXAMPLE Writing in Scientific Notation

2 A supercomputer can perform 135,300,000,000,000 operations per second. Write this quantity in scientific notation.

$135,300,000,000,000 = 1.35,300,000,000,000.$ ← **Move the decimal point 14 places to the left.**

$= 1.353 \times 10^{14}$ ← **Use 14 as the exponent of 10.**

The supercomputer can perform 1.353×10^{14} operations per second.

✓ Quick Check

2. Write 3,476,000 m, the moon's diameter, in scientific notation.

Numbers in scientific notation can have negative exponents. Multiplying a number by 10^n, when n is negative, moves the decimal point n places to the left.

EXAMPLE Negative Exponents

3 **Biology** Fingernails grow about 1.23×10^{-2} centimeters per day. Write this rate in standard form.

$1.23 \times 10^{-2} = .01.23$ ← **Move the decimal point 2 places to the left to make 1.23 less than 1.**

Fingernails grow about 0.0123 centimeters per day.

✓ Quick Check

3. Write 2.5×10^{-4} inches, the diameter of a cell, in standard form.

To write a number that is less than 1 in scientific notation, determine the first factor by moving the decimal point. Then write the second factor as a power of ten with a negative exponent.

EXAMPLE Numbers Less Than 1

4 Write the quantity 0.0000076 in scientific notation.

$0.0000076 = 0.000007.6$ ← **Move the decimal point 6 places to the right to get a factor greater than 1 but less than 10.**

$= 7.6 \times 10^{-6}$ ← **Use −6 as the exponent of 10.**

✓ Quick Check

4. Write 0.0000035 in scientific notation.

1. **Vocabulary** A number is in scientific notation if the first factor is greater than or equal to __?__ and less than 10.

2. **Reasoning** Explain why 1.55×10^6 does not have six zeros when it is written in standard form.

3. **Number Sense** Is 8.1×10^{-5} greater than or less than 0? Explain.

4. When 123.4 and 654.321 are written in scientific notation, will the exponents of 10 be the same? Explain.

Homework Exercises

For more exercises, see Extra Skills and Word Problems.

GO for Help

For Exercises	See Examples
5–9	1
10–14	2
15–19	3
20–25	4

Write each number in standard form.

5. 3.2×10^3 6. 5.08×10^4 7. 4.1×10^8 8. 7.145×10^9

9. **Whales** Write the average weight of a blue whale, 2.6×10^5 lb, in standard form.

Write each number in scientific notation.

10. 4,800   11. 17,200   12. 180,000   13. 343,502

14. **Space Travel** NASA's Apollo program lasted nine years (1963–1972) and included six moon landings. Write the cost of the Apollo project, $25,000,000,000, in scientific notation.

Write each number in standard form.

15. 2.5×10^{-3} 16. 5.12×10^{-5} 17. 1.05×10^{-2} 18. 3.14×10^{-7}

19. Write the size of a grain of very fine sand, about 9.35×10^{-3} cm, in standard form.

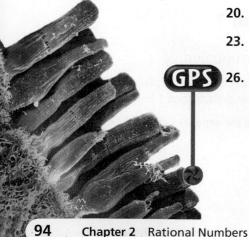

Retina Cells

Write each number in scientific notation.

20. 0.00581   21. 0.00105   22. 0.0000078

23. 0.000027   24. 0.000000132   25. 0.000000009

26. **Guided Problem Solving** The human eye's retina has about 130 million light-sensitive cells. Write this number in scientific notation.
   - What is 130 million written in standard form?
   - Should you move the decimal point to the right or to the left?
   - How many places should you move the decimal point?

Find each value of n.

27. $1.0035 \times 10^n = 100,350,000$ **28.** $56,194 = n \times 10^4$

29. $0.0000083 = 8.3 \times 10^n$ **30.** $n \times 10^{-9} = 0.000000004802$

31. The population of the United States is expected to be 392 million people by 2050. Write this number in scientific notation.

32. Error Analysis Explain how you know that 492×10^5 is not in scientific notation.

33. Astronomy When the sun emits a solar flare, the blast wave can travel through space at 3×10^6 km/h. Use the formula $d = rt$ to find how far the wave will travel in 30 min.

34. Which number is greater, 3.14×10^{99} or 3×10^{100}?

35. Heat For a 10-minute shower, you use about 5,500 kilocalories to heat 50 gallons of water. (The prefix *kilo-* means 1,000 or 10^3.)
a. About how many calories do you use in a 5-minute shower?
b. Write your answer to part (a) in scientific notation.

36. Writing in Math A number written in scientific notation is multiplied by 100. Explain what happens to the exponent of 10.

37. Challenge Write $10^{29} - 10^{28}$ in scientific notation.

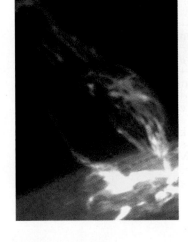

Test Prep and Mixed Review   Practice

Multiple Choice

38. The moon is about 380,000 kilometers from Earth. Which expression represents this measurement in scientific notation?
Ⓐ 3.8×10^3 km   Ⓒ 3.8×10^5 km
Ⓑ 3.8×10^4 km   Ⓓ 3.8×10^6 km

39. In Brett's class, there are $2\frac{1}{2}$ times as many people who eat meat as people who don't. If 10 people in his class eat meat, which equation can be used to find the number of people v who do not?
Ⓕ $v = 2\frac{1}{2} \times 10$ Ⓗ $v = 2\frac{1}{2} \div 10$
Ⓖ $v = 10 \div 2\frac{1}{2}$ Ⓙ $v = 2\frac{1}{2} + 10$

40. Maya wants to find the width of a rectangular trunk using the formula $v = \ell wh$, where $v = 24$ ft^3, $\ell = 4$ ft, and $h = 2$ ft. To solve the formula for w,
Ⓐ Multiply both sides by 6.   Ⓒ Divide both sides by 6.
Ⓑ Multiply both sides by 8.   Ⓓ Divide both sides by 8.

Find each value of y for x = 3.

41. $y = x^3 + x^4 - x^5$ **42.** $y = 3x^3 - 2x^2$ **43.** $y = x^2 - x^3$

Writing Measurements

When you write very large or very small numbers in scientific notation, you write the numbers as multiples of powers of ten. In the metric system of measurement, you can use prefixes to indicate powers of ten. The table shows common prefixes and their meanings.

For example, the prefix *kilo-* means 10^3. You can write 2 kilometers as 2×10^3, or 2,000, meters. Similarly, you can write 4,000 meters as 4×10^3 meters, or 4 kilometers. Note that the symbol for kilo- is k, so the abbreviation for kilometers is km.

Prefix	Symbol	Meaning
micro-	μ	10^{-6}
milli-	m	10^{-3}
centi-	c	10^{-2}
kilo-	k	10^3
mega-	M	10^6

ACTIVITY

1. Use a metric prefix to write 3,100 grams (g) in kilograms (kg).

2. Use a metric prefix to write 0.0052 meters (m) in millimeters (mm).

3. Use a metric prefix to write 64,200,000 bytes (b) in megabytes (Mb).

4. Copy the table below. Fill in each of the facts about Thomson's gazelles using both scientific notation and metric prefixes.

Thomson's Gazelles

Characteristic	Measure	Scientific Notation	Metric Prefixes
Average weight	21,500 g	■ g	■
Average height	0.63 m	■ m	■
Possible diameter of a single hair	0.00005 m	■ m	■
Distance a herd can travel in a day	16,000 m	■ m	■

5. Make a table like the one above for an animal or insect of your choice. Write all measures using both scientific notation and metric prefixes.

6. The average diameter of a human hair is about 80 micrometers. Use scientific notation or measurements with metric prefixes to compare it to the diameter of a gazelle's hair. Explain your choice.

7. Suppose you want to compare the weight of an elephant to the weight of a whale. Would you write the measures in scientific notation or using metric prefixes? Explain your choice.

Writing Short Responses

Short-response questions are usually worth 2 points. To receive full credit, you must give the correct answer (including the appropriate units, if needed), and justify your reasoning or show your work.

EXAMPLE

A parent paid a baby sitter \$33 to baby-sit two children for one night. The sitter watched the children for $5\frac{1}{2}$ hours. Write and solve an equation to find how much the sitter was paid per hour.

To receive full credit, you must (1) set up an equation, (2) solve the equation, and (3) tell how much the sitter was paid per hour. The number of points for different types of answers follow.

Scoring

[2]   The equation and the solution are correct.

[1]   There is no equation. There *is* a method to show the correct solution.
       OR There are an equation and a solution containing minor errors.
       OR The equation and solution are correct. No work is shown.

[0]   There is no response, or the solution is completely incorrect.

Here are three responses with their points.

2 points

Let p = sitter's pay/hour
$$33 = 5\frac{1}{2}p$$
$$33 \div 5\frac{1}{2} = 5\frac{1}{2}p \div 5\frac{1}{2}$$
$$6 = p$$
The sitter was paid \$6/h.

1 point

$$\frac{33}{5\frac{1}{2}} = 6$$
\$6

0 points

$$\frac{33}{5\frac{1}{2}} = 7$$
The sitter was paid \$7/h.

Exercises

1. **Writing in Math** Explain why each response above received the indicated number of points.

2. **Reasoning** How many points does the response at the right deserve? Explain.

3. **Error Analysis** A student uses the equation $p \div 5\frac{1}{2} = 33$ to solve the problem. Explain why the equation is incorrect.

Let p = sitter's pay/hour
$$33 = 5\frac{1}{2}p$$
$$27\frac{1}{2} = 5\frac{1}{2}p$$
$$5 = p$$
The sitter was paid \$5/h.

Chapter 2 Review

Vocabulary Review

 base (p. 86)
composite number (p. 52)
divisible (p. 52)
exponent (p. 86)
factor (p. 52)
formula (p. 81)
greatest common factor (GCF)
  (p. 53)

least common denominator
  (LCD) (p. 62)
least common multiple (LCM)
  (p. 62)
multiplicative inverse (p. 73)
power (p. 86)
prime factorization (p. 53)

prime number (p. 52)
rational number (p. 57)
reciprocals (p. 73)
relatively prime (p. 57)
repeating decimal (p. 58)
scientific notation (p. 92)
terminating decimal (p. 58)

Choose the correct vocabulary term above to complete each sentence.

1. __?__ is used when writing very large or very small numbers.

2. Two numbers whose product is one are called __?__.

3. The __?__ of 15 and 25 is 75.

4. The expression $3^2 \cdot 7$ is the __?__ of 63.

5. An expression like 12^8 is a(n) __?__.

6. A(n) __?__ shows the relationship between two or more quantities.

7. The numbers 8 and 9 are __?__ because 1 is their only common factor.

8. The number 0.3589402 is a __?__.

9. The __?__ of 15 and 25 is 5.

10. The expression 5^3 has a(n) __?__ of 3 and a(n) __?__ of 5.

Go Online
PHSchool.com
For: Online Vocabulary Quiz
Web Code: asj-0251

Skills and Concepts

Lessons 2-1, 2-2
- To identify prime and composite numbers and to find the greatest common factor
- To write equivalent fractions and decimals

The **greatest common factor** of two numbers is the greatest **factor** that is common to both numbers. A **rational number** can be written in the form $\frac{a}{b}$, where a is an integer and b is any nonzero integer.

Use a factor tree to find the prime factorization of each number.

11. 260   12. 700   13. 378   14. 139   15. 7,020

16. **Surveys** In a survey about favorite subjects in school, 0.16 of the students surveyed liked math the most. What fraction of the students surveyed chose math as their favorite subject?

Lesson 2-3

- To use least common denominators, decimals, and number lines to compare and order rational numbers

You can compare rational numbers by rewriting the fractions with a common denominator or by changing each fraction to a decimal.

Compare. Write <, >, or =.

17. $\frac{3}{5}$ ▮ $\frac{7}{9}$ **18.** -4 ▮ $-\frac{14}{3}$ **19.** 0.625 ▮ $\frac{5}{8}$

Lessons 2-4, 2-5

- To add and subtract fractions and mixed numbers and to solve problems involving rational numbers
- To multiply and divide fractions and mixed numbers and to solve problems involving rational numbers

To add or subtract fractions, write equivalent fractions using a common multiple of the denominators or the **least common denominator (LCD).** To multiply fractions, multiply both the numerators and denominators. To divide, multiply by the **reciprocal** of the divisor.

Simplify.

20. $-\frac{7}{8} + \frac{3}{4}$ **21.** $-2\frac{4}{5} - \left(-1\frac{3}{10}\right)$ **22.** $-3\frac{1}{6} + 2\frac{1}{2}$

23. $-\frac{1}{6} \cdot \left(-\frac{3}{8}\right)$ **24.** $2\frac{1}{2} \div \frac{10}{13}$ **25.** $-4\frac{2}{3} \div 2\frac{2}{9}$

26. A carpenter cuts a $7\frac{1}{2}$-ft board into $2\frac{1}{2}$-ft pieces. How many pieces does he have?

Lesson 2-6

- To use formulas to solve problems and to solve a formula for a variable

A **formula** is an equation that shows a relationship between two or more quantities. A common formula for finding distance is $d = rt$.

27. Find the average rate of travel if a car travels 270 miles in 6 hours.

Solve each formula for the variable shown in red.

28. $A = \frac{1}{2}bh$ **29.** $y = mx + b$ **30.** $d = rt$

Lessons 2-7, 2-8

- To write, simplify, and evaluate expressions involving exponents
- To write numbers in both standard form and scientific notation

An **exponent** tells how many times a number, or **base,** is used as a factor. To simplify a numerical expression, use the order of operations.

A number is in **scientific notation** if the first factor is greater than or equal to 1 and less than 10 and the second factor is a **power** of 10.

Simplify each expression.

31. $(4 \cdot 2)^2 - 3$ **32.** $5^2 \cdot 2 + 4$ **33.** $-8 + 2 \cdot 4^2$

Write each number in scientific notation.

34. 3,500   **35.** 801,000   **36.** 0.000205   **37.** 0.000000081

38. The moon is about 3.8×10^8 m from Earth. Write this number in standard form.

Chapter 2 Test

Go Online For: Online chapter test
PHSchool.com Web Code: asa-0252

Find the GCF of each pair of numbers.

1. 12, 16   2. 32, 48   3. 144, 192

Use a factor tree to find the prime factorization of each number.

4. 90   5. 432   6. 47   7. 280

Compare. Write <, >, or =.

8. $\frac{3}{8}$ ▪ 0.4   9. $-\frac{1}{2}$ ▪ $-\frac{5}{12}$

10. -0.89 ▪ $-\frac{9}{10}$ 11. $\frac{4}{9}$ ▪ $0.\overline{4}$

Write each fraction as a decimal. Round to three decimal places.

12. $\frac{2}{5}$ 13. $-\frac{27}{8}$ 14. $\frac{19}{15}$ 15. $\frac{7}{11}$

Write each decimal as a fraction or mixed number in simplest form.

16. 0.64   17. $0.\overline{6}$ 18. 0.471   19. $0.\overline{282}$

20. **Sports** Each time a ball hits the ground, it bounces back to $\frac{2}{3}$ of its previous height. On its second bounce, the ball reaches a height of 12 in. What was the ball's original height?

21. **Running** A runner jogs on a $\frac{1}{4}$-mi track. How many miles does the runner jog in 18 laps?

Simplify each expression. Write the answer as a fraction or mixed number in simplest form.

22. $-\frac{3}{5} - \frac{1}{3}$ 23. $\frac{1}{12} - \frac{5}{12}$

24. $\frac{5}{12} + \frac{5}{9}$ 25. $3\frac{1}{4} - 2\frac{2}{3}$

26. $\frac{11}{12} - \frac{3}{4}$ 27. $2\frac{1}{5} - 3\frac{1}{3}$

28. $-2\frac{3}{4} \cdot \frac{8}{9}$ 29. $\frac{5}{8} \div \left(-\frac{1}{2}\right)$

30. $-\frac{2}{5} \cdot \frac{7}{8}$ 31. $-1\frac{1}{2} \div \frac{5}{12}$

32. $1\frac{1}{4} \cdot -\frac{5}{9}$ 33. $\frac{21}{50} \div \frac{21}{50}$

34. **Writing in Math** Write what you would say to a classmate who asked you to explain why -4^2 is equal to -16.

Simplify each expression.

35. $(-2)^4$ 36. -2^4 37. $3^3 + 5^2$

38. $4^2 \cdot 2 + 8$ 39. $(9 - 3)^2$ 40. $22 - 7^2$

Evaluate each expression for $m = -4$ and $p = 2$.

41. $m^2 - p + 12$ 42. $2p^2 - (m - 1)^2$

43. $3(5m - 1)^2$ 44. $\frac{m^2 + 16}{m^2}$

Write each number in scientific notation.

45. 23,000,000   46. 1,500,000

47. 450,000,000   48. 0.00007

49. 0.0089   50. 0.0401

Write each number in standard form.

51. 4.1×10^5 52. 8.02×10^4

53. 5×10^{-3} 54. 8.8×10^{-6}

55. **Number Sense** Which number is greater, 5×10^{-6} or 6×10^{-5}? Explain.

56. **Aviation** In 2002, Erik Lindbergh, the grandson of aviator Charles Lindbergh, flew 3,756 miles in 17.7 hours. Find his average speed. Use the formula $d = rt$.

57. Find the area of a rectangle with a length of $2\frac{1}{4}$ in. and a width of $\frac{7}{8}$ in. Use the formula $A = \ell w$.

Solve each formula for the variable shown in red.

58. $L = 2\pi rh$ 59. $V = Bh$

60. $S = a + 2b$ 61. $C = -5d + p$

Multiple Choice

Read each question. Then write the letter of the correct answer on your paper.

1. Size B8 paper measures $2\frac{1}{2}$ by $3\frac{1}{2}$ inches. Find the number of square inches in its area.

   Ⓐ $5\frac{3}{4}$ Ⓑ $6\frac{1}{4}$ Ⓒ $8\frac{3}{4}$ Ⓓ $9\frac{1}{4}$

2. The expression $6(x - 2)$ is equivalent to which of the following?

   Ⓕ $6x - 2$ Ⓗ $6x - 12$
   Ⓖ $6x + 2$ Ⓙ $6x + 12$

3. What is the area of the rectangle below?

   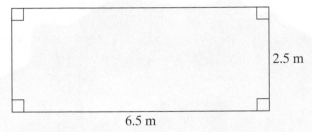
   2.5 m
   6.5 m

   Ⓐ 9 m^2 Ⓒ 16.25 m^2
   Ⓑ 15.5 m^2 Ⓓ 18 m^2

4. Which quotient is between -4 and -5?

   Ⓕ $2\frac{5}{6} \div \left(-\frac{1}{2}\right)$ Ⓗ $-9\frac{1}{3} \div 2$

   Ⓖ $-5\frac{1}{2} \div \left(-1\frac{1}{2}\right)$ Ⓙ $1\frac{2}{3} \div \left(-\frac{1}{2}\right)$

5. Evaluate the expression $3 - 6m$ for $m = 3$.

   Ⓐ -15 Ⓒ 6
   Ⓑ 0 Ⓓ 15

6. The number 66,510 is NOT divisible by which of the following?

   Ⓕ 3 Ⓖ 4 Ⓗ 5 Ⓙ 9

7. Which of the following is the LCM of 24 and 36?

   Ⓐ 2 Ⓑ 4 Ⓒ 12 Ⓓ 72

8. If $a + y = 18$, then $y =$ ■.

   Ⓕ $a - 18$ Ⓗ $18 - a$

   Ⓖ $a + 18$ Ⓙ $\frac{18}{a}$

9. A racing canoeist can paddle 250 feet in $20\frac{1}{2}$ seconds. At that rate, how many feet does the canoeist paddle each second?

   Ⓐ $\frac{41}{500}$ Ⓑ $\frac{121}{41}$ Ⓒ $\frac{500}{82}$ Ⓓ $\frac{500}{41}$

10. There are $3\frac{2}{3}$ times as many birds b as there are trees t. Which equation relates the two variables?

    Ⓕ $b = 3\frac{2}{3}t$ Ⓗ $b = 3\frac{2}{3} + t$

    Ⓖ $t = 3\frac{2}{3}b$ Ⓙ $t = 3\frac{2}{3} + b$

Gridded Response

Record your answer in a grid.

11. Find the value of $\frac{2}{5} + \frac{1}{2}$.

12. Find the GCF of 24 and 40.

Short Response

13. A student had $78. She then earned money baby-sitting. Now she has $116.

    a. Write an equation you can use to find how much the student earned baby-sitting.

    b. How much did the student earn baby-sitting?

Extended Response

14. The area of the figure below is 130,000 yd^2.

    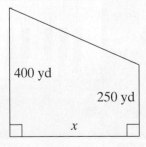
    400 yd
    250 yd
    x

    a. Write an equation that you can use to find the length x.

    b. Find the length of x. Show your work.

Applying Real Numbers

Frequency and Math Vibrations produce sounds. When a series of vibrations makes pleasing combinations of sounds, the result is called music.

The *frequency* of a sound is the number of vibrations, or cycles, per second that produce the sound. The greater the frequency, the higher the pitch. The *period* of a sound is the duration of one cycle in seconds. For example, one part of a telephone's dial tone uses a frequency of 350 cycles per second. This sound has a period of $\frac{1}{350}$ s.

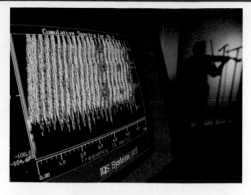

Analyzing Sound

A spectrum analyzer measures the sound of a violin.

Exploding Glass

If you tap a delicate glass, it produces a high-pitched tone. This is the "natural frequency" of the glass. A very steady, very loud sound with this frequency can break the glass by causing it to vibrate until it shatters.

Keyboard

Strings

Tuning pin

Put It All Together

1. a. What is the frequency of a piano string that vibrates 50 times per second?

b. What is the period of the note?

2. Copy and complete the table. Write each period in decimal form.

Sound	Approximate Frequency (cycles per second)	Period (seconds)
Lowest sound audible to humans	20	◼
Lowest note on a guitar	82	◼
Highest note on an oboe	1,568	◼
Highest sound audible to humans	20,000	◼

3. Reasoning People often associate trumpet-like sounds with elephants. Scientists have discovered that elephants communicate using "sounds" with periods as long as $\frac{1}{10}$ s. Why do you think these communications weren't discovered until recently?

4. a. Language Bats use ultrasonic frequencies to help them navigate and locate food. Use a dictionary to find the definition of *ultrasonic*.

b. Open-Ended Give an example of the period of an ultrasonic frequency.

5. Research Prepare a report about animals who make sounds with frequencies that humans cannot hear.

Acoustic Guitar

This acoustic guitar has a hollow body and six strings. Plucking or strumming the strings produces vibrations. The guitar's body amplifies the vibrations.

Hollow body   Strings   Neck   Headstock

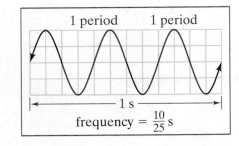

1 period   1 period

1 s

frequency $= \frac{10}{25}$ s

Sound Waves

The period of a sound wave is one complete "wave" of the sound. The frequency is the length, or duration, of the period.

Piano Strings

A grand piano (shown) has 88 keys and about 230 strings running parallel to the floor. The strings of an upright piano run perpendicular to the floor.

Go Online
PHSchool.com

For: Information about sound
Web Code: ase-0253

What You've Learned

- In Chapter 1, you wrote and solved algebraic equations.

- In Chapter 2, you used appropriate operations to solve problems involving rational numbers.

 Check Your Readiness

GO for Help

For Exercises	See Lessons
1–2	1-1
3–5	1-3
6–9	2-2
10–12	2-6
13–15	2-7

Evaluating and Simplifying Expressions

(Algebra) Evaluate each expression for $s = 4$ and $t = -3$.

1. $5s + 16t$

2. $44 - 2st$

Simplify each expression.

3. $-11 + 2$

4. $15 + (-2)$

5. $5 - (-5)$

Fractions and Decimals

Write each fraction as a decimal. Round to three decimal places.

6. $\frac{5}{6}$

7. $\frac{16}{40}$

8. $\frac{21}{13}$

9. $\frac{19}{22}$

Formulas

(Algebra) Solve each formula for the variable indicated in red.

10. $c = a + b$

11. $d = 16t$

12. $s = 200 + T$

Exponents

Simplify each expression.

13. $3^2 + 4^2$

14. $5^2 - 2^2$

15. $9^2 + 10^2$

What You'll Learn Next

- In this chapter, you will approximate the value of irrational numbers and use the Pythagorean Theorem to solve real-world problems.

- You will graph points and lines in the coordinate plane.

- You will translate, reflect, and rotate figures.

 Problem Solving Application On pages 156 and 157, you will work an extended activity on mountain slopes.

🔊 Key Vocabulary

- coordinate plane (p. 124)
- image (p. 136)
- irrational numbers (p. 107)
- linear equation (p. 131)
- ordered pair (p. 124)
- perfect square (p. 106)
- Pythagorean Theorem (p. 112)
- quadrants (p. 124)
- real numbers (p. 107)
- reflectional symmetry (p. 142)
- rotational symmetry (p. 146)
- solution (p. 131)
- square root (p. 106)
- transformation (p. 136)
- translation (p. 136)

Exploring Square Roots and Irrational Numbers

What You'll Learn

To find and estimate square roots and to classify numbers as rational or irrational

🔊 **New Vocabulary** perfect square, square root, irrational numbers, real numbers

Why Learn This?

Not every situation can be modeled using the four basic operations. For example, you need square roots to relate the time and distance a skydiver falls.

A number that is the square of a whole number is a **perfect square.** The **square root** of a number is another number that when multiplied by itself is equal to the given number.

In the diagram at the right, 16 square tiles form a square with 4 tiles on each side. Since $4 \cdot 4 = 16$ and $-4 \cdot (-4) = 16$, 16 has two square roots, 4 and −4. Since $4^2 = 16$, 16 is a perfect square.

$4^2 = 16$

EXAMPLE **Finding Square Roots of Perfect Squares**

Perfect Squares

n	n^2
0	0
1	1
2	4
3	9
4	16
5	25
6	36
7	49
8	64
9	81
10	100
11	121
12	144

1 Find the two square roots of 25.

$5 \cdot 5 = 25$ and $-5 \cdot (-5) = 25$

The square roots of 25 are 5 and −5.

✓ Quick Check

1. Find the square roots of each number.
   a. 36   **b.** 1   **c.** $\frac{1}{16}$

The symbol $\sqrt{}$ means the square root of a number. In this book, $\sqrt{}$ means the positive square root, unless stated otherwise. So $\sqrt{9}$ means the positive square root of 9, or 3, and $-\sqrt{9}$ means the opposite of the positive square root of 9, or −3.

To estimate the square root of a number that is not a perfect square, use the square root of the nearest perfect square.

EXAMPLE Estimating a Square Root

2 Estimate the value of $\sqrt{28}$ to the nearest integer.

$$\overset{\sqrt{25}}{\underset{5}{|}} \quad \overset{\sqrt{28}}{\bullet} \qquad\qquad \overset{\sqrt{36}}{\underset{6}{|}}$$

Since 28 is closer to 25 than it is to 36, $\sqrt{28}$ is closer to 5 than to 6. You can write $\sqrt{28} \approx 5$.

✅ Quick Check

2. Estimate the value of $\sqrt{38}$ to the nearest integer.

Finding a number's square root is the inverse operation of finding the number's square. So $\sqrt{3^2} = 3$.

EXAMPLE Application: Skydiving

3 The formula $d = 16t^2$ represents the approximate distance d in feet a skydiver falls in t seconds before opening the parachute. The formula assumes there is no air resistance. Find the time a skydiver takes to fall 816 feet before opening the parachute.

$$d = 16t^2 \quad \leftarrow \textbf{Use the formula for distance and time.}$$
$$816 = 16t^2 \quad \leftarrow \textbf{Substitute 816 for } d.$$
$$\frac{816}{16} = t^2 \quad \leftarrow \textbf{Divide each side by 16 to isolate } t.$$
$$51 = t^2 \quad \leftarrow \textbf{Simplify.}$$
$$\sqrt{51} = \sqrt{t^2} \quad \leftarrow \textbf{Find the positive square root of each side.}$$

$$\boxed{\sqrt{}}\ 51\ \boxed{=}\ 7.141428429 \quad \leftarrow \textbf{Use a calculator.}$$
$$7.1 \approx t \qquad \leftarrow \textbf{Round to the nearest tenth.}$$

The skydiver takes about 7.1 seconds to fall 816 feet.

✅ Quick Check

3. Find the time a skydiver takes to fall each distance. Round to the nearest tenth of a second.
   a. 480 ft   **b.** 625 ft

Irrational numbers are numbers that cannot be written in the form $\frac{a}{b}$, where a is any integer and b is any nonzero integer. Rational and irrational numbers form the set of **real numbers.**

For: Square Roots Activity
Use: Interactive Textbook, 3-1

GO for Help

For help in using formulas, go to Lesson 2-6, Example 1.

The diagram below shows the relationships among sets of numbers.

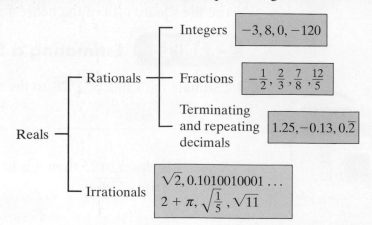

The decimal digits of irrational numbers do not terminate or repeat. The decimal digits of $\pi = 3.14159265359\ldots$ do not terminate or repeat, because π is an irrational number. Irrational numbers can also include decimals that have a pattern in their digits, like $0.02022022202222\ldots$

For any integer n that is not a perfect square, $\sqrt{n}$ is irrational.

EXAMPLE **Classifying Real Numbers**

GO for Help

For help with terminating and repeating decimals, go to Lesson 2–2, Example 3.

④ Is each number *rational* or *irrational*? Explain.

a. $0.818118111\ldots$ Irrational; the decimal does not terminate or repeat.

b. $-0.\overline{81}$ Rational; the decimal repeats.

c. $1\frac{2}{9}$ Rational; the number can be written as the ratio $\frac{11}{9}$.

d. $\sqrt{5}$ Irrational; 5 is not a perfect square.

✓ Quick Check

4. Is $0.\overline{6}$ *rational* or *irrational*? Explain.

✓ Check Your Understanding

Vocabulary Write all the possible names for each number. Choose from the terms at the right.

1. $\sqrt{6}$ **2.** $-0.\overline{6}$

3. $\frac{1}{6}$ **4.** 25

A. rational number
B. irrational number
C. real number
D. perfect square

Find the positive and negative square roots of each number.

5. 4 **6.** $\frac{1}{4}$ **7.** 100 **8.** $\frac{1}{100}$

Homework Exercises

For more exercises, see Extra Skills and Word Problems.

GO for Help

For Exercises	See Examples
9–13	1
14–21	2
22–25	3
26–31	4

Find the square roots of each number.

9. 49 10. 900 11. $\dfrac{1}{36}$ 12. $\dfrac{1}{121}$ 13. $\dfrac{4}{25}$

Estimate the value of each expression to the nearest integer.

14. $\sqrt{3}$ 15. $\sqrt{10}$ 16. $-\sqrt{22}$ 17. $\sqrt{88}$

18. $-\sqrt{54}$ 19. $-\sqrt{105}$ 20. $\sqrt{150}$ 21. $-\sqrt{120}$

Use $s = 20\sqrt{273 + T}$ to estimate the speed of sound s in meters per second for each Celsius temperature T. Round to the nearest integer.

22. $0°C$ 23. $20°C$ 24. $-10°C$ 25. $70°C$

Is each number *rational* or *irrational*? Explain.

26. -0.6 27. $\sqrt{40}$ 28. $0.606606660\ldots$

29. $-\sqrt{144}$ 30. $\sqrt{12}$ 31. $0.0203040506\ldots$

32. **Guided Problem Solving** The area of a square postage stamp is $\dfrac{81}{100}$ in.^{2}. What is the side length of the stamp?
    - What is the formula for the area of a square?
    - How can you use the formula to find the side length of a square?

33. **Boxing** The area of a square boxing ring is 484 ft^2. What is the perimeter of the boxing ring?

GO Online
Homework Video Tutor
Visit: PHSchool.com
Web Code: ase-0301

34. **Geometry** A tile is shown at the right. The area of the larger square is 49 in.^{2}. Find the area of the smaller square.

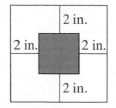

35. **Open-Ended** Give an example of an irrational number that is less than 2 and greater than 1.5. Explain how you know the number is irrational.

36. **Writing in Math** Explain how you can approximate $\sqrt{30}$.

37. The Closure Property states that a set of numbers is closed under a given operation if the result of the operation is in the same set of numbers. For example, the set of rational numbers is closed under addition, because the sum of any two rational numbers is a rational number. Is each set of numbers closed under addition? Explain.
    a. even numbers   b. irrational numbers   c. prime numbers

Find the value of each expression.

38. $(\sqrt{36})^2$ **39.** $\sqrt{(10)^2}$ **40.** $\sqrt{(3.2)^2}$ **41.** $(\sqrt{a})^2$

A number that is used as a factor three times is the cube root of the product. Since $2^3 = 8$, 2 is the cube root of 8. Find each cube root n.

42. $n^3 = 27$ **43.** $n^3 = 64$ **44.** $n^3 = 125$ **45.** $n^3 = -8$

46. The area of a square is $\frac{25}{36}$ in.^{2}. What is the length of its side?

47. Ferris Wheels The formula $d = 1.23\sqrt{h}$ represents the distance in miles d you can see from h feet above ground. On the London Eye Ferris Wheel, you are 450 ft above ground. To the nearest tenth of a mile, how far can you see?

48. Number Sense For what values of n is $\sqrt{n}$ a rational number?

49. Error Analysis A student evaluated the expression $\sqrt{4 + 9}$ and got the answer 5. What error did the student make?

50. Challenge Explain how you know that the number 123,456,789,101,112 cannot be a perfect square. (*Hint:* What is the units digit?)

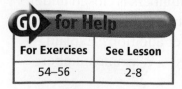

Test Prep and Mixed Review

Practice

Multiple Choice

51. The area of a square is 150 square centimeters. Which best represents the side length of the square?
  Ⓐ 11.7 cm Ⓑ 12.2 cm Ⓒ 2.9 cm Ⓓ 13 cm

52. The diameter of a human hair is about 1.7×10^{-5} meters. Which of the following represents this number in standard notation?
  Ⓕ 0.000017 Ⓖ 0.00017 Ⓗ 17,000 Ⓙ 170,000

53. Which problem situation matches the equation $2x + 5 = 20$?
  Ⓐ Jacob travels 5 more than twice as many miles to work as Carrie travels. If Carrie travels 20 miles to work, how many miles x does Jacob travel?
  Ⓑ Dana's arm is 5 inches longer than Collin's arm. If Dana's arm is 20 inches long, what is twice the length x of Collin's arm?
  Ⓒ Joel made a $20 phone call to Spain. The call cost $2 per minute plus a $5 connection fee. How many minutes x did the call last?
  Ⓓ Alondra invited 20 people to a party. Two people arrived late, and five people could not go. How many people x arrived on time for the party?

GO for Help

For Exercises	See Lesson
54–56	2-8

Write each number in scientific notation.

54. 18,000 **55.** 6,038,000 **56.** 49,700

Exploring the Pythagorean Theorem

ACTIVITY

Step 1 Use centimeter grid paper to draw a right triangle. The right angle should be included between sides that are 3 cm and 4 cm long.

Step 2 Draw a 3-by-3 square along the side that is 3 cm long. Label the square A. Draw a 4-by-4 square along the side that is 4 cm long. Label the square B.

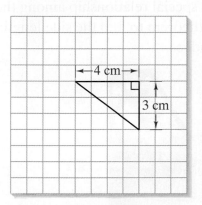

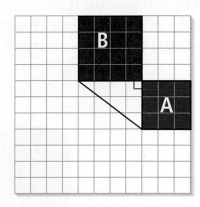

Step 3 Cut out another piece of grid paper to make a square on the side opposite the right angle. Label the square C.

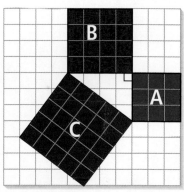

Exercises

1. **a.** Repeat the activity for the triangles shown in the table. Copy and complete the table.

   b. Patterns What is the relationship between the areas of the two smaller squares (A and B) and the area of the largest square (C)?

2. **(Algebra)** Use variables to write an equation that relates the side lengths of a right triangle.

Sides of Triangle	Area of Square A	Area of Square B	Area of Square C
3, 4, 5	9	16	25
5, 12, ▦	▦	▦	▦
6, 8, ▦	▦	▦	▦
9, 12, ▦	▦	▦	▦

The Pythagorean Theorem

Check Skills You'll Need

1. **Vocabulary Review** What is the *square root* of a number?

Estimate the value of each expression to the nearest integer.

2. $\sqrt{60}$ 3. $\sqrt{111}$

4. $\sqrt{80}$ 5. $\sqrt{22}$

GO for Help
Lesson 3-1

What You'll Learn

To use the Pythagorean Theorem to find the length of the hypotenuse of a right triangle

🔊 **New Vocabulary** legs, hypotenuse, Pythagorean Theorem

Why Learn This?

The Pythagorean Theorem describes the special relationship among the sides of a right triangle. You can use the theorem to find the side lengths of right triangles in structures such as bridges.

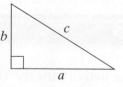

In a right triangle, the two shortest sides are **legs.** The longest side, which is opposite the right angle, is the **hypotenuse.** The **Pythagorean Theorem** is an equation that shows the relationship between the legs and the hypotenuse.

> **KEY CONCEPTS** **The Pythagorean Theorem**
>
> In any right triangle, the sum of the squares of the lengths of the legs is equal to the square of the length of the hypotenuse.
>
> $$a^2 + b^2 = c^2$$
>
>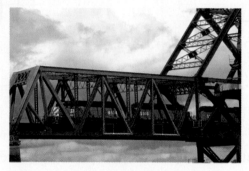

You can use the Pythagorean Theorem to find the length of the hypotenuse of a right triangle if you know the lengths of the two legs.

EXAMPLES Finding the Hypotenuse

① Find the length of the hypotenuse of the triangle below.

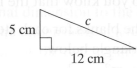

5 cm
12 cm
c

$$a^2 + b^2 = c^2 \qquad \leftarrow \text{Use the Pythagorean Theorem.}$$
$$5^2 + 12^2 = c^2 \qquad \leftarrow \text{Substitute 5 for } a \text{ and 12 for } b.$$
$$25 + 144 = c^2 \qquad \leftarrow \text{Simplify.}$$
$$169 = c^2 \qquad \leftarrow \text{Add.}$$
$$\sqrt{169} = \sqrt{c^2} \qquad \leftarrow \text{Find the positive square root of each side.}$$
$$13 = c \qquad \leftarrow \text{Simplify.}$$

The length of the hypotenuse is 13 cm.

② **Gridded Response** An architect drew the sketch of a bridge shown below. The bridge has 12-ft-long horizontal members and 24-ft-long vertical members. What is the length in feet of each diagonal member? Round to the nearest foot.

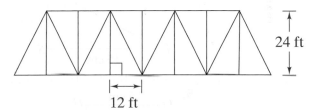

24 ft

12 ft

Each diagonal member is the hypotenuse of a right triangle.

$$a^2 + b^2 = c^2 \qquad \leftarrow \text{Use the Pythagorean Theorem.}$$
$$12^2 + 24^2 = c^2 \qquad \leftarrow \text{Substitute 12 for } a \text{ and 24 for } b.$$
$$144 + 576 = c^2 \qquad \leftarrow \text{Simplify.}$$
$$720 = c^2 \qquad \leftarrow \text{Add.}$$
$$\sqrt{720} = \sqrt{c^2} \qquad \leftarrow \text{Find the positive square root of each side.}$$

$\boxed{\sqrt{}}$ 720 $\boxed{=}$ *26.83281573* ← Use a calculator.

$$27 \approx c \qquad \leftarrow \text{Simplify.}$$

The length of each diagonal member is about 27 ft.

✓ Quick Check

1. Find the length of the hypotenuse of a right triangle with legs of 12 cm and 16 cm.

2. A bridge has 22-ft horizontal members and 25-ft vertical members. Find the length of each diagonal member to the nearest foot.

Video Tutor Help
Visit: PHSchool.com
Web Code: ase-0775

Test Prep Tip

Draw and label a picture of a right triangle like the one below to match the problem situation.

24 ft   ?
12 ft

Squares and Square Roots

To estimate the weight, in pounds, of a large fish, fishermen square the girth, multiply by the length, divide by 800, and then add $\frac{1}{10}$ of that number. What is the weight of the tarpon below?

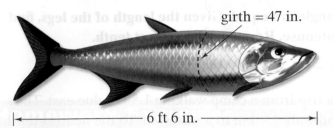

girth = 47 in.

|← 6 ft 6 in. →|

What You Might Think

> What do I know?
> What do I want to find out?

> How do I estimate an answer?

> How do I calculate an answer?

> What is the answer?

> Is the answer reasonable?

What You Might Write

The girth g is 47 inches, and the length ℓ is 6 ft 6 in. or 78 inches. I know the formula is $w = (g^2 \times \ell) \div 800 \times 1\frac{1}{10}$.

Round 47 to 50 and 78 to 80. Then ignore the extra $\frac{1}{10}$ to compensate for rounding up. $(50^2 \times 80) \div 800 = 250$. The fish weighs about 250 pounds.

$$w = (47^2 \times 78) \div 800 \times 1\frac{1}{10}$$
$$= (2{,}209 \times 78) \div 800 \times 1.1$$
$$\approx 236.9$$

The fish weighs about 237 pounds.

Yes; 237 pounds is close to the 250-pound estimate.

Think It Through

1. **Reasoning** Why is multiplying by 1.1 the same as adding $\frac{1}{10}$ of a number to that number?

2. **Number Sense** When you estimated, why did rounding up 47 and 78 compensate for ignoring "add $\frac{1}{10}$"?

Exercises

Solve each problem. For Exercises 3 and 4, answer the questions first.

3. A jogger runs around the city park shown below. Her friend cuts through the park on a diagonal. In miles, how far does each jogger run on a five-lap jog?

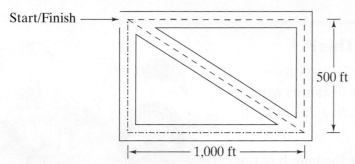

Start/Finish

500 ft

1,000 ft

Jogger's Path – – – –
Friend's Path – – – –
Both ·–·–·–·–

   a. What do you know and what do you want to find out?
   b. How will the Pythagorean Theorem help you?

4. Ignoring air resistance, the distance d in feet an object falls in t seconds is $d = 16t^2$. The Sears Tower is 1,450 ft tall. If a window washer at the top of the tower drops his squeegee, about how much time passes before the squeegee hits the sidewalk below?
   a. What do you know and what do you want to find out?
   b. **Number Sense** To estimate, why might you round 1,450 ft to 1,600 ft? Explain.

5. A car washing business uses the equation $m = -4p^2 + 40p$ to predict the amount of money m they can make with the price p of a car wash. For example, if the price of one wash is \$1, the amount of money they make is $m = -4(1)^2 + 40(1)$, or \$36.
   a. Complete the table at the right.
   b. At which price does the business earn the most money? The least?

Car Wash Business

p (dollars)	1	2	3	4	5	6	7
m (dollars)							

6. Carpenters have a simple way to tell if a wall forms a 90° angle with the floor. They mark a point at the base of the wall. Then they measure 3 ft up the wall and mark a point. They also mark a point on the floor 4 ft away from the base of the wall. If the wall forms a right angle, what is the distance from the point on the wall to the point on the floor? How do you know?

Using the Pythagorean Theorem

✓ Check Skills You'll Need

1. **Vocabulary Review** State the *Pythagorean Theorem*.

Find the length of the hypotenuse given the lengths of the two legs, *a* and *b*. Round to the nearest tenth.

2. $a = 3, b = 4$

3. $a = 7, b = 5$

 **for Help**
Lesson 3-2

What You'll Learn

To use the Pythagorean Theorem to find missing measurements of triangles

Why Learn This?

You can use the Pythagorean Theorem to find distances without measuring, including distances in space.

When you know the length of one leg and the hypotenuse of a right triangle, you can use the Pythagorean Theorem to find the length of the other leg.

EXAMPLE   Finding a Leg of a Right Triangle

1 Find the missing leg length of the triangle below.

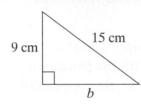

$a^2 + b^2 = c^2$ ← Use the Pythagorean Theorem.

$9^2 + b^2 = 15^2$ ← Substitute 9 for *a* and 15 for *c*.

$81 + b^2 = 225$ ← Simplify.

$b^2 = 144$ ← Subtract 81 from each side.

$\sqrt{b^2} = \sqrt{144}$ ← Find the positive square root of each side.

$b = 12$ ← Simplify.

The length of the other leg is 12 cm.

✓ Quick Check

1. The hypotenuse of a right triangle is 20.2 ft long. One leg is 12.6 ft long. Find the length of the other leg to the nearest tenth.

You can substitute the known leg length for either a or b in the Pythagorean Theorem.

EXAMPLE **Application: Satellites**

2 **Multiple Choice** Satellites that relay television signals to Earth cruise at a distance of about 22,200 miles above Earth's surface. The radius of Earth is about 4,000 miles. Find the distance a from the satellite to point T in the diagram below. Round to the nearest hundred miles.

Ⓐ 22,500 mi   Ⓒ 25,900 mi

Ⓑ 26,000 mi   Ⓓ 670,440 mi

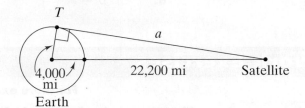

Vocabulary Tip

The *radius* of a circle is a segment that connects the center to the circle.

The diagram above shows a right triangle with a hypotenuse of 22,200 miles + 4,000 miles, or 26,200 miles. The length of the known leg is 4,000 miles. The variable a represents the length of the other leg.

$a^2 + b^2 = c^2$	← Use the Pythagorean Theorem.
$a^2 + 4{,}000^2 = 26{,}200^2$	← Substitute 4,000 for b and 26,200 for c.
$a^2 + 16{,}000{,}000 = 686{,}440{,}000$	← Find $4{,}000^2$ and $26{,}200^2$.
$a^2 = 670{,}440{,}000$	← Subtract 16,000,000 from each side.
$\sqrt{a^2} = \sqrt{670{,}440{,}000}$	← Find the positive square root of each side.
√ 670,440,000 ☰ *25892.85616*	← Use a calculator.
$a \approx 25{,}900$	← Round to the nearest hundred.

Test Prep Tip

You can eliminate Choice D, because the leg of a right triangle cannot be longer than its hypotenuse.

The distance from the satellite to the horizon is about 25,900 mi. The answer is C.

✓ Quick Check

2. **Construction** The bottom of an 18-ft ladder is 5 ft from the side of a house. Find the distance from the top of the ladder to the ground. Round to the nearest tenth.

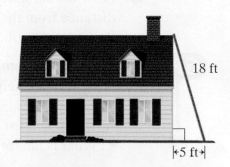

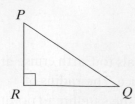

1. **Vocabulary** Name the two legs and the hypotenuse of the triangle at the left.

2. Fill in the blanks for each step to find the missing leg length of the triangle below.

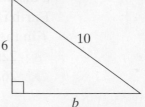

   a. $6^2 + b^2 = \blacksquare^2$
   b. $\blacksquare + b^2 = 100$
   c. $\qquad b^2 = \blacksquare$
   d. $\qquad b = \blacksquare$

Homework Exercises

For more exercises, see Extra Skills and Word Problems.

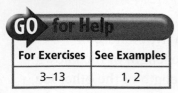

GO for Help

For Exercises	See Examples
3–13	1, 2

Find the missing leg length. For Exercises 7–12, *a* and *b* represent leg lengths and *c* represents the length of the hypotenuse. If necessary, round to the nearest tenth.

3.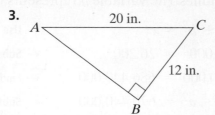

4.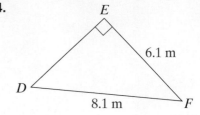

5.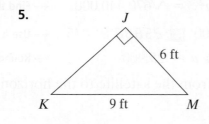

6.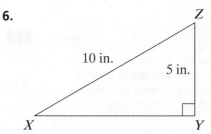

7. $a = 5, c = 12$ 8. $a = 7, c = 25$ 9. $b = 10.5, c = 20.1$

10. $a = 3.4, c = 6.7$ 11. $b = 8.3, c = 16.9$ 12. $b = 11, c = 15$

13. A 10-ft-long slide is attached to a deck that is 5 ft high. Find the distance from the bottom of the deck to the bottom of the slide to the nearest tenth.

14. **Guided Problem Solving** A computer screen has a diagonal length of 17 in. and a height of 9 in. To the nearest tenth, what is the area of the screen?
    • To the nearest tenth, what is the width of the computer screen?
    • What is the formula for the area of a rectangle?

Use the formula $A = \frac{1}{2}bh$ to find the area of a right triangle with a leg of length a and hypotenuse of length c.

15. $a = 4$, $c = 5$ **16.** $a = 8.6$, $c = 10$ **17.** $a = 7.3$, $c = 9.1$

18. Diving A diver swims 20 m under water to the anchor of a buoy that is 10 m below the surface of the water. On the surface, how far is the buoy located from the place where the diver started? Round to the nearest meter.

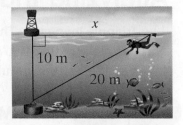

19. Error Analysis One leg of a right triangle is 3 cm and the hypotenuse is 4 cm. A student evaluates $\sqrt{3^2 + 4^2}$ to find the length of the other leg. What error did the student make?

20. The distance from home plate to second base is about 127.3 ft.

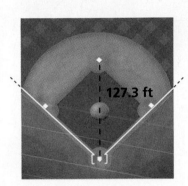

127.3 ft

    a. Writing in Math Explain how you would find the distance between the bases.

    b. Estimation Estimate the distance between the bases to the nearest foot.

    c. When you hit a home run, you run around all the bases. How far do you run?

21. Challenge The sides of a right triangle are labelled a, b, and c. Can $a + b = c$? Explain.

Test Prep and Mixed Review

Practice

Multiple Choice

22. The top of a badminton net is 5 feet high. Ropes connect the top of each pole to stakes in the ground. The ropes are 8.5 feet long. Which is closest to the distance from a stake to the base of a pole?

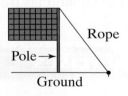

Rope
Pole→
Ground

    Ⓐ 4 ft   Ⓑ 7 ft   Ⓒ 9 ft   Ⓓ 15 ft

23. Which integer is closest to $\sqrt{10}$?

    Ⓕ 2   Ⓖ 3   Ⓗ 4   Ⓙ 5

24. Oliver is buying three items that cost $4.95, $6.99, and $1.05. He gives the cashier a $20 bill. How much change should he receive?

    Ⓐ $5.95   Ⓑ $7.01   Ⓒ $8.06   Ⓓ $12.99

GO for Help

For Exercises	See Lesson
25–28	2-3

Compare. Use $<$, $>$, or $=$.

25. $\frac{5}{6}$ ▇ $\frac{9}{11}$ **26.** $\frac{1}{8}$ ▇ 0.1 **27.** $\frac{4}{20}$ ▇ 0.2 **28.** $\frac{3}{7}$ ▇ $\frac{4}{10}$

Analyzing Triangles

The Triangle Inequality Theorem states that the sum of the lengths of any two sides of a triangle is greater than the length of the third side.

EXAMPLE **Side Measurements of a Triangle**

1 Is it possible to construct a triangle with side lengths 6 in., 10 in., and 20 in.? Explain.

Since $6 + 10 < 20$, it is not possible.

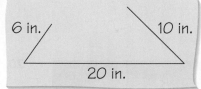

If the equation $a^2 + b^2 = c^2$ is true for the lengths of the sides of a triangle, then the triangle is a right triangle. This is called the converse of the Pythagorean Theorem.

EXAMPLE **Identifying a Right Triangle**

2 Is a triangle with sides 7 in., 25 in., and 24 in. a right triangle? Explain.

$a^2 + b^2 = c^2$ ← Use the Pythagorean Theorem.

$7^2 + 24^2 \stackrel{?}{=} 25^2$ ← The longest side, 25 in., is the hypotenuse. Substitute $a = 7$, $b = 24$, and $c = 25$.

$49 + 576 = 625$ ✓   ← Simplify.

The equation is true, so the triangle is a right triangle.

Exercises

Is it possible for a triangle to have sides with the given lengths? Explain.

1. 15 cm, 35 cm, 40 cm

2. 7 mi, 15 mi, 6 mi

3. $1\frac{1}{2}$ in., $2\frac{1}{2}$ in., $3\frac{1}{2}$ in.

4. Measurement Draw a triangle with side lengths of your choice. Use a ruler to test the Triangle Inequality Theorem.

Is a triangle with the given side lengths a right triangle? Explain.

5. 6 cm, 8 cm, 10 cm

6. 10 in., 24 in., 26 in.

7. 16 km, 63 km, 65 km

8. Number Sense How do you know a triangle with side lengths $\sqrt{1}$, $\sqrt{2}$, and $\sqrt{3}$ is a right triangle? Explain.

1. Estimate the value of $\sqrt{85}$ to the nearest integer.

Is each number *rational* or *irrational*? Explain.

2. $\sqrt{13}$

3. $\frac{13}{28}$

4. $1.231241251261271\ldots$

Find the missing length in each right triangle. If necessary, round to the nearest tenth.

5. leg = 9 cm, leg = 12 cm

6. leg = 8 ft, leg = 21 ft

7. leg = 7 in., hypotenuse = 25 in.

8. leg = 15 m, leg = 19 m

9. **Diving** You stand at the edge of a 4-m-high diving platform. A beach ball is exactly 8 m from the base of the platform. To the nearest tenth of a meter, what is the distance d from the top of the platform to the beach ball?

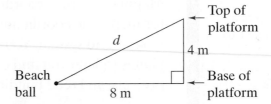

Top of platform

4 m

Base of platform

Beach ball

8 m

MATH AT WORK

Civil Engineer

Civil engineers design and build structures. They specialize in areas such as transportation, construction, and the environment.

Civil engineers who work in transportation use geometry and their knowledge of maps to plan and build roadways. Some, who specialize in construction, design structures such as buildings, bridges, and dams. Civil engineers who work with the environment build facilities such as water treatment plants that make water safe to drink.

Go Online
PHSchool.com
For: Information on Civil Engineers
Web Code: asb-2031

Graphing in the Coordinate Plane

What You'll Learn

To graph points and to use the Pythagorean Theorem to find distances in the coordinate plane

🔊 **New Vocabulary** coordinate plane, *y*-axis, *x*-axis, quadrants, origin, ordered pair, *x*-coordinate, *y*-coordinate

Why Learn This?

Mapmakers use a coordinate grid system for maps. The coordinate plane is another type of grid system. You can use coordinate planes to help you find distances, design projects, and read building plans.

A **coordinate plane** is a grid formed by the intersection of two number lines. You can use a coordinate plane to locate and name points.

The **y-axis** is a vertical number line.

The **x-axis** is a horizontal number line.

The axes divide the plane into four **quadrants.**

O indicates the **origin,** where the axes intersect.

An **ordered pair** (*x*, *y*) gives the coordinates of the location of a point. In the graph above, point *A* has coordinates (2, −4).

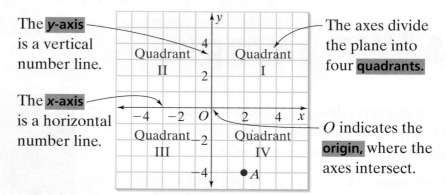

The **x-coordinate** tells the number of horizontal units a point is from the origin.

The **y-coordinate** tells the number of vertical units a point is from the origin.

You can graph a point when you know its coordinates.

Graphing Points

1 Graph point $A\left(2\frac{1}{2}, -3\right)$ on a coordinate plane.

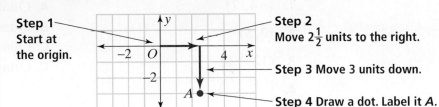

Step 1
Start at
the origin.

Step 2
Move $2\frac{1}{2}$ units to the right.

Step 3 Move 3 units down.

Step 4 Draw a dot. Label it *A*.

✓ Quick Check

1. Graph $R(4, -2)$ and $S\left(-4, 2\frac{1}{2}\right)$ on the same coordinate plane.

You can use the Pythagorean Theorem to find distances in the coordinate plane.

EXAMPLE **Finding Distance on a Coordinate Plane**

2 **Multiple Choice** The library is 5 miles north of your house. The post office is 6 miles east of your house. To the nearest mile, how far is the library from the post office?

Ⓐ 7 mi   Ⓑ 8 mi   Ⓒ 9 mi   Ⓓ 10 mi

Graph the three locations on a coordinate plane. Place your home at the origin. Notice that you can draw a right triangle. The *x*-coordinate and the *y*-coordinate are the lengths of the legs of the right triangle.

$a^2 + b^2 = c^2$ ← Use the Pythagorean Theorem.

$5^2 + 6^2 = c^2$ ← Substitute.

$25 + 36 = c^2$ ← Simplify.

$61 = c^2$ ← Add.

$\sqrt{61} = \sqrt{c^2}$ ← Find the positive square root of each side.

√ 61 ▤ 7.810249676 ← Use a calculator.

$c \approx 8$

The answer is B.

Test Prep Tip

Be careful to follow the order of operations when solving for a variable in the Pythagorean Theorem.

✓ Quick Check

2. Your school is 3 miles south of your house. The general store is 5 miles east of your school. To the nearest mile, how far is your house from the general store?

Vocabulary Match each ordered pair with the appropriate quadrant.

1. $(-4, 2)$

2. $(3, 5)$

3. $(12, -6)$

4. $(-7, -1)$

A. Quadrant I
B. Quadrant II
C. Quadrant III
D. Quadrant IV

Name the coordinates of each point in the graph.

5. A

6. B

7. C

8. D

9. E

10. F

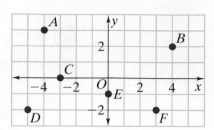

Homework Exercises

For more exercises, see **Extra Skills and Word Problems.**

Graph each point on the same coordinate plane.

GO for Help

For Exercises	See Examples
11–22	1
23	2

11. $A(4, -5)$

12. $B(3, 4)$

13. $C(5, 0)$

14. $D(0, -3)$

15. $E(-5, 1)$

16. $F(-2, -4)$

17. $G(-2, 0)$

18. $H(6, 2)$

Name the point with the given coordinates in the graph at the right.

19. $(3, -2)$

20. $(-3, -2)$

21. $\left(3\frac{3}{4}, 0\right)$

22. $(-2, 1.5)$

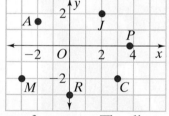

23. Softball A softball diamond has the shape of a square. The distance from home plate to second base is about 85 ft. Find the distance a player would run going from first base to second base.

GPS

24. Guided Problem Solving Find the length of the hypotenuse to the nearest tenth.
- The length of $\overline{AC}$ is ■ units.
- The length of $\overline{BC}$ is ■ units.
- Using the Pythagorean Theorem, the length of $\overline{AB}$ is the square root of $■^2 + ■^2$.

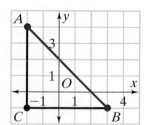

25. a. Graph each of these points on a coordinate plane:

$(-2, -2), (-5, 3), (-3, 3), (-1, 0), (1, 3), (3, 3), (0, -2),$
$(0, -7), (-2, -7), (-2, -2).$

b. Connect the points in order and describe the figure formed.

26. On a graph, the points (4, −2), (7, −2), (9, −5), and (2, −5) are connected in order to form a trapezoid. To the nearest tenth, what is its perimeter?

27. **Geography** Degrees of longitude and latitude indicate locations on a map. The longitude of Chicago is about 88° W, and the latitude is about 42° N. Estimate the longitude and latitude of St. Paul and Lincoln.

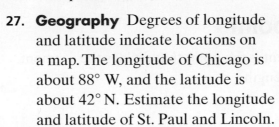

In which quadrant is each point located?

28. (x, y) if $x > 0$ and $y < 0$

29. (x, y) if $x > 0$ and $y > 0$

30. **Writing in Math** Use coordinates to write directions that will get the mouse to the cheese in the maze at the right.

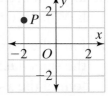

31. **Challenge** Graph and connect the points (3, 2), (−2, 2), (−2, 7), (3, 7), and (3, 2) in order. Then graph and connect the points (3, −2), (−2, −2), (−2, −7), (3, −7), and (3, −2) in order. How are these two figures related?

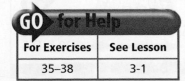
Test Prep and Mixed Review **Practice**

Multiple Choice

32. What are the coordinates of point P at the right?
Ⓐ (1.5, −2)
Ⓒ (−2, 1.5)
Ⓑ (−1.5, 2)
Ⓓ (2, −1.5)

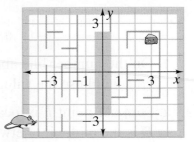

33. Oscar grew 3 inches each year for 5 years, until he was 18 years old. What additional information is necessary to find Oscar's height at age 18?
Ⓕ the average height of an 18-year-old
Ⓖ how quickly he grew from age 0 to age 6
Ⓗ how tall Oscar was when he was 13
Ⓙ Oscar's weight when he turned 18

34. Sarah walks across a rectangular field as shown. Which is the closest to the distance she walks?
Ⓐ 100 ft
Ⓒ 70 ft
Ⓑ 90 ft
Ⓓ 50 ft

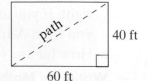

GO **for Help**

For Exercises	See Lesson
35–38	3-1

Find each square root. Where necessary, round to the nearest tenth.

35. $\sqrt{50}$

36. $-\sqrt{\frac{1}{6}}$

37. $\sqrt{7}$

38. $\sqrt{0.18}$

Finding the Midpoint

The **midpoint** of a line segment is the point that divides the segment into two segments of equal length.

ACTIVITY

In the diagram below, the midpoint of $\overline{AC}$ is point B.

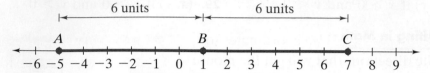

1. On the number line above, the value at point B is 1. Describe how you could use the values at points A and C to find the value at B.

2. Suppose point E is located at 27 on the number line above. Point D is the midpoint between C and E. Use what you learned in Exercise 1 to find the value at point D.

Exercises

For Exercises 1 and 2, use the diagram at the right.

1. **a.** What are the coordinates of the midpoint of $\overline{FG}$?
   b. What are the coordinates of the midpoint of $\overline{FJ}$?

2. Find the coordinates of the midpoints of $\overline{GH}$ and $\overline{HJ}$. Use the same technique you used in Exercise 1, but use it once to find the x-coordinate and once to find the y-coordinate.

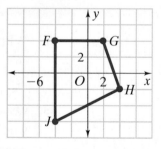

3. The coordinates of the four corners of a square are $(8, 12)$, $(12, 4)$, $(0, 8)$, and $(4, 0)$. Find the coordinates of the midpoint of each side.

4. **a.** Suppose you are traveling from Los Angeles, California to Chicago, Illinois along Route 66. Use the photo at the right. If you are 150 miles from Los Angeles, how far are you from Adrian, Texas?
   b. How far are you from Chicago?

5. **Writing in Math** The coordinates of points W and Z in the coordinate plane are (x_1, y_1) and (x_2, y_2) respectively. Explain how you can find the x- and y-coordinates of the midpoint of $\overline{WZ}$.

Tables and Graphs

Words, data tables, and graphs are three different ways to show the same information. You can use one representation to generate another representation.

ACTIVITY

For Exercises 1 and 2, describe the pattern shown in each graph. Then copy and complete each table.

1. The graph at the right shows how the earnings of a lifeguard change with the number of hours she works.

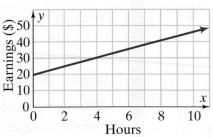

Hours	0	4	8	12	24
Earnings ($)	20	30	40	■	■

2. The graph at the right shows how the total cost of a cookout changes with the number of guests.

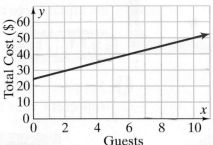

Guests	6	9	12	30	120
Cost ($)	45	55	■	■	■

3. The students in the skateboarding club at Orchard Middle School had a fundraiser to raise money to build a new skate park. The club began with 180 raffle tickets to sell. Every day, they sold 9 tickets.
   a. Copy and complete the table below.

Number of Days	0	1	2	3	■
Tickets Remaining	■	■	■	■	0

   b. Use the data in the table to draw a graph showing how the number of tickets remaining changes with the number of days the club has been selling tickets.

4. **Algebra** You can also use an algebraic equation to represent data. Use Exercise 3 to write an equation relating the number of days the club has been selling tickets to the number of tickets remaining. Let x be the number of days and y be the number of tickets.

Equations, Tables, and Graphs

Check Skills You'll Need

1. **Vocabulary Review**
   What do you call a symbol that stands for one or more numbers?

Evaluate for $a = 4$.

2. $6a - 21$

3. $13 + 2a$

4. $5a + 8$

for Help
Lesson 1-1

What You'll Learn

To use tables, equations, and graphs to solve problems

🔊 **New Vocabulary** solution, linear equation

Why Learn This?

You can use equations, tables, and graphs to represent the same data. For example, you can use a table of values for plant growth to write an equation or make a graph.

Given a word problem, you can sometimes make a table of data. Then you can write an equation to model the situation.

EXAMPLE   Making Tables and Writing Equations

for Help

For help making a table of data, go to Lesson 1-1, Example 4.

1 Suppose you save $3 each week. Make a table and write an equation to represent your total savings after a given number of weeks.

Number of Weeks	Total Savings (dollars)	Expression
0	0	3(0)
1	3	3(1)
2	6	3(2)
3	9	3(3)
w	t	3(w)

↑ Let w represent the number of weeks.

↑ Let t represent your total savings.

← Look for a pattern in the table. Your total savings for a given week is 3 times the number of weeks you have been saving.

The equation $t = 3w$ models your total savings.

Quick Check

1. You buy CDs from a music store. Each CD costs $15. Make a table and write an equation to represent the total cost of buying a given number of CDs.

Any ordered pair that makes an equation true is a **solution** of the equation. For example, $(2, 6)$ is a solution of $y = 3x$ because $6 = 3(2)$. An equation with two variables can have many solutions. You can show these solutions on a graph. An equation is a **linear equation** if all of its solutions lie on a line.

EXAMPLE **Graphing Linear Equations**

Jerrod keeps track of how much dry food is in his cat's feeder. Graph the linear equation $y = -\frac{1}{2}x + 12$, where y represents the cups of food left and x represents the number of days since he filled the twelve-cup feeder.

Step 1 Make a table.

x	$y = -\frac{1}{2}x + 12$
0	$-\frac{1}{2}(0) + 12 = 12$
4	$-\frac{1}{2}(4) + 12 = 10$
9	$-\frac{1}{2}(9) + 12 = 7\frac{1}{2}$
16	$-\frac{1}{2}(16) + 12 = 4$

Step 2 Graph the ordered pairs and draw a line through the points.

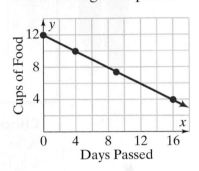

Each point (x, y) on the graph represents a solution of the equation. For example, the point $(4, 10)$ means that after 4 days, 10 cups are left.

Quick Check

2. Graph the linear equation $y = 5x + 50$, where y represents the temperature in °F of a chemical solution after x minutes.

More Than One Way

A plant is 4 cm tall and grows 2 cm per day. Predict how tall the plant will be after 8 days.

Roberto's Method

I can make a table of data.

Height of Plant

Days Passed	0	1	2	3	4	5	6	7	8
Height	4	6	8	10	12	14	16	18	20

After 8 days, the plant will be 20 cm tall.

Jasmine's Method

I can make a graph. Let x represent the number of days that have passed. Let y represent the height of the plant.

Height of Plant

Days Passed (x)	1	2	3
Height (y)	6	8	10

I can make a table of solutions. Three points on the graph are $(1, 6)$, $(2, 8)$, and $(3, 10)$.

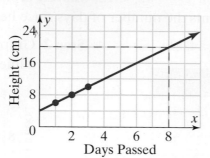

I can draw a line through the points. Then I can use the graph to find the height y when $x = 8$.

After 8 days, the plant will be 20 cm tall.

Choose a Method

A bag of rice weighs 80 oz. If a serving of rice is 2 oz, how much rice will be left after you prepare 10 servings? Explain why you chose the method you used.

✓ Check Your Understanding

1. **Vocabulary** Which statement about linear equations is *not* true?
   - Ⓐ The graph of a linear equation is a line.
   - Ⓑ Every point on the graph of a linear equation is a solution.
   - Ⓒ A point that does not lie on the graph of a linear equation may still be a solution of the equation.
   - Ⓓ You can write solutions of a linear equation as ordered pairs.

2. A leaky pipe loses 0.75 gallons of water every minute. Complete the data table below.

   Water Loss

Number of Minutes (t)	1	2	3	4
Gallons of Water Lost (g)	▪	▪	▪	▪

3. Use the table from Exercise 2. Write a linear equation to represent the amount of water lost from the leaky pipe.

4. Suppose you wanted to graph the equation in Exercise 3. Use the table from Exercise 2 to name four points that lie on the graph.

Homework Exercises

For more exercises, see Extra Skills and Word Problems.

GO for Help

For Exercises	See Examples
5–6	1
7–8	2

5. In 2000, about four babies were born world-wide every second. Make a table and write an equation to represent the total number of babies born over time.

6. The temperature drops 2°F every hour. Make a table and write an equation to represent the total temperature drop over time.

7. For a certain repair, an auto shop charges a $20 fee for materials plus $40 per hour for labor. Graph the linear equation $y = 40x + 20$, where y represents the total cost and x represents the hours of labor.

8. On a 100-point test, each question is worth 5 points. Partial answers receive partial credit. Graph the linear equation $y = 100 - 5x$, where y represents your score and x represents the number of incorrect answers.

9. **Guided Problem Solving** In the design at the right, 12 squares surround a row of 3 circles. Predict the number of squares needed to surround a row of 10 circles.

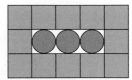

- **Make a Plan** Make a table of values. Graph the ordered pairs from the table and draw a line through the points. Then use the graph to find the answer.
- **Carry Out the Plan** Complete the table below.

Number of Circles (x)	1	2	3	4	5	6
Number of Squares (y)	■	■	■	■	■	■

Graph each linear equation.

10. $y = -\dfrac{2}{3}x + 3$ 11. $y = -\dfrac{3}{5}x - 2$ 12. $y = 1.5x + 4$

13. **Writing in Math** Four of the five points below are solutions of the same linear equation. Which one is not? Explain.
$A(2, 1)$ $B(0, -4)$ $C(1, -2)$ $D(4, 4)$ $E(3, 2)$

GO Online

Homework Video Tutor
Visit: PHSchool.com
Web Code: ase-0305

14. The table below shows the cost of buying class mugs online. Write an equation to model the data.

Number of Mugs	1	2	3	4	5
Total Cost	13	21	29	37	45

15. Engraving a key chain costs $10 plus $1.50 for each engraved letter. You can only spend $20. What is the maximum number of letters you can engrave? Solve by making a table and writing an equation.

16. **Choose a Method** You start an exercise routine by lifting 3 lb and increase the weight by 2 lb per month. Predict how much weight you will lift after 5 months. Explain why you chose the method you used.

17. **Error Analysis** Gina owes her father $200. During each week, she pays $20. They both draw graphs to represent the money she owes. Who is correct? Explain.

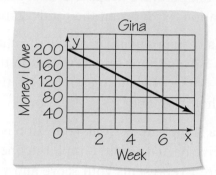

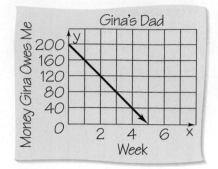

18. **Challenge** A club sells calendars for $4 each. It spends $2 to make each calendar and $20 on film. Write and graph two equations to represent income and expenses. Where do the graphs intersect?

Test Prep and Mixed Review
Practice

Multiple Choice

19. The graph of $y = \frac{1}{2}x + 1$ is shown on the coordinate grid at the right. Which table of ordered pairs contains only points on this line?

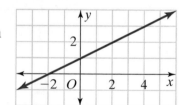

Ⓐ
x	y
−4	1
2	2
3	2.5

Ⓑ
x	y
−2	0
1	1.5
4	3

Ⓒ
x	y
0	−2
1	0
2	2

Ⓓ
x	y
−3	−1.5
0	2
5	3.5

20. Audrey bought a box of cereal and some bananas for $4.69. If the cereal cost $3.99 and the bananas were on sale for $0.28 per pound, how many pounds of bananas did Audrey buy?
    Ⓕ 0.42 lb   Ⓖ 2.2 lb   Ⓗ 2.5 lb   Ⓙ 4.2 lb

21. A ferry travels at 20 knots, which is about 23 miles per hour. How should Sam find the number of miles per hour that equals 1 knot?
    Ⓐ Divide 20 by 23.   Ⓒ Divide 3 by 20.
    Ⓑ Divide 23 by 20.   Ⓓ Divide 3 by 23.

GO for Help

For Exercises	See Lesson
22–24	1-6

Solve each equation.

22. $b + 6 = 10$ 23. $k - 1 = 24$ 24. $-4 + n = 40$

Matching Graphs

Graphs in algebra can tell a story, just as graphs in
the real world do.

EXAMPLE   **Matching Graphs And Descriptions**

Mary and Marty both get the same allowance. Match each description of
how they spend their allowance with one graph shown below. Explain
your choice.

1. Mary gets her allowance once a week and spends it all.
2. Marty gets his allowance once a week. He saves half and spends half.

Graph A   **Graph B**   **Graph C**   **Graph D**

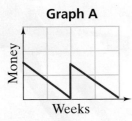   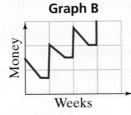   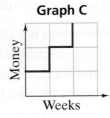   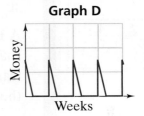

Graph D represents Mary, because during each week, the amount of
money drops to zero. Graph B represents Marty because the graph
shows half the money staying constant before Marty gets his
allowance again.

Exercises

Sketch a graph to match each description. Label the *x*- and *y*-axes.

1. The energy level of a puppy whose family leaves at 8 A.M., returns at
   5 P.M., goes to bed at 10 P.M., and wakes up at 6 A.M. The *x*-axis
   shows the time for three days.

2. The number of students on your school grounds during a typical
   school day. The *x*-axis is labeled 8 A.M., 2 P.M., 10 P.M., and 4 A.M. for
   three days.

3. Your interest level in watching television over a 1-week period
   during the school year. The *x*-axis shows the seven days with times
   each day labeled 8 A.M., 2 P.M., 6 P.M., and 2 A.M.

4. Make a story and graph to match. Pick an activity for which your
   interest level varies over time. Make a graph, label both axes, draw
   the graph, and write a paragraph that explains the graph.

3-6 Translations

Check Skills You'll Need

1. Vocabulary Review
In what *quadrant* is $(-3, 5)$ located?

Name the coordinates of each point.

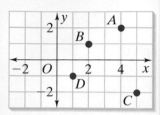

2. A   **3.** B

4. C   **5.** D

GO for Help
Lesson 3-4

What You'll Learn

To graph and describe translations in the coordinate plane

🔊 **New Vocabulary** transformation, translation, image

Why Learn This?

Translations are used in games and in the arts. You can use translations to plan a winning chess strategy or choreograph a figure-skating routine.

A **transformation** is a change in the position, shape, or size of a figure. A **translation** is a transformation that moves each point of a figure the same distance and in the same direction.

The figure you get after a transformation is an **image** of the original figure. To identify the image of point A, use prime notation (A'). You read A' as "A prime."

EXAMPLE   Graphing a Translation

1 **Multiple Choice** If $\triangle PQR$ below is translated 6 units to the right and 3 units down, what are the coordinates of point P'?

Ⓐ $P'(-1, -2)$ Ⓑ $P'(-2, 1)$ Ⓒ $P'(-2, -1)$ Ⓓ $P'(1, -2)$

Vocabulary Tip

Each corner of a triangle is a *vertex*. The plural of vertex is *vertices*.

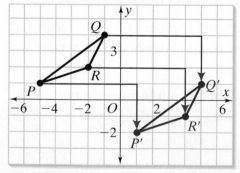

Slide each vertex right 6 units and down 3 units. Label and connect the images of the vertices.

The answer is D.

✓ Quick Check

1. $\triangle JKL$ has vertices $J(0, 2)$, $K(3, 4)$, and $L(5, 1)$. Translate $\triangle JKL$ 4 units to the left and 5 units up. What are the coordinates of J'?

You can use arrow notation to describe the translation in Example 1. The translation of each point is shown below.

$P(-5, 1) \rightarrow P'(1, -2)$ ← Read $P \rightarrow P'$ as "point P goes to point P prime."
$Q(-1, 4) \rightarrow Q'(5, 1)$
$R(-2, 2) \rightarrow R'(4, -1)$

The arrow notation for the translation of the image is
$\triangle PQR \rightarrow \triangle P'Q'R'$.

You can use arrow notation to write a general rule that describes a translation. For example, $(x, y) \rightarrow (x - 1, y + 5)$ shows the ordered pair (x, y) and describes a translation to the left 1 unit and up 5 units.

EXAMPLE   Describing a Translation

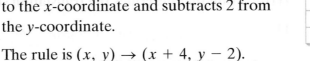

2 Write a rule to describe the translation of the black triangle to the blue triangle.

Each point has moved 4 units to the right and 2 units down. So the translation adds 4 to the x-coordinate and subtracts 2 from the y-coordinate.

The rule is $(x, y) \rightarrow (x + 4, y - 2)$.

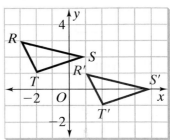

Test Prep Tip
Draw arrows from each original point to its image to help you see the translation.

✓ Quick Check

2. Write a rule that describes the translation shown on the graph at the right.

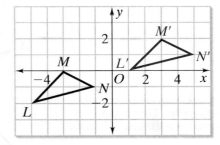

✓ Check Your Understanding

1. **Vocabulary** A (transformation, image) is a change in the position, shape, or size of a figure.

2. **Sports** The graph at the left shows an ice skater moving across the ice. How far and in what direction does the skater move?

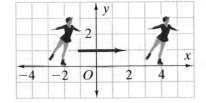

Graph each point and its image after the given translation.

3. $T(1, 3)$, left 2 units

4. $V(-4, 4)$, down 6 units

5. $S(4, 0)$, right 1 unit, down 3 units

6. $X(0, -2)$, right 7 units

What You'll Learn

To graph rotations and to identify rotational symmetry

🔊 **New Vocabulary** rotation, center of rotation, angle of rotation, rotational symmetry

Why Learn This?

When you learn to recognize rotational symmetry, you can see it in everything from art and nature to architecture and science.

A **rotation** is a transformation that turns a figure about a fixed point called the **center of rotation.** A figure has **rotational symmetry** if it can be rotated 180° or less and exactly matches its original figure.

Rotations change the position of a figure but not its size or shape. The **angle of rotation** is the number of degrees the figure rotates. A complete rotation is 360°.

 center of rotation   90°   180°   270°   360°

EXAMPLE   Rotational Symmetry

1 **Nature** Find the angle of rotation of the figure.

The image matches the original after $\frac{1}{5}$ of a complete rotation.

$\frac{1}{5} \cdot 360° = 72°$

The angle of rotation is 72°.

✓ Quick Check

1. If the figure at the right has rotational symmetry, find the angle of rotation. If it does not, write *no rotational symmetry*.

You can use the coordinate plane to graph rotations. In this book, all rotations are counterclockwise.

EXAMPLE Graphing Rotations

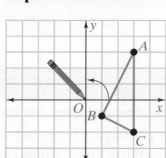

2 Draw the image of △*ABC* after a rotation of 90° about the origin.

Step 1 Draw and trace.

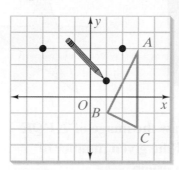

- Draw △*ABC* on a piece of graph paper. Place a piece of tracing paper over your graph.
- Trace the vertices of the triangle, the *x*-axis, and the *y*-axis, as shown in blue.
- Place your pencil at the origin to rotate the paper.

Step 2 Rotate and mark each vertex.

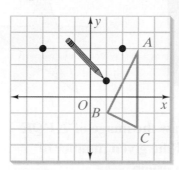

- Rotate the tracing paper 90° counterclockwise. The axes should line up.
- Mark the position of each vertex by pressing your pencil through the paper.

Step 3 Complete the new figure.

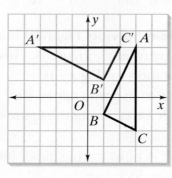

- Remove the tracing paper.
- Draw the triangle.
- Label the vertices to complete the figure.

✓ Quick Check

2. Copy △*ABD*. Draw the image of △*ABD* after a rotation of the given number of degrees about the origin.
   a. 180°
   b. 270°

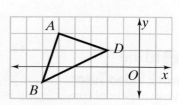

1. **Vocabulary** A figure has rotational symmetry if it can be rotated ▦ degrees or less and exactly match its original figure.

Graph each point. Then rotate it the given number of degrees about the origin. Give the coordinates of the image.

2. $L(3, 3)$, 90°   3. $M(-4, -2)$, 270°   4. $N(3, -5)$, 180°

Homework Exercises

For more exercises, see Extra Skills and Word Problems.

GO for Help

For Exercises	See Examples
5–7	1
8–10	2

Determine whether each figure has rotational symmetry. If it does, find the angle of rotation. Write *no rotational symmetry* if applicable.

5.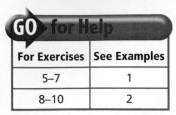

6.

7.

Copy $\triangle PQR$. **Draw the image of** $\triangle PQR$ **after a rotation of the given number of degrees about the origin.**

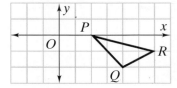

8. 90°   9. 180°   10. 270°

 11. **Guided Problem Solving** Figure B is an image formed by rotating Figure A. Give the angle of rotation for Figure B.
- Draw Figure A on graph paper. Be sure to graph the center of the figure on the origin.
- Trace Figure A onto tracing paper and rotate counterclockwise.

Figure A

Figure B

12. Graph $\triangle JKL$ with vertices $J(1, -3)$, $K(6, -2)$, and $L(6, -4)$. Graph the three images formed by rotating the triangle 90°, 180°, and 270° about the origin.

13. **Error Analysis** A square has rotational symmetry because it can be rotated 180° so that its image matches the original. Your friend says the angle of rotation is 180° ÷ 4 = 45°. What is wrong with this statement?

GO Online
Homework Video Tutor
Visit: PHSchool.com
Web Code: ase-0308

Draw the image of the figure at the right after the following rotations.

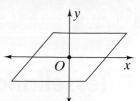

14. 90° **15.** 180° **16.** 270°

17. <u>**Writing in Math**</u> Explain how the design in the tie at the left can be made by using rotations and translations.

Copy each figure. Then draw the image of the figure after the given rotation about the origin.

18. 180°

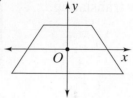

19. 270°

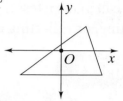

20. **Challenge** Graph △PQR with vertices P(3, 2), Q(1, 0), and R(3, −2). Draw the triangle after it is reflected across the y-axis. How can you get the same image using a rotation? Explain.

Test Prep and Mixed Review   **Practice**

Multiple Choice

21. Look at the pattern. What is the eighth figure in the pattern?

(A)   (B)   (C)   (D)

22. Plastic cups cost $4.50 per bag, plastic plates cost $4.30 per package, and plastic utensils cost $2.25 per box. Scott buys 2 bags of cups, 1 package of plates, and 2 boxes of utensils. How much will he pay after using a coupon for half off his entire purchase?
  (F) $5.53   (G) $8.90   (H) $9.15   (J) $18.30

23. Alejandro wants to buy a digital audio player for $124. His mother will pay $\frac{1}{3}$ of the cost. Alejandro has $32.74. How much more money does he need to make the purchase?
  (A) $8.59   (B) $49.93   (C) $60.84   (D) $74.07

For Exercises	See Lesson
24–25	3-6

For M(0, −3), give the coordinates of its image after each translation.

24. right 2 units and down 1 unit   **25.** left 3 units and up 3 units

Tessellations

A **tessellation** is a repeating pattern of congruent shapes that completely cover a plane without gaps or overlaps. The Dutch artist M. C. Escher (1898–1972) was famous for using tessellations in his art. Many of his designs, like the one at the right, are based on polygons that tessellate.

You can make a tessellation by repeatedly translating, rotating, or reflecting a figure.

EXAMPLE

Show how the figure at the right can form a tessellation.

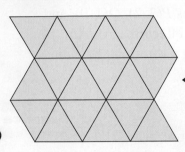

← Rotate, translate, and reflect the figure to cover the plane.

Exercises

Make multiple copies of each figure on graph paper. Determine whether each figure can form a tessellation. If it can, show the tessellation.

1.

2.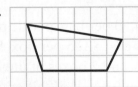

3.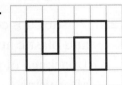

4.

5. The diagrams below show how to construct a repeating figure for a tessellation. Follow the steps shown to make your own tessellation.

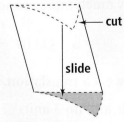

6. **Open-Ended** Make and decorate a tessellation, starting with a square.

Writing Extended Responses

Extended-response questions have multiple parts. To receive full credit, you need to answer each part and show your work or justify your reasoning.

EXAMPLE

A machine to make buttons costs $12, and each blank costs $.50. Each button sells for $2. Write and graph equations to find how many buttons you must sell for income and expenses to be equal, or *to break even*.

Here are four students' responses and the points they received.

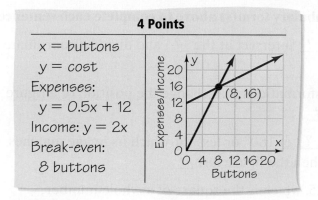

4 Points

x = buttons
y = cost
Expenses:
$y = 0.5x + 12$
Income: $y = 2x$
Break-even:
8 buttons

The equations, the graphs, and the solution are correct.

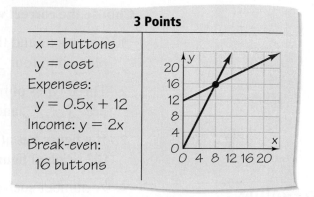

3 Points

x = buttons
y = cost
Expenses:
$y = 0.5x + 12$
Income: $y = 2x$
Break-even:
16 buttons

The equations and graphs are correct, but the solution is incorrect.

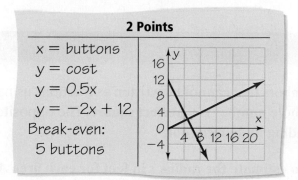

2 Points

x = buttons
y = cost
$y = 0.5x$
$y = -2x + 12$
Break-even:
5 buttons

The equations are incorrect, but the graphs for the student's equations are correct.

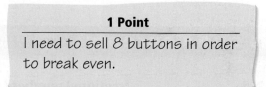

1 Point

I need to sell 8 buttons in order to break even.

The solution is correct, but no work is shown.

For the question to receive 0 points, there is either no response, or it is completely incorrect.

Exercises

1. Tim can type 40 words per min. Bo can type 50 words per min. Tim has already typed 30 words. Write and graph equations to find how many minutes pass before Tim and Bo type the same number of words.

Vocabulary Review

 **angle of rotation** (p. 146)
center of rotation (p. 146)
coordinate plane (p. 124)
hypotenuse (p. 112)
image (p. 136)
irrational numbers (p. 107)
legs (p. 112)
line of reflection (p. 141)
line of symmetry (p. 142)

linear equation (p. 131)
ordered pair (p. 124)
origin (p. 124)
perfect square (p. 106)
Pythagorean Theorem (p. 112)
quadrants (p. 124)
real numbers (p. 107)
reflection (p. 141)
reflectional symmetry (p. 142)

rotation (p. 146)
rotational symmetry (p. 146)
solution (p. 131)
square root (p. 106)
transformation (p. 136)
translation (p. 136)
***x*-axis** (p. 124)
***x*-coordinate** (p. 124)
***y*-axis** (p. 124)
***y*-coordinate** (p. 124)

Choose the correct vocabulary term(s) above to complete each sentence.

1. The *x*-axis and the __?__ intersect at the __?__ and divide a coordinate plane into four __?__.

2. Three types of transformations that change the position of a figure are __?__, __?__, and __?__.

3. If a figure has a(n) __?__ of 180° or less for which its image matches the original figure, then the figure has __?__.

4. A number such as 25, which is the square of a whole number, is a __?__.

5. The __?__ is the longest side of a right triangle.

Go Online
PHSchool.com
For: Online Vocabulary Quiz
Web Code: asj-0351

Skills and Concepts

Lesson 3-1
• To find and estimate square roots and to classify numbers as rational or irrational

Irrational numbers are numbers that cannot be written as fractions using integers. The square of a whole number is a **perfect square.** The opposite of squaring a number is finding its **square root.**

For a circle, use $A = 3r^2$ to estimate the radius r in feet for each area A in square feet. Round to the nearest tenth.

6. 21 square feet   7. 240 square feet   8. 570 square feet

Is each number *rational* or *irrational*? Explain.

9. $\sqrt{196}$ 10. $-\sqrt{\dfrac{25}{36}}$ 11. $\sqrt{57}$ 12. $\sqrt{1.6}$ 13. $\sqrt{225}$

Lessons 3-2, 3-3

- To use the Pythagorean Theorem to find the length of the hypotenuse of a right triangle
- To use the Pythagorean Theorem to find missing measurements of triangles

The **Pythagorean Theorem** states that if a and b are the lengths of the **legs** of a right triangle, and c is the length of the **hypotenuse,** then $a^2 + b^2 = c^2$.

Find the length of the hypotenuse given the lengths of the two legs. If necessary, round to the nearest tenth.

14. $a = 6$, $b = 8$ **15.** $a = 12$, $b = 6$ **16.** $a = 24$, $b = 40$

17. The base of a 24-ft ladder is 6 ft from the base of a house. To the nearest tenth, how far up the house does the ladder reach?

Lesson 3-4

- To graph points and to use the Pythagorean Theorem to find distances in the coordinate plane

An **ordered pair** describes the location of a point on a **coordinate plane.** The first number is the ***x*-coordinate.** The second is the ***y*-coordinate.**

Name the coordinates of each point in the graph at the right.

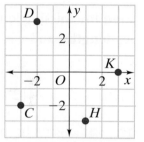

18. C **19.** D **20.** H

In which quadrant or on which axis is each point?

21. $(7, -4)$ **22.** $(0, -2)$ **23.** $(-6, 5)$

Lesson 3-5

- To use tables, equations, and graphs to solve problems

When the values in an ordered pair make an equation with two variables true, the ordered pair is a **solution** of the equation. To graph a **linear equation,** graph several solutions and draw a line through the points.

Graph each linear equation.

24. $y = x + 3$ **25.** $y = \frac{1}{4}x - 1$ **26.** $y = -2x + 1$ **27.** $y = -\frac{2}{3}x$

Lessons 3-6, 3-7, 3-8

- To graph and describe translations in the coordinate plane
- To graph reflections in the coordinate plane and to identify lines of symmetry
- To graph rotations and to identify rotational symmetry

A **transformation** is a change in the position, shape, or size of a figure. The figure you get after a transformation is called the **image.** You can transform figures in a plane by a **translation,** a **reflection,** or a **rotation.**

Copy $\triangle ABC$ for Exercises 28–30. Graph the image of $\triangle ABC$ after each transformation.

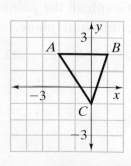

28. translation 2 units left and 1 unit up

29. reflection over the x-axis

30. rotation of 90° about the origin

Find the two square roots of each number.

1. 144   **2.** 256   **3.** 400

Simplify.

4. $\sqrt{100}$ **5.** $\sqrt{0}$ **6.** $-\sqrt{1}$

Determine whether each number is *rational* or *irrational*.

7. $2.\overline{79}$ **8.** $-\sqrt{10}$ **9.** $-1\frac{5}{6}$

10. $0.717117111\ldots$ **11.** $\sqrt{49}$

12. <u>**Writing in Math**</u> Describe the difference between rational and irrational numbers.

Find the missing length, where *a* and *b* are the leg lengths, and *c* is the hypotenuse length.

13. $c = 5,\ a = 3$ **14.** $b = 30,\ c = 34$

15. $a = 5,\ b = 12$ **16.** $a = 48,\ c = 60$

17. Sailboats In the diagram of a sailboat at the right, the length of the luff is 17 ft. The length of the foot is 10 ft. What is the length of the leech to the nearest foot?

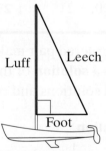

Luff   Leech

Foot

Match each equation with its graph at the right.

18. $y = 3x + 2$

19. $y = -3x - 2$

20. $y = \frac{1}{2}x - 3$

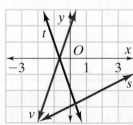

Graph all the points on the same coordinate plane.

21. $A(4, -2)$ **22.** $B(0, 5)$ **23.** $C(-3, 2)$

In which quadrant or on which axis is each point located?

24. $(-4, -2)$ **25.** $(5, -3.7)$ **26.** $(128, 0)$

27. A bowling alley charges $2.00 for shoe rental and $4.00 for each game. Write and graph an equation that represents the total cost to bowl x games.

28. Business You want to make a game. You spend $20 for setup costs and $5 for the materials for each game. Make a table and write an equation to represent the total cost of making x games.

$\triangle JKL$ has vertices $J(4, 5)$, $K(6, 2)$, and $L(3, 2)$. Graph $\triangle JKL$ and its image after each transformation.

29. translation 6 units left

30. translation 3 units left and 3 units down

31. reflection over the y-axis

32. reflection over the line through $(1, -2)$ and $(1, 2)$

33. rotation of $90°$ about the origin

34. rotation of $180°$ about the origin

35. Write a rule to describe the translation at the right.

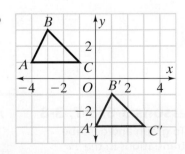

36. Open-Ended Draw and describe a figure that has exactly three lines of symmetry.

37. After a certain reflection, the image of $P(3, -1)$ is $P'(-1, -1)$. What are the coordinates of the image of $Q(-2, 4)$ after the same reflection?

Reading Comprehension

Read each passage and answer the questions that follow.

> **Just Kidding** Mrs. Kidd likes to invite the neighbors for a cookout and then hide the food in various places around the backyard. Guests start at the center of the yard and then follow her clues to find their food. Here is one set of clues: ìMeat at $(3, 3)$. Ve getables at $(-5, -12)$. Beverages at $(5, -12)$. All measurements are in fathoms."

1. Treat the yard as a coordinate plane with the origin at the center. In which quadrant are the vegetables located?
   - A I
   - B II
   - C III
   - D IV

2. Mrs. Kidd also gives this clue: "Dessert is 2 fathoms to the right and 5 fathoms below the meat." What is the location of dessert?
   - F $(2, -5)$
   - G $(5, -2)$
   - H $(-5, 2)$
   - J $(5, 2)$

3. How far must guests walk to go directly from the vegetables to the beverages?
   - A 10 fathoms
   - B 12 fathoms
   - C 24 fathoms
   - D 26 fathoms

4. Mrs. Kidd hints, "Potatoes are at the reflection of the meat over the y-axis." What are the coordinates of the potatoes?
   - F $(-3, 3)$
   - G $(3, -3)$
   - H $(-3, -3)$
   - J $(3, 3)$

> **Piano Movers** The Singhs are deciding where to put a new piano. They take graph paper and draw an outline of the room, using one square to represent 1 foot. With the origin at the center of the room, the room's corners fall at $(8, 10)$, $(8, -10)$, $(-8, 10)$, and $(-8, -10)$. The piano is 5 ft long and 3 ft wide.

5. Mr. Singh wants the piano to be along the left wall, but there is a window from $(-8, 3)$ to $(-8, 6)$ and from $(-8, -6)$ to $(-8, -3)$. Will the piano fit between the windows?
   - A No, there is only 3 ft of space.
   - B No, there is only 4 ft of space.
   - C Barely, there is exactly 5 ft of space.
   - D Easily, there is 6 ft of space.

6. Suppose the piano's corners are at $(0, 0)$, $(5, 0)$, $(5, 3)$ and $(0, 3)$. If the piano is pushed straight back along the y-axis to the wall, where will the $(0, 0)$ corner end up?
   - F $(7, 0)$
   - G $(0, 7)$
   - H $(0, 8)$
   - J $(0, 0)$

7. If one corner of the piano is in the center of the room, which point could NOT be the location of another corner of the piano?
   - A $(5, 0)$
   - B $(3, 5)$
   - C $(-5, -3)$
   - D $(3, 3)$

8. Suppose the piano has the same location that it had at the start of Exercise 6. The $(0, 0)$ corner stays where it is, but the piano is turned to face the opposite direction. Which ordered pair will NOT be the new coordinates of a corner?
   - F $(-5, 0)$
   - G $(0, -3)$
   - H $(-5, -3)$
   - J $(0, 3)$

Applying Rate of Change

Mountain Slopes Mt. Washington, in New Hampshire, is the highest mountain in the northeastern United States. Although it is shorter than many mountains in the western United States, it still offers some challenging hiking. One part of its Great Gulf Trail rises 1,600 ft in 0.8 mi! When you plan a hike, you need to consider elevation gain as well as the length of the trail.

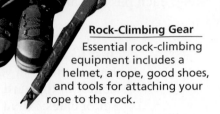

Rock-Climbing Gear

Essential rock-climbing equipment includes a helmet, a rope, good shoes, and tools for attaching your rope to the rock.

Ice on the Mt. Washington Observatory

In certain weather conditions, fog droplets freeze on rocks, trees, and the outside of the observatory. Crystal-like ice deposits can grow as tall as 10 ft! Weather observers break up the ice once an hour to keep it from interfering with the instruments at the observatory.

Windy Weather

Mt. Washington, with an elevation of 6,288 ft, is one of the windiest places on Earth. The annual mean wind speed is 35.1 mi/h, and the mountain holds the world record for greatest wind gust, 231 mi/h (April 12, 1934). Hurricane-force winds occur, on average, 100 days a year.

Go Online
PHSchool.com
For: Information about Mt. Washingon
Web Code: ase-0353

Put It All Together

Materials graph paper, ruler, watch or timer

Routes to the Top of Mount Washington

Route	Distance (mi)	Elevation Gain (ft)	Guidebook Time
Tuckerman Ravine Trail	4.2	4,300	4 h 15 min
Boott Spur Trail	5.4	4,300	4 h 50 min
Ammonoosuc Ravine Trail	4.5	3,800	4 h 10 min
Great Gulf Trail	7.9	5,000	6 h 25 min

SOURCE: Appalachian Mountain Club

1. The table shows four popular routes to the top of Mt. Washington.
   a. Why do some trails have different elevation gains even though they all end up at the top of Mt. Washington?
   b. Why do some trails have the same elevation gain but take different lengths of time to climb?
   c. **Reasoning** What does an elevation gain of 0 mean?

2. Make a graph to show the average elevation gain per hour for each trail. Place time on the x-axis and elevation gain on the y-axis. Label each line.

3. a. **Measurement** Measure the height of a flight of stairs. (*Hint:* If your home is on one level, measure a flight somewhere else.)
   b. Time yourself as you walk up the flight of stairs. How long does it take?
   c. Using your results from part (b), calculate the time it would take to gain 4,000 ft of elevation at the same rate.
   d. Add the stair-climbing data to your graph.
   e. **Writing in Math** How does your stair-climbing rate compare with the guidebook times in the table? Explain any differences.

Helmet

Rope

Rock Climbing

With the correct training and equipment, people can go rock climbing on Mt. Washington three seasons a year.

Rock-climbing shoes

Rock-climbing tools

157

Applications of Proportions

What You've Learned

- In Chapter 1, you used equations to solve problems.
- In Chapter 3, you used the Pythagorean Theorem to find missing measurements in triangles.
- You also graphed translations, reflections, and rotations in the coordinate plane.

Check Your Readiness

GO for Help

For Exercises	See Lessons
1–9	2-2
10–15	2-5
16–18	3-3

Equivalent Forms of Rational Numbers

Write each fraction in simplest form.

1. $\dfrac{34}{68}$ 2. $\dfrac{32}{112}$ 3. $\dfrac{45}{63}$ 4. $\dfrac{66}{120}$

Write each fraction as a decimal. Round to three decimal places.

5. $\dfrac{17}{27}$ 6. $\dfrac{49}{12}$ 7. $\dfrac{10}{31}$ 8. $\dfrac{19}{7}$ 9. $\dfrac{18}{35}$

(Algebra) Multiplying and Dividing Rational Numbers

Solve each equation.

10. $\dfrac{1}{2}k = 28$ 11. $3b = \dfrac{3}{4}$ 12. $\dfrac{3}{4}t = \dfrac{5}{8}$

13. $2y = \dfrac{9}{8}$ 14. $\dfrac{5}{6}r = \dfrac{7}{2}$ 15. $\dfrac{1}{3}x = 10$

The Pythagorean Theorem

Find the missing side length. Round to the nearest tenth.

16.
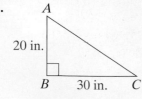

17.
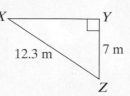

18.
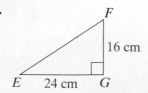

What You'll Learn Next

- In this chapter, you will solve problems involving ratios, rates, and proportions.

- You will use proportions in real-world applications, including scale models and indirect measurements.

- You will graph dilations in the coordinate plane.

 **Key Vocabulary**

- congruent angles (p. 181)
- conversion factor (p. 167)
- cross products (p. 175)
- dilation (p. 187)
- enlargement (p. 188)
- indirect measurement (p. 197)
- proportion (p. 174)
- rate (p. 161)
- reduction (p. 188)
- scale (p. 192)
- scale factor (p. 187)
- scale model (p. 192)
- similar figures (p. 181)
- similar polygons (p. 181)
- unit rate (p. 161)

 Problem Solving Application On pages 206 and 207, you will work an extended activity on burning Calories.

4-1 Ratios and Rates

Check Skills You'll Need

1. **Vocabulary Review**
What is the *least common denominator* of two rational numbers?

Determine which rational number is greater.

2. $\frac{3}{9}, \frac{1}{6}$ 3. $\frac{15}{25}, \frac{4}{5}$

4. $\frac{45}{54}, \frac{2}{3}$ 5. $\frac{4}{7}, \frac{7}{12}$

GO for Help
Lesson 2-3

What You'll Learn

To write ratios and unit rates and to use rates to solve problems

◀)) **New Vocabulary** rate, unit rate

Why Learn This?

When you shop, you make decisions based on both price and quantity. You can use ratios to compare quantities of different products.

KEY CONCEPTS **Ratio**

A ratio is a comparison of two quantities by division. You can write a ratio in three ways.

Arithmetic	**Algebra**
5 to 8 $\frac{5}{8}$ 5 : 8	a to b $\frac{a}{b}$ $a : b$ where $b \neq 0$

To write a ratio in simplest form, first write it as a fraction. Then find the simplest form of the fraction. The simplest form of a ratio can be a whole number.

EXAMPLE **Writing a Ratio in Simplest Form**

1 Write the ratio 50 seconds : 2 minutes in simplest form.

$$\frac{50 \text{ s}}{2 \text{ min}} = \frac{50 \text{ s}}{120 \text{ s}} \quad \leftarrow \text{ Convert minutes to seconds so that both measures are in the same units. Divide the common units.}$$

$$\frac{50}{120} = \frac{50 \div 10}{120 \div 10} \quad \leftarrow \text{ Divide the numerator and the denominator by the GCF, 10.}$$

$$= \frac{5}{12} \quad \leftarrow \text{ Simplify.}$$

The ratio of 50 seconds : 2 minutes is $\frac{5}{12}$.

✓ Quick Check

1. Write the ratio $\frac{30 \text{ s}}{3 \text{ min}}$ in simplest form.

Online active math

For: Exploring Ratios Activity
Use: Interactive Textbook, 4-1

A rate is a ratio that compares quantities measured in different units, such as miles to gallons or feet to seconds. A unit rate is the rate for one unit of a given quantity.

If a car travels 120 mi on 4 gal of gasoline, then the rate is $\frac{120 \text{ mi}}{4 \text{ gal}}$. The unit rate is $\frac{30 \text{ mi}}{1 \text{ gal}}$, or 30 mi/gal.

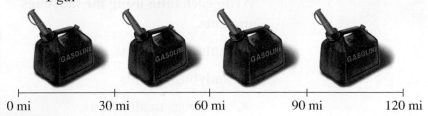

0 mi   30 mi   60 mi   90 mi   120 mi

GO Online

Video Tutor Help
Visit: PHSchool.com
Web Code: ase-0775

EXAMPLE Finding a Unit Rate

2 **Cycling** A team finished the 200-lap Indiana Little 500 race in 2 hours and 4 minutes, or about 2.07 hours. Find the unit rate of laps per hour.

$\frac{\text{number of laps}}{\text{number of hours}} = \frac{200 \text{ laps}}{2.07 \text{ hours}}$ ← Write a rate comparing laps to hours.

$\approx 96.6 \text{ laps/hour}$ ← Divide. Round to the nearest tenth.

The unit rate is about 96.6 laps per hour.

✓ Quick Check

2. Find the unit rate for 52 deliveries in 8 hours.

At a grocery store, the unit rate, or unit cost, is posted for each item. Unit costs help consumers compare prices of items in different sizes.

EXAMPLE Application: Consumer Prices

3 Find the unit cost for each bottle. Which size bottle is the better buy?

$\frac{\$2.99}{64 \text{ oz}}$ ← Write the rates comparing dollars to ounces → $\frac{\$1.59}{12 \text{ oz}}$

$= \$.04671875/\text{oz}$ ← Divide. → $= \$.1325/\text{oz}$

$\approx \$.05/\text{oz}$ ← Round to the nearest cent. → $\approx \$.13/\text{oz}$

The 64-oz bottle has the lower unit cost. This size is the better buy.

Check for Reasonableness $\$.05 \cdot 64 = \$3.20$ and $\$3.20 \approx \$2.99$. Also, $\$.13 \cdot 12 = \$1.56$ and $\$1.56 \approx \$1.59$. The answers are reasonable.

✓ Quick Check

3. The cost of a 20-oz box of cereal is $4.29. A 12-oz box of the same cereal costs $3.59. Which box of cereal is a better buy?

1. **Vocabulary** How do you know that the ratio *6 students out of 23 students* is not a rate?

Write each ratio using the ladybugs and ants.

2. ants to all insects

3. ladybugs to ants

4. ladybugs to all insects

Write each ratio in simplest form.

5. 16 cm : 8 cm

6. 10 s to 2 min

7. $\frac{32 \text{ in.}}{4 \text{ ft}}$

Homework Exercises

For more exercises, see Extra Skills and Word Problems.

For Exercises	See Examples
8–13	1
14–21	2 and 3

Write each ratio in simplest form.

8. 50 m : 30 m

9. $\frac{28 \text{ s}}{2 \text{ min}}$

10. $\frac{80 \text{ yd}}{120 \text{ ft}}$

11. 22 in. to 3 ft

12. 6 ft to 6 yd

13. 36 cm : 132 cm

Find each unit rate.

14. 36 gal in 12 min

15. $42 for 3 books

16. 300 ft in 48 s

17. $21.60 for 12 roses

18. 200 m in 16 s

19. 676 mi in 13 h

20. **Water** A water pump moves 330 gallons of water in 22 minutes. Find the unit rate.

21. **Food** A 32-oz container of yogurt costs $2.69. An 8-oz container of the same yogurt costs $.75. Find the unit cost of each container. Which container of yogurt is the better buy?

22. **Guided Problem Solving** *Apollo 11* traveled about 237,000 miles to the moon in about 103 hours. *Apollo 12* made the same trip in about 123 hours. Find the difference in the rates of travel of the two spacecraft. Round to the nearest whole number.
    • What ratio represents the rate of *Apollo 11*?
    • What ratio represents the rate of *Apollo 12*?

GO Online
Homework Video Tutor
Visit: PHSchool.com
Web Code: ase-0401

23. **Temperature** As you climb a mountain, the temperature of the air around you drops. If the temperature decreases at a rate of $\frac{-6.5°C}{1,000 \text{ m}}$, what is the unit rate of decrease? Round to the nearest thousandth.

Write each ratio as a fraction in simplest form.

24. $11\frac{1}{3}$ out of $50\frac{2}{3}$ **25.** $5\frac{1}{4}$ out of $20\frac{3}{4}$ **26.** $28\frac{1}{2} : 30\frac{1}{4}$

27. Travel During a 7.5-hour drive, a car's mileage indicator starts at 18,560 mi and ends at 18,980 mi. What is the car's rate of travel?

28. Syrup Each year in Vermont, about 1,200 farmers produce about 410,000 gal of maple syrup. A typical farmer collects about 8,750 gal of sap. The sap produces 250 gal of syrup, which sells for about $4.50 per half pint.
  a. Write a ratio, in simplest form, of the number of gallons of sap a grower collects to the number of gallons of syrup produced.
  b. Find the unit rate of the number of gallons of maple syrup produced per year to the number of maple growers in Vermont.
  c. Suppose a gallon of syrup has the same unit cost as a half pint. How much does a gallon of maple syrup cost? (1 gal = 8 pt)

Careers Farmers manage their crops and estimate how much profit they will make.

29. Writing in Math Your friend is 16 years old and her sister is 12 years old. In 3 years, will the ratio of their ages change? Explain.

30. Challenge A bag contains 7 red marbles and 5 black marbles. You add 60 marbles to the bag while keeping the ratio of red marbles to black marbles the same. How many of each color should you add?

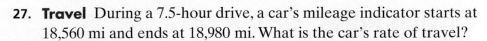

Test Prep and Mixed Review

Practice

Multiple Choice

31. Ryan mows a 4,000-square-foot lawn in 30 minutes. Which is closest to the number of square feet Ryan cuts in 1 minute?

  Ⓐ $133\frac{1}{3}$ ft^2 Ⓑ $133\frac{2}{3}$ ft^2 Ⓒ $134\frac{1}{3}$ ft^2 Ⓓ $134\frac{2}{3}$ ft^2

32. If figure $ABCD$ is translated 3 units to the left and 2 units down, what are the coordinates of point C'?

  Ⓕ $(0, 0)$ Ⓗ $(-1, 1)$
  Ⓖ $(1, -1)$ Ⓙ $(1, 1)$

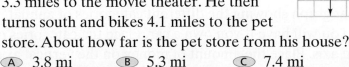

33. Tony leaves his house and bikes west 3.3 miles to the movie theater. He then turns south and bikes 4.1 miles to the pet store. About how far is the pet store from his house?

  Ⓐ 3.8 mi   Ⓑ 5.3 mi   Ⓒ 7.4 mi   Ⓓ 27.7 mi

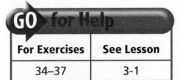

For Exercises	See Lesson
34–37	3-1

Find the positive square root of each number.

34. 225   **35.** $\frac{1}{625}$ **36.** $\frac{25}{400}$ **37.** $\frac{121}{196}$

Finding Rates

In a few years, you will be driving. Suppose your
parents have offered to buy you a used car as long as
you agree to pay for the expenses that go along with
owning a car. You should estimate your expenses so that
you will know what you are getting into.

ACTIVITY

1. Suppose your parents buy a car that gets 24 miles
   per gallon. If you plan to drive about 15,000 miles
   each year, how many gallons of gas would you use each year?

2. What is the cost per gallon of gasoline these days? This is the unit
   rate, or unit cost, for gasoline.

3. To find how much you should expect to spend on gasoline each
   year, multiply the unit rate by the number of gallons you plan on
   using in a year.

4. Suppose four new tires cost $350. The tires will last 60,000 miles.
   How many years will the tires last if you plan on driving
   15,000 miles per year? Use this information to find the cost per
   year for tires.

5. Use all of your calculations and the information in the table below
   to find the amount you will need to pay for all expenses for one
   year (not including the price of the car).

   Annual Car Expenses

Expense	Cost
Registration	$70
Insurance	$1,300
Repairs	$800

6. Make a bar graph showing the different categories of annual
   expenses you will have if you own a car. Place the categories on the
   horizontal axis. Place the amount of money on the vertical axis.

7. Using your bar graph, compare the amount you would spend in each
   category. In which category would you spend the most money each
   year? In which would you spend the least?

8. How much money will you have to earn *per month* to pay for all of
   the expenses for the car?

Choosing Units

When you measure, you need to know which units to use. The table shows some common units of measurement in the customary and metric systems.

Customary Units

	Name	Approximate Comparison
Length	Inch	Length of a soda bottle cap
	Foot	Length of an adult maleís foot
	Yard	Length across a door
	Mile	Length of 14 football fields
Weight	Ounce	Weight of a slice of bread
	Pound	Weight of a loaf of bread
	Ton	Weight of two grand pianos
Capacity	Fluid ounce	Amount in mouthful of mouthwash
	Cup	Amount of milk in a single-serving carton
	Pint	Amount in a container of cream
	Quart	Amount in a bottle of fruit punch
	Gallon	Amount in a large can of paint

Metric Units

	Name	Approximate Comparison
Length	Centimeter	Length of a button
	Meter	Length of a baseball bat
	Kilometer	Length of 11 football fields
Mass	Gram	Mass of a small paper clip
	Kilogram	Mass of 4 videocassettes
Capacity	Milliliter	Amount of water in 2 dewdrops
	Liter	Amount in a bottle of fruit punch—about a quart

EXAMPLES **Customary and Metric Units**

1. Choose an appropriate customary unit for the weight of a truck.

   Since a truck is quite heavy, tons would be the best units to use.

2. Choose an appropriate metric unit for the capacity of a jug of cider.

   A jug of cider is large, so you should use liters.

Exercises

Choose an appropriate customary unit.

1. length of a pencil
2. weight of a plum
3. capacity of a car's gas tank

Choose an appropriate metric unit.

4. distance from Dallas to Reno
5. capacity of a small glass
6. mass of an adult

Check Skills You'll Need

1. **Vocabulary Review**
   What is the product of a number and its *reciprocal*?

Find each product. Write the answer in simplest form.

2. $\frac{10}{3} \cdot \frac{1}{4}$ 3. $\frac{4}{6} \cdot \frac{5}{6}$

4. $\frac{4}{9} \cdot \frac{3}{2}$ 5. $\frac{6}{7} \cdot \frac{8}{3}$

 **for Help**
Lesson 2-5

What You'll Learn

To convert units within and between the customary and metric systems

🔊 **New Vocabulary** conversion factor

Why Learn This?

In 1999, the Mars orbiter was lost because the units of measure used to program the orbiter were not converted.

The table below shows equivalent measurements within the customary and metric systems.

Units of Measurement

Type	Unit	Equivalent
Length (customary)	inch (in.)	
	foot (ft)	1 ft = 12 in.
	yard (yd)	1 yd = 3 ft
	mile (mi)	1 mi = 5,280 ft
Length (metric)	centimeter (cm)	
	meter (m)	1 m = 100 cm
	kilometer (km)	1 km = 1,000 m
Capacity (customary)	fluid ounce (fl oz)	
	cup (c)	1 c = 8 fl oz
	pint (pt)	1 pt = 2 c
	quart (qt)	1 qt = 2 pt
	gallon (gal)	1 gal = 4 qt
Capacity (metric)	milliliter (mL)	
	liter (L)	1 L = 1,000 mL
Weight (customary)	ounce (oz)	
	pound (lb)	1 lb = 16 oz
	ton (t)	1 t = 2,000 lb
Mass (metric)	gram (g)	
	kilogram (kg)	1 kg = 1,000 g

You can change one unit of measure to another by multiplying by a conversion factor. A **conversion factor** is a rate equal to 1. For example, 12 in. = 1 ft, so $\frac{12 \text{ in.}}{1 \text{ ft}} = 1$. Since conversion factors equal 1, multiplying by them does not change the value of a measurement.

EXAMPLE Converting Measurements

1 Convert 1.2 miles to feet.

Since 5,280 ft = 1 mi, use the conversion factor $\frac{5,280 \text{ ft}}{1 \text{ mi}}$.

$$1.2 \text{ mi} = \frac{1.2 \text{ mi}}{1} \cdot \frac{5,280 \text{ ft}}{1 \text{ mi}} \quad \leftarrow \text{Multiply by the conversion factor, } \tfrac{5,280 \text{ ft}}{1 \text{ mi}}.$$

$$= \frac{(1.2)(5,280) \text{ ft}}{1} \quad \leftarrow \text{Simplify.}$$

$$= 6,336 \text{ ft} \quad \leftarrow \text{Simplify.}$$

There are 6,336 ft in 1.2 miles.

Test Prep Tip

Check that the units cancel when you multiply by the conversion factor.

✔ Quick Check

1. Convert $2\frac{1}{4}$ mi to feet.

Sometimes you need to use two or more conversion factors.

EXAMPLE Application: Rowing

2 **Gridded Response** Community Rowing Inc., a nonprofit club, participated in the annual Head of the Charles Regatta rowing race in Boston, Massachusetts. The team completed the 2,000-m course at a rate of about 1.92 m/s. Convert this rate to kilometers per minute (km/min). Round your answer to hundredths.

Multiply by the conversion factors $\frac{60 \text{ s}}{1 \text{ min}}$ and $\frac{1 \text{ km}}{1,000 \text{ m}}$.

$$\frac{1.92 \text{ m}}{1 \text{ s}} = \frac{1.92 \text{ m}}{1 \text{ s}} \cdot \frac{60 \text{ s}}{1 \text{ min}} \cdot \frac{1 \text{ km}}{1,000 \text{ m}}$$

$$= \frac{(1.92)(60)(1) \text{ km}}{(1)(1,000)(1) \text{ min}} \quad \leftarrow \text{Simplify.}$$

$$= 0.1152 \quad \leftarrow \text{Use a calculator.}$$

The team raced at a rate of about 0.12 km/min.

Check for Reasonableness Round 1.92 to 2. Then $2 \cdot 60 \div 1,000 = 0.12$. The answer 0.12 km/min matches the estimate. The answer is reasonable.

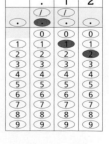

✔ Quick Check

2. You ran at a rate of 0.15 mi/min. Convert the rate to feet per second.

You can estimate conversions by using compatible numbers.

EXAMPLE Converting Using Compatible Numbers

③ Use compatible numbers to estimate the number of cups in 50 fl oz.

The conversion factor for changing fluid ounces to cups is $\frac{1\,c}{8\,fl\,oz}$.

$50\,fl\,oz \approx 48\,fl\,oz$ ← **Round to the nearest number divisible by 8.**

$= \frac{48\,\cancel{fl\,oz}}{1} \cdot \frac{1\,c}{8\,\cancel{fl\,oz}}$ ← **Multiply by the conversion factor, $\frac{1\,c}{8\,fl\,oz}$.**

$= \frac{48}{8}$ cups ← **Simplify.**

$= 6$ cups ← **Divide.**

There are about 6 cups in 50 fl oz.

✓ Quick Check

3. Use compatible numbers to estimate.
   a. 14,120 lb is about ■ t.   b. 9.8 c is about ■ pt.

You can convert between the metric system and the customary system using conversion factors. The table below shows the relationship between measurements in the two systems.

Type	Customary Units and Metric Units
Length	1 in. = 2.54 cm 1 mi ≈ 1.61 km 1 ft ≈ 0.3 m
Capacity	1 qt ≈ 0.94 L
Weight and Mass	1 oz ≈ 28.4 g 1 lb ≈ 0.45 kg

EXAMPLE Converting Between Systems

④ Convert 36 cm to inches. Round to the nearest tenth.

$36\,cm = \frac{36\,\cancel{cm}}{1} \cdot \frac{1\,in.}{2.54\,\cancel{cm}}$ ← **Multiply by the conversion factor, $\frac{1\,in.}{2.54\,cm}$.**

$= \frac{(36)(1)in.}{2.54}$ ← **Simplify.**

$\approx 14.2\,in.$ ← **Divide using a calculator.**

There are about 14.2 in. in 36 cm.

✓ Quick Check

4. Convert 15 L to quarts. Round to the nearest tenth.

1. **Vocabulary** What conversion factor would you use to convert feet to inches?

Choose the correct conversion factor to convert each measure.

2. 130 in. to feet

3. 48 lb to ounces

4. 9 km to meters

5. 36 ft to inches

6. 70 oz to pounds

A. $\dfrac{16 \text{ oz}}{1 \text{ lb}}$

B. $\dfrac{12 \text{ in.}}{1 \text{ ft}}$

C. $\dfrac{1 \text{ lb}}{16 \text{ oz}}$

D. $\dfrac{1,000 \text{ m}}{1 \text{ km}}$

E. $\dfrac{1 \text{ ft}}{12 \text{ in.}}$

Homework Exercises

For more exercises, see Extra Skills and Word Problems.

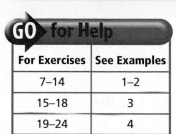

For Exercises	See Examples
7–14	1–2
15–18	3
19–24	4

Convert each measure. Round to the nearest tenth, if necessary.

7. 32 in. = ■ ft

8. 2,500 cm = ■ m

9. 15,000 g = ■ kg

Find an equivalent rate.

10. 90 in./min = ■ ft/min

11. $27/h = $■ /min

12. 12 cm/day = ■ cm/h

13. 12 qt/min = ■ gal/min

14. **Sports** Some pitchers can throw a baseball as fast as 100 mi/h. What is this rate in feet per second?

Estimation Use compatible numbers to estimate.

15. 148 in. is about ■ ft.

16. 82 oz is about ■ lb.

17. 500 min is about ■ h.

18. 3,980 mm is about ■ m.

Convert each measure. Round to the nearest tenth, if necessary.

19. 25 cm = ■ in.

20. 18 qt = ■ L

21. 55 lb = ■ kg

22. 23 in. = ■ cm

23. 10 kg = ■ lb

24. 16 L = ■ qt

25. **Guided Problem Solving** The cheetah can run as fast as 93 ft/s. Estimate the number of meters the cheetah can run in 7 seconds.
    • What conversion factor can you use for changing feet to meters?
    • How can you change the conversion factor to a number compatible with 93?

26. The radius of a wheel is 14 in. Estimate the radius in centimeters.

Convert each measure. Round to the nearest tenth, if necessary.

27. $1\frac{1}{2}$ mi/h = ■ ft/day   **28.** $64\frac{2}{3}$ yd/h = ■ in./s

Use the formulas $F = \frac{9}{5}C + 32$ and $C = \frac{5}{9}(F - 32)$ to convert temperatures between Celsius and Fahrenheit.

29. 28°C   **30.** 14°C   **31.** 32°F   **32.** 0°F

Use the table to match the activity with the Calories burned per minute.

33. 3.8 Cal/min   **34.** 4.4 Cal/min

35. 2.9 Cal/min   **36.** 6.2 Cal/min

37. **Writing in Math** Explain how you would estimate the number of times you blink your eyes in a day and in a week.

Activity	Calories/h
Aerobics (moderate)	371
Cycling (10 mi/h)	262
Dancing (moderate)	171
Jumping rope	342
Running (7 mi/h)	513
Swimming (25 yd/min)	228
Walking (4.5 mi/h)	257

SOURCE: *Principles & Labs*

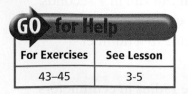

38. **Population** In 2004, about 129,405,000 babies were born in the world.
   a. Find the approximate number of births per day for a 365-day year.
   b. Find the number of births per hour.

39. **Challenge** Simplify 4 ft 7 in. − 3 ft 9 in. + 2 ft 5 in. Write the answer in simplest form.

Test Prep and Mixed Review   **Practice**

Gridded Response

40. Grace is a member of her school's track team. In one race, she ran 10 feet per second. What was her rate in miles per hour? Round to the nearest tenth.

41. Suppose $\triangle ABC$ at the right is reflected over the y-axis. What is the x-coordinate of A'?

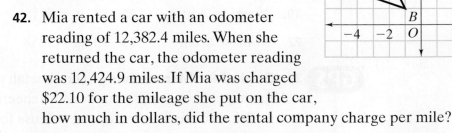

42. Mia rented a car with an odometer reading of 12,382.4 miles. When she returned the car, the odometer reading was 12,424.9 miles. If Mia was charged $22.10 for the mileage she put on the car, how much in dollars, did the rental company charge per mile?

Graph each linear equation.

43. $y = -x + 3$ **44.** $y = \frac{3}{4}x - 5$ **45.** $y = -\frac{2}{5}x - 2$

Checkpoint Quiz 1

Write each ratio in simplest form.

1. $\dfrac{48 \text{ s}}{12 \text{ min}}$

2. 81 in. to 27 ft

3. 90 m : 15 m

4. $\dfrac{18 \text{ yd}}{72 \text{ ft}}$

Find each unit rate.

5. $84 for 7 books

6. 96 m in 8 s

7. 57 gal in 19 min

8. 232 mi in 29 h

Convert each measure. If necessary, round to the nearest tenth.

9. $12/h = $ ■ /min

10. 9 kg = ■ lb

11. 16 L = ■ qt

12. 20 cm = ■ in.

13. The speed limit on some highways is 65 mi/h. What is this rate in kilometers per hour?

14. It costs $38 to have 8 pages of notes typed. Find the unit rate.

15. An airplane is flying at 455 miles per hour. What is its speed in kilometers per minute?

MATH AT WORK

Automotive Mechanic

Automotive mechanics diagnose and repair mechanical problems. An automotive mechanic must inspect a car and analyze its problems to determine the necessary adjustments to make.

The ability to reason is a skill that an auto mechanic uses to diagnose problems quickly and accurately. Mechanics also use estimating skills to determine the approximate cost of repairs. The mechanic wants to make sure that he or she charges enough for the work, yet does not overcharge the customer.

Go Online
PHSchool.com
For: Information on Automotive Mechanics
Web Code: asb-2031

Proportional and Nonproportional Relationships

A relationship is proportional if it can be described by ratios that are equivalent. If the ratios are not equivalent, the relationship is said to be nonproportional.

ACTIVITY

The figure below shows a series of squares drawn on graph paper with some blocks shaded.

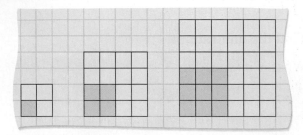

1. Draw an 8-by-8 square on a piece of graph paper. Shade the number of blocks needed to follow the pattern in this series of squares.

2. Complete the table below. Draw the next few squares on your graph paper as needed. Write all ratios in simplest form.

Shaded Blocks	1	4	9	16	25	■
Total Blocks	4	16	36	■	■	144
Ratio $\frac{\text{shaded}}{\text{total}}$	■	$\frac{4}{16} = \frac{1}{4}$	■	■	■	■

3. Look at the ratios you calculated in the table. Is the relationship between the number of shaded blocks and the total number of blocks proportional? Explain.

4. You can also use a graph to determine proportional and nonproportional relationships. Use the ordered pairs (number of shaded blocks, number of total blocks) to draw a graph for this series of squares on a coordinate plane.

5. Describe the graph. What is its shape? Where does it intersect the *y*-axis?

6. Use your graph to predict the total number of blocks in a square with 64 shaded blocks.

A different series of figures is shown below.

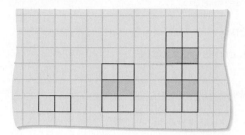

7. Draw a 7-by-2 rectangle on a piece of graph paper. Shade the number of blocks needed to follow the pattern in this series of rectangles.

8. Complete the table below. Draw the next few rectangles on your graph paper as needed. Write all ratios in simplest form.

Shaded Blocks	0	2	4	6	8	▪
Total Blocks	2	6	10	▪	▪	22
Ratio $\frac{\text{shaded}}{\text{total}}$	$\frac{0}{2}=0$	▪	▪	▪	▪	▪

9. Is this relationship between the number of shaded blocks and the total number of blocks proportional? Explain.

10. Use the ordered pairs (number of shaded blocks, number of total blocks) to draw a graph for this series of figures. What is its shape? Where does it intersect the y-axis?

11. Compare the graphs for the two different series of figures. How are the graphs alike? How are they different?

12. Draw a series of figures using shaded blocks. Is the relationship between shaded and total blocks proportional or nonproportional?

Exercises

Tell whether each table represents a proportional or nonproportional relationship. Explain.

1.

Shaded Blocks	1	2	3	10	100
Total Blocks	5	10	15	50	500

2.

Shaded Blocks	3	4	5	9	11
Total Blocks	11	14	17	29	35

4-3 Solving Proportions

Check Skills You'll Need

1. **Vocabulary Review**
Is the fraction $\frac{a+2}{b+2}$ in *simplest form*? Explain.

Write each fraction in simplest form.

2. $\frac{30}{99}$ 3. $\frac{42}{12}$

4. $\frac{132}{602}$ 5. $\frac{70}{25}$

 **for Help**
Lesson 2-2

What You'll Learn

To identify and solve proportions

🔊 **New Vocabulary** proportion, cross products

Why Learn This?

Exchange rates between currencies change daily. You can use equal ratios to find the value of the U.S. dollar at any time.

The rectangles below have the same amount shaded, so the ratios $\frac{12}{32}$ and $\frac{3}{8}$ are equal. The equation $\frac{12}{32} = \frac{3}{8}$ is a proportion.

$\dfrac{12}{32}$ ← shaded
← total

$\dfrac{3}{8}$ ← shaded
← total

KEY CONCEPTS **Proportion**

A **proportion** is an equation stating that two ratios are equal.

Arithmetic

$$\frac{6}{10} = \frac{9}{15}$$

Algebra

$$\frac{a}{b} = \frac{c}{d}, \text{where } b \neq 0 \text{ and } d \neq 0$$

EXAMPLE **Identifying Proportions**

① Do $\frac{4}{5}$ and $\frac{12}{15}$ form a proportion? Explain.

$\dfrac{4}{5} \overset{?}{=} \dfrac{12}{15}$ ← Write as a proportion.

 ← Use number sense to find a common multiplier.

Since $\frac{4}{5} = \frac{12}{15}$, they form a proportion.

✓ Quick Check

1. Do $\frac{6}{7}$ and $\frac{23}{28}$ form a proportion? Explain.

You can use the Multiplication Property of Equality to show an important property of all proportions.

$$\frac{6}{10} = \frac{9}{15}$$
$$\qquad\qquad\qquad\qquad\qquad\qquad\qquad\frac{a}{b} = \frac{c}{d}$$

$$\frac{6}{10}(10 \cdot 15) = \frac{9}{15}(10 \cdot 15)$$ ← Multiply each side by the denominators. → $$\frac{a}{b}(b \cdot d) = \frac{c}{d}(b \cdot d)$$

$$\frac{6 \cdot \cancel{10}^1 \cdot 15}{1\cancel{10}} = \frac{9 \cdot 10 \cdot \cancel{15}^1}{1\cancel{15}}$$ ← Divide the common factors. → $$\frac{a \cdot \cancel{b}^1 \cdot d}{1\cancel{b}} = \frac{c \cdot b \cdot \cancel{d}^1}{1\cancel{d}}$$

$$6 \cdot 15 = 9 \cdot 10$$ ← Simplify. → $$a \cdot d = c \cdot b$$
$$\text{or } 6 \cdot 15 = 10 \cdot 9 \qquad\qquad\qquad\qquad\qquad \text{or } a \cdot d = b \cdot c$$

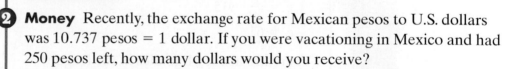

KEY CONCEPTS **Cross Products Property**

The cross products of two ratios are two products found by multiplying the denominator of each ratio by the numerator of the other ratio. In a proportion, the cross products are equal.

Arithmetic

$$\frac{6}{10} = \frac{9}{15}$$
$$6 \cdot 15 = 10 \cdot 9$$

Algebra

$$\frac{a}{b} = \frac{c}{d}, \text{ where } b \neq 0 \text{ and } d \neq 0$$
$$ad = bc$$

You can use cross products to solve a proportion.

EXAMPLE **Using Cross Products**

2 Money Recently, the exchange rate for Mexican pesos to U.S. dollars was 10.737 pesos = 1 dollar. If you were vacationing in Mexico and had 250 pesos left, how many dollars would you receive?

Let d = the number of dollars.

$$\frac{10.737}{1} = \frac{250}{d}$$ ← Write the proportion $\frac{pesos}{dollars}$.

$$10.737 \cdot d = 1 \cdot 250$$ ← Write the cross products.

$$\frac{10.737d}{10.737} = \frac{250}{10.737}$$ ← Divide each side by 10.737.

$$d = 23.28397131$$ ← Use a calculator.

You would receive $23.28.

Check for Reasonableness Round 10.737 to 10. Then $250 \div 10 = 25$. The answer 23.28 is close to the estimate 25. The answer is reasonable.

 Quick Check

2. Recently, the exchange rate for Swiss francs to U.S. dollars was 1.2450 Swiss francs = 1 dollar. If you were leaving Switzerland for the United States with 300 francs left, how many dollars would you receive?

Vocabulary Tip

Read $\frac{6}{10} = \frac{9}{15}$ as "The ratio of 6 to 10 equals the ratio of 9 to 15" or "6 is to 10 as 9 is to 15."

More Than One Way

Hockey In the National Hockey League, the ratio of goalies to the total number of players on a team is about 2 to 30. If the league has 915 players, about how many goalies are in the league?

Daryl's Method

I'll set up a proportion and use the cross products property. I'll let g stand for the number of goalies in the league.

$$\frac{2}{30} = \frac{g}{915}$$
$$2 \cdot 915 = 30 \cdot g$$
$$1{,}830 = 30g$$
$$\frac{1{,}830}{30} = \frac{30g}{30}$$
$$61 = g$$

There are about 61 goalies in the league.

Michelle's Method

I see that 2 out of every 30 players is a fraction of the total. Since there are 915 players in the league, I just need to multiply $\frac{2}{30}$ by 915 to find the number of goalies g in the whole league.

$$g = \frac{2}{30} \cdot 915$$
$$g = 61$$

There are about 61 goalies in the league.

Choose a Method

The ratio of defense players to the total number of players in the National Hockey League is about 9 to 30. If the league has 890 players, about how many defense players are in the league? Explain why you chose the method you used.

Check Your Understanding

1. **Vocabulary** You can find the __?__ of two ratios by multiplying the denominator of each ratio by the numerator of the other ratio.

Number Sense Do the ratios form a proportion? Explain.

2. $\frac{5}{6}$ and $\frac{15}{18}$ 3. $\frac{6}{27}$ and $\frac{2}{9}$ 4. $\frac{3}{13}$ and $\frac{4}{14}$

For more exercises, see Extra Skills and Word Problems.

GO for Help

For Exercises	See Examples
5–12	1
13–21	2

Do the ratios form a proportion? Explain.

5. $\frac{1}{4}$ and $\frac{2}{10}$ **6.** $\frac{30}{4}$ and $\frac{15}{2}$ **7.** $\frac{7}{6}$ and $\frac{28}{24}$ **8.** $\frac{3}{8}$ and $\frac{4}{10}$

9. $\frac{11}{18}$ and $\frac{22}{32}$ **10.** $\frac{25}{40}$ and $\frac{5}{8}$ **11.** $\frac{15}{27}$ and $\frac{5}{9}$ **12.** $\frac{2}{5}$ and $\frac{40}{100}$

Solve each proportion.

13. $\frac{2}{9} = \frac{10}{a}$ **14.** $\frac{k}{4} = \frac{21}{12}$ **15.** $\frac{45}{15} = \frac{y}{1}$ **16.** $\frac{12}{t} = \frac{8}{6}$

17. $\frac{20}{b} = \frac{15}{9}$ **18.** $\frac{12}{9} = \frac{w}{12}$ **19.** $\frac{x}{63} = \frac{9}{14}$ **20.** $\frac{3}{c} = \frac{5}{9}$

21. You are visiting friends in Estonia. Suppose the exchange rate is 12.68 kroons = 1 dollar. How many Estonian kroons will you receive if you have $500?

22. Guided Problem Solving For each crate of apples on display in a market, $\frac{1}{3}$ crate of oranges should be on display. If $2\frac{1}{4}$ crates of apples are on display, how many crates of oranges do you need?
- **Make a Plan** Write a proportion comparing crates of apples and crates of oranges.
- **Carry Out the Plan** Solve the proportion.

GO Online

Homework Video Tutor
Visit: PHSchool.com
Web Code: ase-0403

Recently, the exchange rate for Japanese yen to U.S. dollars was 1 yen = $.0093. Find the number of yen you would receive for each dollar amount.

23. $450   **24.** $40   **25.** $210   **26.** $175

Solve each proportion. Justify each step in the solution.

27. $\frac{x + 3}{2} = \frac{5}{4}$ **28.** $\frac{6}{9} = \frac{x + 4}{12}$

29. Error Analysis In 3 hours, Jim can walk 14 miles. To find the time he would take to walk 25 miles, he wrote the proportion $\frac{3}{14} = \frac{25}{h}$. Explain his error.

30. Determine whether the shaded regions below are proportional.

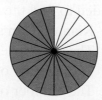 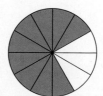

31. Choose a Method A 354-gram box of granola contains 20 grams of fat. The recommended serving size of granola is 55 grams. How many grams of fat does the recommended serving size contain? Explain why you chose the method you used.

Estimate the solution of each proportion.

32. $\frac{k}{20} = \frac{12}{47}$ **33.** $\frac{h}{22.3} = \frac{4}{55}$ **34.** $\frac{1.5}{r} = \frac{3}{4.97}$

35. Money Before a trip to Quebec, you want to exchange 1,500 U.S. dollars to Canadian dollars. The exchange rate for U.S. dollars to Canadian dollars is 0.7975 U.S. dollar = 1 Canadian dollar from one bank and 0.8352 U.S. dollar = 1 Canadian dollar from another bank. How many more Canadian dollars will you get from the first bank than from the second bank?

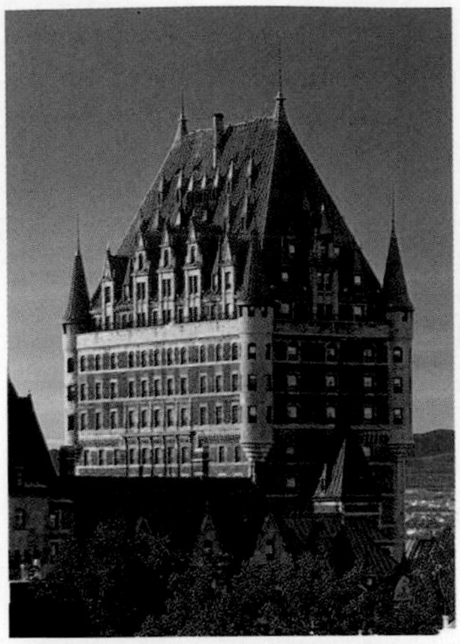

At Quebec's Le Chateau Frontenac hotel, a room can cost $399 in Canadian dollars, or about $321 in U.S. dollars.

Solve each proportion for *x*.

36. $\frac{x}{\frac{1}{2}} = \frac{12}{9}$ **37.** $\frac{8}{x + 1} = \frac{1}{2}$ **38.** $\frac{5}{\frac{1}{3}} = \frac{6}{x}$

39. Writing in Math Explain why the ratios $\frac{x}{y}$ and $\frac{x + z}{y}$ form a proportion only when $z = 0$.

40. Challenge The scale shown at the right is balanced when $a : y = b : x$. Suppose a 50-lb weight rests 29 in. from the fulcrum. How far from the fulcrum must a 30-lb weight be placed to maintain balance?

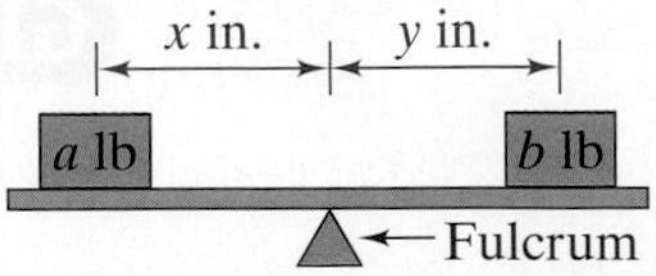

Test Prep and Mixed Review

Practice

Multiple Choice

41. Jocelyn has a 16-page presentation that she needs to give to 5 different teachers. A print shop charges $7.20 for the entire print job. How much does it cost her to print each page?

(A) $0.45 (B) $0.05 (C) $0.09 (D) $1.44

42. Which quadrant only contains points with a positive *x*-coordinate and a negative *y*-coordinate?

(F) Quadrant I
(G) Quadrant II
(H) Quadrant III
(J) Quadrant IV

43. For every 2 points that Lisa's team scored during a basketball game, Kiana's team scored 3 points. What additional information is needed to find the number of points Lisa's team scored?

(A) Kiana's team's score
(B) The score after the first quarter
(C) The number of players on Lisa's team
(D) The number of players on both teams

GO for Help

For Exercises	See Lesson
44–46	1-3

Simplify each expression.

44. $-11 + (-5)$ **45.** $-25 + 6$ **46.** $-13 - 14$

Using Rates and Proportions

You can use unit rates to write and solve equations involving ratios.

The table below shows data for the time it takes to make copies on a new photocopy machine. Use this data to find the amount of time it would take to copy 1,000 pages.

Time (minutes)	25	50	150	250	75
Number of Pages	875	1,750	5,250	8,750	2,625

What You Might Think

What do I know? What do I want to find out?

How can I find the unit rate?

How can I use the unit rate in an equation to find how long it takes to make copies?

How long does it take to copy 1,000 pages?

What You Might Write

I know how long it takes to copy certain numbers of pages. I want to find the amount of time it would take to copy 1,000 pages.

To find the unit rate, I divide time by the number of pages. For the first column, the unit rate is $\frac{25 \text{ min}}{875 \text{ pages}} \approx 0.029$ min/page. The unit rate is the same for all the data, so the unit rate is about 0.029 min/page.

The unit rate multiplied by the number of copies c will give the time t it will take to make a certain number of copies. So my equation is

$t = 0.029c$

$t = 0.029(1,000)$

$t = 29$

It takes 29 minutes to copy 1,000 pages.

Think It Through

1. **Number Sense** How do you know if 29 minutes is reasonable? (*Hint*: Compare it to 1,750 copies in the chart.)

2. Can you use the proportion $\frac{c}{t} = \frac{0.029}{1}$ for the situation above? Explain.

3. How long would it take you to copy 750 pages? 2,000 pages?

Exercises

Solve each problem. For Exercises 4 and 5, answer the questions first.

4. Data from the Council of Better Business Bureaus shows that customers filed approximately 28,000 complaints about cell phones in 2004. About how many complaints would this be per week?
   a. What are you trying to find?
   b. Use the diagram below to write a proportion for this situation.

$0\,x$ 28,000 complaints

$0\,1$ week   52 weeks

5. In an opinion poll, 600 teenagers were asked if basic money management skills should be taught in high school. The ratio of yes to no votes was 4 to 1. How many students voted yes and how many voted no?
   a. Suppose someone says that 4 students voted yes and 1 voted no. Is that the best answer? Explain.
   b. Use the diagram below to write an equation for this situation.

    Yes   No

                 +   =   600 students

6. The graph at the right shows the enrollment in American Sign Language classes in various years. Compared to the number of students in 1995, how many times greater was the number of students that enrolled in American Sign Language classes in 2002?

7. In a study of 6,349 public libraries in 2002, the average spending per person in the community was $30.32. Suppose you live in a community of 25,000 people and the annual budget is $437,500 for the library. Is this above or below the average found in the study? Explain.

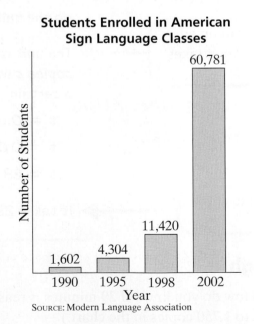

Students Enrolled in American Sign Language Classes

60,781

Number of Students

1,602   4,304   11,420

1990   1995   1998   2002

Year

SOURCE: Modern Language Association

4-4 Similar Figures and Proportions

✓ Check Skills You'll Need

1. **Vocabulary Review**
   What are the *cross products* for
   $\frac{10}{15} = \frac{2}{3}$?

Solve each proportion.

2. $\frac{7}{13} = \frac{21}{t}$

3. $\frac{k}{50} = \frac{22}{10}$

4. $\frac{16}{25} = \frac{324}{m}$

 **for Help**
Lesson 4-3

What You'll Learn

To identify similar figures and to use proportions to find missing measurements in similar figures

🔊 **New Vocabulary** similar figures, congruent angles, similar polygons

Why Learn This?

Sometimes you want an image to be larger or smaller than the original.

Similar figures have the same shape but not necessarily the same size. **Congruent angles** have equal measures. The ratios of the lengths of corresponding sides in similar figures are proportional.

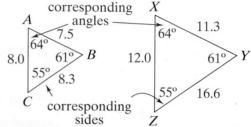

The symbol ~ means "is similar to."
The symbol ≅ means "is congruent to."

If two polygons are **similar polygons**, then corresponding angles are congruent and the lengths of corresponding sides are in proportion.

EXAMPLE Identifying Similar Polygons

1. Is rectangle *LMNO* similar to rectangle *HIJK*? Explain.

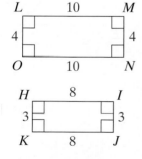

$$\angle L \cong \angle H \quad \angle M \cong \angle I \quad \angle N \cong \angle J \quad \angle O \cong \angle K$$

$\frac{MN}{IJ} \stackrel{?}{=} \frac{LM}{HI}$ ← Write a proportion.

$\frac{4}{3} \stackrel{?}{=} \frac{10}{8}$ ← Substitute.

$4 \cdot 8 \stackrel{?}{=} 3 \cdot 10$ ← Write the cross products.

$32 \neq 30$ ← Simplify.

The corresponding angles are congruent, but the corresponding sides are not in proportion. So the rectangles are *not* similar.

✓ Quick Check

1. Rectangle *EFGH* has side lengths of 18 and 27. Rectangle *LMNO* has side lengths of 36 and 54. Are the rectangles similar? Explain.

You can use proportions to find unknown lengths in similar figures.

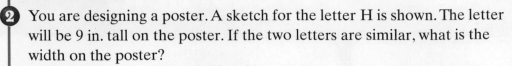

EXAMPLE Application: Design

2 You are designing a poster. A sketch for the letter H is shown. The letter will be 9 in. tall on the poster. If the two letters are similar, what is the width on the poster?

$$\frac{5\text{ in.}}{9\text{ in.}} = \frac{4\text{ in.}}{w} \quad \leftarrow \textbf{Write a proportion.}$$

$$5 \cdot w = 9 \cdot 4 \quad \leftarrow \textbf{Write the cross products.}$$

$$5w = 36 \quad \leftarrow \textbf{Simplify.}$$

$$\frac{5w}{5} = \frac{36}{5} \quad \leftarrow \textbf{Divide each side by 5.}$$

$$x = 7.2 \quad \leftarrow \textbf{Simplify.}$$

5 in.

|← 4 in. →|

The width of the letter is 7.2 inches.

✓ Quick Check

2. If the letter H on the poster has a height of 14 in., what is its width?

When similar figures overlap, you can separate them.

EXAMPLE Overlapping Similar Triangles

3 **Multiple Choice** In the figure at the left, $\triangle ABC \sim \triangle DEC$. Find the value of x.

  Ⓐ 8 ft   Ⓑ 9 ft   Ⓒ 12 ft   Ⓓ 18 ft

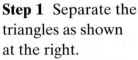

Step 1 Separate the triangles as shown at the right.

Step 2 Write a proportion using corresponding sides of the triangles.

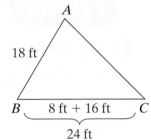
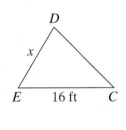

$$\frac{18}{x} = \frac{24}{16} \quad \leftarrow \textbf{Write a proportion.}$$

$$18 \cdot 16 = 24 \cdot x \quad \leftarrow \textbf{Write the cross products.}$$

$$288 = 24x \quad \leftarrow \textbf{Simplify.}$$

$$\frac{288}{24} = \frac{24x}{24} \quad \leftarrow \textbf{Divide each side by 24.}$$

$$12 = x \quad \leftarrow \textbf{Simplify.}$$

The value of x is 12 ft. The correct answer is choice C.

Test Prep Tip

You can reduce $\frac{24}{16}$ in the first step. This uses more steps but makes calculations easier.

✓ Quick Check

3. If DC is 14 ft, what is the length of $\overline{AC}$?

Vocabulary Tip

The notation PQ means the length of $\overline{PQ}$.

1. **Vocabulary** Can a triangle and square be similar figures? Explain.

Complete each statement for the similar figures at the right.

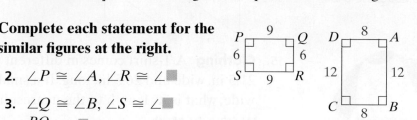

2. $\angle P \cong \angle A$, $\angle R \cong \angle \blacksquare$

3. $\angle Q \cong \angle B$, $\angle S \cong \angle \blacksquare$

4. $\dfrac{PQ}{AB} = \dfrac{\blacksquare}{BC}$

Homework Exercises

For more exercises, see Extra Skills and Word Problems.

GO for Help

For Exercises	See Examples
5–6	1
7–9	2
10–11	3

Are the figures in each pair similar? Explain.

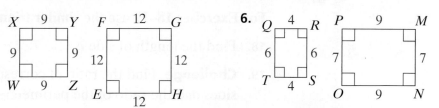

5.

6.

Exercises 7–8 show pairs of similar figures. Find the unknown lengths.

7.

8.

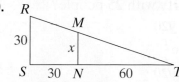

9. **Movies** A frame of movie film is 35 mm wide and 26.25 mm high. The film projects an image 8 m wide. How high is the image?

Exercises 10–11 show similar figures. Find the unknown lengths.

10.

11.

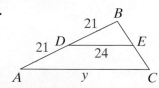

GPS 12. **Guided Problem Solving** You have a class photo that is 10 in. long and 8 in. wide. If you want to enlarge your photo to be 15 in. long, how wide will the photo be?
  - **Understand the Problem** You know the dimensions of the original photo and the length of the enlarged photo. Find the width of the enlarged photo.
  - **Make a Plan** Draw the figures and label their sides.

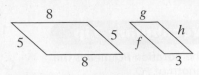
Exercises 13–14 show pairs of similar figures. Find the unknown lengths.

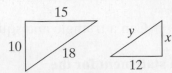

13.

14.

15. **Clothing** A T-shirt comes in different sizes. A large T-shirt is 21.5 in. wide and 26.5 in. long. If a small youth T-shirt is 15.5 in. wide, what is its length to the nearest inch?

16. **Writing in Math** Are squares always similar? Explain.

17. **Multiple Choice** Which statement is *true*?
   Ⓐ Corresponding sides of similar polygons are equal.
   Ⓑ Not all circles are similar.
   Ⓒ Corresponding sides of similar polygons are congruent.
   Ⓓ Not all rectangles are similar.

For Exercises 18–19 use the similar triangles shown below.

18. Find the length of side c.

19. **Challenge** Find the ratio of corresponding sides and the ratio of the perimeters. What do you notice?

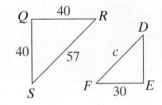

Ⓐ Ⓑ Ⓒ Ⓓ **Test Prep and Mixed Review**   **Practice**

Multiple Choice

20. The figures shown at the right are similar. What is the value of w?
   Ⓐ 4.0   Ⓒ 6.3
   Ⓑ 4.4   Ⓓ 8.0

21. Javier and Daisy threw a dinner party for 38 people. The party cost $920. Which proportion can be used to find the cost c of throwing a similar party with 25 people?
   Ⓕ $\frac{38}{25} = \frac{920}{c}$ Ⓗ $\frac{38}{920} = \frac{c}{25}$
   Ⓖ $\frac{13}{38} = \frac{c}{920}$ Ⓙ $\frac{13}{25} = \frac{c}{920}$

22. Judy spends 3 more than twice as many hours studying for history as she does for math. She studies 4 hours for history. Which equation can be used to find x, the number of hours she studies for math?
   Ⓐ $3x + 3 = 4$ Ⓒ $2x + 2 = 4$
   Ⓑ $3x + 2 = 4$ Ⓓ $2x + 3 = 4$

GO for Help

For Exercises	See Lesson
23–26	2-3

Compare. Use <, >, or =.

23. $\frac{16}{20}$ ■ 0.8   24. $\frac{7}{8}$ ■ 0.85   25. $\frac{18}{12}$ ■ −1.5   26. $\frac{5}{14}$ ■ $0.\overline{3}$

Ratios of Similar Figures

You can use diagrams to determine the relationships between side length, perimeter, and area in similar figures.

ACTIVITY

The figure at the right shows three similar rectangles drawn on graph paper.

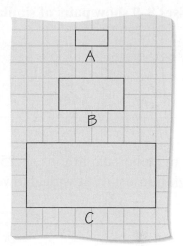

1. Copy and complete the table below.

Rectangle	Length	Perimeter	Area
A	2	6 units	2 units^2
B	■	■	■
C	■	■	■

2. Find the ratios of Length A to Length B, Perimeter A to Perimeter B, and Area A to Area B. Record your answers in a table like the one below.

Ratio	A to B	A to C	B to C
Length : Length	■	■	■
Perimeter : Perimeter	■	■	■
Area : Area	■	■	■

3. Find the ratios needed to complete the table. Write all ratios in simplest form.

4. How does the ratio of the perimeters of any two rectangles in the table compare to the ratio of the lengths of the rectangles?

5. How does the ratio of the areas of any two rectangles in the table compare to the ratio of the lengths of the rectangles?

6. If you draw a rectangle with side lengths five times those of rectangle A, what would you expect the perimeter and area of the new rectangle to be?

7. How does the ratio of the lengths of corresponding sides of any two similar figures compare to the ratio of the perimeters of the figures? Explain.

8. How does the ratio of the lengths of corresponding sides of any two similar figures compare to the ratio of the areas of the figures? Explain.

Solve each proportion.

1. $\dfrac{k}{6} = \dfrac{19}{3}$

2. $\dfrac{15}{t} = \dfrac{5}{7}$

3. $\dfrac{16}{12} = \dfrac{w}{6}$

4. $\dfrac{5}{13} = \dfrac{20}{a}$

5. $\dfrac{2}{5} = \dfrac{n}{15}$

6. $\dfrac{0.7}{m} = \dfrac{7}{28}$

7. Recently, the exchange rate for U.S. dollars to Indian rupees was $1 = 43.43 rupees. How many dollars would you get for 860 rupees?

Exercises 8–9 show pairs of similar polygons. Find the unknown lengths.

8.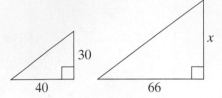

9.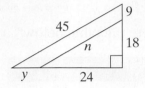

10. A model of a lighthouse is 25 cm wide and 75 cm high. The original lighthouse is 17 ft wide. How high is the original lighthouse?

4-5a Activity Lab

Exploring Dilations

1. Draw triangles using the following instructions.
   - Graph points $A(4, 2)$, $B(8, 2)$, $C(4, 5)$, and $O(0, 0)$ on graph paper. Draw $\triangle ABC$.
   - Use a different color to draw rays $\overrightarrow{OA}$, $\overrightarrow{OB}$, and $\overrightarrow{OC}$.
   - Use a ruler to locate A' on $\overrightarrow{OA}$ so that $\overline{OA} = \overline{AA'}$, as shown.
   - Locate points B' and C'. Then draw $\triangle A'B'C'$.

2. What appears to be true about $\triangle ABC$ and $\triangle A'B'C'$? Explain.

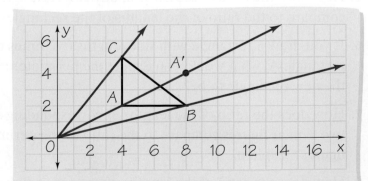

Similarity Transformations

Check Skills You'll Need

1. **Vocabulary Review**
The first coordinate
in an *ordered pair* is
the __?__ - coordinate.

Graph each point on a
coordinate plane.

2. $A(3, 6)$ 3. $B(-2, 7)$

4. $C(5, -1)$ 5. $D(-3, 0)$

 **for Help**

Lesson 3-4

What You'll Learn

To graph dilations and to determine the scale factor of a dilation

New Vocabulary dilation, scale factor, enlargement, reduction

Why Learn This?

Photos can be enlarged or reduced
using scale factors.

A **dilation** is a transformation in which
a figure and its image are similar. The
ratio of a length in the image to the
corresponding length in the original
figure is the **scale factor.**

Vocabulary Tip

Dilate means "to make
wider or larger." In math, a
dilation can enlarge or
reduce a figure.

EXAMPLE Finding a Dilation

1 Find the image of $\triangle ABC$ below after a dilation
with center A and a scale factor of $\frac{1}{2}$.

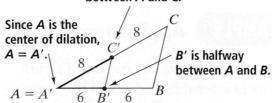

*C′ is halfway
between A and C.*

*Since A is the
center of dilation,
A = A′.*

*B′ is halfway
between A and B.*

$\triangle A'B'C'$ is the image of $\triangle ABC$ after a dilation with a scale factor of $\frac{1}{2}$.

$\triangle ABC \sim \triangle A'B'C'$.

Quick Check

1. Find the image of $\triangle DEF$ with vertices $D(-2, 2)$, $E(1, -1)$, and
$F(-2, -1)$ after a dilation with center D and a scale factor of 2.

Unless otherwise noted, in this text, dilations in a coordinate plane
have $(0, 0)$ as the center of dilation. To find the image of a figure in a
coordinate plane after a dilation, you multiply the x- and y-coordinates
by the scale factor.

EXAMPLE Graphing Dilation Images

② Find the coordinates of the image of quadrilateral *KLMN* after a dilation with a scale factor of $\frac{3}{2}$.

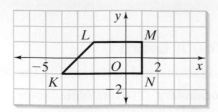

Step 1 Multiply the coordinates of each point by $\frac{3}{2}$.

$$K(-4, -1) \rightarrow K'\left(-6, -\frac{3}{2}\right)$$

$$L(-2, 1) \rightarrow L'\left(-3, \frac{3}{2}\right)$$

$$M(1, 1) \rightarrow M'\left(\frac{3}{2}, \frac{3}{2}\right)$$

$$N(1, -1) \rightarrow N'\left(\frac{3}{2}, -\frac{3}{2}\right)$$

Step 2 Graph the image.

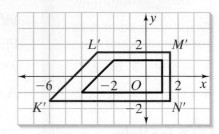

✔ **Quick Check**

2. Find the coordinates of the image of *ABCD* with vertices $A(0,0)$, $B(0,3)$, $C(3,3)$, and $D(3,0)$ after a dilation with a scale factor of $\frac{4}{3}$.

A dilation with a scale factor greater than 1 is called an **enlargement.** The image is bigger than the original. A dilation with a scale factor less than 1 is called a **reduction.** The image is smaller than the original.

EXAMPLE Application: City Planning

③ Figure *TRSV* shows the outline of a park. A city planner dilates the figure to show the area of the park that can be used for concerts. Find the scale factor. Is it an enlargement or a reduction?

$$\begin{array}{c} \text{image} \rightarrow \\ \text{original} \rightarrow \end{array} \frac{T'R'}{TR} = \frac{2}{8} = \frac{1}{4}$$

The scale factor is $\frac{1}{4}$. It is less than 1, so the dilation is a reduction.

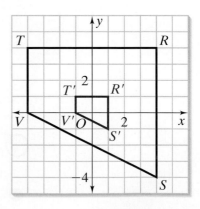

✔ **Quick Check**

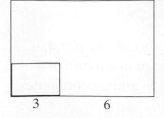

3. The blue figure at the left shows the outline of a yard. The black figure is a doghouse. The blue figure is a dilation of the black figure. Find the scale factor. Is it an enlargement or a reduction?

1. **Vocabulary** A rectangle is dilated with a scale factor of 0.6. Is the image a reduction or an enlargement? Explain.

Use the diagram for Exercises 2 and 3. The blue figure is a dilation of the original figure.

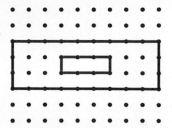

2. Is the blue figure an enlargement or a reduction of the original figure?

3. What is the scale factor?

Homework Exercises

For more exercises, see Extra Skills and Word Problems.

GO for Help	
For Exercises	**See Examples**
4–5	1
6–7	2
8–10	3

In each exercise, find the image of △*ABC* after a dilation with the given center and scale factor.

4. center *C*, scale factor $\frac{1}{2}$

5. center *B*, scale factor 2

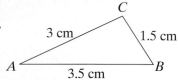

Find the coordinates of the image of quadrilateral *ABCD* after a dilation with the given scale factor. Graph the image.

6. scale factor 2

7. scale factor $\frac{1}{2}$

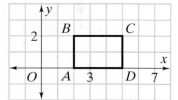

Each blue figure is a dilation of the original figure. Find the scale factor. Classify each dilation as an *enlargement* or a *reduction*.

8.
9.
10.

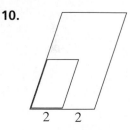

11. **Guided Problem Solving** You are reducing a digital photo that is 2 in. high and 3 in. wide. If the reduced photo is $1\frac{1}{4}$ in. high, what is its width? Write your answer as a mixed number in simplest form.
  - **Understand the Problem** You know the height and width of the original photo and the height of the reduced photo. You want to find the length of the reduced photo.
  - **Make a Plan** Draw and label the original photo and the reduced photo next to each other. Label the missing width *w*.

Graph the coordinates of quadrilateral *EFGH*. Find the coordinates of its image after a dilation with the given scale factor. Graph the image.

12. $E(-2, -1)$, $F(2, 0)$, $G(2, 2)$, $H(-1, 2)$; scale factor of 2

13. $E(-3, 0)$, $F(1, -4)$, $G(5, 0)$, $H(1, 4)$; scale factor of $\frac{1}{2}$

14. $E(3, 0)$, $F(0, -2)$, $G(-3, 1)$, $H(2, 3)$; scale factor of 1.5

15. **Computers** A window on a computer screen is $1\frac{1}{2}$ in. high and 2 in. wide. After you click the "size reduction" button, the window is reduced to $1\frac{1}{8}$ in. high and $1\frac{1}{2}$ in. wide. What is the scale factor?

16. $\triangle A'B'C'$ is the image of $\triangle ABC$ after a dilation. $AB = 7$ cm, $AC = 10$ cm, $A'B' = 28$ cm, and $B'C' = 24$ cm. What is the ratio of the perimeter of $\triangle ABC$ to the perimeter of $\triangle A'B'C'$?

17. **Writing in Math** Explain the steps involved in dilating a figure in a coordinate plane.

18. **Challenge** $\triangle ABC$ has three angles of 60° and three sides that measure 60 cm each. What scale factor should you use to create $\triangle A'B'C'$ with side lengths of 21 cm?

Test Prep and Mixed Review
Practice

Multiple Choice

19. The blue figure is a dilation of the original figure. What is the scale factor?

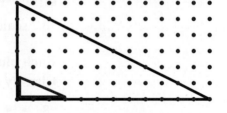

   Ⓐ $\frac{1}{4}$ Ⓒ 2

   Ⓑ $\frac{1}{2}$ Ⓓ 4

20. The number of people a restaurant can hold is proportional to the area of its floor space. A restaurant has a length of 45 feet, a width of 40 feet, and a height of 25 feet. It can hold 115 people. Which information will NOT help find the space needed for 200 people?
   Ⓕ The length of the restaurant
   Ⓖ The number of people the restaurant can hold
   Ⓗ The height of the restaurant
   Ⓙ The width of the restaurant

21. Cory is putting tape along the diagonals of windows to prepare for a storm. Each window is 54 inches high and 40 inches wide. Which is closest to the amount of tape Cory needs to cover 12 windows?
   Ⓐ 11 ft   Ⓑ 67 ft   Ⓒ 134 ft   Ⓓ 185 ft

GO for Help

For Exercises	See Lesson
22–23	3-2

The legs of a right triangle are given. Find the hypotenuse.

22. 16 cm, 12 cm   23. 57 in., 76 in.

Geometry Software and Dilations

You can use the dilation command from geometry software to dilate a figure. The software asks you to specify a center of dilation and a scale factor. Use the origin (0, 0) for the center of dilation.

ACTIVITY

Draw $\triangle ABC$ with the following vertices: $A(0, 0)$, $B(5, 4)$, and $C(6, 1)$. Find the image of $\triangle ABC$ after a dilation with a scale factor of 2. Then find the coordinates of the image of $\triangle ABC$.

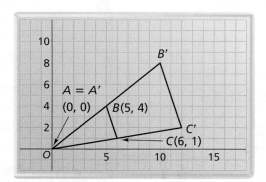

Step 1 Plot points A, B, and C. Construct the triangle.

Step 2 Use the *Dilate* command. Enter 2 for the scale factor. The results are shown at the right.

1. Find the image of $\triangle ABC$ after a dilation with a scale factor of 2.5.

2. Find the coordinates of the image of $\triangle ABC$.

Exercises

Use the figure at the right for Exercises 1–4. Rectangle *HIJK* is shown at the right.

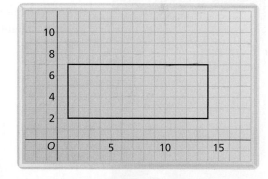

1. Graph the coordinates of rectangle *HIJK* with vertices $H(1, 2)$, $I(1, 7)$, $J(14, 7)$, and $K(14, 2)$. Label the vertices.

2. Find the image of rectangle *HIJK* after a dilation with a scale factor of 0.5. Label the image *LMNO*.

3. Describe the relationship between the perimeters of rectangle *HIJK* and of rectangle *LMNO*. Write a ratio to compare the perimeters.

4. **a.** Use the Area tool to find the areas of *HIJK* and *LMNO*. Write a ratio to compare the areas.
   b. Reasoning What conclusions can you make about the ratio of the areas with a scale factor of 0.5?

Scale Models and Maps

Check Skills You'll Need

1. **Vocabulary Review**
   A *product* is the result of which operation?

Multiply.

2. 4×3.2

3. 7.6×5.9

4. 1.8×22

5. 13×6.5

 **for Help**
Skills Handbook, page 632

What You'll Learn

To use proportions to solve problems involving scale

◄)) **New Vocabulary** scale model, scale

Why Learn This?

When building a large object, such as a car, you can make a scale model first to get an idea of what the object will look like.

A **scale model** is a model similar to the actual object it represents. The **scale** of a model is the ratio of the length of the model to the corresponding length of the actual object.

EXAMPLE Using Proportions to Solve Problems

1 **Museums** The Museum of Science and Industry in Chicago has a scale model of a human heart that is large enough for people to walk through. The height of the model is 16 ft. The scale used is 1 ft : $\frac{9}{32}$ in. What is the height of the actual heart on which the model is based?

Let h = the height of the actual heart.

model height (ft) → $\frac{1}{\frac{9}{32}} = \frac{16}{h}$ ← model height (ft)
actual height (in.) → ← actual height (in.)

$1 \cdot h = 16 \cdot \frac{9}{32}$ ← Write the cross products.

$h = \overset{1}{16} \cdot \frac{9}{\underset{2}{32}}$ ← Divide 16 and 32 by the GCF.

$h = \frac{9}{2}$ ← Simplify.

$h = 4\frac{1}{2}$ ← Write the improper fraction as a mixed number.

The height of the actual heart is $4\frac{1}{2}$ in.

This model heart would fit in a person who is 28 stories tall!

✓ Quick Check

1. In Example 1, suppose the width of the scale model is 10 ft. What is the width of the actual heart?

You can use the scale of a map to find actual distances between locations.

EXAMPLE **Application: Geography**

2 **Multiple Choice** Find the map distance from Columbus, Georgia, to Birmingham, Alabama. Which is closest to the actual distance?

Ⓐ 120 mi   Ⓒ 140 mi

Ⓑ 130 mi   Ⓓ 150 mi

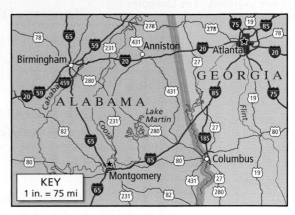

KEY
1 in. = 75 mi

The map distance is about $1\frac{3}{4}$ in., or 1.75 in.

Let x = the actual distance.

map (in.) → $\dfrac{1}{75} = \dfrac{1.75}{x}$ ← map (in.)
actual (mi) →   ← actual (mi)

$1 \cdot x = 75 \cdot 1.75$ ← **Write the cross products.**

$x = 131.25$ ← **Simplify.**

The distance from Birmingham to Columbus is about 130 mi. The correct answer is choice B.

Test Prep Tip ⒶⒷⒸⒹ

You can also solve this problem by multiplying 1.75 by the unit rate $\frac{75\ mi}{1\ in.}$.

✓ **Quick Check**

2. Use the map in Example 2 and an inch ruler. Find the actual distance from Montgomery, Alabama, to Atlanta, Georgia.

✓ **Check Your Understanding**

1. **Vocabulary** What does the scale on a map tell you about map distance and actual distance?

2. **Mental Math** Suppose a distance on the map in Example 2 is 2 in. Find the actual distance without using proportions.

3. **Reasoning** Consider two models of the same object. The models have scales of 1 : 2 and of 1 : 3. Which model is larger? Explain.

The scale of a model car is 1 in. : $2\frac{1}{2}$ ft. The length of the model is 6 in. The width of the model is 2.3 in.

4. Use the proportion $\dfrac{1\ in.}{2\frac{1}{2}\ ft} = \dfrac{\blacksquare\ in.}{x\ ft}$ to find the actual length of the car.

5. Use the proportion $\dfrac{1\ in.}{2\frac{1}{2}\ ft} = \dfrac{\blacksquare\ in.}{y\ ft}$ to find the actual width of the car.

For more exercises, see Extra Skills and Word Problems.

GO for Help

For Exercises	See Examples
6–9	1
10–20	2

A builder wants to make a model of the silo shown at the right. Find the height and diameter of the model silo for each scale.

15 ft

75 ft

6. 1 in. : $2\frac{1}{2}$ ft   **7.** 1 in. : 5 ft

8. 1 in. : $3\frac{1}{3}$ ft   **9.** 1 in. : 6 ft

The scale of a map is 1 in. : 10 mi. How many actual miles does each measurement on the map represent?

10. $3\frac{1}{4}$ in.   **11.** $2\frac{1}{2}$ in.   **12.** 4.4 in.   **13.** 5.3 in.

Suppose you want to make a map with a scale 1 in. : 4 mi. How many inches does each distance occupy on the map?

14. 22 mi   **15.** 86 mi   **16.** 92 mi   **17.** 39 mi

Test Prep Tip

Always choose efficient tools for measuring. This key relates inches to miles, so use an inch ruler.

Maps Use the map below and an inch ruler for Exercises 18–20.

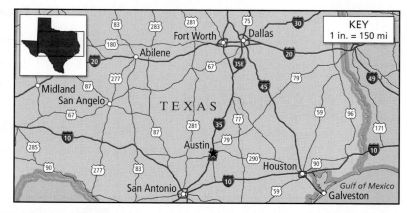

KEY
1 in. = 150 mi

18. **a.** What is the map distance between Abilene and Houston?
   b. Find the actual distance in miles using a proportion.

19. What is the actual distance from Midland to Austin?

20. Which two cities on the map are about 300 mi from Fort Worth?

GPS **21.** **Guided Problem Solving** Model trains built on the HO scale are $\frac{1}{87}$ the size of real trains. Models built on the N scale are $\frac{1}{160}$ the size of real trains. A full-size passenger car is 80 ft long. A model of the car is $\frac{1}{2}$ ft long. On which scale is the model made?
   • Solve the proportion $\frac{1}{87} = \frac{\blacksquare}{80}$ for the HO scale.
   • Solve the proportion $\frac{1}{160} = \frac{\blacksquare}{80}$ for the N scale.

22. **Open-Ended** Make a scale drawing of a calculator or a pen. Be sure to include the scale.

Architecture For Exercises 23–25, use the blueprint and an inch ruler.

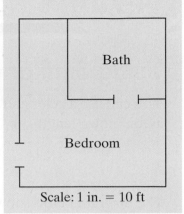

Bath

Bedroom

Scale: 1 in. = 10 ft

23. How many feet wide are the doors leading into the bedroom?

24. What is the actual length of the right wall shared by the bedroom and bath?

25. <u>**Writing in Math**</u> Could a bed 6 ft long and 3 ft wide fit into the narrow section of the bedroom? Explain.

26. **Geometry** You draw a 6 in.-by-8 in. rectangle on a piece of paper to represent the roof of a 300 ft-by-400 ft rectangular building. What is the scale of your drawing?

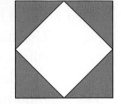

27. **Challenge** Make a scale drawing of the figure at the right for the scale 1 in. : $\frac{1}{3}$ in.

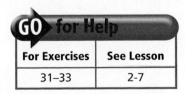

Test Prep and Mixed Review   **Practice**

Multiple Choice

28. An architect made a model building to scale so that 1 inch represents 40 feet. If the height of the model is $3\frac{1}{2}$ inches, what is the height of the actual building?

   Ⓐ 11.4 ft   Ⓒ 125 ft

   Ⓑ 36 ft   Ⓓ 140 ft

29. Which number has the greatest value?

   Ⓕ $-\dfrac{3}{2}$ Ⓗ $-\dfrac{1}{4}$

   Ⓖ -2 Ⓙ -0.38

30. The figures below have a repeating pattern. Which shows a 180° rotation of the 14th figure in the pattern?

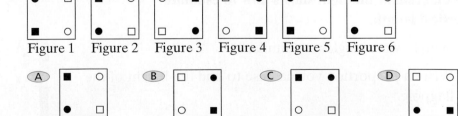

Figure 1   Figure 2   Figure 3   Figure 4   Figure 5   Figure 6

Evaluate each expression for $x = -1$ and $y = 1$.

31. $x^2 - 10(x - y^3)$ **32.** $(x^5 + x^8)(y^7 - y^5)$ **33.** $x + y - x^2 - y^2$

Using Similar Figures

You can use a ruler and similar triangles to estimate an unknown length.

ACTIVITY

The diagram below shows how to measure the length of a pond indirectly.

Step 1 Stand back and close one eye. Use the other hand to hold a ruler away from your face, parallel to the unknown length represented by $\overline{AB}$.

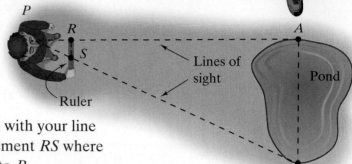

Step 2 Move the ruler until one end lines up with your line of sight to point A. Note the measurement RS where the ruler intersects your line of sight to B.

Step 3 Find the distance PR from your eye to the ruler and the distance PA from you to point A.

1. Which triangle is similar to $\triangle PRS$?

2. Write a proportion you can use to find the length of the pond. Which three of the measurements in this proportion are known?

3. Solve the proportion from Exercise 2 to find the unknown distance if $RS = 0.75$ ft, $PA = 110$ ft, $PR = 1.5$ ft.

Exercises

The diagram at the right shows how to estimate a vertical length.

1. Which two triangles are similar?

2. Write a proportion you can use to find the height of the flagpole.

3. Solve the proportion from Exercise 2 to find the unknown distance if $d_2 = 14$ in., $d_1 = 88$ ft, $XY = 8$ in.

4. In Exercise 3, is it necessary to use the same units for all three measurements? Explain.

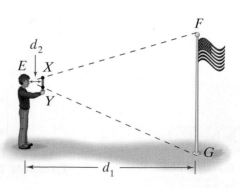

4-7 Similarity and Indirect Measurement

Check Skills You'll Need

1. Vocabulary Review *Similar figures* have the same __?__ but not necessarily the same size.

2. If $\triangle ABC \sim \triangle XYZ$, which angle is congruent to $\angle B$?

for Help
Lesson 4-4

What You'll Learn

To use proportions and similar figures to solve problems

🔊 **New Vocabulary** indirect measurement

Why Learn This?

When measuring large objects, such as trees, it is not practical to use tools such as rulers.

Indirect measurement uses proportions and similar triangles to measure distances that would be difficult to measure directly.

Video Tutor Help
Visit: PHSchool.com
Web Code: ase-0775

EXAMPLE   Measuring Indirectly

1 A student is 5 ft tall and casts a shadow 15 ft long. A nearby tree casts a shadow 75 ft long. Find the height h of the tree.

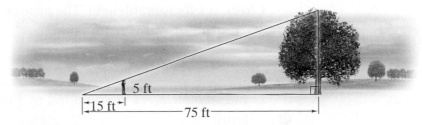

5 ft
15 ft
75 ft

Use similar triangles to set up a proportion.

tree's height → $\dfrac{h}{5} = \dfrac{75}{15}$ ← length of tree's shadow
student's height → $\phantom{\dfrac{h}{5} = \dfrac{75}{15}}$ ← length of student's shadow

$$\dfrac{h}{5} = \dfrac{75}{15}$$ ← Use number sense to find a common multiplier.

$$h = 25$$ ← Use mental math. Since $15 \div 5 = 3$, divide 75 by 3 to find h.

The height of the tree is 25 ft.

✓ Quick Check

1. A school 40 ft high casts a 160-ft shadow. A nearby cellular phone tower casts a 210-ft shadow. Find the height of the tower.

You can use similar triangles to measure distances across canyons and rivers.

Application: Surveying

2 A civil engineer took the measurements shown in the figure at the right, where $\triangle JKL \sim \triangle NML$. Find d, the distance across the river.

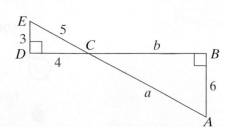

Use similar triangles to set up a proportion.

$$\frac{JK}{NM} = \frac{KL}{ML}$$

Estimate Round 450 and 525 to 500.
Then $\frac{d}{500} = \frac{300}{500}$. So $d \approx 300$.

$$\frac{d}{525} = \frac{300}{450} \quad \leftarrow \text{Substitute using actual measurements.}$$

$$450 \cdot d = 525 \cdot 300 \quad \leftarrow \text{Write the cross products.}$$

$$450d = 157{,}500 \quad \leftarrow \text{Simplify.}$$

$$\frac{450d}{450} = \frac{157{,}500}{450} \quad \leftarrow \text{Divide each side by 450.}$$

$$157{,}500 \; \boxed{\div} \; 450 \; \boxed{=} \; \textit{350} \quad \leftarrow \text{Use a calculator.}$$

The distance across the river is 350 m.

Check for Reasonableness The answer 350 m is close to the estimate 300 m. The answer is reasonable.

✓ Quick Check

2. In Example 2, NL is about 691 m. Find LJ. Round to the nearest tenth.

✓ Check Your Understanding

Vocabulary Which would you use to measure the height of the object—direct measurement or indirect measurement?

1. flagpole   2. lamp   3. Eiffel Tower   4. rabbit

In the figure, $\triangle ABC \sim \triangle EDC$.
Use the figure for Exercises
5 and 6.

5. Use the proportion $\frac{b}{4} = \frac{6}{\blacksquare}$ to find b.

6. Find a using the proportion $\frac{a}{5} = \frac{\blacksquare}{3}$.

Homework Exercises

For more exercises, see **Extra Skills and Word Problems.**

GO for Help

For Exercises	See Examples
7–8	1
9–14	2

7. A tower 15 m high casts a shadow 30 m long. A nearby telephone pole casts a shadow 16 m long. Find the height of the telephone pole.

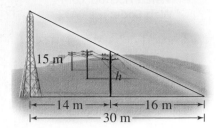

15 m   h
14 m   16 m
30 m

8. A telephone booth 7 ft tall casts a shadow 20 ft long. At the same time, a nearby fire hydrant casts a shadow 8 ft long. Find the height of the fire hydrant.

7 ft   h
8 ft
20 ft

In the figure below, $\triangle PQR \sim \triangle TSR$.

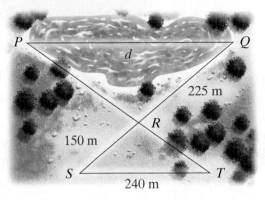

P   d   Q

225 m

R

150 m

S   240 m   T

9. Find d.

10. $PR = 255$ m. Find RT.

In the figure, $\triangle ABC \sim \triangle EDC$. Round each answer to the nearest tenth.

A   C 845 m   D

725 m   d

B 482.5 m   E

11. Find d.

12. $AC = 870$ m. Find CE.

Each figure shows similar triangles. Find h. Round to the nearest tenth.

13.

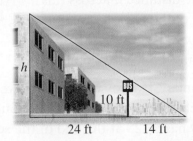

h
BUS
10 ft
24 ft   14 ft

14.

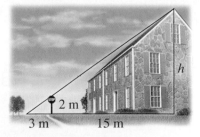

h
2 m
3 m   15 m

GPS **15. Guided Problem Solving** The Washington Monument casts a shadow 200 m long. At the same time, a nearby van that is 2.1 m high casts a shadow 2.5 m long. How tall is the monument?

- **Make a Plan** Draw and label a diagram. Write a proportion.
- **Carry Out the Plan** Solve the proportion $\frac{2.5}{200} = \frac{\blacksquare}{h}$.

16. <u>**Writing in Math**</u> Describe an everyday situation in which you might measure a distance indirectly.

17. **History** The Bunker Hill Monument in Massachusetts is 221 ft tall. When its shadow is 189 ft long, a nearby tree casts a shadow 29 ft long. To the nearest foot, how tall is the tree?

In the diagram of the lake below, $\triangle BDC \sim \triangle AEC$.

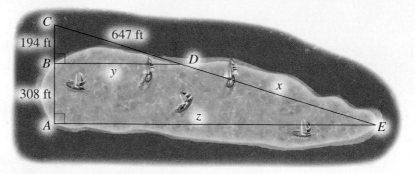

18. Use similar triangles to find the value of x.

19. Use the Pythagorean Theorem to find the value of y.

20. Find the value of z.

For help with the Pythagorean Theorem, go to Lesson 3-3, Example 1.

21. **Challenge** The figure at the right shows a method of indirect measurement. The triangles are similar. Once you have placed the mirror on the ground, how do you know where to stand?

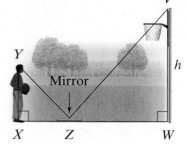

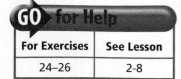

Test Prep and Mixed Review   **Practice**

Multiple Choice

22. In the figure at the right, the triangles shown are similar. Find the distance d across this section of the river basin.

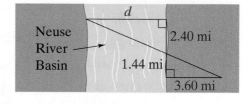

Ⓐ 2 mi   Ⓒ 4.5 mi
Ⓑ 3 mi   Ⓓ 6 mi

23. On Monday, Harvey received his weekly allowance. He spent $3.25 on lunch each day at school. He bought two books for $5.50 each. If Harvey has $2.25 at the end of the school week, which expression can he use to find the amount of money he received on Monday?

Ⓕ $2(3.25) + 5(5.50) + 2.25$ Ⓗ $2(3.25) + 5(5.50) - 2.25$
Ⓖ $5(3.25) + 2(5.50) + 2.25$ Ⓙ $5(3.25) + 2(5.50) - 2.25$

Write each number in standard form.

For Exercises	See Lesson
24–26	2-8

24. 2.02×10^5 25. 5.00×10^{-2} 26. 9.606×10^{-6}

Using a Variable

You can solve many problems by using a variable to represent an unknown quantity. Use the variable to write an equation.

EXAMPLE

You have a copy of your company logo that is 3.8 cm long and 2 cm wide. You need an enlarged copy of the logo that is 6 cm long. How wide must the enlarged copy be?

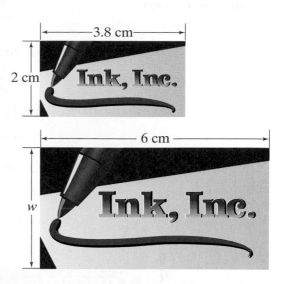

You can use the diagrams at the right to help visualize which side length you are trying to find.

Let w = the width of the enlargement.

Set up a proportion to find w.

$\dfrac{6}{w} = \dfrac{3.8}{2}$ ← length
← width

$2 \cdot 6 = 3.8 \cdot w$ ← Write the cross products.

$12 = 3.8w$ ← Multiply.

$\dfrac{12}{3.8} = \dfrac{3.8w}{3.8}$ ← Divide each side by 3.8.

$3.2 \approx w$ ← Simplify.

The width of the enlargement should be about 3.2 cm.

Exercises

1. A family is on a 400-mi road trip. They have already driven 220 miles in 4 hours. If they continue driving at this rate, about how long will it take them to drive the entire 400 miles?

   A 2 h   B 3 h   C 7 h   D 8 h

2. A map is 15.5 in. wide and 20 in. long. The map is enlarged so it is 32 in. long. Which proportion can you use to find the new width?

   F $\dfrac{15.5}{20} = \dfrac{32}{x}$ H $\dfrac{15.5}{32} = \dfrac{x}{20}$

   G $\dfrac{15.5}{x} = \dfrac{20}{32}$ J $\dfrac{15.5}{x} = \dfrac{32}{20}$

3. A carpenter can build 3 tables in 5 hours. Which equation can he use to find how long it will take him to make 18 tables?

   A $t = 5 \cdot 18$ C $t = 3 \cdot 18$
   B $t = 15 \cdot 18$ D $t = 5 \cdot 6$

Chapter 4 Review

Vocabulary Review

🔊 congruent angles (p. 181)
conversion factor (p. 167)
cross products (p. 175)
dilation (p. 187)
enlargement (p. 188)

indirect measurement (p. 197)
proportion (p. 174)
rate (p. 161)
reduction (p. 188)
scale (p. 192)

scale factor (p. 187)
scale model (p. 192)
similar figures (p. 181)
similar polygons (p. 181)
unit rate (p. 161)

Choose the correct vocabulary term above to complete each sentence.

1. A speed of 30 mi/h is an example of a(n) __?__.

2. A(n) __?__ is an equation stating that two ratios are equal.

3. A model of an office building may have a(n) __?__ of 1 : 200.

4. __?__ helps you to measure the height of very tall objects.

5. A(n) __?__ is a dilation with a scale factor less than one.

6. You can use a(n) __?__ to convert 3.4 miles to feet.

Go Online
PHSchool.com

For: Online vocabulary quiz
Web Code: asj-0451

Skills and Concepts

Lessons 4-1, 4-2
- To write ratios and unit rates and to use rates to solve problems
- To convert units within and between the customary and metric systems

A **rate** is a ratio that compares quantities measured in different units. The rate for one unit of a given quantity is called the **unit rate.**

In both the metric and customary systems, it is important to choose appropriate units. Use **conversion factors** to convert units of measure.

Write each ratio in simplest form.

7. 6 s out of 48 s

8. $\dfrac{10 \text{ m}}{300 \text{ cm}}$

9. 1 ft : 1 yd

Choose a Method Use a calculator, paper and pencil, or mental math to find each unit rate.

10. $42 for 1.5 h

11. 826 mi in 14 h

12. 150 km per 24 L

13. A 36-oz container of ketchup costs $2.52. A 24-oz container of ketchup costs $1.69. Which container of ketchup is the better buy? Explain.

Find an equivalent rate.

14. 33 m/h = ■ cm/h

15. 16 lb/ft = ■ oz/ft

16. 1 L/min = ■ mL/s

17. 3 mi/h = ■ ft/day

18. ■ cm/min = 30 m/h

19. $.30/min = $■/h

Lesson 4-3
- To identify and solve proportions

To solve a **proportion**, you can write the **cross products** and then solve.

Solve each proportion.

20. $\frac{4}{5} = \frac{x}{20}$ **21.** $\frac{6}{a} = \frac{18}{3}$ **22.** $\frac{14}{6} = \frac{28}{t}$ **23.** $\frac{b}{16} = \frac{9}{2}$

24. Recently, the exchange rate for euros to U.S. dollars was 0.81 euros = \$1. How many euros would you receive for \$1,000?

Lessons 4-4, 4-5
- To identify similar figures and to use proportions to find missing measurements in similar figures
- To graph dilations and to determine the scale factor of a dilation

Figures that have the same shape but not necessarily the same size are **similar figures.**

The image of a figure after a **dilation** is similar to the original figure. The **scale factor** of a dilation describes the size of the change from the original figure to its image.

In the figure, $\triangle ACE \sim \triangle BCD$. Find each unknown length.

25. AE **26.** CE **27.** DE

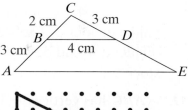

28. The blue figure is a dilation of the original figure. Find the scale factor and classify the dilation as an *enlargement* or a *reduction*.

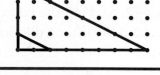

Lessons 4-6, 4-7
- To use proportions to solve problems involving scale
- To use proportions and similar figures to solve problems

Use proportions to solve **scale-model** and **indirect-measurement** problems.

The scale of a map is 1 in. : 7 mi. How many actual miles does each measurement on the map represent?

29. 6.2 in. **30.** 9.5 in. **31.** $4\frac{2}{3}$ in. **32.** $8\frac{1}{5}$ in.

33. Plans The scale of a plan is 1 in. : 8 ft. A room will be 18 ft long by 14 ft wide. Find the dimensions on the plan.

The diagram at the right shows similar triangles.

34. Find x. **35.** Find AS.

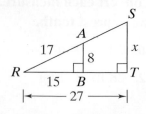

36. A person 5 ft 6 in. tall casts a 21-ft shadow. A nearby building casts a 45-ft shadow. How high is the building?

Go Online For: Online chapter test
PHSchool.com **Web Code:** asa-0452

Write each ratio in simplest form.

1. 16 cm : 60 cm   **2.** 3 ft to 9 in.

3. $\frac{100 \text{ min}}{8 \text{ h}}$ **4.** 6 yd to 36 ft

5. 500 m : 2 km   **6.** $\frac{54 \text{ c}}{6 \text{ oz}}$

Choose a Method Use a calculator, paper and pencil, or mental math to find each unit rate.

7. 200 yd in 5 min   **8.** 700 L in 24 h

9. 30 gal in 5 min   **10.** $2.50 for 10 oz

Find an equivalent rate.

11. $33/h = $■/min   **12.** 3 ft/s = ■ yd/min

Solve each proportion.

13. $\frac{3}{7} = \frac{6}{n}$ **14.** $\frac{25}{a} = \frac{100}{4}$ **15.** $\frac{w}{5} = \frac{30}{13}$

16. Stocks A stock investment of 160 shares paid a dividend of $584. At this rate, what dividend would be paid on 270 shares of stock?

17. $\triangle ABC$ has vertices $A(1, 2)$, $B(4, 3)$ and $C(-2, 5)$. Find the coordinates of the image of $\triangle ABC$ after a dilation with a scale factor of 3.

$\triangle ABC \sim \triangle EDC$. Find each unknown length.

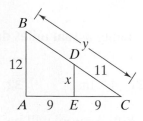

18. x **19.** y

Convert each measure. If necessary, round to the nearest tenth.

20. 9 L = ■ qt   **21.** 4 kg = ■ lb

22. 28 lb = ■ kg   **23.** 25 in. = ■ cm

The scale of a map is 1 in. : 6 mi. How many inches does each distance occupy on the map? Round to the nearest tenth.

24. 23 mi   **25.** 10 mi

26. 45 mi   **27.** 16 mi

The scale of a map is 1 in. : 15 mi. How many actual miles does each measurement on the map represent?

28. 8.6 in.   **29.** $10\frac{1}{3}$ in.

30. $7\frac{3}{5}$ in.   **31.** 11.2 in.

32. <u>**Writing in Math**</u> Suppose you know the coordinates of the vertices of a triangle. Explain how you would find the coordinates of the vertices of its image after a dilation with a scale factor of r.

33. Copy $\triangle ABC$ below. Draw the image of $\triangle ABC$ after a dilation with a scale factor of 2.

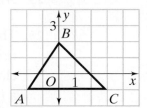

34. Cranes A student is 5 ft tall and casts a shadow 15 ft long. At the same time of day, a nearby crane casts a shadow 90 ft long. What is the height of the crane?

35. In the figure below, $\triangle XBY$ is the image of $\triangle ABC$ after a dilation. What is the scale factor?

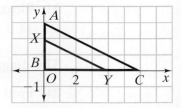

Reading Comprehension

Read the passage and answer the questions that follow.

Paper Money U.S. paper money is 2.61 in. wide and 6.14 in. long. You probably know it is illegal to make an exact copy of money—that is counterfeiting! But did you know you can legally make a perfect copy as long as it is a different size? To be sure the copy does not fool anyone, it must be less than three fourths or more than one and a half times the length and width of the real bill.

1. How long is the diagonal (corner to opposite corner) of a real U.S. dollar bill?
   - Ⓐ 2.95 in.
   - Ⓒ 6.67 in.
   - Ⓑ 4.34 in.
   - Ⓓ 8.75 in.

2. Would a 2 in.-by-4 in. copy of a $10 bill be a legal copy of a real $10 bill?
   - Ⓕ No, the copy would be too long.
   - Ⓖ No, the copy would be too wide.
   - Ⓗ No, the copy would be too long and too wide.
   - Ⓙ Yes

3. A poster-sized copy of a $5 bill is 5.22 ft wide. What is the length of the poster if the copy has the same proportions as the real bill?
   - Ⓐ 12.28 in.
   - Ⓒ 6.14 ft
   - Ⓑ 5.22 ft
   - Ⓓ 12.28 ft

4. What are the smallest dimensions (length and width) that would be legal for a larger-than-life copy of a $100 bill?
   - Ⓕ 4.60 × 1.95 in.
   - Ⓗ 6.45 × 2.74 in.
   - Ⓖ 9.21 × 3.92 in.
   - Ⓙ 10.74 × 4.57 in.

Space Meal Math Space shuttle astronauts can choose from a variety of foods. A dietician reviews the astronauts' menu selections to be sure that the foods are well balanced and that the meals provide the right amount of energy (Calories). Dieticians check the calorie needs with a formula.

Part of the calculation depends on the astronaut's weight. For female astronauts, $E = 9.6 \times W$. For male astronauts, $E = 13.7 \times W$. In this formula, E is the daily food energy in Calories and W is the astronaut's weight in kilograms. (Other formulas consider height and age.)

5. A male and a female astronaut both weigh the same amount. According to the weight formula, what is the ratio of Calories the male will need compared to the female?
   - Ⓐ 13.7 : 9.6
   - Ⓒ 9.6 : 23.3
   - Ⓑ 9.6 : 13.7
   - Ⓓ 13.7 : 23.3

6. A 70-kg male and a 50-kg female astronaut go on a two-week flight. What ratio of the total food supplies would belong to the female, according to the weight formula?
   - Ⓕ $\dfrac{50 \cdot 9.6}{70 \cdot 13.7}$
   - Ⓗ $\dfrac{9.6}{13.7}$
   - Ⓖ $\dfrac{70 \cdot 13.7}{50 \cdot 9.6}$
   - Ⓙ $\dfrac{50 \cdot 9.6}{(50 \cdot 9.6 + 70 \cdot 13.7)}$

Applying Proportions

Food Power Food energy powers the human body, and the human body can power appliances. For example, you could connect a stationary bicycle to a generator and produce electricity when you pedal. Could this replace the power you get from your utility company?

What's a Calorie?
A calorie is the amount of energy needed to heat 1 g of water from 14.5°C to 15.5°C.

Organic Power
Juice in a fresh potato reacts with copper and zinc electrodes to power a digital clock.

Put It All Together

Data File Use the information on these two pages to answer these questions.

Energy Measurement Conversion Factors

1 food Calorie = 1,000 gram-calories (g-cal)
1 g-cal = 0.001162 watt-hours
1 watt-hour = 860.42 g-cal

1. a. A typical sandwich provides about 250 food Calories. How many watt-hours of energy does a sandwich provide?

   b. Your body uses about $\frac{3}{4}$ of the chemical energy in food to maintain itself. The rest is available for activities like pedaling a bicycle. How much energy from the sandwich can you use for pedaling (in watt-hours)?

2. a. Use the energy formula to find how much energy you would need to light a 75-watt light bulb for 10 hours.

Energy Formula

$$\text{energy to run device (watt-hours)} = \text{power used (watts)} \times \text{time running (hours)}$$

   b. How many hours could you light a 75-watt bulb with a bicycle generator using the energy from one sandwich?

   c. How long could you light a 30-watt light bulb? Give your answer in hours and minutes.

3. Suppose you eat about 2,500 food Calories per day.

   a. Using your human-powered generator, how much electrical energy (in watt-hours) can you produce from these Calories?

   b. **Open-Ended** Pick a device from the table and calculate how long you could run it with this energy.

Home Appliance Energy-Use Guide

Appliance	Watts Needed to Run
Computer	1,500
Digital clock	325
Hair dryer	1,200
Microwave	186
Refrigerator	50
Stereo system	30
Television	300
VCR	2

Pedal Power

A college student uses pedal power to operate a blender and make salad dressing.

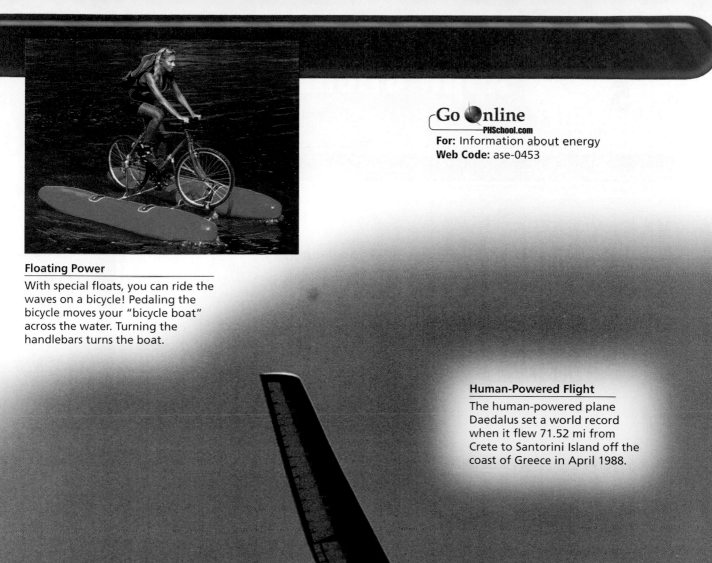

Go Online
PHSchool.com
For: Information about energy
Web Code: ase-0453

Floating Power

With special floats, you can ride the waves on a bicycle! Pedaling the bicycle moves your "bicycle boat" across the water. Turning the handlebars turns the boat.

Human-Powered Flight

The human-powered plane Daedalus set a world record when it flew 71.52 mi from Crete to Santorini Island off the coast of Greece in April 1988.

What You've Learned

- In Chapter 2, you compared and ordered rational numbers.
- In Chapter 4, you wrote and used ratios and rates.
- You found solutions to problems involving proportional relationships.

Check Your Readiness

GO for Help

For Exercises	See Lessons
1–4	1-7
5–8	2-2
9–11	2-5
12–17	4-3

Solving One-Step Equations

Solve each equation.

1. $16 = 0.8p$

2. $2m = 31.82$

3. $0.32x = 76$

4. $95v = 166.25$

Equivalent Forms of Rational Numbers

Write each fraction in simplest form.

5. $\frac{50}{100}$

6. $\frac{25}{40}$

7. $\frac{6}{72}$

8. $\frac{36}{64}$

Multiplying Rational Numbers

Find each product. Write the answer in simplest form or as a mixed number.

9. $\frac{3}{10} \cdot 100$

10. $15 \cdot \frac{17}{30}$

11. $160 \cdot \frac{5}{8}$

Solving Proportions

Solve each proportion.

12. $\frac{7}{12} = \frac{21}{n}$

13. $\frac{k}{45} = \frac{10}{225}$

14. $\frac{18}{t} = \frac{27}{48}$

15. $\frac{1}{4} = \frac{25}{y}$

16. $\frac{5}{3} = \frac{z}{11.4}$

17. $\frac{h}{76} = \frac{9}{8}$

What You'll Learn Next

- In this chapter, you will compare and order integers, percents, fractions, and decimals.

- You will use estimation, proportions, and equations to solve problems involving percents.

- You will use ratios to find probability.

 Problem Solving Application On pages 256 and 257, you will work an extended activity on expenses.

Fractions, Decimals, and Percents

 **Check Skills You'll Need**

1. **Vocabulary Review**
A *rational number* is a number that can be written in the form __?__ .

Write each fraction in simplest form.

2. $\frac{90}{100}$ 3. $\frac{80}{100}$

4. $\frac{35}{100}$ 5. $\frac{25}{100}$

 **for Help**
Lesson 2-2

What You'll Learn

To convert between fractions, decimals, and percents and to order rational numbers

🔊 **New Vocabulary** percent

Why Learn This?

Teachers can write grades in different forms. You may need to convert from one form to another in order to understand your grades better.

Suppose you correctly answer four fifths of the questions on a quiz. You can express this fraction as a percent. A **percent** is a ratio that compares a number to 100.

Sometimes you can use mental math to write percents.

EXAMPLE   **Writing a Fraction as a Percent**

1 Use mental math to write $\frac{4}{5}$ as a percent.

What you think

I can write $\frac{4}{5}$ as an equivalent fraction with a denominator of 100.

$$\overset{\times 20}{\underset{\times 20}{\frac{4}{5} = \frac{80}{100}}}$$ I can rewrite $\frac{80}{100}$ as 80%.

Why it works

$\frac{4}{5} = \frac{4 \cdot 20}{5 \cdot 20}$ ← Multiply the numerator and denominator by 20.

$= \frac{80}{100}$ ← Simplify.

$= 80\%$ ← Write the fraction as a percent.

✓ Quick Check

1. Use mental math to write $\frac{11}{20}$ as a percent.

GO 🌐 **nline**

Video Tutor Help
Visit: PHSchool.com
Web Code: ase-0775

Percents can be between 1% and 100%, greater than 100%, or less than 1%.

EXAMPLE Writing a Decimal as a Percent

2 Write 1.2 as a percent.

$$1.2 = 1\frac{2}{10} = \frac{12}{10}$$ ← Write the decimal as a mixed number and then as a fraction.

$$= \frac{12 \cdot 10}{10 \cdot 10}$$ ← Multiply the numerator and denominator by 10.

$$= \frac{120}{100}$$ ← Write as an equivalent fraction with a denominator of 100.

$$= 120\%$$ ← Write the fraction as a percent.

For help multiplying by powers of 10, go to Lesson 2-8, Example 1.

✓ Quick Check

2. Write 0.08 as a percent.

You can also write percents as fractions.

EXAMPLE Writing a Percent as a Fraction

3 **Nutrition** A brand of daily vitamin supplies $2\frac{1}{2}\%$ of the Recommended Dietary Allowance (RDA) of potassium. Write this percent as a fraction.

$$2\frac{1}{2}\% = \frac{2\frac{1}{2}}{100}$$ ← Write the percent as a fraction with a denominator of 100.

$$= 2\frac{1}{2} \div 100$$ ← Rewrite the fraction as division.

$$= \frac{5}{2} \div 100$$ ← Write the mixed number as an improper fraction.

$$= \frac{1\cancel{5}}{2} \cdot \frac{1}{\cancel{100}_{20}}$$ ← Multiply by the reciprocal of 100. Divide by the GCF.

$$= \frac{1}{40}$$ ← Simplify.

✓ Quick Check

3. A vitamin has 150% of the RDA of vitamin C. Write this percent as a fraction.

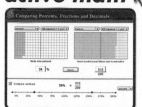

For: Comparing Numbers Activity
Use: Interactive Textbook, 5-1

Another way to write a decimal as a percent is to multiply it by 100, or move the decimal point 2 places to the right. To write a percent as a decimal, divide it by 100, or move the decimal point 2 places to the left.

4 Order 34%, 0.38, $\frac{1}{4}$, and 2 from least to greatest.

$$34\% = 0.34, \quad 0.38 = 0.38 \quad \frac{1}{4} = 0.25 \quad \leftarrow \text{Change each number to a decimal.}$$

Since $0.25 < 0.34 < 0.38 < 2$, $\frac{1}{4} < 34\% < 0.38 < 2$.

✓ Quick Check

4. Order 76%, 0.73, and $\frac{3}{4}$ from least to greatest.

✓ Check Your Understanding

1. **Vocabulary** A percent compares a number to ▦.

Match each fraction or decimal with a percent.

2. 1.0   **A.** 14%

3. $\frac{12}{200}$ **B.** 6%

               C. 40%

4. 0.06   **D.** 100%

5. $\frac{14}{100}$

6. $\frac{10}{25}$

Homework Exercises

For more exercises, see Extra Skills and Word Problems.

GO▶ for Help

For Exercises	See Examples
7–11	1
12–16	2
17–21	3
22–25	4

Mental Math Use mental math to write each fraction as a percent.

7. $\frac{2}{5}$ 8. $\frac{3}{4}$ 9. $\frac{24}{25}$ 10. $\frac{7}{20}$ 11. $\frac{42}{50}$

Write each decimal as a percent.

12. 0.36   13. 0.003   14. 5.2   15. 0.9   16. 0.00007

Write each percent as a fraction in simplest form.

17. 105%   18. 220%   19. $22\frac{2}{9}\%$ 20. $66\frac{2}{3}\%$

21. On a math test, a student received a grade of 135 points out of 150 total points. Write the grade as a percent.

Order each set of numbers from least to greatest.

22. $\frac{1}{3}$, 36%, 0.3, $\frac{3}{8}$ 23. 0.01, 0.09%, $\frac{1}{99}$, 1.01%

24. $\frac{2}{9}$, $\frac{1}{4}$, 0.2, 20.9%   25. 150%, 150, $\frac{9}{5}$, 1.5%

26. Guided Problem Solving The table below shows the results of a student survey about lunch. What percent of students did *not* choose tacos as their favorite food? Round to the nearest percent.

Favorite Food	Hamburgers	Tacos	Sandwiches	Pizza
Number of Students	45	7	19	34

- How many students were surveyed?
- How many students *did* choose tacos as their favorite food?

27. Write the fraction, decimal, and percent that describe the shaded part of the figure.

28. Jobs The average employee in the United States works about 248 days per year and receives about 13 days of paid vacation. Write the number of vacation days as a percent of the total number of days worked. Round to the nearest hundredth of a percent.

29. Jewelry 18-karat gold is 75% pure gold, and 14-karat gold is 58% pure gold. Write each percent as a fraction in simplest form.

A bag contains 9 quarters, 4 dimes, and 12 nickels. Use this information for Exercises 30–32.

30. What percent of the coins are dimes?

31. What percent of the coins are quarters and nickels?

32. What percent of the coins are *not* nickels?

33. Writing in Math Explain why 0.09 is different from 0.09%.

34. Challenge On average, about 60% of an adult's body weight is water. About how many pounds of a 135-lb person are water?

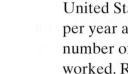

GO Online
Homework Video Tutor
Visit: PHSchool.com
Web Code: ase-0501

GO for Help

For Exercises	See Lesson
37–39	2-1

Test Prep and Mixed Review
Practice

Multiple Choice

35. Which list shows the numbers in order from least to greatest?

Ⓐ $0.63, \frac{25}{42}, 0.6, \frac{1}{2}, 62\frac{1}{2}\%$ Ⓒ $\frac{25}{42}, 0.6, 62\frac{1}{2}\%, 0.63, \frac{1}{2}$

Ⓑ $\frac{1}{2}, 0.63, 0.6, 62\frac{1}{2}\%, \frac{25}{42}$ Ⓓ $\frac{1}{2}, \frac{25}{42}, 0.6, 62\frac{1}{2}\%, 0.63$

36. A scale model of a school is 7 inches high. If 2 inches on the model represents 9 feet on the actual building, how tall will the building be?

Ⓕ 14 ft   Ⓖ 23.5 ft   Ⓗ 27 ft   Ⓙ 31.5 ft

Find the GCF of each pair of numbers.

37. 15 and 39   **38.** 75 and 100   **39.** 18 and 54

5-2   Estimating With Percents

✓ Check Skills You'll Need

1. Vocabulary Review
The *multiplicative inverse* of $\frac{3}{7}$ is ■.

Find each product.

2. $36 \cdot \frac{3}{4}$ **3.** $\frac{2}{3} \cdot 12$

4. $\frac{9}{10} \cdot 60$ **5.** $81 \cdot \frac{5}{9}$

GO for Help
Lesson 2-5

What You'll Learn

To estimate percents using decimals and fractions

Why Learn This?

Estimation is a quick method for calculating numbers that do not need to be exact, such as a restaurant tip.

To find the percent of a number, multiply. You can estimate by using a decimal or fraction that is close to the percent. You can also use compatible numbers when estimating.

Vocabulary Tip

Compatible numbers are easy to compute mentally. The numbers 20 and 4 are compatible, but 37 and 8 are not.

EXAMPLE   Estimating Percents Using Decimals

1 Use decimals to estimate 28% of 191.

     $28\% \approx 0.3$ ← **Use a decimal that is close to 28%.**

       $191 \approx 200$ ← **Round 191 to a number that is compatible with 0.3.**

   28% of $191 \approx 0.3$ of 200

               $= 0.3 \cdot 200$ ← **Multiply to find 0.3 of 200.**

               $= 60$ ← **Simplify.**

28% of 191 is about 60.

✓ Quick Check

1. Use decimals to estimate 18% of 107.

To estimate, you should be familiar with common equivalent fractions.

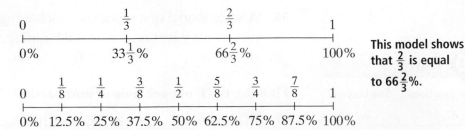

This model shows that $\frac{2}{3}$ is equal to $66\frac{2}{3}\%$.

Careers Many disc jockeys start by working at small events, such as friends' parties.

EXAMPLE **Estimating Percents Using Fractions**

2 A disc jockey says that about 65% of his 238 CDs are pop albums. Using fractions, estimate the number of pop albums he has.

$65\% \approx \frac{2}{3}$ ← Use a fraction that is close to 65%.

$238 \approx 240$ ← Round to a number that is compatible with 3.

65% of $238 \approx \frac{2}{3}$ of 240

$\qquad = \frac{2}{\underset{1}{\cancel{3}}} \cdot \frac{\overset{80}{\cancel{240}}}{1}$ ← Multiply to find $\frac{2}{3}$ of 240. Divide by the GCF.

$\qquad = 160$ ← Simplify.

About 160 CDs in the disc jockey's collection are pop albums.

✓ Quick Check

2. A teacher says that about 35% of the 24 students in a class have blue eyes. Using fractions, estimate the number of blue-eyed students.

You can also estimate percents by using multiples of 10%, which are easy to calculate mentally. This method is useful when computing tips in restaurants.

EXAMPLE **Estimating Tips**

3 You and a friend have a $28.85 restaurant bill. Use mental math to estimate a 15% tip.

What you think

The bill is about $30. I know 10% of 30 is $\frac{1}{10}$ of 30, or 3. Then 5% of 30 is half of 3, or 1.5. A 15% tip is about $3.00 plus $1.50, or $4.50.

Why it works

15% of $30 = 0.15 \cdot 30$ ← Rewrite 15% as 0.15.

$\qquad = (0.10 + 0.05)\,30$ ← Rewrite 0.15 as 0.10 + 0.05.

$\qquad = 0.10(30) + 0.05(30)$ ← Distributive Property

$\qquad = 3 + 1.50$ ← Multiply.

$\qquad = 4.50$ ← Add.

A 15% tip for a $28.85 bill is about $4.50.

✓ Quick Check

3. Mental Math Estimate a 15% tip for a $72.10 restaurant bill.

Estimate Match each expression with the correct estimate.

1. 15% of $38.90
2. 15% of $20.79
3. 15% of $398

A. $3
B. $6
C. $60

4. **Mental Math** Suppose you want to leave a 20% tip for a meal that costs $28. Use a multiple of 10% to calculate the tip.

5. **Number Sense** Use a decimal other than 0.3 to estimate 28% of 191.

Homework Exercises

For more exercises, see Extra Skills and Word Problems.

GO for Help

For Exercises	See Examples
6–11	1
12–15	2
16–22	3

Use decimals to estimate each percent.

6. 9% of 9
7. 63% of 62
8. 15% of 78
9. 52% of 492
10. 38% of 81
11. 68% of 222

Use fractions to estimate each percent.

12. 27% of 39
13. 49.8% of 177
14. 74.5% of 31

15. **Student Government** In a recent student council election, 66% of the 310 students voted for the winning candidate. Use fractions to estimate how many students voted for the winner.

Mental Math Estimate a 15% tip for each restaurant bill.

16. $9.85
17. $12.63
18. $18.20
19. $27.55
20. $31.49
21. $86.96

22. You decide to leave your waiter a 20% tip. Your dinner cost $47.51. Estimate the tip.

23. **Guided Problem Solving** According to a recent census, there were about 115,904,640 housing units in the United States. About 91% of these units were occupied. About 34% of the occupied units were rented. Estimate the number of rented units.
    • About how many units were occupied?
    • Round 34% to a compatible number.

GO Online
Homework Video Tutor
Visit: PHSchool.com
Web Code: ase-0502

24. **Cities** About 41% of the 13 million people in Guatemala live in cities. Use decimals to estimate how many people live in cities.

Back-to-school sale!
30% off
This weekend only!

Long-sleeve T-shirts
$14.89

Watches
$32.49

Backpacks
$29.99

Jeans
$32.99

Sneakers
$45.99

Shopping The ad at the left shows the prices of several items on sale at a store. Estimate the discounted price of each item.

25. a pair of jeans   **26.** a backpack   **27.** a watch

28. Error Analysis Your friend estimates that a 15% tip on a $41.28 bill is $2.50. Is this a reasonable estimate? Explain.

Number Sense Use <, >, or = to complete each statement.

29. 85% ■ $\frac{5}{6}$ **30.** 15% of 24 ■ 20% of 18

31. 10% of 156 ■ 1% of 1,025   **32.** 9% of 57 ■ 5% of 47

33. Blood Types About 40% of Americans have type A blood. Suppose there are about 301,421,900 Americans. Estimate how many Americans have type A blood.

34. **Writing in Math** Explain why it is helpful to estimate with percents even when you are finding the exact answer.

35. Challenge The average person's daily caloric intake is about 2,000 Calories. You have eaten a blueberry muffin (135 Calories) and a banana (105 Calories) for breakfast, and a bag of pretzels for a snack. Suppose you have consumed 24% of your daily caloric intake. Estimate how many Calories were in the bag of pretzels.

Test Prep and Mixed Review   Practice

Multiple Choice

36. In a recent city election, 66.7% of the registered voters in the city voted. If there were 717,449 registered voters in the city, about how many people voted in the election?
  Ⓐ 47,853,848   Ⓑ 1,195,987   Ⓒ 478,538   Ⓓ 238,911

37. Which equation can be represented by the line shown in the graph?
  Ⓕ $y = -3x + 1$
  Ⓖ $y = x - \frac{1}{3}$
  Ⓗ $y = -\frac{1}{3}x + 1$
  Ⓙ $y = 3x + 1$

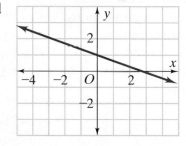

38. Ashley's class is using a microscope to study an insect. The insect is 8.2×10^{-4} meters long. What is this number in standard form?
  Ⓐ 0.000082   Ⓑ 0.00082   Ⓒ 82,000   Ⓓ 820,000

GO for Help

For Exercises	See Lesson
39–40	3-6

A point and its image are given. Write a rule to describe each translation.

39. $Q(-4, -3)$, $Q'(0, 2)$ **40.** $R(6, -5)$, $R'(-7, 0)$

5-3 Percents and Proportions

✓ Check Skills You'll Need

1. **Vocabulary Review**
   Two equal ratios form a _ ? _ .

Solve each proportion.

2. $\frac{4}{b} = \frac{20}{100}$

3. $\frac{8}{12} = \frac{e}{100}$

4. $\frac{240}{n} = \frac{12}{5}$

5. $\frac{s}{4} = \frac{75}{100}$

6. $\frac{6}{y} = \frac{24}{100}$

 **for Help**
Lesson 4-3

What You'll Learn

To use proportions to find part of a whole, a whole amount, or a percent

Why Learn This?

Large groups, such as an orchestra, are divided into sections. Percents and proportions can help you understand the relationship between the size of sections and the whole group.

When using percents, you can use a diagram to show the relationship between a part and the whole.

```
                    part        whole
                     ↓            ↓
Number    0          n           32
          ├──────────┼───────────┤
Percent   0%        45%         100%
```

$\frac{n}{32} = \frac{45}{100}$ ← The part n corresponds to 45%.
          ← The whole 32 corresponds to 100%.

EXAMPLE Finding Part of a Whole

1 Find 45% of 32.

$\frac{n}{32} = \frac{45}{100}$ ← Write a proportion.

$100n = 45 \cdot 32$ ← Write the cross products.

$100n = 1,440$ ← Simplify.

$\frac{100n}{100} = \frac{1,440}{100}$ ← Divide each side by 100.

$n = 14.4$ ← Simplify.

45% of 32 is 14.4.

■ Calculator Tip

When using a calculator to solve the proportion $\frac{n}{32} = \frac{45}{100}$, use the calculator-ready form $n = \frac{45 \cdot 32}{100}$.

✓ Quick Check

1. Use a proportion to find 74% of 95.

Some problems include percents that are greater than 100%. In these cases, the part is greater than the whole.

Video Tutor Help
Visit: PHSchool.com
Web Code: ase-0775

EXAMPLE **Finding Percents Greater Than 100%**

2 **Bills** This month's heating bill is 130% of last month's bill. Last month's bill was $46. Find 130% of 46.

whole part

Number   0   46 n

Percent   0%   100% 130%

← A diagram can help you understand the problem.

$$\frac{n}{46} = \frac{130}{100}$$ ← Write a proportion.

$100n = 130 \cdot 46$ ← Write the cross products.

$100n = 5{,}980$ ← Simplify.

$$\frac{100n}{100} = \frac{5{,}980}{100}$$ ← Divide each side by 100.

$n = 59.8$ ← Simplify.

This month's bill is $59.80.

✓ Quick Check

2. Use a proportion to find 235% of 85.

If you know the percent a part represents, you can find the whole.

EXAMPLE **Finding a Whole Amount**

3 **Orchestra** About 35% of an orchestra's musicians, or 30 members, are violin players. Find the total number of musicians in the orchestra.

part   whole

Number   0   30 w

Percent   0%   35%   100%

← A diagram can help you understand the problem.

$$\frac{30}{w} = \frac{35}{100}$$ ← Write a proportion.

$30 \cdot 100 = 35w$ ← Write the cross products.

$3{,}000 = 35w$ ← Simplify.

$$\frac{3{,}000}{35} = \frac{35w}{35}$$ ← Divide each side by 35.

$w = 85.71428571$ ← Use a calculator.

There are about 86 musicians in the orchestra.

✓ Quick Check

3. About 40% of students in a school, or 110 students, are in an after-school program. How many students are in the school?

Before solving a
problem, check to make
sure you set up the
proportion correctly.

EXAMPLE   Finding a Percent

4 105 is what percent of 200?

part   whole

Number   0   105   200   ← A diagram can help you
                                          understand the problem.
Percent   0% $p\%$ 100%

$$\frac{105}{200} = \frac{p}{100}$$ ← Write a proportion.

$$\frac{105}{200} \overset{\div 2}{\underset{\div 2}{=}} \frac{p}{100}$$ ← Use number sense to find a common divisor.

$$52.5\% = p$$ ← Divide 105 by 2 to find p.

Check for Reasonableness 105 is about 100 and 100 is half of 200. Since
$\frac{1}{2}$ is 50%, which is close to 52.5%, the answer is reasonable. ✔

✓ Quick Check

4. 36 is what percent of 180?

For: Percents and
Proportions Activity
Use: Interactive
Textbook, 5-3

You can use the following proportion to solve percent problems.

$$\frac{\text{part}}{\text{whole}} = \text{percent (written as a fraction)}$$

KEY CONCEPTS   Percents and Proportions

Finding the Part	Finding the Whole	Finding the Percent
What number is 20% of 25?	5 is 20% of what number?	5 is what percent of 25?
$\dfrac{n}{25} = \dfrac{20}{100}$	$\dfrac{5}{w} = \dfrac{20}{100}$	$\dfrac{5}{25} = \dfrac{p}{100}$

✓ Check Your Understanding

1. Draw a diagram to represent the percent of 1.25 that is 1.

Match each problem with the correct proportion.

2. 5 is 42% of what number?

3. What number is 5% of 42?

4. 5 is what percent of 42?

A. $\dfrac{5}{42} = \dfrac{x}{100}$

B. $\dfrac{5}{y} = \dfrac{42}{100}$

C. $\dfrac{z}{42} = \dfrac{5}{100}$

For more exercises, see Extra Skills and Word Problems.

For Exercises	See Examples
5–17	1–2
18–24	3
25–30	4

GO for Help

Use a proportion to find the given percent of each number. A diagram may be helpful.

5. 80% of 72   **6.** 3% of 48   **7.** 60% of 55

8. 38% of 50   **9.** 12% of 46   **10.** 26% of 65

11. 345% of 24   **12.** 200% of 24   **13.** 150% of 3

14. 275% of 60   **15.** 734% of 75   **16.** 195% of 66

17. Shopping Last month you spent $87 on clothing. This month you spent 165% of what you spent last month. Find 165% of $87.

Use a proportion to solve each problem. A diagram may be helpful.

18. 6 is 80% of what number?   **19.** 3 is 60% of what number?

20. 74 is 32% of what number?   **21.** 38 is 4% of what number?

22. 120 is 48% of what number?   **23.** 150 is 25% of what number?

24. In one school, about 56% of the eighth-graders, or 140 students, have brown hair. How many students are in the eighth grade?

Use a proportion to solve each problem. A diagram may be helpful.

25. What percent of 25 is 16?   **26.** 20 is what percent of 160?

27. What percent of 300 is 12?   **28.** 18 is what percent of 45?

29. What percent of 64 is 24?   **30.** What percent of 12 is 96?

31. Guided Problem Solving In an election with two candidates, the winner received about 72.2% of the 214,082 votes cast. By how many votes did the winning candidate win?

- Begin by finding the number of votes cast for the winner.

Words: $\dfrac{\% \text{ of winner's votes}}{\text{total \% of votes}} = \dfrac{\text{number of votes cast for winning candidate}}{\text{total number of votes cast}}$

Proportion: $\dfrac{72.2}{100} = \dfrac{x}{\blacksquare}$

32. Collections The Library of Congress has more than 5 million maps. Maps make up just 3.75% of the library's entire collection of items. How many items does the Library of Congress have?

33. Reasoning Explain how a percent can be greater than 100.

34. Number Sense If $x\%$ of y is 15, then what is $y\%$ of x?

35. Writing in Math Explain why researchers often use percents to report their findings.

GO Online
Homework Video Tutor
Visit: PHSchool.com
Web Code: ase-0503

Use a proportion to solve each problem.

36. Find 0.025% of 120.

37. Find 1,342% of 5,678.

38. 99.6 is 200% of what number?

39. 1.8 is 30% of what number?

40. Find 0.108% of 1,375.

41. Find 234% of 468.

Indiana

UNITED STATES

Rhode Island

42. Geography Rhode Island's area is 1,231 square miles. Indiana's area is about 2,958.6% of Rhode Island's area. Indiana's area is about 0.98% of the area of the United States. Find the area of the United States.

43. Error Analysis A student said that 40 percent of one number plus 30 percent of another number is the same as 70 percent of the sum of the two numbers. Do you agree? Explain.

44. One semester, 27 college students registered for an art history class. After two male students dropped out of the class, 44% of the students in the class were male. What percent of the students in the original class were female? Round to the nearest tenth of a percent.

45. Challenge A meter is what percent of a centimeter?

Test Prep and Mixed Review
Practice

Multiple Choice

46. A recent survey was done of the shopping habits of 500 households. The graph shows the day those surveyed did their major shopping. Based on the results, how many more households did their major shopping on Saturday than on Sunday?

   Ⓐ 10   Ⓒ 100

   Ⓑ 40   Ⓓ 400

Days People Shop

Mon. 15%
Tues. 14%
Wed. 11%
Thurs. 14%
Fri. 13%
Sat. 21%
Sun. 13%

47. A quality-control inspector found that 3 out of every 45 radios produced on his assembly line were defective. About what percent of the radios were NOT defective?

   Ⓕ 7%   Ⓖ 67%   Ⓗ 93%   Ⓙ 135%

48. Jada bought 12 bottles of water for $2.99. Which expression can be used to find the cost of 60 bottles of water?

   Ⓐ 2.99 · 5   Ⓒ 35.88 · 12

   Ⓑ 2.99 · 12   Ⓓ 35.88 · 60

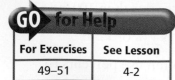

GO for Help

For Exercises	See Lesson
49–51	4-2

Write each ratio in simplest form.

49. 10 cm : 25 m

50. $\frac{16 \text{ in.}}{2 \text{ ft}}$

51. $\frac{35 \text{ oz}}{5 \text{ lb}}$

Percents and Graphs

Graphs and percents can be used to represent and compare information. When you analyze data, you have to be careful that the data are not misrepresented.

ACTIVITY

The bar graph at the right shows the results of a survey of what type of music students listen to. Notice that the horizontal scale does not start at 0.

What Music Do You Listen To?

1. Redraw the graph. Use a vertical scale starting at 0.

2. Explain how the new graph represents the data more clearly.

The table below shows the results of a survey asking students whether they would attend a school barbecue.

Barbecue Survey Results

Answer	Number
Yes	62
Maybe	32
No	26

3. Calculate the percent of student responses for each answer category and use this information to make a bar graph.

4. Suppose 320 students were asked, but only 120 students responded to the survey. Draw a new graph based on the total number of students who were asked.

5. **Reasoning** How does knowing that 200 students didn't respond change your interpretation of the data?

The table at the right shows the number of free throws made by four members of a basketball team.

Free-Throw Results

Player	Shots	Baskets
Anna	50	35
Carla	20	12
Nikki	5	4
Raylene	40	30

6. Calculate the free-throw percentage for each student. Show the results in a bar graph.

7. According to your graph, which player has the best free-throw percentage?

8. **Writing in Math** Is this player necessarily the best free-throw shooter in the group? Explain.

5-4 Percents and Equations

Check Skills You'll Need

1. **Vocabulary Review** Is $2 \cdot 8 = 16$ an *equation* or an *expression*? Explain.

Solve each equation.

2. $0.25p = 10$

3. $12.25 = 9.8x$

4. $24 = 1.6s$

5. $0.64k = 0.02$

GO for Help
Lesson 1-7

What You'll Learn

To use equations to solve problems involving percents

Why Learn This?

The sales tax on an item is a percent of the item's cost. Understanding percents helps you calculate the total price of your purchases.

You can use the relationship between the part and the whole to solve various kinds of problems.

KEY CONCEPTS — Percent Equations

Finding the Part	**Finding the Whole**	**Finding the Percent**
part $= P \cdot$ whole	part $= P \cdot$ whole	part $= P \cdot$ whole
What is 20% of 25?	5 is 20% of what?	5 is what percent of 25?
$n = 0.20 \cdot 25$	$5 = 0.20 \cdot w$	$5 = P \cdot 25$

EXAMPLE — Finding Part of a Whole

① **Sales Tax** A hair dryer costs $22. The sales tax rate is 4.9%. Find the amount of sales tax.

Let $t =$ the amount of sales tax.

$$part = P \cdot whole \quad \leftarrow \text{Use the percent equation.}$$
$$t = 0.049 \cdot 22 \quad \leftarrow \text{Substitute.}$$
$$t = 1.078 \approx 1.08 \quad \leftarrow \text{Simplify. Round to the nearest cent.}$$

The sales tax is about $1.08.

Check for Reasonableness 4.9% of 22 ≈ 5% of 20. Since 5% of 20 is 1, which is close to 1.08, the answer is reasonable. ✔

✓ Quick Check

1. A bike costs $195.99 plus 6% for sales tax. Find the amount of tax.

Test Prep Tip

To write a percent as a decimal, divide the percent by 100, or move the decimal point two places to the left.

EXAMPLE Finding a Whole Amount

2 60 is 48% of what number?

$$60 = 0.48 \cdot w \quad \leftarrow \text{Write a percent equation.}$$

$$\frac{60}{0.48} = \frac{0.48w}{0.48} \quad \leftarrow \text{Divide each side by 0.48.}$$

$$125 = w \quad \leftarrow \text{Simplify.}$$

✓ Quick Check

2. Using an equation, 18% of what number is 16.2?

● More Than One Way

The average American recycles 372.3 lb, or 22.1%, of his or her trash per year. How much trash does the average American generate per year?

Tina's Method

I can use a percent equation. Let t = pounds of trash generated.

$$372.3 = 0.221 \cdot t \quad \leftarrow \text{Write a percent equation.}$$

$$\frac{372.3}{0.221} = \frac{0.221t}{0.221} \quad \leftarrow \text{Divide each side by 0.221.}$$

$$372.3 \;\boxed{\div}\; 0.221 \;\boxed{=}\; \mathit{1684.615385} \quad \leftarrow \text{Use a calculator.}$$

The average American generates about 1,684.6 lb of trash each year.

Kevin's Method

I can use a proportion. Let t = pounds of trash generated.

$$\frac{372.3}{t} = \frac{22.1}{100} \quad \leftarrow \text{Write a proportion.}$$

$$37{,}230 = 22.1t \quad \leftarrow \text{Write the cross product.}$$

$$\frac{37{,}230}{22.1} = \frac{22.1t}{22.1} \quad \leftarrow \text{Divide each side.}$$

$$37{,}230 \;\boxed{\div}\; 22.1 \;\boxed{=}\; \mathit{1684.615385} \quad \leftarrow \text{Use a calculator.}$$

Each year, the average American generates about 1,684.6 lb of trash.

Choose a Method

In a recent year, the population of Arkansas was about 2,675,000. This was 12% of the population of Texas. What was the approximate population of Texas that year? Explain why you chose the method you used.

1. **Mental Math** 12 is 50% of what number?

Use an equation to find each percent.

2. 31% of 82　　　　3. 5% of 28　　　　4. 27% of 16

5. A sales tax is 6 cents on the dollar. What is this tax as a percent?

6. **Reasoning** Suppose that 36 is 20% of some number. Is the unknown number greater than or less than 36? Explain.

Homework Exercises

For more exercises, see Extra Skills and Word Problems.

GO for Help

For Exercises	See Examples
7–8	1
9–14	2

7. **Cell Phones** In 2005, the Pennsylvania sales tax rate was 6%. Find the sales tax paid in Pennsylvania for a $39.99 cellular phone.

8. A college student buys a $19.95 poster for his dorm room. If the sales tax rate is 4.75%, how much sales tax does the student pay?

Use an equation to solve each problem. Round to the nearest hundredth.

9. 2.8 is 4% of what number?　　10. 6 is 92% of what number?

11. 356 is 80% of what number?　　12. 0.777 is 7% of what number?

13. 58.5 is 15% of what number?　　14. 174 is 25% of what number?

15. **Guided Problem Solving** In a recent year, Mississippi's sales tax was 7%. Arizona's tax was 80% of Mississippi's tax. Find the tax on a $25.85 concert ticket in Arizona.
    - The equation (■)(0.07) = p represents Arizona's sales tax p.
    - Use (■)(25.85) = t to find the tax on the ticket in Arizona.

16. In 1980, about 17.7 million households had cable television. This was about 25.8% of the households that had cable in 2000. How many households had cable in 2000?

17. **Royalties** A singer makes 2% royalties on the sales of her album. How much did her album earn in sales if she made $53,000 in royalties?

18. The figure shows the grade levels of students at a middle school. What percent of the students are eighth-graders?

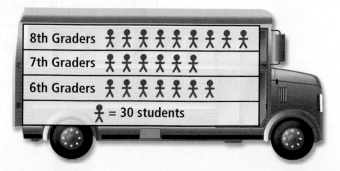

8th Graders 👤👤👤👤👤👤👤👤👤
7th Graders 👤👤👤👤👤👤
6th Graders 👤👤👤👤👤
👤 = 30 students

GO Online
Homework Video Tutor
Visit: PHSchool.com
Web Code: ase-0504

Electronics Use the table below to find the total price (including sales tax) of an $899 television in each state.

19. Kansas

20. North Carolina

21. Virginia

State	Sales-Tax Rate
Kansas	5.3%
North Carolina	4%
Virginia	5%

22. **Agriculture** About 12,457,350 tons of the oranges harvested in the United States in one year were used to make juice. If 13,113,000 tons of oranges were harvested, what percent were used to make juice?

23. **Choose a Method** In 2000, the population of Hawaii was about 1,200,000 people. The population of Florida in 2000 was about 1,333% of the population of Hawaii. What was the approximate population of Florida in 2000? Explain why you chose the method you used.

24. **Writing in Math** Explain two ways you can find 13% of a number.

25. **Challenge** Your neighbor bought a remote-controlled car for 20% off the original price of *x* dollars. The sales tax rate was 6.5%. She later sold the car for 75% of what she paid for it (including the tax). Write an equation for the amount your neighbor received for the car.

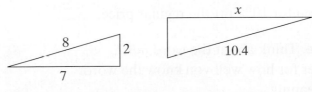

Test Prep and Mixed Review

Practice

Multiple Choice

26. A local television station devotes about 15% of its prime-time programming to commercials. How many minutes of commercials air in each hour of prime-time programming?
    - Ⓐ 4 min
    - Ⓑ 9 min
    - Ⓒ 12 min
    - Ⓓ 15 min

27. Gary bought a couch for $899.99 and a coffee table for $119.99, including tax. He is going to pay the total amount over a 2-year period. What is a reasonable amount for each monthly payment?
    - Ⓕ $43.00
    - Ⓖ $54.00
    - Ⓗ $65.00
    - Ⓙ $85.00

28. The triangles shown below are similar. Find *x*.

    8
    7
    2
    x
    10.4

    - Ⓐ 9.1
    - Ⓑ 9.4
    - Ⓒ 11.4
    - Ⓓ 11.9

GO for Help

For Exercises	See Lesson
29–31	2-3

Determine which number is greater.

29. 1.23, $\frac{15}{12}$

30. -45.78, $-\frac{412}{9}$

31. $\frac{1}{66}$, 0.015

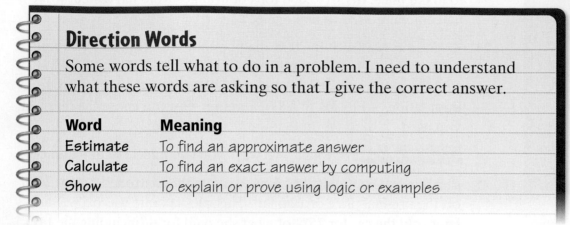

Vocabulary Builder

High-Use Academic Words

High-use academic words are words that you will
see often in textbooks and on tests. These words are
not math vocabulary terms, but knowing them will
help you to succeed in mathematics.

Direction Words

Some words tell what to do in a problem. I need to understand
what these words are asking so that I give the correct answer.

Word	Meaning
Estimate	To find an approximate answer
Calculate	To find an exact answer by computing
Show	To explain or prove using logic or examples

Exercises

1. Estimate your age in days.

2. Calculate your age in days.

3. Show that your birthday will never fall on the same day of the week
   in two consecutive years.

4. Estimate the total you pay if you leave a 15% tip for a restaurant bill
   of $29.42.

Use the table at the right for Exercises 5–6.

5. Calculate the cost of a game plus sales tax at the rate of 8%.

6. Show that $200 is enough money to purchase a tax-free monitor
   if you have a coupon for 10% off the regular price.

Home Arcade

Equipment	Price ($)
Controller	$29.95
Game	$53.25
Monitor	$219.95

7. **Word Knowledge** Think about the word *label*.
   a. Choose the letter for how well you know the word.
      A. I know its meaning.
      B. I've seen it, but I don't know its meaning.
      C. I don't know it.
   b. **Research** Look up and write the definition of *label*.
   c. Use the word in a sentence involving mathematics.

Checkpoint Quiz 1

Write each fraction as a percent. Round to the nearest hundredth of a percent where necessary.

1. $\frac{2}{4}$ 2. $\frac{1}{11}$ 3. $\frac{3}{8}$ 4. $\frac{15}{6}$ 5. $\frac{10}{25}$

Estimate the given percent of each number.

6. 19% of 58   7. 0.66% of 36   8. 137% of 8   9. 1.9% of 2

10. **Population** In 2000, about 25% of the 5,130,632 people living in Arizona were Latino. Find how many Arizona residents were Latino.

Use an equation to solve each problem.

11. 20.5 is 41% of what number?

12. What percent of 320 is 16?

13. Find 3% of 26.

14. 0.08 is 32% of what number?

5-5a   Activity Lab

Describing Change

City	1950 Population	2000 Population
Jacksonville, Florida	204,517	753,617
Virginia Beach, Virginia	5,390	425,257

SOURCE: U.S. Census Bureau. Go to **PHSchool.com** for an update. Web Code: asg-9041

Use the table above for Exercises 1–3.

1. Find the change in population for each city from 1950 to 2000. State whether the change is an increase or a decrease.

2. Write the ratio $\frac{\text{change in population}}{\text{1950 population}}$ for each city. Then write each ratio as a percent to the nearest tenth. This is the percent of change of the population for each city.

3. Does your answer to Exercise 1 or Exercise 2 better describe the population change for each city? Explain.

5-5 Percent of Change

Check Skills You'll Need

1. **Vocabulary Review** A __?__ is a ratio that compares a number to 100.

Write each fraction as a percent. Round to the nearest tenth of a percent.

2. $\frac{9}{8}$ 3. $\frac{6}{22}$

4. $\frac{4}{15}$ 5. $\frac{11}{3}$

 **for Help**
Lesson 5-1

What You'll Learn

To find percent of change and to solve problems involving percent of increase and percent of decrease

🔊 **New Vocabulary** percent of change

Why Learn This?

The U.S. Census is taken every ten years. Percents can help you understand the changes from one census to another.

The percent a quantity increases or decreases from its original amount is the **percent of change.**

$$P = \frac{\text{amount of change}}{\text{original amount}} \quad \leftarrow P \text{ is the percent of change.}$$

EXAMPLE Finding Percent of Increase

1790 ▶
3,929,200
people

2000* ▶
281,421,906
people

🚶=10,000,000
people

*Includes Alaska and Hawaii

Source: U.S. Census Bureau. Go to PHSchool.com for an update. Web Code: asg-9041

1 **Population** When the first U.S. Census was taken in 1790, the population was 3,929,200. In 2000, the population was 281,421,906. Find the percent of increase. Round to the nearest percent.

amount of change = 281,421,906 − 3,929,200 = 277,492,706

$$P = \frac{277,492,706}{3,929,200} \quad \begin{array}{l}\leftarrow \text{amount of change} \\ \leftarrow \text{original amount}\end{array}$$

277,492,706 ÷ 3,929,200 = 70.62320727 ← Use a calculator to divide.

≈ 7,062% ← Write the decimal as a percent. Round to the nearest percent.

The percent of increase in the population was about 7,062%.

Check for Reasonableness 7,062% of 3,929,200 is about 7,000% of 4,000,000. Since 7,000% of 4,000,000 is 280,000,000, which is close to 281,421,906, the answer is reasonable.

✓ Quick Check

1. **Education** In 1995, about 3,748,000 students were enrolled in Texas public schools. In 2010, there will be about 4,475,000 students enrolled. Find the percent of increase to the nearest tenth.

When working with different units of measure, convert all measures to the same units.

EXAMPLE Application: Sports

2 In the 1896 Olympic Games, Ellery Clark of the United States jumped 20 ft 10 in. to win the men's long jump. In a recent Olympic Games, an athlete jumped 28 ft 0.75 in. to win the men's long jump. Find the percent of increase in the length of the men's winning long jump.

For help converting units, see Lesson 4-2, Example 1.

20 ft 10 in. = 20 · 12 + 10 = 250 in. ⎤ ← **Write measures in**
28 ft 0.75 in. = 28 · 12 + 0.75 = 336.75 in. ⎦ ← **the same units.**

amount of change = 336.75 − 250 = 86.75

$P = \dfrac{86.75}{250}$ ← amount of change
← original amount

= 0.347 ← **Simplify.**

= 34.7% ← **Write the decimal as a percent.**

The length of the winning long jump increased by 34.7%.

✓ Quick Check

2. A girl was 4 ft 9 in. tall last year. This year she is 5 ft tall. Find the percent of increase in her height. Round to the nearest tenth.

Percent of decrease is the percent a quantity decreases from its original amount.

EXAMPLE Finding Percent of Decrease

3 In 1967, there were 3,384 drive-in movie theaters in the United States. In 1997, there were 619 drive-in theaters. Find the percent of decrease in the number of theaters. Round to the nearest tenth.

amount of change = 3,384 − 619 = 2,765

$P = \dfrac{2,765}{3,384}$ ← amount of change
← original amount

= 0.817080378 ← Use a calculator.

≈ 81.7% ← Write the decimal as a percent.
Round to the nearest tenth of a percent.

The number of drive-in theaters decreased by about 81.7%.

✓ Quick Check

3. In 1995, the average price of a personal computer was $2,100. In 2001, the average price was $899. Find the percent of decrease in the average price. Round to the nearest tenth.

1. **Vocabulary** The percent of change is the percent a quantity increases or decreases from its __?__ amount.

2. **Shopping** Use the information at the right to find the percent of increase in online shopping sales from 2000 to 2003. Round to the nearest tenth.

Online Shopping
2000 $27.287 BILLION
2003 $40.379 BILLION

Find the percent of change.

3. from 12 to 15

4. from 36 to 27

5. from 9 to 27

Homework Exercises

For more exercises, see Extra Skills and Word Problems.

For Exercises	See Examples
6–12	1
13–15	2
16–22	3

GO for Help

Find each percent of increase. Round your answer to the nearest tenth, if necessary.

6. 75 to 110

7. 10 to 23

8. 4 to 56

9. 20 to 28

10. 15 to 25

11. 50 to 80

12. **Money** In 1950, the minimum hourly wage for non-farm workers was $.75. In 2000, the minimum hourly wage was $5.15. Find the percent of increase. Round to the nearest tenth.

Find each percent of increase. Round your answer to the nearest tenth, if necessary.

13. 36 ft 3 in. to 37 ft 6 in.

14. 16 lb 4 oz to 20 lb 1 oz

15. **Infants** A baby weighed 7 lb 3 oz at birth. Four months later, the baby weighed 13 lb 5 oz. Find the percent of increase. Round to the nearest tenth.

Find each percent of decrease. Round your answer to the nearest tenth, if necessary.

16. 190 to 183

17. 15 to 10

18. 205 to 164

19. 87 to 64

20. 52 to 1

21. 368 to 275

22. **Entertainment** In 1998, there were 824 "easy listening" radio stations. In 2001, there were 299 easy listening stations. Find the percent of decrease. Round to the nearest tenth.

23. Guided Problem Solving In 1990, Mexico and Central America had about 204,450,000 acres of forest. In 2000, the amount of forest had decreased by 18%. Find the number of acres of forest in 2000.

- Find the decrease in the number of acres *a* by using the formula $a = (\blacksquare)(204{,}450{,}000)$.
- Find the number of acres of forest in 2000 by using the formula $204{,}450{,}000 - a = \blacksquare$.

Find each percent of change. Round to the nearest tenth. Label your answer *increase* or *decrease*.

24. 1.4 to 9.6   **25.** 0.8 to 0.2   **26.** 8.7 to 99.9

27. 5 to $1\frac{1}{4}$ **28.** $\frac{7}{5}$ to 130   **29.** $610\frac{1}{3}$ to 81

GO Online
Homework Video Tutor
Visit: PHSchool.com
Web Code: ase-0505

30. Education A middle school increased the length of its school day from 6 h 10 min to 6 h 25 min. Find the percent of increase in the length of the school day. Round to the nearest tenth of a percent.

31. Writing in Math The number 100 is increased by 20%. The result is then decreased by 20%. Is 100 the final result? Explain.

32. Challenge Three weeks ago, a sunflower plant was 1 ft 3 in. tall. Since then, its height has increased by $213\frac{1}{3}\%$. Find the current height of the sunflower in feet and inches.

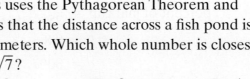

Test Prep and Mixed Review   **Practice**

Multiple Choice

33. The population of Marisa's town increased by 3% from last year to this year. If 30,000 people lived in the town last year, how many people live there this year?

   Ⓐ 900   Ⓑ 9,000   Ⓒ 30,900   Ⓓ 39,000

34. If $\triangle PQR$ is reflected over the *y*-axis, what will be the coordinates of R''?

   Ⓕ (2, −3)   Ⓗ (−2, 3)
   Ⓖ (2, 3)   Ⓙ (−2, −3)

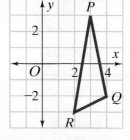

35. Luis uses the Pythagorean Theorem and finds that the distance across a fish pond is $\sqrt{7}$ meters. Which whole number is closest to $\sqrt{7}$?

   Ⓐ 2   Ⓑ 3   Ⓒ 4   Ⓓ 5

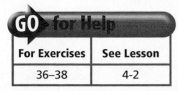

GO for Help

For Exercises	See Lesson
36–38	4-2

Convert each measure. Round to the nearest hundredth, if necessary.

36. 2.25 t = $\blacksquare$ lb   **37.** 6 qt = $\blacksquare$ c   **38.** 240 s = $\blacksquare$ h

5-6 Markup and Discount

Check Skills You'll Need

1. **Vocabulary Review**
   A ? relates a part to the whole.

   Use an equation to solve each problem.

2. What number is 16% of 25?

3. Find 80% of 250.

4. 33 is 3% of what number?

5. 0.55% of what number is 77?

GO for Help
Lesson 5-4

What You'll Learn

To use percent of change to find markup, discount, and selling price

🔊 **New Vocabulary** markup, selling price, discount, sale price

Why Learn This?

Store owners use percents in many ways. Sales flyers advertise a percent of a price. Store owners calculate a percent increase over their cost to make a profit.

Markup is the amount of increase in price. Markup is added to the store's cost for the item to arrive at the **selling price,** the price the store charges.

The percent of increase in the price of an item is called the percent of markup. Use the percent of change equation to find percent of markup.

$$\text{percent of change} = \frac{\text{amount of change}}{\text{original amount}} \qquad \text{percent of markup} = \frac{\text{markup}}{\text{store's cost}}$$

EXAMPLE Finding Percent of Markup

Store's cost

+ Markup

Selling price

1. **Clothing** Find the percent of markup on a sweater that cost a store $25 and has a selling price of $45.

   markup = selling price − store's cost

   $\quad\quad\quad = \$45 - \$25$ ← Substitute.

   $\quad\quad\quad = \$20$ ← Subtract.

   percent of markup $= \dfrac{20}{25}$ ← markup / store's cost

   $\quad\quad\quad\quad\quad\quad\quad\quad = 0.8$ ← Write the fraction as a decimal.

   $\quad\quad\quad\quad\quad\quad\quad\quad = 80\%$ ← Write the decimal as a percent.

✓ Quick Check

1. Find the percent of markup on an item that cost a store $10 and has a selling price of $19.

Managers use the store's cost for an item and percent of markup to calculate the item's selling price.

EXAMPLE Finding Selling Price

2 **Business** A school store sells pens. Each pen costs the store $.79. The store then marks up the price 65%. What is the selling price of each pen?

Method 1 Find the markup first. Then find the selling price.

65% of $.79 equals the markup.

$0.65 \cdot 0.79 = 0.5135$ ← **Multiply to find the markup.**

≈ 0.51 ← **Round to the nearest hundredth.**

$.79 + $.51 = 1.30 ← **store's cost + markup = selling price**

The school store sells each pen for $1.30.

Method 2 Find the selling price directly.

The selling price equals 100% of the store's cost plus a markup of 65% of the store's cost. The selling price of each pen is 100% + 65%, or 165%, of $.79.

165% of $.79 equals the selling price.

$1.65 \cdot 0.79 = 1.3035$ ← **Multiply to find the selling price.**

≈ 1.30 ← **Round to the nearest hundredth.**

The school store sells each pen for $1.30.

✓ Quick Check

2. An item costs a store $89.89. The store then marks the price up 80%. What is the selling price of the item?

Stores also use percents to calculate the prices of items on sale. The amount by which the price of an item on sale is reduced is called the **discount.** The regular price of an item minus the discount equals the **sale price** of the item.

The percent of decrease in the price of an item after a discount is called the percent of discount. Use the percent of change equation to find the percent of discount.

$$\text{percent of change} = \frac{\text{amount of change}}{\text{original amount}} \qquad \text{percent of discount} = \frac{\text{discount}}{\text{regular price}}$$

You can calculate the sale price of an item if you know the regular price and the percent of discount for the item. You can find the regular price of an item when you know the sale price and the percent of discount.

EXAMPLE Finding Sale Price

3 Furniture A furniture store is having a 30%-off sale. What is the sale price of a table that regularly costs $259.98?

Method 1 Find the discount first. Then subtract to find the sale price.

30% of $259.98 equals the discount.

$$0.3 \cdot 259.98 \approx 77.99 \quad \leftarrow \text{Multiply to find the discount. Round to the nearest hundredth.}$$

$$259.98 - 77.99 = 181.99 \quad \leftarrow \text{regular price} - \text{discount} = \text{sale price}$$

The sale price is $181.99.

Method 2 Find the sale price directly.

The sale price is 100% − 30%, or 70%, of $259.98.

$$0.7 \cdot 259.98 \approx 181.99 \quad \leftarrow \text{Multiply. Round to the nearest hundredth.}$$

The sale price is $181.99.

✓ Quick Check

3. An item that regularly sells for $182.75 is on sale for 45% off. Find the sale price to the nearest cent.

EXAMPLE Finding Regular Price

Test Prep Tip

Remember that when an item is discounted, the regular price is more than the sale price.

4 Multiple Choice You buy a pair of in-line skates on sale for $54. This price is 40% off the regular price. Find the regular price.
  Ⓐ $21.60   Ⓑ $32.40   Ⓒ $75.60   Ⓓ $90.00

regular price − 40% of regular price = sale price

Let r = the regular price.

$$r - 0.4r = 54 \quad \leftarrow \text{Substitute. Write the percent as a decimal.}$$

$$(1 - 0.4)r = 54 \quad \leftarrow \text{Distributive Property}$$

$$0.6r = 54 \quad \leftarrow \text{Subtract.}$$

$$\frac{0.6r}{0.6} = \frac{54}{0.6} \quad \leftarrow \text{Divide each side by 0.6.}$$

$$r = 90 \quad \leftarrow \text{Simplify.}$$

The regular price of the skates is $90. The correct answer is choice D.

GO for Help

For help with the Distributive Property, go to Lesson 1-5, Example 4.

✓ Quick Check

4. A stereo is on sale for $99 at 15% off. Find the regular price.

Vocabulary Match each term with its meaning.

1. markup
2. sale price
3. selling price

A. regular price of an item minus the discount
B. cost of the item plus the markup
C. amount of increase in price

4. **Reasoning** Explain why selling price after markup is always greater than selling price after a discount.

Homework Exercises

For more exercises, see Extra Skills and Word Problems.

GO for Help

For Exercises	See Examples
5–8	1
9–11	2
12–14	3
15–17	4

Find each percent of markup.

5. store's cost: $26
   selling price: $39

6. store's cost: $125
   selling price: $168.75

7. store's cost: $75
   selling price: $90

8. **Video Games** A video game costs a store $20. If the store sells the game for $33, what is the percent of markup?

Find each selling price. Round to the nearest cent.

9. store's cost: $118.12
   percent of markup: 60%

10. store's cost: $22.05
    percent of markup: 95%

11. A soccer ball costs a store $29.50. What is the selling price of the ball after a 35% markup? Round to the nearest cent.

Find each sale price. Round to the nearest cent.

12. regular price: $16.99
    percent of discount: 55%

13. regular price: $77.00
    percent of discount: 5%

14. A nursery has a 25%-off sale. Find the sale price of a $200 tree.

Find each regular price. Round to the nearest cent.

15. sale price: $66.30
    percent of discount: 65%

16. sale price: $13
    percent of discount: 20%

17. Employees at a clothing store get a 15% discount. Find the regular price of jeans that cost an employee $24.65.

18. **Guided Problem Solving** A store buys bags for $5.25 and marks them up 80%. Find the sale price of the bags after a 30% discount.
    • What is 80% of $5.25?
    • What is 30% of the selling price?

GO Online
Homework Video Tutor
Visit: PHSchool.com
Web Code: ase-0506

Find each selling price. Round to the nearest cent.

19. store's price: $71.99
percent of markup: $66\frac{2}{3}\%$

20. store's price: $364.38
percent of markup: $37\frac{1}{2}\%$

21. Reasoning A travel agency offers the trip advertised at the left. There is a 10% service fee. Will you do better if the agency adds the service fee and then subtracts the discount, or if the agency subtracts the discount and then adds the service fee? Explain.

22. DVDs are on sale for 40% off the regular price of $22.99. Your friend has $45 to spend. How many DVDs can your friend buy at the reduced price?

23. Writing in Math Write a general rule for finding a store's cost for an item if you know the selling price and the percent of markup.

24. Challenge There is a "buy two, get one free" sale on energy bars that regularly cost $1.25 each. How much do four bars cost?

NEW YORK CITY
$250
10% service fee additional
NOW 30% OFF

Test Prep and Mixed Review

Practice

Multiple Choice

25. Emily saw a dress she liked for $60. The following week, the dress was on sale for $45. By what percent was the dress marked down?

Ⓐ 1.3%   Ⓑ 25%   Ⓒ 33%   Ⓓ 75%

26. Which graph contains all the points represented by the coordinate pairs in the table at the right?

x	-1	$-\frac{1}{2}$	1
y	-3	-2	1

Ⓕ 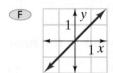   Ⓖ 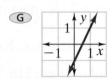   Ⓗ 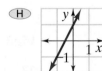   Ⓙ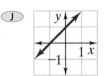

27. Jason bought a 10-pound box of Clementine oranges for $3.99. If navel oranges sell for $0.99 per pound, why did Jason believe that he made the better buy?

Ⓐ Navel oranges are heavier than Clementine oranges.

Ⓑ The cost per pound of Clementine oranges is $0.60 more than the cost per pound of navel oranges.

Ⓒ The cost per pound of Clementine oranges is $0.60 less than the cost per pound of navel oranges.

Ⓓ The cost for all kinds of oranges in 10-pound boxes is the same.

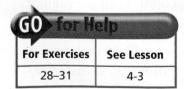

For Exercises	See Lesson
28–31	4-3

Solve each proportion.

28. $\frac{3}{8} = \frac{t}{24}$

29. $\frac{k}{234} = \frac{4}{5}$

30. $\frac{16}{25} = \frac{9.6}{n}$

31. $\frac{10}{f} = \frac{3.4}{8.5}$

Using Percents

Suppose a restaurant meal costs $17 and you want to leave a 15% tip. What is your total cost? You could calculate the exact amount of the tip or you could use estimation and the model below.

ACTIVITY

Step 1 On graph paper, draw a horizontal axis and label it from 0% to 150%. At 100%, draw a vertical axis and label it from $0 to $60.

Step 2 Hold one end of a string at the 0% point on the horizontal axis.

Step 3 To find the total cost of the meal, pull the string tight and move it until it crosses the vertical axis at $17. Then find the point where the string crosses 115%, which represents the cost of the meal (100%) plus tip (15%). Estimate the amount at this point. The total is about $19.00.

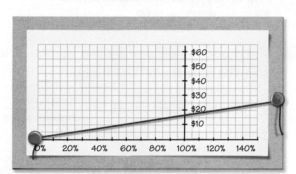

Exercises

Use your model to estimate a value for each exercise.

1. Your purchases cost $55. The sales tax rate is 6%. What is the total?

2. An item costs a store owner $28. She adds 35% to get the selling price. What is the selling price?

3. A CD costs $17 and you have a coupon for 25% off. What is your cost?

4. **Reasoning** The cost of a restaurant meal plus an 18% tip is $25. Explain how you can use your model to find the cost of the meal.

Practice Solving Problems

A sign over a rack reads "40% or more off." A sweater on the rack shows a sale price of $20 and a regular price of $36. Should the sweater be on the sale rack? Explain.

What You Might Think

What do I know?
What do I want to find out?

How can I find the amount of the discount?

How can I use the discount in an equation to find the percent of discount?

Should the sweater be on the sale rack?

What You Might Write

I know the regular price of the sweater is $36 and the sale price is $20. I want to find the percent of discount.

To find the amount of the discount, I subtract the sale price from the regular price. The amount of the discount is $36 − $20 = $16.

The discount divided by the regular price will give the percent of the discount.

$$\text{percent of discount} = \frac{\text{discount}}{\text{regular price}}$$
$$= \frac{16}{36}$$
$$= \frac{4}{9}$$
$$= 0.44444\ldots$$
$$\approx 44.4\%$$

The sweater should be on the sale rack because 44.4% > 40%. The percent of discount on the sweater is greater than 40%.

Think It Through

1. **Reasoning** Could you have solved the problem by dividing the sale price by the regular price? Explain.

2. Does a 25% discount cancel a 25% markup? Explain.

3. Suppose the sweater was discounted by 20% and then discounted by another 20%. Should the sweater still be on the sale rack?

Exercises

Solve each problem. For Exercises 4–5, answer the questions first.

4. Spending by federal, state, and local sources for K–12 public education in 2003 was $440.3 billion. This was a 4.9% increase from 2002. About how much was the total spending in 2002?
   a. What percent of the spending for 2002 is $440.3 billion?
   b. Write an equation, where x equals the spending in 2002.

5. New Jersey spends y% more than the national average of $8,019 per student. Find y.

Per Pupil Spending

State	Amount
District of Columbia	$13,328
New Jersey	$12,202
New York	$12,140
Connecticut	$10,372
Vermont	$10,322
Massachusetts	$10,223

SOURCE: U.S. Census Bureau. Go to **PHSchool.com** for an update. Web Code: asg-9041

   a. How much more did New Jersey spend than the national average?
   b. Find the percent of increase for New Jersey.

For Exercises 6–7, use the graph at the right.

6. By approximately what percent did the average price of a gallon of gasoline increase during the year?

7. Between what two months was the greatest percent of increase in the average price of a gallon of gasoline?

8. During August, the price of a gallon of gasoline in Seattle was about 2.7% higher than in Boston. The price of gasoline in Boston was about 0.6% higher than in Cleveland. The price of gasoline in Cleveland was $2.59 per gallon. What was the price of a gallon of gasoline in Seattle?

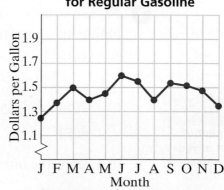

U.S. Retail Prices for Regular Gasoline

SOURCE: Energy Information Administration. Go to **PHSchool.com** for a data update. Web Code: asg-9041

Simple Interest

✓ Check Skills You'll Need

1. **Vocabulary Review**
A __?__ is a rule that shows a relationship between quantities.

Solve each formula for the variable indicated in red.

2. $V = \ell w h$

3. $d = rt$

4. $y = x + b$

5. $V = \frac{1}{3}Bh$

 **for Help**
Lesson 2-6

What You'll Learn

To find simple interest and account balances

🔊 **New Vocabulary** interest, interest rate, principal, simple interest, balance

Why Learn This?

When you deposit money in a bank, the bank pays you for the use of your money. When you borrow money, the bank charges you for the use of its money.

Interest is the amount of money paid for the use of money. Interest is calculated at a certain percentage rate called the **interest rate**. **Principal** is the original amount deposited or borrowed. **Simple interest** is interest calculated only on the principal.

KEY CONCEPTS   Simple Interest

$$I = p \cdot r \cdot t$$

where I is the interest, p is the principal, r is the interest rate per year, and t is the time in years.

EXAMPLE   Finding Simple Interest

1 **Gridded Response** A student deposits $200 in a bank account. The simple interest rate is $6\frac{1}{2}\%$ per year. Find the interest the account earns in 4 years.

$I = p \cdot r \cdot t$ ← simple interest formula

$\quad = 200 \cdot 0.065 \cdot 4$ ← Substitute.

$\quad = 52$ ← Multiply.

In 4 years, the interest earned is $52.00.

Test Prep Tip ⊛⊛⊛⊛

Check the placement of the decimal point in your answer for reasonableness.

✓ Quick Check

1. Find the interest earned on $3,600 invested at $3\frac{1}{2}\%$ simple interest for 5 years.

The principal in an account plus the earned interest is the balance.

EXAMPLE **Finding an Account Balance**

② **Savings** You deposit $120 in an account that earns 5% simple interest. Find the balance in the account after 3 years.

Step 1 Find the interest earned.

$$I = p \cdot r \cdot t$$
$$= 120 \cdot 0.05 \cdot 3 \quad \leftarrow \text{Substitute.}$$
$$= 18 \quad \leftarrow \text{Multiply.}$$

Step 2 Find the balance in the account.

$$\text{principal} + \text{earned interest} = \text{balance}$$
$$120 \quad + \quad 18 \quad = \quad 138 \quad \leftarrow \text{Substitute. Then add.}$$

The final balance in the account is $138.

✓ **Quick Check**

2. A teacher invests $205 in an account that earns 8% simple interest. Find the balance in the account after 10 years.

✓ Check Your Understanding

Vocabulary Match each term with the correct definition.

1. simple interest
2. interest
3. interest rate

A. percent on which savings earnings are based
B. money earned by a depositor or lender
C. money earned based only on the deposit

4. An account with $545 is invested at 5% simple interest for 6 years. What is the final balance in the account?

Homework Exercises

For more exercises, see Extra Skills and Word Problems.

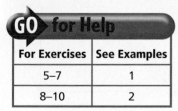

For Exercises	See Examples
5–7	1
8–10	2

Find the interest earned on each account.

5. $970 at $4\frac{1}{4}$% simple interest for 2 years

6. $182 at 6% simple interest for 4 years

7. You deposit $3,500 in an account. Find the interest earned in 5 years at a simple interest rate of $7\frac{1}{2}$% per year.

Find the balance in each account.

8. $198 invested at 4% simple interest for 13 years

9. $535 invested at 6% simple interest for 10 years

10. An electrician deposits $6,000 in a bank account with 7% simple interest. What is the balance after 4 years?

11. **Guided Problem Solving** You deposit $100 into an account that pays 5% simple interest. After 3 years, you move the balance to an account that pays 5.5% simple interest. What is your balance after 4 years in the second account?
    - **Understand the Problem** For 3 years, $100 earns 5% simple interest. For the next 4 years, it earns 5.5% simple interest.
    - **Make a Plan** Find the balance in the first account after 3 years and in the second account after 4 years.

GO Online
Homework Video Tutor
Visit: PHSchool.com
Web Code: ase-0507

12. **Investments** A woman invests $500 in a 36-month certificate of deposit (CD) with a simple interest rate of 5.36%. At the end of the 36 months, the woman redeposits her final balance into another 36-month CD with the same simple interest rate. Find the final balance.

13. **Writing in Math** There are two accounts being offered at your bank. One account pays 1.3% simple interest and has no monthly maintenance fees. The other account pays 2% simple interest but charges a $1 monthly maintenance fee. Into which account would you prefer to deposit $747 for one year? Explain.

14. **Challenge** You deposit $1,000 into an account. At what simple interest rate will the balance be $1,240 after 180 months?

Test Prep and Mixed Review

Practice

Gridded Response

15. Nick deposited $2,500 in an account that earns 6% simple interest. How many dollars will be in the account after 7 years?

16. The boxes shown at the right are similar. What is the value of x, to the nearest tenth?

17. Mrs. Ramirez is sending three students from each homeroom in her school to a conference. If there are 36 homerooms, how many students will attend the conference?

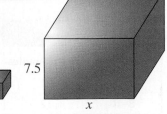

GO for Help

For Exercises	See Lesson
18–19	2-6

Find the area of each figure.

18. square: side = 3.6 cm

19. rectangle: 9 ft by 11.4 ft

Checkpoint Quiz 2

Lessons 5-5 through 5-7

Find each percent of change. Round to the nearest tenth of a percent where necessary. Label your answer *increase* or *decrease*.

1. 14 to 154   **2.** 427 to 420   **3.** 2 to 0.4   **4.** 123 to 456

5. Sports At a track meet, a shot-putter's first throw was 36 ft 3 in. long. The shot-putter's second throw was 37 ft 6 in. long. Find the percent of increase in the length of the throws. Round to the nearest tenth of a percent.

6. Pets A dog owner pays $14.99 for a 20-lb bag of dog food at 35% off. Find the regular price for the dog food. Round to the nearest cent.

7. Shopping Charlene buys a skirt on sale. The regular price is $26.99, but she pays $22.94. What is the percent of discount Charlene gets when she buys the skirt on sale?

Find the simple interest earned on each account.

8. $250 at $3\frac{1}{2}$% for 5 years   **9.** $95 at 6% for 3 years

---

5-8a   Activity Lab

Hands On

Exploring Probability

ACTIVITY

1. Toss a coin. Record whether the coin lands heads or tails.

2. Repeat this process 20 times.

3. Copy and complete the table at the right. Did heads or tails occur more often?

4. Compare your results with those of your classmates. Did the entire class record the same results? Explain why or why not.

5. What results do you think you would get if you tossed the coin 100 times? Explain.

Result	Number of Occurrences
Heads	▦
Tails	▦

245

What You'll Learn

To find probability and the sample space of an event

🔊 **New Vocabulary** outcome, event, probability of an event, sample space

Why Learn This?

Suppose you have six quarters like the ones shown, and you choose one at random. You can find the probability of choosing a quarter from a certain state.

An **outcome** is any of the possible results that can occur. A collection of possible outcomes in an experiment is an **event**. There are three possible events in this experiment: selecting an Indiana quarter, selecting a Tennessee quarter, and selecting an Ohio quarter.

The **probability of an event** E is given by the following formula when outcomes are equally likely.

$$P(E) = \frac{\text{number of favorable outcomes}}{\text{total number of possible outcomes}}$$

EXAMPLE   Finding a Probability

1 Suppose you choose a ball at random from the balls in the bowl at the left. Find $P(\text{red})$.

$$P(\text{red}) = \frac{2}{8} \leftarrow \textbf{2 favorable outcomes}$$
$$\phantom{P(\text{red})} \leftarrow \textbf{8 possible outcomes}$$
$$\phantom{P(\text{red})} = \frac{1}{4} \quad \leftarrow \textbf{Simplify.}$$

The probability of choosing a red ball is $\frac{1}{4}$.

✓ Quick Check

1. Find $P(\text{blue})$.

You can express probabilities as fractions or as percents.

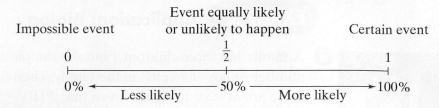

Event equally likely
or unlikely to happen

Impossible event   Certain event

0        $\frac{1}{2}$ 1

0% ← Less likely   50%   More likely → 100%

EXAMPLE   **Application: Surveys**

② **Multiple Choice** The circle graph shows the results of a survey of middle school students. Suppose you choose a student's name at random. Find the probability that the student's favorite music is pop or country.

  (A) 12%   (B) 32%   (C) 44%   (D) 63%

$P(\text{pop or country}) = P(\text{pop}) + P(\text{country})$
$= 32\% + 12\%$ ← **Substitute.**
$= 44\%$ ← **Simplify.**

Since the probability is 44%, the correct answer is choice C.

Test Prep Tip

The phrase "pop or country music" refers to anyone in either group. For this reason, you add the individual percents together.

Favorite Music

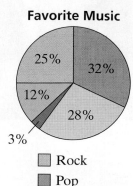

25%   32%
12%
28%
3%

□ Rock
■ Pop
□ Hip-hop
■ Classical
□ Country

✓ Quick Check

2. Find $P(\text{classical or rock})$.

The collection of all possible outcomes in an experiment is called the **sample space.** You can make a table to find the sample space.

EXAMPLE   **Finding a Sample Space**

③ Construct the sample space for rolling two number cubes. Then find the probability that the two number cubes have a product of 12. Express the probability as a fraction and as a percent.

Of the 36 possible outcomes, four outcomes have a product of 12.

$P(\text{product of 12}) = \frac{4}{36}$, or $\frac{1}{9}$

The probability is $\frac{1}{9}$, or about 11.1%.

	1	2	3	4	5	6
1	(1,1)	(2,1)	(3,1)	(4,1)	(5,1)	(6,1)
2	(1,2)	(2,2)	(3,2)	(4,2)	(5,2)	(6,2)
3	(1,3)	(2,3)	(3,3)	(4,3)	(5,3)	(6,3)
4	(1,4)	(2,4)	(3,4)	(4,4)	(5,4)	(6,4)
5	(1,5)	(2,5)	(3,5)	(4,5)	(5,5)	(6,5)
6	(1,6)	(2,6)	(3,6)	(4,6)	(5,6)	(6,6)

✓ Quick Check

3. Find $P(\text{sum is odd})$. Write the answer as a fraction.

You can also use a tree diagram to construct a sample space.

EXAMPLE **Application: Biology**

4 A family has three children. Find the sample space showing the number of boys and girls in the family. Then find the probability that there are at least two girls, given that $P(B) = P(G)$. Express the probability as a fraction.

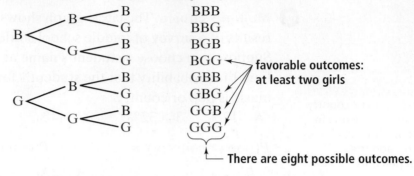

| Child 1 | Child 2 | Child 3 | Sample Space |

BBB
BBG
BGB
BGG ← favorable outcomes: at least two girls
GBB
GBG
GGB
GGG

└─ There are eight possible outcomes.

$P(\text{at least two girls}) = \dfrac{\text{number of outcomes with at least two girls}}{\text{total number of outcomes}}$

$= \dfrac{4}{8}$ ← Substitute.

$= \dfrac{1}{2}$ ← Write the fraction in simplest form.

✓ Quick Check

4. Use the tree diagram from Example 4. Find the probability that a family with three children will have exactly two boys. Express the probability as a fraction.

✓ Check Your Understanding

1. **Vocabulary** Explain the difference between an outcome and an event. Can an outcome be an event?

2. **Reasoning** A jar contains only red, white, and blue marbles. Explain how you know that $P(\text{red, white, or blue}) = 1$.

A dart lands at random within the circle on the game board shown at the right. Find each probability.

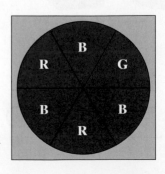

3. $P(\text{red})$

4. $P(\text{blue})$

5. $P(\text{green})$

For more exercises, see Extra Skills and Word Problems.

GO for Help

For Exercises	See Examples
6–11	1
12–14	2
15–20	3
21–25	4

A spinner has eight equal sections labeled 1 through 8. You spin the spinner once. Write each probability as a fraction.

6. $P(6)$

7. $P(3)$

8. $P(\text{even number})$

9. $P(\text{number less than 4})$

10. $P(\text{number greater than 8})$

11. $P(\text{number less than 10})$

Using the graph at the right, find each probability.

What We Prefer to Hear When on Hold

61%

7%

7%

22%

3%

■ Music
■ Silence
■ Talk radio
■ Company ads
■ Other

12. $P(\text{music or silence})$

13. $P(\text{talk or ads})$

14. $P(\text{anything but silence})$

Two spinners have four sections of equal size labeled 1, 2, 3, and 4. Construct the sample space for spinning the two spinners. Write each probability as a fraction.

15. $P(\text{Product is 4.})$

16. $P(\text{Sum is even.})$

17. $P(\text{Difference is 2.})$

18. $P(\text{Sum is 7.})$

19. $P(\text{Difference is odd.})$

20. $P(\text{Sum is 5.})$

For Exercises 21–25, use three coins.

21. Draw a tree diagram to find the sample space. One possible outcome is heads–tails–tails.

22. Find $P(\text{no heads})$.

23. Find $P(\text{exactly one head})$.

24. Find $P(\text{exactly two heads})$.

25. Find $P(\text{three heads})$.

26. Guided Problem Solving A vending machine contains 200 packages of granola bars and crackers. If you pick a package at random, $P(\text{crackers}) = 45\%$. How many packages are granola bars?

- **Make a Plan** Find the number of packages of crackers and subtract that from the total.
- **Carry Out the Plan** The number of packages of crackers is ■. The number of packages of granola bars is $200 -$ ■.

27. Gardening A package of wildflower seeds contains 50 daisy seeds, 80 sunflower seeds, 100 black-eyed Susan seeds, and 20 lupine seeds. Find the probability that a seed selected at random will be a daisy seed.

GO Online

Homework Video Tutor
Visit: PHSchool.com
Web Code: ase-0508

28. Use the graph at the right to find the probability that a person chosen at random in 2065 will be under the age of 40.

Projected 2065 U.S. Population by Age Group

13.2%
25%
13.1%
7.8%
22.9%
18%

☐ 9 years and younger
☐ 10–19 years
☐ 20–39 years
☐ 40–59 years
☐ 60–79 years
☐ 80 years and older

SOURCE: U.S. Census Bureau. Go to **PHSchool.com** for an update. Web Code: asg-9041

Marbles A bag contains 3 purple marbles, 2 orange marbles, 1 black marble, and 4 silver marbles. Find each probability when choosing at random.

29. $P(\text{orange})$

30. $P(\text{silver})$

31. Suppose you choose a silver marble, and you do not put it back in the bag. Find $P(\text{orange})$ if you choose a second marble.

32. Writing in Math Can $\frac{5}{4}$ represent a probability? Explain.

33. Challenge You flip a coin, toss a number cube, and then flip another coin. What is the probability that you will get heads on the first coin, a 3 or a 5 on the number cube, and heads on the second coin?

Test Prep and Mixed Review

Practice

Multiple Choice

34. Rebecca is playing a game with a number cube. If she rolls a number greater than 4, she will win the game. What is the probability that Rebecca will win?

Ⓐ $\frac{1}{6}$ Ⓑ $\frac{1}{3}$ Ⓒ $\frac{1}{2}$ Ⓓ $\frac{2}{3}$

35. Julio is drawing rectangle $ABCD$ on a coordinate grid. What will be the coordinates of point D?

Ⓕ $(2.5, 2.5)$ Ⓗ $(2.5, -2.5)$
Ⓖ $(3.5, 3.5)$ Ⓙ $(3.5, -3.5)$

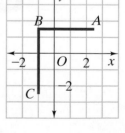

36. About 30% of the 126 students in Tanner's class play a musical instrument. Which proportion can be used to find n, the number of students who play an instrument?

Ⓐ $\frac{n}{100} = \frac{30}{126}$ Ⓑ $\frac{126}{n} = \frac{30}{100}$ Ⓒ $\frac{126}{30} = \frac{100}{n}$ Ⓓ $\frac{n}{126} = \frac{30}{100}$

GO for Help

For Exercises	See Lesson
37–39	4-1

Write each ratio in simplest form.

37. 120 lb : 4 lb

38. $\frac{74 \text{ mi}}{111 \text{ ft}}$

39. 9 h to 127 s

Test-Taking Strategies

Estimating the Answer

Estimating answers may help you find answers, check an answer, or eliminate one or more answer choices.

EXAMPLES

1 A student collects baseball cards. The student bought one card in the collection for $12.07. Five years later, the card was worth $15.98. Find the percent of increase in the value of the baseball card.

Ⓐ 3.91%　　Ⓑ 24.5%　　Ⓒ 32.4%　　Ⓓ 39.1%

Since the beginning value is near $12, and the ending value is near $16, the amount of change is about $4. Using the percent of change equation, you can estimate the percent of increase.

$$P \approx \frac{4}{12} = \frac{1}{3} = 33\frac{1}{3}\%$$

You can eliminate answer choices A, B, and D, which are not close to $33\frac{1}{3}\%$. The correct answer is choice C.

2 In an election, the winning candidate received 88% of the votes. If 558 students voted, how many voted for the winning candidate?

Ⓐ 521　　Ⓑ 491　　Ⓒ 469　　Ⓓ 387

You can estimate the answer by finding 90% of 560. Since $0.9 \cdot 560$ is 504, the correct answer is choice B.

Exercises

Estimate to solve each problem.

1. A football kicker made 21 field goal attempts in one season and was successful about 73% of the time. How many goals did he make?

Ⓐ 20　　Ⓑ 15　　Ⓒ 12　　Ⓓ 5

2. Which is closest to $\frac{78}{643}$?

Ⓕ 10%　　Ⓖ 12.5%　　Ⓗ 20%　　Ⓙ $33\frac{1}{3}\%$

3. During a tour, 44 of a rock band's 49 shows sold out. About what percent of the band's shows sold out?

Ⓐ 85%　　Ⓑ 87.5%　　Ⓒ 90%　　Ⓓ 95%

4. You and a friend have a $23.04 restaurant bill. If you want to leave a 15% tip, about how much should you leave for a tip?

Ⓕ $2.50　　Ⓖ $3　　Ⓗ $3.50　　Ⓙ $4

Vocabulary Review

balance (p. 243)
discount (p. 235)
event (p. 246)
interest (p. 242)
interest rate (p. 242)
markup (p. 234)

outcome (p. 246)
percent (p. 210)
percent of change (p. 230)
principal (p. 242)
probability of an event
  (p. 246)

sale price (p. 235)
sample space (p. 247)
selling price (p. 234)
simple interest (p. 242)

Choose the correct vocabulary term to complete each sentence.

1. __?__ is the amount by which a store increases the price of an item.

2. The original deposit in a bank account is called the __?__.

3. A(n) __?__ is any of the possible results that can occur in an experiment.

4. The amount by which the price of an item on sale is reduced is the __?__.

5. Interest calculated only on the principal of an account is __?__.

Go Online
PHSchool.com
For: Online Vocabulary Quiz
Web Code: asj-0551

Skills and Concepts

Lessons 5-1, 5-2
- To convert between fractions, decimals, and percents and to order rational numbers
- To estimate percents using decimals and fractions

A **percent** is a ratio that compares a number to 100. You can write fractions and decimals as percents. It is often helpful to estimate percents.

Write each fraction as a percent. Round to the nearest hundredth of a percent where necessary.

6. $\frac{7}{8}$ 7. $\frac{13}{12}$ 8. $\frac{5}{16}$ 9. $\frac{27}{6}$

Write each percent as a fraction or a mixed number in simplest form.

10. 36%   11. $33\frac{1}{3}\%$ 12. 124%   13. 27%

Estimate each percent.

14. 24% of 97   15. 15% of $35.07   16. 68% of 89

17. About 13% of the 23 students in a middle school class said that soccer was their favorite sport. Using fractions, estimate how many students said they liked soccer the best.

Lessons 5-3, 5-4

- To use proportions to find part of a whole, a whole amount, or a percent
- To use equations to solve problems involving percents

You can solve a percent problem using a proportion or an equation.

$$\frac{\text{part}}{\text{whole}} = \frac{p}{100} \qquad \text{part} = P \cdot \text{whole}$$

Use a proportion or an equation to solve each problem.

18. 85% of what number is 170?

19. What percent of 2 is 0.8?

20. Find 150% of 12.

21. 26% of what number is 39?

22. Tennis About 7.5% of the eighth-grade students in a middle school, or 12 students, are on the tennis team. How many students are in the eighth grade?

Lessons 5-5, 5-6

- To find percent of change and to solve problems involving percent of increase and percent of decrease
- To use percent of change to find markup, discount, and selling price

You can find the **percent of change** P expressed as a decimal.

$$P = \frac{\text{amount of change}}{\text{original amount}}$$

Markup is a type of percent of increase that stores use to calculate the **selling price** of an item. The amount stores reduce the price of an item to find the **sale price** is called the **discount.**

Find each percent of change. Round your answer to the nearest tenth of a percent where necessary. Label your answer *increase* or *decrease*.

23. 13 to 9   **24.** 2 to 88   **25.** 154 to 155   **26.** 18 to 3

27. Video Games A store is having a 20%-off sale. Find the sale price of a video game system that regularly costs $249.99.

Lesson 5-7

- To find simple interest and account balances

Simple interest is interest calculated only on the principal. To calculate simple interest, use the formula $I = p \cdot r \cdot t$.

Find the balance in each account.

28. $475 at 7% simple interest for 3 years

29. $710 at 2% simple interest for 7 years

30. $3,500 at 7% simple interest for 5 years

Lesson 5-8

- To find probability and the sample space of an event

An **event** is a collection of possible **outcomes** of an experiment. The collection of all possible outcomes is the **sample space.**

$$\text{probability of an event } E = P(E) = \frac{\text{number of favorable outcomes}}{\text{total number of possible outcomes}}$$

31. A swimmer wins 3 gold ribbons, 5 silver ribbons, and 1 bronze ribbon during a season. Suppose she chooses a ribbon from her collection at random. What is the probability that she will choose a silver ribbon?

Go Online For: Online chapter test
PHSchool.com Web Code: asa-0552

Compare. Use <, >, or =.

1. $\frac{5}{8}$ ■ 0.625

2. 0.6% ■ 0.6

3. $\frac{1}{3}$ ■ 0.34

4. $\frac{5}{6}$ ■ 85%

Write each fraction as a percent. Round to the nearest hundredth of a percent.

5. $\frac{11}{13}$

6. $\frac{22}{9}$

7. $\frac{1}{205}$

Estimate each percent. Explain how you made your estimate and why.

8. 76% of 48

9. 20% of $23.87

10. 250% of 29

11. 15% of $61.51

12. **Athletics** More than 7 million high school students in the United States participate in a school sport. Suppose only 98,000 college students receive sports scholarships. Estimate what percent of high school athletes receive college sports scholarships. Round your answer to the nearest tenth of a percent.

Use a proportion to solve each problem.

13. Find 37% of 134.

14. Find 2% of 70.

15. 68 is 5% of what number?

16. 350% of what number is 21,000?

17. About 13% of a school's 782 students walk to school. How many students walk to school?

Use an equation to solve each problem.

18. Find 132% of 65.

19. Find 16% of 3.

20. 6% of what number is 105?

21. 120% of what number is 0.006?

22. How much sales tax would you pay on a skateboard priced at $49.95 in a state that charges 5.5% sales tax?

Find each percent of change. Round the answer to the nearest hundredth of a percent. Label your answer *increase* or *decrease*.

23. 99 to 163

24. 13 to 1

25. 158 to 24

26. 613 to 655

27. **Jobs** Last year, a student earned $6.00 per hour baby-sitting. This year he earns $6.75 per hour. Find the percent of increase.

Find the final price after each markup or discount. Round to the nearest cent.

28. $90.00, 33% discount

29. $19.99, 15% markup

30. **Writing in Math** The Drama Club bought T-shirts for $4 and sold them for $5. A student claims that the markup rate is 20% because $1 is 20% of $5. Explain the student's error and give the correct markup rate.

31. **Savings** Miguel wants to save between 50% and 65% of his allowance to buy a new bike. He receives an allowance of $17 each week. What are the least and the greatest amounts of money he could save each week?

Find the final balance in each account.

32. $250 at $4\frac{1}{2}$% simple interest for 3 years

33. $450 at 6% simple interest for 2 years

34. $800 at 6% simple interest for 3 years

35. Suppose you roll two cubes. Each cube has the numbers 1, 2, 3, 4, 5, and 6 on its faces.
    a. Use a table to find the sample space.
    b. Find *P*(sum greater than 8).
    c. Find *P*(product even).

Multiple Choice
Read each question. Then write the letter of the correct answer on your paper.

1. Which pair of numbers has a GCF of 21?
   - Ⓐ 14 and 21
   - Ⓑ 630 and 126
   - Ⓒ 84 and 105
   - Ⓓ 42 and 84

2. An HO scale model railroad is $\frac{1}{87}$ scale, which means that 1 inch of an HO train is equal to 87 inches of a real train. Find the size of an HO boxcar if a real boxcar is 50 ft long.
   - Ⓕ about 3.5 in.
   - Ⓖ about 15 in.
   - Ⓗ about 7 in.
   - Ⓙ about 7 ft

3. Subtract $4\frac{2}{3} - \left(-3\frac{3}{4}\right)$.
   - Ⓐ $-1\frac{1}{7}$
   - Ⓑ $\frac{11}{12}$
   - Ⓒ $7\frac{11}{12}$
   - Ⓓ $8\frac{5}{12}$

4. Fifteen is 12% of what number?
   - Ⓕ 1.25
   - Ⓖ 1.8
   - Ⓗ 12.5
   - Ⓙ 125

5. Find the length of the hypotenuse.
   - Ⓐ 11
   - Ⓑ 13
   - Ⓒ 17
   - Ⓓ 26

   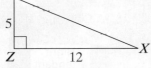

6. A jacket with a regular price of $79.99 is on sale for 35% off. Estimate the sale price of the jacket.
   - Ⓕ $60
   - Ⓖ $53
   - Ⓗ $45
   - Ⓙ $40

7. Which of these is NOT equal to 45%?
   - Ⓐ 0.45
   - Ⓑ $\frac{18}{40}$
   - Ⓒ 4.5
   - Ⓓ $\frac{27}{60}$

8. Solve $n - \frac{5}{6} = -\frac{1}{4}$.
   - Ⓕ $-1\frac{1}{2}$
   - Ⓖ $\frac{7}{12}$
   - Ⓗ $\frac{3}{5}$
   - Ⓙ $4\frac{1}{2}$

9. Solve $x + 7 = -11$.
   - Ⓐ -18
   - Ⓑ -3
   - Ⓒ 3
   - Ⓓ 18

10. Simplify $64 - 4^2 \div 8$.
    - Ⓕ 6
    - Ⓖ 7.5
    - Ⓗ 62
    - Ⓙ 450

11. When $\triangle ABC$ is reflected over the x-axis, what is the y-coordinate of the image of A?

    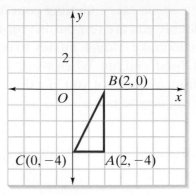

    - Ⓐ -4
    - Ⓑ -2
    - Ⓒ 2
    - Ⓓ 4

Gridded Response
Record your answer in a grid.

12. Suppose you roll a number cube with numbers 1, 2, 3, 4, 5, and 6 on its faces. What is $P(\text{prime number})$?

13. Add $2 + \frac{3}{4} + 7\frac{1}{8}$.

Short Response

14. On a sports team, the ratio of boys to girls is 3 to 2. Set up and solve a proportion to find how many boys are on a team with 8 girls.

15. Calculate the interest earned and the final balance in a savings account that has $150 and earns 5% simple interest over 4 years.

Extended Response

16. The table below contains coordinates of several points on a line.

x	−6	−2	2	6
y	3	1	−1	−3

    a. Write an equation to model the data in the table.

    b. Graph the data in the table. Draw a line through the points.

Applying Percents

Making Ends Meet Getting your first apartment is a big step! Suddenly you are responsible for taking care of yourself. You have to make enough money to cover your basic expenses for rent, food, and fun. When you start looking for a job, you'll want to think about what you like doing, as well as how much money you're going to make.

Paying Bills

People often pay bills monthly for heat, electricity, and water.

Job Fair

At a job fair, people who are looking for jobs meet with people who have jobs to fill. At a career day, students learn about different careers.

Go Online
PHSchool.com
For: Information about careers
Web Code: ase-0553

Put It All Together

1. The list shows your projected monthly expenses.
   a. Find the total.
   b. 25% of your earnings go for taxes. How much will you need to make each month to cover your expenses?

Monthly Expenses

Expense	Cost
Rent	$1,000
Utilities	$60
Food	$150
Transportation	$50
Entertainment	$100
Total	▦

2. One job you consider is selling cars. Your salary would be $400 a month plus a commission of 25% of the dealer's profit on each car you sell.
   a. How much must you make in commission each month?
   b. How much must the dealer's profit from your sales be each month?
   c. The dealer's profit is 6% of the selling price of each car. What will your total monthly sales have to be?
   d. The average selling price of a car is $18,000. How many cars will you have to sell each month?

3. Your second option is to wait tables. The job pays $2.50 per hour plus tips.
   a. If you work 40 hours per week, how much money must you earn in tips each month? (Assume there are four 40-hour working weeks in each month.)
   b. The average bill in this restaurant is $25 per person. Your tips average 15% of each bill. About how many customers will you need to serve in a month? In a week? In an hour?

4. **Writing in Math** Money is only one of the things you need to think about when choosing a job. Write a letter to yourself describing the pros and cons of each job.

Police officer

Nurse

Pilot

Stock broker

Parent

Real estate broker

CHAPTER 6
Equations and Inequalities

What You've Learned

- In Chapter 1, you used integers and the order of operations to solve problems.

- In Chapter 3, you used tables, graphs, and algebraic equations to solve problems.

- In Chapter 4, you selected and used appropriate forms of rational numbers to solve problems.

Check Your Readiness

GO for Help

For Exercises	See Lessons
1–4	1-3
5–11	1-4
12–17	1-5

Adding and Subtracting Integers

Simplify each expression.

1. $8 + 15 + (-25)$ **2.** $6 + 7 - 15$

3. $14 - 8 + 8$ **4.** $120 + (-6) + 9$

Multiplying and Dividing Integers

Simplify each expression.

5. $-12 \div 3$ **6.** $-3 \div (-1)$

7. $3(-2 - 5) \div 7$ **8.** $6 \cdot (-2) \div (-12)$

Evaluate each expression when $a = 2$ and $b = -1$.

9. $\dfrac{ab}{2}$ **10.** $\dfrac{a - 2b}{4}$ **11.** $\dfrac{a - b}{a + b}$

Using the Distributive Property

Find each product.

12. $5(c - 3)$ **13.** $-2(w + 8)$ **14.** $-9(6 - t)$

15. $2(-5 + a)$ **16.** $11(4 - b)$ **17.** $-1(x - 2)$

What You'll Learn Next

- In this chapter, you will simplify algebraic expressions.

- You will solve problems by writing and solving multi-step equations.

- You will write, solve, and graph inequalities.

 Problem Solving Application On pages 298–299, you will work an extended activity about movies.

🔊 Key Vocabulary

- Addition Property of Inequality (p. 282)
- Division Property of Inequality (p. 288)
- inequality (p. 282)
- like terms (p. 266)
- Multiplication Property of Inequality (p. 288)
- Subtraction Property of Inequality (p. 282)
- term (p. 266)

Modeling Multi-Step Equations

You can use algebra tiles to model and solve multi-step equations.

To solve a multi-step equation, get the *x*-tiles alone on one side. Then divide each side into equal groups.

ACTIVITY

Use algebra tiles to solve $2x + 1 = -5$.

Model the equation. ⟶  $2x + 1 = -5$

Add −1 to each side, creating a zero pair on the left side. ⟶  $2x + 1 + (-1) = -5 + (-1)$

Remove the zero pair. ⟶  $2x = -6$

Divide each side into two equal groups. ⟶  $\dfrac{2x}{2} = \dfrac{-6}{2}$

Remove one group from each side. ⟶  $x = -3$

Exercises

Use algebra tiles to solve each equation.

1. $-2x + 5 = 3$ 2. $3x + 2 = -7$ 3. $2x - 4 = -2$

4. $2x - 7 = 5$ 5. $1 + 2x = 5$ 6. $3x - 5 = -11$

7. $-15 - 8x = 25$ 8. $16x + 36 = 100$ 9. $46 - 12x = -62$

10. **Open-Ended** Write two different equations that have the solution modeled at the right.

11. Use algebra tiles to model and solve $2x + 5 = x - 1$. Describe each step.

6-1

Solving Two-Step Equations

Check Skills You'll Need

1. **Vocabulary Review** What does it mean to *isolate* the variable?

Solve each equation.

2. $x + 4 = -3$

3. $c - 5 = 1$

4. $5 + a = 35$

 **for Help**
Lesson 1-6

What You'll Learn

To solve two-step equations and to use two-step equations to solve problems

Why Learn This?

Many real-world situations are modeled by equations with multiple steps.

Suppose you adopt a puppy from an animal shelter and buy 3 bags of dog food. The adoption fee is $125 and you spend a total of $154.97. How much does each bag of dog food cost?

Total cost $154.97	
Adoption fee $125	Bags $3b$

The model at the left shows that you can use the equation $125 + 3b = 154.97$ to represent the problem. This equation requires two steps to solve. Use the order of operations in reverse to choose the operation to undo first.

For: Two-Step Equations Activity
Use: Interactive Textbook, 6-1

EXAMPLE Solving Using Subtraction and Division

1 Solve $125 + 3b = 154.97$.

$$125 + 3b = 154.97$$
$$125 - 125 + 3b = 154.97 - 125 \quad \leftarrow \text{Subtract 125 from each side.}$$
$$3b = 29.97 \quad \leftarrow \text{Simplify.}$$
$$\frac{3b}{3} = \frac{29.97}{3} \quad \leftarrow \text{Divide each side by 3.}$$
$$b = 9.99 \quad \leftarrow \text{Simplify.}$$

Check $125 + 3b = 154.97$

$$125 + 3(9.99) \stackrel{?}{=} 154.97 \quad \leftarrow \text{Substitute 9.99 for } b.$$
$$154.97 = 154.97 \ \checkmark \quad \leftarrow \text{The solution checks.}$$

Quick Check

1. Solve $4g + 11.6 = -23.2$. Check the solution.

Multiple Choice Suppose you buy a slice of pizza for $1.50. You also split the cost of renting a video with two friends. Your total cost is $2.75. Which equation can you use to find the cost of renting the video?

(A) $1.50 + v = 2.75$

(C) $1.50 + \frac{v}{3} = 2.75$

(B) $1.50 + \frac{v}{2} = 2.75$

(D) $\frac{1.50 + v}{3} = 2.75$

Words $\boxed{\text{cost of pizza}}$ plus $\boxed{(\text{cost of video} \div 3)}$ is $\boxed{\$2.75}$

Let v = the cost of the video.

Equation $\boxed{1.50}$ + $\boxed{\frac{v}{3}}$ = $\boxed{2.75}$

The correct answer is C. You can solve the equation to find the cost.

$$1.50 + \frac{v}{3} = 2.75$$

$1.50 - 1.50 + \frac{v}{3} = 2.75 - 1.50$ ← Subtract 1.50 from each side.

$\frac{v}{3} = 1.25$ ← Simplify.

$(3)\frac{v}{3} = (3)1.25$ ← Multiply each side by 3.

$v = 3.75$ ← Simplify.

The cost of renting the video is $3.75.

✓ Quick Check

2. **Telephone Bill** To make a long-distance call, it costs $.50 per call and $.85 per minute. You make a long-distance call that costs $3.90. Write and solve an equation to find the length of the call.

✓ **Check Your Understanding**

Write an equation for each model.

1.

2.

Write the first step in solving each equation.

3. $\frac{t}{-2} - 8 = 10$

4. $-5 = \frac{x}{2} - 5$

5. $4m - 12 = 0$

6. $7q + 9 = 3$

7. **Estimation** Use estimation to solve $10.67 + \frac{x}{1.95} = 38.9$.

For more exercises, see Extra Skills and Word Problems.

GO for Help

For Exercises	See Examples
8–13	1
14–18	2

Solve each equation. Check the solution.

8. $4x + 7 = 3$

9. $1 + 2g = -7$

10. $15 = 3y + 6$

11. $-6b + 10 = -14$

12. $23 + 8b = -4.2$

13. $17 + 2.6b = 30$

14. $7 + \dfrac{x}{4} = 3$

15. $17 + \dfrac{b}{26} = 30$

16. $15 = \dfrac{y}{3} + 6$

Write and solve an equation to answer each question. You may find a model helpful.

17. Leo ordered 4 CDs by mail. Each CD cost the same amount. With a $5 shipping charge, the total cost was $68.96. How much did each CD cost?

18. School Supplies Annamarie bought a notebook for $1.19 and pencils for $.39 each. The total cost was $3.92. How many pencils did she buy?

19. Guided Problem Solving A bag of rice costs $1.99. You buy 1 bag of rice and 6 cans of black beans for a total cost of $7.33. If you have $8.25, can you buy another can of beans? Explain.
- What equation can you use to find c, the cost of a can of beans?
- Knowing c, how can you determine whether you have enough money for another can of beans?

20. Error Analysis Which student's work is correct? Explain.

Wendy

$$-20 = \dfrac{x}{2} + 7$$

$$-20 - 7 = \dfrac{x}{2} + 7 - 7$$

$$(2)(-27) = (2)\left(\dfrac{x}{2}\right)$$

$$-54 = x$$

Ben

$$-20 = \dfrac{x}{2} + 7$$

$$(2)(-20) = \left(\dfrac{x}{2} + 7\right)(2)$$

$$-40 - 7 = x + 7 - 7$$

$$-47 = x$$

GO Online
Homework Video Tutor
Visit: PHSchool.com
Web Code: ase-0601

21. Nutrition According to the Food and Drug Administration, the recommended daily intake of iron is 18 mg. This is 4 less than twice the recommended daily intake of zinc. What is the recommended daily intake of zinc?

22. Estimation Use estimation to check whether 24.27 is a reasonable solution for $6p + 39.95 = 105.65$. Show your work.

23. Solve $7b + 3 = 24$. Justify your steps.

Solve each equation.

24. $\frac{y}{3} - 9 = 30$ **25.** $\frac{n}{1.4} + 1 = 10$ **26.** $-8.2 + \frac{t}{-2} = 1.7$

27. $12 = -6 - 3v$ **28.** $1.2 = 3s - 1.8$ **29.** $10 = 3q - 2.6$

30. a. Jobs Two students want to save $200 each. One student starts with $60 and rakes leaves for $6 per hour. The other student starts with nothing but earns $9 per hour painting houses. Let x represent the number of hours worked. Write and solve two equations to find the number of hours each student will have to work.

  b. Writing in Math Explain why one of the equations from part (a) is a one-step equation and the other is a two-step equation.

31. Challenge Multiply each side of the equation $0.5x + 1.3 = 4.8$ by 10 and solve for x. How does this solution compare to the solution to the original equation? Explain why it is helpful to multiply by 10.

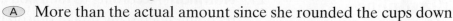

Test Prep and Mixed Review

Practice

Multiple Choice

32. This year, 227 pets were adopted from a shelter. This is 35 fewer than twice the number that were adopted last year. Which equation can you use to find the number of pets adopted last year?

  Ⓐ $n = \frac{227 + 35}{2}$ Ⓒ $n = \frac{227 - 35}{2}$

  Ⓑ $n = 2(227) - 35$ Ⓓ $n = 2(227) + 35$

33. A town's youth soccer teams play on fields as shown in the diagrams at the right. The two fields are similar. If the area of the field for players under 10 years old is 2,400 yd², what is the area of the field for players under 8 years old?

  Ⓕ $1,200$ yd² Ⓗ 600 yd²

  Ⓖ 800 yd² Ⓙ 300 yd²

20 yd

40 yd

Under 8   Under 10

34. A recipe calls for $1\frac{3}{4}$ cups of flour. Sabrina is increasing the recipe by $2\frac{1}{2}$ times. She estimates that she'll need 5 cups of flour. Which of the following best describes her estimate?

  Ⓐ More than the actual amount since she rounded the cups down

  Ⓑ More than the actual amount since she rounded the cups up

  Ⓒ Less than the actual amount since she rounded the cups up

  Ⓓ Less than the actual amount since she rounded the cups down

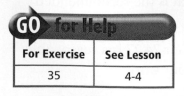

For Exercise	See Lesson
35	4-4

35. Rectangles *ABCD* and *PQRS* are similar. *ABCD* is 4 m long and 9.5 m wide. The length of *PQRS* is 9.6 m. How wide is *PQRS*?

Modeling Expressions

Two students from Garth School bicycled to a game. Three buses of students also went to the game. From Greenly School, four students on bicycles and two buses went to the game. Each bus carried the same number of students. You can model this situation with tiles.

Let represent x, the number of students on a bus.

Let represent a student arriving by bicycle.

The tiles below model the total number of students at the game.

Garth School   Greenly School

Exercises

1. Write two algebraic expressions, one for the number of students from Garth School who went to the game and one for the number of students from Greenly School who went to the game.

2. **a.** How many buses were there in all at the game?
   b. How many students rode bicycles to the game?

3. Use your answers to Exercise 2 to write an algebraic expression that represents the total number of students from the two schools who went to the game.

4. **Reasoning** How are your algebraic expressions in Exercise 1 related to your algebraic expression in Exercise 3?

Copy and complete the algebraic expression for each group of tiles.

5.  $\rightarrow$ ■ $x + 4$

6.  $\rightarrow$ ■ x + ■

7. A student wrote the equation $3x + 2 + 5x + 1 = ■x + 3$. What number should the student use to fill in the blank? Justify your reasoning.

6-2 Simplifying Algebraic Expressions

Check Skills You'll Need

1. **Vocabulary Review**
Is the expression
$5 + 3a - 15$
simplified? Explain.

Simplify each
expression.

2. $-8(r + 3)$

3. $-7(s - 5)$

4. $35(2 - t)$

 **for Help**
Lesson 1-5

What You'll Learn

To combine like terms and to simplify algebraic expressions

New Vocabulary term, like terms

Why Learn This?

Some calculations, such as finding the cost of several items, involve more than one variable. Simplifying expressions first can make calculations easier.

An expression may have one or more terms. A **term** is a number, a variable, or the product of a number and one or more variables. **Like terms** are terms that have exactly the same variable factors.

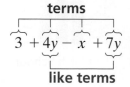

Like Terms	Not Like Terms
-5 and 8	$-5x$ and 8
$2x$ and $-3x$	$2x$ and $-3y$
$2x^2$ and $-3x^2$	$2x^2$ and $-3x$
$2xy$ and $-3xy$	$2x$ and $-3xy$

Vocabulary Tip

Expressions with only integers are always like terms.

Often a variable does not have a number in front of it. In this case, there is an *understood* "1" in front of the variable. For example, b is the same as $1b$ and $-a$ is the same as $-1a$.

When you add or subtract like terms, you are combining like terms.

EXAMPLE Combining Like Terms

1. Combine like terms in the expression $5m + 9m + m$.

$$5m + 9m + m = 5m + 9m + 1m \quad \leftarrow \text{Rewrite } m \text{ as 1m.}$$
$$= (5 + 9 + 1)m \quad \leftarrow \text{Distributive Property}$$
$$= 15m \quad \leftarrow \text{Combine like terms by adding.}$$

Quick Check

1. Combine like terms in the expression $2t + t - 17t$.

When defining variables, it is often helpful to choose letters that remind you of what the variables represent.

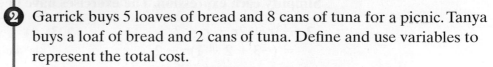 **EXAMPLE** **Application: Picnics**

2 Garrick buys 5 loaves of bread and 8 cans of tuna for a picnic. Tanya buys a loaf of bread and 2 cans of tuna. Define and use variables to represent the total cost.

Words	Garrick:	cost of 5 loaves	plus	cost of 8 cans

Let b = the cost of a loaf of bread.
Let t = the cost a can of tuna.

Expression $5b$ + $8t$

Words	Tanya:	cost of 1 loaf	plus	cost of 2 cans

Expression b + $2t$

Combined Expression $(5b + 8t) + (b + 2t)$

$$(5b + 8t) + (b + 2t) = 5b + b + 8t + 2t \qquad \leftarrow \text{Commutative Property of Addition}$$
$$= (5 + 1)b + (8 + 2)t \qquad \leftarrow \text{Distributive Property}$$
$$= 6b + 10t \qquad \leftarrow \text{Simplify.}$$

✓ Quick Check

2. In one trip to a hardware store, you buy 16 boards, 2 boxes of nails, and a hammer. On a second trip, you buy 10 more boards and a box of nails. Define and use variables to represent the total cost.

When you use the Distributive Property with subtraction, remember to distribute the negative sign.

EXAMPLE **Distributing and Simplifying**

3 Simplify $8c - 3(c + 5)$.

$$8c - 3(c + 5) = 8c + (-3)(c + 5) \qquad \leftarrow \text{Add the opposite of } 3(c + 5).$$
$$= 8c + [-3c + (-15)] \qquad \leftarrow \text{Distributive Property}$$
$$= 8c + (-3c) - 15 \qquad \leftarrow \text{Simplify.}$$
$$= [8 + (-3)]c - 15 \qquad \leftarrow \text{Distributive Property}$$
$$= 5c - 15 \qquad \leftarrow \text{Simplify.}$$

Video Tutor Help
Visit: PHSchool.com
Web Code: ase-0775

✓ Quick Check

3. Simplify the expression $11 - 2(3b + 1)$.

1. **Vocabulary** Are $3x^2y^5z^{11}$ and $5x^2z^5y^{11}$ like terms? Explain.

Simplify each expression. The exercises have been started for you.

2. $-3r + 2r + r - 2$
   $= (-3 + 2 + 1)r - 2$

3. $4x - 2 + 6y + y - 4$
   $= 4x + 6y + y - 4 - 2$

4. $9m + 2(2 + n)$
   $= 9m + 4 + 2n$

5. $3a + 5(3 + a)$
   $= 3a + 15 + 5a$

6. **Mental Math** Combine like terms in the expression $1.3a + 2.4a$.

Homework Exercises

For more exercises, see Extra Skills and Word Problems.

Combine like terms.

GO for Help

For Exercises	See Examples
7–15	1
16–22	2
23–28	3

7. $8b + 3b$

8. $9r + 22r$

9. $34x - 3x$

10. $19z - 24z + 6z$

11. $-25t + 21t - 7t$

12. $-13b - 17b + 32b$

13. $-6a + a + 28a$

14. $19t - t + 6t$

15. $j - 4j - 15j$

Simplify each expression.

16. $3a + 2 + a$

17. $2x + 1 + 3x$

18. $n + 4n - 3$

19. $5n - 6r + 4n + 3r$

20. $2z - 3y - 8z + y$

21. $9 - 7t + 1 + 4t$

22. **Clothing** For the summer, Tia buys 3 T-shirts and 2 pairs of shorts. Her brother buys 4 T-shirts and 1 pair of shorts. Define and use variables to represent the total cost.

Simplify each expression.

23. $3 - 5(a - 4)$

24. $7(t + 8.5) - 5t + 4$

25. $-8(m + 2) - 19m$

26. $4.3(5.6 + c) + 9c$

27. $-5b - 2(b - 1)$

28. $16b - 4(c + 3) - 4b$

GPS 29. **Guided Problem Solving** On Saturday, Simone drove to the mall and back home. Then she drove 10 miles to a flea market and back. On Sunday, she made 2 trips from home to the mall. Define and use a variable to represent the total distance Simone traveled.
   - Draw a diagram showing the trips between the mall, the flea market, and home.
   - What quantity do you need to represent with a variable?

30. **Party Planning** You buy 6 lb of sliced turkey, 3 lb of cole slaw, and 4 lb of cheese for a party. Then you invite more people to the party, so you buy another 4 lb of turkey, 2 lb of cole slaw, and 3 lb of cheese. Define and use variables to represent the total cost.

31. On a shopping trip, Kelly buys 3 barrettes and a headband. Her sister buys 2 barrettes and 2 headbands. Define and use variables to represent the total cost.

Simplify each expression.

32. $7b + 5 - 9b + c$

33. $x + 2(x - y)$

34. $-5u + 6 + u + 4u$

35. $(5x + y) - (4x - 9)$

36. $3(t - 14) - 5(t + 12)$

37. $33.7y + 8.4 - 2.04y$

38. $9(a + 1.4b) + 8(b - 16a)$

39. $4.2x + 8.1x + 1.8x - 2.1x$

40. **Writing in Math** One way to organize a CD collection is by categories of music. Explain how combining like terms is similar to organizing a CD collection by categories.

41. **Open-Ended** Write two different expressions that can be simplified to $3m + 8$. One expression should have three terms, and the other should have four terms.

42. **Reasoning** Does $5a + 5b = 10ab$? Explain.

43. **Challenge** Simplify the expression $2.5(2t - 8v) - 3(3v + 1.5t)$.

Test Prep and Mixed Review

Practice

Multiple Choice

44. The scale factor between two squares is 7. The area of the smaller square is 4 in.^{2}. What is the area of the larger square?
    - Ⓐ 28 in.^{2}
    - Ⓒ 196 in.^{2}
    - Ⓑ 112 in.^{2}
    - Ⓓ 784 in.^{2}

45. Members of the Sylvester family are riding their bikes to a friend's house 20 miles away. If their average speed is 8 miles per hour, how long will they take to reach their destination? [$d = rt$]
    - Ⓕ 2 h
    - Ⓖ 2.5 h
    - Ⓗ 5 h
    - Ⓙ 10 h

46. A square has one vertex at $(0, 3)$ on a coordinate grid. If the square is translated 3 units up and 2 units to the left, what are the new coordinates of this vertex?
    - Ⓐ $(5, 8)$
    - Ⓑ $(2, 6)$
    - Ⓒ $(-2, 0)$
    - Ⓓ $(-2, 6)$

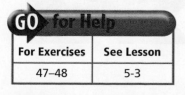

GO for Help

For Exercises	See Lesson
47–48	5-3

Use a proportion to solve each problem.

47. 16 is 80% of what number?

48. What percent of 250 is 160?

Solve each equation.

1. $-7 + 2q = 4$

2. $16 = -2v + 34$

3. $-9 = 3b - 12$

4. $2x + 5 = 11$

5. $49 = 5y - 26$

6. $\frac{m}{-2} + 7 = 21$

7. $\frac{-3.4}{p} = -0.06$

8. $-15 = \frac{z}{2.05} - 2$

9. $-5 = 3a + 4$

10. **Flowers** You buy 6 roses for $2.45 each, 12 carnations for $.99 each, and 9 tulips. Your total cost is $40.08. How much does each tulip cost?

Simplify each expression.

11. $-3m + 4 - 5m + p$

12. $1.7(g - 0.5) - 6.4(-g + 2)$

13. $2h - 4(h - 5)$

14. $-k - 11(-k - 0.01)$

15. $2.9(1.1j - 6.3) - 8j$

16. $28 - 10(a - 14) + 7a$

17. **Camping** You purchase 6 sleeping bags and 4 flashlights for a camping trip. Then you find out that more people are coming on the trip, so you buy 5 more sleeping bags and 3 more flashlights. Define and use variables to represent the total cost.

MATH AT WORK

Research Scientist

Research scientists work in many different areas, such as agriculture, biotechnology, chemical and nuclear technology, manufacturing, and forensic science. They make observations, calculate and record results, and interpret graphs and statistics.

Sometimes research scientists work outside the laboratory, researching plants and animals in their natural habitats. The research may lead to the development of new products and technologies.

Go Online
PHSchool.com
For: Information on Research Scientists
Web Code: asb-2031

6-3 Solving Multi-Step Equations

Check Skills You'll Need

1. Vocabulary Review Identify the *like terms* in $3x + 2x + 8 - x$.

Simplify.

2. $5 - 3m + 7 - 23m$

3. $4(7 - 3r)$

4. $(q + 1)5 + 3q$

GO for Help
Lesson 6-2

What You'll Learn

To write and solve multi-step equations

Why Learn This?

You can model many situations with one- and two-step equations. More complicated situations, such as finding the cost of multiple items, involve multiple steps.

You often need to simplify at least one side of an equation before solving it. To simplify, you combine like terms.

EXAMPLE **Simplifying Before Solving an Equation**

1 Solve $3n + 9 + 4n = 2$.

$3n + 9 + 4n = 2$

$3n + 4n + 9 = 2$ ← Commutative Property

$7n + 9 = 2$ ← Combine like terms.

$7n + 9 - 9 = 2 - 9$ ← Subtract 9 from each side.

$7n = -7$ ← Simplify.

$\dfrac{7n}{7} = \dfrac{-7}{7}$ ← Divide each side by 7.

$n = -1$ ← Simplify.

Check $3n + 9 + 4n = 2$

$3(-1) + 9 + 4(-1) \stackrel{?}{=} 2$ ← Substitute –1 for *n*.

$2 = 2$ ✔ ← The solution checks.

GO for Help

For help combining like terms, see Lesson 6-2, Example 1.

Quick Check

1. Solve $-15 = 5b + 12 - 2b + 6$. Check the solution.

You can use the Distributive Property to simplify an equation.

6-3 Solving Multi-Step Equations **271**

EXAMPLE **Using the Distributive Property**

② **Multiple Choice** Your class hopes to collect 1,200 returnable bottles to raise money for a class trip. During the first week, the 24 students in your class collect an average of 34 bottles each. How many more bottles per student should the class collect?

   Ⓐ 11 bottles   Ⓑ 16 bottles   Ⓒ 49 bottles   Ⓓ 384 bottles

Words 24 students $\cdot \left(\dfrac{34 \text{ bottles}}{\text{per student}} + \dfrac{\text{additional}}{\text{bottles per}}_{\text{student}} \right) = \dfrac{1,200 \text{ bottles}}{\text{per student}}$

Equation Let r = the number of additional bottles.

$$24 \quad \cdot \quad (34 \quad + \quad r) \quad = \quad 1,200$$

$$24(34 + r) = 1,200$$
$$816 + 24r = 1,200 \quad \leftarrow \textbf{Distributive Property}$$
$$816 - 816 + 24r = 1,200 - 816 \quad \leftarrow \textbf{Subtract 816 from each side.}$$
$$24r = 384 \quad \leftarrow \textbf{Simplify.}$$
$$\frac{24r}{24} = \frac{384}{24} \quad \leftarrow \textbf{Divide each side by 24.}$$
$$r = 16 \quad \leftarrow \textbf{Simplify.}$$

Each student should collect 16 more bottles. The correct answer is choice B.

Check for Reasonableness Round 24 to 20 and 34 to 40. The class collected about 20 · 40, or 800 bottles. They need to collect 400 more, or 20 bottles per student. 16 is close to 20. The answer is reasonable.

Test Prep Tip

Be sure to answer the question asked. You need to find the number of bottles each student collects, not the total number.

✓ Quick Check

2. **Class Trips** Your class goes to an amusement park. Admission is $10 for each student and $15 for each chaperone. The total cost is $380. There are 12 girls in your class and 6 chaperones on the trip. How many boys are in your class?

You can also use division to simplify equations. The algebra tiles below model one way to simplify the equation $2(x + 1) = 12$. First, divide each side by 2, grouping the tiles into two equal groups. Then, remove one group from each side. The simplified equation is $x + 1 = 6$.

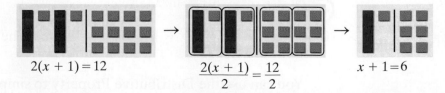

$2(x + 1) = 12 \qquad \dfrac{2(x + 1)}{2} = \dfrac{12}{2} \qquad x + 1 = 6$

● More Than One Way

Solve the equation $5(2.9 + k) = 8.3$.

Eric's Method

I'll use the Distributive Property to eliminate the parentheses.

$$5(2.9 + k) = 8.3$$
$$5(2.9) + 5k = 8.3 \quad \leftarrow \text{Distributive Property}$$
$$14.5 + 5k = 8.3 \quad \leftarrow \text{Simplify.}$$
$$14.5 - 14.5 + 5k = 8.3 - 14.5 \quad \leftarrow \text{Subtract 14.5 from each side.}$$
$$5k = -6.2 \quad \leftarrow \text{Simplify.}$$
$$\frac{5k}{5} = \frac{-6.2}{5} \quad \leftarrow \text{Divide each side by 5.}$$
$$k = -1.24 \quad \leftarrow \text{Simplify.}$$

Jasmine's Method

I'll use division to eliminate the parentheses.

$$5(2.9 + k) = 8.3$$
$$\frac{5(2.9 - k)}{5} = \frac{8.3}{5} \quad \leftarrow \text{Divide each side by 5.}$$
$$2.9 + k = 1.66 \quad \leftarrow \text{Simplify.}$$
$$2.9 - 2.9 + k = 1.66 - 2.9 \quad \leftarrow \text{Subtract 2.9 from each side.}$$
$$k = -1.24 \quad \leftarrow \text{Simplify.}$$

Choose a Method
Solve $3(m - 6.5) = 27$. Explain why you chose the method you used.

✓ Check Your Understanding

1. **Vocabulary** When you simplify an expression, you combine
   __?__ terms.

2. Describe the first step in simplifying the expression $2h - 4(h - 5)$.

Match each equation to the correct solution.

3. $-7 + x = 4$

4. $16 = -2x$

5. $-9 = x - 12$

A. -8
B. 3
C. 11

For more exercises, see Extra Skills and Word Problems.

Solve each equation. Check the solution.

For Exercises	See Examples
6–13	1
14–20	2

6. $5h + 2 - h = 22$

7. $-8 = z + 3z$

8. $3b + b - 8 = 4$

9. $3a + 12 - 6a = -9$

10. $21 = 6 - x - 4x$

11. $2m + 8 - 4m = 28$

12. $-3y + 4 + 5y = -6$

13. $78 = 3c + 12 - c + 4$

14. $4(m + 3) = -32$

15. $14 = 2(s + 5)$

16. $40 = 5(d - 2)$

17. $2(z - 1) = 16$

18. $-2(x - 9) = -24$

19. $7(4 - t) = -84$

20. **Food** You want to buy 4 lb of Cortland apples and some Gala apples. Each variety of apple costs \$1.20/lb. You can spend \$7.20. How many pounds of Gala apples can you buy?

21. **Guided Problem Solving** You mailed 3 identical letters weighing more than 1 oz each. Mailing each letter cost \$.39 for the first ounce, plus \$.24 for each additional ounce. Each letter required \$1.59 postage. How much did each letter weigh, to the nearest ounce?
- **Make a Plan** Write and solve an equation to solve for x, the number of additional ounces.
- **Check the Answer** Be sure you answer the question asked.

22. **Jobs** An employee earns \$7.00 an hour for the first 35 hours worked in a week and \$10.50 for any hours over 35. One week's paycheck (before deductions) was for \$308.00. How many hours did the employee work?

GO Online
Homework Video Tutor
Visit: PHSchool.com
Web Code: ase-0603

Use this information to write an equation for Exercises 23–25. When you count by ones from any integer, you are counting consecutive integers. Using variables, three consecutive integers are n, $n + 1$, and $n + 2$.

23. The sum of two consecutive integers is -45. What are they?

24. The sum of three consecutive integers is 48. What are they?

25. The sum of three consecutive integers is -255. What are they?

26. **Writing in Math** To solve $5y - 2 - 3y = 8$, can you start by adding 2 to each side? Justify your reasoning.

Solve each equation.

27. $15 = -3(c - 1) + 9$

28. $2(1.5n + 4) - 6n = -7$

29. $2(z - 20) + 3z = 10$

30. $5s - 2 + 3(s - 11) = 5$

Write an equation for each diagram. Then find the unknown lengths.

31.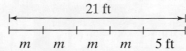

21 ft

| m | m | m | m | 5 ft |

32.

1,000 in.

| y | $2y$ | 505 in. |

33. Choose a Method To make peanut butter and jelly sandwiches for her class, a teacher bought bread for $2.79 per loaf, peanut butter for $3.19 per jar, and jars of jelly. The total cost was $14.56. If the teacher bought two of each item, what was the cost of one jar of jelly? Explain why you chose the method you used.

34. Challenge Solve $1.5 - 0.25(a + 4) = 3 + 3(0.05 - 0.5a)$.

Test Prep and Mixed Review
Practice

Multiple Choice

35. Two classes went to the zoo for $5 per person. The total cost was $200. One class has 19 people. Solve the equation $5(n + 19) = 200$ to find n, the number of people in the other class.

Ⓐ 105   Ⓑ 36   Ⓒ 21   Ⓓ 10

36. An interior designer researched prices and compiled the following data for a particular type of fabric. Which store's prices are based on a constant unit price?

Ⓕ **Materials Unlimited**

Yards	Total Price
2	$10
4	$18
6	$27
8	$32

Ⓗ **The Fab Store**

Yards	Total Price
2	$9
4	$18
6	$27
8	$36

Ⓖ **Haley's Fabric**

Yards	Total Price
2	$8
4	$18
6	$28
8	$38

Ⓙ **We R Fabric**

Yards	Total Price
2	$10
4	$18
6	$27
8	$35

37. Based on her batting average, the probability that Maggie will get a hit in softball is 5 out of 12. Which of the following expresses this probability as a percent?

Ⓐ 2.4%   Ⓑ 29.4%   Ⓒ 41.7%   Ⓓ 70.6%

GO for Help

For Exercises	See Lesson
38–40	6-1

Algebra Solve each equation.

38. $\frac{n}{4} - 1 = 10$ **39.** $\frac{x}{-5} - 7 = 8$ **40.** $\frac{a}{8} + 12 = -4$

6-4 Solving Equations With Variables on Both Sides

Check Skills You'll Need

1. **Vocabulary Review** Operations that undo each other are called __?__.

Simplify.

2. $9(t + 7) - 16$
3. $12 - 6(2r - 8)$
4. $2x - (5x + 7)$.

for Help
Lesson 6-2

What You'll Learn

To write and solve equations with variables on both sides

Why Learn This?

Equations can help you calculate your savings from part-time jobs. An equation shows that two expressions are equal. Because expressions can contain variables, some equations have variables on both sides of the equal sign.

To solve an equation with variables on both sides, bring all the variable terms to one side of the equation.

EXAMPLE Variables on Both Sides

1 Solve $7 + 3h = -1 - 5h$.

$$7 + 3h = -1 - 5h$$
$$7 + 3h + 5h = -1 - 5h + 5h \quad \leftarrow \text{Add 5h to each side.}$$
$$7 + 8h = -1 \quad \leftarrow \text{Combine like terms.}$$
$$7 - 7 + 8h = -1 - 7 \quad \leftarrow \text{Subtract 7 from each side.}$$
$$8h = -8 \quad \leftarrow \text{Simplify.}$$
$$\frac{8h}{8} = \frac{-8}{8} \quad \leftarrow \text{Divide each side by 8.}$$
$$h = -1 \quad \leftarrow \text{Simplify.}$$

Check $7 + 3h = -1 - 5h$
$$7 + 3(-1) \stackrel{?}{=} -1 - 5(-1) \quad \leftarrow \text{Substitute -1 for h.}$$
$$4 = 4 ✔ \quad \leftarrow \text{The solution checks.}$$

Quick Check

1. Solve $7b - 2 = b + 10$. Check the solution.

You may need to use the Distributive Property to simplify an equation before you can bring the variable terms to one side.

EXAMPLE **Using the Distributive Property**

② **Gridded Response** Your science class is doing an experiment. You start with 2 plants. Plant A is 5 cm tall and Plant B is 8 cm tall. Plant A is fertilized and grows 2 cm per day. Plant B is not fertilized and grows 1.5 cm per day. Predict in how many days the plants will be the same height.

Words 5 + 2 cm · number of days = 8 + 1.5 cm · number of days

 Let d = the number of days.

Equation 5 + 2 · d = 8 + 1.5 · d

$$5 + 2d = 8 + 1.5d$$
$$5 + 2d - 2d = 8 + 1.5d - 2d \quad \leftarrow \text{Subtract } 2d \text{ from each side.}$$
$$5 = 8 - 0.5d \quad \leftarrow \text{Simplify.}$$
$$5 - 8 = 8 - 8 - 0.5d \quad \leftarrow \text{Subtract 8 from each side.}$$
$$-3 = -0.5d \quad \leftarrow \text{Simplify.}$$
$$\frac{-3}{-0.5} = \frac{-0.5d}{-0.5} \quad \leftarrow \text{Divide each side by } -0.5.$$
$$6 = d \quad \leftarrow \text{Simplify.}$$

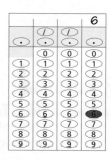

The plants will be the same height in 6 days.

Test Prep Tip

You can also solve the equation at the right by moving all of the variables to the left side.

✓ Quick Check

2. One cell phone plan costs $29.94 per month plus $.10 for each text message sent. Another plan costs $32.99 per month plus $.05 for each text message sent. For what number of text messages will the monthly bill for both plans be the same?

✓ Check Your Understanding

Identify the like terms in each group of expressions.

1. $-\frac{7}{9}, -2.8, 3, 0$

2. xy, x, y, yx

3. $11a, -4.1a^2, a, a^2$

4. Is 7 a solution of the equation $3x + 8 - x = 5x - 4$?

5. **Error Analysis** A student solved an equation as shown at the left. Explain the error the student made. Solve the equation correctly.

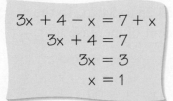

6. **Mental Math** Is the solution of $2x = 3x - 12 - 5x$ a positive or a negative integer? Explain.

For more exercises, see Extra Skills and Word Problems.

GO for Help

For Exercises	See Examples
7–15	1–2

Solve each equation. Check the solution.

7. $2 + 14z = -8 + 9z$

8. $-8 - 5y = 12 - 9y$

9. $22 + 2x = 37 + 6 + x$

10. $6d + 1 = 15 - d$

11. $-k = 9(k - 10)$

12. $7m = 9(m + 4)$

13. $8(4 - a) = 2a$

14. $8 - 3(p - 4) = 2p$

15. At Video Shack, movie rentals cost $3.99 each. The cost of renting three movies and one video game is $.11 less than the cost of renting five video games. How much does renting a video game cost?

16. Guided Problem Solving A croquet ball weighs 460 grams. Together a golf ball and a croquet ball weigh the same as 11 golf balls. How much does one golf ball weigh?
- What quantity will you represent with a variable?
- Write and solve an equation.

17. Efren leaves home at 9 A.M. and walks 4 miles per hour. His brother, Gregory, leaves half an hour later and runs 8.5 miles per hour in the same direction as Efren. Predict the time at which Gregory will catch up to Efren.

GO Online

Homework Video Tutor
Visit: PHSchool.com
Web Code: ase-0604

18. Writing in Math Explain how to solve an equation with the same variable on both sides.

19. Challenge Solve $0.75 + 2(x - 0.5) = 3x - 0.4$.

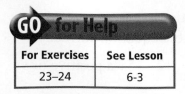# Test Prep and Mixed Review

Practice

Gridded Response

20. The side of a square is $2x + 8$ inches long. The perimeter of the square is $20x + 8$ inches. What is the side length of the square in inches?

21. The trapezoids shown at the right are similar. What scale factor was used to dilate trapezoid *FGHJ* to trapezoid *LMNP*?

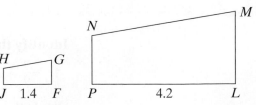

22. The federal minimum wage once rose from $4.25 to $4.75. To the nearest tenth of a percent, what was the percent of increase?

GO for Help

For Exercises	See Lesson
23–24	6-3

Algebra Solve each equation.

23. $6q + 3 - 4q = 9$

24. $7(x + 1) - 1 = 34$

Writing Equations

Ticket Prices Mr. and Mrs. Smith have two children, ages 4 and 8. They are trying to decide whether to buy day passes or a yearly membership to an aquarium. With how many single-day visits would it be better for the Smiths to have a yearly membership?

Aquarium Ticket Prices

Single-Day Tickets

Adults $21.95
Children $10.95

Yearly Membership

Unlimited visits for
2 adults and
2 children (3–12) $175

What You Might Think

What do I know? What do I want to find out?

What equation can I write?

When will the cost of single-day tickets equal the cost of a yearly membership?

Is the answer reasonable?

What You Might Write

I know single-day tickets are $21.95 for adults and $10.95 for children.
Two adult tickets → 2 × $21.95 = $43.90.
Two child tickets → 2 × $10.95 = $21.90.
A yearly membership is $175. I want to find when a yearly membership would be less expensive.

Let d = the number of visits. Then the total cost of d visits is $43.90d + 21.90d$.

$$43.90d + 21.90d = 175$$
$$65.80d = 175$$
$$d \approx 2.66$$

Since you cannot have 2.66 visits, round the answer up to 3. So for three or more visits it would be better to have the yearly membership.

The cost for single-day tickets is about $40 + $20 or $60. 3 × $60 = $180. So 3 visits is a reasonable answer.

Think It Through

1. **Reasoning** Can an answer to this problem be 2 visits? Explain.

2. Can you use the following equation to solve this problem? Explain.
   $21.95d + 21.95d + 10.95d + 10.95d = 175$

Exercises

Solve each problem. For Exercises 3 and 4, answer parts (a) and (b) first.

3. The cost of a membership at a health club last year was 75% of the cost at the club this year. This year's membership costs $20 more than last year's membership. Find the cost of a membership last year and the cost of a membership this year.
   a. Let x = the cost of last year's membership. Then $x + 20$ = the cost of this year's membership.
   b. Represent the cost of last year's membership as $0.75(x + 20)$. To find the value of x, solve $x = 0.75(x + 20)$.

4. A camp counselor buys granola bars and juice drinks for the campers. She decides to buy 3 times as many drinks as granola bars. Predict how many of each she can buy on a budget of $24.

   a. Let x = the number of granola bars the counselor buys and let $3x$ = the number of juice drinks she buys. What is the cost of x granola bars? The cost of $3x$ juice drinks?
   b. Use your answers to part (a) to write and solve an equation to find how many of each the camp leader can buy.

5. In a random survey of adults and children, children were found to have 23% more snacks between meals each year than adults. Altogether, the adults and children in this survey had 3,000 snacks between meals in one year. About how many snacks did the children in this survey have in one year? (*Hint:* Let x = the number of between-meal snacks the adults in this survey had in one year.)

6-5a Activity Lab

Graphing Inequalities

An *inequality* is a mathematical sentence that contains
<, >, ≤, ≥, or ≠. The **graph of an inequality**
shows all the solutions that satisfy the inequality.

Inequality	Graph	Word Sentence
$x < 3$	⊕ open dot at 3, shaded left, 0 1 2 3 4	x is less than 3.
$x \leq 3$	● closed dot at 3, shaded left, 0 1 2 3 4	x is less than or equal to 3.
$x > 3$	⊕ open dot at 3, shaded right, 0 1 2 3 4	x is greater than 3.
$x \geq 3$	● closed dot at 3, shaded right, 0 1 2 3 4	x is greater than or equal to 3.
$x \neq 3$	⊕ open dot at 3, shaded both ways, 0 1 2 3 4	x is *not* equal to 3.

EXAMPLES Graphing Inequalities

1 Graph $x < 2$.

An open dot means 2 is *not* a solution.

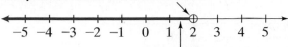

Shade the numbers less than 2.

2 Graph $-3 \leq x$.

A closed dot means -3 is a solution.

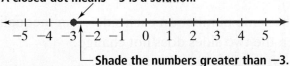

Shade the numbers greater than -3.

Exercises

Graph each inequality.

1. $x < -5$ **2.** $-4 \leq x$ **3.** $x > 1$ **4.** $0 \geq x$ **5.** $x \neq 2$

Write an inequality for each word sentence.

6. y is less than -4. **7.** p has a minimum of -5. **8.** k is no more than 7.

9. Reasoning Is 6 a possible value for w in the word sentence "w is
more than 6"? Explain.

6-5

Solving Inequalities by Adding or Subtracting

✓ Check Skills You'll Need

1. Vocabulary Review
An __?__ is a mathematical sentence with an equal sign.

Solve each equation.

2. $x + 15 = -3$

3. $y + 22 = 9$

4. $a - 28 = -4$

for Help

Lesson 1-6

What You'll Learn

To write and solve inequalities

🔊 **New Vocabulary** inequality, Addition Property of Inequality, Subtraction Property of Inequality

Why Learn This?

You can use inequalities to describe restrictions such as the maximum weight for luggage or the minimum height to ride a roller coaster. An **inequality** is a mathematical sentence that contains $<, \leq, >, \geq$, or $\neq$.

Some inequalities, such as $x < 3$ and $x \geq 3$, contain a variable. You can graph inequalities on number lines.

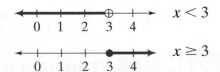

You can see from the number line below that if you add 2 to each side of the inequality $-5 \leq -1$, the resulting inequality, $-3 \leq 1$, is also true.

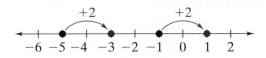

KEY CONCEPTS   Addition and Subtraction Properties of Inequalities

If you add or subtract the same number on each side of an inequality, the relationship between the two sides does not change.

Arithmetic	Algebra
$8 < 12$, so $8 + 3 < 12 + 3$, and $8 - 4 < 12 - 4$.	If $a < b$, then $a + c < b + c$, and $a - c < b - c$.
$10 > 7$, so $10 + 5 > 7 + 5$, and $10 - 2 > 7 - 2$.	If $a > b$, then $a + c > b + c$, and $a - c > b - c$.

Vocabulary Tip

You can think of the $\geq$ symbol as $>$ and $=$ combined. You can think of the $\leq$ symbol as $<$ and $=$ combined.

You solve an inequality involving addition or subtraction by using inverse operations to isolate the variable. An inequality sometimes has an infinite number of solutions, making it impossible to check them all. Instead, check your computations and the direction of the inequality symbol.

EXAMPLE Solving Inequalities by Adding

1 Solve $q - 7 < -2$. Graph the solutions.

$$q - 7 < -2$$
$$q - 7 + 7 < -2 + 7 \quad \leftarrow \text{ Isolate the variable. Use the Addition Property of Inequality.}$$
$$q < 5 \quad \leftarrow \text{ Simplify.}$$

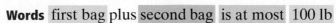

$$\xleftarrow{\qquad} \quad -3 \; -2 \; -1 \; \; 0 \; \; 1 \; \; 2 \; \; 3 \; \; 4 \; \; 5 \; \; 6 \; \; 7 \quad \xrightarrow{\qquad}$$

Check

Step 1 Check whether your answer is a solution to the related equation.

$$q - 7 = -2 \quad \leftarrow \text{ Write the related equation.}$$
$$5 - 7 \overset{?}{=} -2 \quad \leftarrow \text{ Substitute 5 for } q.$$
$$-2 = -2 \; \checkmark$$

Step 2 Check the inequality symbol by substituting into the inequality.

$$q - 7 < -2$$
$$4 - 7 < -2 \quad \leftarrow \text{ Substitute a number less than 5 for } q.$$
$$-3 < -2 \; \checkmark$$

Steps 1 and 2 both check, so $q < 5$ is the solution of $q - 7 < -2$.

✓ Quick Check

1. Solve $1 \leq u - 4$. Graph the solutions.

EXAMPLE Solving Inequalities by Subtracting

2 **Luggage** An airline restricts checked baggage to 100 lb per person. You pack one 39-lb bag. How much can your second bag weigh?

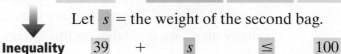

Words first bag plus second bag is at most 100 lb

Let s = the weight of the second bag.

Inequality $39 \quad + \quad s \quad \leq \quad 100$

$$39 + s \leq 100$$
$$39 + s - 39 \leq 100 - 39 \quad \leftarrow \text{ Isolate the variable. Use the Subtraction Property of Inequality.}$$
$$s \leq 61 \quad \leftarrow \text{ Simplify.}$$

Your second bag can weigh as much as 61 lb.

✓ Quick Check

2. A school auditorium has 300 seats. If 89 people have tickets for the school play, how many more people can attend?

1. **Vocabulary** What is the difference between an inequality and an equation? Explain.

Write an inequality for each word sentence.

2. n is at least -2.

3. 0.6 is no greater than x.

4. y minus 4 is greater than -4.

5. $y - 4$ is a negative number.

Write an inequality to represent each situation.

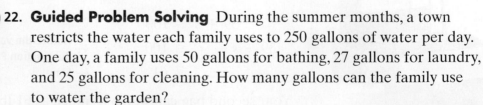

GENERAL ADMISSION	9.00
SENIOR CITIZENS	6.00
CHILDREN UNDER 12	6.00
BARGAIN MATINEE	6.00
GIFT CERTIFICATES	20.00

6. The ages of people who pay children's admissions.

7. People at least 65 years old receive a senior citizen discount.

Homework Exercises

For more exercises, see Extra Skills and Word Problems.

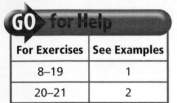

For Exercises	See Examples
8–19	1
20–21	2

Solve each inequality. Graph the solutions.

8. $x - 8 > 18$

9. $m - 1 < -3$

10. $a - 13 > 1$

11. $2 \le n - 5$

12. $-11 > w - 1$

13. $p - 12 < -12$

14. $x + 12 \ge 1$

15. $3 + t \le 1$

16. $m + 1 \ge 22$

17. $w + 1 < 2$

18. $5 + b \ge 1$

19. $u + 10 < 0$

Write and solve an inequality to answer each question.

20. Eighteen is subtracted from a number. The result is at least 5. What numbers are solutions?

21. **Electricity** You plug a microwave oven into a 20-ampere (amp) electrical circuit. The microwave uses as much as 12.5 amps. How many amps are available on this circuit for other appliances?

22. **Guided Problem Solving** During the summer months, a town restricts the water each family uses to 250 gallons of water per day. One day, a family uses 50 gallons for bathing, 27 gallons for laundry, and 25 gallons for cleaning. How many gallons can the family use to water the garden?
    - How much water is used for bathing, laundry, and cleaning?
    - Write and solve an inequality for the total water usage. Use a variable to represent the amount of water not used.

23. <u>Writing in Math</u> Describe how the solution of an inequality and the solution of an equation are alike. How are they different?

Write an inequality for each graph.

24.
$$\begin{array}{c} \longleftrightarrow\!\!+\!\!+\!\!\oplus\!\!+\!\!+\!\!+\!\!+\!\!\longrightarrow \\ -3\ -2\ -1\ \ 0\ \ 1\ \ 2\ \ 3 \end{array}$$

25.
$$\begin{array}{c} \longleftrightarrow\!\!+\!\!+\!\!+\!\!\bullet\!\!+\!\!+\!\!+\!\!+\!\!\longrightarrow \\ -3\ -2\ -1\ \ 0\ \ 1\ \ 2\ \ 3 \end{array}$$

26. Banking A bank offers free checking for accounts with a balance greater than $500. You have a balance of $516.46 and you write a check for $26.47. Write an inequality to represent how much you would need to deposit to have free checking.

Reasoning Write > or < to make each statement true.

27. If $x > y$ and $y > z$, then x ▇ z. **28.** If $a > b$, then b ▇ a.

Use the inequality $1.2 < x < 6.9$ to answer each question.

29. What is the greatest integer that is a solution of the inequality?

30. What is the least integer that is a solution of the inequality?

31. How many integers are solutions of the inequality?

32. Challenge Solve the inequality $2(y + a) - y > a$ for y.

 Test Prep and Mixed Review **Practice**

Multiple Choice

33. Anita has $15. She plans to save $6 a week. Which equation can she use to find w, the number of weeks it will take her to save $45?

Ⓐ $6(w + 15) = 45$ Ⓒ $\frac{w}{6} + 15 = 45$

Ⓑ $6w - 15 = 45$ Ⓓ $6w + 15 = 45$

34. Five European countries and their land areas are shown in the table. Which country's land area is 97,066 km² more than Sweden's land area?

Country	Area (km²)
Ukraine	603,700
France	547,030
Spain	504,750
Sweden	449,964
Germany	357,021

Ⓕ France   Ⓗ Spain
Ⓖ Germany   Ⓙ Ukraine

35. In two more years, 5 times Solana's age will be the age of her grandfather, who will be 60. Which equation can be used to find n, Solana's age now?

Ⓐ $5n - 2 = 60$ Ⓒ $5n + 2 = 60$

Ⓑ $5(n - 2) = 60$ Ⓓ $5(n + 2) = 60$

GO for Help

For Exercises	See Lesson
36–38	2-4

Find each sum or difference. Write your answer in simplest form.

36. $\frac{1}{5} + \frac{2}{9}$ **37.** $\frac{3}{4} - \frac{1}{3}$ **38.** $\frac{7}{11} + \frac{1}{2}$

Vocabulary Builder

High-Use Academic Words

High-use academic words are words that you will see often in textbooks and on tests. These words are not math vocabulary terms, but knowing them will help you to succeed in mathematics.

Direction Words

Some words tell what to do in a problem. I need to understand what these words are asking so that I give the correct answer.

Word	Meaning
Define	To show that you understand what a term means by giving an accurate meaning of it
Solve	To work out a solution to a problem
Combine	To join things together

Exercises

1. Define "jigsaw puzzle."

2. Solve the puzzle at the right by drawing the missing piece.

3. Copy the jigsaw pieces below. Combine them to make a picture.

4. Define "like terms."   5. Solve the equation $3x - 8 = 325$.

6. Combine like terms: $x + 2x + 3x + 4x + 5y - 4y + 3y - 2y$

7. **Word Knowledge** Think about the word *infinite*.
   a. Choose the letter for how well you know the word.
      A. I know its meaning.
      B. I've seen it, but I don't know its meaning.
      C. I don't know it.
   b. **Research** Look up and write the definition of *infinite*.
   c. Use the word in a sentence involving mathematics.

Checkpoint Quiz 2

Write an inequality for each graph.

1.
$$\begin{array}{cccccccc} -3 & -2 & -1 & 0 & 1 & 2 & 3 \end{array}$$

2.
$$\begin{array}{cccccccc} -3 & -2 & -1 & 0 & 1 & 2 & 3 \end{array}$$

Solve each equation or inequality.

3. $-3.5 - 4f = 10 - 2.5f$

4. $-z - (z - 6) = 8$

5. $\frac{m}{-2} + 7 = 21$

6. $a + 3.4 \geq -2.6$

7. $g + 1.5 \leq 2.5$

8. $y - (-1) < -22$

Write and solve an equation or inequality to answer each question. Round to the nearest hundredth, if necessary.

9. **Food** A pineapple costs $4.99. Together one banana and one pineapple cost the same as 13 bananas. What does one banana cost?

10. A truck weighs 28,500 lb. The total weight limit for the truck is 64,000 lb. What is the maximum load weight the truck can carry?

6-6a Activity Lab

Inequalities and Negative Numbers

ACTIVITY

1. **Mental Math** Simplify each side of each inequality at the right. Then replace each ■ with $<$, $=$, or $>$.

2. **a. Patterns** What happens to the direction of the inequality symbol as you multiply or divide each side by a positive number?
   b. What happens as you multiply or divide each side by a negative number?

3. **Reasoning** Suppose a is larger than b. What is the relationship between $2a$ and $2b$? $-2a$ and $-2b$?

$6(3) < 12(3)$	$\frac{6}{3} < \frac{12}{3}$
$6(2) \; ■ \; 12(2)$	$\frac{6}{2} \; ■ \; \frac{12}{2}$
$6(1) \; ■ \; 12(1)$	$\frac{6}{1} \; ■ \; \frac{12}{1}$
$6(0) \; ■ \; 12(0)$	
$6(-1) \; ■ \; 12(-1)$	$\frac{6}{-1} \; ■ \; \frac{12}{-1}$
$6(-2) \; ■ \; 12(-2)$	$\frac{6}{-2} \; ■ \; \frac{12}{-2}$
$6(-3) \; ■ \; 12(-3)$	$\frac{6}{-3} \; ■ \; \frac{12}{-3}$

Solving Inequalities by Multiplying or Dividing

Check Skills You'll Need

1. **Vocabulary Review** Is the definition "*Negative numbers* are numbers less than or equal to zero" correct? Explain.

Solve each equation.

2. $4x = -16$

3. $-8p = 808$

4. $-2u = -12.4$

5. $1 = \dfrac{t}{-8}$

for Help
Lesson 1-7

What You'll Learn

To write and solve inequalities using multiplication and division

 **New Vocabulary** Multiplication Property of Inequality, Division Property of Inequality

Why Learn This?

Suppose you want to find the minimum number of people needed for a project or the maximum number of hours for a trip. To solve these problems, you can use the properties of inequalities.

The number line below shows the effect of multiplying the inequality $-1 < 2$ by a positive number, 3.

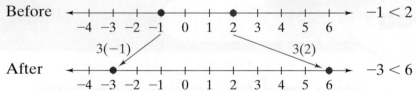

Before $\quad -1 < 2$

$3(-1) \qquad 3(2)$

After $\quad -3 < 6$

KEY CONCEPTS **Multiplication and Division Properties of Inequalities**

Using Positive Numbers to Multiply or Divide
When you multiply or divide each side of an inequality by a positive number, the relationship between the two sides does not change.

		Multiplication	**Division**
Arithmetic	$6 > 5,$	so $6(3) > 5(3)$	and $\dfrac{6}{2} > \dfrac{5}{2}$
	$4 < 10,$	so $4(5) < 10(5)$	and $\dfrac{4}{2} < \dfrac{10}{2}$
Algebra	If $a > b$ and $c > 0,$	then $ac > bc$	and $\dfrac{a}{c} > \dfrac{b}{c}$
	If $a < b$ and $c > 0,$	then $ac < bc$	and $\dfrac{a}{c} < \dfrac{b}{c}$

Note that these relationships are also true for $\leq$ and $\geq$.

Dividing by a Positive Number

1 **Business** An Internet service provider is advertising the special offer below. The company's goal is to make at least an additional $450,000. How many new customers must the company attract to meet its goal?

NEW CUSTOMER SPECIAL!
Unlimited Monthly Internet Access
@ only **$15** per month
Click for more information.

Words new customers times $15 is at least $450,000

⬇

Let n = the number of new customers.

Inequality n · 15 ≥ 450,000

$$15n \geq 450{,}000$$
$$\frac{15n}{15} \geq \frac{450{,}000}{15} \quad \leftarrow \text{Isolate the variable. Use the Division Property of Inequality.}$$
$$n \geq 30{,}000 \quad \leftarrow \text{Simplify.}$$

The company must attract at least 30,000 new customers.

Check for Reasonableness The answer makes sense because 30,000 · 15 is 450,000, and any number over 30,000 multiplied by 15 is a number greater than 450,000.

✔ Quick Check

1. A hotel elevator has a weight limit of 2,000 lb. Suppose the average weight of a passenger is 160 lb. How many passengers should the elevator safely hold?

The number line below shows the effect of multiplying an inequality by a negative number.

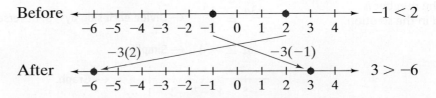

When the inequality $-1 < 2$ is multiplied by -3, the result is $3 > -6$. Notice that the direction of the inequality is reversed. The number lines suggest the following properties of inequalities.

KEY CONCEPTS **Multiplication and Division Properties of Inequalities**

Using Negative Numbers to Multiply or Divide

When you multiply or divide each side of an inequality by a negative number, *reverse* the direction of the inequality sign.

		Multiplication	**Division**
Arithmetic	$6 > 5,$	so $6 \cdot (-3) < 5 \cdot (-3)$	and $\frac{6}{-2} < \frac{5}{-2}$
	$4 < 10,$	so $4 \cdot (-5) > 10 \cdot (-5)$	and $\frac{4}{-2} > \frac{10}{-2}$
Algebra	If $a > b$ and $c < 0,$	then $ac < bc$	and $\frac{a}{c} < \frac{b}{c}$
	If $a < b$ and $c < 0,$	then $ac > bc$	and $\frac{a}{c} > \frac{b}{c}$

Note that these relationships are also true for $\leq$ and $\geq$.

EXAMPLE **Multiplying by a Negative Number**

2 Solve $\frac{x}{-2} < 1$. Graph the solutions.

$$\frac{x}{-2} < 1$$

$$-2 \cdot \left(\frac{x}{-2}\right) > -2 \cdot 1 \quad \leftarrow \begin{array}{l}\textbf{Multiply each side by } -2. \\ \textbf{Reverse the direction of the inequality.}\end{array}$$

$$x > -2 \quad \leftarrow \textbf{Simplify.}$$

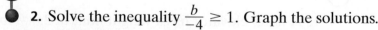 $\leftarrow$ **Graph.**

Quick Check

2. Solve the inequality $\frac{b}{-4} \geq 1$. Graph the solutions.

EXAMPLE **Dividing by a Negative Number**

3 Solve $-3a \leq 12$. Graph the solutions.

$$-3a \leq 12$$

$$\frac{-3a}{-3} \geq \frac{12}{-3} \quad \leftarrow \textbf{Divide each side by } -3. \textbf{ Reverse the direction of the inequality.}$$

$$a \geq -4 \quad \leftarrow \textbf{Simplify.}$$

$\leftarrow$ **Graph.**

Quick Check

3. Solve the inequality $-2p \geq 34$. Graph the solutions.

1. **Vocabulary** Explain how the Multiplication Property of Inequality differs for positive and negative numbers.

2. **Mental Math** Does the solution of $\frac{z}{-3} \geq 4$ include any positive numbers? Explain.

Solve each inequality. The exercises have been started for you.

3. $\frac{d}{3} > 4$

  $(3)\frac{d}{3} > 4(3)$

4. $2b < 8$

  $\frac{2b}{2} < \frac{8}{2}$

Homework Exercises

For more exercises, see Extra Skills and Word Problems.

For Exercises	See Examples
5–12	1
13–21	2–3

GO ▶ for Help

Solve each inequality.

5. $\frac{y}{2} > 0$

6. $-4 < \frac{r}{5}$

7. $5c < 10$

8. $4y \leq -20$

9. $6w \leq -54$

10. $-18 \leq \frac{x}{2}$

Write and solve an inequality to answer each question.

11. The luncheon special at Little Jimmy's costs $4.89. The math club has $23.50 in its treasury. How many luncheon specials can the club buy?

12. **Carpentry** A CD case is 0.375 in. thick. You are building a shelf 36 in. long. How many CD cases can you fit on the shelf?

Solve each inequality. Graph the solutions.

13. $\frac{r}{-2} \leq 3$

14. $\frac{m}{-2} > 0$

15. $\frac{z}{-12} \leq -8$

16. $-20 \geq \frac{b}{-7}$

17. $6 < \frac{x}{-2}$

18. $-6x \leq 24$

19. $-2w < -14$

20. $-15 > -3q$

21. $27 \geq -0.9r$

22. **Guided Problem Solving** There are 157 students and 8 teachers going on a field trip. Each bus can seat at most 48 passengers. How many buses should the school reserve?
    • What is the total number of passengers going on the trip?
    • Write and solve an inequality to find x, the number of buses that should be reserved.

GO ● nline
Homework Video Tutor
Visit: PHSchool.com
Web Code: ase-0606

23. **Reasoning** What number is *not* a solution of $x < -3$ or $-x < 3$?

24. **Writing in Math** Explain how solving $5x < 20$ is different from solving $-5x < 20$.

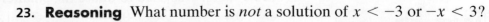

What values of *a* and *b* make each inequality true?

25. $-ab > 0$ **26.** $ab < 0$ **27.** $a^2b > 0$ **28.** $\frac{a}{b} > 0$

29. Child Care In Virginia, for every group of 5 two-year-olds in day care, there must be at least 1 teacher. If there are 19 two-year-olds in a class, how many teachers must the center have?

30. Your brother wants to buy a new multi-disc DVD player for $182.89. He earns $6.85 per hour working at a theater. How many hours will he need to work to earn enough money for the player?

31. Challenge A student solved $\frac{a}{b} > 2$ for *a* and got the solution $a > 2b$. Is the student's answer correct for all values of *b*? Explain.

Careers Child-care workers perform a combination of basic care and teaching duties.

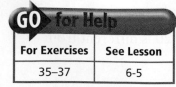 **Test Prep and Mixed Review**   **Practice**

Multiple Choice

32. At one store, a DVD is on sale for 25% off $26.99. At another store, the same DVD is on sale for 30% off $29.99. Why should Rueben buy the DVD at the first store?

Ⓐ 30% is more than 25%.

Ⓑ $26.99 is less than $29.99.

Ⓒ 25% of $26.99 is less than 30% of $29.99.

Ⓓ 75% of $26.99 is less than 70% of $29.99.

33. A pattern of equations is shown below. Which statement best describes this pattern of equations?

$$64\% \text{ of } 25 = 16$$
$$16\% \text{ of } 100 = 16$$
$$4\% \text{ of } 400 = 16$$
$$1\% \text{ of } 1600 = 16$$

Ⓕ When the percent is divided by 4, and the other number is multiplied by 4, the answer is 16.

Ⓖ When the percent is multiplied by 4, and the other number is divided by $\frac{1}{4}$, the answer is 16.

Ⓗ When the percent is divided by 4, and the other number is divided by 4, the answer is 16.

Ⓙ When the percent is multiplied by 4, and the other number is multiplied by 4, the answer is 16.

34. Two banners are similar. The height of the smaller banner is 24 inches, while the height of the larger banner is 60 inches. What scale factor was used to dilate the smaller banner to the larger one?

Ⓐ 0.4   Ⓑ 0.6   Ⓒ 1.4   Ⓓ 2.5

GO for Help

For Exercises	See Lesson
35–37	6-5

Algebra Solve each inequality. Graph the solutions.

35. $y + 3 \le 29$ **36.** $a - 7 > 15$ **37.** $w - 6 \ge 9$

Reading for Understanding

Reading-comprehension questions are based on a passage. Read the questions carefully *before* reading the passage. Then, as you read, look for the information you need to answer the questions.

EXAMPLE

Legislative Math

When a majority of the members of the Senate and a majority of the members of the House of Representatives vote in favor of a bill, the bill goes to the White House for the President's signature.

But the President can veto a bill to prevent it from becoming law. The President's veto outweighs the combined votes of the 100 members of the Senate and the 435 members of the House of Representatives.

Congress can override the veto, however. Two thirds of the members of the Senate and two thirds of the members of the House present at the vote must vote to override the veto. The bill then automatically becomes law.

If all senators are present at the vote, how many must vote in favor of an override of a presidential veto for the override to pass?

Two thirds of the members of the Senate present at the vote must vote to override a veto. There are 100 members of the Senate.

$$\text{number of senators needed} = \frac{2}{3} \cdot 100 = 66.\overline{6}$$

At least 67 senators must vote to override a presidential veto.

Exercises

Use the passage in the example for the following exercises.

1. If all members of the House of Representatives are present, how many votes are required to override a presidential veto?

2. In 1845, President John Tyler's veto was overridden by Congress. There were 42 members of the Senate and 157 members of the House present at the vote. How many had to vote against the veto for it to be overridden?

3. Can you find the total number of Senate and House members required for an override by adding the members of the Senate and the House and then taking two thirds of the total? Explain.

Chapter 6 Review

Choose the correct term to complete each sentence.

1. (Terms, Like terms) have the same variables.

2. An (equation, inequality) is a mathematical sentence that contains $<$, $>$, $\leq$, $\geq$, or $\neq$.

3. A (solution, term) is a number, a variable, or the product of a number and a variable.

4. When you use the (Addition Property of Inequality, Multiplication Property of Inequality), you may need to reverse the direction of the inequality sign.

5. To solve the inequality $x - 5 < 7$, use the (Addition Property of Inequality, Subtraction Property of Inequality).

Go Online
PHSchool.com

For: Online Vocabulary Quiz
Web Code: asj-0651

Skills and Concepts

Lesson 6-1

• To solve two-step equations and to use two-step equations to solve problems

To solve two-step equations, first undo the addition or subtraction. Then undo the multiplication or division.

Solve each equation. Check the solution.

6. $2n - 5 = 19$

7. $4 + 3q = -7$

8. $-1 = \frac{b}{5} + 2$

9. $\frac{c}{-3} - 1 = 2$

10. $12s + 2 = -8$

11. $\frac{w}{4} + 10 = 20$

12. You bought cat food for $1.79 per can and a bag of rabbit food for $6.59. The total cost was $33.44. How many cans of cat food did you buy?

13. At the mall, you spent a total of $170.86. You bought 2 pairs of jeans for $39.95 each, a jacket for $45.99, and shirts for $14.99 each. How many shirts did you buy?

Lesson 6-2
- To combine like terms and simplify algebraic expressions

The parts of an algebraic expression are **terms. Like terms** have exactly the same variable factors. You simplify an expression by combining like terms.

Simplify each expression.

14. $4 - 3(f - 1)$ **15.** $3(a + 2) + 5$ **16.** $8x + 3(x - 4)$

Lessons 6-3, 6-4
- To write and solve multi-step equations
- To write and solve equations with variables on both sides

When simplifying an equation, combine like terms. If an equation has variables on each side, use the addition or subtraction property of equality to isolate the variable.

Solve each equation. Check the solution.

17. $4a + 3 - a = -7 + 2 + a$ **18.** $2b - 8 = -b + 7$

19. $18 = 2(3k + 1) - k$ **20.** $3(c + 4) - 7 = -10$

21. Marsha buys 3 pounds of cheddar cheese and some Swiss cheese. Both cheeses cost $4.50 per pound. The total cost is $24.75. How many pounds of Swiss cheese did Marsha buy?

Lesson 6-5
- To write and solve inequalities using addition and subtraction

An **inequality** is a mathematical sentence that contains $<, \le, >, \ge$, or $\ne$. Any value of the variable that makes an inequality true is a solution. You can graph all the solutions of an inequality on a number line. You can solve an inequality using the addition and subtraction properties of inequality.

Solve each inequality. Graph the solutions.

22. $g - 7 > 12$ **23.** $u + 3 \le 5$ **24.** $4 + t \ge -7$

Write an inequality for each word sentence.

25. The jacket costs less than $75.   **26.** You must raise at least $150.

Lesson 6-6
- To write and solve inequalities using multiplication and division

When you multiply or divide an inequality by a positive number, the relationship between the two sides does not change. Multiplying or dividing an inequality by a negative number, however, reverses the direction of the inequality sign.

Solve each inequality. Graph the solutions.

27. $4x < -12$ **28.** $-17y \ge 34$ **29.** $-6a > -42$

30. $\frac{w}{8} \le 16$ **31.** $\frac{c}{-2} > 10$ **32.** $\frac{z}{-4} < -3$

Simplify each expression.

1. $9 - 4r - 7$

2. $5 + (-12t) + 8t$

3. $2(3m - 5) + 6$

4. $-4(7a + 2a) - 5$

5. $4v + 17 - 9v$

6. $13s - (-6 - 4s)$

Solve each equation.

7. $x + 7 = 18 - 2x$

8. $2 + y = -7 + 2y$

9. $\frac{6z}{7} = -30$

10. $\frac{a}{-2} = 2.5 - 3a$

11. $4m - 9 = 27$

12. $-2c + 5 = 9$

13. $-3(h + 7) = -18$

14. $\frac{r}{-5} - 3 = 14$

15. $6 + 2d = 3d - 4$

16. $5 = 3(4 - b) + 2$

17. $5t - 1 = 7t - 5$

18. $2(c + 1) = c - 7$

19. A quilter is making a quilt that will be 48 in. wide. The border will be 2 in. at each end. Each quilt block is 4 in. wide. How many quilt blocks does the quilter need across the width of the quilt?

20. **Groceries** You buy 15 apples and a $2.75 block of cheese. The bill is $6.20. How much does each apple cost?

21. **Bowling** You and your friend go bowling. Your score is 6 more than twice your friend's score. If your score is 212, what is your friend's score?

22. A cricket bat weighs 42 oz. Together, two cricket balls and a cricket bat weigh the same as eight cricket balls plus 9 oz. How much does a cricket ball weigh?

23. **Open-Ended** Write a problem you could represent with the equation $3k - 12 = 6$. Solve the equation and show your solution.

Define a variable and write an inequality to describe each situation.

24. Each driver must be at least 16 years old.

25. You can have no more than five passengers in a car.

26. There are fewer than three weeks until vacation.

27. There are at most 75 tickets to the play still available.

28. Your essay must be at least four pages long.

Write and solve an inequality to answer each question.

29. When a number is multiplied by -3, the result is at least 15. What is the greatest value the number can have?

30. **Shopping** You have $15 to buy a sketch pad and some pens. The sketch pad you want costs $11, and pens cost $.40 each. How many pens can you buy?

31. **Postage** You want to send a package. First-class mail costs $.39 for the first ounce and $.24 for each additional ounce. You can spend at most $3.00 on postage. What is the maximum weight of your package? Round down to the nearest ounce.

Solve each inequality. Graph the solutions.

32. $18 > w + 3$

33. $y - 12 > -7$

34. $\frac{z}{3} \le 5$

35. $-4s \ge 64$

36. $3m < 12$

37. $-2t \ge -3$

38. $4b \le 16$

39. $-9c > 81$

40. **Writing in Math** Describe how solving an inequality is like solving an equation. Describe how it is different. Include examples.

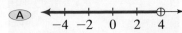 **Test Prep** Practice

Multiple Choice

For Exercises 1–9, choose the correct letter.

1. Which graph shows the solution of $9y < 36$?

   Ⓐ ⟵———|—|—|—⊕—|—⟶
          −4 −2 0 2 4

   Ⓑ ⟵—|—|—|—|—⊕—⟶
          −4 −2 0 2 4

   Ⓒ ⟵⊕—|—|—|—|—⟶
          −4 −2 0 2 4

   Ⓓ ⟵—⊕—|—|—|—⟶
          −4 −2 0 2 4

2. The perimeter of a rectangle is 28 cm. Its length is 10 cm more than its width (w). Which equation can be used to find the dimensions?

   Ⓕ $w + (w + 10) = 28$
   Ⓖ $2w + 2(w + 10) = 28$
   Ⓗ $w(w + 10) = 28$
   Ⓙ $2w(2w + 20) = 28$

3. If $a - by = c$, then $y = \blacksquare$.

   Ⓐ $\dfrac{a - c}{b}$ Ⓑ $\dfrac{c - a}{b}$ Ⓒ $\dfrac{c}{b} - a$ Ⓓ $a - \dfrac{c}{b}$

4. Which numbers are all solutions of the inequality $x - 3 < -1$?

   Ⓕ $-2, -1, 0$ Ⓗ $0, 1, 2$
   Ⓖ $-1, 0, 2$ Ⓙ $1, 2, 3$

5. Which variable expression is NOT equivalent to $2(y + 3)$?

   Ⓐ $2(y) + 2(3)$ Ⓒ $(y + 3) + (y + 3)$
   Ⓑ $2y + 3$ Ⓓ $6 + 2y$

6. The solution of which inequality is represented by the graph below?

   ⟵⊕—|—|—|—|—|—|—⟶
    −5 −4 −3 −2 −1 0 1 2

   Ⓕ $25 > -5w$ Ⓗ $3x \geq -15$
   Ⓖ $-4y > -20$ Ⓙ $2z < -10$

7. What can the expression $12k$ represent?

   Ⓐ the cost (in cents) of a dozen cans of juice if each can costs 12 cents
   Ⓑ the cost (in cents) of k photocopies if each photocopy costs 12 cents
   Ⓒ the time it took Alana to run 1 mi if she ran 12 mi in k min
   Ⓓ Darrin's age, if Darrin is k years older than his 12-year-old brother

8. The variables x, y, and z represent integers other than zero. You know that $x > y$ and $y > z$. Which statement must be true?

   Ⓕ $z > x$ Ⓖ $z < x$ Ⓗ $x \leq z$ Ⓙ $\dfrac{x}{y} > \dfrac{y}{z}$

9. In professional ice hockey, a team earns 2 points for a win, 1 point for a tie, and 0 points for a loss. One season a team earned 31 points and had 10 losses and 7 ties. Which equation can be used to determine the number of wins (w) this team had?

   Ⓐ $w + 7 = 31$ Ⓒ $2w + 7 = 31$
   Ⓑ $10 + 7 + w = 31$ Ⓓ $31 - 10 = 2w$

Gridded Response

10. You want a copy of a poster and copies of a flier. It costs $6.00 for a poster and $.08 for each copy of the flier. You have $10.00. How many copies of the flier can you make?

Short Response

11. Define a variable and write an inequality to model the word sentence "There will be at most three tests this year."

Extended Response

12. Eli is on a diet and loses 2 lb a month. When he began his diet, he weighed 190 lb.
    a. Write an expression to model what Eli's weight will be after x months.
    b. How much will Eli weigh after 8 months? Show your work.

Problem Solving Application

Applying Equations

Coming to Life Making movies is very expensive. It involves many people as well as many different stages. Some of the people who help make a movie are the producer, the director, the screenwriters, the animators, and many different types of artists.

Technical Wizardry

One of the first films to explore the possibilities of matte painting was *The Wizard of Oz* (1939).

Matte Paintings

Two-dimensional paintings on glass, or mattes, provide background detail when blended with live-action footage. Matte painting also saves time and money by eliminating travel to distant locations, expensive sets, and miniature models.

Before the Matte

The crew filmed the actors in *Jurassic Park III* on a simple set piece.

After the Matte

A digital matte painting makes a steep canyon blocking the characters' path.

Put It All Together

Data File Use the information on these two pages and on page 647 to answer these questions.

Materials: 2 number cubes

1. Suppose you're a screenwriter with a movie idea that you're trying to sell to a Hollywood producer.
   a. Make up a title for your movie. It can be silly or serious.
   b. Your movie needs a budget. To determine the cost of your movie, roll two number cubes and let x = the sum of the two numbers. Find your movie's cost in dollars by evaluating the expression

   $$3,000,000x + 10,000,000.$$

2. You can use the following equation to model the profit from a movie.

   $$\text{profit} = \text{money from ticket sales} - \text{cost}$$

   a. Suppose a movie studio makes a $4 profit on every ticket sold. Let t = the number of tickets to your movie that will be sold. Write an equation to calculate the profit.
   b. Use your equation to make a table showing how the profit depends on the number of tickets sold. Calculate the profit for every million tickets from 1 million to 15 million.

3. a. Choose a movie from the list on page 647. Calculate its cost per minute.
   b. Estimate the number of ticket sales needed before the movie can start making a profit.

Go Online
PHSchool.com
For: Information about movie-making
Web Code: ase-0653

Making the Matte

1. In the documentary *Manassas: End of Innocence*, about the Civil War, actors in period costumes walk by a church "acting" as a church in Washington, D.C.

2. A digital technician used wire-frame technology to build the church steeple and the Capitol in three dimensions. An artist painted the trees, the lamppost, and the nearby buildings in two dimensions.

3. The final composite shows a street scene in Washington, D.C. The Capitol dome was under construction in 1861.

What You've Learned

- In Chapter 2, you used formulas to solve problems.
- In Chapter 4, you used proportions to find missing measurements in triangles.
- In Chapter 6, you wrote and solved equations and inequalities.

Check Your Readiness

For Exercises	See Lessons
1–3	1-1
4–7	1-6
8–11	1-7
12–14	2-6

GO for Help

Evaluating Expressions

Evaluate each expression.

1. $\frac{1}{2}bh$ for $b = 9$ and $h = 8$

2. $2(3.14)r$ for $r = 16$

3. $\frac{1}{2}a(b + c)$ for $a = 4$, $b = 3$, and $c = 17$

Solving One-Step Equations

Solve each equation.

4. $25 = 17 + m$ 5. $b + 13 = 56$ 6. $44 + s = 41$ 7. $10 = p - 22$

8. $4.2g = 63$ 9. $16 = 14k$ 10. $\frac{w}{3.5} = 24$ 11. $5.1 = \frac{c}{7}$

Using Formulas to Solve Problems

Find the area of each figure.

12.
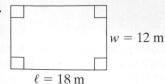
$w = 12$ m
$\ell = 18$ m

13.
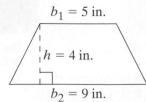
$b_1 = 5$ in.
$h = 4$ in.
$b_2 = 9$ in.

14.
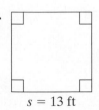
$s = 13$ ft

What You'll Learn Next

- In this chapter, you will use the properties of pairs of angles and parallel lines to find angle measures.

- You will find the areas of geometric figures, including parallelograms, triangles, trapezoids, and circles.

- You will construct congruent angles and parallel lines using a compass and straightedge.

 Problem Solving Application On pages 350 and 351, you will work an extended activity on sailing.

◀)) Key Vocabulary

- alternate interior angles (p. 307)
- area (p. 328)
- compass (p. 341)
- complementary (p. 304)
- congruent polygons (p. 312)
- corresponding angles (p. 307)
- parallelogram (p. 319)
- perpendicular lines (p. 304)
- quadrilateral (p. 319)
- rectangle (p. 319)
- regular polygon (p. 325)
- rhombus (p. 319)
- right triangle (p. 318)
- square (p. 319)
- supplementary (p. 304)
- trapezoid (p. 319)

Exploring Pairs of Angles

ACTIVITY

1. Draw two intersecting lines. Number the angles as shown at the right.

2. Use a protractor. Measure the angles in your drawing. Record the results.

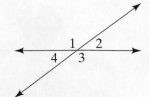

3. Draw three different pairs of intersecting lines.

4. For each pair, compare $m\angle 1$ and $m\angle 3$. Then compare $m\angle 2$ and $m\angle 4$.

5. **Patterns** Make a conjecture about these pairs of angles.

6. For each pair of lines, find the sum of $m\angle 1$ and $m\angle 2$.

7. For each pair of lines, find the sum of $m\angle 2$ and $m\angle 3$.

8. **Patterns** Make a conjecture about these pairs of angles.

ACTIVITY

Navigation The pilot of a ship uses a navigational tool called a parallel rule to plot routes on charts. Recall that parallel lines lie in the same plane and do not intersect. In the diagram, m is parallel to t, and r is parallel to s.

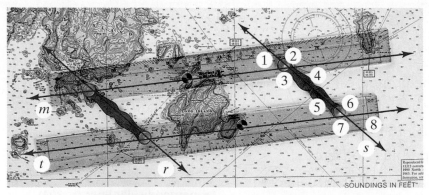

9. Use a protractor. Find the measures of the numbered angles.

10. Identify all the congruent pairs of angles.

11. Make a conjecture about the angles formed when a line intersects two parallel lines.

12. Check your conjecture by measuring other angles in the diagram. Is your conjecture correct? Explain.

7-1 Pairs of Angles

Check Skills You'll Need

1. Vocabulary Review What is the *inverse operation* of addition?

Solve each equation.

2. $a + 14 = 32$

3. $b - 5 = 26$

4. $10 + c = -31$

5. $-48 = d - 19$

for Help
Lesson 1-6

Vocabulary Tip

The *vertex* of an angle is the point of intersection of two sides of an angle or figure.

Test Prep Tip

You can name the angle below in four ways.

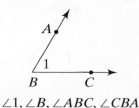

$\angle 1, \angle B, \angle ABC, \angle CBA$

What You'll Learn

To identify types of angles and to find angle measures using the relationship between angles

🔊 **New Vocabulary** vertical angles, adjacent angles, supplementary, complementary, perpendicular lines

Why Learn This?

City streets cross each other in certain ways. Understanding angles can help you read and draw maps.

Vertical angles are formed by two intersecting lines and are opposite each other. Vertical angles are congruent. They have the same measure.

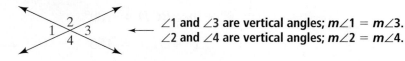

∠1 and ∠3 are vertical angles; $m\angle 1 = m\angle 3$.
∠2 and ∠4 are vertical angles; $m\angle 2 = m\angle 4$.

Adjacent angles have a common vertex and a common side, but no common interior points.

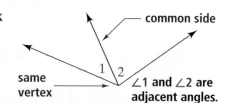

common side

same vertex

∠1 and ∠2 are adjacent angles.

EXAMPLE Identifying Adjacent and Vertical Angles

1. City Planning Name a pair of adjacent angles and a pair of vertical angles in the photo at the right. Find $m\angle JBT$.

∠DBJ and ∠JBT are adjacent angles.

∠DBY and ∠JBT are vertical angles.

Vertical angles are congruent, so $m\angle JBT = m\angle DBY$. So $m\angle JBT$ is 80°.

Quick Check

1. Name another pair of vertical angles and another pair of adjacent angles in the photo.

If the sum of the measures of two angles is 180°, the angles are **supplementary.** If the sum of the measures of two angles is 90°, the angles are **complementary.**

In the diagram below, ∠C and ∠WYZ are both supplements of ∠XYW. ∠C and ∠VSR are both complements of ∠VST.

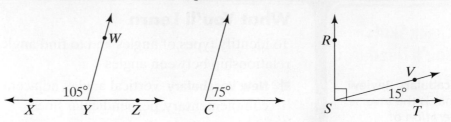

You can solve equations to find the measures of supplementary and complementary angles.

EXAMPLE   Finding Supplementary Angles

2 **(Algebra)** Suppose m∠BCD = 121°. Find the measure of its supplement.

Let x° = the measure of the supplement of ∠BCD.

$$x° + m∠BCD = 180°$$ ← The sum of the measures of supplementary angles is 180°.

$$x° + 121° = 180°$$ ← Substitute 121° for m∠BCD.

$$x° + 121° - 121° = 180° - 121°$$ ← Subtract 121° from each side.

$$x° = 59°$$ ← Simplify.

The measure of the supplement of ∠BCD is 59°.

✓ Quick Check

2. An angle has a measure of 47°. Find the measure of its supplement.

Perpendicular lines are two lines that intersect to form a right angle. Recall that a right angle has a measure of 90°.

◑nline
active math

For: Investigating Angle
     Theorems Activity
Use: Interactive
     Textbook, 7-1

EXAMPLE   Finding Angle Measures

3 In the diagram at the right, m∠5 = 58°. Find the measures of ∠1 and ∠2.

$$m∠1 + 58° = 90°$$ ← ∠1 and ∠5 are complementary.

$$m∠1 = 32°$$ ← Subtract 58° from each side.

Since ∠1 and ∠2 are vertical angles, m∠2 = 32°.

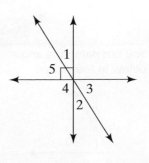

✓ Quick Check

3. Find the measures of ∠3 and ∠4 in Example 3.

Vocabulary Are ∠3 and ∠4 adjacent angles? Explain.

1. 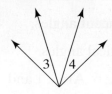　　**2.** 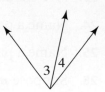　　**3.**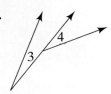

4. Reasoning Does every angle have a complement? Explain.

Homework Exercises

For more exercises, see **Extra Skills and Word Problems.**

GO for Help

For Exercises	See Examples
5–7	1
8–12	2
13–15	3

Name a pair of vertical and adjacent angles in each figure. Find $m∠1$**.**

5. 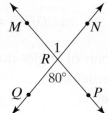　**6.** 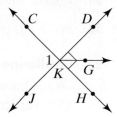　**7.**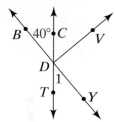

Find the measure of the supplement of each angle.

8. 14°　　**9.** 24°　　**10.** 145°　　**11.** 39°　　**12.** 116°

Find the measure of each numbered angle.

13. 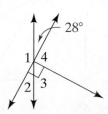　　**14.** 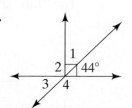　　**15.**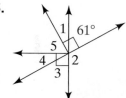

 **16. Guided Problem Solving** Route 43 is perpendicular to Devon Avenue. Find the measure of the acute angle formed by Route 43 and Northwest Highway.
- What kinds of angles do perpendicular lines form?
- What special pairs of angles do you see?

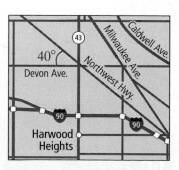

Find the measure of the complement and the supplement of each angle.

17. 32°　　**18.** 77°　　**19.** 85.9°　　**20.** 42.3°　　**21.** 6.1°

Art Use the stained glass window below for Exercise 22–26.

22. Are ∠1 and ∠7 adjacent? Explain.

23. Are ∠2 and ∠3 vertical? Explain.

24. Name a pair of adjacent angles.

25. Name a pair of vertical angles.

26. Suppose $m\angle 1 = m\angle 6$. Are ∠1 and ∠5 supplementary? Explain.

27. **Writing in Math** Can two supplementary angles have the same measure? Explain.

Use the diagram for Exercises 28–31.

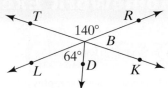

28. ∠LBD and ∠TBL are ___?___ angles.

29. ∠RBT and ∠___?___ are vertical angles.

30. $m\angle KBL = \blacksquare°$ 31. $m\angle DBK = \blacksquare°$

32. **Challenge** Which pair of angles does NOT exist? Explain.
    Ⓐ adjacent supplementary   Ⓒ complementary vertical
    Ⓑ vertical adjacent   Ⓓ congruent complementary

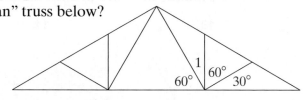
Test Prep and Mixed Review   **Practice**

Multiple Choice

33. A truss is part of the roof of a house. What is the measure of ∠1 in the "fan" truss below?

    Ⓐ 30°   Ⓑ 45°   Ⓒ 60°   Ⓓ 90°

34. Which problem situation matches the equation $18 = 40x$?
    Ⓕ A credit card charges 18% interest on purchases. Debra bought a $40 item. What is x, the amount of interest charged?
    Ⓖ Isabella made 18 out of 40 paper snowflake decorations. What is x, the percent of the snowflakes Isabella made?
    Ⓗ Johannes gave the waitress an 18% tip. The cost of the meal was $40. What is x, the amount of the tip?
    Ⓙ Out of 40 free throw attempts, Rohit made 22 and missed 18. What is x, the percent of free throws he made?

35. **Shopping** A department store is having its annual 30%-off sale. A jacket is on sale for $63. What was the jacket's regular price?

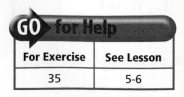

For Exercise	See Lesson
35	5-6

What You'll Learn

To identify parallel lines and the angles formed by parallel lines and transversals

Why Learn This?

Carpenters must know about angles and parallel lines in order to make correct measurements and cuts.

A line that intersects two other lines at different points is a **transversal.** In the diagrams below, line *t* is a transversal. Some pairs of angles formed by two lines and a transversal have special names.

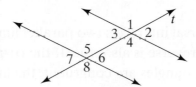

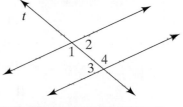

Corresponding angles lie on the same side of the transversal and in corresponding positions.

∠1 and ∠5   ∠2 and ∠6
∠3 and ∠7   ∠4 and ∠8

Alternate interior angles lie within a pair of lines and on opposite sides of the transversal.

∠1 and ∠4   ∠2 and ∠3

EXAMPLE   Identifying Angles

1 Identify a pair of corresponding angles and a pair of alternate interior angles.

∠1 and ∠3 are corresponding angles.

∠2 and ∠7 are alternate interior angles.

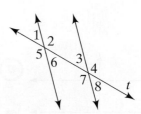

✓ Quick Check

1. Use the diagram in Example 1. Identify each pair of angles as *corresponding, alternate interior,* or *neither.*
   a. ∠3, ∠6   **b.** ∠5, ∠7   **c.** ∠1, ∠8

KEY CONCEPTS **Transversals and Parallel Lines**

When a transversal intersects two parallel lines,
- corresponding angles are congruent, and
- alternate interior angles are congruent.

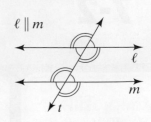

$\ell \parallel m$

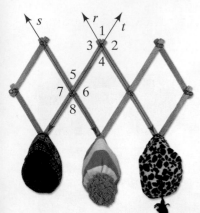

EXAMPLE **Finding Angle Measures**

2 **Gridded Response** A carpenter wants to make the hat rack at the left and needs to find all the angle measurements. She knows that line r is parallel to line s, and $m\angle 4 = 63°$. What is $m\angle 5$ measured in degrees?

$m\angle 5 = m\angle 4 = 63°$ ← **Alternate interior angles are congruent.**

The correct answer is 63 degrees.

✓ Quick Check

2. In Example 2, $m\angle 3 = 117°$. Find $m\angle 6$ and $m\angle 7$.

When a transversal intersects two parallel lines, some pairs of angles are congruent. The reverse is also true. If the corresponding angles or the alternate interior angles are congruent, the lines are parallel.

If $\overleftrightarrow{AB}$ is parallel to $\overleftrightarrow{CD}$, you write $\overleftrightarrow{AB} \parallel \overleftrightarrow{CD}$.

EXAMPLE **Identifying Parallel Lines**

3 In the diagram at the right, $m\angle 1 = 60°$, $m\angle 2 = 60°$, and $m\angle 3 = 60°$. Explain how you know $\overleftrightarrow{LP} \parallel \overleftrightarrow{MN}$ and $\overleftrightarrow{LM} \parallel \overleftrightarrow{PN}$.

$\overleftrightarrow{LP} \parallel \overleftrightarrow{MN}$ because $\angle 1$ and $\angle 2$ are congruent corresponding angles. $\overleftrightarrow{LM} \parallel \overleftrightarrow{PN}$ because $\angle 1$ and $\angle 3$ are congruent alternate interior angles.

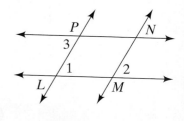

✓ Quick Check

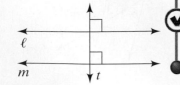

3. Transversal t at the left is perpendicular to lines ℓ and m. Explain how you know $\ell \parallel m$.

The reasoning used in Example 3 is called *deductive reasoning*. Deductive reasoning is the logical process of drawing conclusions from given facts.

In the diagram at the right, $\overleftrightarrow{PQ} \parallel \overleftrightarrow{ST}$.

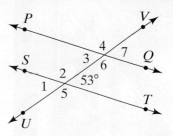

1. Name a pair of corresponding angles.

2. Name a pair of alternate interior angles.

3. Which line is the transversal?

4. What other angles have measures of 53°?

5. **Reasoning** Is the following statement *true* or *false*? Corresponding angles can also be alternate interior angles. Explain.

Homework Exercises

For more exercises, see Extra Skills and Word Problems.

GO for Help

For Exercises	See Examples
6–13	1
14–19	2
20–22	3

Identify the angles as *corresponding*, *alternate interior*, or *neither*.

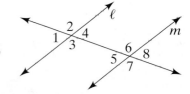

6. ∠6, ∠3   7. ∠8, ∠4

8. ∠2, ∠1   9. ∠2, ∠4

10. ∠1, ∠5   11. ∠2, ∠7

12. ∠3, ∠5   13. ∠4, ∠3

In the diagram, $\ell \parallel m$. If $m\angle 3 = 122°$, find the measure of each angle.

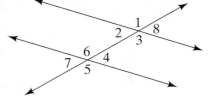

14. ∠4   15. ∠2   16. ∠6

17. ∠7   18. ∠8   19. ∠5

For each diagram, explain how you know $a \parallel b$.

20.
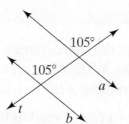

21.
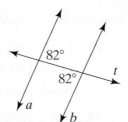

22.
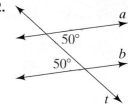

GPS 23. **Guided Problem Solving** Two lines are cut by a transversal. The corresponding angles are not congruent. Are the two lines parallel?
- **Understand the Problem** If a transversal cuts two parallel lines, corresponding angles are congruent. The question is, are two lines parallel if corresponding angles are not congruent?
- **Make a Plan** Draw pictures of corresponding angles that are not congruent. Conclude whether or not the two lines are parallel.

24. Architecture The railings in the photo at the left are parallel. If $m\angle 1 = 138°$, find $m\angle 2$ and $m\angle 3$.

Which pairs of lines, if any, are parallel? Explain.

25.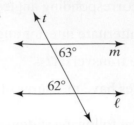

26.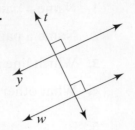

27.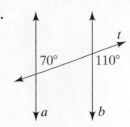

28. <u>**Writing in Math**</u> A transversal t cuts parallel lines m and n. If t is perpendicular to m, what is the relationship between t and n?

Use the diagram at the right for Exercises 29–30.

29. Find the measure of each numbered angle.

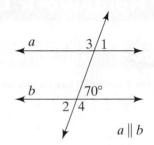

30. *Alternate exterior angles* lie outside a pair of lines and on opposite sides of a transversal. What do you notice about the measures of alternate exterior angles of parallel lines?

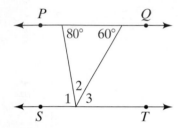

31. a. In the diagram at the left, $\overleftrightarrow{PQ} \parallel \overleftrightarrow{ST}$. Find the measure of each numbered angle.
   b. What is the sum of the angle measures of the triangle?

32. Challenge Which pair of angles is always congruent?
   A alternate interior angles   C corresponding angles
   B vertical angles   D alternate exterior angles

Test Prep and Mixed Review
Practice

Gridded Response

33. In the diagram at the right, triangle ABC is similar to triangle ADE. What scale factor was used to reduce triangle ABC to triangle ADE?

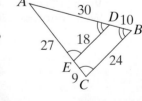

34. The equation $c = 17t + 5$ models the total cost c of a tomato garden, where t is the cost of each tomato plant. Find the total cost, in dollars, if each plant costs $0.50.

35. A punch recipe calls for 3 quarts of pineapple juice, 2 quarts of orange juice, 3 cups of grapefruit juice, and 3 cups of cranberry juice. How many quarts of punch does the recipe make?

For Exercises	See Lesson
36–39	5-4

Use an equation to find each percent.

36. 23% of 55   **37.** 78% of 41   **38.** 14% of 36   **39.** 62% of 199

7-2b Activity Lab

Algebra Thinking

Solving Angle Equations

You can use what you know about solving equations
to find angle measures.

EXAMPLE Solving Angle Equations

Find the measure of each angle in the diagram at the right.

$(3x + 40)° + (6x + 50)° = 180°$ ← adjacent supplementary angles

$9x + 90 = 180$ ← Combine like terms.

$9x + 90 - 90 = 180 - 90$ ← Subtract 90 from each side.

$9x = 90$ ← Simplify.

$\dfrac{9x}{9} = \dfrac{90}{9}$ ← Divide each side by 9.

$x = 10$ ← Simplify.

To find the measure of each angle in the diagram, substitute 10 for x.
$3(10) + 40 = 70$ and $6(10) + 50 = 110$. So the angle measures are
70° and 110°.

Exercises

Find the measures of the two angles in each diagram.

1.

$(2x + 45)°$

$(3x + 15)°$

2.

$(3x + 45)°$

$(2x + 15)°$

3. Find the measure of ∠1 in the figure below.

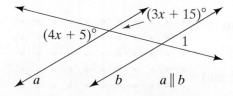

$(4x + 5)°$ $(3x + 15)°$

1

a b $a \parallel b$

Use the figure at the right.

4. Find the measure of the obtuse angles.

5. Find the measure of the acute angles. Then write
an algebraic expression for that measure.

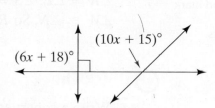

$(10x + 15)°$

$(6x + 18)°$

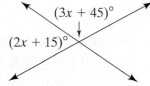

Activity Lab   Solving Angle Equations   **311**

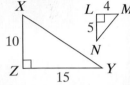

What You'll Learn

To identify congruent figures and use them to solve problems

🔊 **New Vocabulary** congruent polygons

Why Learn This?

Land surveyors measure angles and distances on land. To survey land, it is helpful to know about congruent polygons.

Congruent polygons are polygons that have the same size and shape. When two polygons are congruent, you can slide, flip, or turn one so that it fits exactly on top of the other one.

Corresponding angles and corresponding sides of congruent polygons are congruent. The two polygons below are congruent.

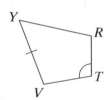 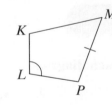

$\angle T$ corresponds to $\angle L$.

$\overline{YV}$ corresponds to $\overline{MP}$.

R corresponds to K.

You can write $VTRY \cong PLKM$.

The tick marks in the diagram tell you which sides are congruent. The arcs tell you which angles are congruent. When you name congruent polygons, you must list the corresponding vertices in the same order.

EXAMPLE Writing Congruence Statements

1. Write a congruence statement for the congruent figures at the right.

   $\angle R \cong \angle L$, $\angle S \cong \angle K$, $\angle T \cong \angle J$, and $\angle W \cong \angle N$. So $RSTW \cong LKJN$.

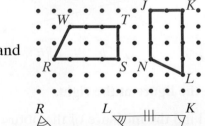

✓ Quick Check

1. Write a congruence statement for the congruent figures at the right.

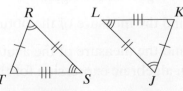

You can use corresponding parts of triangles to show that two triangles are congruent. You do not need to know that *all* the corresponding parts are congruent to show congruent triangles. You can show congruence in several ways.

KEY CONCEPTS **Showing Triangles Are Congruent**

To demonstrate that two triangles are congruent, show that the following parts of one triangle are congruent to the corresponding parts of the other triangle.

| Side-Side-Side (SSS) | Side-Angle-Side (SAS) | Angle-Side-Angle (ASA) |

 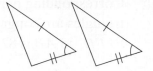 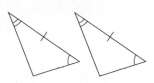

Vocabulary Tip

The abbreviations SSS, SAS, and ASA are easy ways to remember how to show triangles are congruent.

The order of the angles and sides is important in deciding whether two triangles are congruent.

EXAMPLE **Congruent Triangles**

2 Show that each pair of triangles is congruent.

a.

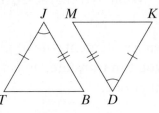

$\overline{TJ} \cong \overline{KD}$ **S**ide

$\angle J \cong \angle D$ **A**ngle

$\overline{BJ} \cong \overline{MD}$ **S**ide

$\triangle TJB \cong \triangle KDM$ by SAS.

b.

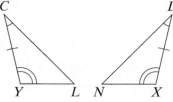

$\angle C \cong \angle D$ **A**ngle

$\overline{CY} \cong \overline{DX}$ **S**ide

$\angle Y \cong \angle X$ **A**ngle

$\triangle CYL \cong \triangle DXN$ by ASA

✓ Quick Check

2. Show that each pair of triangles is congruent.

a.

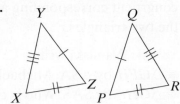

b.

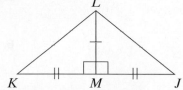

You can use corresponding parts of congruent figures to find distances.

EXAMPLE **Application: Surveying**

3 A surveyor drew the picture below. A bridge will be built across the river from point *A* to point *B*. Show that the two triangles are congruent. Then find *AB*.

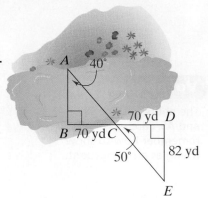

$\angle B \cong \angle D$ ← Both are right angles.

$BC = DC$ ← Both measure 70 yd.

$\angle ACB \cong \angle ECD$ ← They are vertical angles.

So $\triangle ABC \cong \triangle EDC$ by ASA.

Corresponding parts of congruent triangles are congruent. $\overline{AB}$ corresponds to $\overline{ED}$, so AB is 82 yd.

✓ Quick Check

3. Use the diagram in Example 3 to find each measure.
   a. $m\angle E$ **b.** $m\angle ACB$

✔ Check Your Understanding

1. **Vocabulary** What two characteristics do congruent polygons have in common?

2. Is the following statement *true* or *false*? When two polygons are congruent, you can translate, reflect, or rotate one so that it fits on top of the other one.

State whether each pair of triangles is congruent by SSS, SAS, or ASA.

3.
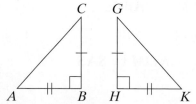

4.
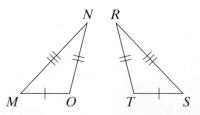

Use the two congruent triangles below for Exercises 5 and 6.

5. List the congruent corresponding angles and sides of the two triangles.

6. **Error Analysis** Vanessa writes $\triangle EFH \cong \triangle GFH$ by ASA. Michael writes $\triangle EFH \cong \triangle GHF$ by SAS. Who is correct?

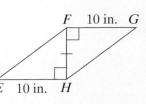

For more exercises, see Extra Skills and Word Problems.

GO for Help

For Exercises	See Examples
7–8	1
9–10	2
11–18	3

Write a congruence statement for each pair of congruent figures.

7.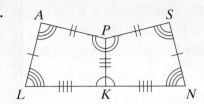

8.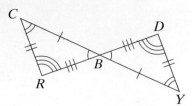

Show that each pair of triangles is congruent.

9.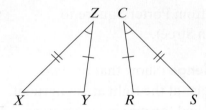

10.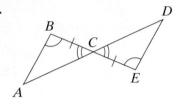

In the diagram below, *LMRC ≅ TXND*. Find each measure.

11. $m\angle N$

12. $m\angle T$

13. RM

14. ND

15. $m\angle C$

16. $m\angle M$

17. XT

18. CL

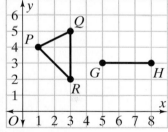

GPS **19.** **Guided Problem Solving** Use rotations and translations to find a point *F* such that $\triangle PQR \cong \triangle FGH$.

- Using the congruence statement, you know that $\overline{QR} \cong$ ■.
- $\triangle FGH$ is the exact image of $\triangle PQR$ after a rotation of ■° about point *R* followed by a translation ■ units to the right and ■ units up.

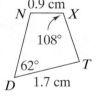

Is each pair of triangles congruent? Explain.

20.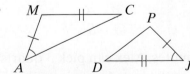

21.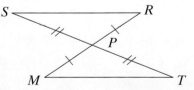

22. **Writing in Math** Explain the difference between similar triangles and congruent triangles.

23. **Reasoning** Can you show that two triangles are congruent by Angle-Angle-Angle? Draw figures to support your answer.

Maps Use the map at the right for Exercises 24–27.

24. Show that the triangles in the map are congruent.

25. Copy the triangles. Mark the sides and angles to show congruent corresponding parts.

26. How far is Porter Square from the intersection of Lee Street and Washington Road?

27. Find the distance along the road from Porter Square to Green Street.

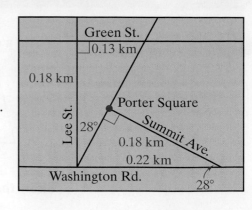

28. **Challenge** Show that the two triangles at the right are congruent. Then find the missing measures.

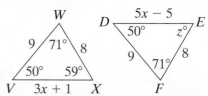

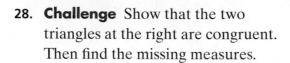

Test Prep and Mixed Review

Practice

Multiple Choice

29. James wants to buy a textbook. The price at University Bookstore is 12% off of $24.50. Carson Books is selling the same book for 20% off of $28. Why should James go to the University Bookstore?

   Ⓐ The cost of the book after the discount was $0.84 more at Carson Books.

   Ⓑ The cost of the book after the discount was $0.84 more at University Bookstore.

   Ⓒ The price before the discount was less at University Bookstore.

   Ⓓ The percent of discount was more at Carson Books.

30. Which point on the graph at the right has the x-coordinate with the largest value?

   Ⓕ P Ⓗ R

   Ⓖ Q Ⓙ S

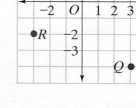

31. In 40 minutes, Alex can pick 3 quarts of berries. If 4 people work at that rate, how long will they take to pick 15 quarts?

   Ⓐ 30 min   Ⓑ 50 min   Ⓒ 160 min   Ⓓ 200 min

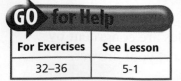
For Exercises	See Lesson
32–36	5-1

Write each percent as a decimal.

32. 15%   33. 3.72%   34. 180%   35. 0.015%   36. 0.49%

Identify each pair of angles as *adjacent, corresponding, alternate interior,* or *vertical.*

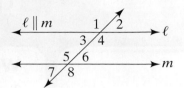

ℓ ∥ m

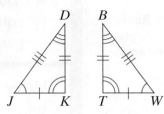

1. ∠6, ∠7   **2.** ∠4, ∠5   **3.** ∠2, ∠6

4. ∠3, ∠4   **5.** ∠1, ∠5   **6.** ∠7, ∠8

7. Show that the pair of triangles at the right is congruent.

8. Let $m\angle C = 67°$. Find the measures of the complement and the supplement.

In the diagram below, *APKS* ≅ *OFND*. Find each measure.

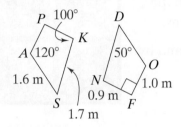

9. $m\angle N$ **10.** $m\angle P$ **11.** $m\angle O$

12. PK **13.** DO **14.** DN

MATH AT WORK

Dancers

Modern dance allows for freedom of movement and self-expression. Other types of dance include folk, classical ballet, ethnic, tap, and jazz.

You might wonder how math applies to dance. Dancers often perform as a group. The choreography, or arranged movements of the dance, often consists of repeated steps. Knowledge of patterns helps dancers memorize the steps and synchronize themselves with the other dancers.

Go Online
PHSchool.com
For: Information on Dancers
Web Code: asb-2031

Classifying Triangles and Quadrilaterals

What You'll Learn

To classify triangles and quadrilaterals

🔊 **New Vocabulary** acute triangle, obtuse triangle, right triangle, equilateral triangle, isosceles triangle, scalene triangle, quadrilateral, parallelogram, trapezoid, rhombus, rectangle, square

Why Learn This?

When you understand the properties of shapes, you can make designs such as quilt patterns.

You can classify triangles by their angles and by their sides.

acute triangle
three acute angles

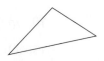
obtuse triangle
one obtuse angle

right triangle
one right angle

equilateral triangle
three congruent sides

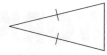
isosceles triangle
at least two congruent sides

scalene triangle
no congruent sides

EXAMPLE Classifying Triangles

1 **Signs** Classify the triangle in the sign at the right by its sides and its angles.

The triangle has three sides that are not congruent, and a right angle. It is a scalene right triangle.

✓ Quick Check

1. Classify each triangle by its sides and its angles.

a.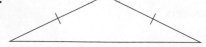

b.

You can classify quadrilaterals by their sides and angles. Arrowheads on the sides of quadrilaterals tell you which sides are parallel.

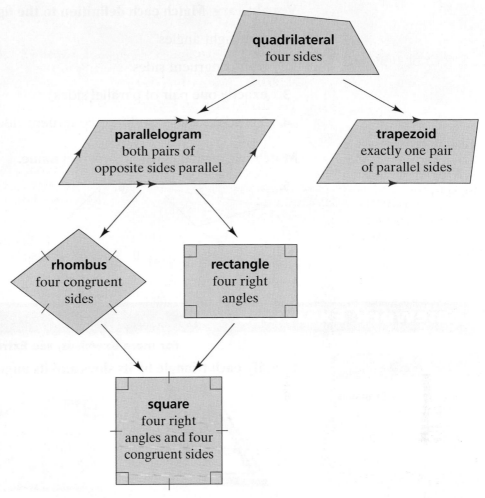

You name quadrilaterals by listing their vertices in consecutive order.

EXAMPLE **Classifying Quadrilaterals**

2 **Multiple Choice** What is the best name for parallelogram *DGHJ* at the right?

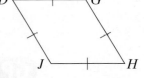

    Ⓐ trapezoid   Ⓒ rectangle

    Ⓑ rhombus   Ⓓ square

DGHJ has two pairs of opposite sides that are parallel, so it is a parallelogram. It has four congruent sides, so it is a rhombus. The best answer is choice B.

✓ Quick Check

2. What is the best name for each quadrilateral? Explain.

    a.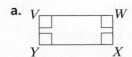
    b.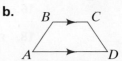

Vocabulary Match each definition to the figure it best describes.

1. four right angles

2. four congruent sides

3. exactly one pair of parallel sides

4. four right angles and four congruent sides

A. square
B. rhombus
C. rectangle
D. trapezoid

Match each triangle with its correct name.

5.

6.

7.

A. isosceles acute   **B.** scalene obtuse   **C.** isosceles right

Homework Exercises

For more exercises, see Extra Skills and Word Problems.

GO for Help

For Exercises	See Examples
8–10	1
11–14	2

Classify each triangle by its sides and its angles.

8.

9.

10.

What is the best name for each quadrilateral? Explain.

11.

12.

13.

14.

GPS 15. **Guided Problem Solving** The perimeter of an equilateral triangle is 36 cm. You stick two equilateral triangles together to make a rhombus. Find the perimeter of the rhombus.
   • What do you know about the sides of an equilateral triangle?
   • How many of these sides would make a rhombus?

Draw and label a figure to fit each description.

16. isosceles right triangle   17. trapezoid with a right angle

18. rectangle with four congruent sides

19. trapezoid with two congruent sides

20. Give an example of each type of triangle or quadrilateral you see in the diagram at the right.

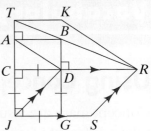

21. **Writing in Math** Why is a square both a rectangle and a rhombus?

22. The coordinates of three vertices of a parallelogram are $(3, 5)$, $(8, 5)$, and $(1, -1)$. Find the coordinates for the fourth vertex.

You can turn around "if-then" statements. Reverse each statement and decide whether the result is still a true statement.

SAMPLE If a quadrilateral is a rhombus, then it is a parallelogram.

If a quadrilateral is a parallelogram, then it is a rhombus. This statement is not true.

23. If a quadrilateral is a parallelogram, then it has two pairs of opposite sides that are parallel.

24. If a rectangle has four congruent sides, then it is a square.

25. If a triangle is equilateral, then it is an isosceles triangle.

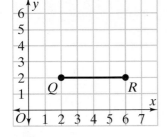

26. **Challenge** Name the coordinates of a point P in the graph at the left such that $\triangle PQR$ fits each description.
  a. isosceles obtuse   **b.** scalene acute   **c.** isosceles right

---

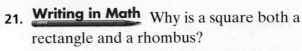

Test Prep and Mixed Review — **Practice**

Multiple Choice

27. Which of the polygons listed CANNOT have four right angles?
  Ⓐ rectangle   Ⓑ rhombus   Ⓒ square   Ⓓ trapezoid

28. Two banners for advertising a new store are similar. The height of the letters on the smaller banner is 6 inches. The height of the letters on the larger banner is 15 inches. What scale factor was used to dilate the smaller banner to the larger one?
  Ⓕ 0.4   Ⓖ 0.6   Ⓗ 1.4   Ⓙ 2.5

29. Which list shows the numbers $\frac{3}{5}$, $\frac{5}{8}$, 0.58, and 0.65 in order from least to greatest?
  Ⓐ $0.58, \frac{3}{5}, \frac{5}{8}, 0.65$ Ⓒ $\frac{3}{5}, 0.58, \frac{5}{8}, 0.65$
  Ⓑ $0.58, 0.65, \frac{3}{5}, \frac{5}{8}$ Ⓓ $0.58, \frac{3}{5}, 0.65, \frac{5}{8}$

GO for Help

For Exercises	See Lesson
30–33	5-5

Find each percent of change. Round to the nearest tenth of a percent. Label your answer *increase* or *decrease*.

30. 500 to 450   **31.** 11 to 18   **32.** 9.95 to 6.65   **33.** 12 to 13.52

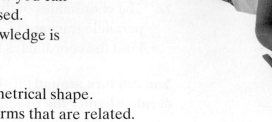

Using Concept Maps

Concept maps are visual tools that show how you can relate different ideas and terms you have used. Connecting new knowledge to existing knowledge is important in understanding mathematics.

To build a concept map, follow these steps:

- Place each concept or term inside a geometrical shape.
- Draw lines connecting the concepts or terms that are related.

EXAMPLE

In this chapter, you learned how different triangles can be classified by their angle measures or side lengths. You can show the relationships among these terms with the concept map below.

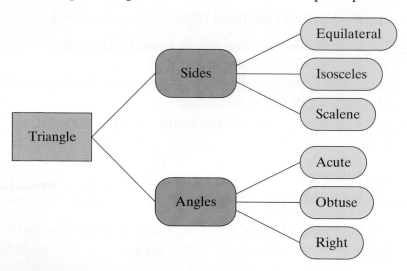

Exercises

1. Make a concept map for "Properties of Equality" using the following properties and examples from Chapter 1.

   - Addition Property of Equality
   - $12 = 4(3)$, so $\frac{12}{2} = \frac{4(3)}{2}$
   - $6 = 3(2)$, so $6 + 4 = (3)(2) + 4$
   - Multiplication Property of Equality
   - $6 = 3(2)$, so $6 - 4 = 3(2) - 4$
   - Subtraction Property of Equality
   - Division Property of Equality
   - $4 = \frac{12}{3}$, so $3(4) = 3\left(\frac{12}{3}\right)$

2. Use the terms from Lesson 7-4 that are related to quadrilaterals. Make a concept map showing the relationships among the terms.

Angle Sums

What is the sum of the measures of the angles of a figure
such as a STOP sign? You can find the answer by
drawing diagonals from one vertex to make triangles.

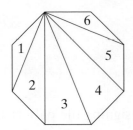

The diagonals form six triangles. The sum of
the measures of all the angles of a triangle is
180°. The sum of the angles for a STOP sign
is 6 × 180° = 1,080°.

ACTIVITY

You can develop a formula for finding the sum of the angles of a polygon.

1. Draw polygons with 4, 5, 6, and 7 sides. Draw all the diagonals from
   one vertex of each figure. Count the number of triangles formed.

2. Copy and complete the table below.

Number of Sides	Number of Triangles Formed	Sum of All Angle Measures
3	1	180°
■	■	■
■	■	■
■	■	■
■	■	■

3. a. **Patterns** Describe how the sum of the angle measures changes
      as the number of sides of a polygon increases by 1.
   b. **Reasoning** What relationship do you notice between the
      number of sides of a polygon and the number of triangles
      formed? Explain.

4. a. An *exterior angle of a polygon* is an angle formed by a side and an
      extension of an adjacent side. ∠1, ∠2, ∠3, and ∠4 at the right
      are exterior angles of a polygon. Draw polygons with 3, 4, 5, and
      6 sides. Draw and measure the exterior angles of each polygon.
   b. Find the sum of the measures of the exterior angles of each
      polygon. Record your information in a table.
   c. Make a conjecture about the sum of the exterior angles of
      a polygon.

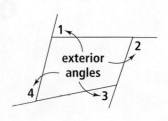

Angles and Polygons

Check Skills You'll Need

1. **Vocabulary Review**
   How do you *evaluate* an algebraic expression?

Evaluate each expression for $a = 8$.

2. $3(a + 1)$

3. $\dfrac{5a + 8}{a}$

4. $(a - 2)6$

for Help
Lesson 1-1

What You'll Learn

To find the angle measures of a polygon

🔊 **New Vocabulary** regular polygon

Why Learn This?

Polygons often appear in art and architecture. In designing tile patterns, it helps to know about the angles of polygons.

Here is a list of common polygons.

Polygon Name	Number of Sides
Triangle	3
Quadrilateral	4
Pentagon	5
Hexagon	6
Heptagon	7

Polygon Name	Number of Sides
Octagon	8
Nonagon	9
Decagon	10
Dodecagon	12

Two consecutive sides of a polygon form one interior angle. The sum of the measures of the interior angles depends on the number of sides.

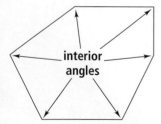

interior angles

KEY CONCEPTS **Polygon Angle Sum**

For a polygon with n sides, the sum of the measures of the interior angles is $(n - 2)180°$.

EXAMPLE **The Sum of Angle Measures of a Polygon**

1 What is the sum of the measures of the interior angles of a nonagon?

$(n - 2)180° = (9 - 2)180°$ ← A nonagon has nine sides. Substitute 9 for *n*.

$= 1,260°$ ← Simplify.

The sum of the angle measures of a nonagon is $1,260°$.

✓ Quick Check

1. What is the sum of the measures of the interior angles of a heptagon?

You can use the same formula to find angle measures in a polygon.

EXAMPLE **Angle Measures of a Polygon**

2 (**Algebra**) Find the missing angle measure in the pentagon at the right.

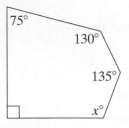

Step 1 Find the sum of the angle measures.

$(n - 2)180° = (5 - 2)180°$ ← **Substitute 5 for *n*.**

$= 540°$ ← **Simplify.**

Step 2 Write an equation. Let x = the missing angle measure.

$540° = 90° + 75° + 130° + 135° + x°$ ← **Write an equation.**

$540° = 430° + x°$ ← **Simplify.**

$110° = x°$ ← **Subtract 430° from each side.**

The missing angle measure is 110°.

✓ **Quick Check**

2. A hexagon has five angles with measures of 142°, 84°, 123°, 130°, and 90°. What is the measure of the sixth angle?

A **regular polygon** is a polygon with all sides congruent and all angles congruent. To find the measure of each angle of a regular polygon, divide the sum of the angle measures by the number of angles.

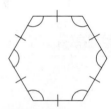

EXAMPLE **Angle Measures of a Regular Polygon**

3 **Multiple Choice** A carpenter wants to know the angle measures of the window at the right in order to cut out the correct space in a wall. If the window is a regular octagon, what is the measure of each angle?

(A) 85°   (B) 135°   (C) 142°   (D) 156°

$(n - 2)180° = (8 - 2)180°$ ← **Substitute 8 for *n*.**

$= 1,080°$ ← **Simplify.**

$1,080° ÷ 8 = 135°$ ← **Divide the sum by the number of angles.**

Each angle of a regular octagon has a measure of 135°. The correct answer is choice B.

✓ **Quick Check**

3. Find the measure of each angle of a regular polygon with 5 sides.

1. **Vocabulary** What is a regular polygon?

Classify each polygon by the number of its sides.

2.
3.
4.
5.

6. **Error Analysis** Jason knows the sum of the angle measures of a hexagon is 720°. To find the sum of the angle measures of a dodecagon, he multiplies 720° by 2 since 12 = 6 · 2. Miranda multiplies 180° by 10. Who is correct? Explain.

Homework Exercises

For more exercises, see Extra Skills and Word Problems.

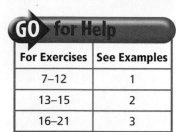

For Exercises	See Examples
7–12	1
13–15	2
16–21	3

Find the sum of the measures of the interior angles of each polygon.

7. pentagon   8. octagon   9. hexagon

10. decagon   11. triangle   12. dodecagon

(**Algebra**) **Find the missing angle measure in each figure.**

13.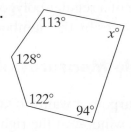

14.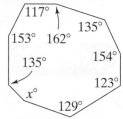

15.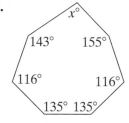

16. **Coins** The Australian 50-cent coin at the left is a regular dodecagon. What is the measure of each interior angle of the coin?

Find the measure of each angle of a regular polygon with the given number of sides. Round to the nearest tenth.

17. 7   **18.** 10   **19.** 14   **20.** 15   **21.** 18

GPS 22. **Guided Problem Solving** The measure of each interior angle of a regular polygon is 157.5°. How many sides n does the polygon have?
- What two expressions can you write for the sum of the measures of the interior angles of the polygon?
- What is the solution for n when you set the two expressions equal to each other?

23. Reasoning What is another name for a regular quadrilateral?

Algebra Find the missing angle measures in each figure.

24.
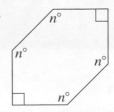

25.
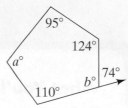

26.
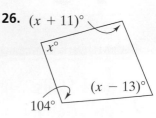

27. Writing in Math An irregular polygon is a polygon that is *not* regular. Explain why you cannot find the measure of each angle in an irregular polygon by dividing the sum of the angle measures by the number of angles.

28. The measures of six angles of a heptagon are 145°, 115°, 152°, 87°, 90°, and 150°. Find the measure of the seventh angle.

29. Baseball In the home plate at the left, ∠1 ≅ ∠2. Find $m\angle 1$.

30. Challenge A polygon is chosen at random from five regular polygons with 3, 4, 5, 6, and 8 sides. What is the probability that the measure of each angle of the polygon is a multiple of 30°?

Test Prep and Mixed Review
Practice

Multiple Choice

31. The following statements are true about △*ABC*.
- $m\angle A$ is less than $m\angle B$.
- $m\angle B$ is less than $m\angle C$.
- $m\angle C$ is less than 90°.
- Each angle measure is divisible by 3.

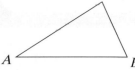

Which are possible measures of angles *A*, *B*, and *C*?

Ⓐ $m\angle A = 33°, m\angle B = 66°, m\angle C = 99°$
Ⓑ $m\angle A = 33°, m\angle B = 66°, m\angle C = 81°$
Ⓒ $m\angle A = 81°, m\angle B = 66°, m\angle C = 33°$
Ⓓ $m\angle A = 30°, m\angle B = 60°, m\angle C = 90°$

32. The area of a square is 275 square feet. Which is closest to the side length of the square?
Ⓕ 15.8 ft   Ⓖ 16.1 ft   Ⓗ 16.4 ft   Ⓙ 16.6 ft

33. A distributor places a coupon for a free subscription inside 2 of 15,978 daily newspapers. What percent of the newspapers have a coupon?
Ⓐ 12.5%   Ⓑ 1.3%   Ⓒ 0.125%   Ⓓ 0.013%

For Exercises	See Lesson
34–37	7-1

Find the measure of the supplement of each angle.

34. 65°   **35.** 48°   **36.** 127°   **37.** 153°

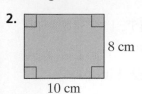
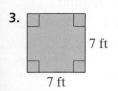

What You'll Learn

To find the areas of parallelograms, triangles, and trapezoids

🔊 **New Vocabulary** area

Why Learn This?

People who work in fields such as construction and engineering must calculate area to find how much material they need for a job. The 15 square tiles at the right cover 15 square units of area.

The **area** of a figure is the number of square units the figure encloses.

The formula for the area of a parallelogram is $A = bh$, where b is the base, and h is the perpendicular distance between the bases.

KEY CONCEPTS **Area of a Parallelogram**

The area of a parallelogram equals the product of any base length b and the corresponding height h.

$$A = bh$$

A diagonal divides a parallelogram into two congruent triangles. The area of each triangle is *half* the area of the parallelogram.

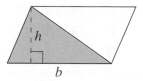

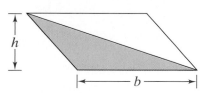

Any side of a triangle can be the base. The height of a triangle is the perpendicular distance between the base and the opposite vertex.

KEY CONCEPTS **Area of a Triangle**

The area of a triangle equals half the product of any base length b and the corresponding height h.

$$A = \frac{1}{2}bh$$

EXAMPLE · Finding the Area of a Triangle

1 Architecture An architect plans to cover the front triangular section of a townhouse with cedar shingles. Find the area of the triangle at the left.

$$A = \frac{1}{2}bh \qquad \leftarrow \text{Use the formula for the area of a triangle.}$$

$$= \frac{1}{2} \cdot 24 \cdot 16 \qquad \leftarrow \text{Substitute 24 for } b \text{ and 16 for } h.$$

$$= 192 \qquad \leftarrow \text{Multiply.}$$

The area is 192 ft^2.

✓ Quick Check

1. Find the area of the triangle below.

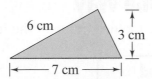

A trapezoid has two parallel sides, or bases, b_1 and b_2. The height h of a trapezoid is the perpendicular distance between the two bases.

You can use the diagram below to develop the formula for the area of a trapezoid. You can arrange two congruent trapezoids to form a parallelogram.

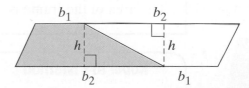

Area of parallelogram $= bh$ $\leftarrow$ Use the formula for the area of a parallelogram.

$$= (b_1 + b_2)h \qquad \leftarrow \begin{array}{l}\text{Substitute for } b \text{ and } h. \text{ The base of}\\ \text{the parallelogram is } b_1 + b_2; \text{ the}\\ \text{height is } h.\end{array}$$

Area of trapezoid $= \frac{1}{2}(b_1 + b_2)h$ $\leftarrow \begin{array}{l}\text{The area of one of the trapezoids}\\ \text{is half the area of the parallelogram.}\end{array}$

KEY CONCEPTS · Area of a Trapezoid

The area of a trapezoid is one half the product of the height and the sum of the lengths of the bases.

$$A = \frac{1}{2}h(b_1 + b_2)$$

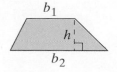

EXAMPLE **Finding the Area of a Trapezoid**

2️⃣ Find the area of the trapezoid at the right.

$$A = \frac{1}{2}h(b_1 + b_2)$$ ←Use the formula.

$$= \frac{1}{2}(3)(9 + 5)$$ ← Substitute 3 for h, 9 for b_1, and 5 for b_2.

$$= 21$$ ← Simplify.

The area of the trapezoid is 21 cm².

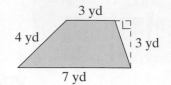

✓ **Quick Check**

2. Find the area of the trapezoid at the right.

More Than One Way

Find the area of the picture frame at the left.

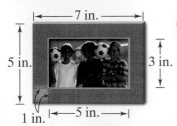

Nicole's Method

I will divide the frame into four rectangles. Then I will find the area of each rectangle and add the areas together.

Rectangles 1 and 3	Rectangles 2 and 4
$A = bh$	$A = bh$
$= (7)(1) = 7$	$= (1)(3) = 3$

The area of the frame is $2(7) + 2(3)$, or 20 in.².

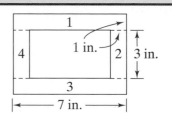

Roberto's Method

I will subtract the inner rectangle's area from the outer rectangle's area.

Outer Rectangle	Inner Rectangle
$A = bh$	$A = bh$
$= (7)(5) = 35$	$= (5)(3) = 15$

The area of the frame is $35 - 15$, or 20 in.².

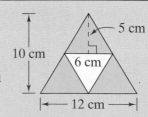

Choose a Method

The four smaller triangles are congruent. Find the area of the shaded regions. Explain why you chose the method you used.

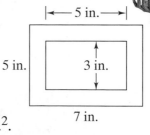

1. **Vocabulary** Which unit *cannot* be used to express area?
   - Ⓐ square centimeters
   - Ⓒ feet
   - Ⓑ square inches
   - Ⓓ square yards

Identify which polygon area each formula represents.

2. $A = bh$

3. $A = \frac{1}{2}bh$

4. $A = \frac{1}{2}h(b_1 + b_2)$

5. Find the area of the parallelogram at the left.

6 cm 5 cm 10 cm

For more exercises, see Extra Skills and Word Problems.

GO ▸ for Help

For Exercises	See Examples
6–8	1
9–11	2

Find the area of each triangle.

6.
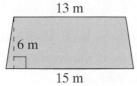
5 in. 9.4 in. 8 in.

7.
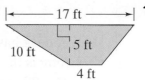
16 m 12 m 9.6 m 20 m

8.
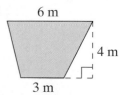
22 mm 15 mm 24 mm

Find the area of each trapezoid.

9.
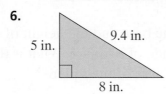
13 m 6 m 15 m

10.
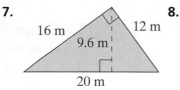
17 ft 10 ft 5 ft 4 ft

11.
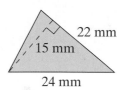
6 m 4 m 3 m

12. **Guided Problem Solving** The perimeter of a rectangular garden is 54 yd. One side has a length of 15 yd. Find the area of the garden.
    - What do you need to know to find the area of the garden?
    - How can you use the perimeter and one side to find the area?
    - What is the length of the other side of the garden?

13. **Engineering** The plan for a new parking lot at the left uses parallelograms for parking spaces. Find the area of each parking space and the total area of the unpaved sections.

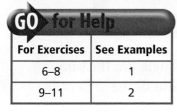

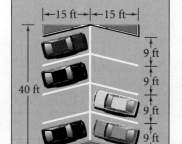
|←15 ft→|←15 ft→| 9 ft 9 ft 9 ft 9 ft 40 ft

14. **Open-Ended** On graph paper, draw two different parallelograms with the same area. What are the lengths of their bases and heights?

Choose a Method Find the area of each shaded region.

15.
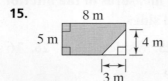
8 m 5 m 4 m 3 m

16.
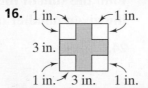
1 in. 1 in. 3 in. 1 in. 3 in. 1 in.

17.
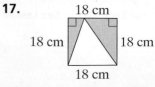
18 cm 18 cm 18 cm 18 cm

18. a. **Construction** Your cousin wants to retile a kitchen floor. The floor plan of the kitchen is shown at the right. Find the area of the floor.

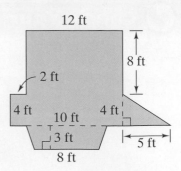

   b. One case of tiles covers 44 ft². How many cases are needed?

   c. Each case of tiles costs $39.16. What is the total cost of the tiles?

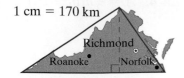

1 cm = 170 km

19. **Geography** Use the map at the left. Estimate the area of Virginia.

20. **Writing in Math** Use the diagram below to explain why the formulas for the area of a parallelogram and the area of a rectangle are the same.

21. **Challenge** The base and the height of a triangle are the same length as the side of a square. What is the ratio of the area of the triangle to the area of the square?

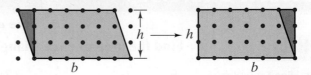

Test Prep and Mixed Review   **Practice**

Multiple Choice

22. A desk has a rectangular top with an area of 966 square inches. How long is the desktop if the width is 42 inches?
    Ⓐ 23 in.   Ⓑ 42 in.   Ⓒ 882 in.   Ⓓ 924 in.

23. A soup recipe calls for these ingredients:

    > 2 16-ounce cans of beans
    > 32 ounces chicken broth
    > $3\frac{1}{2}$ cups cooked chicken
    > $\frac{1}{2}$ cup chopped carrots
    > 5 cups cooked pasta

    What is the smallest pan that will hold all the ingredients?
    Ⓕ a 4-quart pan   Ⓗ a 6-quart pan
    Ⓖ a 5-quart pan   Ⓙ a 7-quart pan

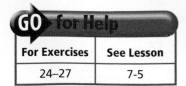
GO for Help

For Exercises	See Lesson
24–27	7-5

Find the sum of the measures of the interior angles of a polygon with the given number of sides.

24. 3 sides   25. 8 sides   26. 16 sides   27. 25 sides

Geoboard Area

Louise designed a pendant on a geoboard for her math team, the X-Factors. She had the front of each pendant gold-plated at a cost of $1.25 per square inch. If the pegs on the geoboard are 1 in. apart, how much did it cost to gold-plate 8 pendants?

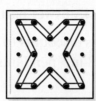

What You Might Think

What do I know? What do I want to find out?

How do I find the area?

What numerical expression represents the area A?

What numerical expression represents the cost C?

What is the answer?

What You Might Write

I know the cost per square inch. I need to find the area of the pendant, multiply the area by the cost, and then multiply the product by 8.

I can draw a square around the entire figure. I can remove two small triangles from the top and the bottom and two larger triangles from the left and right sides to find the area of the pendant.

$$A = \text{area of square} - 2 \times \text{area of small } \triangle - 2 \times \text{area of large } \triangle$$
$$= 16 - 2(\tfrac{1}{2})(2)(1) - 2(\tfrac{1}{2})(4)(1)$$
$$= 16 - 2 - 4$$
$$= 10$$

$$C = 8 \times 1.25 \times A$$
$$= 8 \times 1.25 \times 10$$
$$= 100$$

It cost $100 to gold-plate 8 pendants.

Think It Through

1. **Reasoning** Is there another way to find the area of the pendant by separating it into simpler figures? Explain.

2. **Number Sense** Suppose the geoboard pegs were $\frac{1}{2}$ inch apart instead of 1 inch apart. Would the cost of gold-plating the pendants be half of $100? Explain.

Exercises

Solve each problem. For Exercises 3 and 4, answer parts (a) and (b) first.

3. Aurora Gold-Plating Company offers discounts to customers based on the table at the right. How many 8-in.² pendants would you have to plate to get a 5% discount?
   a. What do you know and what do you want to find out?
   b. What is the minimum number of square inches needed to get a 5% discount?

Aurora Gold-Plating Company Discounts

Area (in.²)	Discount
100–199	5%
200–399	10%
400–599	15%
600–900	20%

4. Sixth- and seventh-graders are in training for the X-Factors. They are called the Ys Team and the Z-Z-Z Team. The cost of silver-plating is about $\frac{3}{4}$ the cost of gold plating. The cost of copper-plating is about $\frac{1}{2}$ the cost of gold plating. How much would it cost to silver-plate 10 pendants for the Ys Team? How much would it cost to copper-plate 12 pendants for the Z-Z-Z Team?

   a. What do you know and what do you want to find out?
   b. Find the cost to gold-plate each pin. Then find a fraction of each cost.

5. The formula for the area of a circle is $A = \pi r^2$. An approximate circle is shown on the geoboard below. Find the difference between the area of a circle with a radius of 2 in. and the area of the shape on the geoboard. How close is the approximation?

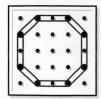

6. One pound of gold will make a thin wire about 900 mi long. A cubic mile of seawater contains about 25 tons of gold. The distance around the earth at the equator is about 25,000 mi. If the gold from a cubic mile of seawater were made into a thin wire, about how many times could the wire go around the equator of the earth?

Determine the best name for each polygon. Then find the area.

1.
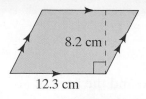
8.2 cm
12.3 cm

2.
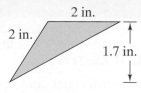
2 in.
2 in.
1.7 in.

3.
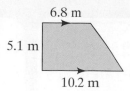
6.8 m
5.1 m
10.2 m

4. Find the missing angle measure in the figure at the right.

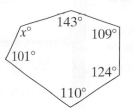
143°
109°
x°
101°
124°
110°

Draw and label a figure to fit each description.

5. a scalene obtuse triangle

6. an equilateral triangle

7-7a   Activity Lab

Hands On

Estimating Area

If you cut a pizza into equal pieces you can form a figure resembling a parallelogram.

r

$\frac{1}{2}$ circumference

1. Use a compass and an inch ruler. Make a circle with a radius of 4 in. Use a protractor to divide your circle into eight equal sections with interior angles of 45°. Cut out the sections.

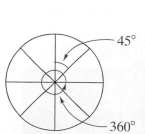
45°
360°

2. Arrange the sections of your circle as in the pizza diagram above.

3. a. Estimation Measure the base and the height of the parallelogram you made. Use the formula $A = b \cdot h$ to estimate the area of the parallelogram. What does this area represent?

b. (Algebra) Write a formula to relate the radius of a circle to the area of a circle. Recall that $C = 2\pi r$.

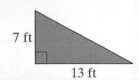

What You'll Learn

To find the circumference and area of a circle and the area of irregular figures

Why Learn This?

When making sporting equipment, such as an archery target, knowing the circumference and area of circles is important.

Below are four terms related to a circle.

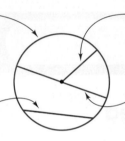

Circumference is the distance around the circle.

A **radius** is a segment that has one endpoint at the center and the other endpoint on the circle.

A **chord** is a segment with endpoints on the circle.

A **diameter** is a chord that passes through the center of the circle.

Pi (π) is the special name for the ratio of the circumference C of a circle to the diameter d of the circle.

$$\pi = \frac{C}{d}$$

If you solve this equation for C, you get $C = \pi d$, a formula for the circumference of a circle. The formula for the area of a circle is $A = \pi r^2$. Approximate values for π are $\frac{22}{7}$ and 3.14.

GO Online

Video Tutor Help
Visit: PHSchool.com
Web Code: ase-0775

KEY CONCEPTS **Circumference and Area of a Circle**

The circumference of a circle is the product of π and the diameter d.

$$C = \pi d \text{ or } C = 2\pi r$$

The area of a circle is the product of π and the square of the radius r.

$$A = \pi r^2$$

EXAMPLE Finding the Measures of a Circle

1 **Sports Equipment** Find the circumference and area of the basketball hoop at the right.

45 cm

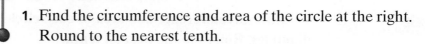

Calculator Tip

If you use 3.14 for π to find the circumference, the rounded result is 141.3, not 141.4. The calculator key $\boxed{\pi}$ gives a more accurate value for π.

$C = \pi d$ ← Use the formula for circumference.

$= \pi(45)$ ← Substitute 45 for d.

$\boxed{\pi}\ \boxed{\times}\ 45\ \boxed{=}\ 141.3716694$ ← Use a calculator.

The circumference is about 141.4 cm.

$A = \pi r^2$ ← Use the formula for the area of a circle.

$= \pi(22.5)^2$ ← The radius is 45 ÷ 2, or 22.5. Substitute 22.5 for r.

$\boxed{\pi}\ \boxed{\times}\ 22.5\ \boxed{x^2}\ \boxed{=}\ 1590.43128$ ← Use a calculator.

The area is about 1,590 cm².

✓ **Quick Check**

1. Find the circumference and area of the circle at the right. Round to the nearest tenth.

25 in.

Sometimes you can separate an irregular figure into simpler figures.

EXAMPLE Finding the Area of an Irregular Figure

2 Find the area of the front of the mailbox.

Step 1 Find the area of the half circle.

$A = \frac{1}{2}\pi r^2$ ← Multiply the formula for the area of a circle by $\frac{1}{2}$.

$= \frac{1}{2}\pi(5)^2$ ← Substitute 5 for r.

≈ 39.3 ← Multiply. Round to the nearest tenth.

10 in.

7 in.

U.S. MAIL

Step 2 Find the area of the rectangle.

$A = bh$ ← Use the formula for the area of a rectangle.

$= 10 \cdot 7 = 70$ ← Substitute 10 for b and 7 for h.

Step 3 Add the two areas: $39.3 + 70 = 109.3$.

The area of the front of the mailbox is about 109.3 in.².

✓ **Quick Check**

2. Find the area of the shaded region at the right. Round to the nearest tenth.

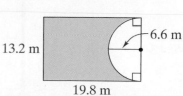

13.2 m

6.6 m

19.8 m

Careers The U.S. Postal Service hires over 300,000 mail carriers to collect, sort, and deliver the mail.

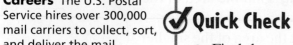

1. **Vocabulary** What is the perimeter of a circle called?

2. How would you separate the figure at the right into simpler figures to find its area?

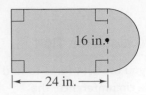
16 in.
24 in.

3. **Reasoning** Show that the two formulas for circumference, $C = \pi d$ and $C = 2\pi r$, are equivalent.

Mental Math Find the circumference of a circle with the given radius or diameter. Use $\frac{22}{7}$ for π.

4. $d = 21$ cm   5. $r = 7$ km   6. $r = 3.5$ m   7. $d = 28$ in.

Homework Exercises

For more exercises, see Extra Skills and Word Problems.

GO for Help

For Exercises	See Examples
8–16	1
17–22	2

Find the circumference and area of each circle with the given radius or diameter. Round to the nearest tenth.

8.
12 m

9.
5 cm

10.
14 yd

11. $d = 9.2$ in.   12. $r = 4.5$ cm   13. $r = 17.6$ mm

14. $d = 8.1$ yd   15. $r = 10.5$ cm   16. $d = 6.4$ ft

GO for Help

For help with finding the area of a triangle, go to Lesson 7-6, Example 1.

Find the area of each shaded region to the nearest tenth.

17.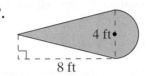
4 ft
8 ft

18.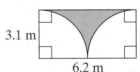
3.1 m
6.2 m

19.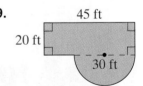
45 ft
20 ft
30 ft

20.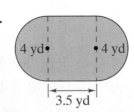
4 yd
4 yd
3.5 yd

21.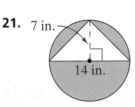
7 in.
14 in.

22.
11.8 ft

23. **Guided Problem Solving** Find the area of the shaded ring to the nearest square centimeter.

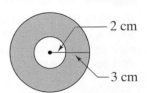
2 cm
3 cm

* **Make a Plan** Subtract the area of the smaller circle from the area of the larger circle.
* **Carry Out the Plan** The area of the larger circle is ▪. The area of the smaller circle is ▪. The difference between the two areas is ▪.

24. Basketball A part of a basketball court is shown at the right. Find the area of the purple shaded region.

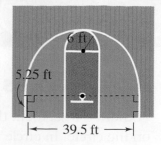

6 ft

5.25 ft

|← 39.5 ft →|

25. Writing in Math Compare the area of a circle with diameter 2 in. to the area of a square with side length 2 in.

Find the radius and diameter of each circle with the given circumference. Round to the nearest hundredth.

26. 22.35 cm   **27.** 1.71 in.   **28.** 50.94 ft   **29.** 62.83 m

30. Recreation The circumference of a pool is about 63 ft. What is the area of the bottom of the pool? Round to the nearest tenth.

31. Food A large pizza has a total diameter of 14 in. and a crust that is 1 in. wide. What is the area of the crust? Round to the nearest tenth.

32. a. Number Sense The ratio of the radii of two circles is 3 : 1. What is the ratio of their areas?

   b. (**Algebra**) The ratio of the radii of two circles is $a : b$. Write the ratio of their areas in terms of a and b.

33. The area of a circle is 432 ft². Estimate its radius.

34. Challenge The area of the shaded wedge at the right is about 64 cm². To the nearest tenth, what percent of the area of the circle is the wedge?

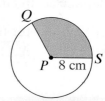

Q

P   8 cm   S

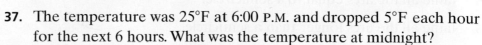

Test Prep and Mixed Review   **Practice**

Multiple Choice

35. Malcolm rode a Ferris wheel and traveled about 785 feet in one full rotation. What was the diameter of the wheel to the nearest foot?

   Ⓐ 63 ft   Ⓑ 125 ft   Ⓒ 225 ft   Ⓓ 250 ft

36. Which procedure can be used to find the number of degrees in $\angle B$ at the right?

   Ⓕ Divide 180 by 3.
   Ⓖ Divide 150 by 2.
   Ⓗ Subtract the sum of 120 and 30 from 360.
   Ⓙ Subtract the sum of 120 and 30 from 180.

C   30°

120°

A   B

37. The temperature was 25°F at 6:00 P.M. and dropped 5°F each hour for the next 6 hours. What was the temperature at midnight?

   Ⓐ −30°F   Ⓑ −25°F   Ⓒ −5°F   Ⓓ 5°F

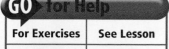
Mental Math Estimate a 15% tip for each restaurant bill.

38. $28.55   **39.** $64.82   **40.** $13.97   **41.** $108.16

Arcs, Chords, and Semicircles

A chord is a segment that has both endpoints on the circle. In circle F, $\overline{AB}$ is a chord.

An arc is part of a circle. In circle F, $\overset{\frown}{CD}$ and $\overset{\frown}{DE}$ are arcs. An arc that is half the circumference of a circle is called a semicircle. $\overset{\frown}{CDE}$ is a semicircle. You use three letters to name a semicircle or an arc longer than a semicircle. Note that $\overset{\frown}{CDE}$ has the same endpoints as diameter $\overline{CE}$.

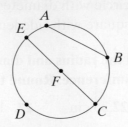

EXAMPLES

1 Name all the chords in circle O.

The chords are $\overline{PQ}, \overline{QR}, \overline{RS}, \overline{SP},$ and $\overline{QS}$.

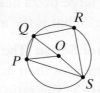

2 Name an arc that is shorter than, equal to, and longer than a semicircle in circle W.

$\overset{\frown}{XY}$ is shorter than a semicircle. $\overline{XZ}$ is a diameter, so $\overset{\frown}{XYZ}$ is a semicircle. $\overset{\frown}{XZY}$ is longer than a semicircle.

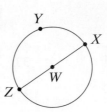

Exercises

Name all the chords in each circle.

1.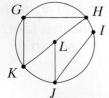

2.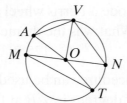

3.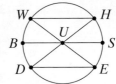

Use the circle at the right for Exercises 4–6.

4. Name all the arcs shorter than a semicircle.

5. Name all the arcs equal to a semicircle.

6. Name all the arcs longer than a semicircle.

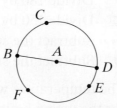

7. Reasoning Is a diameter a chord? Is a radius a chord? Explain.

8. What is the length of a semicircle of a circle with a diameter of 8 cm? Express your answer in terms of π.

Constructions

✓ Check Skills You'll Need

1. **Vocabulary Review** How are *congruent polygons* the same?

List the congruent parts of each pair of congruent figures.

2. $\triangle PQR \cong \triangle TUV$

3. $ABCD \cong LMNO$

GO for Help
Lesson 7-3

What You'll Learn

To construct congruent angles and parallel lines

🔊 **New Vocabulary** compass

Why Learn This?

Marine pilots use tools, such as compasses and rulers, to map the paths of ships. To navigate accurately, they construct angles and lines.

A **compass** is a tool used to draw circles and parts of circles called *arcs*. A straightedge is a ruler with no markings on it.

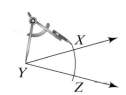

EXAMPLE Constructing Congruent Angles

1 Construct $\angle S$ congruent to $\angle Y$ shown at the left.

Step 1 Draw a ray with endpoint S.

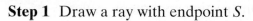

Step 2 Put the compass tip at Y and draw an arc that intersects the sides of $\angle Y$. Label the points of intersection X and Z.

Step 3 Keep the compass open to the same width. Put the compass tip at S. Draw an arc that intersects the ray at a point T.

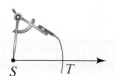

Step 4 Adjust the compass so that the tip is at Z and the pencil is at X. Using this compass opening, put the tip at T. Draw an arc to determine point R. Draw $\overrightarrow{SR}$.

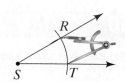

$\angle S$ is congruent to $\angle Y$.

✓ Quick Check

1. Draw an obtuse angle, $\angle F$. Construct $\angle N$ congruent to $\angle F$.

You can construct congruent angles to help construct parallel lines.

EXAMPLE **Constructing Parallel Lines**

② Construct a line parallel to line n at the right.

Step 1 Draw line m that intersects line n at A. Label the angle formed ∠1. Then label point B on line m.

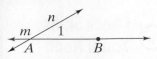

Step 2 Construct an angle at B that is congruent to ∠1.

$\overleftrightarrow{BF}$ is parallel to line n.

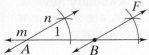

✓ Quick Check

2. Draw a line d. Construct a line e parallel to line d.

Check Your Understanding

1. **Vocabulary** A compass is a tool used to draw ___?___.

2. **Reasoning** Do you need to know the measure of an angle to construct a congruent angle? Explain.

3. Describe the step in constructing congruent angles that is shown at the right.

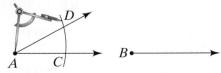

4. **Multiple Choice** To construct parallel lines, which pair of angles do you construct?

  Ⓐ alternate interior   Ⓒ supplementary

  Ⓑ corresponding   Ⓓ vertical

Homework Exercises

For more exercises, see Extra Skills and Word Problems.

GO▶ for Help

For Exercises	See Examples
5–6	1
7–8	2

Copy each angle. Then construct a congruent angle.

5.

6.

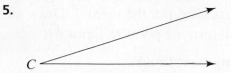
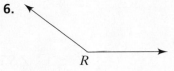

Draw each line. Then construct a line parallel to it.

7. a horizontal line   8. a vertical line

9. **Guided Problem Solving** Use a compass and straightedge to construct a parallelogram.
   - **Make a Plan** Draw a line *a*. Draw a line *b* that intersects line *a*. Construct line *c* parallel to line *a*. To draw the fourth side, connect the points where the arcs intersect lines *a* and *c*.
   - **Check the Answer** Check that opposite sides and opposite angles are congruent.

10. **Multiple Choice** Which is *not* a step in constructing $\angle E$ congruent to $\angle A$?

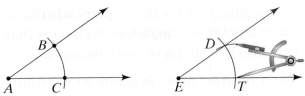

A Adjust the compass width to the distance between *B* and *C*.
B Draw a ray with endpoint *E*.
C Draw an arc that intersects both sides of $\angle A$.
D Adjust the compass width to the distance between *A* and *B*.

11. **Writing in Math** How could you construct a trapezoid?

12. **Challenge** Draw a triangle $\triangle ABC$. Construct a triangle with the same angle measures as $\triangle ABC$.

GO **Online**
Homework Video Tutor
Visit: PHSchool.com
Web Code: ase-0708

Test Prep and Mixed Review

Practice

Multiple Choice

13. A triangular traffic sign has an area of 390 square inches. If the height of the triangle is 26 inches, what is the length of its base?
    A 14 in.   B 15 in.   C 30 in.   D 52 in.

14. Which of the following is an expression for the area in square meters of the figure at the right?
    F $4(4\pi) + 4$ H $4 + 4\pi$
    G 8π J $2\pi + 2(2)$

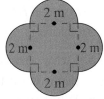

15. The cost *c* to install rain gutters on a house can be found using the equation $c = 70 + 2n$, where *n* represents the number of feet of gutters needed. If the cost was $262, how many feet of gutters were needed?
    A 61 ft   B 96 ft   C 166 ft   D 594 ft

Probability Find each probability if you spin the spinner once. A spinner has 26 sections of equal size. Each section is labeled with a different letter of the alphabet. Express each probability as a fraction.

16. *P*(M, A, T, or H)   17. *P*(a letter before I)   18. *P*(a letter after Q)

GO **for Help**

For Exercises	See Lesson
16–18	5-8

Online lesson quiz, PHSchool.com, Web Code: asa-0708

7-8 Constructions   **343**

Chapter 7 Review

Vocabulary Review

🔊 acute triangle (p. 318)
adjacent angles (p. 303)
alternate interior angles (p. 307)
area (p. 328)
compass (p. 341)
complementary (p. 304)
congruent polygons (p. 312)
corresponding angles (p. 307)
equilateral triangle (p. 318)

isosceles triangle (p. 318)
obtuse triangle (p. 318)
parallelogram (p. 319)
perpendicular lines (p. 304)
quadrilateral (p. 319)
rectangle (p. 319)
regular polygon (p. 325)
rhombus (p. 319)

right triangle (p. 318)
scalene triangle (p. 318)
square (p. 319)
supplementary (p. 304)
transversal (p. 307)
trapezoid (p. 319)
vertical angles (p. 303)

Choose the correct vocabulary term to complete each sentence.

1. A (transversal, compass) intersects two lines at different points.

2. A triangle with no congruent sides is (isosceles, scalene).

3. The measures of (complementary, supplementary) angles add up to 180°.

4. A (rhombus, trapezoid) has four congruent sides.

5. All the sides and angles of a (congruent polygon, regular polygon) are congruent.

Go Online
PHSchool.com
For: Online Vocabulary Quiz
Web Code: asj-0751

Skills and Concepts

Lessons 7-1, 7-2
• To identify types of angles and to find angle measures using the relationship between angles
• To identify parallel lines and the angles formed by parallel lines and transversals

Vertical angles are congruent. The sum of the measures of a pair of **supplementary** angles is 180°. The sum of the measures of a pair of **complementary** angles is 90°.

If two parallel lines are cut by a **transversal,** the **corresponding angles** are congruent, and the **alternate interior angles** are congruent.

Find the measures of ∠1 and ∠2 in each diagram.

6.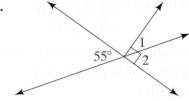

7.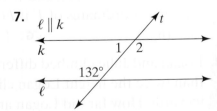

Lessons 7-3, 7-4

- To identify congruent figures and use them to solve problems
- To classify triangles and quadrilaterals

Congruent polygons have exactly the same size and shape. You can use SAS, ASA, or SSS to decide whether two triangles are congruent. You can classify triangles by angle measures or by the number of congruent sides. You can classify quadrilaterals by their sides and angles.

Classify each triangle by its sides and its angles.

8.   9.   10.

Write a congruence statement and show that the triangles are congruent.

11. 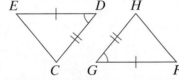   12.

Lesson 7-5

- To find the angle measures of a polygon

For a polygon with n sides, the sum of the measures of the interior angles is $(n - 2)180°$. The measure of each angle of a **regular polygon** equals the sum of the angle measures divided by the number of angles.

Find the measure of each angle of a regular polygon with the given number of sides.

13. 6   14. 8   15. 12   16. 18

Lessons 7-6, 7-7

- To find the areas of parallelograms, triangles, and trapezoids
- To find the circumference and area of a circle and the area of irregular figures

Area formulas: **parallelogram** $A = bh$ **triangle** $A = \frac{1}{2}bh$

         trapezoid $A = \frac{1}{2}h(b_1 + b_2)$ **circle** $A = \pi r^2$

The distance around a circle is the **circumference** of the circle.

$C = \pi d$ or $C = 2\pi r$

Find the area of each figure. If necessary, round to the nearest tenth.

17. 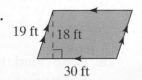   18. 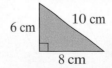   19.

Lesson 7-8

- To construct congruent angles and parallel lines

You can construct congruent angles and parallel lines using a **compass.**

20. Draw an acute $\angle P$. Then construct $\angle T$ congruent to $\angle P$.

21. Draw a vertical line a. Construct a line b parallel to a.

Identify each pair of angles in the diagram below as *adjacent*, *corresponding*, *alternate interior*, *vertical*, or *none of these*.

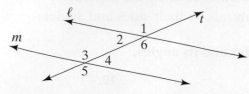

1. $\angle 2$, $\angle 4$ 2. $\angle 1$, $\angle 5$

3. $\angle 1$, $\angle 3$ 4. $\angle 3$, $\angle 4$

5. $\angle 4$, $\angle 6$ 6. $\angle 3$, $\angle 5$

7. Find the measures of the numbered angles in the diagram below.

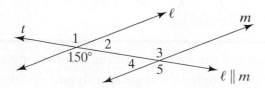

$\ell \parallel m$

The measure of $\angle D$ is 68°.

8. Find the measure of its supplement.

9. Find the measure of its complement.

Reasoning Write *true* or *false*. Explain.

10. An obtuse triangle can be a right triangle.

11. A scalene triangle can be an acute triangle.

12. A rhombus can have four right angles.

Determine the best name for each figure. Explain.

13. 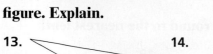   14.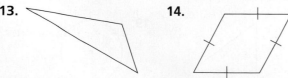

15. **Writing in Math** Explain the difference between a rectangle and a parallelogram.

16. What is the measure of each interior angle of a regular pentagon?

Determine whether each pair of triangles is congruent. If so, write a congruence statement and explain how you know the triangles are congruent.

17.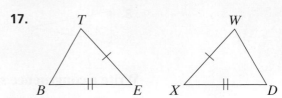

18.

Draw and label a figure to fit each description.

19. a scalene right triangle

20. an equilateral triangle

21. a parallelogram that is not a rectangle

22. a rectangle that is a rhombus

Find the sum of the measures of the interior angles of a polygon with the given number of sides.

23. 4 sides   24. 7 sides   25. 15 sides

Find the area of each figure.

26.   8 in.   27.
                                                                 10 cm
6.5 in.   6 in.   6 cm
                                                                 9 cm

28. **Food** Find the circumference and the area of a pancake with a diameter of 15 cm. Round your answers to the nearest tenth.

29. Draw an obtuse angle and label it $\angle G$. Construct $\angle H$ congruent to $\angle G$.

Multiple Choice
For Exercises 1–10, choose the correct letter.

1. Which square root lies between the whole numbers 11 and 12?
   - Ⓐ $\sqrt{101}$
   - Ⓑ $\sqrt{120}$
   - Ⓒ $\sqrt{135}$
   - Ⓓ $\sqrt{144}$

2. Aleisha can read four pages in 12 min. Which proportion can she use to figure out how long it will take her to read an 18-page chapter?
   - Ⓕ $\frac{4}{12} = \frac{x}{18}$
   - Ⓗ $\frac{4}{18} = \frac{12}{x}$
   - Ⓖ $\frac{12}{18} = \frac{4}{x}$
   - Ⓙ $\frac{4}{x} = \frac{18}{12}$

3. Write $3\frac{1}{2}\%$ as a fraction in simplest form.
   - Ⓐ $\frac{7}{2}$
   - Ⓑ $\frac{7}{20}$
   - Ⓒ $\frac{7}{200}$
   - Ⓓ $\frac{3.5}{100}$

4. What is the circumference of a circle with an area of 36π in.²?
   - Ⓕ 6π in.
   - Ⓗ 18π in.
   - Ⓖ 12π in.
   - Ⓙ 36π in.

5. Which power is equivalent to $5^3 \cdot 5^2$?
   - Ⓐ 5^5
   - Ⓑ 5^6
   - Ⓒ 25^5
   - Ⓓ 25^6

6. Which is a pair of corresponding angles?

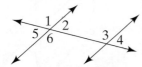

   - Ⓕ $\angle 1$ and $\angle 6$
   - Ⓗ $\angle 3$ and $\angle 6$
   - Ⓖ $\angle 1$ and $\angle 4$
   - Ⓙ $\angle 2$ and $\angle 4$

7. A job pays $160 for 25 hours. At this rate, what would it pay for 40 hours?
   - Ⓐ $216
   - Ⓒ $640
   - Ⓑ $256
   - Ⓓ $1,000

8. Which algebraic expression is NOT equivalent to $2(x + 5)$?
   - Ⓕ $2(x) + 2(5)$
   - Ⓗ $(x + 5) + (x + 5)$
   - Ⓖ $2(5 + x)$
   - Ⓙ $5 + 2x$

9. $S'(-3, -2)$ is the image after a translation of 6 units to the left and 2 units up. What are the coordinates of the original point?
   - Ⓐ $(9, -2)$
   - Ⓒ $(1, 2)$
   - Ⓑ $(3, 2)$
   - Ⓓ $(3, -4)$

10. Choose the step you should complete first to construct $\angle E$ congruent to $\angle M$.
    - Ⓕ Put the compass tip at M.
    - Ⓖ Draw a ray with endpoint E.
    - Ⓗ Draw an arc that intersects the sides of $\angle M$.
    - Ⓙ Put the compass tip at E.

Gridded Response
Record your answer in a grid.

11. A painter needs 15 gallons of violet paint. The formula for mixing violet paint is 3 parts blue to 2 parts red. How many gallons of blue paint does the painter need?

Short Response

12. Farmer Hoyle usually takes the shortcut across his rectangular field. How much distance does he save by taking the shortcut instead of walking along two sides of the field? Justify your answer.

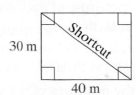

Extended Response

13. On the first day of gym class, students do 6 push-ups. The number of push-ups the students do will increase by 2 each time they come to class.
    a. Write an equation that represents the number of push-ups p the class does after c classes.
    b. How many push-ups will the class do on the ninth day of class? Justify your answer.

Problem Solving Application

Applying Geometry

You Can't Get There From Here For a sailboat, the shortest distance between two points is not always a straight line. Sailboats cannot travel directly into the wind (upwind). They can head about 45° from the direction of the wind, but not closer. To get to a specific point upwind, the sailboat has to follow a zigzag course, as shown below. This is called tacking.

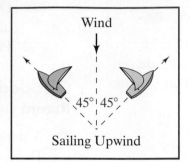

Wind

45° 45°

Sailing Upwind

Safe-Water Buoy
Buoys are floating aids that mark channels and warn sailors of obstructions in the water.

Put It All Together

Materials ruler, protractor

Three sailboats are racing upwind toward the finish line, 3 mi away. One crew tacks twice, another tacks three times, and the third crew tacks four times. Their courses create isosceles right triangles where they intersect the dashed lines.

1. Copy the sailing diagram. For each course, find the length of the hypotenuse of each triangle.

2. **Writing in Math** In the triangle diagram below, point D is the midpoint of $\overline{BC}$, so $\overline{BD} \cong \overline{DC}$. Explain how you know that $\triangle ADC \cong \triangle ADB$.

3. **a.** Find the measures of the angles in $\triangle ABC$, $\triangle ADC$, and $\triangle ADB$. What do you notice?
   b. What are the measures of the three angles of an isosceles right triangle? Explain.

4. **a.** Suppose $DC = 100$ yd. How long is $\overline{AD}$? Explain.
   b. Reasoning Suppose the hypotenuse of $\triangle ABC$ measures 10 mi. How long is $\overline{AC}$? Explain.

5. **a.** Find the course length for each boat. Which boat follows the shortest course?
   b. Patterns If a boat tacks ten times, what will its course length be?

6. **Reasoning** Why might the skipper of a sailboat crew decide to tack more times? Fewer times?

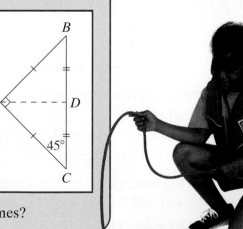

Wind

Tacking Toward the Mark

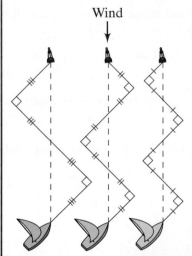

B

A ◇- - - - D

45°

C

350

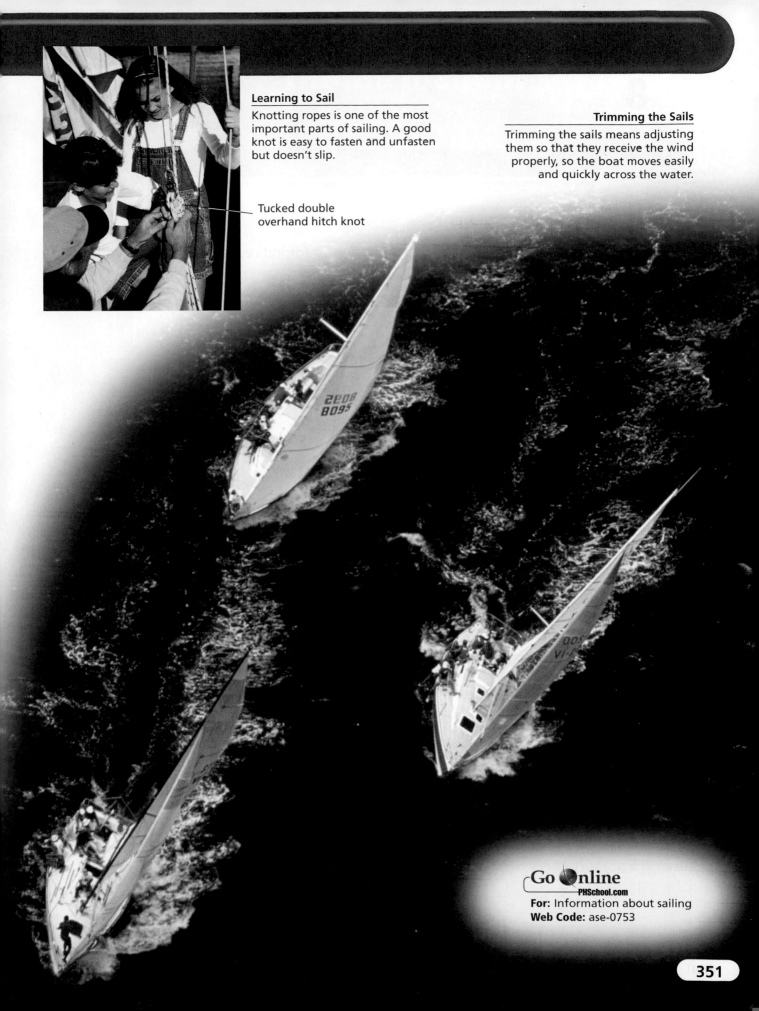

Learning to Sail
Knotting ropes is one of the most important parts of sailing. A good knot is easy to fasten and unfasten but doesn't slip.

Tucked double
overhand hitch knot

Trimming the Sails
Trimming the sails means adjusting them so that they receive the wind properly, so the boat moves easily and quickly across the water.

Go Online
PHSchool.com
For: Information about sailing
Web Code: ase-0753

What You've Learned

- In Chapter 4, you used proportions and similar figures for indirect measurement.
- In Chapter 7, you found the areas of parallelograms, triangles, trapezoids, and circles.
- You classified two-dimensional figures based on their properties.

Check Your Readiness

GO for Help

For Exercises	See Lesson
1–2	7-7
3–6	7-6
7–10	4-3

Finding Area

Find the area of each figure. Round to the nearest square unit.

1.
3 ft

2.
2 m

3.
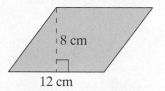
8 cm
12 cm

4.
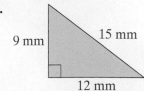
9 mm · 15 mm · 12 mm

5.
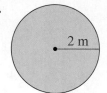
7 in. · 5 in. · 8 in.

6.
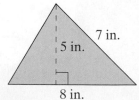
8 cm · 5 cm · 4 cm · 3 cm

Solving Proportions

Solve each proportion.

7. $\frac{x}{4} = \frac{15}{20}$

8. $\frac{a}{9} = \frac{21}{27}$

9. $\frac{26}{5} = \frac{13}{b}$

10. $\frac{10}{h} = \frac{30}{36}$

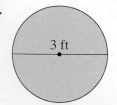
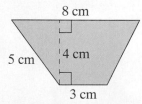

What You'll Learn Next

- In this chapter, you will classify and draw three-dimensional figures.

- You will find the surface areas and volumes of prisms, cylinders, pyramids, cones, and spheres.

- You will use proportions to find missing measurements in similar solids.

 Problem Solving Application On pages 408 and 409, you will work an extended activity on wingspans.

🔊 Key Vocabulary

- base plan (p. 358)
- cone (p. 354)
- cylinder (p. 354)
- isometric view (p. 359)
- lateral area (p. 369)
- net (p. 364)
- polyhedron (p. 354)
- prism (p. 354)
- pyramid (p. 354)
- similar solids (p. 398)
- skew lines (p. 355)
- slant height (p. 374)
- solids (p. 354)
- sphere (p. 393)
- surface area (p. 368)
- volume (p. 380)

Check Skills You'll Need

1. **Vocabulary Review**
What does it mean to say that two triangles are *congruent*?

Determine the best name for each figure.

2.

3.

GO for Help
Lesson 7-4

What You'll Learn

To identify solids, parts of solids, and skew line segments

🔊 **New Vocabulary** solids, prism, pyramid, cylinder, cone, polyhedron, skew lines

Why Learn This?

Our world is made up of largely three-dimensional figures, or solids. Artists use three-dimensional figures in sculptures.

Solids are objects that do not lie in a plane. They have length, width, and height. Below are some common solids.

A **prism** is a solid with two parallel bases that are congruent polygons. The lateral faces are parallelograms.

A **pyramid** is a solid with exactly one base, which is a polygon. The lateral faces are triangles.

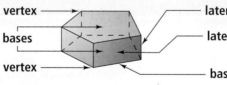

vertex · lateral edge · vertex
bases · lateral face · base
vertex · base edge

A prism is named for the shape of its bases. The prism above is a pentagonal prism.

A pyramid is named for the shape of its base. The pyramid above is a square pyramid.

A **cylinder** is a solid with two bases that are parallel, congruent circles.

A **cone** is a solid with exactly one circular base and one vertex.

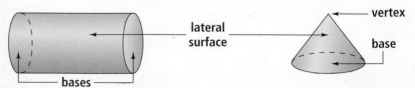

lateral surface

bases

vertex

base

Vocabulary Tip

Polyhedron means "many surfaces."

A **polyhedron** is a solid whose faces are polygons. Of the solids above, only prisms and pyramids are polyhedrons.

EXAMPLE **Naming Solids and Their Parts**

1 Refer to the figure at the right. Describe the base, name the figure, and name $\overline{RL}$.

The only base is a circle. The figure is a cone. $\overline{RL}$ is a diameter.

✓ Quick Check

1. Refer to the figure at the right. Name the figure, $\overline{JK}$, and the points J and K.

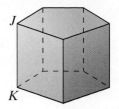

Common solids are everywhere. Often, solids form complex structures.

EXAMPLE **Recognizing Solids**

2 **Set Design** A stage crew for the school play constructed the ramp shown. Name the three solids used to construct the ramp.

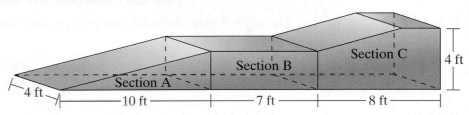

Section A is a triangular prism. Section B is a rectangular prism. Section C is a pentagonal prism.

✓ Quick Check

2. Name two solids that can be used to make up Section C.

Skew lines are lines that do not intersect and are not parallel. Unlike parallel or intersecting lines, skew lines do not lie in the same plane.

EXAMPLE **Identifying Skew Line Segments**

3 Name a pair of skew line segments and a pair of parallel line segments in the figure at the right.

$\overline{AF}$ and $\overline{ED}$ are skew. $\overline{BC}$ and $\overline{FG}$ are parallel.

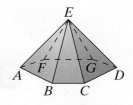

✓ Quick Check

3. **Open-Ended** Name a pair of intersecting line segments in the figure above. Are they skew line segments?

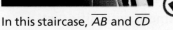

In this staircase, $\overline{AB}$ and $\overline{CD}$ are skew line segments.

1. **Vocabulary** What is the difference between parallel lines and skew lines?

Use the figure at the right for Exercises 2–4.

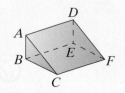

2. The bases are two __?__.

3. The figure is a __?__ prism.

4. $\overline{CF}$ is a (lateral face, lateral edge).

5. The three solids that make up the pencil shown below are a hexagonal prism, a cone, and a __?__.

For more exercises, see **Extra Skills and Word Problems.**

For each figure, describe the base, name the figure, and name $\overline{PQ}$.

GO for Help	
For Exercises	**See Examples**
6–8	1
9	2
10–12	3

6.

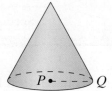

7.

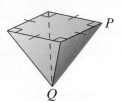

8.

9. **Models** For an art project, you are building a model like the one at the right out of balsa wood. What solids will you use to construct your model?

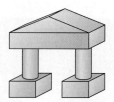

For each figure, name a pair of skew line segments and a pair of parallel line segments.

10.

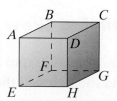

11.

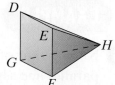

12.

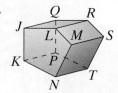

13. **Guided Problem Solving** A figure has exactly four lateral faces that are triangles. What name best describes this solid?
   - Use the strategy *Draw a Picture*. Experiment with different drawings. Do you have a figure with four triangular lateral faces?
   - What is the name of your solid?

Use the rectangular pyramid at the right. State whether each pair of line segments is *intersecting*, *parallel*, or *skew*.

14. $\overline{CO}, \overline{CE}$ **15.** $\overline{OR}, \overline{CE}$ **16.** $\overline{CT}, \overline{ER}$

17. Design You are asked to help design the skating terrain for a local skate park. Explain which common solids you would choose to make the terrain challenging and fun for all skaters.

18. Writing in Math Kenji says the figure at the right is a trapezoidal prism. Esther says it is a triangular prism and rectangular prism combined. Are they both correct? Explain.

19. A figure has three lateral faces that are rectangles. Name the figure.

20. Challenge Describe one way the solid below can be made from three different types of prisms.

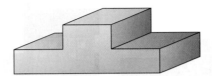

 Test Prep and Mixed Review   **Practice**

Multiple Choice

21. The area of a swimming pool is 336 square feet. What is the length of the pool if the width is 28 feet?

  Ⓐ 12 ft   Ⓒ 14 ft

  Ⓑ 56 ft   Ⓓ 84 ft

$A = 336 \text{ ft}^2$

|← 28 ft →|

22. The three leading consumers of oil in millions of barrels per day are the United States with $20\frac{1}{2}$, China with $6\frac{1}{2}$, and Japan with $5\frac{2}{5}$. How many more million barrels does the United States consume than China and Japan combined?

  Ⓕ $10\frac{2}{5}$ Ⓖ 10   Ⓗ $9\frac{2}{5}$ Ⓙ $8\frac{3}{5}$

23. A parallelogram has four congruent sides but no right angles. Which statement about the figure is true?

  Ⓐ The figure could be a trapezoid.

  Ⓑ The formula for the area of the figure is $A = bh$.

  Ⓒ The measures of the interior angles are the same.

  Ⓓ A diagonal of the figure divides the shape into two rhombuses.

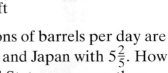

For Exercises	See Lesson
24–26	5-2

Estimate each product.

24. 15% of 506   **25.** 60% of 38   **26.** 94% of 440

For help with the area and circumference of a circle, go to Lesson 7-7, Example 1.

KEY CONCEPTS — Lateral Area and Surface Area of a Cylinder

The lateral area L.A. of a cylinder is the product of the circumference of the base and the height of the cylinder.

$$L.A. = 2\pi rh$$

The surface area S.A. of a cylinder is the sum of the lateral area and the area of the bases.

$$S.A. = L.A. + 2B$$

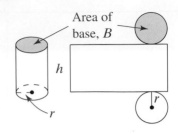

Area of base, B

h

r

EXAMPLE   Finding Surface Area of a Cylinder

3 Find the surface area of the can at the right to the nearest square centimeter.

7 cm

BAKING POWDER

11.5 cm

Estimate Use 3 for π, 4 cm for the radius, and 11 cm for the height.

$$L.A. \approx 2(3)(4)(11) = 264$$

$$B \approx 3(4)^2 = 48$$

$$B \approx 3(4)^2 = 48$$

S.A. $\approx 48 + 264 + 48$. The surface area is about 360 cm².

Test Prep Tip

You can estimate to find whole-number approximations of expressions that use π.

The radius is 7 cm ÷ 2, or 3.5 cm. Use the cylinder surface area formula.

S.A. = L.A. + 2B	← surface area formula
$= 2\pi rh + 2(\pi r^2)$	← Use $2\pi rh$ for L.A. and πr^2 for B.
$= 2\pi(3.5)(11.5) + 2\pi(3.5)^2$	← Substitute 3.5 for r and 11.5 for h.
$= 105\pi$	← Simplify.
≈ 329.8672286	← Use a calculator.

The surface area of the can is about 330 cm².

Check for Reasonableness The answer 330 cm² is close to the estimate of 360 cm². The answer is reasonable.

✓ Quick Check

3. Find the surface area of the cylinder at the right to the nearest square meter.

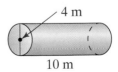

4 m

10 m

1. **Vocabulary** What is the difference between the lateral area of a prism and the surface area of a prism?

The net for a rectangular prism is shown at the right. Find each area.

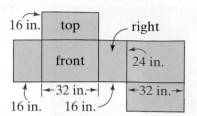

16 in. top right
front 24 in.
32 in. 32 in.
16 in. 16 in.

2. front face   3. right face

4. top face   5. lateral area

Homework Exercises

For more exercises, see Extra Skills and Word Problems.

Use a net to find the surface area of each prism.

GO for Help

For Exercises	See Examples
6–7	1
8–11	2
12–13	3

6.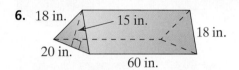

18 in. 15 in. 18 in.
20 in. 60 in.

7.
4 cm
4 cm 4 cm

8. The shed at the right needs to be painted. Find the lateral area of the shed including the door and windows.

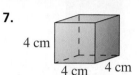

10 ft
10 ft 12 ft

Use a formula to find the surface area of each figure.

9.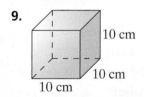
10 cm
10 cm
10 cm

10.
5 in.
7 in.
4 in. 3 in.

11.
10 ft
10 ft 2 ft
8 ft
6 ft

Find the surface area of each cylinder. Round to the nearest square unit.

12. radius: 4 in., height: 6 in.   13. diameter: 7 cm, height: 9 cm

14. **Guided Problem Solving** A cleaning company is hired to clean the windows of the building shown. Estimate the area that needs to be cleaned.

45 ft
126 ft
105 ft

- **Understand the Problem** The windows are on the four sides of the building. To estimate the area that needs to be cleaned, find the ? area of a ? .
- **Carry Out the Plan** What is the perimeter p of the base? What is the height h? Find $p \times h$ to determine the area.

15. Which will require more cardboard to make: a box 9 cm by 5.5 cm by 11.75 cm, or a box 8 cm by 6.25 cm by 10.5 cm? Explain.

16. **Writing in Math** You can draw a net or use a formula to find the surface area of a solid. Which way do you prefer? Explain.

17. a. **Lighthouses** Explain how you can estimate the lateral area of Cape Hatteras Lighthouse, shown at the left.

   b. **Estimation** One gallon of paint covers 350 square feet. Estimate the number of gallons of black paint and the number of gallons of white paint necessary to repaint the lighthouse.

Find the lateral and surface areas of each figure to the nearest square unit.

18.
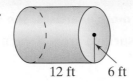

19.
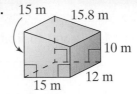

20.
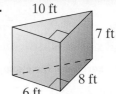

21. **Challenge** In the drawing, the surface area of cube A was 150 cm² before cube B was removed. The surface area of cube B is 24 cm². What effect did removing cube B have on the surface area of cube A? Explain.

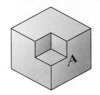

 Test Prep and Mixed Review **Practice**

Multiple Choice

22. A painter uses the roller shown. To the nearest square inch, what is the area covered by one complete revolution of the roller?
    Ⓐ 28 in.² Ⓒ 57 in.²
    Ⓑ 38 in.² Ⓓ 75 in.²

23. The average cost of gasoline increased $0.34 per gallon, or 16%. What was the original average cost per gallon?
    Ⓕ $2.41   Ⓖ $2.13   Ⓗ $1.99   Ⓙ $1.83

24. What is the width x of the kite at the right to the nearest inch?
    Ⓐ 12 in.   Ⓒ 21 in.
    Ⓑ 17 in.   Ⓓ 30 in.

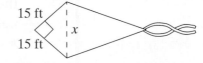

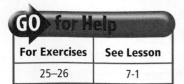
Find the measure of each angle.

25. the supplement of 62°

26. the complement of 78°

Use the figure at the right for Exercises 1 and 2.

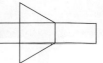

1. What three-dimensional figure will this net form?

2. Name the shapes that make up the lateral faces of this figure.

Use the figure at the right for Exercises 3 and 4.

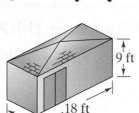

3. Draw a base plan for the figure.

4. Draw the top, front, and right views for the figure.

5. **Painting** A softball team wants to paint the equipment shed shown at the right. Find the lateral area of the shed including the doors.

9 ft
18 ft
8 ft

8-5a   Activity Lab

Hands On

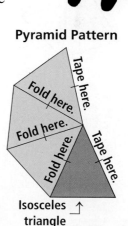

Surface Area of a Pyramid

Step 1 Draw an isosceles triangle on a piece of cardboard.

Step 2 Duplicate your triangle three times. Each triangle should share one side with another triangle, as in the diagram at the right.

Step 3 Cut out your pattern along its outside edge. Fold the pattern along the long sides of the triangles. Tape it together.

Step 4 Cut a square to be the base of the pyramid. Tape it in place.

Pyramid Pattern

Tape here.
Fold here.
Fold here.
Fold here.
Tape here.
Isosceles triangle

1. Measure the height and base of one of the triangles. Calculate the area of the triangle.

2. The lateral area of the square pyramid is the sum of the areas of the four lateral triangular surfaces. Calculate the lateral area.

3. Find the area of the base of the pyramid. Calculate the total surface area of the pyramid.

4. **Reasoning** Write a formula to find the surface area of a pyramid.

Surface Areas of Pyramids and Cones

Check Skills You'll Need

1. **Vocabulary Review** The longest side of a right triangle is the __?__.

2. Find the area of the figure below to the nearest whole unit.

5 ft

4 ft

for Help

Lesson 7-6

What You'll Learn

To find surface areas of pyramids and cones using nets and formulas

🔊 **New Vocabulary** slant height

Why Learn This?

When you can find the surface area of pyramids and cones, you can find the amount of materials you need for projects as large as roofing a house or as small as making a funnel.

The height of a pyramid is different from the height of its lateral faces. For this reason, the height of a pyramid's lateral faces is called the slant height and is indicated by the symbol ℓ.

height (h)   slant height (ℓ)

You can draw a net to find the surface area of a square pyramid. The four triangular faces are congruent isosceles triangles.

EXAMPLE Using a Net to Find Surface Area

1 Find the surface area of the square pyramid at the left.

6 in.

5 in.

Step 1 Draw a net of the pyramid.

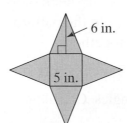

6 in.

5 in.

Step 2 Find the area of the faces and the base.

$$\text{S.A.} = \frac{\text{area of}}{\text{triangles}} + \frac{\text{area of}}{\text{square}}$$

$$= 4 \cdot \frac{1}{2}bh + s^2$$

$$= 4 \cdot \frac{1}{2}(5 \cdot 6) + 5^2 \quad \leftarrow \begin{array}{l}\text{Substitute 5 for } b,\\ \text{6 for } h, \text{ and 5 for } s.\end{array}$$

$$= 60 + 25 \qquad \leftarrow \text{Simplify.}$$

$$= 85 \qquad\qquad \leftarrow \text{Add.}$$

The surface area is 85 in.^{2}.

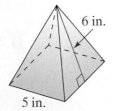

for Help

For help with nets, go to Lesson 8-3, Examples 1 and 2.

✓ Quick Check

1. Draw a net of the square pyramid at the right. Then find its surface area.

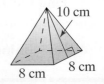

10 cm

8 cm   8 cm

You can also use a formula to find the surface area of a square pyramid.

KEY CONCEPTS **Lateral Area and Surface Area of a Square Pyramid**

The lateral area L.A. of a square pyramid is four times the area of one of the lateral faces.

$$\text{L.A.} = 4 \cdot \left(\tfrac{1}{2}b\ell\right) = 2b\ell$$

The surface area S.A. of a square pyramid is the sum of the lateral area and the area of the base.

$$\text{S.A.} = \text{L.A.} + B$$

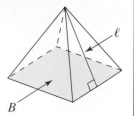

EXAMPLES **Finding Lateral and Surface Area**

2 **Architecture** The photo at the right shows the Pyramid Arena in Tennessee. Find the lateral area to determine the amount of siding material it needs.

L.A. $= 2b\ell$ ← lateral area formula

$= 2(450)(367)$ ← Substitute 450 for *b* and 367 for ℓ.

$= 330{,}300$ ← Simplify.

The lateral area of the Pyramid Arena is 330,300 ft².

3 Find the surface area of the Pyramid Arena.
S.A. $= \text{L.A.} + B$ ← surface area formula

$= 2b\ell + b^2$ ← Use $2b\ell$ for L.A. and b^2 for B.

$= 2(450)(367) + 450^2$ ← Substitute 450 for *b* and 367 for ℓ.

$= 330{,}300 + 202{,}500$ ← Simplify.

$= 532{,}800$ ← Add.

The surface area is 532,800 ft².

✓ Quick Check

2. Find the lateral area of the Great Pyramid of Khufu, shown at the right.

3. Find the surface area of the Great Pyramid of Khufu.

611 ft

755 ft

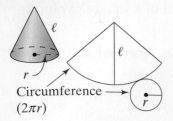

The curved surface of a cone is its lateral surface. In the net at the left, the cone's lateral surface may remind you of a triangle.

The height of the lateral surface is the slant height ℓ. The length of the base of the surface is the circumference of the circular base, $2\pi r$.

You can substitute ℓ and $2\pi r$ in the formula for area of a triangle to find the lateral area of a cone.

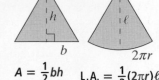

$$\text{L.A.} = \tfrac{1}{2}bh \quad \leftarrow \text{area of a triangle}$$

$$= \tfrac{1}{2}(2\pi r)\ell \quad \leftarrow \text{Substitute } 2\pi r \text{ for } b \text{ and } \ell \text{ for } h.$$

$$= \pi r\ell \quad \leftarrow \text{Simplify.}$$

$A = \tfrac{1}{2}bh$ L.A. $= \tfrac{1}{2}(2\pi r)\ell$

KEY CONCEPTS   **Lateral Area and Surface Area of a Cone**

The lateral area L.A. of a cone is one half the product of the circumference of the base and the slant height.

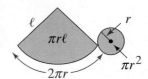

$$\text{L.A.} = \tfrac{1}{2}(2\pi r)\ell = \pi r\ell$$

The surface area S.A. of a cone is the sum of the lateral area and the area of the base.

$$\text{S.A.} = \text{L.A.} + B$$

EXAMPLE   **Using the Cone Surface Area Formula**

4 Find the surface area of the cone at the right to the nearest square meter.

$$\text{S.A.} = \text{L.A.} + B \quad \leftarrow \text{surface area formula}$$

$$= \pi r\ell + \pi r^2 \quad \leftarrow \text{Use } \pi r\ell \text{ for L.A. and } \pi r^2 \text{ for } B.$$

$$= \pi(7)(30) + \pi(7^2) \quad \leftarrow \text{Substitute 7 for } r \text{ and 30 for } \ell.$$

$$= 210\pi + 49\pi \quad \leftarrow \text{Use the order of operations.}$$

$$= 259\pi \quad \leftarrow \text{Simplify.}$$

$$\approx 813.6724973 \quad \leftarrow \text{Use a calculator.}$$

The surface area of the cone is about 814 m^2.

30 m

14 m

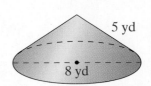

Test Prep Tip

Be sure that you understand each variable in a formula so you can substitute in the formula correctly.

✓ Quick Check

4. Find the surface area of the cone at the right to the nearest square yard.

5 yd

8 yd

1. **Vocabulary** Describe the difference between the lateral area of a square pyramid and the surface area of a square pyramid.

2. **Mental Math** A square pyramid has a lateral area of 10.25 m² and a base area B of 5.3 m². Find its surface area.

Use the cone at the right.

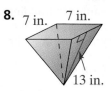

3. The slant height ℓ is ▇ m.

4. Write an expression for lateral area using π.

5. Write an expression you can simplify to find the surface area.

14 m
8 m

Homework Exercises

For more exercises, see Extra Skills and Word Problems.

GO▶for Help	
For Exercises	**See Examples**
6–8	1
9–11	2–3
12–14	4

Use a net to find the surface area of each pyramid.

6.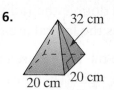
32 cm
20 cm 20 cm

7.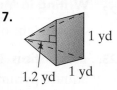
1 yd
1.2 yd 1 yd

8.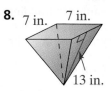
7 in. 7 in.
13 in.

Use formulas to find the lateral and surface areas of each pyramid.

9.
50 in.
30 in.
30 in.

10.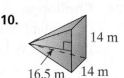
14 m
16.5 m 14 m

11.
3 cm 3 cm
3 cm
4 cm

Find the surface area of each cone to the nearest square unit.

12.
4 ft
11 ft

13.
6 m
8 m

14.
7.5 in.
7 in.
7 in.

GPS 15. **Guided Problem Solving** The roof of the doghouse at the right is a square pyramid. If shingles cost $1.25 to cover one square foot, how much would it cost to put new shingles on the roof of the doghouse?
- What is the lateral area of the roof?
- What operation would you use to find the cost?

4 ft
Spike
5 ft 5 ft

16. Error Analysis A student tried to find the lateral area of the cone at the right. Explain the student's mistake. Then find the correct solution.

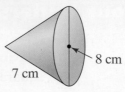

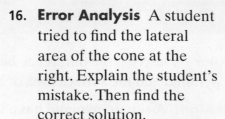

L.A. $= \pi r \ell$
$= \pi(8)(7)$
$= 56\pi$
≈ 175.93
L.A. ≈ 176 cm^2

17. Buildings Use the photo caption at the left.
  a. Find the slant height of the Transamerica Building.
  b. Find the lateral area of the Transamerica Building.

Find the lateral area of each cone to the nearest square unit.

18.

18 yd
8 yd

19.

25 cm
16 cm

20.

5 ft
3 ft

The Transamerica Building in San Francisco is roughly a square pyramid with height of 853 ft and base-edge length of 145 ft.

21. (**Algebra**) Corey uses the formula S.A. $= \pi r(r + \ell)$ to find the surface area of a cone. Will this always work? Explain.

22. Writing in Math You double the radius of a cone and divide the slant height by 2. Does the lateral area stay the same? Explain.

23. Estimation Estimate the lateral area of the square pyramid at the right. Then find the actual lateral area to the nearest square meter.

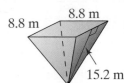
8.8 m
8.8 m
15.2 m

24. Challenge A cone and a pyramid have the same slant height. The areas of both bases are the same. Which has the larger surface area? Explain.

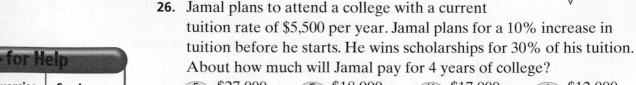

Test Prep and Mixed Review   **Practice**

Multiple Choice

25. The net for a square pyramid is at the right. Use a centimeter ruler to measure the dimensions. Which of the following is closest to the surface area of the pyramid?
  Ⓐ 9 cm^2 Ⓒ 5 cm^2
  Ⓑ 8 cm^2 Ⓓ 3 cm^2

26. Jamal plans to attend a college with a current tuition rate of $5,500 per year. Jamal plans for a 10% increase in tuition before he starts. He wins scholarships for 30% of his tuition. About how much will Jamal pay for 4 years of college?
  Ⓕ $27,000   Ⓖ $18,000   Ⓗ $17,000   Ⓙ $12,000

27. Draw an obtuse $\angle K$. Construct $\angle L$ congruent to $\angle K$.

Modeling Volume

The volume of a rectangular prism depends on its
height and its base area. You can use this relationship
to find the volume of nonrectangular prisms.

ACTIVITY

1. Use cubes to build each prism below. Copy and complete
   the table.

Prism	Height	Base Area	Volume (total number of cubes)
■ base ■	■	■	■
■ base ■	■	■	■

2. **Writing in Math** Explain how you can find the volume of a prism
   using its height and the area of its base.

3. Use the figures in the table below. Copy and complete the table.

Figure	Height	Base area	Volume (total number of cubes)
■ base ■	■	■	■
■ base ■	■	■	■
■ base ■	■	■	■

4. **Algebra** Write a formula to find the volume of a cylinder using
   its height and the radius of its base.

8-6 Volumes of Prisms and Cylinders

✓ Check Skills You'll Need

1. **Vocabulary Review**
   Is a *cylinder* also a *prism*? Explain.

Find the surface area of each figure to the nearest square unit.

2.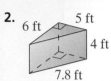
   6 ft   5 ft
   4 ft
   7.8 ft

3.
   8 m
   6 m

GO for Help
Lesson 8-4

What You'll Learn

To find the volumes of prisms and cylinders

🔊 **New Vocabulary** volume

Why Learn This?

When you pack a bag or load a car, you must consider the amount of space, or volume, each object occupies.

Volume is the number of unit cubes, or cubic units, needed to fill a solid. In the prism above, each layer has 2 × 4, or 8, cubes. The prism has 3 layers, so its volume is 8 × 3, or 24, cubic units.

KEY CONCEPTS **Volume of a Prism**

The volume *V* of a prism is the product of the base area *B* and the height *h*.

$$V = Bh$$

EXAMPLE **Finding Volume of a Triangular Prism**

1 **Camping** The tent at the left approximates a triangular prism. Find its volume.

Step 1 Find the area *B* of the base.

$$B = \frac{1}{2}bh \quad \leftarrow \text{area of a triangle}$$
$$= \frac{1}{2} \cdot 5 \cdot 4 \quad \leftarrow \text{Substitute.}$$
$$= 10 \quad \leftarrow \text{Multiply.}$$

Step 2 Use the base area to find the volume.

$$V = Bh \quad \leftarrow \text{volume of a prism}$$
$$= 10 \cdot 7.5 \quad \leftarrow \text{Substitute.}$$
$$= 75 \quad \leftarrow \text{Multiply.}$$

The volume of the tent is 75 ft³.

✓ Quick Check

1. Find the volume of the prism at the right.

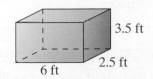
3.5 ft
6 ft   2.5 ft

You can think of a cylinder with height h as having h layers of circles stacked on top of each other. Then the volume of the cylinder is the product of its base area and its height.

Since the bases of cylinders are circles, you can use the formula for the area of a circle to find a cylinder's base area.

KEY CONCEPTS **Volume of a Cylinder**

The volume V of a cylinder is the product of the base area B and the height h.

$$V = Bh$$

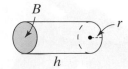

EXAMPLE **Finding Volume of a Cylinder**

2 Find the volume of the cylinder below to the nearest cubic centimeter.

10 cm

80 cm

Estimate Use 3 for π. The area of the base is about 3×5^2 cm^2, or 75 cm^2. The volume is about 75×80 cm^3, or 6,000 cm^3.

Step 1 Find the area of the base.

$$B = \pi r^2 \quad \leftarrow \text{area of a circle}$$
$$= \pi(5^2) \quad \leftarrow \text{Substitute.}$$
$$= 25\pi \quad \leftarrow \text{Simplify.}$$

Step 2 Use the base area to find the volume.

$$V = Bh \qquad\qquad \leftarrow \text{volume of a cylinder}$$
$$= 25\pi \cdot 80 \qquad \leftarrow \text{Substitute } 25\pi \text{ for } B \text{ and } 80 \text{ for } h.$$
$$= 2,000\pi \qquad \leftarrow \text{Simplify.}$$
$$\approx 6283.185307 \quad \leftarrow \text{Use a calculator.}$$

The volume of the cylinder is about 6,283 cm^3.

Check for Reasonableness The answer 6,283 cm^3 is close to the estimate of 6,000 cm^3. The answer is reasonable.

The AquaDom in Berlin is the world's largest cylindrical aquarium. It is over 52 ft high and has a diameter of 36 ft.

✓**Quick Check**

2. a. Estimation Estimate the volume of the cylinder at the right. Use 3 for π.
   b. Find the volume of the cylinder to the nearest cubic millimeter.

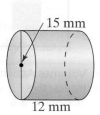

15 mm

12 mm

19. **Number Sense** Which has a greater effect on the volume of a cylinder, doubling the radius or doubling the height? Explain.

20. A store keeps about 240 boxes of crayons in its inventory.
    a. If each box measures 6 in. by 2.5 in. by 4 in., how many cubic inches of storage space does the store need for the crayons?
    b. One cubic foot is equal to $(12\ in.)^3$, or $1{,}728\ in.^3$. Find the number of cubic feet necessary for storing 240 boxes of crayons.

Find the volume of each prism.

21.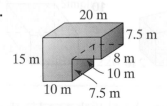

22.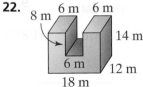

23. **Writing in Math** Explain how you would find the radius of a cylinder with a height of 20 in. and a volume of $565.5\ in.^3$.

24. **Food** You cut a 3-in. circle in the center of a 3-in.-high cake and served the outer ring. The cake had a diameter of 12 in. How much cake did you serve?

25. **Challenge** A rectangular prism has square bases and a height of 11 ft. Its lateral area is $308\ ft^2$. Find its volume.

Test Prep and Mixed Review

Practice

Multiple Choice

26. A refrigerator is 30 inches wide, 30 inches deep, and 5 feet 6 inches tall. Which is closest to the volume of the refrigerator in cubic feet?
    - Ⓐ $10.5\ ft^3$
    - Ⓑ $34\ ft^3$
    - Ⓒ $55\ ft^3$
    - Ⓓ $75\ ft^3$

27. A cylindrical paperweight has the net shown at the right. Which is the closest to the lateral surface area of the paperweight?
    - Ⓕ $9\ in.^2$
    - Ⓗ $23\ in.^2$
    - Ⓖ $27\ in.^2$
    - Ⓙ $50\ in.^2$

    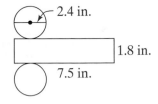

28. A pair of jeans is on sale for 20% off the original price. A student buys the jeans on sale and saves $12. What was the regular price of the jeans?
    - Ⓐ $14.40
    - Ⓒ $60.00
    - Ⓑ $48.00
    - Ⓓ $240.00

GO for Help

For Exercises	See Lesson
29–31	5-5

Find each percent of decrease. Round to the nearest tenth of a percent.

29. 34 to 22

30. 456 to 92

31. 100 to 86

Using Formulas

The surface area of an adult's skin is about 2,500 in.^{2}. The adult is
5 ft 5 in. tall. Consider the person a cylinder with no top or bottom.
What is the diameter of a cylinder with this surface area?

What You Might Think

What do I know? What do I want to find out?

How can I estimate the answer?

How can I find the answer?

Is the answer reasonable?

What You Might Write

The adult's height is 5 ft 5 in., or 65 in. The formula for the lateral area of a cylinder is $2\pi rh$. I need to solve $2,500 = 2\pi rh$ for r and then double r to get the diameter.

I will use 3 for π and compatible numbers.

$$2,500 = 2\pi rh$$
$$2,500 \approx 2(3)r(65)$$
$$2,500 \approx 390r$$
$$2,400 \approx 400r$$
$$6 \approx r$$

I estimate a 6-in. radius or 12-in. diameter.

I will substitute exact values in the formula.

$$2,500 = 2\pi rh$$
$$2,500 = 2\pi r(65)$$
$$2,500 = 130\pi r$$
$$6.121343965 \approx r$$

The diameter is about 2×6.12 in., or 12.24 in.

Since 12.24 in. is close to 12 in., the answer is reasonable.

Think It Through

1. **Reasoning** Justify each step in solving $2,500 = 2\pi rh$ for r.

2. **Estimation** What compatible numbers were used in the estimate?

Precision and Significant Digits

When you add or subtract measurements, your results can be only as precise as the least precise measurement. The measurement with the smaller units is more precise.

When you multiply or divide measurements, you use significant digits to determine how precise your result should be. Round your answer to match the measurement with the fewest significant digits.

Type of Number	Which Zeros Are Significant	Example
Decimal numbers between 0 and 1	Zeros to the left of *all* the nonzero digits are not significant. All other zeros are significant.	Significant digits 0.006040 Not significant digits
Positive integers	Zeros to the right of *all* the nonzero digits are not significant. Zeros between nonzero digits are significant.	Significant digits 203,400 Not significant digits
Noninteger decimal numbers greater than 1	All zeros are significant.	Significant digits 350,070.50

EXAMPLES **Calculating With Measurements**

1 Add 20.08 km + 5.2 km.

20.08 km + 5.2 km = 25.28 km ← **Add.**

$\approx$ 25.3 km ← **Since 5.2 is less precise than 20.08, round to the nearest tenth.**

2 Find the area of a plot of land that is 115.6 ft by 81.2 ft.

115.6 · 81.2 = 9,386.72 ← **Multiply.**
↑ ↑
4 significant digits **3 significant digits**

Since the least number of significant digits in the measurement is 3, round the answer to 3 significant digits. The area is about 9,390 ft^2.

Exercises

Compute.

1. 34 ft + 16.9 ft

2. 1.1 cm + 1.01 cm

3. 60 in. − 22.80 in.

4. 42.00 m^2 − 21.0 m^2

5. 372 mi × 278 mi

6. 189.9 km × 5.40 km

7. 6 yd ÷ 0.0569 yd

8. 124.6 m ÷ 8.101 m

Eliminating Answers

Before solving a multiple-choice problem, you can usually eliminate some answer choices. This can save you time and help you to make an "educated" guess if you do not actually know how to find the answer.

EXAMPLE

Find the volume of the square pyramid below.

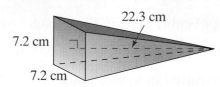

22.3 cm

7.2 cm

7.2 cm

Ⓐ 36.528 cm³   Ⓒ 320.724 cm³

Ⓑ 385.344 cm³   Ⓓ 3,187.367 cm³

Underestimate and overestimate the answer using compatible numbers.

Underestimate   Overestimate

$V = \frac{1}{3}Bh \approx \frac{1}{3}(48)(20) = 320$ $V = \frac{1}{3}Bh \approx \frac{1}{3}(50)(24) = 400$

The correct answer is between 320 and 400. Since choices A and D are not between 320 and 400, you can eliminate them. Choice C is very close to the underestimate, so you can make an educated guess that choice B is the most likely answer.

Exercises

1. To the nearest square meter, what is the surface area of a cone with a radius of 3 m and a slant height of 4 m?
   Ⓐ 21 m²   Ⓑ 66 m²   Ⓒ 83 m²   Ⓓ 120 m²

2. A cell measures 1.3×10^{-5} mm in length. Which number represents this measurement in standard form?
   Ⓕ 130,000   Ⓖ 13   Ⓗ 0.013   Ⓙ 0.000013

3. A gift box is 24 inches long, 8 inches wide, and 6 inches high. Which is closest to the volume of the box in cubic feet?
   Ⓐ $\frac{1}{2}$ ft³   Ⓑ $2\frac{1}{2}$ ft³   Ⓒ 3 ft³   Ⓓ 6 ft³

Chapter 8 Review

Vocabulary Review

🔊 **base plan** (p. 358)
cone (p. 354)
cylinder (p. 354)
isometric view (p. 359)
lateral area (p. 369)
net (p. 364)

polyhedron (p. 354)
prism (p. 354)
pyramid (p. 354)
similar solids (p. 398)
skew lines (p. 355)

slant height (p. 374)
solids (p. 354)
sphere (p. 393)
surface area (p. 368)
volume (p. 380)

Go Online
PHSchool.com

For: Online vocabulary quiz
Web Code: asj-0851

Choose the correct vocabulary term above to complete each sentence.

1. The __?__ of an object is the number of cubic units in the object.

2. A(n) __?__ has one base and one vertex, but it is not a polyhedron.

3. Both __?__ area and __?__ area are measured in square units.

4. Both a(n) __?__ and a(n) __?__ have two parallel, congruent bases.

5. A(n) __?__ shows all the surfaces of a solid in one view.

Skills and Concepts

Lesson 8-1
• To identify solids, parts of solids, and skew line segments

Solids are any objects that have a length, a width, and a height. If all the faces of a solid are polygons, the figure is a **polyhedron. Prisms** and **pyramids** are polyhedrons. **Cylinders** and **cones** are not polyhedrons.

For each solid, describe the shape of the base(s) and the lateral surface(s).

6. rectangular prism   7. square pyramid   8. cylinder

Lessons 8-2, 8-3
• To draw views of three-dimensional figures, including base plans and isometric views
• To identify nets of solids

A **base plan** shows the shape of the base and the height of each part of a solid. Top, front, and right views show a solid from three different perspectives. A **net** is a pattern that can be folded to form a solid.

Draw a base plan and top, front, and right views of each figure.

9.    10.    11.

Identify the solid formed by each net.

12. 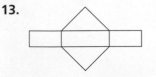   13. 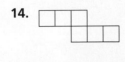   14.

Lessons 8-4, 8-6

- To find surface areas of prisms and cylinders using nets and formulas
- To find the volumes of prisms and cylinders

Lateral area L.A. is the sum of the areas of all of a solid's surfaces except the base(s). **Surface area** S.A. is the sum of the areas of all of the surfaces of a solid. **Volume** V is the number of cubic units in a solid.

Formulas for prisms	Formulas for cylinders	Volume formula for prisms and cylinders
L.A. = ph	L.A. = $2\pi rh$	
S.A. = L.A. + $2B$	S.A. = L.A. + $2B$	$V = Bh$

Find the surface area and volume to the nearest whole number.

15.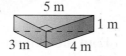
5 m, 1 m, 3 m, 4 m

16.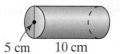
5 cm, 10 cm

17.
13 in., 13 in., 13 in.

Lessons 8-5, 8-7

- To find surface areas of pyramids and cones using nets and formulas
- To find the volumes of pyramids and cones

The **slant height** ℓ of a pyramid or a cone is the distance from the figure's vertex to its base edge b. It is used to find the lateral area or surface area.

Formulas for pyramids	Formulas for cones	Volume formula for pyramids and cones
L.A. = $2b\ell$	L.A. = $\pi r\ell$	
S.A. = L.A. + B	S.A. = L.A. + B	$V = \frac{1}{3}Bh$

Find the surface area and volume to the nearest whole number.

18.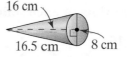
9.2 m, 4 m, 9 m, 4 m

19.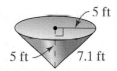
16 cm, 16.5 cm, 8 cm

20.
5 ft, 5 ft, 7.1 ft

Lesson 8-8

- To find the surface area and volume of a sphere

A **sphere** is the set of all points in space that are the same distance from a center point. The formula for the surface area of a sphere is S.A. = $4\pi r^2$. The formula for volume is $V = \frac{4}{3}\pi r^3$.

21. The earth has a diameter of about 13,000 km. Estimate the earth's surface area and volume.

Lesson 8-9

- To use proportions to find missing measurements of similar solids, including surface area and volume

Similar solids have the same shape and proportional corresponding dimensions. If the ratio of their corresponding dimensions is $\frac{a}{b}$, the ratio of their surface areas is $\frac{a^2}{b^2}$, and the ratio of their volumes is $\frac{a^3}{b^3}$.

For each solid, find the surface area and volume of a similar solid whose dimensions are $\frac{4}{5}$ of those given. Round to the nearest whole number.

22.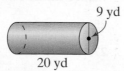
9 yd, 20 yd

23.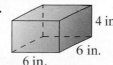
4 in., 6 in., 6 in.

24.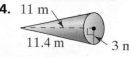
11 m, 11.4 m, 3 m

Chapter 8 Test

Name each solid and describe its base(s).

1.

2.

3.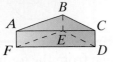

4.

For each figure, name a pair of skew line segments and a pair of parallel line segments.

5.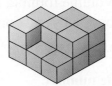

B

A *C*

E

F *D*

6.

I

G *H* *J*

K

Draw a base plan for each solid.

7.

8.

Draw a top, front, and side view of each solid.

9.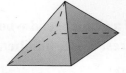

10.

Identify the solid formed by each net.

11.

12.

Draw a net of each solid.

13.

14.

Find the lateral area and surface area of each solid to the nearest square unit.

15.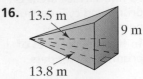
5 yd
7.5 yd
10 yd

16.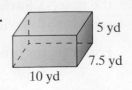
13.5 m
9 m
13.8 m

17.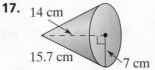
14 cm
15.7 cm
7 cm

18.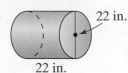
22 in.
22 in.

Find the volume of each solid. When using π, round to the nearest cubic unit.

19.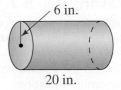
1 ft
0.9 ft
0.75 ft

20.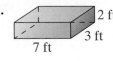
6 in.
20 in.

21.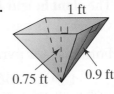
7.5 m
7 m

22.
2 ft
3 ft
7 ft

23. Writing in Math The formulas for surface area and volume of a cylinder involve $\pi r^2 h$ and $2\pi rh + 2\pi r^2$. Explain how to tell which expression goes with which formula.

24. The figures below are similar solids. Find the measures of all missing lengths.

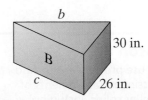
40 in.
20 in.
A
28 in.
a
b
30 in.
B
c
26 in.

Find the surface area and volume of a sphere with the given radius or diameter to the nearest whole number.

25. $r = 2$ in.

26. $r = 5$ ft

27. $d = 6$ m

28. $d = 8$ cm

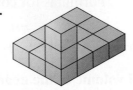

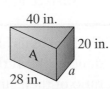

Reading Comprehension

Read each passage and answer the questions that follow.

CD Players Compact disc players read the data on CDs as the discs spin, moving from the center to the outer edge of the disc. Some CD players spin at a steady rate. They read a different amount of data because the data circle gets larger with each revolution. Other CD players read data at a constant rate. Their discs spin at a variable rate, changing the speed as the circumference of the data circle changes.

1. How does the amount of data read per second change for a CD player that spins at a steady rate?
   - (A) less data per second as the circles grow
   - (B) less data per second as the circles shrink
   - (C) more data per second as the circles grow
   - (D) more data per second as the circles shrink

2. For a disc of radius r, which expression gives the length of a data circle located halfway from the center to the disc's outer edge?
   - (F) $\frac{1}{2}\pi r^2$
   - (H) πr
   - (G) $\frac{1}{2}\pi r$
   - (J) $2\pi r$

3. How does the rate of spin change for a CD player that reads a constant amount of data per second?
   - (A) spins faster as the data circles grow
   - (B) spins faster as the data circles shrink
   - (C) spins slower as the data circles grow
   - (D) spins slower as the data circles shrink

4. For a variable-speed CD player, the speed halfway to the outer edge is what percent of the speed at the outer edge?
   - (F) 25%
   - (H) 100%
   - (G) 50%
   - (J) 200%

Airplanes Why do wings work? The top of a typical wing is curved. The underside is relatively flat. As a plane flies, air molecules sliding over a wing have as much as 15% farther to travel to reach the wing's trailing edge than molecules passing under the wing. Even so, molecules passing over the wing reach the trailing edge first. The wing shape speeds up air flowing over the wing and forces it downward. In turn, the air reacts by pushing upward on the wing, resulting in the lift needed to keep the plane aloft.

5. Which inequality is reasonable for the speed of molecule a passing above the wing and the speed of molecule u passing under it?
   - (A) $a < u + 0.15a$
   - (C) $0.15a > u$
   - (B) $a < 0.15u$
   - (D) $a > 1.15u$

6. If the surface area of the top of a wing is $16\ m^2$, what might the surface area of the bottom of the wing be?
   - (F) $8\ m^2$
   - (H) $16\ m^2$
   - (G) $14\ m^2$
   - (J) $19\ m^2$

Applying Measurement

For The Birds Did you know that not all birds can fly? Although people usually think of birds as airborne, there are more than 40 species of flightless birds. The Australian emu, New Zealand kiwi, African ostrich, and South American rhea are all birds that cannot fly. Although some birds are simply too large or heavy to get off the ground, they have learned other skills—ostriches can run up to 40 mi/h, and penguins spend most of their lives in the ocean and use their wings as flippers.

Ostriches
At 5.7 to 9 ft tall, the ostrich is the largest living bird. Its normal walking pace is 2.5 mi/h, but it can run at speeds of up to 45 mi/h.

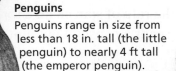

Penguins
Penguins range in size from less than 18 in. tall (the little penguin) to nearly 4 ft tall (the emperor penguin).

Kiwis
The kiwi, the national bird of New Zealand, is about the size of a chicken and weighs between 2.6 and 8.6 lb. Kiwi eggs are large and can weigh up to a pound!

Go Online
PHSchool.com
For: Information about birds
Web Code: ase-0853

Put It All Together

Use the information on these two pages and on page 647 to answer these questions.

Materials construction paper, ruler or straightedge, tape

Copy and cut out the patterns in Figures 1 and 2 for a bird body and two bird wings. Assemble your bird.

1. Examine your bird. Think about what would happen to your bird's body and wings if it grew. Sketch a larger bird by doubling all the dimensions of the original pattern.

2. Copy and complete the table.

3. The upward force that keeps birds (and planes) in the air is called lift. The amount of lift needed to get off the ground is proportional to the weight of the bird. Using volume as an estimate for weight, how many times more lift will the larger bird require than the smaller bird?

Size of Bird	Volume	Wing Area	Ratio	$\frac{volume}{wing\ area}$
Small	▪	▪		▪
Large	▪	▪		▪

4. The amount of lift from a bird's wings is proportional to the area of the wings. How many times more lift will the larger bird's wings provide than the smaller bird's?

5. **Writing in Math** Use your answers to Questions 3 and 4 to explain why the larger bird will have a harder time getting off the ground than the smaller bird.

6. **Open-Ended** Choose a bird from the table on page 647. Compare it to the two birds in the activity. How does it compare in terms of weight (volume)? How does it compare in terms of lift?

Rheas

Male rheas sit on their nests and incubate the eggs laid by females. The average clutch, or group of eggs, is about 25.

Dodos

About the size of turkeys, dodos have been extinct since the 1700s, so there are no photographs of them, only illustrations.

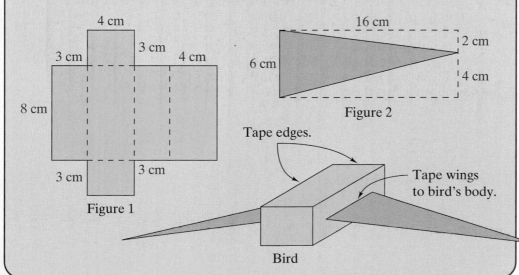

Figure 1

Figure 2

Tape edges.

Tape wings to bird's body.

Bird

Using Graphs to Analyze Data

What You've Learned

- In Chapter 3, you located and named points on a coordinate plane using ordered pairs of rational numbers.

- You also used tables, graphs, and equations to solve problems.

Check Your Readiness

GO for Help

For Exercises	See Lessons
1–9	3-4
10–13	4-3
14–22	5-1

Graphing Points

Graph each point on the same coordinate plane.

1. $(2, 5)$ **2.** $(8, 0)$ **3.** $(-5, 4)$

4. $(3, -1)$ **5.** $(-6, -8)$ **6.** $(-4, 0)$

7. $(3, 7)$ **8.** $(-3, -6)$ **9.** $(0, 4)$

Solving Proportions

Solve each proportion.

10. $\frac{8}{9} = \frac{16}{x}$ **11.** $\frac{a}{24} = \frac{14}{12}$

12. $\frac{6}{3} = \frac{s}{12}$ **13.** $\frac{3}{m} = \frac{75}{125}$

Fractions, Decimals, and Percents

Write each percent as a fraction in simplest form.

14. 26% **15.** 48% **16.** 13%

17. 72% **18.** 20% **19.** 47%

20. 50% **21.** 10% **22.** 5%

What You'll Learn Next

- In this chapter, you will use different types of graphs to represent and analyze data.

- You will make predictions using trends in scatter plots.

- You will read graphs critically and choose an appropriate graph to display a set of data.

 Problem Solving Application On pages 466 and 467, you will work an extended activity on food production.

🔊 Key Vocabulary

- box-and-whisker plot (p. 438)
- circle graph (p. 450)
- frequency (p. 418)
- histogram (p. 419)
- line plot (p. 418)
- mean (p. 412)
- measure of central tendency (p. 412)
- median (p. 412)
- mode (p. 412)
- outlier (p. 413)
- quartiles (p. 438)
- range (p. 413)
- scatter plot (p. 444)
- stem-and-leaf plot (p. 433)
- trend line (p. 445)
- Venn diagram (p. 424)

Finding Mean, Median, and Mode

✓ Check Skills You'll Need

1. **Vocabulary Review** What is the *inverse operation* of addition?

Solve each equation.

2. $a + 14 = 32$

3. $b - 5 = 26$

4. $10 + c = -31$

5. $-48 = d - 19$

 **for Help**
Lesson 1-6

What You'll Learn

To describe data using mean, median, mode, and range and to choose an appropriate measure of central tendency

🔊 **New Vocabulary** measure of central tendency, mean, median, mode, range, outlier

Why Learn This?

Statistics like the mean are used to calculate scores and averages in sports.

A measure of central tendency is a single value that summarizes how a set of data is centered. Mean, median, and mode are measures of central tendency.

The mean is the sum of the data values divided by the number of data items.

The median is the middle value when the data values are arranged in numerical order. For an even number of data values, the median is the mean of the two middle items.

The mode is the item with the greatest frequency. A data set may have no mode, one mode, or more than one mode.

EXAMPLE Finding Mean, Median, and Mode

Vocabulary Tip

In math, the word *average* usually refers to the mean.

1 **Golf** Players in a tournament have scores −4, −3, −5, −5, +2, −5, −4, −2, −2, and −2. Find the mean, median, and mode of the scores.

Mean:

$$\frac{(-4)+(-3)+(-5)+(-5)+2+(-5)+(-4)+(-2)+(-2)+(-2)}{10} = \frac{-30}{10} = -3$$

Add. ↓   Divide. ↓

Median:

−5 −5 −5 −4 −4 −3 −2 −2 −2 2 ← Order the data.

$\frac{-4 + (-3)}{2} = -3.5$ ← Find the mean of the middle two numbers.

Mode: There are two modes, −5 and −2.

✓ Quick Check

1. Find the mean, median, and mode of 11, 19, 11, 15, 16, 18, and 8.

For: Data Set Activity
Use: Interactive
    Textbook, 9-1

The range of a set of data is the difference between the greatest and least values in the set. Range is a measure of how spread out the data in a set are.

EXAMPLE Finding Range

② Find the range of the data: 4.2, 8.1, −2.7, 6, −3.9, 7.2, 5.1, 8.3, −2.5.

The greatest value is 8.3. The least value is −3.9.

$8.3 - (-3.9) = 12.2$ ← **Subtract.**

The range is 12.2.

✓ Quick Check

2. Find the range of the data: −24.9, −26.5, −33.1, −24.2, −31.4, −32.1, −28.4, −30.

If one data item is much higher or lower than the other data items, it is an **outlier.** Outliers can have a great effect on the mean of a set of data. They usually have very little effect on the median and mode.

EXAMPLE Outliers

③ **Wages** A juice stand hires students for the summer. The students' hourly wages are listed below, in dollars. How does the outlier affect the mean?

    7.25 7.25 7.25 7.25 7.25 8.00 8.00
    8.00 8.25 9.00 9.00 9.00 15.00

15 is an outlier. It is 15 − 9, or 6, away from the closest data value.

To find the mean with the outlier, find the sum of all data values and divide by the number of data values, 13.

$\dfrac{110.5}{13} = 8.5$ ← **Find the mean with the outlier.**

To find the mean without the outlier, find the sum of the data values excluding the outlier. Then divide by 12, the number of data values not including the outlier.

$\dfrac{95.5}{12} \approx 7.96$ ← **Find the mean without the outlier.**

The outlier raises the mean about 8.5 − 7.96 = 0.54, or $.54.

✓ Quick Check

3. Find an outlier in each data set and tell how it affects the mean.
   a. 11, 14, 9, 1, 12, 15, 12, 13
   b. −5, −3, 0, 2, −1, −18, −6, 3, −2

Test Prep Tip Ⓐ Ⓑ Ⓒ Ⓓ

To save time in your calculations, you can drop zeros after decimal points when they are not followed by any other numbers.

For the same set of data, the values of the mean, median, and mode can vary significantly. Before you choose which statistic to report, ask yourself what you want to show about the data.

EXAMPLE **Choosing a Measure of Central Tendency**

4 **Multiple Choice** A meteorologist recorded the temperature at a local airport at 5:00 P.M. every day last week. The temperatures in degrees Fahrenheit (°F) were 45, 78, 75, 80, 78, 61, and 58. Which measure would make the temperature seem most warm?

Ⓐ Mode   Ⓑ Median   Ⓒ Mean   Ⓓ Range

45 58 61 75 78 78 80   ← **Order the data.**

The mode is 78.

The median is 75.

The mean is (45 + 78 + 75 + 80 + 78 + 61 + 58) ÷ 7 ≈ 67.9.

The range is 80 − 45 = 35.

The greatest measure is the mode, so the correct answer is choice A.

GO for Help

For help with ordering integers, go to Lesson 1-2, Example 2.

✓ Quick Check

4. Your scores on the last six math tests were 82, 84, 88, 72, 91, and 72. Which measure of data would make your scores seem greatest— mean, median, mode, or range?

✓ Check Your Understanding

1. **Vocabulary** Does the following set of data have a mode? Explain.
   1 3 7 5 9 8 6 4 2 10

Use the table below for Exercises 2–6.

2. What is the sum of the temperatures?

3. How many data values are in the set?

4. Use your answers to Questions 2 and 3. Find the mean of the data.

Minimum Daily Temperatures (°F)

Date	Temperature	Date	Temperature
12/20	−3	12/26	1
12/21	−2	12/27	15
12/22	−9	12/28	6
12/23	−8	12/29	11
12/24	2	12/30	7
12/25	0	12/31	11

5. List the data in order from least to greatest. Find the median and the mode.

6. Find the greatest and least values.

For more exercises, see Extra Skills and Word Problems.

Find the mean, median, mode, and range of each data set.

For Exercises	See Examples
7–12	1–2
13–15	3
16	4

7. hits per game:

0 0 0 0 1 1 2 2 3

8. test scores:

70 80 84 90 92 100

9. hours of sleep:

7 8 8 9 9 9 9 10 10

10. number of movies seen

0 1 1 2 2 3 3 3 4 6

11. **Change in Numbers of Endangered U.S. Bird Species**

Year	Change
1997	2
1998	0
1999	−2
2000	4
2001	0
2002	0
2003	0
2004	−1

SOURCE: U.S. Fish and Wildlife Service. Go to **PHSchool.com** for a data update. Web Code: asg–9041.

12. **Minimum Daily Temperatures**

Date	Temperature (°F)
1/23	−1
1/24	16
1/25	7
1/26	8
1/27	7
1/28	14
1/29	8
1/30	−3
1/31	−9

Whooping cranes are an endangered species.

For Exercises 13–15, find an outlier and tell how it affects the mean.

13. 1, 0, 3, 10, 0, 2, 4, 1

14. 28, 12, 37, 36, 30, 32, 35

15. **Wages** A park hires students for the summer. The students' hourly wages are $8.00, $7.50, $8.00, $8.00, $8.00, and $20.50.

16. **Jobs** A company reports the following salaries for its employees: $20,000; $22,000; $34,000; $42,000; $43,000; $50,000; and $80,000. Which measure of central tendency would make you most want to apply for a job with this company?

17. **Guided Problem Solving** A data set has nine values. The mean of the set is 5. When a tenth value is added, the mean becomes 6. What is the tenth value?
  • What is the sum of the original 9 data values?
  • **Make a Plan** Write and solve an equation to find the tenth value.

18. **Homework** The number of hours that Olivia spent on homework in the last five days was 2.75, 1.75, 1.25, 3.00, and 2.75. Which measure of central tendency could Olivia use to most impress her parents?

Complete each data set so that the mean is 8.

19. 11, 5, 11, 5, ■   **20.** 7, 7, 7, 7, ■   **21.** 18, 0, 18, 6, ■

Use the data at the right.

22. Find the mean, median, and mode.

23. **Writing in Math** Is the data value for the United States an outlier? Explain.

24. **Reasoning** You have one more test to take. The scores you have already received are 89, 92, 78, 83, and 83.
 a. What score must you get to raise the mean to 87?
 b. What score must you get to raise the median by 2 points?

25. **Challenge** The median of three numbers is 7. The range is 14. The mean is 11. What are the three numbers?

| Average Number of Vacation Days per Year ||
Country	Days
Italy	42
France	37
Germany	35
Brazil	34
Canada	26
Korea	25
Japan	25
United States	13

Test Prep and Mixed Review   **Practice**

Multiple Choice

26. The bar graph shows the number of rainy days in Cleveland. Which measure of data makes the weather in Cleveland appear the least rainy?
 Ⓐ Mean   Ⓒ Mode
 Ⓑ Median   Ⓓ Range

Rainy Days in Cleveland

Number of Days

16 14 15 15 13 11

Jan. Feb. Mar. Apr. May June

SOURCE: National Oceanic and Atmospheric Administration.
Go to **PHSchool.com** for a data update.
Web Code: asg–9041.

27. A cube has a surface area of 337.5 ft². What is the length of any one side?
 Ⓕ 7.5 ft   Ⓗ 28 ft
 Ⓖ 18 ft   Ⓙ 56 ft

28. An interior designer saved $29 on a pair of window blinds. If the sale price was 20% off the regular price, what was the regular price of the blinds?
 Ⓐ $345   Ⓑ $145   Ⓒ $69   Ⓓ $36

GO for Help

For Exercises	See Lesson
29–32	1-4

Simplify each expression.

29. $15(-20)$ **30.** $-7(-11)$ **31.** $\dfrac{-120}{-6}$ **32.** $\dfrac{60}{-4}$

Comparing Mean and Median

When you use a measure of central tendency, you choose one number to represent an entire set of data. This is like choosing one adjective to describe your pet, so choose carefully! The characteristics of a data set can help you choose an appropriate measure.

ACTIVITY

Work in a group.

1. Write each group member's height in inches. Calculate the group's mean and median height.

2. Suppose a person whose height is 7 ft 2 in. joins your group. Calculate the new mean and median height for the group.

3. Which measure, the mean or the median, was more affected by the new data? Explain why this happened.

4. Which measure of central tendency, mean or median, better describes the height of your group with the additional person? Give reasons for your choice.

ACTIVITY

5. Calculate the mean body length for the rodent species in the table at the right.

6. Write the range of the data. Explain why the range tells you more about the data than the mean does.

Body Length of Some Rodents

Rodent	Body Length (in.)
Capybara	48
Flying squirrel	9
Gray squirrel	10
Harvest mouse	3
Porcupine	26
Woodchuck	18

Exercises

Collect group data for each question. Then calculate the mean, median, and range for each data set. Choose either the mean or the median as the best measure of central tendency for each set of data. Explain your choice.

1. How long (in seconds) can you stand on one leg?

2. How many states in the United States have you visited?

3. How many pets have you had?

4. What is the length of your hair?

Displaying Frequency

What You'll Learn

To use line plots, frequency tables, and histograms to represent data

🔊 **New Vocabulary** frequency, line plot, frequency table, histogram

Why Learn This?

You can use a frequency table or line plot to display data such as body temperatures of cats. Line plots are useful for comparing amounts, finding the most common value in a data set quickly, or identifying outliers.

Body Temperatures of Cats (°F)
101, 102, 101, 100, 102, 103
102, 101, 101
104, 101, 102

The number of times a data item occurs is the **frequency** of the item. You can display frequency in a line plot. A **line plot** displays data with ✗ marks above each data value on a number line.

EXAMPLE Making a Line Plot

① **Biology** The table above shows the body temperatures of some cats. Use the data to make a line plot.

Body Temperatures of Cats

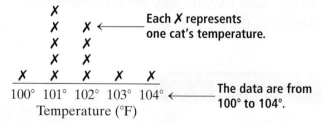

Each ✗ represents one cat's temperature.

The data are from 100° to 104°.

✓ Quick Check

1. Make a line plot for these human body temperatures (°F):
98, 98, 99, 97, 98, 96, 99, 98, 97, 100, 99, 98, 99.

You can find the mean, median, and mode of a set of data using a line plot. Use the frequency of each data item to find the sum of the items and the total number of items.

To find the mean of data in a frequency table or line plot, first multiply each data value by its frequency.

EXAMPLE Using a Line Plot

② Find the mean of the data in the line plot in Example 1.

Multiply each data value by its frequency.
↓

$$\frac{(1 \cdot 100) + (5 \cdot 101) + (4 \cdot 102) + (1 \cdot 103) + (1 \cdot 104)}{1 + 5 + 4 + 1 + 1}$$

↑

Add the frequency of each item to find the total number of items.

$$\frac{1,220}{12} \approx 101.7 \quad \leftarrow \text{Simplify. Then round to the nearest tenth.}$$

✓ Quick Check

2. Use the line plot in Example 1. Find the median and mode.

A frequency table lists the frequency of each item in a set of data. To display the data visually, make a histogram. A histogram is a special type of bar graph with no spaces between bars. The height of each bar shows the frequency of data within that interval. The intervals of a histogram are of equal size and do not overlap.

EXAMPLE Making a Histogram

③ **Energy** Some brands of batteries last longer than others. Make a frequency table and histogram for the data on hours of battery life: 12, 9, 10, 14, 10, 11, 10, 18, 21, 10, 14, 22.

Make a frequency table. The data range from 9 to 22. Use equal-sized intervals that begin with multiples of 5. Then make a histogram.

Battery Life

Hours	Tally	Frequency
0–4		0
5–9	/	1
10–14	𝚻𝚮𝚰 ///	8
15–19	/	1
20–24	//	2

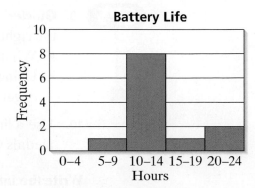

✓ Quick Check

3. Make a frequency table and histogram for the data on the cost of a movie: $5.00, $6.00, $8.50, $9.00, $5.50, $7.00, $7.00, $7.50, $6.00, $7.50, $4.00, $9.00, $8.00, $5.50

1. **Vocabulary** How is a histogram different from a bar graph?

Use the line plot below for Exercises 2 and 3.

2. **Reasoning** Explain why the number line for the line plot at the right starts at 25 instead of 0.

3. Find the mean of the data set.

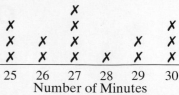

Number of Minutes

Homework Exercises

For more exercises, see Extra Skills and Word Problems.

For Exercises	See Examples
4–5	1
6–7	2
8	3

Make a line plot for each set of data.

4. hours spent on homework:
2 2 3 1 1 2 0 3 2 0
4 2 1 3 1 3 1 4 2 2

5. hard-drive sizes (gigabytes):
8 10 8 12 16 20 18 16
12 14 18 24 12 8

Find the mean, median, and mode of the data to the nearest tenth.

6.

```
                        X
              X         X
      X       X         X
  X   X   X   X         X
  X   X   X   X   X   X
  0   1   2   3   4   5
```

7.

```
              X   X           X
              X   X           X
  X           X   X           X
  X   X   X   X   X   X
  X   X   X   X   X   X
 -2  -1   0   1   2   3
```

8. Make a histogram for the data.
Low temperatures in February (°F):
-2 -1 0 -2 -1 -4 2 3 0 -1 2 -3
-1 0 1 2 3 2 -2 3 4 2 1 5 6 4 3 1

9. **Guided Problem Solving** Use the table at the right. Make a histogram for the data.
- What intervals will you use?
- Using those intervals, how will you organize the data?

10. Use a line plot to display the frequency of medals won at the 2002 Winter Olympics.

Write the intervals described in each statement.

11. intervals that are multiples of 10 for data that range from 58 to 100

12. intervals that are multiples of 20 for data that range from 305 to 458

Distribution of Gold Medals at the 2002 Winter Olympics

Country	Medals
Germany	12
Norway	11
United States	10
Canada	6
Russian Federation	6
Finland	4
France	4
Italy	4

SOURCE: *The World Almanac*

Make a line plot for each data set. Then find the mean, median, and mode of the data.

13. cars sold per month:
24 25 23 26 28 29 21 27 31 28 26 24

14. ages of members of the Seniors Hiking Club (years):
62 73 78 66 67 67 60 73 76 62 78 78 60 67 75 62

15. keystrokes in computer passwords:
8 7 8 6 6 5 6 7 7 8 8 8 6 5 5 6 5 6 7 7 6 5 5

Make a frequency table and histogram for each data set. Use intervals of equal sizes to group the data.

16. televisions sold at a store each day:
7 8 9 13 14 18 5 9 11 16 5 6 14 12 10 9 7 9 2 21

17. golf scores:
0 −2 −1 0 3 −1 0 2 1 −2 3 0 1 −5 4 3
4 5 −2 0 −1 4 0 −2 3 2 3 1 4 0 −2 1

18. monthly car payments (dollars):
205 190 305 346 452 325 140 376 289 368 512 337 254 398

19. **Writing in Math** How does the appearance of a histogram change when you use many small intervals instead of a few large intervals?

Families Use the line plots below for Exercises 20–22. The Bakers and the Smiths are each having a family reunion. The line plots below show the number of children attending from each family.

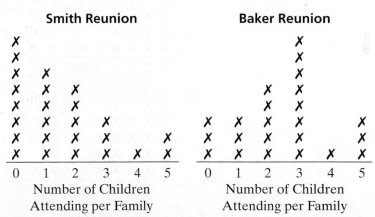

20. Which reunion, the Bakers or the Smiths, has more families without children?

21. Which reunion, the Bakers or the Smiths, has more large families attending?

22. Find the mean, median, and mode for each line plot. Round to the nearest tenth.

23. Challenge Use equal intervals to make a frequency table and histogram of the number of cars per 100 people.

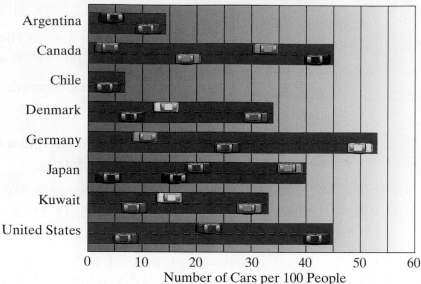

Who's on the Road?

Number of Cars per 100 People

Source: *Ward's Motor Vehicle Facts & Figures*

Test Prep and Mixed Review

Practice

Multiple Choice

24. Which line plot best represents the following data?

2 1 5 4 1 3 7 8 2 2 3 4 1 6
8 9 1 1 2 4 5 4 3 5 4 3 2 1

(A)
```
X
X
X                   X
X X                 X
X X   X       X X
X X X X X X X X X
1 2 3 4 5 6 7 8 9
```

(C)
```
X   X   X   X
X   X   X   X
X   X   X   X
X X X X   X X X
X X X X   X X X
1 2 3 4 5 6 7 8 9
```

(B)
```
X
X X   X
X X X X
X X X X
X X X X       X
X X X X X X X X X
1 2 3 4 5 6 7 8 9
```

(D)
```
X
X X
X X X X X
X X X X X
X X X X       X
X X X X X X X X X
1 2 3 4 5 6 7 8 9
```

25. Sixteen percent of the executives in a company are women. What fraction of executives are women?

(F) $\frac{4}{25}$ (G) $\frac{16}{25}$ (H) $\frac{8}{5}$ (J) $\frac{25}{4}$

GO for Help

For Exercises	See Lesson
26–28	5-1

Write each percent as a fraction in simplest form.

26. 20%   **27.** $33\frac{1}{3}\%$ **28.** 1.75%

Making Histograms

A graphing calculator can help you make histograms.

ACTIVITY

Off the coast of Hawaii, a researcher recorded the
following wave heights (in feet): 6.0, 6.5, 6.6, 6.3, 6.7,
7.4, 7.2, 7.4, 7.0, 7.2, 7.2, 7.3, 6.8, 7.3, 7.7, 7.8, 7.5, 7.2, 7.6,
7.3, 7.3, 7.1, 7.5, 6.9, and 6.8. Make a histogram of these data.

Step 1 Press $\boxed{\text{LIST}}$. Enter the 25 data values into L_1.

Step 2 Use the PLOT feature. Select the first plot. Select **On**. Select
the type of graph that looks like a histogram. Set Xlist = L_1.

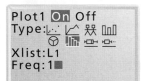

Step 3 Press $\boxed{\text{ZOOM}}$. Select ZoomStat.

Step 4 Press $\boxed{\text{WINDOW}}$. To make the intervals on the horizontal
axis 0.1, set Xscl = 0.1.

Step 5 Press $\boxed{\text{GRAPH}}$ to see the histogram.

Step 6 Press $\boxed{\text{TRACE}}$ and move the cursor across the histogram to
see the frequency of each interval.

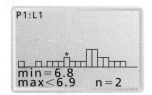

Step 7 Sketch a histogram of the data values.

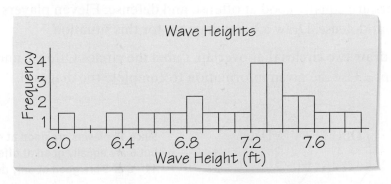

Exercises

Graph a histogram for each data set using a graphing calculator. Then sketch
the histogram.

1. 9, 12, 11, 14, 12, 11, 13, 14, 13, 11, 14, 14, 15, 11, 14, 16, 12, 12, 13, 11

2. 100, 120, 140, 160, 120, 180, 180, 280, 260, 240, 220, 220, 200, 200,
   260, 240, 240, 120, 140, 160, 160

Venn Diagrams

✓ Check Skills You'll Need

1. **Vocabulary Review**
   Two numbers whose sum is 0 are __?__.

Simplify.

2. $10 - (-6)$

3. $-4 + 3$

4. $16 + (-9)$

 **for Help**
Lesson 1-3

What You'll Learn

To use Venn diagrams to represent relationships between data

🔊 **New Vocabulary** Venn diagram

Why Learn This?

You can use Venn diagrams to describe the skills of the players on a sports team.

A **Venn diagram** is a diagram that uses regions, usually circles, to show how sets of numbers or objects are related.

EXAMPLE Using a Venn Diagram

1 A soccer coach is working on the lineup for the next game. The team has 15 players. Ten players on the team are good at offense. Six of those players are equally good at offense and defense. Eleven players are good at defense. Draw a Venn diagram for this situation.

First draw two circles that overlap. Label the circles Offense and Defense. Use the given information to complete the diagram.

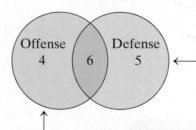

Since 11 players are good at defense but 6 are equally good at offense, 11−6 or 5 are good at only defense.

Since 10 players are good at offense but 6 are equally good at defense, 10−6 or 4 players are good at only offense.

✓ Quick Check

1. A softball team has 18 players. Fourteen players bat right-handed. Two players can bat left- or right-handed. Four players bat only left-handed. Draw a Venn diagram for this situation.

1. **Vocabulary** In a Venn diagram, what does the region of the overlapping circles represent?

2. Use the Venn diagram at the right. How many dogs are brown and have a long tail?

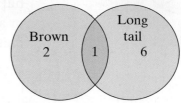

3. Of 120 students surveyed, 72 listen to pop music, 45 listen to country music, and 12 listen to both. How many students listen to only pop music?

Homework Exercises

For more exercises, see Extra Skills and Word Problems.

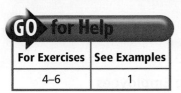

For Exercises	See Examples
4–6	1

Draw a Venn diagram for each situation.

4. 18 students play a sport.
   15 students are in the band.
   11 do both activities.

5. 12 red shapes
   12 triangles
   8 non-red triangles

6. 75 people are downhill skiers.
   51 people are cross-country skiers.
   26 ski both downhill and cross-country.

7. **Guided Problem Solving** At a summer camp, 20 campers try canoeing or climbing. Suppose 13 campers try canoeing and 15 try climbing. Of those 15 campers, 7 try only climbing. How many campers try only canoeing?
   - Place the information in a Venn diagram. Use two circles.
   - How many students try both activities?

Solve each problem by drawing a Venn diagram.

8. What is the greatest common factor of 30 and 40?

9. Between 1 and 20, there are 10 odd numbers and 8 prime numbers. Three odd numbers are not prime. How many prime numbers are *not* odd?

10. **School** Of 15 students in summer school, 11 take math and 9 take English. Of the students taking English, 5 also take math. What is the probability that a randomly-selected student takes only math?

11. **Reasoning** A Venn diagram has two circles that do not overlap. What conclusion can you draw about the categories of data?

Online Homework Video Tutor
Visit: PHSchool.com
Web Code: ase-0903

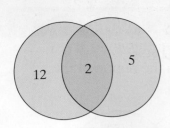

12. **Writing in Math** Write a problem that you could solve using the Venn diagram at the left.

13. **Challenge** The Venn diagram below shows the results of a survey of the types of pets in 580 households. The area within the rectangle but outside the circles represents households that do not have a dog or a cat. Find the probability that a household chosen at random has neither a cat nor a dog.

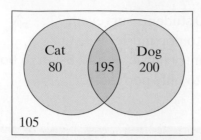

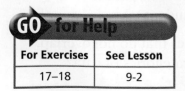
Test Prep and Mixed Review   **Practice**

Multiple Choice

14. Use the Venn diagram at the right. How many more employees work in the stock room than at the register?

    Ⓐ 3   Ⓒ 5
    Ⓑ 4   Ⓓ 6

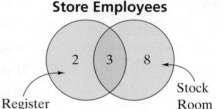

15. A circular fountain has a radius of 5 feet. The circular center of the fountain does not hold water and has a diameter of 3 feet. The outer part of the fountain that holds water is 2.5 feet deep. About how much water does the outer part hold?

    Ⓕ 18 ft³   Ⓖ 125 ft³   Ⓗ 178 ft³   Ⓙ 196 ft³

16. Manuella is planning a garden 80 feet wide and 125 feet long. The garden will have a square fountain, 8 feet on a side. It will also have 2,500 square feet of paths. The rest of the garden is reserved for plants. What is the area of the garden that is reserved for plants?

    Ⓐ 7,436 ft²   Ⓒ 7,492 ft²
    Ⓑ 7,484 ft²   Ⓓ 10,000 ft²

Make a frequency table and a histogram for each data set. Use intervals of equal size to group the data.

17. lengths of wood (cm):
    23 26 25 26 23 25 25 24 21 21 22 23

18. weekly earnings (dollars):
    260 270 260 300 290 300 250 270 320 260

For Exercises	See Lesson
17–18	9-2

Reading Graphical Displays

The manager of a store made the graphs below as part of
a report to the corporate office. At first glance, things
seem to be going well. Sales went up from January to
September, and expenses increased only a small amount.

ACTIVITY

1. Use the Monthly Sales Record graph at the right. Calculate the
   increase in sales from January to September. What
   percent of the January sales is this increase?

2. **Reasoning** Explain how the manager drew the Monthly
   Sales graph to make the increase in sales seem to be greater
   than it is.

3. Use the graph below to calculate the percent of increase in
   operating expenses from January to September.

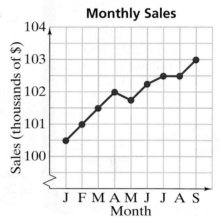

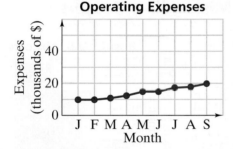

4. **Reasoning** Explain how the manager drew the Operating Expenses
   graph to make the increase in operating expenses seem to be less
   than it is.

5. **Writing in Math** Write a report that better describes the store's sales
   and operating expenses. Include the percent changes you calculated
   in Questions 1 and 3. Include new graphs that remove the distortions
   you described in Questions 2 and 4.

Exercises

1. Find a graph in a newspaper or magazine that you think
   misrepresents or distorts the numerical data it was meant to
   represent. Explain why the data are not represented fairly.

2. Make a new graph that shows the data more fairly.

Reading Graphs Critically

Check Skills You'll Need

1. **Vocabulary Review** What does a *bar graph* show?

2. The following data show the number of students in a class who prefer each primary color. Red: 12; Yellow: 3; Blue: 10. Make a bar graph of this data.

 **for Help**

Skills Handbook
p. 641

What You'll Learn

To recognize misleading graphs and to choose appropriate scales

Why Learn This?

You can analyze graphs of real-world data to compare passenger activity at various airports.

The same set of data may be graphed in several different ways. Sometimes, however, a graph can give a misleading visual impression.

EXAMPLE Recognizing Misleading Graphs

① **Multiple Choice** The graph gives the impression that Chicago O'Hare Airport is four times as busy as Los Angeles International Airport. Which statement explains why?

Ⓐ The graph should be a line graph.

Ⓑ The intervals are not equal.

Ⓒ The intervals on the vertical axis are too small.

Ⓓ The scale on the vertical axis does not start at 0.

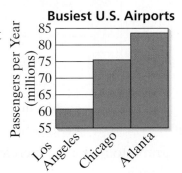

The bar for Chicago appears to be four times as long as the bar for Los Angeles because the scale on the vertical axis does not start at 0. The correct answer is choice D.

✓ Quick Check

1. Explain why the graph at the right is more clear than the graph in Example 1.

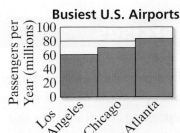

When some of the values on an axis of a graph have been left out, the graph should have a break symbol, $\lessgtr$, to alert the reader.

EXAMPLE Selecting an Appropriate Scale

② **Education** Using different scales, make two line graphs for the data at the left. Use a break symbol in only one of the graphs.

The highest projected college enrollment is 18.2 million. Label the vertical axis with multiples of 5 from 0 to 20.

Projected U.S. College Enrollment

The data start at 17 million. Label the vertical axis with multiples of 0.5, beginning with 16. Use a break symbol.

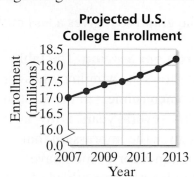

Projected U.S. College Enrollment

Year	Students (millions)
2007	17.0
2008	17.2
2009	17.4
2010	17.5
2011	17.7
2012	17.9
2013	18.2

Projected U.S. College Enrollment

SOURCE: U.S. National Center for Educational Statistics

✔ Quick Check

2. Which graph above shows the data more clearly? Explain.

✔ Check Your Understanding

1. **Vocabulary** What features can make a graph misleading?

Use the graph at the right.

2. In which year does it appear that the winning fish weighed twice as much as the 2001 winning fish?

3. Do you think the graph represents the data fairly? Explain.

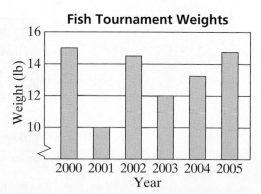

Fish Tournament Weights

For more exercises, see **Extra Skills and Word Problems.**

Publishing Use the graph below for Exercises 4–7.

GO for Help

For Exercises	See Examples
4–6	1
7	2

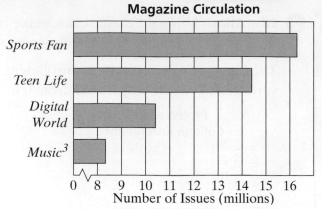

Magazine Circulation

Sports Fan

Teen Life

Digital World

Music³

0 8 9 10 11 12 13 14 15 16
Number of Issues (millions)

4. Which magazine appears to have about twice the circulation of *Music³*?

5. Which magazine actually has about twice the circulation of *Music³*?

6. Explain why the graph gives a misleading impression of the data.

7. Redraw the graph so it gives a less misleading impression of the data.

GPS

8. Guided Problem Solving The table at the right shows the winning times for men and women runners in the Boston Marathon for several years. Draw a graph that gives the impression that the winning times for women have decreased to less than one third of what they were in 1970.

- Write the minutes as fractions of an hour.
- Decide what vertical scale to use.

Boston Marathon Winning Times

Year	Men	Women
1970	2:10:30	3:05:07
1975	2:09:55	2:42:24
1980	2:12:11	2:34:28
1985	2:14:05	2:35:06
1990	2:08:09	2:25:23
1995	2:09:22	2:25:11
2000	2:09:47	2:26:11
2005	2:11:45	2:25:13

Jean Driscoll won the women's wheelchair division of the Boston Marathon a record eight times.

Using different scales, make either two line graphs or two bar graphs for each set of data. Use a break symbol in only one of the graphs. Explain which graph shows the data more clearly.

9. **Top Films**

Film	Total (millions)
Titanic	$601
Star Wars	$461
Shrek 2	$436.7
E.T., The Extra-Terrestrial	$435

SOURCE: *Variety*

10. **Population Density**

Year	Population/mi²
1	50.6
2	57.4
3	64.0
4	70.3
5	79.6

Recycling Use the table below for Exercises 11–13.

11. Make a line graph to show that the recycling rate of drink containers stayed about the same.

12. Make a line graph to show that the recycling rate has varied.

13. **Writing in Math** Explain how the scale you chose for each graph gives the visual impression you want to create.

Recycling of Drink Containers

Year	Percent
1998	62.8%
1999	62.5%
2000	62.1%
2001	55.4%
2002	53.4%
2003	50.0%
2004	51.2%

Use the table at the left for Exercises 14–16.

14. You want to encourage the school board to approve the hiring of more teachers. Graph the data in a way that would show a big change in school enrollment.

15. Graph the data to show very little change in the school enrollment over the years.

16. **Reasoning** Which of the graphs you drew more fairly presents the data? Explain.

17. **Challenge** A graph uses the following labels at equal intervals along the horizontal axis: 1940, 1945, 1955, 1975, 2015.
    a. What are the intervals being used?
    b. Is this an appropriate scale? Explain.
    c. **Patterns** Is there a pattern in the scale? Explain.

Public School Enrollment in the United States

Year	Enrollment (thousands)
1970	52,322
1975	53,654
1980	50,335
1985	48,901
1990	52,061
1995	55,933
2000	58,976
2005	61,090

SOURCE: U.S. Census Bureau. Go to **PHSchool.com** for a data update.
Web Code: asg–9041

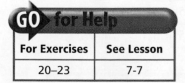

Test Prep and Mixed Review
Practice

Multiple Choice

18. The stated size of computer monitors is based on the measurement of the diagonal of the screen. If the height of a screen is 9.75 inches and the width is 12.75 inches, what is the best estimate of the stated size of the monitor?
    Ⓐ 8.5 in.   Ⓑ 15 in.   Ⓒ 16 in.   Ⓓ 22 in.

19. Rachel is making three aprons for a school play. Each apron uses $2\frac{1}{4}$ yards of fabric. If Rachel has $7\frac{1}{2}$ yards of fabric, how much will be left after she makes the aprons?
    Ⓕ $\frac{1}{4}$ yd   Ⓖ $\frac{3}{4}$ yd   Ⓗ $5\frac{1}{4}$ yd   Ⓙ $6\frac{3}{4}$ yd

Geometry Find the area of a circle with the given radius. Round to the nearest tenth.

20. $r = 8$ cm   21. $r = 14$ in.   22. $r = 9.6$ m   23. $r = 1.2$ ft

GO for Help

For Exercises	See Lesson
20–23	7-7

9-4b Activity Lab

Data Analysis

Making Graphs to Tell a Story

Visitors to National Parks

Year	1998	1999	2000	2001	2002	2003	2004
Number of Visitors (millions)	435.7	436.3	429.9	424.3	421.3	413.9	427.7

SOURCE: National Park Service. Go to **PHSchool.com** for a data update. Web Code: asg-9041

1. Make a graph that gives the visual impression of a sizeable annual change in the number of visitors.

2. Make a second graph that gives the visual impression of a modest annual change in the number of visitors.

3. Compare your graphs. Which graph do you think more fairly represents the data in the table? Explain.

Checkpoint Quiz 1

Lesson 9-1 through 9-4

For Exercises 1–4, use these temperatures for 11 days in July:
80 83 88 88 90 106 100 101 110 109 85

1. Find the mean.　　2. Find the median.　　3. Find the mode.　　4. Find the range.

For Exercises 5–7, use these math test scores:
93 75 87 83 99 75 80 90 72 77 95 98 82 87 100 91 68

5. Make a frequency table. Use intervals of equal size.

6. Make a line plot.

7. Use the frequency table from Exercise 5 to make a histogram.

8. Make two bar graphs for the set of data at the right. In one of the graphs, use a break symbol. Explain which graph shows the data more clearly.

Average Number of Students per Computer

High School	10.5
Middle School	12.75
Elementary School	13.25

Stem-and-Leaf Plots

Check Skills You'll Need

1. **Vocabulary Review**
What does a *line plot* display?

Use the line plot for Exercises 2–4.

2. Find the mean.
3. Find the median.
4. Find the mode.

GO for Help
Lesson 9-2

What You'll Learn

To represent and interpret data using stem-and-leaf plots

◀)) **New Vocabulary** stem-and-leaf plot

Why Learn This?

A stem-and-leaf plot is an efficient way to compare prices of digital music players.

A **stem-and-leaf plot** is a graph that shows numerical data arranged in order. Each data item is broken into a stem and a leaf.

The stem is the digit or digits on the left and the leaf is the digit or digits on the right.

Prices of Digital Music Players (dollars)
189, 214, 200, 195, 190, 192, 193, 211, 201, 196, 195, 194, 205, 198, 208, 201

$1|0$ ← leaf
↑
stem

$5.|52$ ← leaf
↑
stem

$5.5|2$ ← leaf
↑
stem

EXAMPLE Making Stem-and-Leaf Plots

1 Make a stem-and-leaf plot for the data in the table above.

Step 1 Choose the stems. The least value is 189; the greatest value is 214. For this data use the first two digits as the stems. The stems in this case are 18, 19, 20, and 21.

Step 2 Draw the stem-and-leaf plot. Include a key.

stems   leaves
↓   ↓

18	9
19	0 2 3 4 5 5 6 8
20	0 1 1 5 8
21	1 4

The leaves are the ones place written in increasing order.

Key: 19 | 2 means $192

The key explains what the stems and leaves represent.

High Temperatures (°F) Death Valley, California
87 91 101 111 120
125 134 126 120
113 97 86

✓ Quick Check

1. At the left are the monthly high temperatures for Death Valley, California. Make a stem-and-leaf plot for the data.

Because stem-and-leaf plots display data items in numerical order, they are useful tools for finding median and mode.

More Than One Way

The table shows the annual percent change in the United States Consumer Price Index. The Consumer Price Index measures the average change in how much you pay for things. Find the median and mode.

United States Consumer Price Index

Year	Percent Change
1993	3.0
1994	2.6
1995	2.8
1996	3.0
1997	2.3
1998	1.6
1999	2.2
2000	3.4
2001	2.8
2002	1.6
2003	2.3
2004	2.7

SOURCE: Bureau of Labor Statistics. Go to **PHSchool.com** for a data update. Web Code: asg-9041

Michelle's Method

A stem-and-leaf plot is an appropriate way to organize the data to find the median and mode.

```
1 | 6 6
2 | 2 3 3 6 7 8 8
3 | 0 0 4
```

Key: 3 | 0 means 3.0%

$\frac{2.6 + 2.7}{2} = 2.65$ ← There are 12 leaves in the stem-and-leaf plot. So the median is the mean of the sixth and seventh leaves.

The median change in the United States Consumer Price Index is 2.65%. The modes are 1.6%, 2.3%, 2.8%, and 3.0%.

Eric's Method

To find the median and mode, I need to put the data items in order.

1.6 1.6 2.2 2.3 2.3 2.6 2.7 2.8 2.8 3.0 3.0 3.4

The median is the mean of the sixth and seventh items, which is 2.65.

The median change in the United States Consumer Price Index is 2.65%. The modes are 1.6%, 2.3%, 2.8%, and 3.0%.

Choose a Method

The table shows the average amount of time drivers in different cities spend in traffic annually. Find the median and mode of the data. Explain why you chose the method you used.

City	Hours	City	Hours
Los Angeles	56	Denver	45
Phoenix	31	Houston	50
Seattle	53	New York	34
Las Vegas	21	Miami	42
Chicago	34	Detroit	41

SOURCE: Time Almanac

When you compare two sets of the same type of data, use back-to-back stem-and-leaf plots.

EXAMPLE **Application: Gas Mileage**

2 The back-to-back stem-and-leaf plot below shows the city mileage and the highway mileage of seven new cars. Compare the city mileage to the highway mileage by using the mode of each data set.

New Car Mileage (mi/gal)

City		Highway
9 8 8	1	
7 4 2	2	4 5 7 8
0	3	3 3
	4	0

Key: means $27 \leftarrow 7 \mid 2 \mid 8 \rightarrow$ means 28

The mode for city mileage is 18 mi/gal. The mode for highway mileage is 33 mi/gal. This measure of central tendency gives the impression that the highway mileage of the new cars is higher than the city mileage.

✓ Quick Check

2. Compare city mileage to highway mileage using the mean and the median.

✓ Check Your Understanding

Online active math

For: Stem-and-Leaf Plot Activity
Use: Interactive Textbook, 9-5

1. **Vocabulary** Identify the stem and the leaf in the number 6.7.

Use the stem-and-leaf plot below for Exercises 2–5.

2. What numbers make up the stems?

3. What are the leaves for the first stem?

4. How many data items are shown in the stem-and-leaf plot?

5. Find the median and mode of the data.

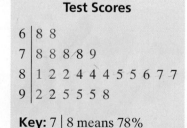

Test Scores

6	8 8
7	8 8 8 8 9
8	1 2 2 4 4 4 5 5 6 7 7
9	2 2 5 5 5 8

Key: 7 | 8 means 78%

6. Make a stem-and-leaf plot for the data below. Find the median and the mode.

    18 19 27 8 19 20 19 6 18 27 16 13 12 7
    8 18 19 11 10 19 18 18 8 17 16 12

For more exercises, see Extra Skills and Word Problems.

GO for Help

For Exercises	See Examples
7–9	1
10–11	2

Make a stem-and-leaf plot for each set of data.

7. 54 48 52 53 67 61 68 49 40 50 69 73 74 76 78

8. 124 129 131 116 138 107 105 116 122 137 138 134

9. 3.7 5.0 6.9 3.2 4.5 6.3 6.7 5.8 5.2 6.9 5.0 4.3 4.1

Use the stem-and-leaf plot below for Exercises 10 and 11.

Vocabulary Tip

In a stem-and-leaf plot of two sets of data, 8|6|5 means that both 8 and 5 are leaves of the stem 6.

10. **Health** The plot at the right shows the blood pressure of 40 men and women of the same age. Find the mean and median of each data set.

11. **Reasoning** What conclusions can you draw about men's blood pressure compared to women's blood pressure? Explain.

Blood Pressure

Men		Women
8	6	5 5 6 8
9 7 7 6	7	0 1 1 2 5 6 8 8 9
9 9 8 7 4 4 1	8	0 0 3 5 6
8 5 4 2 0 0	9	0 1
2 0	10	

Key: means 94 ← 4 | 9 | 1 → means 91

12. **Guided Problem Solving** Make a back-to-back stem-and-leaf plot for the data sets below. Then find the median and mode.

Length of Wood Boards (in.)

Saw A	Saw B
64 58 63 57 54 61 52 54	72 63 52 57 64 49 45 43

- For Saw B, make a stem-and-leaf plot.
- For Saw A, add any missing stems to the existing list of stems. Draw a vertical line to the left of the stems. Write each leaf for Saw A to the left of its stem.

13. **Golf** In golf, a player's score is based on the total number of strokes needed to get the ball into the holes. The player with the lowest score is the winner. Use the mean, median, and mode of each set of data below to compare men's scores to women's scores in a four-round tournament.

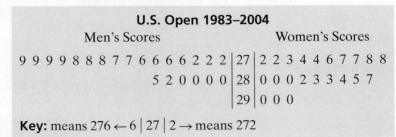

U.S. Open 1983–2004

Men's Scores		Women's Scores
9 9 9 9 8 8 8 7 7 6 6 6 6 2 2 2 2	27	2 2 3 4 4 6 7 7 8 8
5 2 0 0 0 0	28	0 0 0 2 3 3 4 5 7
	29	0 0 0

Key: means 276 ← 6 | 27 | 2 → means 272

Source: *Sports Illustrated 2005 Almanac*

GO Online
Homework Video Tutor
Visit: PHSchool.com
Web Code: ase-0905

14. a. Animals Use the data below on the life spans of different animals (in years) to make a stem-and-leaf plot.

1 10 3 10 4 12 13 15 15 20 40 6 7 10 15 18 22 20
25 7 12 5 15 20 25 20 15

b. Number Sense If you add the data values 13.2, 14.5, 13.5, 15.6, 18.2, 19.7, 21.3, 35.6, 40.2, 13.7, and 12.8, why might you choose different stems in your stem-and-leaf plot?

15. **Writing in Math** A set of data contains numbers in the 30s, 40s and 60s only. Is it necessary to put a 5 on the stem of a stem-and-leaf plot? Justify your answer.

16. Challenge The data sets below have the same mean, median, mode, and range. Copy and complete the back-to-back stem-and-leaf plot.

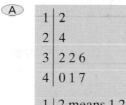

```
        7 6 ■ │3│ 1 2 3
  6 5 4 3 1 │4│ 2 ■ ■ 6
        ■ 0 │5│ 0 0 1
```

Key: means 3■ ← ■│3│1 → means 31

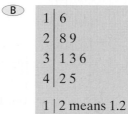 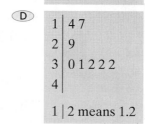

Test Prep and Mixed Review **Practice**

Multiple Choice

17. Which stem-and-leaf plot has a median of 3.2?

Ⓐ
```
1 │ 2
2 │ 4
3 │ 2 2 6
4 │ 0 1 7

1│2 means 1.2
```

Ⓒ
```
1 │ 8
2 │ 0 0 2
3 │ 2
4 │ 7 8 9

1│2 means 1.2
```

Ⓑ
```
1 │ 6
2 │ 8 9
3 │ 1 3 6
4 │ 2 5

1│2 means 1.2
```

Ⓓ
```
1 │ 4 7
2 │ 9
3 │ 0 1 2 2 2
4 │

1│2 means 1.2
```

18. Students recorded the number of hours of sleep they got Monday night. Which list shows the data in order from least to greatest?

Ⓕ 9.25, $9\frac{1}{3}$, $9\frac{5}{6}$, 10, $10\frac{1}{6}$

Ⓖ 9.25, $9\frac{1}{3}$, $9\frac{5}{6}$, $10\frac{1}{6}$, 10

Ⓗ 10, 9.25, $9\frac{1}{3}$, $10\frac{1}{6}$, $9\frac{5}{6}$

Ⓙ $9\frac{1}{3}$, 9.25, $9\frac{5}{6}$, 10, $10\frac{1}{6}$

Find the mean, median, mode, and range of each set of data.

19. 178 179 180 182 177 183 185 180 180 179

20. 4 2 4 8 10 12 10 6 4 8 4 6 8 4 6 8 10

For Exercises	See Lesson
19–20	9-1

What You'll Learn

To represent and interpret data using box-and-whisker plots

🔊 **New Vocabulary** box-and-whisker plot, quartiles

Why Learn This?

You can use box-and-whisker plots to organize very large data sets or to make comparisons between data sets.

A **box-and-whisker plot** is a graph that summarizes a data set along a number line. To make a box-and-whisker plot, you use values called quartiles. **Quartiles** divide data into four equally-sized groups.

Box-and-Whisker Plot

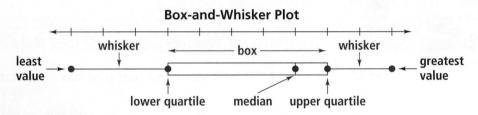

EXAMPLE Comparing Two Sets of Data

1 **Shopping** The two box-and-whisker plots show the prices for clothing at two stores. Write a paragraph comparing the data.

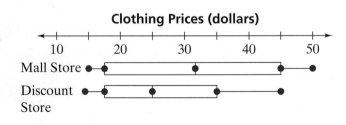

The mall store's prices vary more than the discount store's. The discount store's shorter box means that its prices are less spread out.

✓ Quick Check

1. Write a paragraph comparing the data below.

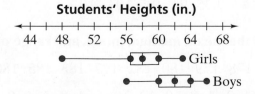

Before you draw a box-and-whisker plot, you need to find the quartiles of the data.

The lower quartile is the median of the lower half of data. The middle quartile is the median of the entire data set. The upper quartile is the median of the upper half of data.

EXAMPLE Making Box-and-Whisker Plots

2) Travel Make a box-and-whisker plot for the data below.

Average Amount Spent by Visitors to the United States (per person)

Country	Amount	Country	Amount
Canada	$483	France	$2,688
Mexico	$562	Brazil	$3,389
Japan	$2,341	Italy	$2,726
United Kingdom	$2,142	South Korea	$3,405
Germany	$2,466	Australia	$3,618

SOURCE: *The World Almanac*

Step 1 Arrange the data from least to greatest. Find the median.

483 562 2,142 2,341 2,466 2,688 2,726 3,389 3,405 3,618

The median is $\frac{2,466 + 2,688}{2}$, or 2,577.

Step 2 Find the lower quartile and the upper quartile.

483 562 **2,142** 2,341 2,466 2,688 2,726 **3,389** 3,405 3,618

The lower quartile is 2,142, and the upper quartile is 3,389.

Step 3 Draw a number line that spans all of the data values. Mark points below the number line at the least and greatest values, at the median, and at the lower and upper quartiles.

Use the lower and upper quartiles to form a box. Mark the median. Then draw whiskers from the box to the least and greatest values.

Amount Spent by Visitors to the United States (dollars per person)

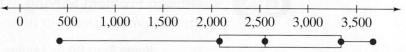

✓ Quick Check

2. Make a box-and-whisker plot for the data below.

   10 16 24 11 35 26 29 31 4 53 47 12 21 24 25 26

Check Your Understanding

1. **Vocabulary** The _?_ is the middle quartile of a data set.

Match each term with the correct point *A, B, C, D,* or *E*.

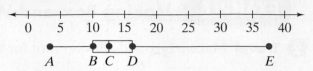

2. median   3. greatest value   4. lower quartile

Homework Exercises

For more exercises, see Extra Skills and Word Problems.

GO for Help

For Exercises	See Examples
5–6	1
7–8	2

For each box-and-whisker plot, write a paragraph to compare the data.

5. **On-Time Flight Arrivals and Departures in 2004 (percent per day)**

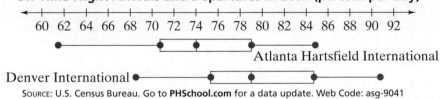

SOURCE: U.S. Census Bureau. Go to **PHSchool.com** for a data update. Web Code: asg-9041

6. **Median Income for Men and Women 1984 to 2003 (thousands of dollars)**

SOURCE: U.S. Census Bureau. Go to **PHSchool.com** for a data update. Web Code: asg-9041

Make a box-and-whisker plot for each set of data.

7. lengths of snakes at a zoo (ft):

   2 9 5 6 8 5 4 6 13 5 8 11 6 14 10 9 13 8 5 7 6 18 9 12

8. bowling scores:

   229 152 161 267 193 184 271 199 161 273 221 180

9. **Guided Problem Solving** Which league in the table below had the greater range in number of home runs hit by league leaders?

Home Runs Hit by League Leaders (2004 Season)

American League	43	41	41	39	38	36	36	34	32
National League	48	46	46	45	42	42	39	38	37

SOURCE: *Sports Illustrated 2005 Almanac*

- Draw box-and-whisker plots on the same number line.
- How can you use the plots to compare the ranges?

Use the box-and-whisker plot below to find each value.

Test Scores

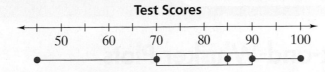

10. the median   **11.** the lower quartile   **12.** the range

13. **Writing in Math** Describe what it means when the median is not exactly in the middle of the box in a box-and-whisker plot.

Racing Use the table below for Exercises 14 and 15.

Average Speed of Daytona 500 Winners

Year	1998	1999	2000	2001	2002	2003	2004	2005
Speed (mi/h)	173	162	156	162	143	134	156	135

Source: NASCAR

14. Make a box-and-whisker plot for the data.

15. **Number Sense** Would the size of the box in your plot change if the average speed were 192 mi/h in 2003? Explain.

16. **Challenge** A scientist has 10 pieces of data in order. The median is 60.5. The sixth piece of data is 71. What is the fifth piece of data?

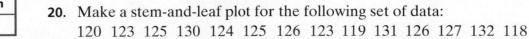

Test Prep and Mixed Review   **Practice**

Multiple Choice

17. What is the median in the box-and-whisker plot at the right?

- Ⓐ 100
- Ⓑ 90
- Ⓒ 67
- Ⓓ 51

18. The base of an isosceles triangle is 3 centimeters longer than its leg. If the perimeter is 18 centimeters, you can use the equation $18 - 2n = n + 3$ to find the length n of each leg. What is the length of each leg?

- Ⓕ 15 cm
- Ⓖ 7.5 cm
- Ⓗ 7 cm
- Ⓙ 5 cm

19. Tasha rolled out dough to make a pie. Which of the following is closest to the area her rolling pin at the right will cover in one complete rotation?

- Ⓐ 36 in.²
- Ⓑ 57 in.²
- Ⓒ 113 in.²
- Ⓓ 226 in.²

20. Make a stem-and-leaf plot for the following set of data:
120 123 125 130 124 125 126 123 119 131 126 127 132 118

Making Box-and-Whisker Plots

A graphing calculator can help you make
box-and-whisker plots.

ACTIVITY

The heights of the twenty largest giant sequoia trees in
feet are 275, 255, 268, 241, 256, 243, 269, 253, 223, 270, 248,
255, 251, 248, 244, 244, 273, 236, 246, and 286. Make a
box-and-whisker plot of these data values

Step 1 Press [LIST]. Enter the 20 values into L_1.

Step 2 Use the PLOT feature. Select the first plot. Select **On**. Select
the type of graph that looks like a box-and-whisker plot. Set
Xlist = L_1.

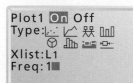

Step 3 Press [ZOOM]. Select ZoomStat.

Step 4 Press [WINDOW]. Set Xscl = 1.

Step 5 Press [GRAPH] to see the box-and-whisker plot.

Step 6 Press [TRACE]. Move the cursor to see the minimum, first
quartile, median, third quartile, and maximum values.

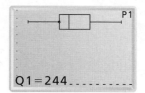

Step 7 Sketch a box-and-whisker plot of the data.

Giant Sequoia Heights (ft)

Exercises

**Graph a box-and-whisker plot for each set of data using a graphing
calculator. Then sketch the box-and-whisker plot.**

1. 46, 45, 36, 36, 52, 35, 38, 44, 53, 50, 44, 35, 37, 37

2. 7, 2, 5, 12, 13, 10, 6, 3, 4, 11, 12, 13, 10, 5, 8, 8, 9, 3, 4, 6

Scatter Plots

Is the length of your arm span (from fingertip to fingertip) related to your height? Graphing data in a scatter plot can help you decide whether one thing is related to another.

ACTIVITY

1. Have a classmate measure and record your height in centimeters.

2. Arm span is the greatest possible distance between the tips of your index fingers when your arms are stretched outward. To measure your arm span, hold one end of a tape measure in one hand and stretch your arms outward as the other hand slides along the tape measure. Measure your arm span in centimeters.

3. Write your data as an ordered pair: (height, arm span).

4. Exchange ordered pairs with your classmates. Record the ordered pairs in a table like the one below.

Height (cm)				
Arm span (cm)				

5. Make a graph of the ordered pairs. Label the horizontal axis Height (cm) and the vertical axis Arm Span (cm). Choose an appropriate scale.

6. **Writing in Math** What do you notice about the graph? Can you predict a person's arm span based on the person's height? Explain.

7. Suppose a person 176 cm tall joins your class. About how long would you expect his or her arm span to be? Explain.

8. Plot a few points on your graph where height and arm span are equal. Draw a line through these points.

9. Look at the points that lie above the line you drew. Describe the relationship between height and arm span for these points.

10. Look at the points that lie below the line. Describe the relationship between height and arm span for these points.

Check Skills You'll Need

1. **Vocabulary Review** What is an *ordered pair*?

Graph each point on a coordinate plane.

2. $A(1, -2)$

3. $B(-3, 5)$

GO for Help
Lesson 3-4

What You'll Learn

To make scatter plots and to use trends to make predictions

🔊 **New Vocabulary** scatter plot, positive trend, negative trend, no trend, trend line

Why Learn This?

You can use a scatter plot to determine whether the age of a car is related to what the car is worth.

A **scatter plot** is a graph that displays two sets of data as ordered pairs. It can help you decide whether two sets of data are related.

EXAMPLE Making Scatter Plots

1. **Cars** Make a scatter plot for the data in the table below.

	What's a Car Worth? Average Value of a Midsize Sedan (dollars)		
Age (yr)	Value	Age (yr)	Value
3	11,000	1	15,000
2	12,000	4	8,000
7	3,000	5	7,000
8	1,000	3	6,000
2	10,000	6	6,000

Step 1 Use the horizontal scale to represent the age of the car. Use the vertical scale to represent the car's value.

Step 2 Plot each data pair. (3, 11,000) represents a data pair.

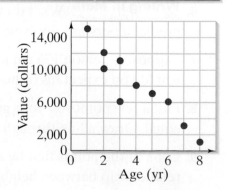

Quick Check

1. Make a scatter plot for the data below.

Age (yr):	1	15	6	19	12	3	5	13	20	6
Sleep Time (h):	15	8.5	9.5	7	9.25	12	11	9	7	9.75

Vocabulary Tip

A trend can also be a current style, as in fashion.

The three scatter plots below show the types of relationships, or trends, two sets of data may have.

Positive trend

As one set of values increases, the other set tends to increase.

Negative trend

As one set of values increases, the other set tends to decrease.

No trend

The points show no relationship.

A **trend line** is a line you draw on a graph to approximate the relationship between the data sets. If there is no trend to the data, you cannot draw a trend line.

You can use trend lines to make predictions about data values that do not appear on a scatter plot.

EXAMPLE Drawing Trend Lines

② **Gridded Response** The table below shows the circumference and height of a variety of trees. Use a scatter plot to predict the height of a tree that has a circumference of 175 in.

Tree Height and Circumference

Height (ft)	19	32	57	43	75	97	110
Circumference (in.)	10	63	72	111	150	185	214

Step 1 Plot each data pair.

Step 2 The plotted points go up from left to right. This scatter plot shows a positive trend.

Step 3 Draw a line with positive slope. Make sure there are about as many points above the line as there are below it.

Step 4 Find 175 on the horizontal axis. Move up to the trend line. Then move left to the vertical axis.

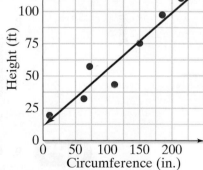

A tree with a circumference of 175 in. should have a height of about 88 ft.

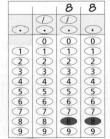

✓ Quick Check

2. Copy the scatter plot from Example 1 and draw a trend line.

1. **Vocabulary** Which type of graph is used to compare two sets of data—a line plot or a scatter plot?

Match each scatter plot with a trend: *positive, negative,* or *no trend.*

2.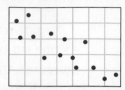

3.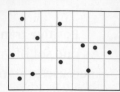

4.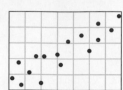

Homework Exercises

For more exercises, see Extra Skills and Word Problems.

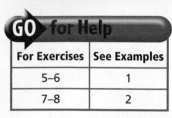

For Exercises	See Examples
5–6	1
7–8	2

Make a scatter plot for each set of data.

5. roommates: 3   2   3   2   4
   Rent (per person): $400 $900 $500 $700 $300

6. Hits: 7 8 4 11 8 2 5 9 1 4
   Runs: 3 2 2 7 4 2 1 3 0 1

Make a scatter plot for each set of data. If possible, draw a trend line and describe the trend.

7.
Life Expectancy

Current Age (yr)	10	15	20	25	30	35	40	45
Life Expectancy (yr)	67.4	62.5	57.7	53.0	48.2	43.5	38.8	34.3

SOURCE: U.S. Census Bureau. Go to **PHSchool.com** for a data update. Web Code: asg-9041

8.
Farm Sizes in the United States

Number of Farms (millions)	6.30	6.10	5.39	3.96	2.95	2.44	2.15	2.17
Average Size (acres)	157	175	216	297	373	426	460	434

SOURCE: U.S. National Agricultural Statistics. Go to **PHSchool.com** for a data update.
Web Code: asg-9041

9. **Guided Problem Solving** Estimate the world production of oil when the United States produced 12% of the world's oil.
   - Draw a scatter plot and a trend line.
   - Find 12% on the vertical axis. Move horizontally to the trend line. Then move down to the horizontal axis.

Oil Production 1960–2000 (billion barrels)

World Oil Production	U.S. Percent of World Oil Production
45.9	21
52.8	16
59.9	13
68.3	9
72.5	7

SOURCE: U.S. Energy Information Administration

For each topic, decide which type of trend a scatter plot of the data would likely show. Explain your choice.

10. age of owner and number of pets currently owned

11. outdoor temperature and layers of clothing

12. **Writing in Math** Do you think predictions made from a trend line will always be accurate? Explain.

13. **a. Baseball** Make a scatter plot for the data at the right.
    b. Draw a trend line.
    c. How many hits would a player be expected to have with 500 at-bats?
    d. How many at-bats would a player with 250 hits have?

Name	At-Bats	Hits
T. Hunter	564	147
I. Rodriguez	442	136
C. Beltran	617	189
G. Anderson	672	194
R. Sierra	344	100
B. Daubach	407	107
J. Liefer	254	65

SOURCE: Major League Baseball Association

14. **Challenge** As the number of women holding jobs increased, the record time in the women's 200-m run decreased. Does this negative trend mean that one set of data *caused* the other to occur? Explain.

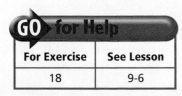

Test Prep and Mixed Review Practice

Gridded Response

15. Use the scatter plot below to predict the cost in dollars for five people to dine out.

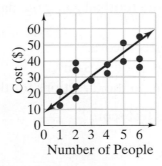

Number of People

16. Find the median of the following data.
    67 72 69 75 81 69 66 85 57

17. An astronomical unit, or AU, is the average distance from Earth to the sun. One AU is 149,597,870.691 kilometers. In scientific notation, this number is about 1.496×10^x. What is the value of x?

18. Make a box-and-whisker plot for the following data.
    number of questions answered correctly on a 10-question pop quiz:
    9 8 1 8 7 6 3 7 9 8 6 4 7 8 9 10 10

Plotting a Strategy

In scatter plots, the relationship between the variables is important. Analyze the clues to solve each problem.

ACTIVITY

The scatter plot at the right shows the number of cellular telephones in each of five families.

- DeWayne's family has three times as many members as cellular phones.
- Tom's family has more cellular phones than any other family.
- Each person in Rita's family has a cellular phone.
- Jack's family has six people in it.
- Manny's family has one extra cellular phone.

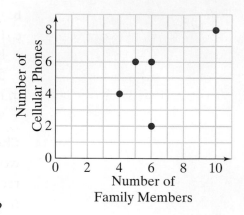

1. How many cellular phones does each person's family own?

ACTIVITY

The scatter plot at the right shows the grades of five students on the last English test and the length of their hair.

- Art's grade is his hair length times a multiple of 10.
- Sam shaved his head for the football game the day before the test.
- DeeDee got her usual perfect score.
- Barb's score was almost as good as Sam's.
- Wilma didn't pay attention to the directions for the test.

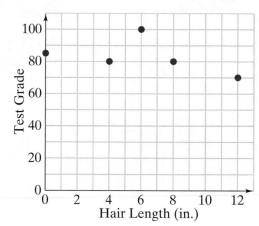

2. What was each student's test score?

ACTIVITY

3. Write five clues to describe how much time five friends spent doing homework last night. Draw a scatter plot to go with your clues.

4. Exchange problems with someone in your class and solve each other's problems.

Make a stem-and-leaf plot for each set of data.

1. test scores:
   68 98 91 100 87 75 82 95 77 93 72 90 80 75 99 83 87

2. current ages of World War II veterans:
   83 86 91 91 75 76 73 88 89 92 95 95 79 80 73 74 87

3. Make a box-and-whisker plot for the following set of data.
   number of hours spent practicing a musical instrument per week:
   1 2 8 5 9 12 4 7 5 8 11 13 8 9 2 7 6 12 11

4. Make a scatter plot for the data in the table below. Describe the type
   of trend: *positive*, *negative*, or *no trend*. Draw a trend line.

Electoral Vote Data

State	CA	FL	AZ	TX	DE	AL	PA
Population (millions)	33.9	16.0	5.1	20.9	0.8	4.4	12.3
Electoral Votes	55	27	10	34	3	9	21

SOURCE: *The World Almanac*

MATH GAMES

Frequent Spinner

What You'll Need
- 2 spinners, each with three equal sections numbered 1, 2, and 3
- a copy of the number line at the right.

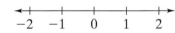

How to Play
- Player A chooses a number between −2 and 2. Player B chooses a different number.
- Each player spins a spinner. Subtract Player B's result from Player A's result. Record the difference on the number line with an ✗.
- Repeat until the ✗ marks for one player's chosen number reach a frequency of 6. That player wins the game.
- Repeat the game with Player B choosing the first number.

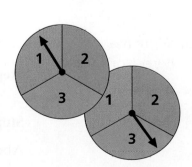

Circle Graphs

Check Skills You'll Need

1. **Vocabulary Review** How are *ratios* and *proportions* related?

Solve each proportion.

2. $\frac{2}{3} = \frac{16}{y}$

3. $\frac{s}{12} = \frac{5}{2}$

4. $\frac{7}{3} = \frac{r}{12}$

5. $\frac{25}{p} = \frac{75}{125}$

GO for Help
Lesson 4–3

What You'll Learn

To represent and interpret data using circle graphs

🔊 **New Vocabulary** circle graph, central angle

Why Learn This?

You can use a circle graph to display the ages of people who use food pantries. A circle graph shows how parts of a data set relate to the whole.

A circle graph is a graph of data in which an entire circle represents a whole. Each wedge, or sector, in the circle represents part of the whole. The total of the data must equal 100%, or 1.

EXAMPLE Reading Circle Graphs

1 **Food Pantries** About 21.3 million people in the United States use food pantries each year. The circle graph below shows their ages. How many people who use food pantries are 17 or younger?

Ages of People Using Food Pantries

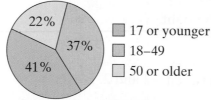

22%
37%
41%

- ▨ 17 or younger
- ▨ 18–49
- ▨ 50 or older

SOURCE: America's Second Harvest

Step 1 Use the key. Pink represents people 17 or younger. This means 41% of the people who use food pantries are 17 or younger.

Step 2 21,300,000 · 41% = 21,300,000 ✕ 0.41 ENTER *8733000*

About 8,733,000 people 17 or younger use food pantries.

Quick Check

1. How many people who use food pantries are 50 or older?

To make a circle graph, you must find the measure of each central angle. A **central angle** is an angle whose vertex is the center of a circle. The sum of the measures of the central angles of a circle is 360°. Use this total to set up proportions for finding the measure of each central angle.

EXAMPLE Making Circle Graphs

② Environment Make a circle graph for the data in the table at the left.

Step 1 Find the total number of species.

$$342 + 273 + 126 + 115 + 72 + 48 + 94 = 1{,}070 \quad \leftarrow \text{Add.}$$

Step 2 Use proportions to find the measures of the central angles.

$$\frac{342}{1{,}070} = \frac{m}{360°}, \text{ so } m \approx 115° \qquad \frac{273}{1{,}070} = \frac{b}{360°}, \text{ so } b \approx 92°$$

$$\frac{126}{1{,}070} = \frac{f}{360°}, \text{ so } f \approx 42° \qquad \frac{115}{1{,}070} = \frac{r}{360°}, \text{ so } r \approx 39°$$

$$\frac{72}{1{,}070} = \frac{c}{360°}, \text{ so } c \approx 24° \qquad \frac{48}{1{,}070} = \frac{i}{360°}, \text{ so } i \approx 16°$$

$$\frac{94}{1{,}070} = \frac{o}{360°}, \text{ so } o \approx 32°$$

Step 3 Use a compass to draw a circle. Mark the center of the circle and draw a radius. Construct the central angles with a protractor.

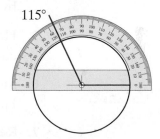

Step 4 Calculate the percents of each group by dividing the number of species by the total number, 1,070.

Step 5 Label each sector and title your graph. Set up a key to make the graph easier to read.

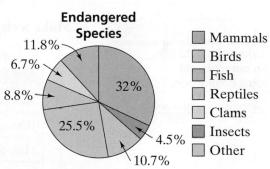

✓ Quick Check

2. Make a circle graph for the data below.

**Fuel Used by Types of Vehicles
(billions of gallons)**

Cars	Vans, Pickups, SUVs	Trucks	Other
75	55	37	1

Source: U.S. Census Bureau. Go to **PHSchool.com** for a data update. Web Code: asg-9041

Endangered Species

Group	Number of Species
Mammals	342
Birds	273
Fish	126
Reptiles	115
Clams	72
Insects	48
Other	94

Source: U.S. Fish and Wildlife Service. Go to **PHSchool.com** for a data update. Web Code: asg-9041

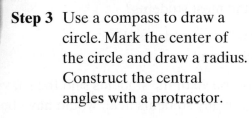

Check Your Understanding

1. **Vocabulary** What is the sum of the measures of the central angles of a circle?

2. Use the circle graph. How much money does the graph allow for lunch?

3. **Reasoning** Explain why the key on a circle graph is important.

$50 Spending Money

$10.84 $12.50
$10.00
$16.66

☐ Gas
☐ CD
☐ Movie
☐ Lunch

Homework Exercises

For more exercises, see Extra Skills and Word Problems.

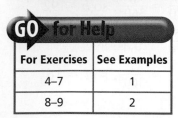

For Exercises	See Examples
4–7	1
8–9	2

Survey A survey asked 200 students about their favorite sport. The circle graph shows the results.

4. Which sport was chosen by the most students?

5. How many students chose each sport?

6. Suppose 90 of the students said their favorite sport was football. How many students in all would have been surveyed?

7. **Reasoning** If the percents were not written on the graph, could you still find the sport that had the least percent of votes? Explain.

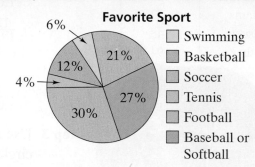

Favorite Sport

6%
21%
12%
4%
27%
30%

☐ Swimming
☐ Basketball
☐ Soccer
☐ Tennis
☐ Football
☐ Baseball or Softball

Make a circle graph for each set of data.

Test Prep Tip

When the data are in percents, set up a proportion.

$$\frac{percent}{100} = \frac{central\ angle}{360°}$$

8. **Favorite Books**

Book Type	People
Adventure	82
Romance	86
Horror	22
Science Fiction	10

9. **Vehicles Owned**

Vehicle Type	Percent
Small	28
Mid-size	48
Large	7
Luxury	17

10. **Guided Problem Solving** A doctor surveyed patients who ran a mile or more each day. Display the data in a circle graph.

Miles	More than 6	6	5	4	3	Less than 3
Number of Patients	34	29	41	73	65	98

● Find the total number of patients.
● Use proportions to find the measures of the six central angles.

Careers Graphic artists paste up layouts and photos to get magazines ready to be printed.

11. **Food** Ella surveyed 81 students in the cafeteria about their favorite school lunch. Display the results in a circle graph.

pizza: 35   spaghetti: 20   hamburger: 18   grilled cheese: 8

12. **Writing in Math** If the data for a budget is given in percents rather than dollars, would you make a circle graph or a bar graph of the data? Explain your choice.

13. **Publishing** A magazine conducted a survey about the kinds of images women prefer to see on magazine covers. Out of 400 women surveyed, 17.7% preferred images of models, 37.4% preferred images of athletes, and 44.9% preferred images of other celebrities.
a. Display the results in a circle graph.
b. About how many women surveyed preferred images of athletes?
c. How many women did *not* prefer images of other celebrities?

14. **Challenge** The bar graph shows the results of a survey that asked, "What color is your cell phone cover?" Display the data in a circle graph. Which graph do you think is a more appropriate display of the data? Explain.

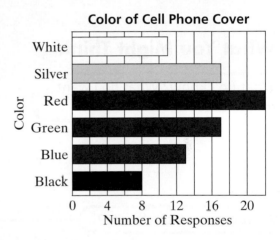

Color of Cell Phone Cover

15. The table shows a budget. Which graph best represents the data?

Multiple Choice

15. The table shows a budget. Which graph best represents the data?

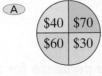
(A) $40 | $70 / $60 | $30

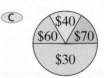
(C) $40 / $60 / $70 / $30

(B) $40 / $70 / $60 / $30

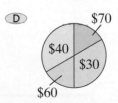
(D) $70 / $40 / $30 / $60

Weekly Budget

Item	Amount
Meals	$70
Recreation	$30
Bills	$60
Savings	$40

16. What type of trend would you expect to see in a scatter plot comparing mosquito population and the sale of insect repellent?
(F) positive   (G) negative   (H) none   (J) opposite

17. Make a scatter plot of the data set. If possible, draw a trend line.

height (in.): 56 52 55 47 58 60 50 39 58 45 54 61 45 34
weight (lb): 78 63 67 52 81 92 60 34 83 47 73 98 45 31

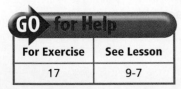
GO for Help

For Exercise	See Lesson
17	9-7

Equations and Graphs

Sports The percent of mountain bike accidents that happen on downhill slopes is 5 times the percent that happen on uphill slopes. The percent that happen on flat areas is two thirds of the percent that happen on uphill slopes. What percent should you use for each part of a circle graph representing this data?

Location of Mountain Bike Accidents

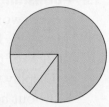

What You Might Think

> What do I know? What do I want to find out?

> What equation can I write?

> What is the answer?

> Is the answer reasonable?

What You Might Write

The downhill percent is 5 times the uphill percent. The flat percent is $\frac{2}{3}$ of the uphill percent. The total for a circle graph is 100%. I need to find the percents for each part of the graph.

Let x = uphill percent. Then, $5x$ = downhill percent and $\frac{2}{3}x$ = flat percent.

uphill + downhill + flat = 100 percent
$$x + 5x + \frac{2}{3}x = 100$$
$$6\frac{2}{3}x = 100$$
$$x = 15$$

The percents for the circle graph are:
uphill: 15%
downhill: $5 \times 15\% = 75\%$
flat: $\frac{2}{3} \times 15\% = 10\%$.

The sum of the percents is $15 + 75 + 10 = 100$. The numbers make sense for the size of the sections of the graph. The answer is reasonable.

Think It Through

1. How was 15 found in the work shown?

2. **Reasoning** What does it mean to say that the numbers make sense for the size of the sections in the graph?

Exercises

3. **Fishing** The percent of fish in a lake that are smallmouth bass is twice the percent that are white perch. The percent of fish that are sunfish is one third the percent that are white perch. What percent should you use for each part of a circle graph representing this data?

Types of Fish

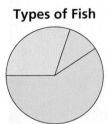

Use the table below for Exercises 4–6.

Available Drink Sizes at a Convenience Store

Year	Sizes Available (oz)
1973	12, 20
1976	12, 16, 20
1978	12, 16, 20, 32
1983	12, 16, 20, 32, 44
1988	12, 16, 20, 32, 44, 64
2003	12, 20, 32, 44, 64
2005	20, 32, 44, 64

4. Make a scatter plot of the data. Use the year on the horizontal scale and the number of ounces on the vertical scale.

5. Describe the trend in the data.

6. **Writing in Math** Predict the largest available drink size in the year 2010. Is this a realistic drink size? Explain.

7. The data below show the largest major earthquakes around the world over a ten-year period, measured on the Richter Scale.

    7.1 7.8 7.3 7.2 6.8 6.9 8.1 7.3 6.5 7.3

   Make a box-and-whisker plot. About how many data values fall between the lower and upper quartiles?

Choosing an Appropriate Graph

What You'll Learn

To choose appropriate graphs to represent different data

Why Learn This?

You can use graphs to describe the population in a city and how it changes over time. To do this effectively, you must be able to choose the appropriate graph.

EXAMPLE   Choosing an Appropriate Graph

1 You want to graph data on the percent of city dwellers in the United States every decade since 1900. Which is more appropriate for displaying the data, a line graph or a circle graph? Explain your choice.

A circle graph shows percents, but it does not show change over time. A line graph shows change over time.

Since the percent of city dwellers in the United States changes over time, a line graph is more appropriate than a circle graph.

✓ Quick Check

1. Choose the appropriate graph to display each set of data. Explain your choice.
   a. life spans of selected animals: bar graph or scatter plot?
   b. average household income and number of cars: histogram or scatter plot?
   c. price of a gallon of gas over a twelve-month period: line graph or circle graph?

When presenting data, the idea you want to express influences the type of graph you choose.

Meteorologists use graphs to analyze atmospheric data.

For help making histograms, go to Lesson 9-2, Example 3.

EXAMPLE Application: Weather

2. The table shows the number of hurricanes that have struck the mainland of the United States in past decades. Decide which type of graph would be most appropriate to illustrate the frequency of these hurricanes over time. Explain your choice. Then draw the graph.

Hurricanes in the United States

Decade	1900s	1910s	1920s	1930s	1940s	1950s	1960s	1970s	1980s	1990s
Number of Hurricanes	15	20	15	17	23	18	15	12	16	14

SOURCE: *The Weather Almanac*

The table divides the data into intervals. It also describes the frequency of hurricanes. A histogram is the most appropriate graph.

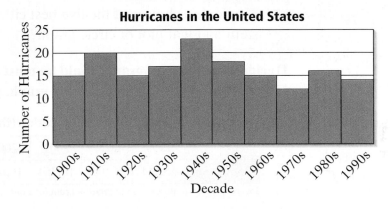

Quick Check

2. Decide which type of graph would be most appropriate for the data in the table. Explain your choice. Then draw the graph.

Weekly Budget

Budget Item	Lunch	Recreation	Clothes	Savings
Amount	$27.00	$13.50	$31.50	$18.00

Check Your Understanding

Vocabulary Summarize the types of graphs by following these steps.

1. Make a three-column table. In the first column, list the types of graphs you have studied in this chapter.

2. In the second column, sketch an example of each type of graph.

3. In the third column, list the different purposes for which you can use each graph. These may include showing frequency, comparing sets of data, showing changes over time, and showing parts of a whole.

For more exercises, see Extra Skills and Word Problems.

For Exercises	See Examples
4–7	1
8–10	2

Choose the appropriate graph for each data set. Explain your choice.

4. inches of rain and the temperature each day for a given city: histogram or scatter plot?

5. **Percent of Total Music Sales Made Up by Country Music**

Year	1997	1998	1999	2000	2001	2002	2003
Percent	14.4	14.7	10.8	10.7	10.5	10.7	10.4

SOURCE: Recording Industry Association of America

line graph or scatter plot?

6. number of boys and number of girls who use a park each day: box-and-whisker plot or double bar graph?

7. 40 people's choices of the five best cities to visit: stem-and-leaf plot or circle graph?

Decide which type of graph would be most appropriate for the data. Explain your choice. Then draw the graph.

8. **Florida's Resident Population (thousands)**

Year	1999	2000	2001	2002	2003	2004
Population	15,111	16,049	16,354	16,681	16,999	17,397

SOURCE: U.S. Census Bureau. Go to **PHSchool.com** for a data update. Web Code: asg-9041

9. height (in.) of students in an eighth-grade class:
63 60 58 56 52 53 57 57 56 55 56 57 56 67 56 58 57 61

10. ages of 15 corporate executives:
31 62 51 44 61 47 49 50 40 52 60 51 67 47 63

11. Guided Problem Solving
The table shows the number of hourly workers in the United States who earn less than or more than $10 per hour. Draw a graph for the data.

Number of Workers Paid Hourly Rates in the United States (millions)

Age	Less Than $10	$10 or More
16 to 24	12.1	4.2
25 to 34	5.8	10.0
35 to 44	5.0	12.2
45 to 54	3.9	9.9
55 to 64	2.3	4.3
65 and older	1.1	0.9

SOURCE: *The World Almanac*

- List the types of graphs you can use to compare two data sets.
- Choose one of these types, and draw the graph.

GO Online

Homework Video Tutor
Visit: PHSchool.com
Web Code: ase-0909

For each graph listed, describe a set of data that would be appropriate.

12. scatter plot **13.** circle graph **14.** line plot

Percent of Homes in the United States With Personal Computers

Year	Percent
1994	33
1996	40
1998	44
2000	56
2002	61
2004	68

SOURCE: Consumer Electronics Association

15. The table at the left and the circle graph at the right show the percent of homes in the United States with personal computers in various years.

   a. **Error Analysis** Explain why using a circle graph for this set of data is not appropriate.

   b. Choose an appropriate graph for the data and then draw the graph. Explain your choice.

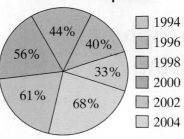

Percent of Homes in the United States With Personal Computers

44% 40% 56% 33% 61% 68%

☐ 1994
☐ 1996
☐ 1998
☐ 2000
☐ 2002
☐ 2004

16. **Writing in Math** Describe data you can collect and display in both a bar graph and a circle graph.

17. **Challenge** Which type of graph might you choose when you have too large a set of data to graph each item? Explain.

Test Prep and Mixed Review

Practice

Multiple Choice

18. The data below show the average lengths, to the nearest quarter inch, of some species of beetles. Which type of graph is most appropriate to represent the data?

   0.5 1.5 3.25 2.5 1.25 3.0 6.0 2.75 2.0 0.25 1.5 1.0
   0.5 1.0 1.5 0.75 0.25 1.75 1.25 0.25 0.75 0.25

   Ⓐ Line graph   Ⓒ Circle graph
   Ⓑ Bar graph   Ⓓ Box-and-whisker plot

19. The graph below shows the results of a read-a-thon. Which conclusion best reflects the data in the histogram?

   Ⓕ Almost half of the participants read between 6 and 11 books.

   Ⓖ Participants between the ages of 9 and 11 read the most books.

   Ⓗ Most of the participants read between 9 and 11 books.

   Ⓙ About one-third of the participants read between 9 and 11 books.

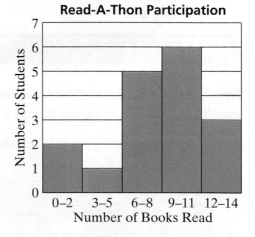

Read-A-Thon Participation

Number of Students (vertical axis, 0–7)

Number of Books Read: 0–2, 3–5, 6–8, 9–11, 12–14

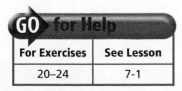

GO for Help

For Exercises	See Lesson
20–24	7-1

Find the measure of the supplement of each angle.

20. 37°   **21.** 95°   **22.** 42°   **23.** 170°   **24.** 64°

Graphing Data Using Spreadsheets

You can use a spreadsheet program to make many types of graphs.

ACTIVITY

The data at the right show the lengths and masses of different birds' eggs.

Step 1 Enter the data into the spreadsheet.

Step 2 Choose an appropriate type of graph from the spreadsheet program. Since you are comparing two related sets of data, a scatter plot is appropriate.

	A	B
1	Length (cm)	Mass (g)
2	2.5	3.6
3	3.1	9
4	3.6	14
5	3.9	20.7
6	4.0	19

A spreadsheet has no title.

Row 1 contains the type of data being compared.

Each row represents the size of one egg. Column A is the egg's length. Column B is the egg's mass.

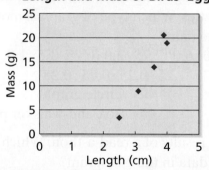

Length and Mass of Birds' Eggs

Exercises

Enter each set of data into a spreadsheet. Choose an appropriate type of graph and use the program to make each graph.

1. **Annual Spending per Child by Middle Income Families in 2004**

Age (yr)	0–2	3–5	6–8	9–11	12–14	15–17
Dollars Spent	9,840	10,120	10,030	9,910	10,640	10,900

SOURCE: U.S. Department of Agriculture. Go to **PHSchool.com** for a data update. Web Code: asg-9041

2. **Bedrooms in New One-Family Houses**

Number of Bedrooms	Two or Fewer	Three	Four or More
Percent of Homes	11	51	37

SOURCE: U.S. Census Bureau. Go to **PHSchool.com** for a data update. Web Code: asg-9041

Measuring to Solve

Some test questions ask you to measure with a centimeter ruler before solving the problem.

EXAMPLE

The net at the right forms a cylinder. Measure its dimensions in centimeters. Which is closest to the surface area of the cylinder?

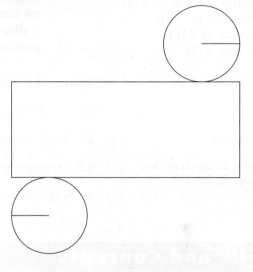

A 6 cm^2

C 16 cm^2

B 11 cm^2

D 22 cm^2

Use a centimeter ruler to measure the width of the rectangle and the radius of one of the circles. To find the surface area, use the formula for surface area of a cylinder. Use 3.14 for π.

$$\text{S.A.} = 2\pi rh + 2\pi r^2$$
$$= 2(3.14)(1)(2.5) + 2(3.14)(1)^2$$
$$= 21.98$$

The surface area of the cylinder is about 22 cm^2. The correct answer is choice D.

Exercises

1. A square bead has the net shown at the right. Measure the dimensions of the net. Which is closest to the lateral surface area of the bead?

A 0.5 cm^2

B 1 cm^2

C 1.5 cm^2

D 2 cm^2

2. Measure the net of the square pyramid below.

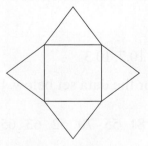

Which is closest to the total surface area of the pyramid?

F 2.5 cm^2

G 3.75 cm^2

H 5.25 cm^2

J 5.5 cm^2

Chapter 9 Review

Vocabulary Review

◀)) **box-and-whisker plot** (p. 438)
central angle (p. 451)
circle graph (p. 450)
frequency (p. 418)
frequency table (p. 419)
histogram (p. 419)
line plot (p. 418)
mean (p. 412)

measure of central tendency
(p. 412)
median (p. 412)
mode (p. 412)
negative trend (p. 445)
no trend (p. 445)
outlier (p. 413)
positive trend (p. 445)

quartiles (p. 438)
range (p. 413)
scatter plot (p. 444)
stem-and-leaf plot (p. 433)
trend line (p. 445)
Venn diagram (p. 424)

Choose the correct vocabulary term to complete each sentence.

1. __?__ divide a data set into four equal parts.

2. A __?__ displays two sets of data as ordered pairs.

3. An angle whose vertex is the center of the circle is a __?__ .

4. A display that shows numeric data in order is a __?__ .

Go **Online**
PHSchool.com
For: Online Vocabulary Quiz
Web Code: asj-0951

Skills and Concepts

Lessons 9-1, 9-2
- To describe data using mean, median, mode, and range and to choose an appropriate measure of central tendency
- To use line plots, frequency tables, and histograms to represent data

The **mean** of a set of numbers is the sum of the numbers divided by the number of data items. The **median** is the middle value in a set of numbers in numerical order. The **mode** is the data item that occurs most often. The **range** is the difference between the greatest and least values. An **outlier** is a value that is much higher or much lower than the other values in a set.

A **frequency table** lists the frequency of each item in a set of data. A **histogram** is a special type of bar graph used to show the frequency of data.

Find the mean, median, mode, and range of each set of data. Round to the nearest hundredth where necessary.

5. 15, 12, 10, 16, 24, 16, 12, 15, 18, 14, 15

6. 9.1, 10.2, 9.5, 10.3, 10.5, 9.1, 9.0, 9.8, 9.9, 9.4, 10.7, 10.3

7. Make a frequency table and a histogram for the data set below. Use intervals of equal size to group the data.
   53 57 78 64 68 72 77 58 60 78 80 81 55 70 52 63 65 79

Lessons 9-3, 9-4

- To use Venn diagrams to represent relationships between data
- To recognize misleading graphs and to choose appropriate scales

Sometimes a graph can give a misleading visual impression.

8. **Art** Out of 25 artists, 22 are painters and 8 are sculptors. How many artists are both painters and sculptors?

9. Make two line graphs for the set of data. In one of the graphs, use a break. Explain which graph shows the data more clearly.

School Chorus Members

Year	1	2	3	4	5
Girls	35	32	35	34	32
Boys	41	40	43	37	39

Lessons 9-5, 9-6

- To represent and interpret data using stem-and-leaf plots and box-and-whisker plots

A **stem-and-leaf plot** shows numeric data arranged in order. A **box-and-whisker plot** shows the distribution of data along a number line.

The data listed show different juice prices (in cents) at various stores.

89 79 85 79 85 67 75 99 79 63 90 72 78 65 78

10. Make a stem-and-leaf plot. Then find the mode and median.

11. Find the quartiles. Then make a box-and-whisker plot.

Lesson 9-7

- To make scatter plots and to use trends to make predictions

A **scatter plot** is a graph that displays two sets of data as ordered pairs. It shows any relationship, or trend, that may exist between the sets of data. To show a trend, draw a trend line. A **trend line** is a line you draw on a graph to approximate the data.

12. **Rivers** Make a scatter plot and draw a trend line for the data at the right.

Length (mi) and Water Flow (1,000 ft³/s) of Rivers

Length	Flow	Length	Flow
2,540	76	1,040	57
1,980	225	886	68
1,460	41	774	67
1,420	58	724	67
1,290	56	659	41

Lessons 9-8, 9-9

- To represent and interpret data using circle graphs
- To choose appropriate graphs to represent different data

A **circle graph** is a graph of data in which the entire circle represents the whole. Each section in the circle represents part of the whole. When choosing a graph, consider the data and the idea you want to convey.

Decide which type of graph would be the most appropriate for the data. Explain your choice and then draw the graph.

13.

Students Wearing Jackets

Temperature (°F)	55	57	63	68	70	73	80
Number of Students	10	11	8	5	4	2	0

14. hours a student worked each week at a summer job:
29 23 21 20 17 16 15 33 30

Go Online PHSchool.com For: Online chapter test Web Code: asa-0952

Find the mean, median, mode, and range of each data set. Round to the nearest hundredth where necessary.

1. −1 9 −2 3 −1 5 −3 7

2. 5.8 5.9 6.3 6.5 5.7 6.2 6.4 6.0 6.3

3. Tell how the outlier affects the mean: 12, 10, 14, 18, 2, 15, 12, 12, 16.

Movies In a survey, twenty students were asked how many movies they saw in a month. The results are 2 3 2 2 1 0 1 2 5 7 2 1 0 3 4 4 3 0 1 2.

4. Make a frequency table.

5. Make a line plot.

6. Find the mean, median, and mode.

Make a frequency table and a histogram for each data set. Use intervals of equal size to group the data.

7. hours of sleep per night:
5 7 8 8 9 8 9 10 11 7 6 5 8 9 8 7 7

8. monthly salaries (in dollars) at local store:
600 780 750 1,200 1,500 1,000 1,100 850 900 425 832 700 900 1,000

Jobs Six hundred high school students were surveyed about the types of jobs they hold. Use the graph for Exercises 9–11.

Students' Jobs

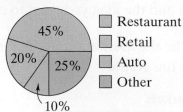

- Restaurant
- Retail
- Auto
- Other

45% 25% 20% 10%

9. How many students work in a restaurant?

10. How many students work in retail sales?

11. What percent of the students do not work at a restaurant? How many students is that?

12. **Television** Make a stem-and-leaf plot for the number of subscribers (in millions) of ten cable television networks: 81.8, 81.3, 81.3, 81.0, 82.5, 83.3, 82.1, 81.9, 81.8, 81.0.

13. a. **Golf** The data below show the career earnings in millions of dollars of the top male and female golfers. Use a single number line to make a box-and-whisker plot for each set of data.

Male: 21.9 18.0 17.8 15.3 14.6 14.5 14.7
Female: 10.2 8.5 7.6 7.3 6.9 6.7 6.3

b. **Writing in Math** Write a paragraph comparing the sets of data.

Decide which type of graph would be most appropriate for each set of data below. Explain your choice and then draw the graph.

14.

Leading U.S. Clothing Businesses

Company	Earnings (billions of dollars)
Nike	10.7
VF	5.2
Jones Apparel Group	4.4
Liz Claiborne	4.2
Reebok International	3.5

Source: *The World Almanac*

15.

Percent of Music Sold on CDs

Year	1999	2000	2001	2002	2003	2004
Percent	83.2	89.3	89.2	90.5	87.8	90.3

Source: Recording Industry Association of America

16. per capita freshwater use (gallons per day): Florida, 509; California, 1,130; Ohio, 944; Kentucky, 1,150; Oregon, 2,520; Alaska, 350

17. In a recent survey of 100 mothers, 67 said they had a daughter. If 23 mothers said they had both a son and a daughter, how many mothers had only a son?

Multiple Choice
Read each question. Then write the letter of the correct answer on your paper.

1. Find the median and the mode of the data in the line plot.
   - A. 7 and 8
   - B. 7.5 and 7
   - C. 7.5 and 8
   - D. 8 and 9

   ```
           X
           X           X
           X    X      X
      X    X    X      X
      ─────────────────────
      6    7    8      9
   ```

2. Which measure of central tendency would you use to describe the data on your classmates' favorite brand of sneakers?
   - F. mode
   - G. range
   - H. median
   - J. mean

3. At a middle school gymnastics competition, the scores for the floor exercises were 5.1, 5.6, 5.3, 5.1, 4.8, 4.6, and 5.2. Find the mean (to the nearest tenth) and the median.
   - A. 5.1 and 5.3
   - B. 5.1 and 5.1
   - C. 5.2 and 5.1
   - D. 5.2 and 5.2

4. Which object is not an example of a prism?
   - F. a shoe box
   - G. a file cabinet
   - H. a domino
   - J. a soup can

5. Describe the trend in the scatter plot at the right.
   - A. positive trend
   - B. negative trend
   - C. no trend
   - D. positive and negative trend

6. Which type of graph shows how a category changes over time?
   - F. histogram
   - G. circle
   - H. line plot
   - J. line graph

7. At the Armstrong School, the student-to-teacher ratio is 12 : 1. There are 30 teachers in the school. How many students are there?
   - A. 42
   - B. 250
   - C. 300
   - D. 360

8. The sum of three consecutive integers is 42. What is the value of the least integer?
   - F. 25
   - G. 18
   - H. 13
   - J. 9

9. What are the missing numbers in the pattern?

   $-2, -3, -5, -8, -12, \blacksquare, -23, \blacksquare, \ldots$
   - A. -18 and -28
   - B. -17 and -30
   - C. -15 and -26
   - D. -19 and -26

10. A rectangular skateboard park has 7 curbs and 4 ramps. The width of the park is $2x$ and the length is $3x$, where x equals 48 meters. What are the dimensions of the park?
    - F. 48 m and 72 m
    - G. 96 m and 144 m
    - H. 100 m and 4 m
    - J. 65 m and 35 m

Gridded Response
Record your answer in a grid.

11. Round 3.0481 to the nearest hundredth.

12. A cubit was a measure used in ancient times. There are about 2 cubits in a yard. How many inches are in a cubit?

Short Response

13. Leana had $50.00 before she went shopping. She bought three books that all cost the same price, and a hat for $18.99, including tax. After shopping, she had $7.04 left. How much was each book? Show your work.

Extended Response

14. The ages of the players on a basketball team are below. Find the lower quartile, median, and upper quartile for their ages. Use a box-and-whisker plot to display the data. Show your work.

    23 25 34 25 19 24 25 25 26 40 33
    21 27 29 31 26 33

Problem Solving Application

Applying Data Analysis

Conic Cuisine Graphic designers often use pictures to present data. You can read that people eat 35,000 tons of pineapples every day, but seeing a pile of pineapples drawn to the size of a large hotel gives you a better sense of how many pineapples this is. The drawings on these pages show the volumes of various crops that the people of the world eat or produce each day.

Potatoes
We dig up 801,000 tons of potatoes every day.

Put It All Together

Materials scale or balance, ruler, food sample

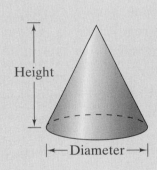

Height

|← Diameter →|

1. Weigh a serving of one of the foods shown on these pages. Remember to subtract the weight of the container if there is one. Use the conversion tables in the back of the book to convert the weight to pounds.

2. Estimate the volume of your food sample in cubic inches.

3. How many tons of your food does the world eat or produce each day? Convert this amount to pounds. Write your answer in scientific notation.

4. Suppose you piled the amount of the food eaten or produced each day into a cone. Find the volume of the cone. (*Hint:* 1,728 in.^{3} = 1 ft^3)

5. Suppose the diameter and the height of the cone are equal.
   a. Use the formula $V = \frac{2}{3}\pi r^3$ and *systematic guess and check* to estimate the radius of the cone.
   b. Calculate the diameter and the height of the cone in feet.

6. **Reasoning** What would the cone of food weigh? Explain.

The world produces 58,000 tons of cucumbers every day.

The world's daily onion harvest weighs 98,000 tons, as much as the ocean liner *Queen Elizabeth*.

For: Information about food
Web Code: ase-0953

Wheat is one of the world's major food crops. The world eats 1.6 million tons of wheat in one day, enough to make a loaf of bread as heavy as four Empire State Buildings.

Rice
The Chinese lead the world in rice production. They eat rice at every meal, consuming about 402,000 tons every day.

Every day people harvest 1.8 million tons of corn, and the world eats enough of it to equal the weight of 300,000 African elephants.

Oranges
The orange is probably the world's most popular fruit—176,000 tons are picked every day.

The tomatoes eaten in one day weigh 234,000 tons.

The world's daily apple harvest is 148,000 tons.

The world produces 35,000 tons of pineapples every day.

The world avocado harvest weighs in at 5,500 tons a day.

In one day, the world produces 43,000 tons of carrots.

467

What You've Learned

- In Chapter 4, you used ratios to solve problems.

- In Chapter 5, you used ratios and percents to describe probabilities.

- In Chapter 9, you used scatter plots to make predictions.

Check Your Readiness

GO for Help

For Exercises	See Lessons
1–6	2-5
7–8	4-1
9–14	5-8

Multiplying Rational Numbers

Find each product.

1. $\frac{3}{7} \cdot \frac{1}{2}$

2. $\frac{1}{6} \cdot \frac{24}{25}$

3. $\frac{9}{14} \cdot \frac{7}{12}$

4. $\frac{8}{9} \cdot \frac{12}{32}$

5. $\frac{27}{34} \cdot \frac{2}{3}$

6. $\frac{10}{17} \cdot \frac{1}{5}$

Writing Ratios

Write three ratios that each diagram can represent.

7.

8.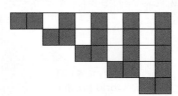

Finding Probabilities

**Suppose you spin the spinner once. Find each probability.
Express each probability as a fraction.**

9. $P(\text{yellow})$

10. $P(\text{green})$

11. $P(\text{purple})$

12. $P(\text{green or blue})$

13. $P(\text{blue or yellow})$

14. $P(\text{green or purple})$

What You'll Learn Next

- In this chapter, you will use theoretical and experimental probabilities to make predictions and decisions.

- You will use permutations and combinations to count outcomes.

- You will evaluate methods of sampling and identify biased and unbiased survey questions.

🔊 Key Vocabulary

- biased questions (p. 481)
- combination (p. 496)
- counting principle (p. 492)
- dependent events (p. 487)
- experimental probability (p. 470)
- factorial (p. 492)
- independent events (p. 486)
- odds in favor (p. 471)
- odds against (p. 471)
- permutation (p. 491)
- population (p. 480)
- random sample (p. 480)
- sample (p. 480)
- theoretical probability (p. 471)

 Problem Solving Application On pages 508 and 509, you will work an extended activity on animal population.

Theoretical and Experimental Probability

10-1

Check Skills You'll Need

1. **Vocabulary Review** A collection of all the possible outcomes in an experiment is a(n) ? .

Suppose you roll a number cube.

2. What are the possible outcomes?

3. Find $P(4)$.

4. Find P(even number).

5. Find P(3 or 4).

for Help
Lesson 5-8

What You'll Learn

To find theoretical probability, experimental probability, and odds

🔊 **New Vocabulary** experimental probability, theoretical probability, odds in favor, odds against

Why Learn This?

You can use probabilities to estimate the likelihood of events. For example, you can estimate the probability of having homework on a Friday.

Probability based on experimental data is called **experimental probability.** You find the experimental probability of an event by using the results of an experiment, or trial, repeated many times.

KEY CONCEPTS **Experimental Probability**

$$P(\text{event}) = \frac{\text{number of times event occurs}}{\text{total number of trials}}$$

EXAMPLE **Finding Experimental Probability**

1 **Science** The scientist Gregor Mendel crossbred green-seed plants and yellow-seed plants. Out of 8,023 crosses, 6,022 plants had yellow seeds and 2,001 had green seeds. Find the probability that a plant had green seeds.

$P(\text{green}) = \dfrac{\text{number of plants with green seeds}}{\text{total number of crossbred plants}}$ ← **Write the probability ratio.**

$= \dfrac{2,001}{8,023}$ ← **Substitute.**

≈ 0.249 ← **Divide.**

The probability that a plant had green seeds is about 0.249.

✓ Quick Check

1. Use the table at the left. Find the experimental probability of getting heads.

Heads	⊬⊬ ///
Tails	⊬⊬ ⊬⊬ //

Video Tutor Help
Visit: PHSchool.com
Web Code: ase-0775

You can toss a coin to find the experimental probability of getting heads. You can find the theoretical probability without using trials because both possible outcomes (heads or tails) are equally likely. To find the theoretical probability, use the formula from Chapter 5.

$$\text{theoretical probability} = \frac{\text{number of favorable outcomes}}{\text{total number of possible outcomes}}$$

The experimental probability of getting a heads is likely to get closer to the theoretical probability the more times you toss the coin.

EXAMPLE **Identifying the Type of Probability**

2 Voting The table shows the results of a survey. Does 55% represent *experimental* or *theoretical* probability?

Survey of Town Voters

Number of People Surveyed	Number of People in Favor	Probability of Voting in Favor
200	110	55%

The survey records actual responses from town voters. 55% represents experimental probability.

✓ Quick Check

2. A bag contains two red cubes and three white cubes. Does $P(\text{red}) = \frac{2}{5}$ represent *experimental* or *theoretical* probability?

Sometimes probabilities are expressed in the form of a ratio called odds. The statement "There's a 2 to 1 chance of rain" uses odds.

KEY CONCEPTS **Odds**

• **Odds in favor** of an event is the ratio
  number of favorable outcomes : number of unfavorable outcomes.
• **Odds against** an event is the ratio
  number of unfavorable outcomes : number of favorable outcomes.

EXAMPLE **Determining Odds**

3 Miniature Golf Suppose you select a ball at random from the golf balls shown at the left. What are the odds in favor of selecting a yellow ball?

Two balls are yellow and five are orange. The odds of selecting a yellow ball at random are 2 : 5.

✓ Quick Check

3. What are the odds against selecting a yellow ball at random?

1. **Vocabulary** Suppose you conduct trials to gather data. Are you finding experimental probability or theoretical probability?

Using the data shown in the table, find each probability.

Cereals in a Food Store	
Type	Number of Brands
With nuts	16
With fruit	40
With whole grains	24
Total	**80**

2. P(cereal with nuts)

3. P(cereal with whole grains)

4. A baseball team has a record of 63 wins and 42 losses. Sam says the odds of winning the next game are 3 to 2. Explain his reasoning.

Homework Exercises

For more exercises, see Extra Skills and Word Problems.

GO for Help

For Exercises	See Examples
5–7	1
8–9	2
10	3

Find each experimental probability. You planted 250 seeds from a bag. All the seeds grew, and there were 68 marigolds, 94 alyssum, 8 poppies. The rest were zinnias.

5. P(marigold)   6. P(alyssum)   7. P(zinnia)

Decide whether each probability is experimental or theoretical.

8. You toss two pennies 20 times. P(2 heads) is $\frac{3}{20}$.

9. A spinner is divided into six equal sections. Three sections are green and three sections are blue. P(green) is $\frac{1}{2}$.

10. A 12-sided solid has faces numbered 1 to 12. The probability of any side facing upward when the solid is rolled is the same. What are the odds in favor of rolling a 7?

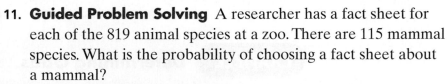

11. **Guided Problem Solving** A researcher has a fact sheet for each of the 819 animal species at a zoo. There are 115 mammal species. What is the probability of choosing a fact sheet about a mammal?
    - How many outcomes are possible?
    - How many outcomes are favorable?

12. The probability of an event is $\frac{1}{4}$. What are the odds in favor of the event occurring?

13. **Writing in Math** The odds in favor of an event are 2 : 3. Does this mean the probability of the event occuring is $\frac{2}{3}$? Explain.

Data Analysis In a survey, 171 children were asked what time they go to bed. The results are shown below. Find the experimental probability that a randomly selected child goes to bed at a certain time.

Bedtimes of Children

Time (P.M.)	7:30	8:00	8:30	9:00	9:30
Number	24	31	38	42	36

14. $P(9:30)$ **15.** $P(8:30)$ **16.** $P(7:30–8:30)$

17. $P(\text{not } 9:00)$ **18.** $P(\text{after } 8:30)$ **19.** $P(\text{before } 9:30)$

20. Challenge To win a game, you have to toss a coin that lands in the green area of the game board at the right. Suppose the center of the coin lands on the board. What is the theoretical probability that the center of the coin will land in the green area?

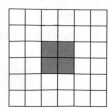

Test Prep and Mixed Review

Practice

Multiple Choice

21. Tammy selected a marble from a bag, recorded the color, and returned the marble to the bag. She did this several times. She got a green marble 8 times and a blue marble 7 times. There are 20 marbles in the bag. Predict the number of green marbles.

 Ⓐ 41 Ⓑ 11 Ⓒ 8 Ⓓ 6

22. The net for an eraser is shown at the right. Measure the dimensions of the net in inches. Which of the following is closest to the total surface area of the eraser?

 Ⓕ 0.25 in.^{2} Ⓗ 2.00 in.^{2}
 Ⓖ 0.75 in.^{2} Ⓙ 2.5 in.^{2}

23. The formula $h = 222(A - D)$ can be used to find the height h in feet of the base of a cumulus cloud. Air temperature A and dew-point temperature D are in degrees Fahrenheit. Find the height if the air temperature is 75°F and the dew-point temperature is 65°F.

 Ⓐ 212 ft Ⓑ 232 ft Ⓒ 1,110 ft Ⓓ 2,220 ft

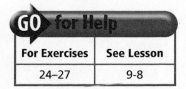

GO for Help

For Exercises	See Lesson
24–27	9-8

Find the measure of the central angle that could represent each percent in a circle graph.

24. 25% **25.** 10% **26.** 20% **27.** 15%

Fair Games

In the World Series, two baseball teams play as many as 7 games. The series ends when a team wins 4 games.

Your friend's favorite team is ahead of your favorite team in the World Series, 3 games to 1. Since his team has won three times as many games as yours, he offers you this deal: If his team wins, you will do his chores for a week. If your team wins, he will do your chores for *three* weeks.

ACTIVITY

Assume that the two teams are evenly matched. You can toss a coin to simulate the outcome of each game.

1. Simulate the remaining games of the World Series by tossing a coin until one team has won a total of 4 games.

2. Repeat the simulation 40 times. Record the number of series wins for each team.

3. Write the ratio of series wins for Team H to series wins for Team T. Compare this to the deal your friend offered.

4. Explain why the only possible outcomes of a simulation for the end of the series are H, T-H, T-T-H, and T-T-T.

5. Complete the tree diagram below to show all the possible outcomes of three consecutive games.

victory for Team H, your friend's team

victory for Team T, your team

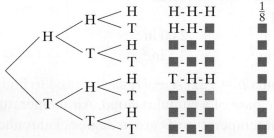

		Outcome	Probability
H	H	H-H-H	$\frac{1}{8}$
	T	H-H-■	■
	H	■-■-■	■
	T	■-■-■	■
T	H	T-H-H	■
	T	■-■-■	■
	H	■-■-■	■
	T	■-■-■	■

6. Use the completed tree diagram to find P(Team H wins the series) and P(Team T wins the series).

7. Should you accept your friend's deal? If not, for how many weeks should he be willing to do your chores if your team wins? Justify your answer.

10-2   Making Predictions

What You'll Learn

To make predictions based on theoretical and experimental probabilities

Why Learn This?

If you know the probability that it will rain, you can decide whether to wear rain gear. In a similar way, business people make predictions and decisions about how to market their products by relying on both surveys and theoretical probability.

When you use probability to make predictions, the actual outcome may differ from your prediction. The prediction only indicates what is *likely* to happen.

EXAMPLE   Using Probability

1. According to game rules, the probability that a bottled-water cap can be redeemed for a prize is $\frac{1}{24}$. If a store stocks 500 bottles of water, about how many winning caps are likely?

```
              0                    500
   Number     |▮▮▮▮▮▮▮▮▮▮▮▮▮▮▮▮▮|      A diagram can help
   Probability |▮                |   ←  you understand
              0 1               1       the problem.
               24
```

$\frac{1}{24} \cdot 500 = \frac{1}{24} \cdot \frac{500}{1}$ ← Find $\frac{1}{24}$ of 500.

$\qquad = \frac{1}{\underset{6}{24}} \cdot \frac{\overset{125}{\cancel{500}}}{1}$ ← Divide the numerator and denominator by the GCF, 4.

$\qquad = \frac{125}{6}$ ← Simplify.

$\qquad = 20\frac{5}{6}$ ← Write the fraction as a mixed number.

About 21 winning caps are likely.

✓ Quick Check

1. Suppose the probability that a bottle has a prize-winning cap is only 1 out of 40. How many winning caps are likely among 500 bottles?

2 **Gridded Response** In a random survey of town voters, 36 out of 60 people say they plan to vote for Mrs. Islas for mayor. If 1,200 people vote in the election, about how many votes will Mrs. Islas receive?

Method 1 Write a proportion.

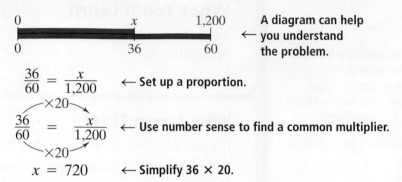

A diagram can help you understand the problem.

$$\frac{36}{60} = \frac{x}{1,200} \quad \leftarrow \text{Set up a proportion.}$$

$$\frac{36}{60} \overset{\times 20}{=} \frac{x}{1,200} \quad \leftarrow \text{Use number sense to find a common multiplier.}$$

$$x = 720 \quad \leftarrow \text{Simplify } 36 \times 20.$$

Mrs. Islas is likely to receive 720 votes.

Method 2 From the survey, find the probability that a voter will vote for Mrs. Islas. Apply this probability to all the voters.

$$\frac{36}{60} = \frac{6}{10}, \text{ or } 60\% \quad \leftarrow \begin{array}{l}\text{The event "vote for Mrs. Islas" occurred} \\ \text{in 36 out of 60 trials.}\end{array}$$

Find 60% of 1,200.

$$60\% \text{ of } 1,200 = 0.6 \times 1,200 \quad \leftarrow \text{Find 60\% of 1,200.}$$

$$= 720 \quad \leftarrow \text{Simplify.}$$

Mrs. Islas is likely to receive 720 votes.

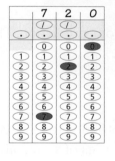

✓ Quick Check

2. In the same survey, 19 out of 60 people said they would vote for Mr. Chiu. Predict how many votes Mr. Chiu will receive in the election.

✓ Check Your Understanding

1. At an auto factory, $\frac{3}{100}$ of the cars produced have a minor defect. If the factory produces 600 cars, about how many are likely to have a defect?

Use theoretical probability to predict the number of heads when a fair coin is tossed each number of times.

2. 10	3. 60	4. 300	5. 599

For more exercises, see Extra Skills and Word Problems.

For Exercises	See Examples
6–11	1
12–17	2

GO for Help

Predict how many times the given outcome will occur for each number of spins. A spinner has sections labeled A, B, C, D, E, F, and 0. The probability the spinner lands on each letter is $\frac{3}{20}$ and the probability it lands on 0 is $\frac{1}{10}$.

6. outcome D; 60 spins

7. outcome D; 600 spins

8. outcome B; 12,000 spins

9. outcome F; 54 spins

10. outcome 0; 80 spins

11. outcome A; 95 spins

Use the table below. A hot dog company surveyed 100 people in a town of 12,000 to find their favorite grilled foods. Predict how many people in the town prefer each grilled food.

Favorite Grilled Foods

Type	Number of Responses
Hot dogs	22
Hamburgers	20
Steak	19
Chicken	17
Fish	12
Other	10

12. hot dogs

13. hamburgers

14. steak

15. fish

16. chicken

17. other

18. Guided Problem Solving From past experience, Marguerite knows that 1 out of 4 beans that she plants will not grow. How many beans should she plant in order for it to be likely that at least 24 bean plants will grow?
  • What is the probability that a planted bean *will* grow?
  • Do 24 plants represent favorable outcomes or all outcomes?
  • Write a proportion using probability and predicted outcomes.

19. The probability of a wooden baseball bat being defective is $\frac{1}{250}$. In a shipment of 1,400 bats, how many are likely to be defective?

20. Transportation The probability that a flight on a certain airline will be on time is $\frac{4}{5}$. At an airport, the airline has 125 flights leaving each day. Predict how many of these flights will be on time.

For Exercises 21–24, use the table at the right. Suppose 9,000 people vote in the election. Predict the number of votes each candidate will receive.

21. Araujo

22. Beech

23. Ciardi

24. <u>**Writing in Math**</u> On the day of the election, Araujo received the most votes. Explain why your prediction may have been incorrect.

Election Poll	
Candidate	Number of Votes
Araujo	50
Beech	15
Ciardi	58
Undecided	27
Total	**150**

The probability that a randomly selected student fits a description is given. Use the probability to predict the number of students in a school of 600 who will be in that category.

25. The probability a student wears contact lenses is 16%.

26. The probability a student has a brother is 45%.

27. The probability a student has a sister is 48%.

28. The probability a student has a brother and a sister is 23%.

29. **Challenge** Suppose the probability of being an eighth-grader at Sunrise Middle School is $\frac{1}{3}$. The probability of an eighth-grader being in Mr. Shelton's math class is $\frac{2}{7}$. Predict how many of the school's 630 students are in Mr. Shelton's eighth-grade math class.

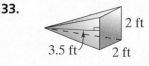

Test Prep and Mixed Review

Practice

Gridded Response

30. The probability that an adult in America is lactose intolerant is $\frac{1}{4}$. About how many people would be lactose intolerant in a group of 450 adult Americans?

31. The two triangles below are similar. Find the length of *FD*.

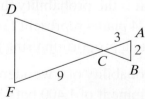

GO for Help

For Exercises	See Lesson
32–33	8-5

Find the lateral area of each figure to the nearest square unit.

32. 32 yd

8 yd

33. 2 ft

3.5 ft 2 ft

Complements and Probability

The complement of an event is the opposite of that event. For example, in a coin toss, heads is the complement of tails. The sum of the probabilities of an event and its complement is 1.

EXAMPLE

Find the probability of *not* rolling a 5 with a number cube.

Since *not rolling a 5* and *rolling a 5* are complements, first find $P(5)$.

$P(5) = \frac{1}{6}$ ← Rolling a 5 is one of six equally likely outcomes.

$1 - \frac{1}{6} = \frac{5}{6}$ ← P(not 5) is the complement of P(5), so P(not 5) + P(5) = 1. Subtract P(5) from 1.

The probability of *not* rolling a 5 is $\frac{5}{6}$.

Exercises

A spinner is divided into 12 equal sections numbered from 1 to 12. You spin the spinner once. Find each probability. Write it as a fraction.

1. P(complement of 2)　　　**2.** P(not odd)　　　**3.** P(not 3, 5, or 10)

 ## Checkpoint Quiz 1

Lessons 10-1 through 10-2

Use the table at the right for Exercises 1–3. Find the probability that a randomly selected student ate each meal.

1. P(dinner)　　　**2.** P(lunch)　　　**3.** P(breakfast)

4. Do your answers to Exercises 1–3 represent theoretical or experimental probability? Explain.

5. The probability that a fair coin lands on heads is 50%. Predict the number of heads you will toss in 20 trials.

6. The probability that a toy is defective is $\frac{1}{630}$. Predict how many defective toys will be in a shipment of 5,670 toys.

Meals Eaten by 1,493 Students

Meals	Number of Students
Breakfast	1,150
Lunch	1,403
Dinner	1,413
Snack	1,329

Conducting a Survey

✔ Check Skills You'll Need

1. **Vocabulary Review** How do *theoretical* and *experimental* probability differ?

There are 9 blue, 5 red, and 4 green pencils in a bag. Find the probability of randomly selecting each color.

2. *P*(blue)

3. *P*(green)

4. *P*(red)

 **for Help**
Lesson 10-1

What You'll Learn

To identify random samples and biased questions and to judge conclusions based on survey results

🔊 **New Vocabulary** population, sample, random sample, biased questions

Why Learn This?

Television program ratings are based on a sample of households from across the United States. You can use random samples to make conjectures about larger groups.

Statisticians use surveys to collect information about specific groups. Any group of objects or people in a survey is called a **population.**

Sometimes a population includes too many objects or people to survey. You can use a sample of the population to find the characteristics of the population. A **sample** is a part of the population.

In a **random sample,** each object or person in the population has the same chance of being selected.

EXAMPLE Determining Random Samples

❶ Determine whether each survey uses a random sample. Describe the population of the sample.

a. Game Shows At a game show, five people in the audience are selected to play by drawing seat numbers.

   This is a random sample. The population is the audience.

b. Surveys A student interviews several people in his art class to determine the movie star most admired by the students at school.

   This is not a random sample. The students in the art class may not represent the views of all the students at school. The population is the students at school.

✔ Quick Check

1. To find out the type of music people in a city prefer, you survey people from 18 to 30 years old. Is the sample random? Explain.

Unfair questions in a survey are **biased questions**. They make assumptions that may not be true. Biased questions can also make one answer seem better than another.

EXAMPLE Identifying Bias in Questions

2 Look at the clipboard at the right. Determine whether the first two questions are biased.

Question 1 is unbiased. It does not try to persuade you one way or the other.

Question 2 is biased. It makes rink A seem more appealing than rink B.

> 1. Do you like to in-line skate?
>
> 2. Would you prefer to skate at the popular rink A or the old-fashioned rink B?
>
> 3. Which do you prefer, in-line skating or ice skating?

✓ Quick Check

2. What bias is there in Question 3? Revise the question to be unbiased.

Using biased questions or poor sampling techniques leads to invalid conclusions.

EXAMPLE Judging Valid Conclusions

3 **Multiple Choice** Julie conducted a survey of people entering a women's clothing store.

From the results at the right, she concluded that shopping for clothes was the favorite shopping trip for people in her town. Which of the following best describes the reason her conclusion may not be valid?

A The survey should have been done on several days.

B The survey should have included more choices.

C The survey should have included people in a variety of stores.

D The survey should have included only women.

Favorite Shopping Trip

Type	Number of Responses
Music	9
Clothing	26
Groceries	3
Books	2
Cars	1
Other	9
Total	**50**

Julie surveyed only people entering a clothing store. She did not get a random sample of all shoppers. The correct answer is choice C.

✓ Quick Check

3. Suppose Julie had surveyed only women. Would her conclusion be more valid? Explain why or why not.

Test Prep Tip

Consider all the answer choices before choosing one. Think about how each change to the survey could affect the results.

Check Your Understanding

1. **Vocabulary** Why do researchers use samples?

2. Explain why this sample is not random: To find how much time students spend traveling to school, you interview students as they get off one school bus.

3. Rewrite this question to be unbiased: Do you like entertaining reality television or boring homework?

4. Why should you avoid using biased questions in a survey?

Homework Exercises

For more exercises, see Extra Skills and Word Problems.

GO for Help

For Exercises	See Examples
5–8	1
9–11	2
12	3

Determine whether each survey uses a random sample. Describe the population of the sample.

5. Your teacher puts the names of the students in your class into a box. He selects class representatives by drawing names out of the box.

6. You survey 25 friends about student support of school sports teams.

7. You want to know how often middle school students buy clothes. You survey every tenth student who arrives at a middle school.

8. Your principal wants to find out what foods to serve at school. The principal interviews 30 students in the eighth grade.

Determine whether each question is biased. Explain your answer.

9. Do you like putrid carnations or sweet-smelling roses?

10. Do you prefer the green chair or the blue chair?

11. What types of movies have you seen?

12. A local market surveys every twentieth customer to determine whether customers think the store's cashiers are friendly and helpful. Is this a good sample? Explain.

13. **Guided Problem Solving** Suppose you survey people walking on the street in a city. Of those surveyed, 60% think the city is a wonderful place to visit. Should you conclude that there is a high probability that a visitor will enjoy the city? Explain.
    - What is the population you are trying to survey?
    - What population did you actually survey?

14. **Writing in Math** How do biased surveys affect probability and statistics?

GO Online

Homework Video Tutor
Visit: PHSchool.com
Web Code: ase-1003

15. Market Research A market research company interviews randomly selected people who register a car during the year to recommend fair purchase prices of cars at a local dealership.

Recommended Purchase Price

Price Range	Frequency
$10,000–$14,999	15
$15,000–$19,999	8
$20,000–$24,999	12
$25,000–$29,999	6

    a. What is the population used in the survey?

    b. Find the experimental probability of a customer choosing the $20,000–$24,999 range.

Careers Market researchers analyze data to make recommendations and predictions to companies about their products.

Open-Ended **Rewrite each biased question as an unbiased question.**

16. Would you rather watch a long baseball game or an exciting figure skating competition?

17. Do you prefer swimming in a closed-in area, such as a pool, or a more open and challenging area, such as a lake or an ocean?

18. Challenge Explain why this question is biased: How do you like your eggs cooked?

 Test Prep and Mixed Review   **Practice**

Multiple Choice

19. One Tuesday, Kristy asked every fifth person who entered the local pool whether he or she prefers swimming in a pool or the ocean. She concluded that most people prefer swimming in a pool. Which is the best explanation for why her conclusion might NOT be valid?

   Ⓐ The survey should have been done on a Saturday.

   Ⓑ The survey should have been done with children only.

   Ⓒ The sample only represents people who swim at the pool.

   Ⓓ The pool is only open during the summer.

20. Katie has read 19 books this year and plans to read two books each week for the rest of the year. Which procedure can she use to find how many books she will have read after six more weeks?

   Ⓕ Multiply 19 by 2 and subtract 6.

   Ⓖ Multiply 19 by 2 and add 6.

   Ⓗ Multiply 6 by 2 and subtract 19.

   Ⓙ Multiply 6 by 2 and add 19.

21. Kim has $30. School lunch costs $2 each day. Which equation can she use to find y, the money she has left after x days of buying school lunches?

   Ⓐ $y = 30 + 2x$ Ⓒ $y = 2 + 30x$

   Ⓑ $y = 30 - 2x$ Ⓓ $y = 2 - 30x$

GO for Help

For Exercise	See Lesson
22	10-1

22. You roll a number cube. Find the odds in favor of rolling a number less than 5.

Simulations With Random Numbers

You can generate random numbers with a graphing calculator or a computer to simulate some situations.

To generate a group of ten digits on a graphing calculator, select the **rand** option from the PRB menu. Each time you press ENTER you will get a different random number. If a random number contains nine digits, use 0 for the tenth digit. When reordering random numbers, ignore the decimal point.

rand	
	.606334928
rand	
	.9518983326
rand	
	.2209784733
rand	
	.5972865589

EXAMPLE

Blood Types About 10% of people in the United States have type-B blood. Find the experimental probability that exactly one of the next two donors at a hospital will have type-B blood.

Since 10% of the people have type-B blood, let 10%, or one out of ten digits, represent this group of people. Let 0 represent type-B blood and the remaining nine digits represent the other blood types.

Group the digits of a random number into pairs to represent two donors.

60	63	34	92	80
95	18	98	33	26
22	09	78	47	33
59	72	86	55	89

Any pair with exactly one 0 represents one of two people with type-B blood. There are three such pairs in this list.

Based on 20 trials, the experimental probability is $\frac{3}{20}$, or 15%.

Exercises

Generate random numbers to simulate each problem.

1. **Blood Types** About 40% of people in the United States have type-A blood. Find the experimental probability that exactly one of the next two donors at a blood drive will have type-A blood.

2. Choose *coin, number cube, spinner,* or *calculator* to simulate each probability. Justify your choice.
   a. 30% chance of rain
   b. random date is Saturday
   c. 1 in 3 chance of winning

Comparing Types of Events

You can conduct an experiment with more than one event. Sometimes the outcome of the second event does not depend on the outcome of the first event. In other cases the first event affects the probability of the second event.

ACTIVITY

1. Place three blue cubes, four green cubes, and three yellow cubes in a bag.

2. Find the theoretical probability of drawing a green cube.

3. Suppose you draw a green cube and replace it. What is the theoretical probability of drawing a green cube on a second draw?

4. Suppose you draw a green cube and do *not* replace it. What is the theoretical probability of drawing a green cube on the second draw?

5. **Number Sense** Is the probability of drawing a green cube on the second draw with replacement *greater than, less than,* or *equal to* the probability without replacement?

6. Copy and extend the table below for 20 trials. For each trial, draw a cube from the bag, record the color, return the cube to the bag, and draw a second cube. Then return the second cube to the bag.

Trial	First Draw	Second Draw
1	?	?
2	?	?

7. Use your results to find the experimental probability of drawing two green cubes when the first cube is drawn and replaced.

8. Complete another table for 20 trials. For each trial, draw a cube from the bag, record the color, do not return the cube to the bag, and draw a second cube. Then return both cubes to the bag.

9. Use your results to find the experimental probability of drawing two green cubes when the first cube drawn is not replaced.

10. **Writing in Math** Compare your answers for Exercises 7 and 9.

11. **Reasoning** You draw two cubes from a bag of 20 cubes of varying colors, including yellow. Will *P*(both yellow) be greater *with* or *without* replacement? Justify your answer.

Independent and Dependent Events

Check Skills You'll Need

1. **Vocabulary Review** How can you use *theoretical probability* to make predictions?

You roll a number cube 50 times. Predict how many times the given outcome will occur.

2. 2   3. 5

4. 8   5. odd

 **for Help**
Lesson 10-2

What You'll Learn

To find the probabilities of independent and dependent events

◀⁣)) **New Vocabulary** independent events, dependent events

Why Learn This?

As people buy different items, a store's stock changes. The chances of finding your favorite team's jersey will change if the store does not replace its stock.

Compound events are two or more related events. Two events are **independent events** if the occurrence of one event does not affect the probability of the occurrence of the other.

> **KEY CONCEPTS** **Independent Events**
>
> If A and B are independent events, then $P(A, \text{then } B) = P(A) \cdot P(B)$.

EXAMPLE Probability of Independent Events

1 **Inventory** The table shows colors for 20 shirts. A clerk selects one shirt from a rack at random, puts a price tag on it, replaces it, and selects again. Find the probability that the first shirt is blue and the second is red.

Because the first shirt is replaced, these are independent events.

Color	Number of Shirts
Blue	6
Red	4
Black	3
Orange	7

$$P(\text{blue, then red}) = P(\text{blue}) \cdot P(\text{red})$$
$$= \frac{6}{20} \cdot \frac{4}{20} \quad \leftarrow \text{Substitute.}$$
$$= \frac{24}{400} = \frac{3}{50} \quad \leftarrow \text{Multiply and simplify.}$$

The probability of choosing a blue and then a red shirt is $\frac{3}{50}$.

Online active math

For: Compound Events Activity
Use: Interactive Textbook, 10-4

✔ Quick Check

1. Use the data in Example 1 to find $P(\text{orange, then black})$.

When the outcome of one event does affect the outcome of a second event, the events are dependent events.

> ### KEY CONCEPTS Dependent Events
>
> If A and B are dependent events, $P(A, \text{then } B) = P(A) \cdot P(B \text{ after } A)$.

EXAMPLE Probability of Dependent Events

2 **Multiple Choice** Two girls and three boys volunteer to speak at a school assembly. One student is selected at random to speak. Then another student is selected. What is the probability of selecting two girls?

Ⓐ $\frac{2}{5}$ Ⓑ $\frac{1}{5}$ Ⓒ $\frac{1}{10}$ Ⓓ $\frac{1}{25}$

First student $P(\text{girl}) = \frac{2}{5}$ ← Two of the five volunteers are girls.

Second student $P(\text{girl after girl}) = \frac{1}{4}$ ← One girl is left of four volunteers.

$P(\text{girl, then girl}) = P(\text{girl}) \cdot P(\text{girl after girl})$ ← Use the formula for dependent events.

$\qquad\qquad\qquad\; = \frac{2}{5} \cdot \frac{1}{4}$ ← Substitute.

$\qquad\qquad\qquad\; = \frac{2}{20} = \frac{1}{10}$ ← Multiply and simplify.

The probability of selecting two girls is $\frac{1}{10}$. The correct answer is choice C.

Test Prep Tip

When answering probability questions, first decide whether the events are independent or dependent.

✓ Quick Check

2. Find the probability that first a boy and then a girl are selected.

EXAMPLE Dependent or Independent Events?

State whether the events are dependent or independent. Explain.

3 **a.** Select a croquet ball. Do not replace it. Then select another ball.

After the first ball is chosen, the collection of remaining items has changed. These are dependent events.

b. Roll a number cube. Then roll the number cube again.

The result of the first roll will have no effect on how the number cube rolls the second time. These are independent events.

✓ Quick Check

3. Are the events dependent or independent? Explain.
  a. Flip a coin and then flip it again.
  b. Pick a name from a hat. Without replacing it, pick another.

✓ Check Your Understanding

1. **Vocabulary** How can you distinguish between independent and dependent events?

Are the events dependent or independent? Explain.

2. Toss a coin. Then roll a number cube.

3. Select a card. Do not replace it. Then select another card.

4. You choose an apple from two green apples and three red apples and eat it. Then you choose and eat another apple. Find P(green, then red).

5. You roll a number cube and then roll it again. Find P(3, then 4).

Homework Exercises

For more exercises, see Extra Skills and Word Problems.

GO for Help

For Exercises	See Examples
6–9	1
10–13	2
14–16	3

Find each probability. A different letter of the alphabet appears on each of 26 cards. You choose a card at random and then replace it. Then you choose a second card. Vowels are A, E, I, O, and U.

6. P(A, then B)

7. P(C, then X)

8. P(I, then a vowel)

9. P(vowel, then a vowel)

Find each probability. A bag contains the following marbles: 6 red, 4 orange, 3 yellow, 2 blue, and 5 green. You choose a marble at random and do not replace it. Then you select another marble.

10. P(red, then blue)

11. P(red, then yellow)

12. P(orange, then blue)

13. P(red, then red)

Are the events dependent or independent? Explain.

14. Select a card. Replace it. Then select another card.

15. Spin a spinner once. Then spin it again.

16. Select a marble from a bag. Put it aside. Then select another marble.

17. **Guided Problem Solving** Your family plans to visit two amusement parks. You have three favorite parks. Your sister has two different favorites. You write the name of each of the five parks on slips of paper. Then you select two parks at random. Find the probability that both parks selected are among your favorites.
   - How does the problem indicate replacement or not? Explain.
   - Find the probability for each of the two drawings. Then multiply.

Find each probability. Suppose you roll a number cube and spin the spinner at the right. Express your answer as a fraction in simplest form.

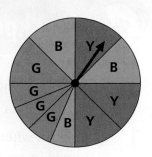

18. $P(3, \text{then green})$ **19.** $P(\text{prime, then blue})$

20. $P(5, \text{then yellow})$ **21.** $P(8, \text{then yellow})$

22. $P(\text{an even number, then green})$

23. **School Carnival** For a carnival game, a cube is rolled. Each of its six faces has a different color. To win, you must select the color rolled. You play the game twice. Find the probability of winning both times.

24. **Writing in Math** What is the difference between independent and dependent events? Explain.

25. **Challenge** Suppose two events, A and B, are dependent. You know that $P(A, \text{then } B) = \frac{2}{15}$ and $P(B \text{ after } A) = \frac{1}{3}$. Find $P(A)$.

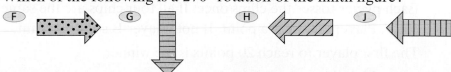

Test Prep and Mixed Review   **Practice**

Multiple Choice

26. A study indicates that the probability of a man being colorblind is $\frac{1}{20}$ and the probability of a woman being colorblind is $\frac{1}{200}$. What is the probability that two women chosen at random are colorblind?

Ⓐ $\dfrac{1}{400,000}$ Ⓒ $\dfrac{1}{400}$

Ⓑ $\dfrac{1}{40,000}$ Ⓓ $\dfrac{11}{200}$

27. The figures shown below have a repeating pattern.

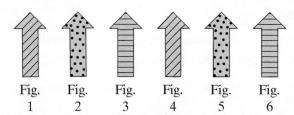

Fig. 1   Fig. 2   Fig. 3   Fig. 4   Fig. 5   Fig. 6

Which of the following is a 270° rotation of the ninth figure?

Ⓕ   Ⓖ   Ⓗ   Ⓙ

Make a stem-and-leaf plot for each set of data.

28. 13, 14, 11, 9, 10, 10, 25, 14, 14, 14, 16, 22, 20, 19, 17

29. 6.4, 5.0, 6.5, 5.5, 5.5, 5.7, 6.8, 5.2, 6.1, 6.1, 5.7, 5.6, 7.0

30. 122, 125, 136, 100, 102, 105, 151, 144, 129, 128, 133, 156, 100, 100

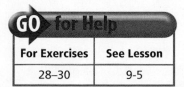

For Exercises	See Lesson
28–30	9-5

1. To find out the types of books young readers prefer, you survey people at random at a local music store. Is this a good sample? Explain.

2. Explain whether the question "Do you prefer watching an exciting movie or reading a dull book?" is biased.

Find each probability. You place 10 cards marked with the letters of the word SIMULATION in a box and select one card at random. You return the card and select again.

3. P(I, then N)

4. P(I, then vowel)

5. P(N, then vowel)

6. P(A, then not U)

Find each probability. You place 14 cards marked with the numbers 0–13 in a box and select one card at random. You put the card aside and select again.

7. P(3, then 0)

8. P(3, then even)

9. P(5, then odd)

10. P(2, then not 11)

MATH GAMES

Yellow Up

What You'll Need

- a set of four chips, with red on one side and yellow on the other side of each chip, as shown at the right

How to Play

- Decide who is Player A and who is Player B.
- Each player tosses the chips once. If all four chips are the same color, Player A scores a point. If not, Player B scores a point.
- The first player to reach 20 points is the winner.

Do you think this game is fair? Explain.

You can evaluate the fairness of the game. Make an organized list of all possible outcomes. Which is more likely: exactly 1, exactly 2, exactly 3, or exactly 4 red sides up?

Does this change your decision about the fairness of the game? Explain.

Permutations

Check Skills You'll Need

1. **Vocabulary Review** What is a *sample space*?

Find the number of possible outcomes in each situation.

2. Roll a number cube and toss a coin.

3. Roll two number cubes.

4. Toss two coins.

GO for Help
Lesson 5-8

What You'll Learn

To find the number of permutations of a set of objects

 **New Vocabulary** permutation, counting principle, factorial

Why Learn This?

In a track meet, six runners compete in the 200-meter dash. The order in which the runners finish matters because it affects the scoring of the meet.

Sometimes, the order of objects in an arrangement is important. A **permutation** is an arrangement of a set of objects in a particular order. You can use a tree diagram to find the number of permutations of objects.

EXAMPLE Permutations Using a Diagram

1 In how many ways can Ryan, Emily, and Justin line up in gym class?

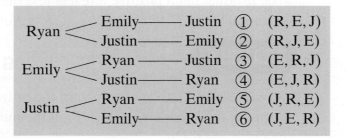

← Draw a tree diagram.

Ryan, Emily, and Justin can line up in six different ways. This means that there are six permutations.

Quick Check

1. Use a tree diagram to find the number of permutations.
   a. You arrange five books on a shelf. In how many ways can you arrange the books?
   b. Four geese fly in line. In how many different orders can they fly?

The tree diagram in Example 1 illustrates the counting principle.

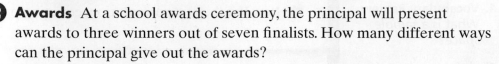

The Counting Principle

Suppose there are *m* ways of making one choice and *n* ways of making a second choice. Then there are *m · n* ways to make the first choice followed by the second choice.

EXAMPLE Using the Counting Principle

2 **Awards** At a school awards ceremony, the principal will present awards to three winners out of seven finalists. How many different ways can the principal give out the awards?

There are seven ways to give out the first award, six ways to give out the second, and five ways to give out the third.

$7 \cdot 6 \cdot 5 = 210$ ← Use the counting principle.

There are 210 different ways to give out the awards.

✔ Quick Check

2. Suppose the principal gives out four awards. How does this affect the number of different ways to give out the awards?

📱 Calculator Tip

Some calculators have a factorial key. Look on the PRB menu for the ! option.

If the principal in Example 2 gave awards to all seven finalists, then there would be $7 \cdot 6 \cdot 5 \cdot 4 \cdot 3 \cdot 2 \cdot 1$ different ways to give out the awards. This solution involves the product of all the integers from 7 to 1.

The product of all positive integers less than or equal to a number is a **factorial.** Write 7!, which you read as "seven factorial."

EXAMPLE Permutations Using Factorials

3 **Music** Many CD players can vary the order in which songs are played. Suppose a CD has eight songs. Find the number of orders in which you can play the songs.

$8! = 8 \cdot 7 \cdot 6 \cdot 5 \cdot 4 \cdot 3 \cdot 2 \cdot 1 = 40{,}320$ ← Simplify.

The songs can be played in 40,320 different orders.

✔ Quick Check

3. Simplify each expression.
   a. 2!   b. 6!   c. 4!

If you only want to play three songs from the CD in Example 3, there are $8 \cdot 7 \cdot 6 = 336$ ways to choose any three songs. You can write this as $_8P_3$.

Vocabulary Tip

KEY CONCEPTS **Permutation Notation**

The expression $_nP_r$ represents the number of permutations of n objects chosen r at a time.

Example $_{25}P_2 = 25 \cdot 24 = 600$
                              ↑   ↑
                    25 objects   groups of 2 (two factors)

● More Than One Way

At a school science fair, ribbons are given for first, second, and third place. There are 20 exhibits in the fair. How many different arrangements of three winning exhibits are possible?

Tina's Method

I can use permutation notation.

$_nP_r = {_{20}P_3}$ ← There are 20 exhibits; 3 of the exhibits will be selected in order.

      $= 20 \cdot 19 \cdot 18$ ← Simplify $_{20}P_3$.

      $= 6{,}840$ ← Simplify.

There are 6,840 different arrangements.

Roberto's Method

I can use a calculator.

Enter 20. Find the PRB menu. Select $_nP_r$.

Enter 3. Press **ENTER**. The display shows *6840*.

There are 6,840 different arrangements.

Choose a Method

How many permutations are there if the school also awards fourth place? Explain why you chose the method you used.

✓ Check Your Understanding

1. **Vocabulary** What is a permutation?

Simplify each expression.

2. $6 \cdot 5 \cdot 4$ 3. $10 \cdot 9 \cdot 8$ 4. $3!$ 5. $_{10}P_2$

For more exercises, see Extra Skills and Word Problems.

GO for Help

For Exercises	See Examples
6–7	1
8–9	2
10–15	3

Use a tree diagram to find the number of permutations.

6. Four students are in line to see the school nurse. In how many different ways can the students be positioned in the line?

7. Suppose you rent a thriller, a drama, and a comedy from a video store. In how many different orders can you watch the videos?

Use the counting principle to find the number of permutations.

8. **Education** Your English teacher gives you a summer reading list of ten books. You must read three of them. In how many different orders can you select three books?

9. There are six finalists in a poetry contest. In how many different orders can three winning poems be read?

Simplify each expression.

10. $5!$ **11.** $7!$ **12.** $9!$ **13.** $10!$ **14.** $11!$

15. An organizer is made up of six sections. If you have six items, in how many different ways can you place them in the organizer?

16. **Guided Problem Solving** From a list of ten artists, students were asked to list their favorite four in order of preference. In how many different ways can the artists be listed?
   • How many choices are there for a student's favorite artist?
   • How many choices are there for the second favorite artist?
   • Complete this multiplication to solve the problem: ■ · ■ · ■ · ■.

GO Online

Homework Video Tutor

Visit: PHSchool.com
Web Code: ase-1005

Simplify each expression.

17. $_{25}P_3$ **18.** $_{18}P_2$ **19.** $_{32}P_3$ **20.** $_8P_4$ **21.** $_{400}P_2$

A bag contains ten blocks. Each block is a different color. Find how many ways you can select each number of blocks.

22. 3   **23.** 5   **24.** 7   **25.** 9   **26.** 10

27. **Dog Shows** Twenty-five dogs enter a dog show. The show awards prizes for first, second, and third places. How many different arrangements of three winners are possible?

28. A picture frame comes in four colors and three sizes. Use the counting principle to find the number of different styles of frames.

29. **Choose a Method** A music class has 21 students. In how many different orders can the teacher choose six students to perform in a concert? Explain why you chose the method you used.

30. <u>Writing in Math</u> Describe two different ways you can use a calculator to compute 12!.

31. Challenge You color rows of eight squares on graph paper, using a different color for each square in a row. It takes 45 seconds to color a row. You use the same eight colors for each row. How many hours will it take you to color all possible arrangements of colors?

Multiple Choice

32. A survey of Americans shows that 78% get to work by driving alone, 9% use a carpool, 5% use mass transporation, 5% use other methods such as walking or biking, and 3% work at home. Find the central angle for the carpool sector in a circle graph of the data.

    Ⓐ 9°   Ⓑ 24°   Ⓒ 32.4°   Ⓓ 90°

33. Which graph shows a rhombus with 3 vertices in the second quadrant and a vertex with an *x*-coordinate of −3?

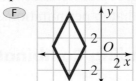
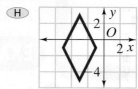
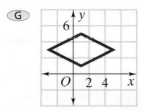
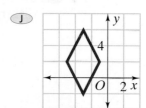

34. Emily borrowed money from her brother for a new CD player with a regular price of $55. The player was on sale for 25% off and the sales tax was 8%. If Emily pays her brother back in four equal payments, what is the approximate amount of each payment?

    Ⓐ $11.00   Ⓑ $12.00   Ⓒ $12.50   Ⓓ $13.75

Choose the appropriate graph for each data set. Explain your choice.

GO for Help

For Exercises	See Lesson
35–36	9-9

35. Computer Use by 12-Year-Olds

Types of Use	Time (min)
Games	17
Web sites	13
E-mail	5
Chat rooms	4
Other	22

Source: The Kaiser Family Foundation Report

36. Florida Orange Production

Year	Boxes of Oranges (thousands)
1960	82,700
1970	142,300
1980	172,400
1990	151,600
2000	223,300

Source: Florida Agricultural Statistics Service

✓ Check Skills You'll Need

1. **Vocabulary Review**
   An arrangement of objects in a certain order is a   ? .

Simplify each expression.

2. $7 \cdot 6$ 3. $4!$

4. $_{10}P_2$ 5. $_{101}P_3$

 **for Help**
Lesson 10-5

What You'll Learn

To find the number of combinations of a set of objects using lists and combination notation

🔊 **New Vocabulary** combination

Why Learn This?

The pair of yogurt toppings *raisins and nuts* is the same as the pair of toppings *nuts and raisins*. When you eat them, they form the same combination.

A **combination** is a group of items in which the order of the items is *not* considered. Recall that in permutations, order does matter.

EXAMPLE   Finding Combinations

① **Food** The table below contains four yogurt toppings. How many different ways can you choose two toppings?

Yogurt Toppings

Topping	Raisins	Nuts	Blueberries	Granola
Letter	R	N	B	G

Use letters to represent the four possible toppings.

Step 1 Make an organized list of all the possible groups of toppings.

RN	RB	RG
NR	NB	NG
BR	BN	BG
GR	GN	GB

Step 2 Cross out any group that is a duplicate of another.

RN	RB	RG
N̶R̶	NB	NG
B̶R̶	B̶N̶	BG
G̶R̶	G̶N̶	G̶B̶

Step 3 Count the number of groups that remain.

There are six different ways to choose two toppings.

> **Vocabulary Tip**
>
> A group of toppings that contains the same items as another group is a *duplicate*. Since NR is the same as RN, NR is a duplicate.

✓ Quick Check

1. Make an organized list to find the number of different groups of three tutors your teacher can choose from four students.

GO Online

Video Tutor Help
Visit: PHSchool.com
Web Code: ase-0775

In Example 1, you found the number of combinations by using a list. You can also use permutations to find combinations.

Since order does not matter, the permutation *raisins and nuts* and the permutation *nuts and raisins* represent the same group of toppings. To remove all the duplicate groups, divide by 2!, the number of ways to arrange two toppings.

$$\text{combinations} = \frac{\text{total number of permutations}}{\text{number of permutations of 2 toppings}} = \frac{4 \cdot 3}{2 \cdot 1} = 6$$

You can write the number of combinations of four yogurt toppings chosen two at a time as $_4C_2$.

KEY CONCEPTS **Combination Notation**

The expression $_nC_r$ represents the number of combinations of *n* objects chosen *r* at a time.

$$_nC_r = \frac{_nP_r}{r!}$$

Example $\quad _7C_3 = \frac{_7P_3}{3!} = \frac{7 \cdot 6 \cdot 5}{3 \cdot 2 \cdot 1} = 35$

The notation can look difficult. The next example shows how the numerator counts all possible arrangements and the denominator "divides out" the repeated combinations.

EXAMPLE **Using Combination Notation**

2 **Fishing** A fishing boat uses 5 fishing lines. Each line holds one lure. There are 12 different lures. How many different combinations of lures can be used at one time on the boat?

Find the number of ways you can choose 5 lures from 12.

The numerator shows the number of ways to arrange 5 lures out of 12.

$$_{12}C_5 = \frac{_{12}P_5}{5!}$$

The denominator shows there are 5! arrangements of each group of 5 lures.

$$= \frac{12 \cdot 11 \cdot 10 \cdot 9 \cdot 8}{5 \cdot 4 \cdot 3 \cdot 2 \cdot 1} \quad \leftarrow \text{Simplify } _{12}P_5 \text{ and 5!}.$$

$$= 792 \quad \leftarrow \text{Simplify.}$$

There are 792 different combinations of lures.

 **Quick Check**

2. Simplify each expression.
   a. $_7C_5$ b. $_8C_4$ c. $_5C_3$

1. **Vocabulary** Explain the difference between a permutation and a combination.

In each situation, tell whether order matters. Then decide if the situation describes a permutation or a combination.

2. First-, second-, and third-prize winners will be selected.

3. Three types of nuts will be selected to go into a snack mix.

4. Seven students are chosen to be on the Student Council.

Find each number of combinations.

5. Ways to choose four of five books

6. Ways to choose four of nine colors

Homework Exercises

For more exercises, see Extra Skills and Word Problems.

Make an organized list to find the number of combinations.

GO ▶ for Help

For Exercises	See Examples
7–8	1
9–19	2

7. **Food** You are buying a pizza with two toppings. The store offers nine toppings. In how many ways can you choose your two toppings?

8. **Committees** A school committee has five members. The principal wants to form a subcommittee of three people. How many different groups of three can be formed from the five committee members?

Simplify each expression.

9. $_4C_3$ 10. $_4C_2$ 11. $_4C_1$ 12. $_6C_5$ 13. $_6C_4$

14. $_{10}C_1$ 15. $_{10}C_9$ 16. $_7C_4$ 17. $_3C_1$ 18. $_9C_6$

19. You can bring three people to a party. You have ten friends. How many different groups of three people can you bring?

20. **Guided Problem Solving** Sixteen listeners call a radio station, and each person requests a different song. The disc jockey only has time to play ten songs. How many different groups of ten songs can the disc jockey play?
    • There are ▪ songs to choose from. The disc jockey will pick ▪.
    • Does this situation describe a permutation or a combination?

GO ●nline
Homework Video Tutor
Visit: PHSchool.com
Web Code: ase-1006

Decide whether the situation describes a permutation or a combination.

21. A president and a vice president will be elected from club members.

22. A salad bar offers eight choices of vegetables.

23. **Sports** Ten teams enter a volleyball tournament. Each team plays every other team once. How many different games are played?

24. **Travel** A group of six tourists arrives at an airport gate 15 minutes before flight time, but only two seats are available.
    a. How many different groups of two can get on the airplane?
    b. How many different groups of four *cannot* get on the airplane?

25. **Writing in Math** What is the difference between the number of permutations and the number of combinations of *n* objects chosen *r* at a time? Explain.

26. **Error Analysis** Sanjay can take two of his five sweaters on a trip. He reasons that he has five choices for his first sweater and four choices for his second. Using the counting principle, he thinks he has 20 ways to choose his sweaters. Is Sanjay correct? Explain.

27. **Challenge** A designer chooses three colors from the palette below for a customer's logo. She picks the three colors in a specific order. What is the probability that another customer, choosing at random, picks the same three colors in the same order?

Multiple Choice

28. A pack of juice boxes contains 4 apple, 4 cherry, 4 orange, and 4 grape juice boxes. If two people select a juice box at random, what is the probability that they will both get grape?

    Ⓐ $\frac{3}{64}$ Ⓑ $\frac{1}{20}$ Ⓒ $\frac{1}{16}$ Ⓓ $\frac{1}{4}$

29. The Venn diagram shows how many of the 40 members in a Girl Scout troop can meet on Monday, Wednesday, or Thursday. What is the probability that a member chosen at random will NOT be able to meet on Monday?

    Available Meeting Days

    Monday 12, 1, Wednesday 15, 2, 1, 3, 6, Thursday

    Ⓕ $\frac{3}{10}$ Ⓗ $\frac{11}{20}$

    Ⓖ $\frac{21}{40}$ Ⓙ $\frac{27}{40}$

GO for Help

For Exercises	See Lesson
30–33	2-8

Write each number in scientific notation.

30. 153,000   31. 45   32. 53,200,000   33. 8,693

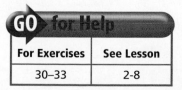

Vocabulary Builder

Understanding Vocabulary

Many words have an everyday meaning, as well as a specific meaning in mathematics. Knowing the everyday meaning can help you understand the math meaning.

EXAMPLE

Give the everyday meaning and math meaning of each of the following words: population, sample, and combination.

Word	Everyday Meaning	Math Meaning
Population	The total number of people living in a region	The total group of people or objects being studied
Sample	A representative item from a larger group	A part of the population
Combination	Two or more things put together	A group of items in which the order of items is *not* considered

Exercises

Copy and complete the table below. Use a dictionary to look up the everyday meanings of words, if necessary.

	Word	Everyday Meaning	Math Meaning
1.	Permutation	A complete rearrangement	?
2.	?	?	Based on all the outcomes when the outcomes are equally likely
3.	Independent	?	?
4.	Biased	Having a strong opinion	?
5.	Random	?	Having the same chance of being selected
6.	Experimental	?	Based on a number of trials
7.	?	Relying on something for support	Outcome of one event affects the outcome of the other

Permutations, Combinations, and Probability

You often need to find the number of permutations or combinations of a set of objects before finding probability.

Teams Cathie, Karla, and Shizuka are on a gymnastics team. There are six members on the team. Three team members are chosen at random to represent the school at the State Olympics. What is the probability that these three girls will be selected?

What You Might Think

What do I know? What do I want to find out?

First I need to find how many different groups are possible.

I can find the probability.

What You Might Write

Three gymnasts are being selected at random from six gymnasts. I want to find the probability that three specific gymnasts will be selected.

Since the order that the gymnasts are selected does not matter, I want to find the number of combinations.

$$_6C_3 = \frac{_6P_3}{3!}$$

$$= \frac{6 \times 5 \times 4}{3 \times 2 \times 1}$$

$$= 20$$

There are 20 ways to select three gymnasts.

I only want the probability of selecting Cathie, Karla, and Shizuka. This is just one arrangement out of 20. So, the probability is $\frac{1}{20}$.

Think It Through

1. What does $_6C_3$ mean in this situation?

2. Is the selection of the second gymnast an independent or dependent event? Explain.

3. Why was $6 \cdot 5 \cdot 4$ divided by $3 \cdot 2 \cdot 1$?

Exercises

Solve each problem. For Exercises 4 and 5, answer parts (a) and (b) first.

4. Carlos and Kareem are two of five members on a bowling team. Two team members are randomly chosen to compete in a Wednesday night tournament. What is the probability that Carlos and Kareem will be selected?
   a. List what you know.
   b. Find the number of combinations.

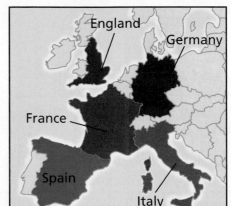

5. Your family makes a list of five European countries to visit on your vacation. You all decide that Italy will be one of the countries you visit. Of the remaining four countries, you decide to choose two at random. What is the probability that you choose to visit Germany?
   a. List what you know.
   b. Find the number of combinations.

6. A vendor makes tacos topped with lettuce, tomatoes, cheese, sour cream, and guacamole. If you order a taco with three randomly chosen toppings, what is the probability you will get one with guacamole?

7. Ten events in a track and field meet take place over two days.

Track and Field Events

Day 1	Day 2
100-m run	1,500-m run
Shot put	Discus throw
High jump	150-m hurdles
Long jump	Pole vault
400-m run	Javelin throw

Each event must be completed on the designated day. In how many ways can the meet director arrange the events?

8. On a certain game show, six numbers are chosen at random from the numbers 1 through 53. Suppose your chances of getting hit by lightning are about 1 in 3,000. Are your chances of getting hit by lightning greater or less than the chances of winning the game show? Explain.

Test-Taking Strategies

Answering the Question Asked

When answering a multiple-choice question, be sure to answer the question asked. Some answer choices may be answers to related questions. Read the question carefully and check that you have answered it.

EXAMPLE

Santo spins the spinner at the right and tosses a coin. What is the probability that he will spin the color blue and the coin will land with tails side up?

(A) $\frac{1}{6}$　　　(B) $\frac{1}{3}$　　　(C) $\frac{1}{2}$　　　(D) $\frac{2}{3}$

The question is, "What is the probability of spinning blue and getting tails?" The probability of spinning blue is $\frac{1}{3}$. The probability of getting tails is $\frac{1}{2}$. Since the two events are independent, multiply the probabilities.

$P(\text{blue, then tails}) = \frac{1}{3} \cdot \frac{1}{2}$　←　Since spinning blue and getting tails are independent, multiply the probabilities.

$= \frac{1}{6}$　←　Simplify.

The probability of spinning blue and getting tails is $\frac{1}{6}$. The correct answer is choice A.

Exercises

1. Ty is equally likely to pick any one of his friends to be on his basketball team. He has seven friends who want to play. What is the probability that he will pick Jana first and then Cooper?

   (A) $\frac{1}{49}$　　　(B) $\frac{1}{42}$　　　(C) $\frac{2}{13}$　　　(D) $\frac{2}{7}$

2. A company makes 8 oz packages of snack mix. The probability of a package being lighter than 8 oz is $\frac{2}{25}$. The company makes 300 packages of snack mix in one day. Predict how many will be underweight.

   (F) 6　　　(G) 12　　　(H) 24　　　(J) 80

3. If you roll a number cube five times, what is the probability of rolling all ones?

   (A) $\frac{1}{7,776}$　　　(B) $\frac{1}{3,125}$　　　(C) $\frac{1}{6}$　　　(D) $\frac{5}{6}$

Vocabulary Review

 **biased questions** (p. 481)
combination (p. 496)
counting principal (p. 492)
dependent events (p. 487)
**experimental
  probability** (p. 470)

factorial (p. 492)
independent events (p. 486)
odds in favor (p. 471)
odds against (p. 471)
permutation (p. 491)

population (p. 480)
random sample (p. 480)
sample (p. 480)
theoretical probability (p. 471)

Choose the correct vocabulary term to complete each sentence.

1. (Experimental probability, Theoretical probability) describes how likely it is that an event will happen based on all the possible outcomes.

2. People often conduct surveys using a (population, random sample) so that each object in the population has the same chance of being selected.

3. To calculate the number of ways a class can line up, you need to find the number of possible (permutations, combinations).

4. When the outcome of an event *does* affect the outcome of a second event, the events are (dependent events, independent events).

Go Online
PHSchool.com
For: Online Vocabulary Quiz
Web Code: asj-1051

Skills and Concepts

Lessons 10-1, 10-2
- To find theoretical probability, experimental probability, and odds
- To make predictions based on theoretical and experimental probabilities

You can find the **experimental probability** of an event with this formula:

$$P(\text{event}) = \frac{\text{number of times event occurs}}{\text{total number of trials}}.$$

You can find the **theoretical probability** of an event with this formula:

$$P(\text{event}) = \frac{\text{number of favorable outcomes}}{\text{total number of possible outcomes}}.$$

You can use probabilities to make predictions.

You have 5 one-dollar bills, 3 five-dollar bills, and 1 ten-dollar bill in your pocket. You select a bill at random. Find the odds in favor of selecting each type of bill.

5. one-dollar bill   6. five-dollar bill   7. ten-dollar bill

8. The probability of a CD case being defective is $\frac{1}{520}$. If the factory makes 7,800 cases per week, how many are likely to be defective?

9. In a random survey, 8 out of 18 students would rather go to an amusement park than to the zoo. In a group of 225 students, how many students can you expect to prefer the amusement park?

Lesson 10-3
• To identify random samples and biased questions and to judge conclusions based on survey results

A **sample** is part of the population, or group, being studied. In a **random sample,** each item has the same chance of being selected. **Biased questions** are unfair questions that may influence the answers in a survey.

A mayor wants to see if there is support for building a skate park in the city. Tell whether or not the surveys use random samples.

10. Randomly interview 50 residents walking on the street.

11. Interview every fifth person who buys a skateboard at a local sporting goods store.

Lesson 10-4
• To find the probabilities of independent and dependent events

When the outcome of one event *does not* affect the outcome of a second event, the events are **independent.**

$$P(A, \text{ then } B) = P(A) \cdot P(B)$$

If the outcome of one event *does* affect the outcome of a second event, the events are **dependent.**

$$P(A, \text{ then } B) = P(A) \cdot P(B \text{ after } A)$$

Are the events dependent or independent? Explain.

12. Roll a number cube. Then roll it again.

13. Pick an item from a bag. Without replacing it, pick another item.

Lessons 10-5, 10-6
• To find the number of permutations of a set of objects
• To find the number of combinations of a group of objects using lists and combination notation

A **permutation** is an arrangement of a set of objects in a certain order.

$$_9P_4 = 9 \cdot 8 \cdot 7 \cdot 6$$

A **combination** is a group of items in which the order of the items is not important.

$$_9C_4 = \frac{_9P_4}{4!}$$

14. If 12 people are playing in a tournament and each person plays every other person, how many games will be played?

15. In how many different ways can you choose two magazines from a shelf of ten magazines in a convenience store?

Chapter 10 Test

Go Online For: Online chapter test
PHSchool.com Web Code: asa-1052

Food Find each probability. A supermarket polled its customers to see which brand of salsa they prefer. The table below shows the results from the survey.

Preference	Number of Votes
Brand X	92
Brand Y	80
Brand Z	120
No preference	108
Total	**400**

1. $P(\text{Brand X})$
2. $P(\text{Brand Y})$

3. **Repairs** On a recent day, a mechanic found that out of 126 fenders, 7 had cracks. What is the experimental probability that a fender selected at random does *not* have a crack?

4. **School** Every day, Nora's teacher randomly selects a row of students to organize the classroom. There are six rows of students. What is the probability that the teacher selects Nora's row two days in a row?

A number from 1 to 100 is selected at random. Find each theoretical probability.

5. $P(85)$
6. $P(105)$
7. $P(\text{number divisible by 9})$
8. $P(\text{number containing a 4})$

Find each probability. Lucinda has 5 yellow pencils, 6 blue pencils, and 9 green pencils. She picks 1 pencil at random and does not replace it. Then she picks another pencil.

9. $P(\text{yellow, then blue})$
10. $P(2 \text{ green})$
11. $P(\text{green, then blue})$
12. $P(2 \text{ yellow})$

13. Suppose you roll a number cube 25 times. Predict the number of times you will roll a 4.

Simplify each expression.

14. $8!$
15. $5!$
16. $_4P_3$
17. $\frac{6!}{2!}$
18. $_{18}C_2$
19. $_{10}C_7$

20. At a school, 50 students were asked whether they brought lunch to school or bought it in the cafeteria. The results are in the table.

Lunch Survey

Response	Number
Bring lunch	17
Buy lunch	33

There are 235 students in the school. About how many of them bring lunch?

Determine whether each survey uses a random sample. Describe the population.

21. **Entertainment** A movie theater surveys every tenth person to determine what types of movies its patrons like.

22. **Games** A computer game company surveys its teenage customers to determine its most popular games.

Is each expression equivalent to $_{12}C_3$? Write *yes* or *no* and explain your answer.

23. $_{12}C_9$
24. $\frac{12!}{9!}$
25. $\frac{12 \cdot 11 \cdot 10}{3!}$
26. $_{12}P_3$

27. **School Supplies** Suppose you want to buy five different colored notebooks. There are eight colors from which to choose. How many combinations of notebooks are possible?

28. **Writing in Math** Explain why there are fewer combinations than permutations for a group of more than 1.

Reading Comprehension

Read each passage and answer the questions that follow.

> **Mathematical Notes** Have you ever wondered how there can still be any songs left to be written? After all, people have been writing music for a very long time, and many songs are limited to the eight notes in the octave of a major or minor scale. Doesn't it seem as though all the new melodies should have been written by now?

For Exercises 1–4, you can use the same note more than once.

1. Suppose you plan to write a song. You use the notes in an octave of a scale. How many different outcomes are there for the first two notes of the song?
   - Ⓐ 8
   - Ⓑ 16
   - Ⓒ 56
   - Ⓓ 64

2. In how many different ways can you choose the first three notes of a song from the notes in an octave of a scale?
   - Ⓕ 6
   - Ⓖ 24
   - Ⓗ 336
   - Ⓙ 512

3. What is the general formula for the number of ways you can write n notes of music choosing from the notes in an octave?
   - Ⓐ $8 \cdot 7 \cdot 6 \cdot 5 \cdot 4 \cdot 3 \cdot 2 \cdot 1$
   - Ⓑ $(n)(n - 1) \ldots (3)(2)(1)$
   - Ⓒ n^8
   - Ⓓ 8^n

4. In how many ways can you choose from eight possible notes to write the first ten notes of a song?
   - Ⓕ 8^{10}
   - Ⓖ 10^8
   - Ⓗ $10 \cdot 9 \cdot 8$
   - Ⓙ 1×10^8

> **Ecology Club** The ecology club at school has 20 members. When the club selects officers, the order of selection matters. When the club selects members to study either recycling, water, land surface, or waste disposal, order does not matter.

5. In how many different ways can the ecology club choose a president, a vice president, and a coordinator?
   - Ⓐ 380
   - Ⓑ 1,140
   - Ⓒ 6,840
   - Ⓓ 8,000

6. The club plans to go on a field trip. Each member must have a buddy. Which expression represents the number of different ways n members can pair off?
   - Ⓕ $(n)(n - 1)$
   - Ⓗ $(n)(n - 1) \ldots 1$
   - Ⓖ n^2
   - Ⓙ $\dfrac{(n)(n - 1)}{2}$

7. The club selects 4 people to lead the curriculum groups. How many ways can the club select 4 people?
   - Ⓐ 116,280
   - Ⓑ 4,845
   - Ⓒ 80
   - Ⓓ 5

8. Suppose the club gets four more members. In how many more ways can the club select 4 group leaders than in Exercise 7?
   - Ⓕ $_{24}P_4 - {}_{20}P_4$
   - Ⓗ $_{24}C_4 - {}_{20}C_4$
   - Ⓖ $_{24}C_4 + {}_{20}C_4$
   - Ⓙ $_{24}P_4 + {}_{20}P_4$

Problem Solving Application

Applying Probability

Animal Census Suppose you want to know how many polar bears live in Alaska, or how many cheetahs live in the Serengeti desert. Since it is nearly impossible to count an animal population directly, scientists use a capture–recapture method to estimate populations.

Monitoring the Albatross
Scientists tag albatrosses to study how commercial fishing ventures affect them.

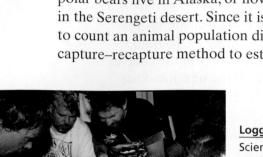

Loggerhead Sea Turtles
Scientists use tags to track sea turtles' movements after nesting, including migration paths and feeding habitats.

King Penguins
Researchers tagged king penguin pairs in a colony of 40,000 penguins to find out how the penguin parents communicated with each other as they incubated their eggs.

Put It All Together

Materials paper bag, dried white beans, permanent marker, graph paper

Work with a partner or in a small group.

- Count out between 250 and 400 beans.
- Record the number and place the beans in the paper bag.
- Exchange bags with another group of students.

1. Use the capture–recapture method to sample the population. Copy and extend the table. Record your results.

2. **a.** Make a scatter plot comparing the probability of recapturing a marked bean to the sample size.

   b. Based on your graph, what percent of the total population do you think is marked?

   c. Estimation Estimate the population in the bag.

   d. Writing in Math Compare your estimate with the number of beans recorded by the group that gave you the bag. Explain any differences.

3. **Reasoning** What real-life factors might make capture–recapture less accurate in the wild? How might scientists control these factors?

Trial Number	Sample Size	Number Recaptured	Percent Recaptured
1	10	2	20%
2	10	▢	▢
3	10	▢	▢
4	10	▢	▢
5	10	▢	▢
6	20	▢	▢
7	20	▢	▢

Capture–Recapture

Step 1 For the capture, take a random sample of 50 beans. Mark each bean with the permanent marker. Return the beans to the bag and shake it.

Step 2 For the recapture, take a random sample of the beans. Record the size of the sample and the number of recaptured beans in a table.

Step 3 Calculate the experimental probability of recapturing a bean. Record the probability as a percent.

Step 4 Repeat Steps 2 and 3 for five samples each of 10, 20, 30, 40, 50, and 60 beans.

Go Online
PHSchool.com
For: Information about animal populations
Web Code: ace-1053

CHAPTER 11

Functions

What You've Learned

- In Chapter 3, you graphed points using ordered pairs of rational numbers.
- You used tables, graphs, and equations to solve problems.
- In Chapter 6, you wrote and solved multi-step equations and inequalities.

Check Your Readiness

GO for Help

For Exercises	See Lessons
1–6	1-4
7–11	3-4
12–14	3-5

Dividing Integers

Simplify each expression.

1. $\dfrac{35}{-7}$

2. $\dfrac{-72}{12}$

3. $\dfrac{-54}{9}$

4. $\dfrac{-40}{5}$

5. $\dfrac{-24}{-6}$

6. $\dfrac{63}{-21}$

Graphing in the Coordinate Plane

Graph each point on the same coordinate plane.

7. $(0, 3)$

8. $(-1, 5)$

9. $(6, -8)$

10. Which vertex of the figure at the right is in the second quadrant?

11. What are the coordinates of point S?

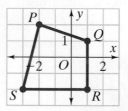

Graphing Equations with Two Variables

Graph each linear equation.

12. $y = \dfrac{3}{4}x + 2$

13. $y = -7x - 14$

14. $y = \dfrac{6}{7}x - 4$

What You'll Learn Next

- In this chapter, you will identify types of sequences and describe them using verbal descriptions and algebraic expressions.

- You will calculate the slopes of lines and use slope to write equations and draw graphs.

- You will identify and describe linear and nonlinear functions.

 Problem Solving Application On pages 556 and 557, you will work an extended activity on setting prices.

◀))) Key Vocabulary

 **Sequences**

What You'll Learn

To write rules for sequences and to use the rules to find terms in a sequence

New Vocabulary sequence, term, inductive reasoning, arithmetic sequence, common difference, geometric sequence, common ratio

Why Learn This?

You can find patterns in data just as a detective finds patterns in evidence. In some problems, you are given a set of numbers and asked to find the pattern. Once you have found the pattern, you can write an algebraic expression to find other numbers.

A **sequence** is a set of numbers that follows a pattern. Here are three different sequences that begin with the numbers 2 and 6.

2, 6, 10, 14, . . .

2, 6, 18, 54, . . .

2, 6, 8, 14, . . .

Each number in a sequence is called a **term.** You can often find additional terms in a given sequence by figuring out the pattern of the sequence. You are using **inductive reasoning** when you make conclusions based on patterns you observe.

EXAMPLE Finding Terms of a Sequence

1 Find the next three terms in the sequence 2, 6, 10, 14, . . .

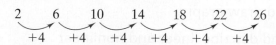

You find each term by adding 4 to the previous term.

The next three terms are 18, 22, and 26.

Quick Check

1. Find the next three terms in each sequence.
   a. 5, 12, 19, 26, . . . **b.** 4, 9, 14, 19, . . . **c.** 2, 12, 22, 32, . . .

Vocabulary Tip

You pronounce *arithmetic sequence* as "ar ith MET ik SEE kwuns."

The sequence in Example 1 is an arithmetic sequence. An **arithmetic sequence** is a sequence in which each term differs from the next by a fixed number, called the **common difference.**

You can use an algebraic expression for a sequence. The expression gives the nth term, where n is the term's position in the sequence.

EXAMPLE **Evaluating Algebraic Expressions**

2 **Multiple Choice** Find the first four terms of the sequence represented by the expression $4 + 3n$.

Ⓐ 2, 5, 8, 11   Ⓒ 5, 7, 9, 11

Ⓑ 7, 10, 13, 16   Ⓓ 4, 6, 9, 12

Test Prep Tip Ⓐ Ⓑ Ⓒ Ⓓ

Make a table like the one shown here, using the counting numbers 1, 2, 3, and 4.

Position, n	1	2	3	4
$4 + 3n$	$4 + 3 \cdot 1$	$4 + 3 \cdot 2$	$4 + 3 \cdot 3$	$4 + 3 \cdot 4$
Term	7	10	13	16

Write the sequence as 7, 10, 13, 16, . . . The correct answer is choice B.

✓ Quick Check

2. Find the first four terms of the sequence represented by $3(n - 1)$.

A table can help you write an algebraic expression for a sequence.

EXAMPLE **Writing an Algebraic Expression**

3 Write an algebraic expression for the sequence 5, 10, 15, . . . Then find the 20th term in the sequence.

Make a table that pairs each term's position with its value.

Position, n	1	2	3	. . .	20
	↓ · 5	↓ · 5	↓ · 5	↓ · 5	↓ · 5
Term	5	10	15	. . .	■

You find a term in the sequence by multiplying the term's position number by 5. The algebraic expression $5n$ represents the sequence.

$5n = 5(20)$ ← Substitute 20 for n to find the 20th term.

$= 100$ ← Simplify.

The 20th term in the sequence is 100.

✓ Quick Check

3. Write an algebraic expression for the sequence $-2, -4, -6, -8, . . .$ Then find the 20th term.

The sequence 2, 6, 18, 54, ... is a geometric sequence. A **geometric sequence** is a set of numbers in which each term is found by *multiplying* the previous term by a fixed number. This fixed number is called the **common ratio.**

The common ratio in the sequence below is 3.

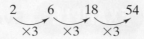

You can describe the sequence as *Start with 2 and multiply by 3 repeatedly.*

EXAMPLE **Describing a Geometric Sequence**

4 **Sports** The first round of a soccer tournament includes 128 teams. The following rounds have 64 teams, 32 teams, 16 teams, and so on. Describe the geometric sequence formed by the tournament. Then find the next three terms.

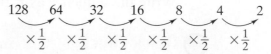

The common ratio is $\frac{1}{2}$. You can describe the sequence as *Start with 128 and multiply by $\frac{1}{2}$ repeatedly.* The next three terms are 8, 4, and 2.

✓ Quick Check

4. Find the common ratio in the sequence 0.1, 1, 10, 100, . . . Describe the sequence and find the next three terms.

✓ Check Your Understanding

1. **Vocabulary** Explain the difference between a common difference and a common ratio.

Find the common difference for each arithmetic sequence.

2. 0, 2, 4, 6, . . .

3. 0, −1, −2, −3, . . .

4. Write a sequence that has the common difference $\frac{1}{2}$.

Find the common ratio for each geometric sequence.

5. 100, 200, 400, 800, . . .

6. 1, 3, 9, 27, . . .

7. A sequence is described as *Start with 2 and multiply by 4 repeatedly.* Write the first three terms in the sequence.

For more exercises, see Extra Skills and Word Problems.

Find the next three terms in each sequence.

8. $7.5, 11.5, 15.5, \ldots$ **9.** $2\frac{3}{4}, 1\frac{3}{4}, \frac{3}{4}, \ldots$ **10.** $11, 18, 25, \ldots$

Find the first four terms of the sequence represented by each expression.

11. $5 + 2n$ **12.** $2 - 2n$ **13.** $-7n$ **14.** $5n + 6$

Write an algebraic expression for each sequence. Then find the 20th term.

15. $3, 6, 9, 12, \ldots$ **16.** $\frac{1}{2}, 1, 1\frac{1}{2}, 2, \ldots$ **17.** $-4, -8, -12, \ldots$

Describe each geometric sequence and find the next three terms.

18. $750, 75, 7.5, 0.75, \ldots$ **19.** $1, 4, 16, 64, \ldots$ **20.** $1, \frac{1}{2}, \frac{1}{4}, \frac{1}{8}, \ldots$

21. $3, 6, 12, 24, \ldots$ **22.** $0.12, 0.36, 1.08, \ldots$ **23.** $125, 25, 5, 1, \ldots$

GPS **24.** **Guided Problem Solving** Use the pattern below. Each side of each pentagon is one unit long. Write an algebraic expression to represent the perimeter of each figure in the pattern.

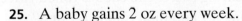

- Write a sequence based on the number of outer edges in each figure. The common difference d is .
- How many times do you add d to 5 to get the second term? How many times do you add d to 5 to get the third term?
- How many times should you add d to 5 to get the nth term?

Tell whether each situation produces an *arithmetic sequence*, a *geometric sequence*, or *neither*.

25. A baby gains 2 oz every week.

26. The time a person bikes each day varies between 30 and 45 minutes.

27. **Writing in Math** Will an arithmetic sequence that has a negative common difference always contain negative numbers? Explain.

Identify each sequence as *arithmetic, geometric,* or *neither.* Find the next three terms of the sequence.

28. $2, 2.3, 2.6, 2.9, \ldots$ **29.** $2, 5, 10, 17, \ldots$ **30.** $21, 15, 9, 3, \ldots$

31. $2, 6, 18, 54, \ldots$ **32.** $1.1, 1.01, 1.001, \ldots$ **33.** $2, 1, 0.5, 0.25, \ldots$

Many of the special effects in *The Incredible Shrinking Man* were created by using split screens and oversized props.

Use the following information for Exercises 34–36. In the 1957 movie *The Incredible Shrinking Man*, the main character mysteriously starts shrinking. Suppose his original height is 6 ft and he shrinks 3 in. every day.

34. How tall is the man at the end of one week?

35. How many days would it take for the man to shrink to half his original height?

36. What type of sequence is the series of numbers representing his height? Write a verbal description for the sequence.

Each table shows four terms of an arithmetic sequence. Write an expression for each sequence. Then find the 20th term in the sequence.

37.

Position, n	1	2	3	4
Term	12.5	9.5	6.5	3.5

38.

Position, n	1	2	4	8
Term	7	11	19	35

39. a. **Geometry** Find the volumes of cubes with side lengths of 2, 3, 4, and 5.
   b. These volumes form a sequence. How do you find each term?
   c. Write an expression for the sequence.

40. **Challenge** Evaluate the expression $400 \cdot \left(\frac{1}{2}\right)^{n-1}$ for $n = 1, 2, 3,$ and 4. Is the sequence formed *arithmetic, geometric,* or *neither*?

Test Prep and Mixed Review
Practice

Multiple Choice

41. Which expression represents the sequence $2, 2.3, 2.6, 2.9, \ldots$?
   - Ⓐ $2(0.3)^n$
   - Ⓑ $2 + 0.3n$
   - Ⓒ $2 + 0.3(n - 1)$
   - Ⓓ $0.3 + 2^{(n-1)}$

42. A number cube has faces labeled 1, 2, and 3, with each number appearing twice. The cube is rolled twice. What is the probability of rolling a 1 and then rolling a 1 or 3?
   - Ⓕ $\frac{1}{18}$
   - Ⓖ $\frac{1}{9}$
   - Ⓗ $\frac{2}{9}$
   - Ⓙ 1

43. The chess club deposits $245 in an account that earns 7.5% simple interest per year. How much interest will be earned in 3 years?
   - Ⓐ $18.38
   - Ⓑ $55.13
   - Ⓒ $61.25
   - Ⓓ $183.75

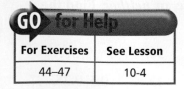

For Exercises	See Lesson
44–47	10-4

Find each probability. A bag contains 7 black paper clips, 2 blue paper clips, and 10 red paper clips. One paper clip is chosen at random and is not replaced. Then a second paper clip is chosen.

44. P(black, then red)

45. P(red, then blue)

46. P(blue, then blue)

47. P(blue, then black)

Exploring Sequences

You can use a graphing calculator to generate sequences.

EXAMPLE

1 Find the first five terms of this sequence: *Start with 100 and add 0.9 repeatedly.*

Step 1 Press 100 [ENTER] .

Step 2 Press [+] 0.9 [ENTER] .

Step 3 Press [ENTER] repeatedly.

The first five terms are 100, 100.9, 101.8, 102.7, and 103.6.

```
100
                 100
Ans+0.9
              100.9
              101.8
              102.7
              103.6
```

You can use the table feature on a graphing calculator to list the terms of a sequence.

EXAMPLE

2 Find the sequence of y-values for $y = 3x + 2$ and $x = 1, 2, 3, 4,$ and 5. Then write a verbal description for the sequence.

Step 1 Press [Y=] and enter the formula.

```
Plot1   Plot2   Plot3
\Y1 ▤ 3X+2
\Y2 =
\Y3 =
\Y4 =
```

Step 2 Use the TBLSET feature.

```
TABLE SETUP
  TblStart=1
  △Tbl=1
Indpnt: Auto Ask
Depend: Auto Ask
```

Step 3 Use the TABLE feature.

X	Y1	
1	5	
2	8	
3	11	
4	14	
5	17	
6	20	
7	23	
X=1		

The sequence is 5, 8, 11, 14, and 17. The verbal description is *Start with 5 and add 3 repeatedly.*

Exercises

Find the first five terms of each sequence.

1. Start with -3.5; add 0.7 repeatedly.

2. Start with 900; subtract 83 repeatedly.

For each formula, find the sequence of y values for $x = 1, 2, 3, 4,$ and 5. Then write a verbal description for the sequence.

3. $y = x + 4$

4. $y = 5 \cdot 3^x$

5. $y = -4x + 30$

6. $y = 2x + 4$

11-2 Relating Graphs to Events

Check Skills You'll Need

1. **Vocabulary Review** What type of data sets do *line graphs* best display?

Describe a set of data that is appropriate for each graph.

2. line plot

3. bar graph

 **for Help**
Lesson 9-9

nline active math

For: Graph Activity
Use: Interactive Textbook, 11-2

What You'll Learn

To interpret and sketch graphs that represent real-world situations

Why Learn This?

Newspapers, books, and magazines often use graphs to display data. A graph shows complex relationships between variables in a simple, visual way.

Drawing a graph makes it easier to see trends and changes in data. You can use a line graph to show how data such as speed or distance change over time.

EXAMPLE Interpreting a Graph

1 **Transportation** The line graph below shows the speed of a commuter train as it makes a morning run.

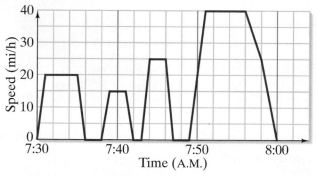

a. How long did the train's trip take?

Time is shown on the *x*-axis. The trip lasted 30 minutes, from 7:30 to 8:00.

b. Between which two times did the speed increase the most?

Between 7:49 and 7:51, the speed increased from 0 to 40 mi/h.

Quick Check

1. Use the graph in Example 1. What was the train's fastest speed?

When you draw a graph without actual data, you are making a sketch.

EXAMPLE **Sketching a Graph**

② **Fitness** Kim measured her pulse rate occasionally during a 45-min workout. The workout included a 10-min warmup period and a 10-min cool-down period. Sketch and label a graph showing her pulse rate during her workout.

The graph below shows that as Kim warmed up, her pulse rate increased. While she was in the middle of her workout, her pulse rate was high, but stable. The cool-down brought her pulse rate down again.

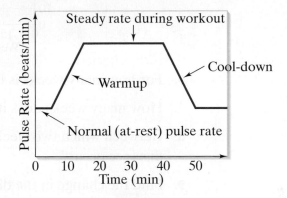

Test Prep Tip

After you sketch a graph, check to be sure it makes sense in relation to the problem.

✓ Quick Check

2. You walk to your friend's house. For the first 10 min, you walk from home to a park. For the next 5 min, you watch a ball game in the park. For the last 5 min, you run to your friend's house. Sketch and label a graph showing your distance from home during your trip.

✓ Check Your Understanding

Use the following information for Exercises 1–5. A student wants to sketch a graph that shows the distance of a bus from the transit center during the morning commute. The trip includes three stops where people get on and a highway where the bus travels at 50 mi/h.

1. **Vocabulary** Why should the student use a line graph?

2. What label should the student put on the horizontal scale? What label should be on the vertical scale?

3. When is the line on the graph parallel to the horizontal axis?

4. When is the line farthest away from the horizontal axis?

5. **Reasoning** Which section of the graph should be steeper, the section for the bus on the highway or the section for the bus in the city? Explain.

For more exercises, see Extra Skills and Word Problems.

For Exercises	See Examples
6–9	1
10–11	2

Swimming Use the graph below for Exercises 6–9.

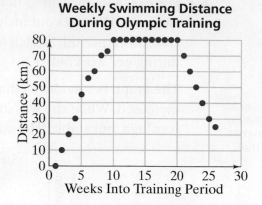

Weekly Swimming Distance During Olympic Training

6. For how many weeks is the swimming distance 80 km/wk?

7. How many weeks does it take to reach the peak training level?

8. Between which two weeks does the greatest increase in swimming distance occur?

9. Find the change in the distance from week 24 to week 25.

10. **Temperature** In general, air temperature rises during the day and drops during the night. Sketch and label a graph showing the temperature during a 24-hour period.

11. **Pets** Haley took her dog to the park. She walked slowly to the park and then sat with a friend. Haley and her dog ran home together. Sketch a graph showing their distance from home throughout the trip.

GPS

12. **Guided Problem Solving** Abel, Ben, and Cam left the computer lab at 2:30 P.M. Cam walked the fastest and Abel the slowest. At the same time, Dan and Erin were walking toward the lab. Erin was walking faster than Dan but slower than Cam. Sketch a graph of each student's distance from the computer lab over time.
   - For which students does distance from the lab increase with time?
   - Which student is represented by the steepest line in the graph?

Use the graph at the right for Exercises 13–16.

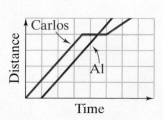

13. Who started the race later?

14. Who finished the race first?

15. Who stopped to tie his shoe?

16. **Writing in Math** Describe the outcome of the race.

GO Online

Homework Video Tutor

Visit: PHSchool.com
Web Code: ase-1102

17. **Chemistry** Water is poured at a constant rate into the container at the left. Sketch a graph of the water level as the container is filled.

18. A boat travels at low speed for 3 min while leaving a harbor. Then it travels at a constant cruising speed for 15 min. Finally, it travels at low speed for 5 min while entering another harbor. Sketch a graph that shows the boat's speed during the trip.

19. **Geometry** As the length of the side of a square increases, the area of the square increases. Sketch a graph that shows the area of the square as the side length changes.

20. **Challenge** You throw a ball into the air. It lands four seconds later. Sketch and label a graph showing the ball's height during this time.

Test Prep and Mixed Review

Practice

Multiple Choice

21. Maritza walks home from school, stopping at a friend's house on the way. Which graph could describe the total distance she walked?

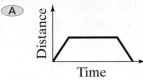
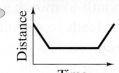
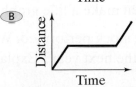
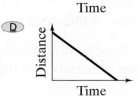

22. Triangle *ABC* was dilated to make triangle *DEF*. What is the scale factor used in the dilation?

F. $\frac{1}{2}$ H. $\frac{5}{4}$

G. $\frac{4}{5}$ J. 2

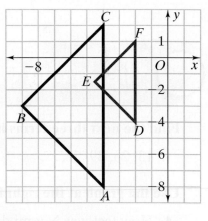

23. The algebraic expression $2 + 3n$ represents a sequence of numbers in which n is the number's position in the sequence. Which sequence does the expression represent?

A. 1, 5, 11, 29, 83, ... C. 3, 5, 11, 29, 83, ...
B. 3, 5, 7, 9, 11, ... D. 5, 8, 11, 14, 17, ...

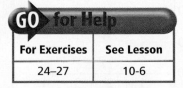

For Exercises	See Lesson
24–27	10-6

Simplify each expression.

24. $_9C_3$ 25. $_7C_5$ 26. $_5C_2$ 27. $_7C_3$

Line Graphs

One type of line graph is called a "stock chart." It records the value of a company's stock over time.

ACTIVITY

1. The line graph shows the value of a company's stock as it changed over one year.
   a. How much did the value increase in one year?
   b. Between which two consecutive months was the greatest increase?

2. Suppose you buy a share of stock in a company for $30. Toss a coin and roll a number cube to simulate the month-to-month gains and losses in the stock value. Heads represents a loss in the stock value and tails represents a gain. The number on the number cube determines the value of the gain or loss. Record the value of the stock for 12 months. Then make a line graph.

3. Write a paragraph summarizing how the stock performed. Would you buy more stock in the company for the next year? Explain.

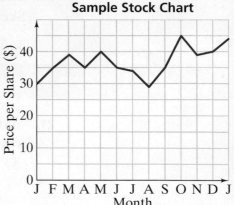

Sample Stock Chart

Checkpoint Quiz 1

Lessons 11-1 through 11-2

Find the next three terms in each sequence.

1. 13, 26, 39, 52, . . .

2. $\frac{3}{4}$, $1\frac{1}{2}$, $2\frac{1}{4}$, 3, . . .

3. −7, −14, −21, −28, . . .

Use the graph at the right for Exercises 4–8.

4. How fast was Naomi driving during the first hour of her trip?

5. How many miles did she travel at this speed?

6. When did Naomi's speed first increase?

7. To what speed did it increase?

8. What was Naomi's final speed at the end of the 4 hours?

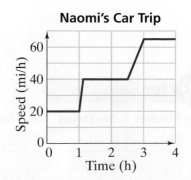

Naomi's Car Trip

11-3 Functions

What You'll Learn

To represent functions with equations, tables, and function notation

 **New Vocabulary** function, function rule

Why Learn This?

The time it takes you to get to your destination is a function of how fast you travel. Your speed affects how long the trip will take.

A **function** is a relationship that assigns exactly one output value to each input value. A **function rule** is an equation that describes a function.

To encourage recycling, some states require a five-cent deposit on drink containers. The total deposit you pay depends on how many containers you buy. You can describe this relationship with a function rule.

$$d = 0.05c \leftarrow \text{input variable } c = \text{number of containers}$$
$$\uparrow$$
output variable d = deposit

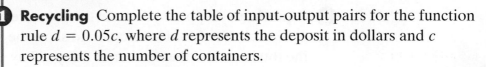

EXAMPLE — Representing Functions

1 **Recycling** Complete the table of input-output pairs for the function rule $d = 0.05c$, where d represents the deposit in dollars and c represents the number of containers.

Input *c* (number of containers)	Output *d* (dollars)	
6	■	← 0.05 × 6 = 0.30
12	■	← 0.05 × 12 = 0.60
24	■	← 0.05 × 24 = 1.20

✓ Quick Check

1. The deposit on a drink container is $.10 in the state of Michigan. Use the function rule $d = 0.1c$. Make a table of input-output pairs to show the total deposits on 5, 10, and 15 containers.

Function notation is a shorter way of writing word descriptions.

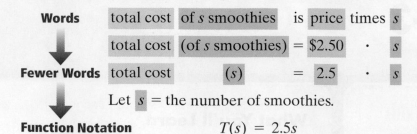

Words	total cost	of s smoothies		is	price	times	s
	total cost	(of s smoothies)	=	$2.50	·	s
Fewer Words	total cost	(s)	=	2.5	·	s

Let s = the number of smoothies.

Function Notation $\qquad T(s) = 2.5s$

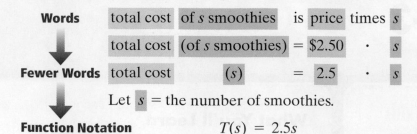

Vocabulary Tip

Read $T(s)$ as "T of s."

EXAMPLE Evaluating a Function Rule

2 Gridded Response A smoothie costs $2.50. Use the function rule $T(s) = 2.5s$. Find the total cost of three smoothies by finding the output value $T(3)$.

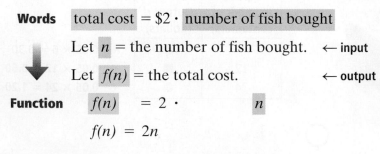

$T(s) = 2.5s$ ← **Write the function rule.**

$T(3) = 2.5(3)$ ← **Substitute the input value for s.**

$\quad\ = 7.5$ ← **Simplify.**

The total cost of three smoothies is $7.50.

Test Prep Tip

To evaluate a function rule, substitute the input value for the variable inside the parentheses.

✓ Quick Check

2. Use the function rule $f(x) = -4x + 12$.
   Find $f(-7)$ and $f(3)$.

$T(3)$ means "total cost of 3 smoothies." Notice that $T(3)$ does *not* mean the product of T and 3. It means the output of the function when the input is 3.

EXAMPLE Using Function Notation

3 Aquariums Suppose you go to the pet store and buy several fish at $2 each. Use function notation to show the relationship between the total cost and the number of fish you buy. Identify the variables you use.

Words	total cost	=	$2 ·	number of fish bought

Let n = the number of fish bought.   ← **input**

Let $f(n)$ = the total cost.   ← **output**

Function	$f(n)$	=	2 ·		n

$f(n) = 2n$

✓ Quick Check

3. Use the function in Example 3. Find $f(6)$. What does $f(6)$ represent?

✓ Check Your Understanding

1. **Vocabulary** How are a function and a function rule related?

2. If $f(n)$ is a function, can $f(2) = 4$ and $f(2) = 5$ both be true? Explain.

3. **Number Sense** If the input value is negative, is the output value of $f(z) = -4z + 12$ always positive or always negative? Explain.

4. Complete the input-output table for the function $f(n) = 3 + n$.

Input n	0	1	2	3
Output $f(n)$	3	■	■	■

Homework Exercises

For more exercises, see Extra Skills and Word Problems.

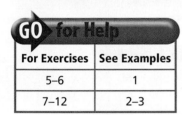

GO for Help

For Exercises	See Examples
5–6	1
7–12	2–3

5. **Hockey** Copy and complete the table of input-output pairs for the function rule $t = \frac{n}{11}$. The variable t represents the number of teams formed in a hockey league. The variable n represents the number of people signed up for the league.

Input n (number of people)	Output t (number of teams)
44	■
132	■
165	■

6. The function rule $p = 1.5 + 2m$ represents the taxi fare p in dollars for a ride that is m miles long. Make a table of input-output pairs to show the fare for rides of 2, 6, and 13 miles.

Use the function rule $f(x) = 2x + 3$. Find each output.

7. $f(0)$ 8. $f(-2)$ 9. $f(2)$ 10. $f(10)$ 11. $f(-16.7)$

12. **Energy** Each hour a stereo is on, it uses 0.4 kilowatt-hours of energy. Complete the function rule $E(h) = \underline{\ ?\ }$ to describe the relationship between the total energy $E(h)$ used by the stereo and the number of hours h the stereo is on.

13. **Guided Problem Solving** Paint brushes cost $1.79 each. Use function notation to show the total cost as a function of the number of paint brushes you buy. Use the rule to find the cost of 27 brushes.
    - Let c represent the total cost and p the number of paint brushes.
    - Find c when $p = 27$.

Reasoning Tell whether the data in each table are values of a function.

14.

Input	2	3	4	5	6
Output	5	5	5	5	5

15.

Input	1	2	2	3	3
Output	1	3	6	9	12

GO Online

Homework Video Tutor

Visit: PHSchool.com
Web Code: ase-1103

16. **Water Use** The function $w = 40\ell$ describes the number w of gallons of water used to wash ℓ loads of laundry in a washing machine.
    a. Find the value of w when $\ell = 6$. What does this represent?
    b. The *domain* of a function is all possible input values. The *range* of a function is all possible output values. Which variable, w or ℓ, represents the domain in part (a)? Explain.
    c. The input variable is also called the *independent variable.* The output variable is the *dependent variable,* because it depends on the input variable. Which is the dependent variable, w or ℓ?

17. **Writing in Math** Find several solutions of the equation $y = 3x - 2$. Explain how these solutions are related to input-output pairs for the function $f(x) = 3x - 2$. Write each solution using function notation.

Copy and complete the table of input-output pairs for each function.

18. $y = 4x$

Input x	Output y
5	■
7	■
9	■
11	■

19. $d = 50t$

Input t	Output d
1	■
2	■
3	■
■	200

20. Fruit smoothies cost $1.50 each plus $.50 for each fruit mixed into the smoothie. Use function notation to find the cost of a smoothie with 4 different fruits mixed in.

21. **Challenge** For each function, find $f(1), f(2), f(3)$, and $f(4)$. Identify each sequence as *arithmetic, geometric,* or *neither.*
    a. $f(n) = 100 - 4n$
    b. $f(n) = n(4 - n)$

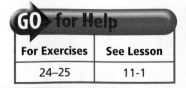

Test Prep and Mixed Review

Practice

Gridded Response

22. An ad in the newspaper costs $52 plus $2.50 for each line of the ad. What is the cost in dollars of placing a 7-line ad?

23. Two similar cylinders are shown. The volume of the larger cylinder is 3,375 cubic centimeters. What is the volume of the smaller cylinder in cubic centimeters?

GO for Help

For Exercises	See Lesson
24–25	11-1

Write an algebraic expression for each sequence and find the next three terms.

24. 4, 8, 12, 16, . . .

25. −1, −2, −3, −4, . . .

Rate of Change

You know that in 1 yard, there are 3 feet. In 2 yards, there are 6 feet.

The table at the right shows that the number of feet changes by 3 as the number of yards changes by 1. You can represent this relationship with a ratio:

$$\frac{\text{change in number of feet}}{\text{change in number of yards}} = \frac{3}{1}$$

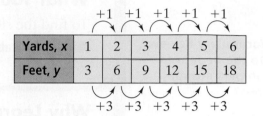

This comparison of two quantities that are changing is called a **rate of change.** As the value of one quantity changes, the value of the other quantity also changes. The rate of change of feet to yards is $\frac{3}{1}$, or 3.

You can find the rate of change from a graph such as the one at the right. Notice that rate of change is the ratio of the vertical change to the horizontal change.

$$\text{rate of change} = \frac{\text{vertical change}}{\text{horizontal change}} = \frac{3}{1}$$

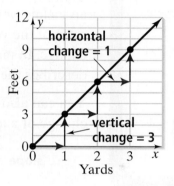

Exercises

Find the rate of change from each table or graph. Explain what the rate of change means in each problem situation.

1.
Age (yr)	8	9	10	11	12
Height (in.)	51	53	55	57	59

2.
Time (h)	1	2	3	4	5
Rainfall (mm)	3	6	9	12	15

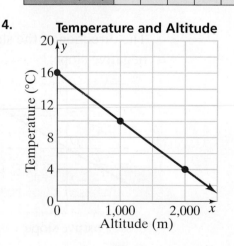

11-4 Understanding Slope

Vocabulary Tip

A *ratio* is the comparison of two quantities by division.

What You'll Learn

To find the slope of a line from a graph or table

🔊 **New Vocabulary** slope, slope of a line

Why Learn This?

You can use slope to describe the steepness of an incline or hill. The steepness of a ramp is the ratio of the vertical change to the horizontal change. In math, slope is a number that describes the steepness of a line.

You can also use slope to describe rate of change of a quantity.

$$\text{slope} = \frac{\text{vertical change}}{\text{horizontal change}} \quad \begin{array}{l} \leftarrow \text{rise} \\ \leftarrow \text{run} \end{array}$$

Slope describes the steepness of lines in the coordinate plane. You can find the slope of a line by subtracting the coordinates of any two points on the line.

KEY CONCEPTS **Slope of a Line**

$$\text{slope of a line} = \frac{\text{change in } y\text{-coordinates}}{\text{change in } x\text{-coordinates}} \quad \begin{array}{l} \leftarrow \text{rise} \\ \leftarrow \text{run} \end{array}$$

The direction of the slant of a line indicates a positive or a negative slope.

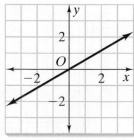

Positive slope

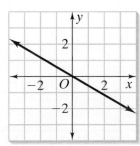

Negative slope

When you find the slope of a line, the first *y*-coordinate you use for the rise must belong to the same point as the first *x*-coordinate you use for the run.

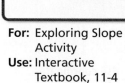

For: Exploring Slope
Activity
Use: Interactive
Textbook, 11-4

EXAMPLE Finding the Slope of a Line

1. Find the slope of the line in the graph below.

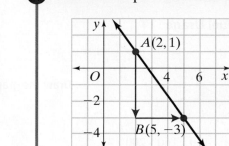

slope = $\dfrac{\text{change in } y\text{-coordinates}}{\text{change in } x\text{-coordinates}}$

$= \dfrac{-3 - 1}{5 - 2}$ ← **Subtract coordinates of A from coordinates of B.**

$= \dfrac{-4}{3}$ or $-\dfrac{4}{3}$ ← **Simplify.**

✓ Quick Check

1. Find the slope of each line.

   a.
   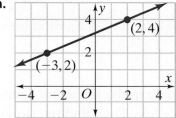

   b.

Some lines have slopes that are neither positive nor negative.

EXAMPLE Slopes of Horizontal and Vertical Lines

Vocabulary Tip

Do not confuse the terms *zero* and *undefined*. The slope of a horizontal line is zero. The slope of a vertical line is undefined.

2. Find the slope of each line. State whether the slope is zero or undefined.

   a.
   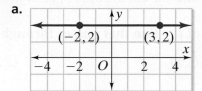

   b.
   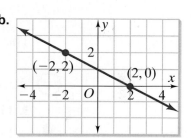

slope = $\dfrac{2 - 2}{3 - (-2)} = \dfrac{0}{5} = 0$

The slope of a horizontal line is zero.

slope = $\dfrac{1 - (-2)}{-5 - (-5)} = \dfrac{3}{0}$

Division by zero is undefined. So, the slope of a vertical line is undefined.

✓ Quick Check

2. Find the slope of a line through the points $(3, 1)$ and $(3, -2)$. State whether the slope is zero or undefined.

When you graph some data, all the points lie on a line. For such data, you can find slope, or rate of change, using a table.

EXAMPLE **Finding Slope From a Table**

Miles Traveled	Fuel Used (gallons)
80	4
120	6
160	8
200	10

3 Graph the fuel-usage data at the left. Connect the points with a line. Then find the rate of change.

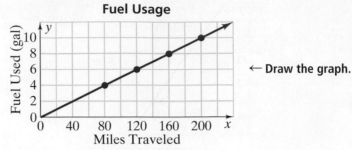

← Draw the graph.

$$\text{rate of change} = \text{slope} = \frac{\text{change in } y}{\text{change in } x} = \frac{10 - 4}{200 - 80}$$ ← Use coordinates of two points.

$$= \frac{6}{120} = \frac{1}{20}$$ ← Subtract and simplify.

The amount of fuel used is 1 gallon for every 20 miles traveled.

✓ Quick Check

3. Graph the data in the table and connect the points with a line. Then find the slope.

x	−1	0	1	2
y	2	0	−2	−4

✓ Check Your Understanding

1. **Vocabulary** The slope of a line is the rise over the __?__.

2. Draw one line for each slope: 0, undefined, +1, and −1.

Find the slope of the line that passes through each pair of points.

3. (0, 3) and (6, 1)
4. (2, 2) and (6, −1)

Homework Exercises

For more exercises, see Extra Skills and Word Problems.

GO for Help

For Exercises	See Examples
5–7	1–2
8–9	3

Find the slope of each line.

5.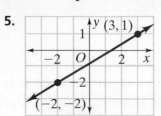

6.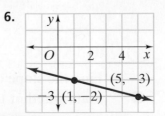

7.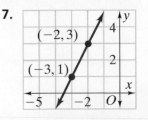

Graph the data in each table and connect the points with a line. Then find the slope of the line.

8.

x	4	5	6	7
y	−2	0	2	4

9.

x	−2	−1	0	1
y	3	2	1	0

GPS

10. **Guided Problem Solving** The graph at the right shows the amount of rice a store has in stock at different times. Use the slope to describe how the amount of rice changes over time.
   - How is the rate of change related to the slope?

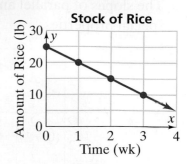

Stock of Rice

11. **Error Analysis** Your classmate said that the slope of a line through (1, 3) and (7, 5) is 3. What error did your classmate make?

12. Which roof is steeper: a roof with a rise of 12 and a run of 7 or a roof with a rise of 8 and a run of 4?

13. **Writing in Math** Point $A(-2, 3)$ lies on a line with a slope of 2. Describe how to find two points on the line on either side of A.

14. **Challenge** Determine whether this statement is *true* or *false*. If the statement is false, rewrite it to make it true. If two lines have the same slope, their equations describe the same line.

GO Online
Homework Video Tutor
Visit: PHSchool.com
Web Code: ase-1104

Test Prep and Mixed Review

Practice

Multiple Choice

15. Chloe wants to graph the distance traveled on a bike ride versus time. Which type of graph should she use?
   - (A) Line graph
   - (B) Circle graph
   - (C) Scatter plot
   - (D) Bar graph

16. At the end of March, Alvin's bank account balance was $54. He deposited $75 a month in April, May, June, and July. He made a car payment of $94 in each of those months. What was his bank balance at the end of July?
   - (F) −$22
   - (G) −$12
   - (H) $76
   - (J) $130

17. A farmer has 35 square miles of land in the shape of a square. Which is closest to the measure of each side of the farm?
   - (A) 6 mi
   - (B) 9 mi
   - (C) 18 mi
   - (D) 36 mi

GO for Help

For Exercises	See Lesson
18–21	3-4

Graph each point on the same coordinate plane.

18. $A(6, -4)$ 19. $B(0, -3)$ 20. $C(-2, 5)$ 21. $D(-8, -1)$

Parallel and Perpendicular Lines

The slopes of parallel and perpendicular lines have special properties.

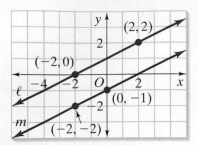

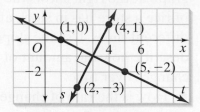

slope of $\ell = \dfrac{2-0}{2-(-2)} = \dfrac{2}{4} = \dfrac{1}{2}$

slope of $m = \dfrac{-1-(-2)}{0-(-2)} = \dfrac{1}{2}$

slope of $s = \dfrac{1-(-3)}{4-2} = \dfrac{4}{2} = \dfrac{2}{1}$

slope of $t = \dfrac{-2-0}{5-1} = \dfrac{-2}{4} = -\dfrac{1}{2}$

product of slopes $= \dfrac{2}{1} \cdot \left(-\dfrac{1}{2}\right) = -1$

Parallel lines have the same slope.

The product of the slopes of perpendicular lines is -1.

EXAMPLE

Line AB has slope $\frac{1}{3}$. Find the slope of a line that is parallel to $\overleftrightarrow{AB}$ and the slope of a line that is perpendicular to $\overleftrightarrow{AB}$.

A line parallel to $\overleftrightarrow{AB}$ has a slope of $\frac{1}{3}$.

Let m represent the slope of a line perpendicular to $\overleftrightarrow{AB}$.

$\dfrac{1}{3} \cdot m = -1$ ← The product of the slopes of perpendicular lines is -1.

$m = -3$ ← Multiply each side by 3.

A line perpendicular to $\overleftrightarrow{AB}$ has a slope of -3.

Exercises

Are lines with the given slopes *parallel*, *perpendicular*, or *neither*?

1. $\dfrac{2}{3}, -\dfrac{3}{2}$

2. $5, -5$

3. $\dfrac{3}{4}, \dfrac{4}{3}$

4. $\dfrac{1}{12}, -12$

5. $\dfrac{3}{9}, \dfrac{1}{3}$

6. $\dfrac{2}{7}, \dfrac{12}{42}$

Find the slope of a line parallel to $\overleftrightarrow{PQ}$ and a line perpendicular to $\overleftrightarrow{PQ}$.

7. $P(1, 2), Q(3, 4)$

8. $P(-5, 1), Q(-1, 2)$

9. $P(3, -2), Q(-2, 1)$

Graphing Equations

You can use a graphing calculator to graph equations and to find solutions.

EXAMPLE

Graph $y = \frac{1}{2}x + 1$. Make a table of solutions for values of x from -3 to 3.

Step 1 Press **Y=**
Enter $\frac{1}{2}x + 1$.

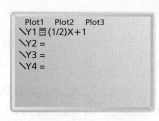

Step 2 Press **ZOOM** 6 to graph your equation with the standard viewing window.

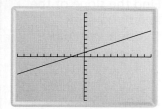

Step 3 Use the TBLSET feature. Set TblStart = -3 and $\triangle$Tbl = 1. The x-values start at -3 and increase by increments of 1.

TABLE SETUP
TblStart = -3
$\triangle$Tbl = 1
Indpnt: Auto Ask
Depend: Auto Ask

Step 4 Use the TABLE feature to see solutions.

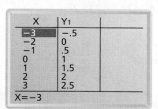

Step 5 Sketch the graph and copy the table of solutions.

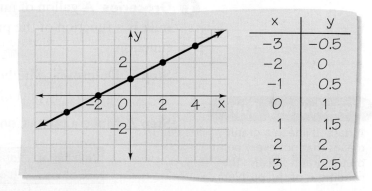

Exercises

Graph each equation using a graphing calculator. Sketch the graph and make a table of solutions for values of x from -3 to 3.

1. $y = 2x - 3$ **2.** $y = 2x + 3$ **3.** $y = -\frac{2}{3}x - 2$ **4.** $y = 5x - 2$

5. Compare the graphs of Exercises 1 and 2. What do you notice?

6. Explain how the graphs of Exercises 3 and 4 are different.

Graphing Linear Functions

✓ Check Skills You'll Need

1. **Vocabulary Review** Explain how to find the *slope* of a line.

Find the slope of the line that passes through each pair of points.

2. (2, 4), (−5, 10)

3. (0, 0), (6, 0)

4. (2, 1), (1, 2)

 **for Help**
Lesson 11-4

What You'll Learn

To use tables and equations to graph linear functions

🔊 **New Vocabulary** discrete data, continuous data, *y*-intercept, slope-intercept form, linear function

Why Learn This?

Graphs can help you quickly see the relationship between two sets of data, such as the price of milk and the total cost of milk for your family.

Different types of data are graphed differently. **Discrete data** are data that involve a count of items, such as numbers of people or cars. For discrete data, plot the data points and connect them with a dashed line.

Continuous data are data where numbers between any two data values have meaning. Examples of continuous data include measurements of height, length, or weight. Use a solid line to indicate continuous data.

EXAMPLE Graphing Discrete Data

1 **Groceries** A gallon of milk costs $2.59. The total cost of *g* gallons of milk is a function of the price of one gallon. Make a table and graph the function.

Step 1 Determine whether the data are discrete or continuous. You cannot buy part of a gallon container, so the data are discrete.

Vocabulary Tip

A dashed line in a graph means that not every point on the graph satisfies the conditions of the problem.

Step 2 Make a table. Connect the points with a dashed line.

Number of Gallons	Total Cost (dollars)
1	$2.59
2	$5.18
3	$7.77
4	$10.36

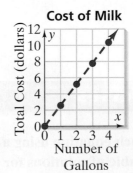

Cost of Milk

✓ Quick Check

1. **Tickets** The function $c = 15t$ represents the cost (in dollars) of *t* adult tickets to a museum. Make a table and graph the function.

EXAMPLE **Graphing Continuous Data**

2️⃣ **Fitness** During one hour of walking, you burn about 257 Calories. The total number of Calories burned is a function of the number of hours walked. Make a table and graph the function.

You can walk for part of an hour, so the data are continuous. Plot the data and connect the data points with a solid line.

Time (hours)	Number of Calories
1	257
2	514
3	771

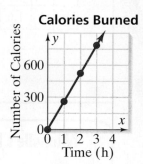

Calories Burned

✓ Quick Check

2. **Sky Diving** The function $h = 4{,}000 - 600m$ gives the height h of a sky diver in feet after she has been falling for m minutes. Make a table and graph the function.

The **y-intercept** is the point where the graph crosses the y-axis.

$$y = -\frac{3}{4}x + 5$$

↑ slope   ↑ y-intercept

Below is the graph of $y = -\frac{3}{4}x + 5$.

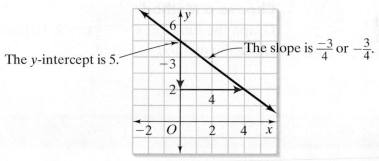

The y-intercept is 5.

The slope is $\frac{-3}{4}$ or $-\frac{3}{4}$.

GO ●nline

Video Tutor Help
Visit: PHSchool.com
Web Code: ase-0775

Notice that the slope and y-intercept may be part of the equation of a line.

An equation written in the form $y = mx + b$ is in **slope-intercept form.** The graph is a line with slope m and y-intercept b.

A **linear function** is a function with points that lie on a line. You can write a linear function in the form $f(x) = mx + b$, or $y = mx + b$. Then you can use the slope and y-intercept to graph the function.

More Than One Way

Graph the function $y = \frac{3}{5}x + 1$.

Kevin's Method

First I will make a table. Then I will graph the points.

x	0	1	2	3	4	5
y	1	1.6	2.2	2.8	3.4	4

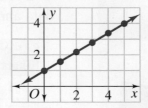

Michelle's Method

I can use slope-intercept form to graph the equation. The y-intercept is 1 and the slope is $\frac{3}{5}$.

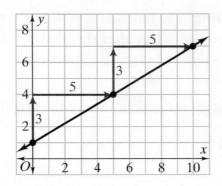

Choose a Method

Graph the function $y = -\frac{2}{3}x - 2$. Explain why you chose the method you used.

Check Your Understanding

1. **Vocabulary** Explain the difference between discrete data and continuous data.

2. Does the graph at the left show discrete data or continuous data?

For each function, find the slope and the y-intercept.

3. $y = 4x - 1$

4. $y = x + 4$

5. Make a table for the function $y = 3x$. Then graph the function.

For more exercises, see Extra Skills and Word Problems.

GO for Help

For Exercises	See Examples
6–8	1–2

Determine whether the data for each function are *discrete* or *continuous*. Then make a table and graph for the function.

6. The function $d = 40 - 15x$ represents the amount of money d (in dollars) you have left after buying x CDs.

7. **Scuba Diving** The deeper a scuba diver descends, the more pressure the diver feels. The function $p = 1 + 0.03x$ represents the approximate pressure p (in atmospheres) at x feet below sea level.

8. The function $y = 1.8x + 32$ represents the equivalent temperature y in degrees Fahrenheit for a temperature of x degrees Celsius.

GPS

9. **Guided Problem Solving** A woman makes necklaces and sells them at a jewelry show. She pays $10.00 to have a table at the show and makes $20.25 for each necklace she sells. Write a function for the money she earns and graph the function.
   - What is the input variable? What is the output variable?
   - What is the slope of this function? What is the y-intercept?

Graph each linear function.

10. $y = -2x + 5$

11. $y = \frac{2}{3}x - 1$

12. $y = -\frac{3}{5}x - 2$

13. $y = 3x - 7$

14. $y = -6x - 1$

15. $y = x + 4$

16. **Writing in Math** Describe a relation in your daily life that is a function. Explain why it is a function and define the input and the output.

17. **Science** The height of a burning candle depends on how long the candle has been burning. For one type of candle, the function $h = 8 - \frac{1}{2}t$ gives the candle's height h (in centimeters) as a function of the time t the candle has burned (in hours).
   a. Graph the function.
   b. What was the original height of the candle?
   c. What is the greatest amount of time the candle can burn?

18. **Nutrition** The label at the right shows the nutrition facts for a package of crackers. Find how many Calories are in one cracker. The number of Calories consumed is a function of the number of crackers eaten. Make a table and a graph for the function.

Nutrition Facts	
Serving Size: 8 crackers (31g)	
Servings Per Container: about 15	
Amount Per Serving	
Calories 140	Calories from Fat 35
	% Daily Value
Total Fat 4g	6%
Saturated Fat 1g	5%
Monounsaturated Fat 1.5g	

GO Online

Homework Video Tutor
Visit: PHSchool.com
Web Code: ase-1105

19. Graph the functions $y = 2x + 1$ and $y = 2x - 1$ on the same coordinate grid. What do you notice about the two lines?

20. Internet Company A charges a fee of $5.00 per month plus $2.00 for each hour of Internet use. Company B charges $10.00 per month plus $1.00 for each hour of Internet use. Write and graph two functions to show how the total cost each month depends on the hours of usage for each company.

21. Challenge Suppose gasoline costs $2.30 per gallon at one gas station and $2.35 at another. Write and graph two functions showing how the cost to fill a car's gas tank depends on the number of gallons of gas it needs. For how many gallons of gasoline is there a price difference of $0.30 between the two functions?

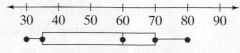

Test Prep and Mixed Review

Practice

Multiple Choice

22. Which of the following is a graph of the equation $y = 2x - 1$?

Ⓐ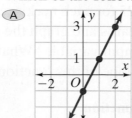

Ⓒ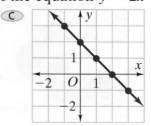

Ⓑ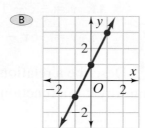

Ⓓ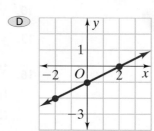

23. A rectangular room that measures 72 inches by 90 inches is to be finished in square tiles. What is the largest size of square tile that can be used without any being cut?

Ⓕ 6 in.^{2} Ⓖ 9 in.^{2} Ⓗ 18 in.^{2} Ⓙ 36 in.^{2}

24. A spinner is spun 50 times. It lands on red 8 times, yellow 12 times, green 20 times, and blue 10 times. Based on the results, what is the experimental probability of landing on green or yellow?

Ⓐ $\frac{6}{25}$ Ⓑ $\frac{2}{5}$ Ⓒ $\frac{3}{5}$ Ⓓ $\frac{16}{25}$

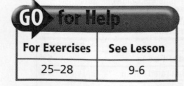

For Exercises	See Lesson
25–28	9-6

Use the box-and-whisker plot below to find each value.

25. the median

26. the lower quartile

27. the upper quartile

28. the least value

Use the function rule $f(x) = -3x - 2$. Find each output.

1. $f(-1)$ **2.** $f(5)$ **3.** $f(0)$ **4.** $f(-10)$

5. Suppose potatoes cost \$.99 per pound. Complete the function rule $C(p) = \underline{\ ?\ }$ to describe the relationship between the total cost $C(p)$ and the number of pounds of potatoes p you buy.

Find the slope of each line in the graph at the right.

6. line a **7.** line b **8.** line c

9. Number Sense Explain which hill is steeper: a hill with a rise of 5 and a run of 3 or a hill with a rise of 3 and a run of 5.

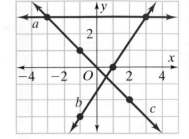

10. Your cousin works at a bookstore and earns \$7 per hour. Make a table to show your cousin's earnings as a function of the hours she works. Graph the data.

MATH GAMES

What's My Rule?

How To Play

- Player 1 writes a function rule on paper. The other players are not allowed to see this function.
- Make a table like the one at the right. Player 1 writes an input-output pair in the table for the other players to see.

What's My Rule?

Input	Output
▦	▦
▦	▦
▦	▦
▦	▦

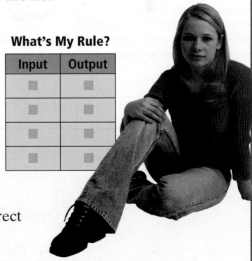

- In turn, each of the other players gives an input and guesses the corresponding output.
- If a player guesses the output correctly, the player gets a point and is allowed to guess the function.
- If the player guesses the function correctly, the player gets another point and starts a new round of play.
- Player 1 gets one point each time a player makes an incorrect guess at the function.
- The player with the most points wins.

11-6 Writing Rules for Linear Functions

Check Skills You'll Need

1. **Vocabulary Review** What is *slope-intercept form*?

For each function, find the slope and *y*-intercept.

2. $y = 3x - 2$

3. $y = x + 5$

4. $y = 8x$

 GO for Help
Lesson 11-5

What You'll Learn

To write function rules from words, tables, and graphs

Why Learn This?

Businesses have toll-free numbers to encourage customers to use their services. A business owner can calculate the cost of a toll-free number if she can write a rule for the function.

Just as you can translate words to an equation, you can also translate words to a function rule. When writing a function rule, be sure to identify the input and the output.

EXAMPLE Writing a Function Rule From Words

1 Multiple Choice Suppose the rate for a toll-free telephone number is $2.95 per month plus $.10 per minute of use. Which function rule correctly represents the monthly cost?

Ⓐ $y = 0.1 + 2.95x$ Ⓒ $y = 2.95 - 0.1x$

Ⓑ $y = 2.95 + 0.1x$ Ⓓ $y = 0.1x - 2.95$

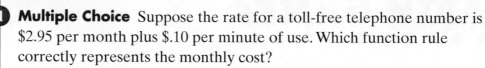

Words   monthly cost = $2.95 plus $0.10 times number of minutes

Let x = the number of minutes.   ← input

Let y = the monthly cost.   ← output

Function y = 2.95 + 0.1   · x

$y = 2.95 + 0.1x$

The function rule $y = 2.95 + 0.1x$ represents the monthly cost for x minutes of use. The correct answer is choice B.

Quick Check

1. A school orchestra is buying music stands. The group has $298 in its treasury. Each stand costs $42. Write a function rule to show how the balance in the treasury depends on the number of stands bought.

Test Prep Tip

The form of each of these answer choices is similar to slope-intercept form. In order to identify the correct answer easily, write your answer in a similar form.

If the ratios of the changes in inputs and outputs of a function are the same for all values, then the function is linear.

EXAMPLE Writing a Rule From a Table

2 Do the values in the table below represent a linear function? If so, write a function rule.

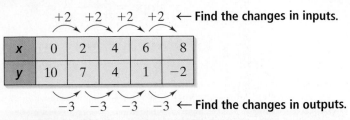

+2 +2 +2 +2 ← Find the changes in inputs.

x	0	2	4	6	8
y	10	7	4	1	−2

−3 −3 −3 −3 ← Find the changes in outputs.

$\dfrac{\text{change in } y}{\text{change in } x}$ ⟶ $\dfrac{-3}{2}$ $\dfrac{-3}{2}$ $\dfrac{-3}{2}$ $\dfrac{-3}{2}$ ← Compare the changes as ratios.

Since each ratio is the same, the function is linear. The slope is $-\frac{3}{2}$.

The point $(0, 10)$ lies on the graph of the function. So the y-intercept is 10. Use slope-intercept form to write a function rule.

$$y = -\frac{3}{2}x + 10 \quad \leftarrow \text{Substitute } -\frac{3}{2} \text{ for } m \text{ and 10 for } b.$$

GO for Help

For help with slope-intercept form, go to Lesson 11-5, Example 2.

✓ Quick Check

2. Do the values in the table represent a linear function? If so, write a function rule.

x	0	1	2	3
y	2	4	7	8

The slope of a line can be expressed by the equation $\frac{y - y_1}{x - x_1} = m$. You can rewrite this equation as $y - y_1 = m(x - x_1)$. If you know two points on a line, or the slope and any point, you can find the equation of the line.

EXAMPLE Writing an Equation From a Graph

3 Find the equation of the line in the graph at the left.

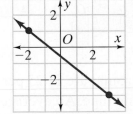

Step 1 Find the slope. Use the points $(3, -3)$ and $(-2, 1)$.

slope $= \dfrac{1 - (-3)}{-2 - 3} = -\dfrac{4}{5}$

Step 2 Use the slope and one point to write an equation.

$y - y_1 = m(x - x_1)$

$y - (-3) = -\dfrac{4}{5}(x - 3)$ ← Use $(3, -3)$ for (x_1, y_1).

$y + 3 = -\dfrac{4}{5}(x - 3)$

Using the point $(3, -3)$, the equation of the line is $y + 3 = -\frac{4}{5}(x - 3)$.

✓ Quick Check

3. Use the point $(-2, 1)$ to write an equation for the line in Example 3.

1. **Vocabulary** How is slope-intercept form related to a linear function rule?

2. Use the graph at the right to find the slope and complete the equation for the line.

   a. slope $= \dfrac{y_2 - y_1}{x_2 - x_1} = \blacksquare$

   b. $y - y_1 = m(x - x_1)$
   $y - \blacksquare = \blacksquare(x - \blacksquare)$

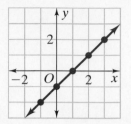

Homework Exercises

For more exercises, see Extra Skills and Word Problems.

GO for Help

For Exercises	See Examples
3–4	1
5–6	2
7–8	3

3. **Sales** Mrs. Savin receives a weekly base salary of $500, plus a commission of $1,200 on each car that she sells. Write a function rule relating her total weekly pay p to cars she sells c.

4. **Ecology** Water flows over a dam at a rate of 500 gallons per minute. Write a function rule relating the amount of water a that flows over the dam to the number of minutes m that have passed.

Do the values in each table represent a linear function? If so, write a function rule.

5.
x	−2	−1	0	1
y	8	5	2	−1

6.
x	0	1	2	3
y	8	6	4	2

Use the slope and two points to write an equation for each line.

7.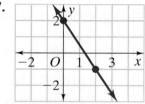

8.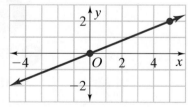

9. **Guided Problem Solving** Prices at a laundromat are $1.25 per load of wash and $.75 per 20 minutes of drying time. An average load takes 1 hour to dry. Write a function rule to describe the total cost of washing and drying as a function of the number of loads.
   - What is the cost for one load of laundry to be washed and dried?
   - Let n be the number of loads. Let C be the cost of n loads.

GO Online
Homework Video Tutor
Visit: PHSchool.com
Web Code: ase-1106

10. **Writing in Math** Explain how to determine whether a function is linear by analyzing an input-output table.

Caricatures are pictures of people in which certain features are exaggerated for comic effect.

11. **Art** At a fair, an artist draws caricatures. He pays the fair $30 for space to set up his table, and $2 for each drawing that he sells.
   a. Write a function rule to represent the artist's total payment to the fair as a function of the number of drawings he sells.
   b. **Reasoning** What input is paired with the output $54? What does this input represent? Express the input-output pair in the form $f(\blacksquare) = \blacksquare$.

Find the equation of each line with the given slope and point.

12. slope $= \frac{3}{4}$; $(2, -5)$

13. slope $= -\frac{1}{2}$; $(4, -1)$

14. Write the equation in Exercise 13 in slope-intercept form.

15. **Challenge** A water theme park charges a $15 entrance fee and $1 per ride. The park also offers a plan with a $30 admission fee and a charge of $.50 per ride. Write and graph a function rule to show the total cost C for r rides for each plan. Which is the best plan for someone who intends to go on many rides? Explain.

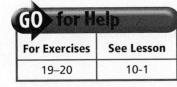

Test Prep and Mixed Review   Practice

Multiple Choice

16. The graph shows the relationship between hours worked h and Gomez Plumbing's total bill b, when materials cost $100. Which of the following is the equation represented by the graph?
   Ⓐ $h = 50b + 100$
   Ⓑ $h = 100b + 50$
   Ⓒ $b = 100h + 50$
   Ⓓ $b = 50h + 100$

Plumbing Costs

17. A piece of siding is in the shape of a trapezoid that is 6 inches high with bases 18 inches long and 24 inches long. Find the area of the trapezoid.
   Ⓕ 54 in.^{2} Ⓖ 63 in.^{2} Ⓗ 126 in.^{2} Ⓙ 252 in.^{2}

18. Which group of numbers lists the integers in order from least to greatest?
   Ⓐ $-5, 4, -2, 1$
   Ⓑ $-5, -2, 1, 4$
   Ⓒ $1, -2, 4, -5$
   Ⓓ $1, 4, -2, -5$

For Exercises	See Lesson
19–20	10-1

Decide whether each probability is experimental or theoretical.

19. A six-sided number cube is tossed 250 times. P(rolling a 4) is $\frac{37}{250}$.

20. A bag contains 8 pens and 18 pencils. P(choosing a pen) is $\frac{4}{13}$.

Linear Functions

For each rental plan, represent the relationship between the number of miles (from 20 to 45) and the cost. Use a linear function, a table of ordered pairs, and a graph (using the same coordinate grid). What conclusions can you draw about these plans?

Car Rental Plan 1
$15 per day
plus
$.25 per mile

Car Rental Plan 2
$8 per day
plus
$.45 per mile

What You Might Think

> What do I know? What do I want to find out?

> How can I write a function rule for each plan?

> How can I make a table and graph?

> What conclusions can be stated?

What You Might Write

Plan 1 costs $15 plus $.25 per mile. Plan 2 costs $8 plus $.45 per mile. I want to compare the two plans using function rules, tables, and graphs.

Let m = the number of miles driven. Let C = the cost of the rental in dollars.

Plan 1: $C_1 = \$.25m + 15$

Plan 2: $C_2 = \$.45m + 8$

I can use the function rule to get data points for the table. Then I can graph those points.

m	C_1	C_2
20	20	17
30	22.5	21.5
35	23.75	23.75
45	26.25	28.25

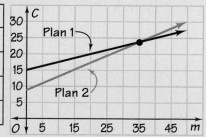

The lines intersect at (35, 23.75). Plan 2 is better if you drive less than 35 miles; otherwise, Plan 1 is better.

Think It Through

1. Could you have used other values for m in the table? Explain.

2. How was the conclusion arrived at? Are there other conclusions?

Exercises

Solve each problem. For Exercises 3 and 4, answer the questions first.

3. **Population** Assume the relationship between the year and number of senior citizens is a linear function. Use the data at the right to predict the number of senior citizens in the United States in 2020.
   a. Using the ordered pairs in the graph as endpoints, make a line graph showing years and number of senior citizens.
   b. Find the slope of the line and then write a function rule for the line. Use the rule to solve the problem.

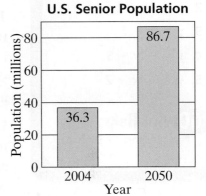

U.S. Senior Population

4. A certain airplane can climb 3,000 feet for every mile it travels horizontally. If it maintains this rate of ascent, how far will the plane have traveled horizontally when it reaches 5 miles in altitude?
   a. What is the rate of ascent in feet per mile?
   b. Let m be the number of miles traveled horizontally and A be the altitude. Write a function rule relating the number of miles traveled and the altitude. Be sure to use the correct units.

5. Student council members are raising funds by selling hats. They take a survey to see how many students will buy the hats at different prices. The results are below.

Price (dollars)	2	4	6	8	10	12
Number of Buyers	400	325	250	175	100	25

   Graph the data. Use the graph to estimate the number of hats that will be sold at $5.

6. **Landfill** A county landfill already contains 20,000 tons of trash. It is gaining 500 tons per month. How many months will it be until the landfill contains 50,000 tons of trash? Write a function rule and make a graph to solve the problem.

11-7 Quadratic and Other Nonlinear Functions

Check Skills You'll Need

1. **Vocabulary Review**
   How do you know if a function is *linear*?

Graph each function.

2. $y = 3x - 1$

3. $y = x + 7$

4. $y = -2x - 5$

5. $y = -4x + 2$

 **for Help**
Lesson 11-5

What You'll Learn

To graph and write quadratic functions and other nonlinear functions

🔊 **New Vocabulary** quadratic function, parabola

Why Learn This?

Think of a juggler's ball being tossed up in the air and falling back down. As the ball rises, its speed decreases. Then it falls, and the speed increases. The relationship between speed and time is not always the same.

In cases like this, nonlinear functions are needed to describe how variables are related. Nonlinear functions are functions whose graphs are not straight lines. A **quadratic function** is a function in which the greatest exponent of a variable is 2.

The graph of a quadratic function is a U-shaped curve called a **parabola**. The curve may open upward or downward. When you throw a ball into the air, the path it follows is a parabola.

EXAMPLE   Graphing a Quadratic Function

1. Make a table and graph the quadratic function $y = 4t - t^2$. Use integers from 0 to 4 for inputs. Connect the points with a smooth curve.

t	$4t - t^2$			=	y
0	$4(0) - (0)^2$	=	$0 - 0$	=	0
1	$4(1) - (1)^2$	=	$4 - 1$	=	3
2	$4(2) - (2)^2$	=	$8 - 4$	=	4
3	$4(3) - (3)^2$	=	$12 - 9$	=	3
4	$4(4) - (4)^2$	=	$16 - 16$	=	0

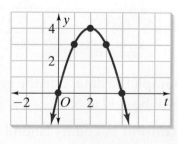

Online active math

For: Quadratic Functions Activity
Use: Interactive Textbook, 11-7

✓ Quick Check

1. Make a table and a graph for the function $y = 2x^2 - 5$.

Other types of nonlinear functions also have curved graphs.

EXAMPLE Graphing Other Nonlinear Functions

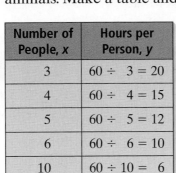

Careers Animal rescue workers go to the aid of wildlife and pets.

2 **Animal Rescue** Suppose it takes a total of 60 hours of work to clean wildlife damaged by an oil spill. The function $y = \frac{60}{x}$ represents the number of hours y each person must work if x people work to clean the animals. Make a table and graph the function.

Number of People, x	Hours per Person, y
3	$60 \div 3 = 20$
4	$60 \div 4 = 15$
5	$60 \div 5 = 12$
6	$60 \div 6 = 10$
10	$60 \div 10 = 6$

Time for Wildlife Cleanup

The data are discrete, so the curve is dashed.

Quick Check

2. The function $y = \frac{200}{s}$ relates the time y (in hours) for a 200-mile trip to the speed traveled s (in miles per hour). Make a table showing speed and number of hours traveled. Then graph the data.

You can write function rules for quadratic functions and other nonlinear functions.

EXAMPLE Writing a Quadratic Function Rule

x	y
0	3
2	7
3	12
5	28

3 Write a rule for the quadratic function shown in the table at the left.

Input x	(Input)^2 x^2	Output y
0	0	3
2	4	7
3	9	12
5	25	28

← Compare each output to (input)^2. Each output is greater than (input)^2 by 3.

So the function rule is $y = x^2 + 3$.

Quick Check

3. Write a quadratic function rule for the data in the table below.

x	-3	-1	0	2	4
y	7	-1	-2	2	14

1. **Vocabulary** Explain how a quadratic function differs from a linear function.

2. Sketch a parabola.

3. Make a table of values for the function $y = 2x^2 - 1$. Use only positive values for x.

Homework Exercises

For more exercises, see Extra Skills and Word Problems.

GO for Help

For Exercises	See Examples
4–9	1
10–13	2
14–17	3

Make a table and graph each quadratic function. Use integers from −3 to 3 for inputs.

4. $y = -x^2$
5. $y = 2x^2$
6. $y = -8x^2$

7. $y = x^2 + 2$
8. $y = -4x^2$
9. $y = 9 + 2x^2$

Make a table and a graph for each function. Use only positive values for x.

10. $y = \dfrac{10}{x}$
11. $y = \dfrac{8}{x}$
12. $y = \dfrac{20}{x}$
13. $y = \dfrac{16}{x}$

Write a quadratic function rule for the data in each table.

14.

x	−10	−5	0	5	10
y	80	5	−20	5	80

15.

x	0	1	2	3	4
y	0	−1	−4	−9	−16

16.

x	0	1	2	3	4
y	5	6	9	14	21

17.

x	−2	−1	0	1	4
y	0	−3	−4	−3	12

18. **Guided Problem Solving** The number of bushels of walnuts y that one acre of trees produces (output) is a function of the number of trees x planted per acre (input). The function rule is $y = -0.01x^2 + 0.8x$. Graph the function and use the graph to explain how the number of trees planted per acre affects walnut production.
    • Complete a table of input-output pairs to represent the data.
    • Graph the data in the table.

19. **Gardening** Suppose you have 12 yards of fencing to enclose a rectangular garden plot. Complete the table at the right to show area as a function of the garden's width. Then graph the function.

Width w	Length	Area A
1	5	■
2	4	■
3	■	■
4	■	■
5	■	■

Make a table and a graph for each quadratic function.

20. $y = -x - 3x^2$ **21.** $y = 2x^2 + 2x + 2$ **22.** $y = x - x^2$

23. **a.** Graph $y = n^2$ and $y = n^3$ on the same coordinate grid.
    b. **Writing in Math** Describe the similarities and differences between the graphs of the two functions.

For Exercises 24–26, match each function to its graph at the left.

24. $y = 3x - 2$ **25.** $y = 3x^2 + 2$ **26.** $y = 2 + 2^x$

Copy and complete the table for each function. Then graph the data.

27. $y = x^2 - 2$ **28.** $y = \dfrac{7}{x} + 2$ **29.** $y = 3 \cdot 2^x$

x	$x^2 - 2 = y$
0	■
1	■
2	■
3	■

x	$\dfrac{7}{x} + 2 = y$
1	■
2	■
3	■
4	■

x	$3 \cdot 2^x = y$
1	■
2	■
3	■
4	■

30. **Challenge** Make a table and a graph for each function. Then compare the graphs.
    a. $y = 3^x$ **b.** $y = 3^{x-2}$ **c.** $y = 3^{x+2}$ **d.** $y = -3^x$

Test Prep and Mixed Review   Practice

Multiple Choice

31. Which graph best represents the equation $d = -16s + 125$?

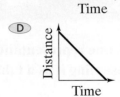

32. A house includes a rectangular door that is 3 ft wide and 7 ft tall and a window of the same width above the door in the shape of a semicircle. Which is closest to the area of the door and the window?
    F 14 ft^2 **G** 24.5 ft^2 **H** 28 ft^2 **J** 74 ft^2

Use the function rule $f(x) = 2x + 5$. Find each output.

33. $f(2)$ **34.** $f(-2)$ **35.** $f(13)$ **36.** $f(27)$

GO for Help

For Exercises	See Lesson
33–36	11-3

Changing Representations

You can use words, graphs, tables, or equations to show algebraic relationships. Learning how to translate among these representations can help solve problems.

EXAMPLE

Food Drive A class collected cans for a food drive for a local shelter. The teacher brought in 15 cans to start the collection. Beginning the next day, the class brought in 6 cans every day. The table below shows the number of cans collected for the first week. Use these data to make a graph and write an equation describing the number of cans c collected in d days.

Number of Days, d	0	1	2	3	4	5
Number of Cans, c	15	21	27	33	39	45

Graph: Make a graph of the data with the number of days on the horizontal axis and the number of cans on the vertical axis.

Since the number of cans must be a whole number, the data are discrete. Connect the points with a dashed line.

Function Rule: The function is linear because the graph is a line. The y-intercept is 15, and the slope is $\frac{21 - 15}{1 - 0} = 6$. So the linear function rule is $c = 6d + 15$.

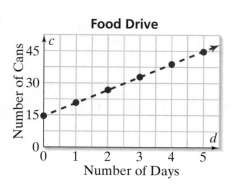

Food Drive

Exercises

In Exercises 1–3, one representation of a relation is given. Translate each relation by representing it as a table, as a graph, and as a function rule.

1.

2. $P = 5 \cdot 3^n$

3.

Input	Output
0	10
1	18
2	26
3	34

4. Reasoning When might it be more useful to use a graph rather than a function rule? A function rule rather than a graph?

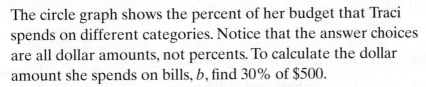

Test-Taking Strategies

Interpreting Data

Many questions involve interpreting data in a table or a graph. Before you answer the question, be sure you understand the information the graph or table is displaying.

EXAMPLE

1 The circle graph shows Traci's monthly budget. If Traci earns $500 a month, how much does she spend on bills each month?

- **A** $150
- **B** $600
- **C** $750
- **D** $2,500

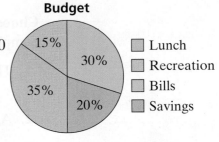

Budget

- Lunch
- Recreation
- Bills
- Savings

The circle graph shows the percent of her budget that Traci spends on different categories. Notice that the answer choices are all dollar amounts, not percents. To calculate the dollar amount she spends on bills, b, find 30% of $500.

$$b = 30\% \text{ of } 500$$
$$= 0.3 \cdot 500 \quad \leftarrow \textbf{Change the percent to a decimal. Then multiply by 500.}$$
$$= 150$$

Traci spends $150 on bills each month. The correct answer is choice A.

Exercises

Use the scatter plot below for Exercises 1–3.

1. Predict the mean temperature for a city at 25° north latitude.
   - **A** 45°F
   - **B** 55°F
   - **C** 65°F
   - **D** 75°F

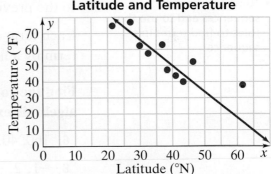

Latitude and Temperature

2. Which of the following is NOT supported by the data in the graph?
   - **F** As latitude increases, so does temperature.
   - **G** As latitude increases, temperature decreases.
   - **H** This graph has a negative trend.
   - **J** The temperature is higher at lower latitudes.

3. At approximately what latitude is the temperature 60°F?
   - **A** 0° N
   - **B** 15° N
   - **C** 35° N
   - **D** 40° N

Vocabulary Review

 arithmetic sequence (p. 513)
common difference (p. 513)
common ratio (p. 514)
continuous data (p. 534)
discrete data (p. 534)
function (p. 523)

function rule (p. 523)
geometric sequence (p. 514)
inductive reasoning (p. 512)
linear function (p. 535)
parabola (p. 546)
quadratic function (p. 546)

sequence (p. 512)
slope (p. 528)
slope of a line (p. 528)
slope-intercept form (p. 535)
term (p. 512)
y-intercept (p. 535)

Choose the vocabulary term from the column on the right that completes the sentence.

1. The U-shaped graph of an equation like $y = x^2 - 2$ is a __?__ .

2. A function whose points lie on a line is a __?__ .

3. A __?__ is a set of numbers that follows a pattern.

4. Each number in a sequence is called a __?__ .

5. A __?__ is a relationship that assigns exactly one output to each input value.

A. sequence
B. function
C. term
D. linear function
E. parabola

Go Online
PHSchool.com
For: Online Vocabulary Quiz
Web Code: asj-1151

Skills and Concepts

Lesson 11-1
• To write rules for sequences and to use the rules to find terms in a sequence

Each term of an **arithmetic sequence** is found by *adding* a fixed number to the previous term. This fixed number is called the **common difference.**

Each term of a **geometric sequence** is found by *multiplying* the previous term by a fixed number. This fixed number is called the **common ratio.**

Find the common difference or ratio in each sequence. Write an algebraic expression for the sequence and find the next three terms.

6. $160, 40, 10, 2.5, \ldots$

7. $14, 21, 28, 35, \ldots$

8. $-1, 2, -4, 8, \ldots$

9. $13, 17, 21, 25, \ldots$

Find the first four terms of the sequence represented by each expression.

10. $14 - 11n$

11. $\frac{1}{4}n$

12. $23 + n$

Lessons 11-2, 11-3
- To interpret and sketch graphs that represent real-world situations
- To represent functions with equations, tables, and function notation

A graph can show complex relationships between variables in a simple, visual way. A **function** is a relationship that assigns exactly one output value to each input value. In **function notation,** $f(3)$ represents the output of function f when the input is 3.

13. **Baseball** A baseball player gets a hit and runs to second base. The next two batters strike out. When the next player hits the ball, the player on second base runs home. Sketch a graph showing the first player's distance from home plate during the inning.

Use the function rule $f(x) = 4x - 7$. Find each output.

14. $f(3)$ 15. $f(0)$ 16. $f(-5)$ 17. $f\left(\frac{1}{2}\right)$

Lessons 11-4, 11-5
- To find the slope of a line from a graph or table
- To use tables and equations to graph linear functions

The **slope of a line** is the steepness of the line. An equation written in the form $y = mx + b$ is in **slope-intercept form.** The graph is a line with slope m and **y-intercept** b. A **linear function** is a function whose points lie on a line.

Find the slope of the line that passes through each pair of points.

18. $(1, 2)$ and $(-3, 2)$ 19. $(5, 1)$ and $(0, -7)$

20. $(-4, 9)$ and $(10, 6)$ 21. $(8, -2)$ and $(-2, 8)$

Graph each linear function.

22. $y = 2x - 5$ 23. $y = -4x + 7$

Lessons 11-6, 11-7
- To write function rules from words, tables, and graphs
- To graph and write quadratic functions and other nonlinear functions

You can write a rule for linear and nonlinear functions from words, a table, or a graph. A **quadratic function** is a function in which the greatest exponent of a variable is 2. Its graph is a U-shaped curve called a **parabola.** Other nonlinear functions also have curved graphs.

Do the data in each table represent a linear function? If so, write a rule for the function.

24.

x	−4	−2	0	2	4
y	−1	0	1	2	3

25.

x	0	1	2	3	4
y	10	7	4	1	−2

Make a table and a graph for each function. Use only positive values for x in Exercises 28 and 29.

26. $y = 2x^2 - 4$ 27. $y = -x^2 + 2$

28. $y = \dfrac{7}{x}$ 29. $y = \dfrac{5}{x} + 2$

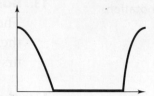
For Exercises 1–3, tell whether each situation produces an *arithmetic* or *geometric sequence*. Give the *common difference* or *ratio*.

1. A house gains $4,500 in value each year.

2. A clock loses 30 seconds each hour.

3. The number of bacteria in a pond triples each day.

4. A sequence has a common difference of $-\frac{1}{2}$ and a first term of 125. Find the next three terms.

For Exercises 5–7, find each output for the equation $f(x) = -x^2 - 3x$.

5. $f(-6)$ 6. $f(3)$ 7. $f(0)$

8. The population of a town is described by $p = 400t + 5,000$. The population is p and the time in years is t. Make a table and find the population after 10 years.

Graph each function. For Exercise 12, use only positive integers as input values.

9. $y = \frac{1}{2}x - 3$ 10. $y = x^2$

11. $y = 5 - x^2$ 12. $y = \frac{12}{x} + 2$

Match each function with its graph.

13. $y = -x - 1$ 14. $y = x^2 + 1$

15. $y = x - 1$ 16. $y = \frac{1}{2}x$

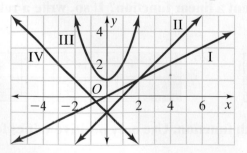

17. Which is steeper, a line with a slope of 7 or a line with a slope of −10? Explain.

18. a. A nickel's mass is about 5 grams. Write a function rule for the mass of n nickels.
    b. What is the mass of $1.00 in nickels?

19. **Writing in Math** Describe a situation that the following graph could represent.

Find the slope of the line that passes through each pair of points.

20. $(-4, 10)$ and $(6, 13)$ 21. $(2, 3)$ and $(9, -3)$

22. $(5, 7)$ and $(-12, 4)$ 23. $(1, -1)$ and $(5, 6)$

24. Write a rule for the quadratic function in the table below.

x	−2	−1	0	1	2
y	5	2	1	2	5

25. A person drops a stone from 40 feet above ground. The equation $d = -16t^2 + 40$ describes the distance in feet the stone is from the ground after t seconds. Make a table, graph the equation, and find how long it takes the stone to hit the ground.

Find the slope of each line

26.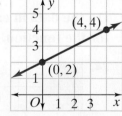

27.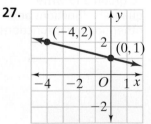

28. Does the data in the table below represent a function? Explain.

Input	0	8	5	3	8
Output	−1	4	7	9	−2

Test Prep Practice

Reading Comprehension

Read each passage and answer the questions that follow.

Our Changing America The 1990 U.S. Census gave the populations of the four largest racial groups as White: 199,686,000; African American: 29,986,000; Latino: 22,354,000; and Asian American: 6,909,000. By 2000, the White population increased to 211,461,000, the African American population increased to 34,658,000, the Latino population increased to 35,306,000, and the Asian American population increased to 10,243,000. The entire population of the United States in 2000 was about 2.82×10^8 people.

1. How would you write the 2000 Latino population in scientific notation?
   - Ⓐ $3 \times 10^8 + 5 \times 10^7 + 3 \times 10^6 + 6 \times 10^4$
   - Ⓑ 3.5306×10^7
   - Ⓒ 35.306×10^6
   - Ⓓ 3.5306×10^6

2. In 2000, about what percent of the population was non-White?
   - Ⓕ 2.5　　Ⓖ 7.5　　Ⓗ 25　　Ⓙ 75

3. What was the approximate percent of increase in the Asian American population from 1990 to 2000?
   - Ⓐ 4　　Ⓑ 29　　Ⓒ 48　　Ⓓ 71

4. About what percent of the population was Latino in 2000?
   - Ⓕ 1.25　　　　　　Ⓗ 25
   - Ⓖ 12.5　　　　　　Ⓙ 1.25×10^7

What a Difference! The tides in the Bay of Fundy are world famous. The difference between the water level at low tide and at high tide averages 39.4 ft, but it can be as much as 53 ft. Situated in Canada between New Brunswick and Nova Scotia, the Bay of Fundy is about 170 mi long and is about 35 mi wide on average. Scientists believe that the bay's long, narrow shape accounts for the extreme variation in its tidal range.

5. Which type of graph would best describe the height of the water throughout the day?
   - Ⓐ circle graph　　Ⓒ bar graph
   - Ⓑ scatter plot　　Ⓓ line graph

6. Which of the following is the best approximation of the area of the Bay of Fundy?
   - Ⓕ 215 mi²　　　　Ⓗ 7,092 mi²
   - Ⓖ 5,950 mi²　　　Ⓙ 12,600 mi²

7. Which equation can be used to find the percent of increase from the average tidal range to the maximum tidal range?
   - Ⓐ $\dfrac{39.4 - 53}{39.4} \times 100$
   - Ⓑ $\dfrac{39.4 - 53}{53} \times 100$
   - Ⓒ $\dfrac{53 - 39.4}{53} \times 100$
   - Ⓓ $\dfrac{53 - 39.4}{39.4} \times 100$

Applying Quadratic Functions

Product Pricing Suppose you make and sell portable CD/DVD players. You want the price to be high enough for you to make a profit, yet low enough that people will want to buy. Interpreting functions can come in handy when choosing the right price.

Portable Drive

In a CD player, a drive motor spins the disc. A laser system reads the bumps on the CD, and a tracking mechanism moves the laser's beam along the spiral track.

TV Bank

People use banks of TVs to monitor more than one TV station at a time or to see one enlarged image.

Put It All Together

1. The equation $n = -2.5p^2 + 39,400$ models the relationship between the price, p, of each CD/DVD player and the number sold, n. Copy and extend the table to a price of $100. Complete the table.

Price p	Number Sold n	Sales Income s
$30	37,150	$1,114,500
$35		
$40		

2. Add a column to your table for income from sales, $s = p \times n$, for each price in the table. Record the income for each price.

3. Make a scatter plot comparing the number sold to income.

4. **Writing in Math** Decide on the best price to charge for your CD/DVD player. Find the number you can expect to sell and the income at that price. Explain your choice.

5. **a.** The prices your competitors charge affect your sales. Make adjustments to the price you chose in Exercise 4 based on the prices you think two competitors will charge. Write down your final price.
   b. Exchange prices with two classmates. Calculate the mean of the three prices.
   c. Use your answer to part (b) and the function from Exercise 1. Find the total number of CD/DVD players your three companies will sell.
   d. Assume that the company with the lowest price makes 40% of the sales from part (c), the company with the highest price makes 25% of the sales, and the third company makes 35% of the sales. Calculate the units sold and the total sales for each company. Which company is the most successful? Explain.

Go Online
PHSchool.com
For: Information about product pricing
Web Code: ase-1153

CHAPTER 12 Polynomials and Properties of Exponents

What You've Learned

- In Chapter 2, you used exponents and the order of operations to evaluate expressions.
- You wrote numbers in scientific notation.
- In Chapter 6, you wrote and simplified algebraic expressions.

 Check Your Readiness

GO for Help

For Exercises	See Lesson
1–12	6-2
13–24	2-7

Simplifying Algebraic Expressions

Simplify each expression.

1. $13d + 9d - 4$
2. $4v + 65 - 11v + 8$
3. $2w - 42 - 7(1 - 9w)$
4. $6f - 23g + 3 + 37f$
5. $8r + 34 - 2r + 30r$
6. $7t - 6 - 15t + x$
7. $5 + 4(a - 3)$
8. $-2b - 7(b - 3)$
9. $-8(f + 11) + 44f$
10. $6x - 9(2x + 5)$
11. $7.3(2.8 + c) - 13c$
12. $20y - (15y + 5)$

Using Exponents

Write using exponents.

13. $7 \cdot 7 \cdot 7 \cdot 7 \cdot 7$
14. $5 \cdot 5 \cdot c \cdot c$
15. $a \cdot a \cdot b \cdot b \cdot b$
16. $x \cdot y \cdot x \cdot y \cdot x$
17. $(3x) \cdot (3x) \cdot (3x)$
18. $c \cdot d \cdot g \cdot d \cdot g$

Simplify each expression.

19. 4^2
20. $(-4)^2$
21. -4^2
22. $-(-2)^5$
23. 10^2
24. 10^3

What You'll Learn Next

- In this chapter, you will write and simplify polynomial expressions.

- You will add, subtract, and multiply polynomials.

- You will use exponent rules to simplify expressions involving powers with the same base.

 Key Vocabulary

- binomial (p. 576)
- coefficient (p. 566)
- constant (p. 561)
- monomial (p. 576)
- polynomial (p. 561)

Problem Solving Application On pages 596 and 597, you will work an extended activity on sizes of animals.

Write an algebraic expression for each model.

1.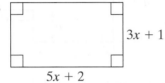

2.

3.

Use properties to simplify each polynomial.

4. $-2 - 6x + 5x^2 - 2x + 6$

5. $9x^2 + 3 - 10x - 3 + 7x^2$

Add or subtract.

6. $(3a^2 + 2a - 1) + (-3a^2 - 9)$

7. $(11b^2 - 7) + (15b^2 - b)$

8. $(c^2 - 9c - 5) - (-c^2 - 8c - 10)$

9. $(2d^2 - 9d) - (-4d^2 + 20d + 17)$

Write the perimeter of each figure as a polynomial. Simplify.

10.

$3x + 1$

$5x + 2$

11.

$10x - 7$ $7x - 3$

$5x$

12-3a Activity Lab

Exploring Exponents

1. Copy and complete the table.

2. a. **Patterns** Look at the first row in the table. What relationship do you see between the sum of the exponents in the first cell and the exponent in the last cell?

   b. Does this relationship hold for the other rows in the table?

Two Exponents	Product as a Repeated Factor	Standard Form	Single Exponent
$2^1 \cdot 2^1$	$2 \cdot 2$	4	2^2
$2^1 \cdot 2^2$	■	■	■
$2^2 \cdot 2^2$	$2 \cdot 2 \cdot 2 \cdot 2$	16	■
$2^2 \cdot 2^3$	■	■	■

3. Write a rule that you can use to find the product of two exponents such as $a^m \cdot a^n$.

12-3 Exponents and Multiplication

What You'll Learn

To multiply powers with the same base and to multiply numbers in scientific notation

Why Learn This?

Astronomers use scientific notation when they work with very large numbers. To calculate using scientific notation, you must know how to multiply with exponents.

You can write the expression $3^2 \cdot 3^4$ using a single exponent.

$$3^2 \cdot 3^4 = (3 \cdot 3)(3 \cdot 3 \cdot 3 \cdot 3) = 3^6$$

The two factors of 3 together with four factors of 3 give a total of six factors of 3. Notice that the exponent 6 is equal to the sum of the exponents 2 and 4.

KEY CONCEPTS — Multiplying Powers With the Same Base

To multiply numbers or variables with the same base, add the exponents

Arithmetic

$3^2 \cdot 3^7 = 3^{(2 + 7)} = 3^9$

Algebra

$a^m \cdot a^n = a^{(m + n)}$

EXAMPLE — Multiplying Powers

1 Write the expression $(-2)^3 \cdot (-2)^5$ using a single exponent.

$(-2)^3 \cdot (-2)^5 = (-2)^{(3 + 5)}$ ← Add the exponents.

$= (-2)^8$ ← Simplify the exponent.

✓ Quick Check

1. Write each expression using a single exponent.
   a. $6^2 \cdot 6^3$ b. $(-4) \cdot (-4)^7$ c. $m^1 \cdot m^{11}$

The rule for multiplying powers with the same base applies to multiplying numbers in scientific notation.

For help with scientific notation, go to Lesson 2-8, Example 2.

EXAMPLE Multiplying With Scientific Notation

2 Multiply $(5 \times 10^6)(9 \times 10^3)$. Write the product in scientific notation.

$(5 \times 10^6)(9 \times 10^3) = (5 \times 9) \times (10^6 \times 10^3)$ ← Use the associative and commutative properties.

$= 45 \times (10^6 \times 10^3)$ ← Multiply 5 and 9.

$= 45 \times 10^9$ ← Add the exponents of the powers of 10.

$= 4.5 \times 10^1 \times 10^9$ ← Write 45 in scientific notation.

$= 4.5 \times 10^{10}$ ← Add the exponents.

✓ **Quick Check**

2. Multiply. Write each product in scientific notation.
   a. $(2 \times 10^6)(4 \times 10^3)$ **b.** $(3 \times 10^5)(2 \times 10^8)$ **c.** $12(8 \times 10^{20})$

You can multiply numbers in scientific notation to find solutions to real-world problems. Multiplying large or small numbers in scientific notation is easier than multiplying the same numbers in standard form.

EXAMPLE Application: Science

Video Tutor Help
Visit: PHSchool.com
Web Code: ase-0775

3 **Multiple Choice** A light-year, the distance light travels in one Earth year, is about 5.9×10^{12} miles. A mile is 5.28×10^3 feet. How many feet are in a light-year?

   Ⓐ 31.2×10^{15} Ⓒ 3.12×10^{15}
   Ⓑ 31.2×10^{16} Ⓓ 3.12×10^{16}

$(5.9 \times 10^{12})(5.28 \times 10^3)$ ← Multiply by the conversion factor.

$(5.9 \times 5.28) \times (10^{12} \times 10^3)$ ← associative and commutative properties

$31.2 \times (10^{12} \times 10^3)$ ← Multiply 5.9 and 5.28. Round to the nearest tenth.

31.2×10^{15} ← Add the exponents of the powers of 10.

$(3.12 \times 10^1) \times 10^{15}$ ← Write 31.2 in scientific notation.

3.12×10^{16} ← Add the exponents.

Since there are about 3.12×10^{16} feet in a light-year, the correct answer is choice D.

✓ **Quick Check**

3. **Astronomy** The speed of light is about 3.0×10^5 kilometers/second. Use the formula $d = r \cdot t$ to find the distance light travels in an hour, which is 3.6×10^3 seconds.

For Exercises 1 and 2, fill in the blank.

1. $(8)^3 \cdot (\blacksquare^4) = 8^7$

2. $5^3 \cdot 5^{\blacksquare} = 5^6$

Write each expression using a single exponent.

3. $(-6)^2 \cdot (-6)^2$

4. $(-2)^8 \cdot (-2)^3$

5. $7^2 \cdot 7^8$

6. $4^5 \cdot 4^6$

7. **Error Analysis** A student simplified $5^2 \cdot 5^4$ as 25^6. Explain the student's error.

8. **Mental Math** Multiply 4.17×10^{20} by 10^3.

Homework Exercises

For more exercises, see Extra Skills and Word Problems.

GO for Help

For Exercises	See Examples
9–16	1
17–22	2
23	3

Write each expression using a single exponent.

9. $y^3 \cdot y^5$

10. $m^{10} \cdot m^{100}$

11. $3.4^3 \cdot 3.4^{10}$

12. $12^5 \cdot 12^{50}$

13. $4.5^{10} \cdot 4.5^{10}$

14. $(-5)^5 \cdot (-5)$

15. $0.4^5 \cdot 0.4^{10}$

16. $x \cdot x^0$

Multiply. Write each product in scientific notation.

17. $(2 \times 10^3)(4 \times 10^6)$

18. $(7 \times 10^2)(9 \times 10^5)$

19. $90(8 \times 10^9)$

20. $(3 \times 10^5)(5 \times 10^7)$

21. $(9 \times 10^5)(5 \times 10^9)$

22. $(5.1 \times 10^4)(2 \times 10^7)$

23. **Earth Science** There are about 4.8×10^{19} ft^3 of water on Earth. One cubic foot of water contains about 9.47×10^{26} water molecules. Approximately how many water molecules are there on Earth?

GPS 24. **Guided Problem Solving** Einstein's famous equation states that $E = mc^2$. E represents energy, m represents mass, and c represents the speed of light. Find the value of E (in joules) when m is equal to 1 kilogram and c is equal to 3.0×10^8 meters per second.
- How can you write Einstein's law without using exponents?
- Evaluate c^2 for $c = 3.0 \times 10^8$.

25. **Open-Ended** Give three different ways to write 4^{12} as the product of two powers.

26. **Writing in Math** Explain why you *cannot* write $5^3 \cdot 7^9$ as $(35)^{12}$.

27. Double the number 3.4×10^{12}. Write the answer in scientific notation.

Write each expression using a single exponent.

28. $4^x \cdot 4^t$

29. $3^m \cdot 3^n$

30. $1.5^8 \cdot 1.5^t$

31. $(-4)^x \cdot (-4)^y$

32. $2^3 \cdot 2 \cdot 2^8$

33. $a^5 \cdot a^4 \cdot a$

34. $9^{12} \cdot 9^6 \cdot 9^3$

35. $3^a \cdot 3^{2a} \cdot 3^{3a}$

36. $xy \cdot x^2y^3$

37. $c^2d \cdot cd^3$

38. $x \cdot x^3 \cdot x^5$

39. $3x^2 \cdot x^5 \cdot x$

40. **Geography** The Sahara is a desert of about 3.5 million square miles. There are about 2.79×10^7 square feet in a square mile. About how many square feet does the Sahara cover? Write your answer in scientific notation.

Use <, >, or = to complete each statement.

41. $4^6 \blacksquare 4^3 \cdot 4^2$

42. $36 \blacksquare 6^2 \cdot 6^2$

43. $5^{16} \blacksquare 5^8 \cdot 5^2$

44. The radius of Venus is about 6.05×10^3 km. Use the formula S.A. $= 4\pi r^2$ to approximate the surface area of Venus.

45. **Challenge** If $(h + h) \cdot (h \cdot h) = 16$, what is the value of h?

Test Prep and Mixed Review **Practice**

Multiple Choice

46. Look for a pattern in the table at the right. Based on the pattern in the table, what value of x makes the statement $4^{15} = 2^x$ true?

Ⓐ 15

Ⓒ 30

Ⓑ 20

Ⓓ 7.5

Powers of 4	Powers of 2
$4^2 = 16$	$2^4 = 16$
$4^3 = 64$	$2^6 = 64$
$4^4 = 256$	$2^8 = 256$
$4^5 = 1024$	$2^{10} = 1024$

47. On a typing test, Lana typed 900 words in 5 minutes. Sierra typed 980 words in 7 minutes. Which of the following statements is true?

Ⓕ Lana's average typing rate was 67 words per minute faster than Sierra's average rate.

Ⓖ Sierra's average typing rate was 80 words per minute faster than Lana's average rate.

Ⓗ Lana's average typing rate was 40 words per minute faster than Sierra's average rate.

Ⓙ Lana's average typing rate was the same as Sierra's average typing rate.

GO **for Help**

For Exercises	See Lesson
48–50	4-1

Find each unit rate.

48. $75 for 15 books

49. 150 mi in 3.5 h

50. $150 for 250 lb

Scientific Notation

Calculators use scientific notation as a shorthand way to write very large numbers. If you enter a number with too many digits for a calculator to display, the calculator will use scientific notation to display the rounded number.

2346549887051 [ENTER] $2.3465498871E12$ ← **The display shows the number rounded.**

The number in the display is $2.346549887 \times 10^{12}$. The 12 after the E is the exponent on 10.

You can use your calculator to simplify expressions in scientific notation.

EXAMPLES **Calculating With Scientific Notation**

1 Use a calculator to find $(7.6 \times 10^6)(3.52 \times 10^3)$.

$(7.6 \times 10^6) \, (3.52 \times 10^3)$

7.6 [EE] 6 [X] 3.52 [EE] 3 ← **Use [EE] to enter the exponent of the power of 10.**

$2.6752E10$

The product is 2.6752×10^{10}.

2 Use a calculator to find $(2.8 \times 10^{12}) + (4.9 \times 10^{15})$.

2.8 [EE] 12 [+] 4.9 [EE] 15

$4.9028E15$

The sum is 4.9028×10^{15}.

Exercises

Use a calculator to simplify. Write your answer in scientific notation.

1. $(3.5 \times 10^{12})(2.3 \times 10^9)$

2. $(2.99 \times 10^{16})(4.36 \times 10^{12})$

3. $(2.75 \times 10^4)^2$

4. $(5.54 \times 10^6) + (1.38 \times 10^6)$

5. $(4.02 \times 10^{13}) - (2.01 \times 10^{13})$

6. $(9.22 \times 10^{11})^3$

7. Mental Math Simplify 10^{20}. Check your answer with a calculator.

8. Find the area of a square with side length 1.5×10^4 units.

12-4 Multiplying Polynomials

✓ Check Skills You'll Need

1. **Vocabulary Review**
The expression $2^3 \cdot 2^5$ can be simplified by adding the ___?___ .

Simplify using a single exponent.

2. $x^4 \cdot x^5 \cdot x^6$

3. $(-a)^3 \cdot (-a)^7$

GO for Help
Lesson 12-3

What You'll Learn

To multiply monomials and binomials

🔊 **New Vocabulary** monomial, binomial

Why Learn This?

Builders use formulas to find quantities such as the area of a foundation. When formulas involve more than one unknown value, you may need to multiply polynomials.

A polynomial with only one term, such as $4a^3$, is a **monomial.** To multiply monomials, multiply the coefficients and use the properties of exponents.

EXAMPLE Multiplying Monomials

❶ Simplify $(4a^3)(-5a^2)$.

$$(4a^3)(-5a^2) = (4)(-5) \cdot a^3 \cdot a^2 \quad \leftarrow \text{Use the Commutative Property of Multiplication to rearrange the factors.}$$
$$= -20 \cdot a^3 \cdot a^2 \quad \leftarrow \text{Multiply coefficients.}$$
$$= -20 \cdot a^5 \quad \leftarrow \text{Add exponents.}$$

✓ Quick Check

1. Simplify $(2y^3)(4y)$.

Vocabulary Tip

The prefix *mono-* means "one." The prefix *bi-* means "two."

A **binomial** is a polynomial with two terms. You can use an area model to find the product of a monomial and a binomial.

This model shows the product of $3x$ and $2x + 3$.

Since the array of tiles forms a rectangle, the area is the product of the height and the base, or $3x(2x + 3)$. The area is also the sum of the tiles, or $6x^2 + 9x$.

So $3x(2x + 3) = 6x^2 + 9x$.

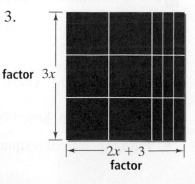

factor $3x$

$\leftarrow$ $2x + 3$ $\rightarrow$
factor

You can also use the Distributive Property to find the product of a monomial and a binomial.

EXAMPLE **Multiplying a Monomial and Binomial**

② **Multiple Choice** An architect is planning the foundation of a new house. The house must have certain dimensions to fit on the home lot. Which expression can he use to find the area of the foundation?

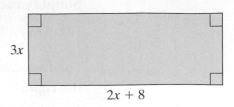

$3x$

$2x + 8$

Ⓐ $5x^2 + 8$　　Ⓑ $5x^2 + 24x$　Ⓒ $6x + 24$　　Ⓓ $6x^2 + 24x$

To find the area, multiply the length, $3x$, times the width, $2x + 8$.

$$A = \ell \cdot w = 3x(2x + 8)$$
$$= 3x \cdot 2x + 3x \cdot 8 \quad \leftarrow \textbf{Use the Distributive Property.}$$
$$= 6x^2 + 24x \quad\quad\quad \leftarrow \textbf{Simplify.}$$

Since $3x(2x + 8) = 6x^2 + 24x$, the correct answer is choice D.

✓**Quick Check**

2. Your neighbor is building an addition to her house. The expression $3r(5r + 5)$ represents the planned area of the house after it is remodeled. Simplify the polynomial to find the total area of the house, including the addition.

You can use an area model to find the product of two binomials.

EXAMPLE **Using Area Models to Multiply Binomials**

③ Simplify $(2x + 1)(3x + 2)$.

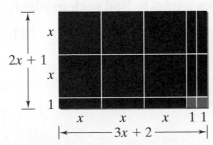

$2x + 1$

x

x

1

x　x　x　$1\ 1$

$\leftarrow$ —— $3x + 2$ ——$\rightarrow$

Count each type of tile.

There are six x^2 tiles.

There are seven x tiles.

There are two unit tiles.

So $(2x + 1)(3x + 2) = 6x^2 + 7x + 2$.

✓**Quick Check**

3. Draw an area model or use algebra tiles to simplify each expression.
   a. $(x + 2)(2x + 3)$　　**b.** $(3x + 4)(2x + 1)$　　**c.** $(x + 1)(2x + 5)$

GO ●nline

Video Tutor Help
Visit: PHSchool.com
Web Code: ase-0775

1. **Vocabulary** How are a monomial and a binomial different?

Simplify each expression.

2. $(-8y)(2y)$ 3. $5a \cdot 3a$ 4. $x^5 \cdot x$

For Exercises 5–6, use the area model at the right.

5. Write the factors shown in the model.

6. Find the product of these factors.

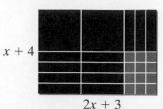

$x + 4$

$2x + 3$

For more exercises, see **Extra Skills and Word Problems.**

Simplify each expression.

For Exercises	See Examples
7–12	1
13–19	2
20–21	3

7. $(-3t^2)(-4t^3)$ 8. $4g^4 \cdot 3g^3$ 9. $(-z^3)(6z^2)$

10. $(7x^2)(-2x^3)$ 11. $(10s^2)(-4s)$ 12. $(5c^3)(-4c^4)$

Simplify each expression.

13. $a(a - 3)$ 14. $2m(m - 7)$

15. $7(3s^2 + 1)$ 16. $-3y(y^2 - 6y)$

17. $2k(5k - 1)$ 18. $-3d^2(d - 4)$

19. The length of a rectangle is four more than twice the width. The product $x(2x + 4)$ represents the area of the figure. Simplify this product.

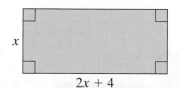

x

$2x + 4$

Use the area model to find each product.

20.

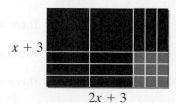

$x + 3$

$2x + 3$

21.

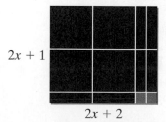

$2x + 1$

$2x + 2$

22. **Guided Problem Solving** An architect is planning a deck. It will be $2(2x + 4)$ ft long and $3(x - 4)$ ft wide. Write an expression for the area of the deck when it is completed.
   • Use the area formula $A = \ell w$.
   • Simplify the expression.

Find the area of each figure.

23.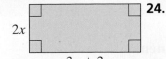
$2x$
$3x + 2$

24.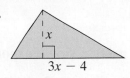
x
$3x - 4$

25.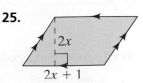
$2x$
$2x + 1$

26. Use the Distributive Property to simplify $-w^2(w^2 + 2w - 4)$.

27. **Writing in Math** Explain how to multiply $(x + 1)$ and $(x + 2)$ using an area model.

State whether each expression is best described as a *monomial*, a *binomial*, a *polynomial*, or *none of these*.

28. $2n^4 + 3n$ 29. $-5n^4$ 30. $6n^2 + n - 2$ **31.** 5

32. **Challenge** Find the factors of each polynomial by finding the GCF of the terms of the polynomial.

   Sample $2a^2 + 6a = 2a \cdot a + 2a \cdot 3 = 2a(a + 3)$

   a. $3x^2 + 9$ **b.** $5y^2 + 10y$ **c.** $8a^3 + 4a^2 + 12a$

Test Prep and Mixed Review   Practice

Multiple Choice

33. Andrea is twice as tall as Jordan. Caitlin is half as tall as Harry. Harry is 4 inches taller than Alec. Alec is 5 feet 10 inches tall. Jordan is 2 inches shorter than Caitlin. How tall is Andrea?

   Ⓐ 4 ft 5 in.   Ⓑ 4 ft 6 in.   Ⓒ 5 ft 5 in.   Ⓓ 5 ft 10 in.

34. The top and side views of a solid figure are shown. Which of the following is the solid figure represented by these views?

Top View

Side View

Ⓕ
Side

Ⓗ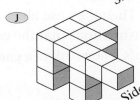
Side

Ⓖ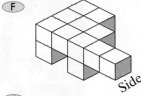
Side

Ⓙ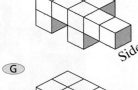
Side

Graph each linear function.

35. $y = 7 - 3x$ 36. $y = 8x + 10$ 37. $y = -x + 2$

Write each expression using a single exponent.

1. $4.7^6 \cdot 4.7^{15}$

2. $(-4a)^2(-4a)^2$

3. $xy^5 \cdot x^3y^7$

Multiply. Write each product in scientific notation.

4. $50(6 \times 10^3)$

5. $(3 \times 10^7)(5 \times 10^4)$

6. $(4 \times 10^4)(9 \times 10^2)$

Simplify each expression.

7. $7f^5 \cdot 4f^3$

8. $(3.1g^6)(5g^2)$

9. $(-8h^8)(2.2h^{10})$

10. $-5j(j^2 - 9j)$

11. $6k(k - 1)$

12. $10m^2(3m - 4)$

Use the area model to find each product.

13.

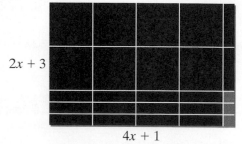

$2x + 3$

$4x + 1$

14.

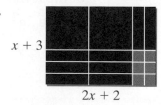

$x + 3$

$2x + 2$

 **Video Game Programmers**

Video game programmers write the code that drives the actions in video games.

Video game programmers need a strong background in mathematics and computer programming. They use logic to design their programs. Then they use algebra to write the detailed instructions that the computer understands. The result is a game that is fun to play.

 **For:** Information about video game programmers
Web Code: asb-2031

Check Skills You'll Need

1. **Vocabulary Review**
Is the expression x^5 an *exponent* or a *power*?

Write each expression using exponents.

2. $7 \cdot 7 \cdot 7 \cdot 7$

3. $4 \cdot 4 \cdot 4$

4. $5 \cdot 5$

5. $1 \cdot 1 \cdot 1 \cdot 1 \cdot 1$

for Help
Lesson 2-7

What You'll Learn

To divide powers with the same base and to simplify expressions with negative exponents

Why Learn This?

Nanorobots are microscopic machines that may soon be used to fight illness inside the human body. When working with very small numbers, such as the length of a nanorobot, you often divide expressions with exponents.

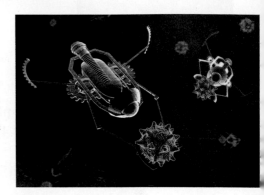

You can divide powers with the same base by writing out all the factors.

$$\frac{7^5}{7^3} = \frac{\cancel{7}^1 \cdot \cancel{7}^1 \cdot \cancel{7}^1 \cdot 7 \cdot 7}{{}_1\cancel{7} \cdot {}_1\cancel{7} \cdot {}_1\cancel{7}} = \frac{7 \cdot 7}{1} = 7^2$$

Notice that $5 - 3 = 2$. This example suggests the following rule.

KEY CONCEPTS **Dividing Powers With the Same Base**

To divide nonzero numbers or variables with the same nonzero base, subtract the exponents.

Arithmetic	**Algebra**
$\dfrac{8^5}{8^3} = 8^{(5-3)} = 8^2$	$\dfrac{a^m}{a^n} = a^{(m-n)}$, where $a \neq 0$

EXAMPLE **Dividing Powers**

1 Write $\dfrac{m^{12}}{m^5}$ using a single exponent.

$$\frac{m^{12}}{m^5} = m^{(12-5)} \quad \leftarrow \text{Subtract exponents with the same base.}$$

$$= m^7 \quad \leftarrow \text{Simplify.}$$

Quick Check

1. Write $\dfrac{w^8}{w^5}$ using a single exponent.

The rule for dividing powers with the same base applies to dividing numbers in scientific notation.

EXAMPLE Dividing Numbers in Scientific Notation

2 Gridded Response The distance between the sun and a comet is about 2.79×10^8 miles. Light travels about 1.1×10^7 miles per minute.

Use the formula time $= \frac{\text{distance}}{\text{speed}}$ to estimate how many minutes sunlight takes to reach the comet. Write your answer in standard form and round to the nearest tenth.

$$\text{time} = \frac{\text{distance}}{\text{speed}} \qquad \leftarrow \text{Use the formula for time.}$$

$$= \frac{2.79}{1.1} \times \frac{10^8}{10^7} \qquad \leftarrow \begin{array}{l}\text{Substitute. Write as a} \\ \text{product of quotients.}\end{array}$$

$$= \frac{2.79}{1.1} \times 10^1 \qquad \leftarrow \text{Subtract exponents.}$$

$$\approx 2.54 \times 10^1 \qquad \leftarrow \text{Divide.}$$

Sunlight takes about 2.54×10^1 minutes, or 25.4 minutes, to reach the comet.

✓ Quick Check

2. **Astronomy** The distance between the sun and Earth is about 9.3×10^7 miles. Light travels about 1.1×10^7 miles per minute. Use the formula time $= \frac{\text{distance}}{\text{speed}}$ to estimate how long sunlight takes to reach Earth. Write your answer in standard form and round to the nearest tenth.

What does the exponent 0 mean? Consider finding the quotient $\frac{3^5}{3^5}$.

If you subtract exponents, $\frac{3^5}{3^5} = 3^{(5-5)} = 3^0$.

If you write factors, $\frac{3^5}{3^5} = \frac{\cancel{3}^1 \cdot \cancel{3}^1 \cdot \cancel{3}^1 \cdot \cancel{3}^1 \cdot \cancel{3}^1}{{}_1\cancel{3} \cdot {}_1\cancel{3} \cdot {}_1\cancel{3} \cdot {}_1\cancel{3} \cdot {}_1\cancel{3}}$

$$= \frac{1}{1} = 1.$$

Notice that $\frac{3^5}{3^5} = 3^0$ and $\frac{3^5}{3^5} = 1$. This suggests the following rule.

Vocabulary Tip

Read 3^0 as "3 to the zero power."

KEY CONCEPTS Zero as an Exponent

For any nonzero number a, $a^0 = 1$.

Example $9^0 = 1$

Expressions With a Zero Exponent

3 Simplify each expression.

a. $(-8)^0$ **b.** $3m^0$

$(-8)^0 = 1$ ← **Simplify.** → $3m^0 = 3 \cdot 1 = 3$

✓ Quick Check

3. Simplify each expression.

a. $(-9)^0$ **b.** $(2r)^0$ **c.** $2r^0$

To understand negative exponents, consider finding the quotient $\frac{6^2}{6^5}$.

If you subtract exponents, $\frac{6^2}{6^5} = 6^{(2-5)} = 6^{-3}$.

If you write factors, $\frac{6^2}{6^5} = \frac{\cancel{6}^1 \cdot \cancel{6}^1}{_1\cancel{6} \cdot {_1}\cancel{6} \cdot 6 \cdot 6 \cdot 6}$

$$= \frac{1}{6 \cdot 6 \cdot 6} = \frac{1}{6^3}.$$

Notice that $\frac{6^2}{6^5} = 6^{-3}$ and $\frac{6^2}{6^5} = \frac{1}{6^3}$. This suggests the following rule.

KEY CONCEPTS   **Negative Exponents**

For any nonzero number a and integer n, $a^{-n} = \frac{1}{a^n}$.

Example $8^{-5} = \frac{1}{8^5}$

To simplify an expression with negative exponents, first write the expression with a positive exponent.

EXAMPLE **Expressions With Negative Exponents**

4 Simplify each expression.

a. 3^{-2} **b.** $(y)^{-6}$

$3^{-2} = \frac{1}{3^2}$ ← **Use a positive exponent.** → $(y)^{-6} = \frac{1}{y^6}$

$= \frac{1}{9}$ ← **Simplify.**

✓ Quick Check

4. Simplify each expression.

a. 3^{-1} **b.** w^{-4} **c.** $(-2)^{-3}$

1. **Reasoning** Is $(-1)^0$ a positive or a negative number? Explain.

2. **Mental Math** Find the value of $\frac{123^5}{123^4}$.

Write out the factors of each expression. Then simplify using a single exponent. Exercise 3 has been started for you.

3. $\frac{2^6}{2^5} = \frac{2 \cdot 2 \cdot 2 \cdot 2 \cdot 2 \cdot 2}{2 \cdot 2 \cdot 2 \cdot 2 \cdot 2}$

4. $\frac{3^4}{3^2}$

5. $\frac{8^5}{8^2}$

Homework Exercises

For more exercises, see Extra Skills and Word Problems.

Write each expression using a single exponent.

GO for Help

For Exercises	See Examples
6–13	1
14	2
15–22	3–4

6. $\frac{a^5}{a^3}$

7. $\frac{x^9}{x^5}$

8. $\frac{c^7}{c^2}$

9. $\frac{(-1)^5}{(-1)^4}$

10. $\frac{23^{12}}{23^8}$

11. $\frac{135^{10}}{135^1}$

12. $\frac{(-7)^{99}}{(-7)^{98}}$

13. $\frac{(-9)^{32}}{(-9)^{15}}$

14. **Astronomy** The distance from the sun to Saturn is about 8.88×10^8 miles. The speed of light is about 1.1×10^7 miles per minute. Use the formula time $= \frac{\text{distance}}{\text{speed}}$ to estimate how long sunlight takes to reach Saturn. Round the answer to the nearest tenth.

Simplify each expression.

15. 4^0

16. $(-3)^0$

17. u^0

18. $(3t)^0$

19. 10^{-2}

20. b^{-6}

21. x^{-4}

22. 7^{-1}

GPS 23. **Guided Problem Solving** China has about 1.3×10^9 people. One of the world's smallest nations, the Marshall Islands, has a population of just 5.9×10^4 people. How many times greater is China's population than the Marshall Islands' population?
- **Make a Plan** Write a ratio comparing China's population to the Marshall Islands' population.
- **Carry Out the Plan** Divide and write the quotient in scientific notation. Simplify.

24. The sun's diameter is 1.39×10^6 kilometers. Earth's diameter is 1.28×10^4 kilometers. How many times greater is the sun's diameter than Earth's diameter?

Complete each equation.

25. $\frac{4^{\blacksquare}}{4^2} = 4^{10}$

26. $\frac{x^6}{x^{\blacksquare}} = x^4$

27. $\frac{14x^5}{7x^3} = 2x^{\blacksquare}$

28. $\frac{1}{c^7} = c^{\blacksquare}$

GO Online

Homework Video Tutor
Visit: PHSchool.com
Web Code: ase-1205

Use $w = -1$ and $x = 2$. Simplify each expression.

29. $(w + x)^{-4}$ **30.** x^w **31.** $-2^{w + 2x}$ **32.** $(2x)^{w + 1}$

33. Speed of Sound At sea level, the speed of sound is about 761 miles per hour, or $\dfrac{4.02 \times 10^6 \text{ feet}}{3.6 \times 10^3 \text{ seconds}}$. What is this speed in feet per second? Write your answer in scientific notation.

Writing in Math Is each statement *true* or *false*? Explain your reasoning.

34. $4^0 = 4^{-1}$ **35.** $8^{-1} = (-8)^1$ **36.** $2^1 \cdot 2^{-1} = 2^0$ **37.** $(-2)^{-1} = 2$

38. Space Travel The space probe *Pioneer 10* was 12.1×10^9 km from Earth in 2002. Its radio signal traveled at 3.0×10^5 km/s. How many hours did its signal take to reach Earth?

39. Challenge You can divide a polynomial by a monomial by dividing each term of the numerator by the denominator.

Sample $\dfrac{6x^4 + 10x^3}{2x^2} = \dfrac{6x^4}{2x^2} + \dfrac{10x^3}{2x^2}$
$$= 3x^2 + 5x$$

a. $\dfrac{6n^5 - 12n^2}{3n^2}$ **b.** $\dfrac{4m^9 + 6m^6 + 2m^3}{2m^3}$

Careers Test pilots often fly airplanes faster than the speed of sound. When they fly near the speed of sound, a cloud of condensation may form because of a rapid drop in air pressure and temperature.

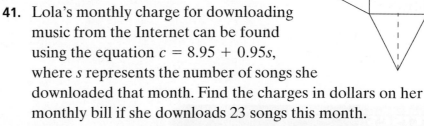

Test Prep and Mixed Review   **Practice**

Gridded Response

40. The net for a square pyramid is shown at the right. Use a centimeter ruler to measure the dimensions. Find the lateral surface area of the pyramid in square centimeters.

41. Lola's monthly charge for downloading music from the Internet can be found using the equation $c = 8.95 + 0.95s$, where s represents the number of songs she downloaded that month. Find the charges in dollars on her monthly bill if she downloads 23 songs this month.

42. A square is dilated with a scale factor of 3. If the area of the original square is 12 square inches, how many square inches is the area of the dilated square?

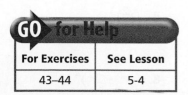

For Exercises	See Lesson
43–44	5-4

Use an equation to solve each problem. Round to the nearest hundredth.

43. What percent of 58 is 17?   **44.** What is 12.5% of 34.50?

Power Rules

You can use the rules for multiplying exponents to simplify an expression such as $(4^3)^2$.

$$(4^3)^2 = 4^3 \cdot 4^3$$
$$= 4^{(3 + 3)} = 4^6$$

Since $6 = 3 \cdot 2$, $(4^3)^2 = 4^{(3 \cdot 2)} = 4^6$. This suggests that to raise a power to a power, you multiply the exponents.

EXAMPLE   Raising a Power to a Power

1 Write each expression using a single exponent.

a. $(3^{-4})^5$

$(3^{-4})^5 = 3^{(-4 \cdot 5)}$

$\qquad = 3^{-20}$

b. $(x^{-2})^{-3}$

$(x^{-2})^{-3} = x^{(-2 \cdot -3)}$

$\qquad = x^6$

You can raise a product to a power using repeated multiplication.

$(2w)^3 = (2w) \cdot (2w) \cdot (2w)$ ← **Write out the factors of the power.**

$\qquad = 2 \cdot 2 \cdot 2 \cdot w \cdot w \cdot w$ ← **Use the commutative property to rearrange the factors.**

$\qquad = 2^3 \cdot w^3 = 2^3 w^3$ ← **Write the factors as a product.**

Notice that $(2w)^3 = 2^3 w^3$. This suggests that to raise a product to a power, you raise each factor to the power.

EXAMPLE   Raising a Product to a Power

2 Simplify $(3y^3)^2$.

$(3y^3)^2 = 3^2(y^3)^2$

$\qquad = 3^2 y^6 = 9y^6$

Exercises

Write each expression using a single exponent.

1. $(3^3)^7$

2. $(9^2)^{-5}$

3. $(w^{-2})^{-6}$

4. $(r^2)^3$

Simplify each expression.

5. $(3x)^2$

6. $(a^2 b^3)^4$

7. $(10x^5)^2$

8. $(y^2 \cdot 2^2)^4$

GPS Guided Problem Solving

Solving Equations

Rectangles based on the Golden Ratio ($1.618w : w$, where w is the width of the rectangle) are pleasing to the eye. Suppose you want a rectangular tiled patio using the Golden Ratio for a circular hot tub with a diameter that is one half of the rectangle's width. How many square feet of patio will be tiled if the patio's width is 25 feet?

What You Might Think

> What do I know? What am I trying to find out?

> How can I visualize the problem?

> How can I write an equation for the area of the patio that needs to be tiled?

> What is the area when $w = 25$?

What You Might Write

The patio has a length to width ratio of $1.618w : w$. A circle with diameter $\frac{1}{2}w$ is removed. I want to find the area of the patio when $w = 25$ feet.

Draw a diagram.

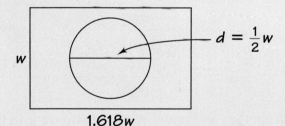

$$1.618w$$

Find the rectangle's area and subtract the circle's area. The radius of the circle is half the diameter. Use 3.14 for π.

$$\ell w - \pi r^2 = (1.618w)(w) - \pi(\tfrac{1}{4}w)^2$$

$$= 1.618w^2 - (3.14)\frac{w^2}{16}$$

$$1.618(25)^2 - (3.14)\frac{25^2}{16} = 888.59375$$

I will need about 889 square feet of tile.

Think It Through

1. In buying tile, you should buy 10% more than the area to be covered. Will 1,000 square feet be enough? Explain.

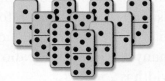

Exercises

Solve each problem. For Exercises 2 and 3, answer the questions first.

2. Wanda likes to set up and knock down dominoes arranged as shown at the right. She says you can find out how many dominoes you need for n rows by adding $1 + 2 + 3 + \ldots + n$. Jake says you can find it by evaluating $\frac{1}{2}(n^2 + n)$. Who is correct?
   a. What are you trying to find?
   b. Try both expressions for the first ten rows. What do you notice?

3. **Science** Gravitational pull varies among the different planets in our solar system. Since your weight depends on gravitational pull, it also varies from planet to planet. Use the table below to find your weight on Jupiter if you weigh 110 lbs on Earth.

Planet	Gravitational Pull (compared to Earth)
Mercury	0.38
Venus	0.91
Mars	0.38
Jupiter	2.36
Saturn	0.91
Uranus	0.89
Neptune	1.12

   a. What do you know? What do you want to find out?
   b. How is your weight on Jupiter related to your weight on Earth?

4. On a clear day, the distance d in miles you can see across the ocean from a height of h feet is given by $h = \frac{2}{3}d^2$. Jaime is learning to parasail with his friends. If beginning parasailers usually go up about 150 feet, how far can Jaime see when he is in the air?

5. Suppose your father goes skydiving for his birthday. He jumps from a plane at 10,000 feet and opens his parachute at 5,000 feet. How much time passes before he opens his parachute? Use the equation $t = 0.25\sqrt{d}$, where t is the time in seconds a falling object takes to fall d feet.

Working Backward

In multiple-choice tests, the correct answer is among the choices. To determine which answer is correct, you can use the problem-solving strategy *Work Backward*.

EXAMPLES

1 A bus can hold 72 passengers. A school uses the equation $b = \frac{n}{72}$ to calculate the number of buses needed to transport n students. What is the greatest number of students 6 buses can hold?

   Ⓐ 288   Ⓑ 360   Ⓒ 432   Ⓓ 504

You can answer the question without solving the equation. Substitute each answer choice for the variable until you find the solution.

    Let $n = 288$. Then $\frac{288}{72} = 4$. Since $4 \neq 6$, choice A is wrong.

    Let $n = 360$. Then $\frac{360}{72} = 5$. Since $5 \neq 6$, choice B is wrong.

    Let $n = 432$. Then $\frac{432}{72} = 6$. Since $6 = 6$, the correct answer is choice C.

You do not need to try choice D.

2 Which expression is equivalent to $12x^2 - 28x$?

   Ⓐ $12x(x - 2)$ Ⓑ $4x(3x - 7)$ Ⓒ $4x^2(3 - 7)$ Ⓓ $6(2x^2 - 4)$

You can multiply each of the answer choices to answer the question.

    $12x(x - 2) = 12x^2 - 24x$ This is not equal to $12x^2 - 28x$, so choice A is wrong.
    $4x(3x - 7) = 12x^2 - 28x$ Choice B is correct.

You do not need to test the other two choices.

Exercises

Solve each of the following by working backward.

1. The equation $m = 33g$ describes the number of miles m a car can travel on g gallons of gas. For which value of g does $m = 297$?

   Ⓐ 4   Ⓑ 6   Ⓒ 9   Ⓓ 14

2. Jorge wants to run a half-marathon (13.1 miles). About how many miles per hour should he run to complete the half-marathon in 1.5 hours? Use the equation $d = rt$.

   Ⓕ 5.2   Ⓖ 8.7   Ⓗ 9.6   Ⓙ 19.6

Vocabulary Review

Choose the correct vocabulary term above to complete each sentence.

1. $6x^2 + 3x - 2$ is an example of a ___?___.

2. A term that does not contain a variable is a ___?___.

3. A polynomial such as $4y$ is called a ___?___.

4. In the polynomial $5z^2 + 2$, 5 is a ___?___.

5. A ___?___ is a polynomial with two terms.

Skills and Concepts

Lessons 12-1, 12-2
- To write algebraic expressions and to simplify polynomials
- To add and subtract polynomials

A **polynomial** is an expression such as $2x^2 - 3x$. A term in a polynomial that does not contain a variable is a **constant**.

To simplify a polynomial, combine like terms. You can use algebra tiles or the properties of numbers to simplify a polynomial.

Write a variable expression for each model.

6.

7.

Use properties of numbers to simplify each polynomial.

8. $5x^2 + 6 - 4x + 9x^2 + 17x$

9. $8 - 3x + 11x^2 + 2x^2 - 10 + 7x$

10. $4 - 3x^2 + 2x - x^2 + 3$

11. $-x^2 + 4x + 7 - 2x + 9x$

Find each sum.

12. $(2x - 5) + (14x + 10)$

13. $(-4x^2 + 7x) + (x^2 - 7x + 3)$

14. $(8x^2 - 7x + 3) + (3x^2 + x - 5)$

15. $(5x^2 + 3) + (2x^2 - 3x - 1)$

Find each difference.

16. $(5x - 4) - (9x + 3)$

17. $(2x^2 - 4x - 8) - (x^2 - 5x + 3)$

18. $(7x^2 + 6) - (2x - 7)$

19. $(5x^2 + 9x - 7) - (2x^2 + 3x)$

Lesson 12-3

- To multiply powers with the same base and to multiply numbers in scientific notation

To multiply numbers with the same base, add the exponents. Use this same property to multiply numbers in scientific notation.

Write each expression using a single exponent.

20. $8^{10} \cdot 8^9$

21. $(-3)^4 \cdot (-3)^9$

22. $2.6^{12} \cdot 2.6^{12}$

23. $11^5 \cdot 11^6$

Multiply. Write each product in scientific notation.

24. $(3 \times 10^6)(2 \times 10^{12})$

25. $5(1.4 \times 10^6)$

26. $(6 \times 10^9)(5 \times 10^4)$

27. $(2.1 \times 10^7)(7 \times 10^{12})$

Lesson 12-4

- To multiply monomials and binomials

To multiply **monomials,** rearrange the factors and use the properties of exponents. To multiply a monomial and a **binomial,** use the Distributive Property. Use an area model to find the product of two binomials.

Simplify each expression.

28. $(-6x)(3x^3)$

29. $(-2x)(-7x)$

30. $-10x(3x - 2)$

31. $5x(x^2 - 3x)$

Use the area model to find each product.

32.

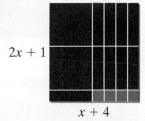

$2x + 1$

$x + 4$

33.

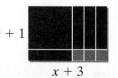

$x + 1$

$x + 3$

Lesson 12-5

- To divide powers with the same base and to simplify expressions with negative exponents

To divide numbers with the same base, subtract the exponents. Any nonzero number with a zero exponent equals 1. For any nonzero number a and integer n, $a^{-n} = \frac{1}{a^n}$.

Write each expression using a single exponent.

34. $\dfrac{5^{10}}{5^7}$

35. $\dfrac{(-8)^{12}}{(-8)^2}$

36. $\dfrac{76^{11}}{76^5}$

37. $\dfrac{1.8^6}{1.8^5}$

Simplify each expression.

38. 8^0

39. $(-16)^0$

40. g^0

41. $(8b)^0$

42. 5^{-4}

43. x^{-9}

44. 9^{-2}

45. h^{-8}

Chapter 12 Test

Go Online For: Online chapter test
PHSchool.com Web Code: asa-1252

For Exercises 1–4, use tiles or properties of numbers to simplify each polynomial.

1. $3x + 12 - 4 + 9x$

2. $4x^2 - 6 + x^2 + 5x - 10$

3. $4 - 2x + 9 + 3x^2 + 7x - 6x^2$

4. $14x - 1 + 5x^2 + 10x^2 - 4$

5. Write and simplify the polynomial represented by the model below.

Find each sum.

6. $(5x^2 - 4x + 2) + (3x^2 - 3x - 5)$

7. $(x^2 - 3x + 5) + (-x^2 + 4x + 4)$

8. $(2x^2 + 7x - 6) + (4x^2 + 3x - 2)$

Find each difference.

9. $(7x^2 - x + 2) - (x^2 + 4x - 4)$

10. $(2x^2 + 3x + 4) - (2x - 7)$

11. $(9x^2 + 5x - 10) - (-2x^2 + 4x + 3)$

12. a. Find the perimeter of the figure below.

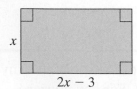

x

$2x - 3$

b. Find the area of the figure.

Write each expression using a single exponent.

13. $10^7 \cdot 10^6$

14. $a^5 \cdot a^2$

15. $3.4^3 \cdot 3.4^6$

16. $(-h)^5 \cdot (-h)^8$

17. $2^3 \cdot 2^6 \cdot 2^5$

18. $r^3 \cdot r^4 \cdot r^{10}$

Simplify each expression.

19. $(-9x)(2x)$

20. $x(3x + 5)$

21. $x^2(x + 17)$

22. $2x(x^2 - 6x)$

Multiply. Write each product in scientific notation.

23. $5(7 \times 10^4)$

24. $11(8 \times 10^2)$

25. $(9 \times 10^5)(3 \times 10^{12})$

26. $(12 \times 10^7)(2 \times 10^6)$

27. $(6 \times 10^3)(6 \times 10^{10})$

Write each expression using a single exponent.

28. $t^{23} \cdot t^0$

29. $\dfrac{(-3)^5}{(-3)^2}$

30. $\dfrac{14^8}{14^4}$

31. $\dfrac{c^6}{c^2}$

32. Use the area model below to find the product.

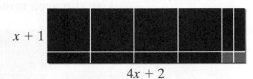

$x + 1$

$4x + 2$

Simplify each expression.

33. 2^0

34. r^0

35. 7^0

36. d^0

37. 4^{-5}

38. a^{-8}

39. r^{-2}

40. 9^{-4}

41. x^{-6}

42. 6^{-3}

43. **Writing in Math** Write what you would say to a classmate who asked you to explain why 5^0 is equal to 1.

44. **Biology** The human eye blinks about 4.2×10^6 times each year. About how many times has the eye of a 14-year-old blinked? Write your answer in scientific notation.

592 Chapter 12 Chapter Test

Multiple Choice
Choose the correct letter.

Go Online For: Online end-of-chapter test
PHSchool.com Web Code: asa-1254

1. You have a set of data that has five items. The median is 14, the mean is 14.8, the mode is 14, and the range is 4. Which could be the correct data set?
   Ⓐ 14, 14, 14, 16, 18   Ⓒ 13, 14, 14, 16, 17
   Ⓑ 12, 14, 14, 15, 20   Ⓓ 12, 13, 14, 16, 16

2. Which proportion could NOT be represented by the model at the right?

   Ⓕ $\frac{12}{15} = \frac{8}{10}$
   Ⓖ $\frac{2}{10} = \frac{3}{15}$
   Ⓗ $\frac{3}{10} = \frac{2}{15}$
   Ⓙ $\frac{4}{5} = \frac{8}{10}$

3. Which number could NOT be a value of y if $y = 2x^2 - 3$?
   Ⓐ 15   Ⓑ 5   Ⓒ -3   Ⓓ -5

4. The graph below represents which inequality?

   Ⓕ $-\frac{x}{3} < 1$ Ⓗ $2 + y \le -1$
   Ⓖ $6z > 18$ Ⓙ $-2w \ge -6$

5. Tia has art class every 6th day of school (Monday through Friday). How often does she have art class on Monday?
   Ⓐ every week   Ⓒ every 6th week
   Ⓑ every 5th week   Ⓓ every 7th week

6. Tate bought 500 grams of hamburger. How many kilograms is this?
   Ⓕ 0.05 kg   Ⓗ 5 kg
   Ⓖ 0.5 kg   Ⓙ 50 kg

7. A right triangle has legs of lengths 3 in. and 4 in. What is the length of the hypotenuse?
   Ⓐ 2 in.   Ⓑ 4 in.   Ⓒ 5 in.   Ⓓ 7 in.

8. Which algebraic expression is NOT equivalent to $2(x - 3)$?
   Ⓕ $2(x) - 2(3)$ Ⓗ $(x - 3) + (x - 3)$
   Ⓖ $2(-3) + 2x$ Ⓙ $2x - 3$

9. Which set of ordered pairs describes the image of the vertices of $\triangle ABC$ after a translation 2 units left and 3 units down?

   Ⓐ $A'(-4, -1), B'(-1, -2), C'(-1, -4)$
   Ⓑ $A'(0, -1), B'(3, -2), C'(3, -4)$
   Ⓒ $A'(0, 5), B'(3, 4), C'(3, 2)$
   Ⓓ $A'(-4, 5), B'(-1, 4), C'(-1, 2)$

10. How many integers have an absolute value less than 3?
    Ⓕ 3   Ⓖ 4   Ⓗ 5   Ⓙ 6

11. Deidre has 4 red shirts, 3 blue shirts, and 2 green shirts. If she chooses a shirt at random, what is the probability it is green?
    Ⓐ $\frac{7}{9}$ Ⓑ $\frac{2}{7}$ Ⓒ $\frac{2}{9}$ Ⓓ $\frac{1}{9}$

12. Estimate the shaded area.
    Ⓕ 0.7 units^2
    Ⓖ 7 units^2
    Ⓗ 17 units^2
    Ⓙ 27 units^2

13. There are about 10,550 radio stations in the United States. How is this number written in scientific notation?
    Ⓐ 1.055×10^3 Ⓒ 10.55×10^3
    Ⓑ 1.055×10^4 Ⓓ 10.55×10^4

14. In how many different orders can 5 out of 8 people be seated in a row of 5 chairs?
　Ⓕ 40,320　Ⓖ 6,720　Ⓗ 120　Ⓙ 56

15. In a circle graph, what is the measure of the central angle of a sector that represents 24% of the whole?
　Ⓐ 2.4°　Ⓑ 8.64°　Ⓒ 24°　Ⓓ 86.4°

16. Which of the following CANNOT be found by looking at a box-and-whisker plot?
　Ⓕ range　　　Ⓗ median
　Ⓖ mode　　　Ⓙ upper quartile

17. In the figure below, the triangles are similar. Find the unknown length h.

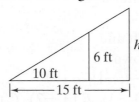

10 ft　6 ft　h　15 ft

　Ⓐ 30 ft　Ⓑ 9 ft　Ⓒ 6 ft　Ⓓ 3 ft

18. Jim had $500 in his bank account on Monday. He wrote checks for $200 and $400 on Tuesday and Wednesday. Which of these amounts represents the balance in his account on Thursday?
　Ⓕ −$100　　　Ⓗ $300
　Ⓖ $100　　　Ⓙ $1,100

19. Which of the following is NOT an example of a prism?
　Ⓐ a shoe box　　Ⓒ a domino
　Ⓑ a file cabinet　Ⓓ a soup can

20. Describe the relationship in the scatter plot at the right.
　Ⓕ no trend
　Ⓖ positive trend
　Ⓗ negative trend
　Ⓙ positive and negative trend

Gridded Response

Use the table below for Exercises 21–23.

How Long Students Studied Last Night

Number of Hours	Less than 1	1	2	3	More than 3
Number of Students	15	12	8	3	5

21. How many students were surveyed?

22. How many students studied 1 hour or less?

23. What percent of the students surveyed studied more than 2 hours? Round to the nearest tenth of a percent.

24. Jake received these grades on his math tests: 83, 86, 95, 95, 90, 82, 85, 82, 87, 82. What is his median test score?

25. Evaluate $-3 + x - y$ for $x = -4$ and $y = -8$.

26. An equilateral triangle has a perimeter of $5\frac{1}{4}$ cm. What is the length of one side in centimeters?

27. Find the area of the figure below in mm^2.

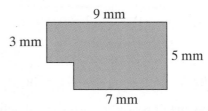

9 mm　3 mm　5 mm　7 mm

28. A diving board is 4 ft above a pool that is 15 ft deep. The total vertical distance of a person's dive is 10 ft. How many feet below the surface of the water did the person dive?

29. A copy center charges $.08 per copy. How much would it cost in dollars to make a copy of a one-page song for 250 students?

30. A rectangular pyramid has a base area of $126\ cm^2$ and a height of 23 cm. Find the volume of the pyramid in cm^3.

Short Response

31. Find the lateral area of the square pyramid below. Then find the surface area.

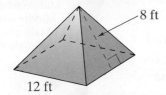

8 ft

12 ft

32. Find the percent of markup on a T-shirt that has a store cost of $4.87 and a selling price of $15.95. Show your work.

33. a. Graph the function $y = -3x - 1$.
b. What value of x will give $y = 11$?

34. According to the graph shown, when did the stock fund earn the most? Explain.

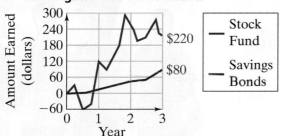

Earnings of Two Investments

Amount Earned (dollars)

Year

Stock Fund — $220

Savings Bonds — $80

35. Which has a greater volume: a cone with radius 2 cm and height 6 cm, or a cone with height 2 cm and radius 6 cm? Explain.

36. a. What is the next term in the sequence 4, 12, 36, 108, . . . ?
b. What is the common ratio?

37. Find the circumference and the area of the circle. Round to the nearest tenth.

14 cm

38. Karen swam for a half hour on Monday. She increased her workout by the same number of minutes each day. On Friday, she swam for one hour. Write and solve an equation to find the number of minutes by which Karen increased her workout each day.

Extended Response

39. It costs $3.99 to connect and $3.99 per minute to use an in-flight phone.
a. Write a function rule for the cost of a call using an in-flight phone.
b. Find the cost of a 10-minute in-flight call. Explain your work.
c. Graph the function.

40. a. Draw a net for a cylinder that has a diameter of 4 yd and a height of 7 yd. Label the diameter and height.
b. Find the surface area of the cylinder to the nearest yd^2. Show your work.

41. Boise wants to buy a scanner for $349. He has $34 and plans to save $15 each week.
a. Write an equation to show how many weeks Boise must save before he can buy the scanner. Define the variables you use.
b. How long will Boise need to save money for the scanner? Justify your reasoning.

42. The diagram below is a plan for a room. The scale is 1 in. = 20 ft.

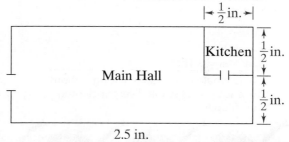

$\frac{1}{2}$ in.

Kitchen $\frac{1}{2}$ in.

Main Hall $\frac{1}{2}$ in.

2.5 in.

a. How long will the 2.5-in. side be in the real building? Justify your reasoning.
b. Find the area of the actual floor. Show your work.

43. A store pays $3.50 for a water bottle. The store sells each water bottle for $6.00.
a. Find the percent of markup on the water bottle. Show your work.
b. How many water bottles can you buy with $15.00? Show your work.

Applying Scientific Notation

Wild Exponents Would a giraffe 5.79×10^3 mm tall fit in your bedroom? Should you be afraid of a lobster that weighs 7.5×10^{-4} t? Could you outrun a rabbit that hopped 5.55×10^9 ft per decade? Scientific notation is convenient for expressing and comparing numbers, but it can also mislead you into thinking the numbers are wilder than they actually are. Often you can tame them by turning them back into a more familiar form.

Average Heights

Middle school boy: 156 cm
Middle school girl: 157 cm
Male giraffe: 530 cm
Female giraffe: 430 cm

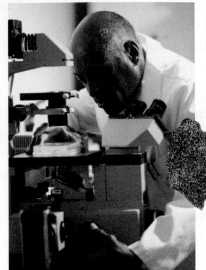

Small Packages

Amoebas, small, transparent organisms, flow outward to move. It's easy to overlook them because they're only about 0.003 mm long!

How Many Is That?

A blue whale can be 33.5 m long—about the length of 18 scuba divers, including their flippers.

Go Online
PHSchool.com
For: Information about animals
Web Code: ase-1253

Put It All Together

1. Warm Up Use the information in the introductory paragraph.
   a. How tall is the giraffe in meters?
   b. How much does the lobster weigh in pounds?
   c. How fast does the rabbit hop in miles per hour?

The goal of this game is to identify an animal when given its common dimensions in uncommon ways.

What You'll Need

• 3 to 5 index cards per student

• **Research** Choose an animal for each card. Consider animals that range in size from microscopic to gigantic. Find three numerical facts about each animal.

• Convert each fact to scientific notation, using units of measure that make the animal look especially large or small. Some numbers should have positive exponents and others should have negative exponents.

• Write these facts, or clues, on the front of the card.

• Illustrate the back of the card with a picture of the animal.

How to Play

2. Exchange cards with another student. Looking only at the clues, and *not* at the back of the card, change each into standard notation. Write your answers on a piece of paper.

3. Check your partner's answers while he or she checks yours. Correct any mistakes. Take turns asking questions about each animal until you guess what it is.

Sample Card (Zebra)

Who Am I?

1. Shoulder height up to 1.5×10^{-2} km

2. Weight up to 4×10^5 g

3. Adult female has 1×10^0 foal per year.

Length Conversions

1 micron = 1×10^{-6} m
1 mm = 1×10^{-3} m
1 km = 1×10^3 m
1 ft = 3.048×10^{-1} m
1 mi = 5.28×10^3 ft
1 light-year = 5.879×10^{12} mi

Weight Conversions

1 mg = 1×10^{-3} g
1 kg = 1×10^3 g
1 kg = 2.2 lb
1 oz = 28.35 g
1 lb = 16 oz
1 t = 2×10^3 lb

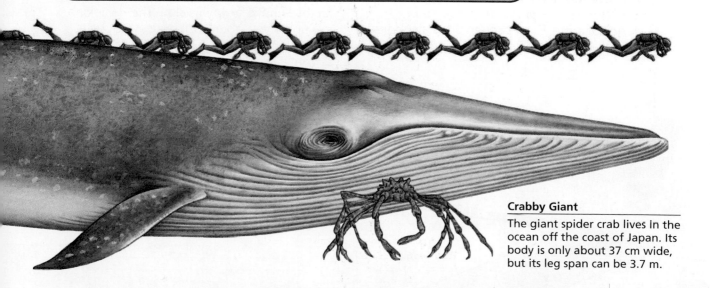

Crabby Giant
The giant spider crab lives in the ocean off the coast of Japan. Its body is only about 37 cm wide, but its leg span can be 3.7 m.

Chapter Projects

Weather or NOT

Would you go swimming in 32° water? Is −2° a good temperature setting for a home freezer? The answer to both questions is "That depends!"

Are you using the Celsius or Fahrenheit scale? Water at 32°C feels like a bath! As for a freezer, −2°C is barely below freezing, while −2°F is a deep freeze! People living in North America use both the Fahrenheit and the Celsius scales, so it pays to know the difference.

Chapter 1 Integers and Algebraic Expressions

Prepare a Report For the chapter project, you will examine weather data for a state or region of your choice. Your final project will be a report on temperature data, using both scales.

Go Online
PHSchool.com
For: Information to help you complete your project
Web Code: asd-0161

A swirling dragon marks the start of the Chinese New Year. The Chinese calendar is one of several calendars used throughout the world. Each calendar is a unique solution to the problem of how to keep track of time. Even though the calendars are all different, they all work quite well.

Chapter 2 Rational Numbers

Invent a New Calendar For the chapter project, you will invent a new calendar, defining weeks and months as you wish. Will your calendar have 10 months per year? Might it have 5-day weeks? The decisions are up to you. Your final project will be a new calendar and a description of the advantages of your new system.

Go Online
PHSchool.com
For: Information to help you complete your project
Web Code: asd-0261

 **StepRight UP!**

Have you ever been to a carnival or fair? "Hit the bull's-eye and win a prize!" Is it skill? Or is it luck?

Design a Game Suppose your class is putting on a fair to raise money for a class trip. For the chapter project, you will invent a game in which a ball rolls down a ramp and comes to rest in a target area of your own design. Does a bull's-eye score 10, or maybe

Chapter 3 *Real Numbers and the Coordinate Plane*

100? Can the players vary the slope of the ramp? You decide, since you make up the rules! Your final project will be the game, along with written rules to play by.

Go Online
PHSchool.com
For: Information to help you complete your project
Web Code: asd-0361

 **Larger Than LIFE**

Mount Rushmore is an example of a scale model that is larger than the objects on which it is based—much larger! Other types of scale models, such as toy trains, dollhouses, and other toys, are smaller than the objects on which they are based.

Build a Scale Model For the chapter project, you will build your own scale model. First, you will choose an object to model. Use your imagination! Your model can be larger or smaller than the actual object—

Chapter 4 *Applications of Proportions*

you choose the scale. Then you will select building materials and assemble the model. Your final project will be to present the model to your class, explaining the scale and how you chose the item to model.

Go Online
PHSchool.com
For: Information to help you complete your project
Web Code: asd-0461

Invest in a WINNER

You've won! You entered a quiz contest thinking you didn't have a chance, and now you're $5,000 richer! You are looking for a way to double your money in five years. Is that possible?

Explore Ways to Invest Money For the chapter project, you will explore different investments, looking for the best one for your money. Your final project will be to prepare an oral and visual presentation describing your investment choice.

For: Information to help you
complete your project
Web Code: asd-0561

ACT

Mobiles are a popular form of art that you may see anywhere: in people's homes, in large office buildings, and in parks. The objects on a mobile float gently on currents of air. American sculptor Alexander Calder (1898–1976) first popularized mobiles. Calder is considered the founder of kinetic art, or art that is in motion.

Make a Mobile For the chapter project, you will explore techniques for constructing a mobile and use equations to model the relationships involved in the mobile. Your final project will be a finished mobile, along with a written summary telling what you have learned.

Go **Online**
PHSchool.com
For: Information to help you
complete your project
Web Code: asd-0661

As the summer sun goes down on another hot day, you just have to get outside. Where do you go? To the park! For generations, people in towns and cities have used parks as places to escape. When properly planned, a park can be the perfect place to relax, meet friends, skate, and be surrounded by natural beauty.

Chapter 7 *Geometry*

Design a Park For the chapter project, you will design a small park and be prepared to present your plan to the town council. Your final project will be a detailed plan of the park.

Go Online
PHSchool.com
For: Information to help you complete your project
Web Code: asd-0761

A BETTER Way

Stop by the cereal section of your local supermarket. There are dozens of brands! Now check out the packaging. Most cereals are packaged in the same way: in cardboard rectangular boxes that are high and wide, but not deep.

Is this a waste of cardboard? Can you design a better package? You can . . . because now, you're in charge!

Chapter 8 *Measurement*

Design Packaging for Cereal For the chapter project, you will redesign the packaging of your favorite cereal. Your final project will be a new and different-shaped cardboard package that still holds the same volume as the original.

Go Online
PHSchool.com
For: Information to help you complete your project
Web Code: asd-0861

NEWS Flash

What type of news catches your eye? Do you notice graphs and charts in news magazines and newspapers? If a picture is worth a thousand words, a graph is worth a thousand numbers! Reporters use graphs to summarize data and to tell a story clearly and simply. Do they always do it accurately?

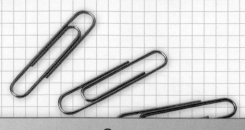

Chapter 9 *Using Graphs to Analyze Data*

Make a Graph for a News Article For the chapter project, you will analyze graphs and charts that appear in the news. For your final project, using a topic that you choose, you will write a news article and illustrate it with an appropriate graph.

Go Online
PHSchool.com
For: Information to help you complete your project
Web Code: asd-0961

Start With the STATS

There are fifteen seconds to go in a close basketball game. Should you foul intentionally? What is the probability that the player you foul will make both free throws? Statistics are everywhere in sports: field-goal percentages, batting averages, and so on. Coaches and players use these statistics to assess probabilities and make decisions.

Prepare a Stat Sheet Suppose you are a statistician for a basketball team. Pick any team—school, professional, or even fictional.

Chapter 10 *Probability*

For the chapter project, you will gather data on five key players from the team. For your final project, you will present a statistical report that summarizes these basketball players' season last year.

Go Online
PHSchool.com
For: Information to help you complete your project
Web Code: asd-1061

How Much Dough?

Chapter 11 *Functions*

How much should a pizza cost? Many restaurants sell pizzas in a variety of sizes and types, with many different kinds of toppings. Do restaurants base their prices on what they think their customers will be willing to pay for different sizes? Or do they take a mathematical approach and figure their costs using area formulas?

Set Prices for a Product For the chapter project, you will investigate prices for a product that is available in many sizes. You will look for patterns in the prices and describe the patterns mathematically. Then you will use this analysis to decide on prices for new products. Your final project will be a written proposal for setting pizza prices.

For: Information to help you complete your project
Web Code: asd-1161

One Small STEP

Chapter 12 *Polynomials and Properties of Exponents*

"That's one small step for man, one giant leap for mankind." In July of 1969, Neil Armstrong was the first man to touch the moon's surface. Since then, space travel has exploded, with new missions being launched almost monthly.

Can you even imagine what the space program will be like in 30 more years? How about in 100 years? Take a small step into the future. Pretend you are a travel agent—one who specializes in space travel!

Create a brochure For the chapter project, you will collect information about two planets, including travel between them, and calculate the approximate distance from Earth to each of them. Your final project will be to design a space-travel brochure that includes interesting and enticing information about travel between the two planets.

Go Online
PHSchool.com
For: Information to help you complete your project
Web Code: asd-1261

CHAPTER 1

Extra Practice

Skills

● **Lesson 1-1** Evaluate each expression for $n = 2$, $m = 3$, and $t = 5$.

1. $3t - 4n$
2. $13 - (m + n)$
3. $\dfrac{m + t}{n}$
4. $4.7 + mt$

● **Lesson 1-2** Compare. Write <, =, or >.

5. $-7 \ \blacksquare\ 7$
6. $32 \ \blacksquare\ |-32|$
7. $|-9| \ \blacksquare\ -3$
8. $|-8| \ \blacksquare\ |-6|$

● **Lessons 1-3 and 1-4** Simplify each expression.

9. $-6 + 4$
10. $-4 + (-5)$
11. $-2 - 6$
12. $-8 - (-5)$
13. $15 - (-8)$
14. $99 + (-101)$
15. $-3 \cdot 4$
16. $-15 \cdot (-5)$
17. $2 \cdot (-7) \cdot 5$
18. $\dfrac{-12}{6}$
19. $\dfrac{-80}{-16}$
20. $\dfrac{16}{-8}$

● **Lesson 1-5** Identify each property.

21. $2(11) + 2(4) = 2(11 + 4)$
22. $(3 + 4) + 5 = 3 + (4 + 5)$
23. $2n + p = p + 2n$
24. $(3 + m)(-7) = -21 - 7m$
25. $(12 \cdot 5) \cdot 100 = 12 \cdot (5 \cdot 100)$
26. $c + 0 = c$

● **Lessons 1-6 and 1-7** Solve each equation.

27. $x - 6 = -15$
28. $-12 = m + 8$
29. $1.5 = m - 3.2$
30. $x + 10 = 10$
31. $\dfrac{b}{7} = 9$
32. $-3w = 360$
33. $144 = 6k$
34. $20 = \dfrac{h}{-10}$

Word Problems

● **Lesson 1-1**

35. The depth of Lake Huron is 855 ft less than the depth of Lake Chelan. Lake Chelan is 1,605 ft deep. How deep is Lake Huron?

36. **Sales** A store sells one model of bicycle for $250. If you buy more than one bicycle, the store will take $10 off the price of the first bicycle, $20 off the price of the second, $30 off the price of the third, and so on. If you buy 5 bicycles, how much will you pay?

Lesson 1-2

37. A teacher asks 15 students to estimate an answer to a question. The answers are 1, 5, 5, 6, 7, 8, 10, and 12. The correct estimate is 7. The teacher wants to calculate how far off the estimates were by finding the absolute value of the difference between each estimate and the answer. Which estimate was off by the most?

Lessons 1-3 and 1-4

38. Stock Market A stock worth $34 at the beginning of the day lost $15 in value by the end of the day. What was the price at the end of the day?

39. A balloon is floating 47 feet above a lake. The bottom of the lake is 128 ft below the surface. How high above the lake bottom is the balloon?

40. Coupons A store sells 12 shirts for $20.00 each. Seven of the shirts are purchased with $5 coupons. Use the equation $20s - 5c$, where s is the number of shirts sold and c is the number of coupons to find the total cost. Evaluate the expression for $s = 12$ and $c = 7$.

41. Over a 3-hour period a subway line carries 7,200 passengers. What is the number of passengers per hour?

Lesson 1-5   In Exercises 42–45, use the Distributive Property to find each total cost.

42. 3 loaves of bread at $1.99 each

43. 6 cans of tuna at $.97 each

44. 4 bags of berries at $1.98 each

45. 5 boxes of rice at $2.95 each

Lesson 1-6

46. School Between 7:30 A.M. and 8:00 A.M. the number of students in a school increased by 73. There were 152 students in the school at 8:00 A.M. How many students were in school at 7:30 A.M.?

47. The movie *Antz* has a run time that is 33 minutes shorter than *Fantasia*'s run time. *Fantasia*'s run time is 120 minutes. Find the run time of *Antz*.

Lesson 1-7   Write and solve an equation for each situation.

48. Three students eat lunch five days in a row. They spend a total of $60. The students spend the same amount of money for each lunch. What is the cost of one lunch?

49. A group of twelve volunteers raises $144 for three charities. Each charity gets the same amount. How much money does each charity get?

Skills

● **Lesson 2-1** **Find the GCF of each pair of numbers using prime factorization.**

1. 9, 33 **2.** 7, 15 **3.** 6, 24 **4.** 4, 18

5. 22, 121 **6.** 17, 51 **7.** 42, 165 **8.** 18, 60

● **Lesson 2-2** **Write each fraction in simplest form.**

9. $\frac{20}{25}$ **10.** $\frac{7}{77}$ **11.** $\frac{40}{48}$ **12.** $-\frac{15}{35}$

13. $-\frac{9}{42}$ **14.** $\frac{36}{63}$ **15.** $-\frac{26}{65}$ **16.** $\frac{34}{51}$

Write each decimal as a mixed number or fraction in simplest form.

17. 0.45 **18.** 12.2 **19.** 8.6 **20.** $0.\overline{8}$

● **Lesson 2-3** **Compare. Write <, =, or >.**

21. $\frac{25}{36}$ ■ $0.69\overline{4}$ **22.** 2.7 ■ $\frac{10}{3}$ **23.** -4.3 ■ -4.2 **24.** $-\frac{17}{5}$ ■ -15.9

● **Lessons 2-4 and 2-5** **Simplify. Write each answer in simplest form.**

25. $-\frac{3}{8} + \frac{7}{8}$ **26.** $-\frac{5}{18} + \left(-\frac{1}{6}\right)$ **27.** $12\frac{1}{3} - 6\frac{2}{3}$ **28.** $3\frac{1}{2} - \left(-\frac{11}{14}\right)$

29. $-\frac{3}{7} \cdot \frac{5}{9}$ **30.** $-4\frac{5}{24} \cdot (-6)$ **31.** $-2\frac{1}{2} \div 6$ **32.** $-25 \div \frac{5}{7}$

● **Lesson 2-6** **Solve each formula for the variable indicated in red.**

33. $V = \frac{1}{3}Bh$ **34.** $I = prt$ **35.** $C = 44a + b$ **36.** $E = mc^2$

● **Lesson 2-7** **Simplify or evaluate each expression.**

37. $-3^2 - (-8)$ **38.** $(-2)^3 + 4 \div 2 - 3$ **39.** $(3 - 4)^5 - 17 + 1^{12}$

40. $2r^2 + 6r + 3$ for $r = -6$ **41.** $-c^3 + 2c^2 - c + 8$ for $c = 3$

● **Lesson 2-8** **Write each number in scientific notation.**

42. 400,000,000 **43.** 8,750,000 **44.** 40,000 **45.** 19,000,000

Word Problems

● **Lesson 2-1**

46. Two frogs hop around a circular track that is 60 inches around. First the larger frog jumps 13 in. and then the smaller frog jumps 11 in. If they take turns jumping, how many inches from the start will they be when they once again are at the same point?

● **Lesson 2-2**

47. A bag of beads for a craft project weighs 6 oz. The project uses 5 bags. Express the total weight of the beads in pounds as a decimal.

● **Lesson 2-3**

48. **Science** Two students are measuring the amount of water in 2 liquids. One student finds that $\frac{10}{17}$ of the first liquid is water. The other finds that 0.6 of the second liquid is water. Which of the two liquids has the higher fraction of water?

● **Lessons 2-4 and 2-5**

49. Find the perimeter of a square whose sides measure $4\frac{7}{8}$ in.

50. A small room has a floor space that measures 48.75 square feet. In one corner of the room a cabinet will be set. The rest of the room will be carpeted. If the cabinet takes up $4\frac{2}{3}$ square feet, how much carpeting is needed?

51. Three quarters of a pound of honey sold at a roadside stand costs $4. How much honey can you get for $6?

52. A bag of nuts weighs $2\frac{1}{4}$ oz. In making a recipe a chef uses $3\frac{1}{2}$ bags. How many ounces of nuts are used in the recipe?

● **Lessons 2-6 and 2-7**

53. An African driver ant queen can lay as many as 4 million eggs in a 25-day period. What is this rate in eggs per hour?

54. **Geometry** The formula for the area of a square is $A = s^2$. What is the area of a square whose sides measure 12 cm?

● **Lesson 2-8**

55. An electronic counter increases by 1 every second. If it starts at 0, what will the count be after 50 days? Express your answer in scientific notation.

Skills

● **Lesson 3-1** Identify each number as *rational* or *irrational*.

1. 1.020304 …   **2.** $\sqrt{25}$ **3.** $\sqrt{26}$ **4.** 5.63663

● **Lessons 3-2 and 3-3** Use the Pythagorean theorem to find the hypotenuse of the right triangle from the given lengths of the two legs.

5. 3, 4   **6.** 10, 24   **7.** 7, 13   **8.** 6, 11

9. $\sqrt{2}$, $\sqrt{7}$ **10.** 1.2, 1.6   **11.** 21, 22   **12.** 13, 31

Given leg ℓ and hypotenuse h determine the length of the missing leg of the right triangle.

13. $\ell = 7$, $h = 25$ **14.** $\ell = 7.5$, $h = 12.5$ **15.** $\ell = 23$, $h = 44$ **16.** $\ell = 50$, $h = 76$

● **Lesson 3-4** Name the coordinates of each point in the graph.

17. C **18.** D

19. K **20.** M

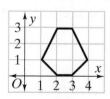

● **Lesson 3-5** Graph each linear equation.

21. $y = 3x + 3$ **22.** $y = -2x - 3$ **23.** $y = \frac{1}{3}x - \frac{2}{3}$ **24.** $y = -\frac{3}{4}x + 1$

● **Lessons 3-6 to 3-8** Copy the figure shown below for Exercises 25–28. Then draw its image after each transformation.

25. translation 3 units right and 1 unit down

26. reflection over the *y*-axis

27. rotation 270° about the origin

Word Problems

● **Lesson 3-1**

28. Open-Ended Name a rational number whose square root is a number between 0 and 1.

29. A square has an area of 240.25 in.². What are the lengths of its sides?

Lessons 3-2 and 3-3

30. The hypotenuse of a right triangle is 5 cm. The lengths of both legs are equal. Find the lengths of the legs. Round to the nearest tenth.

31. A tree forms a right angle with the ground. If you place the base of a 12-ft ladder 3 ft from the tree, how high up the tree will it reach?

Lesson 3-4

32. Designers use coordinates to make graphics. On a computer screen a point is called a pixel. Name the coordinates of each orange pixel shown below. What do these coordinates have in common?

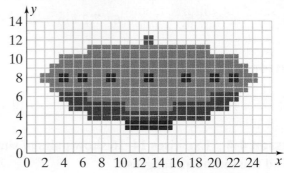

Lesson 3-5

33. Population A country's population is currently about 20 million. The population increases by about 1.2 million people per year. The equation for the population p in millions after y years is $p = 1.2y + 20$. Graph the equation and predict how many people there will be in 19 years.

Lesson 3-6

34. Point Z is translated using the rule $(x, y) \rightarrow (x - 4, y + 11)$. The coordinates of Z' are $(4, -11)$. What are the coordinates of point Z?

Lesson 3-7

35. The vertices of $\triangle RST$ are $R(0, 4)$, $S(0, 0)$, and $T(-4, 0)$. Graph $\triangle RST$ on a coordinate plane. What are the coordinates after a reflection over the y-axis?

Lesson 3-8

36. Rotate the figure at the right 90° clockwise about the origin. What are the coordinates of point Q'?

37. Geometry A regular polygon has all sides and all angles equal. All regular polygons have rotational symmetry. A certain regular polygon has an angle of rotation of 72°. How many sides does this polygon have?

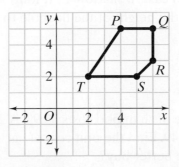

Skills

● **Lesson 4-1** **Find each unit rate.**

1. 240 mi on 8 gal
2. $3.50 for 10 oz
3. 450 mi in 9 h
4. $18 for 12 cans

● **Lesson 4-2** **Convert each measure.**

5. 3.5 mi = ■ ft
6. 7.2 km = ■ m
7. 80 oz = ■ lb
8. 120 fl oz = ■ gal

● **Lesson 4-3** **Solve each proportion.**

9. $\frac{4}{7} = \frac{x}{21}$
10. $\frac{3}{x} = \frac{18}{9}$
11. $\frac{x}{10} = \frac{8}{15}$
12. $\frac{3}{5} = \frac{2}{x}$

● **Lesson 4-4** **Exercises 14–16 show pairs of similar polygons.
Find the unknown lengths.**

13.
14.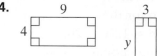
15.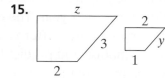

● **Lesson 4-5** **Find the image of $\triangle ABC$ at the right after
a dilation with the given center and scale factor.**

16. center B, scale factor of 3

17. center A, scale factor of $\frac{1}{2}$

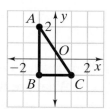

● **Lesson 4-6** **The scale of a map is 1 in. : 30 mi. How many actual
miles does each measurement on the map represent?**

18. 3 in.
19. $2\frac{2}{3}$ in.
20. $\frac{1}{4}$ in.
21. 5 in.
22. $6\frac{1}{2}$ in.

● **Lesson 4-7**

23. A students is 5 ft tall and casts a shadow 12 ft long. A flagpole casts a
shadow 25 ft long. Find the height of the flagpole to the nearest tenth.

Word Problems

● **Lesson 4-1**

24. **Shampoo** A 12-oz bottle of shampoo costs $3.99. A 25.4-oz bottle of the
same shampoo costs $7.49. Find the unit cost of each bottle. Which
bottle of shampoo is the better buy?

Lesson 4-2

25. The world's fastest elevators are located in a building in Taiwan. At top speed, the elevators can go as fast as 37.6 mph. What is this rate in feet per second?

Lesson 4-3

26. Florence can knit 3 scarves in 7 days. Write a proportion to find how long it will take her to knit 10 scarves for a school fundraiser.

Lesson 4-4   An Antonov An-225 airplane model has a wingspan of 22.5 cm. The actual wingspan of an An-225 is 88.4 m.

27. If the actual length of an An-225 is 84 m, what is the length of the airplane model in decimal form?

28. Suppose another model of the An-225 has a scale of 1 cm to 36 m. What is the wingspan of this model in cm?

Lesson 4-5

29. **Photography** Jorge is enlarging a digital photo that is 4 in. high by 6 in. wide. If the enlarged photo is $18\frac{1}{2}$ in. high, find its width.

Lesson 4-6

30. **Sports** A tennis court is 36 ft wide and 78 ft long. Use an inch ruler to measure the green section of the court as shown below. Find the scale used.

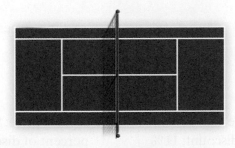

Lesson 4-7

31. The tallest unsupported flagpole in the world is in Amman, Jordan. It casts a shadow 550.6 ft long. At the same time, a nearby man who is 6 ft tall casts a shadow 8 ft long. How tall is the flagpole? Round to the nearest foot.

Skills

● **Lesson 5-1** Write each number as a decimal, a fraction, and a percent.

1. 0.3 **2.** 21% **3.** 3.47 **4.** 0.004

5. $\frac{3}{20}$ **6.** $\frac{1}{3}$ **7.** 0.62% **8.** $2\frac{1}{2}$

● **Lesson 5-2** Estimate each percent.

9. 28% of 99 **10.** 7% of 93 **11.** 48% of 32 **12.** 125% of 84

Estimate a 15% tip for each restaurant bill.

13. $15.50 **14.** $27.89 **15.** $33.07 **16.** $52.31

● **Lessons 5-3 and 5-4** Solve each problem.

17. 6% of 51 **18.** 117% of 22 **19.** 2.5% of 78

20. 145 is 15% of ■. **21.** 0.4 is ■% of 5. **22.** 215% of 20 is ■.

● **Lesson 5-5** Find each percent of change. Round your answer to the nearest tenth of a percent where necessary.

23. 16 to 20 **24.** 320 to 542 **25.** 1 to 4

26. 13 ft 5 in. to 17 ft 4 in. **27.** 8 qt 3 pt to 6 qt 6 pt **28.** 10 lb 4 oz to 14 lb 1 oz

● **Lesson 5-6** Find each percent of markup

29. store's cost: $16; selling price: $20 **30.** store's cost: $43; selling price: $57.19

31. store's cost: $24.50; selling price: $34.79

Find each sale price. Round to the nearest cent.

32. regular price: $14.49
percent of discount: 6%

33. regular price: $28
percent of discount: 11%

34. regular price: $61.25
percent of discount: 18%

● **Lesson 5-7** Find the balance in each account to the nearest cent.

35. $165 at $4\frac{1}{2}$% simple interest for 2 years **36.** $350 at $5\frac{1}{4}$% simple interest for 3 years

● **Lesson 5-8** Suppose you toss a coin twice. Find each probability.

37. $P(\text{no heads})$ **38.** $P(\text{exactly one head})$ **39.** $P(\text{at least one head})$

Word Problems

Lesson 5-1

Household Pets

Animal	Number of Students
Bird	3
Cat	35
Dog	42
Rabbit	8

40. Pets The table at the right shows the results of a survey asking students what pets they have at home. What percent of students have a dog at home?

Lesson 5-2

41. Food A restaurant's appetizers are $\frac{1}{3}$ off on Thursdays. Your bill comes to $17.25. How much should you leave for a 15% tip if you base your tip on the cost before the discount?

Lessons 5-3 and 5-4

42. States The area of Iowa is about 55,869 square miles. Missouri's area is about 123.3% of Iowa's area. What is the area of Missouri?

43. Cars Suppose a car salesperson makes a $3\frac{1}{2}$% commission on each car she sells. What is the salesperson's commission on a $34,285 car?

Lesson 5-5

44. Weather During January 2005, 2.27 inches of precipitation fell in Maine. Only 0.90 inches of precipitation fell in Maine during January 2004. Find the percent of change. Round your answer to the nearest tenth of a percent if necessary.

Lesson 5-6

45. Daniel ordered a shipment of $18.00 sunglasses for his store. He marked them up 50%. After a few weeks, he marked them down to $22.95. What was the percent of discount?

Lesson 5-7

46. Fundraising Your track team deposits money they make from fundraisers during the school year. The team deposits $250 in September at 2.3% simple interest. What is the balance nine months later?

Lesson 5-8

47. Bowling The probability of a professional bowler getting a perfect score of 300 in one year of bowling is 1 out of 4,001. Express this probability as a percent.

Extra Practice

Skills

● **Lesson 6-1**   Write an equation for each model.

1.

2.

Solve each equation.

3. $6n + 3 = 21$

4. $10 = \frac{m}{5} + 2$

5. $-b + 2 = -\frac{1}{2}$

6. $7g - 4 = 10$

7. $-10 = 2 + 6w$

8. $5d + 10 = 25$

9. $15 = -k + 18$

10. $4x - 2 = 8$

● **Lesson 6-2**   Simplify each expression.

11. $6x + 4 - 3x$

12. $7(h - 5)$

13. $2(x + 1) + 5$

14. $-5 + 3p - p$

15. $13q + 91 - 13q$

16. $-(8z + 2z - 1)$

17. $47 - 11r - 7r$

18. $-15h - (23 - 9h)$

● **Lessons 6-3 and 6-4**   Solve each equation.

19. $16 = -(2 - 2b)$

20. $k = 1.5(7 - k)$

21. $-8(3a - 5) = 56a$

22. $123 = 9y + 4 - 7y$

23. $-9 - 3y = 19 + y$

24. $30 - 5(p - 10) = 11p$

25. $14 - 2w = 18w - 26$

26. $4(2.2d - 1) - 0.8d = 23$

27. $4.1x + 1.4 - 5.1x = 6.6$

● **Lesson 6-5**   Solve each inequality. Graph the solution.

28. $x - 2 \le 10$

29. $f + 21 \le 12$

30. $p - 1 > -1$

31. $5 + a \ge -5$

32. $-12 \ge -2 + y$

33. $m + 4 < 16$

Write an inequality for each graph.

34.
$-3\ -2\ -1\quad 0\quad 1\quad 2\quad 3$

35.
$-3\ -2\ -1\quad 0\quad 1\quad 2\quad 3$

● **Lesson 6-6**   Solve each inequality.

36. $7p \le -35$

37. $-4y < 28$

38. $\frac{q}{-6} < 3.1$

39. $\frac{x}{3} < 0$

40. $\frac{z}{-1} > -11$

41. $26 \ge -2.5t$

Word Problems

● **Lesson 6-1**

42. Claudia bought 3 movie passes and a large box of popcorn. The total cost was $33.49. The popcorn cost $4.99. How much did each movie pass cost?

43. **Clothes** You bought socks for $4.99 a pair and a belt for $29.99. The total cost was $59.93. How many pairs of socks did you buy?

● **Lesson 6-2**

44. Seth bought lunch three times and breakfast twice last week. This week Seth bought lunch four times and breakfast once. Define and use variables to represent the total cost.

● **Lessons 6-3 and 6-4**

45. **Fruit** You buy 5 pounds of Bartlett pears and some Bosc pears. Each variety of pears costs $1.09 per pound. The total cost is $10.36. About how many pounds of Bosc pears did you buy?

46. **Boats** A marina charges $175 for materials and $15 per foot to paint the bottom of a boat. It cost $595 to paint a boat. What is the length of the boat?

47. **Savings** Hugo received $100 for his birthday. He then saved $20 each week until he had a total of $460. How many weeks did it take him to save the money?

● **Lesson 6-5**

48. You have only $100 spending money this week. You put $39.85 worth of gas into your car. You spend $56.14 at the grocery store. Do you have enough money to get an oil change for $24.99? Write and solve an inequality to solve this problem.

● **Lesson 6-6**

49. There are 47 children going to a birthday party at a family entertainment center. If a minivan can transport 6 children in a vehicle, how many vans are needed to transport all the children?

50. A school rowing team needs to earn at least $1,250 for new equipment. The team decides to sell raffle tickets for $7 per ticket. How many tickets must the team sell in order to meet their goal?

Skills

● **Lesson 7-1** For Exercises 1–3, use the diagram at the right.

1. Find the measure of the complement of ∠PLK.

2. Name a pair of vertical angles.

3. Find the measures of ∠LPM and ∠MPN.

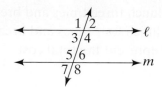

● **Lesson 7-2** In the diagram at the right, ℓ ∥ m.

4. Identify a pair of alternate interior angles.

5. If m∠1 = 108°, find the measure of each numbered angle.

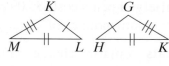

● **Lesson 7-3** Explain why each pair of triangles is congruent.

6. 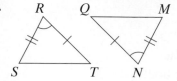   7. 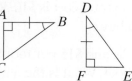   8.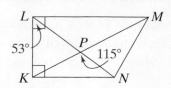

● **Lesson 7-4** Determine the best name for each quadrilateral.

9.   10.   11.   12.

● **Lesson 7-5** Find the sum of the measures of the interior angles of each polygon.

13. rhombus   14. hexagon   15. triangle   16. pentagon   17. trapezoid

● **Lessons 7-6 and 7-7** Find the area of each figure. Round to the nearest tenth.

18.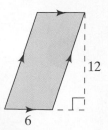

19.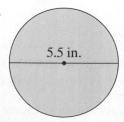

● **Lesson 7-8**

20. Draw an angle and label it ∠A. Construct ∠B congruent to ∠A.

Word Problems

● **Lesson 7-1**

21. **Trees** Suppose a leaning tree makes an angle of 88.5° with the ground as shown in the diagram at the right. What is the measure of angle 1?

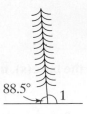

● **Lesson 7-2** **Which pairs of lines, if any, are parallel? Explain.**

22.
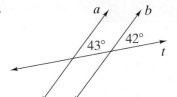

23.
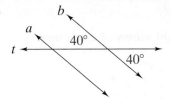

24.
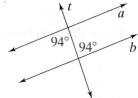

● **Lesson 7-3**

25. Use rotations and translations to find a point *P* such that △*ABC* ≅ △*MNP* in the figure at the right.

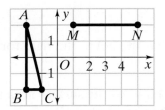

● **Lesson 7-4**

26. **Jewelry** Andrea has a piece of paper with a green shape on it. The shape has exactly two parallel sides. Name the shape.

● **Lesson 7-5**

27. Find the measure of the interior angles of an octagonal stop sign.

● **Lessons 7-6 and 7-7**

28. **Wallpaper** Two walls on the top floor of Louis' house are trapezoidal in shape. The walls are 10 feet wide at the floor and 8.5 feet wide at the ceiling. The walls are 8 feet high. How much wallpaper would Louis need to cover these two walls?

29. A circular sports arena has a diameter of 710 feet. As a security guard, Farrah patrols around the outside edges of the arena. If she walks around the entire stadium three times during each shift, how far has she walked?

● **Lesson 7-8**

30. Describe how to construct two parallel lines.

Skills

● **Lesson 8-1** For each figure, describe the base(s), name the figure, and name the part labeled $\overline{PQ}$.

1.

2.

3.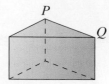

● **Lesson 8-2** Draw the top, front, and right views of each figure.

4.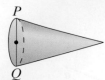

5.

6.

● **Lesson 8-3**

7. Identify the solid that the net at the right forms.

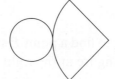

● **Lessons 8-4 and 8-6** Find (a) the surface area and (b) the volume of each figure. Round to the nearest whole unit.

8. cube with edge length 1.2 m

9. rectangular prism 10 cm × 15 cm × 18 cm

10. cylinder with radius 1 ft and height 8 ft

11. cylinder with diameter 6 in. and height 4 in.

● **Lessons 8-5 and 8-7** Find (a) the surface area and (b) the volume of each figure with the given characteristics. Round to the nearest whole unit.

12. a square pyramid with a height of 4 in., a slant height of 5 in., and a base area of 36 in.^{2}

13. a cone with a diameter of 12 cm, a height of 8 cm, and a slant height of 10 cm

● **Lesson 8-8**

14. Find the surface area and volume of a sphere with diameter 18.2 cm. Round to the nearest whole unit.

● **Lesson 8-9**

15. Find the volume of the smaller similar solid at the right.

$V = 3,570 \text{ m}^3$

14 m   7 m

Word Problems

Lesson 8-1

16. Name the common solids that make up the structure at the right.

Lesson 8-2

17. Describe a situation in which drawing the base plan of an object would be more useful than drawing the top, front, or right view.

Lesson 8-3

18. **Moving** Gwen is moving to college. She has boxes that are 24 in. wide by 18 in. long by 18 in. high. Draw a net to represent one of the boxes.

Lessons 8-4 and 8-6

19. **Baking** For a cake recipe, Donnie needs to cover the inside of the cake pan at the right with parchment paper. How much parchment paper will he need to cover the inside of the cake pan (including the bottom)? Round to the nearest square inch.

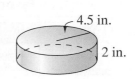

20. If the cake batter exactly fills the cake pan, what is the volume of cake batter Donnie has before baking the cake? Round to the nearest cubic inch.

Lessons 8-5 and 8-7 Jai's office has a water cooler that dispenses conical paper cups like the one at the right.

21. How much paper is used in creating one of the paper cups?

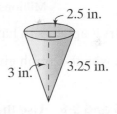

22. How much water can each of the paper cups hold? Round to the nearest cubic inch.

Lessons 8-8 and 8-9

23. Mercury has a radius of about 2,440 km. Find the volume and surface area to the nearest unit.

24. A can of tomatoes has a volume of 245 mL and a diameter of 5 cm. Find the volume of a similar can with a diameter of 6 cm.

25. A cone has a radius of 4 ft and a surface area of 150 ft^2. Find the surface area of a similar cone with a radius of 7 ft.

Skills

● **Lesson 9-1**   **Find the mean, median, mode, and range of each data set.**
   Where necessary, round to the nearest hundredth.

   1. goals per game: 1 1 1 2 2 2 4 4

   2. golf scores: −2 −3 2 5 0 3 7

● **Lessons 9-2 and 9-3**

   3. Make a frequency table, histogram, and line plot for the data set.
   Hours spent waiting: 1.8 1.7 1.4 1.2 1.7 1.7 1.5 1.9 1.6 1.5 1.3 1.4 1.7 1.7 1.6

   4. Draw a Venn diagram for the situation: 10 blue shapes, 5 circles,
   2 blue circles.

● **Lesson 9-4**   **Use the graph below for Exercises 6–7.**

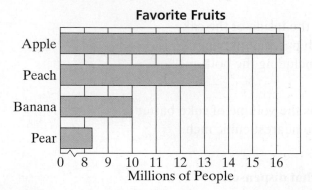

   5. Which fruit appears to have about half the popularity of a banana?

   6. Explain why the graph gives a misleading visual impression of the data.

● **Lessons 9-5 and 9-6**   **Use the stem-and-leaf plot for Exercises 7–8.**

   7. Find the mode and median of the data set.

   8. Make a box-and-whisker plot for the data set.

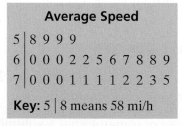

Average Speed		
5	8 9 9 9	
6	0 0 0 2 2 5 6 7 8 8 9	
7	0 0 0 1 1 1 1 2 2 3 5	

Key: 5 | 8 means 58 mi/h

● **Lesson 9-7**   **In each scatter plot, describe the type of trend.**

   9.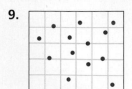

   10.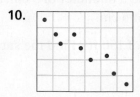

   11.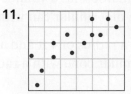

**U.S. Service Academy
2001 Enrollment**

School	Enrollment
Army	4,152
Navy	4,297
Air Force	4,365
Coast Guard	919
Merchant Marine	931

SOURCE: *College Board Handbook*

● **Lesson 9-8**

12. Make a circle graph for the set of data at the right.

● **Lesson 9-9** **Choose the appropriate graph to display each set of data.**

13. circle graph or scatter plot? parts of a monthly budget

14. box-and-whisker plot or double bar graph? number of girls and number of boys in three classes

Word Problems

● **Lesson 9-1**

15. A student bused tables for the summer. His tips for one week were $15, $45, $51, $66, $39, $49, and $78. How does the outlier affect the mean?

● **Lessons 9-2, 9-3, and 9-4**

16. Make a frequency table and histogram to display the data. Ages of members of the ski team: 17 15 14 15 16 14 17 14 13 14 16

17. In a class of 21 students, 14 take Spanish, 10 take French, and 5 take both languages. Use a Venn diagram to find how many students do not take either language.

Farm Animals

Type of Animals	Number of Animals
Cow	12
Pig	38
Horse	5
Chicken	100

18. Make two bar graphs for the data at the right. Use a break symbol in only one graph. Explain which graph shows the data more clearly.

● **Lessons 9-5, 9-6, and 9-7**

19. Make a stem-and-leaf plot and a box-and-whisker plot for the data set. gymnastics scores: 6.9 9.1 2.7 7.5 6.6 8.3 7.2 10.0 5.4 6.3

20. Make a scatter plot for the minimum wage data shown at the right. If possible, draw a trend line.

Minimum Wage (1975–2005)

Year	1975	1980	1985	1990	1995	2000	2005
Minimum Wage	$2.10	$3.10	$3.35	$3.80	$4.25	$5.15	$5.15

SOURCE: U.S. Dept. of Labor. Go to **PHSchool.com** for a data update. Web Code: asg-9041

● **Lesson 9-8**

21. Dana surveyed 125 students about their favorite subject in school. Display the results, shown at the right, in a circle graph.

Favorite Academic Subject

Subject	Number of Students
English	30
Math	15
Science	23
Social Studies	57

● **Lesson 9-9**

22. Is a stem-and-leaf plot or a bar graph appropriate to display the number of students at three schools? Explain your choice.

Skills

● **Lesson 10-1** **Find each experimental probability.**
Suppose you write North, South, East, and West on separate pieces of paper and put them in a hat. You select a piece of paper at random, record the result, replace the paper, and select again. The results of 20 trials are shown.

Location	Number Selected
North	7
South	5
East	3
West	5

1. P(West)
2. P(South or East)
3. P(not North)

4. What is the theoretical probability of selecting North?

5. Which event or events have the same experimental probability as the theoretical probability?

● **Lesson 10-2** **The table shows the results from a survey of 50 students at Green Middle School. The school has 670 students.**

Favorite Elective Class	Number of Students
Music	12
Art	8
Woodshop	7
Graphic Design	23

6. Predict how many students in the school enjoy music class the most.

7. About how many students in the school would choose art class as their favorite elective?

8. Predict how many students in the school like either wood shop or graphic design class the best.

● **Lesson 10-3** **Determine whether each question is biased or not. Explain.**

9. What is your favorite food?
10. How much homework do you do each night?

● **Lesson 10-4** **Find each probability.** A spinner is divided into 26 equal sections. Each section is labeled with a letter of the alphabet. Suppose you spin the spinner once and then roll a number cube. Assume Y is a consonant.

11. P(M, then 2)
12. P(C, then prime)
13. P(vowel, then odd)
14. P(consonant, then 5)

● **Lessons 10-5 and 10-6** **Simplify each expression.**

15. $4!$
16. $8!$
17. $_6P_3$
18. $_{17}P_2$
19. $_{24}P_4$
20. $_{18}P_5$
21. $_7C_4$
22. $_{16}C_2$
23. $_{19}C_7$
24. $_{24}C_2$

25. You need to choose a team of 5 players from 15 potential players. In how many ways can you do this?

Word Problems

● **Lesson 10-1**   **A bag contains 33 green marbles and 25 blue marbles. You select a marble at random from the bag.**

26. Find the theoretical probability of selecting a green marble.

27. Find the theoretical probability of selecting a blue marble.

28. The table at the right shows the results of selecting a marble from the bag, recording the color, and returning the marble to the bag. Find the experimental probability of each color based on the table.

Outcome	Occurrences
Green	41
Blue	35

● **Lessons 10-2 and 10-3**   **A company surveys 100 bicycle riders and asks whether they would be more likely to purchase a mountain bicycle, a road bicycle, or a hybrid bicycle. According to the survey, 67 people would buy a mountain bicycle, and 11 would buy a road bicycle.**

29. If the company sells 500 bikes per month, predict how many of those customers will purchase a mountain bicycle.

30. The company sells 750 bicycles one busy July. About how many of those bikes should be hybrid bicycles?

31. **Transportation** A company is doing a survey on the satisfaction of people who use public transportation. The company surveys every sixth customer at a gas station. Is this a random sample? Explain.

● **Lesson 10-4**   **Jacques has 9 brothers and sisters. His mother makes 5 turkey, 2 roast beef, 2 tuna fish, and 1 cheese sandwiches for lunch.**

32. If Jacques chooses a sandwich at random, what is the probability he will get a roast beef sandwich?

33. Suppose Jacques takes a roast beef sandwich, and then his sister Eva selects her sandwich. What is the probability that she will choose a tuna fish sandwich?

● **Lesson 10-5**   **An eighth-grade class of 144 students elects a president, a vice-president, and a treasurer.**

34. In how many different ways can the class officers be chosen?

35. What is the probability of a teacher choosing the same officers at random?

● **Lesson 10-6**

36. **Research** You have 12 Web sites you can use to write a research paper. How many different combinations of 3 sites can you select?

Skills

● **Lesson 11-1** Find the common difference or ratio in each sequence. Write the rule for each sequence and find the next three terms.

1. $4, 16, 64, \ldots$ 2. $-5, -3, -1, \ldots$ 3. $1, \frac{5}{6}, \frac{2}{3}, \frac{1}{2}, \ldots$ 4. $12, 6, 3, \ldots$

● **Lesson 11-2** Use the graph at the right for Exercises 5–7.

5. What is the rate for the first hour of parking?

6. What is the cost to park for $3\frac{1}{2}$ hours?

7. What is the maximum cost to park for up to 12 hours?

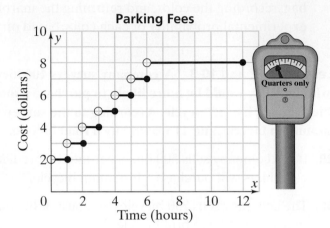

Parking Fees

● **Lesson 11-3** Use the function rule $f(x) = 2x - 1$. Find each output.

8. $f(1)$ 9. $f(0)$ 10. $f(-3)$ 11. $f\left(\frac{1}{2}\right)$

● **Lesson 11-4** Use the table to find the slope. Then graph the data and each line.

12.

x	0	1	2	3	4
y	1	3	5	7	9

13.

x	-2	0	2	4	6
y	10	7	4	1	-2

14.

x	-4	-1	2	5	8
y	-5	0	5	10	15

● **Lesson 11-5** Make a table of input-output pairs for each function. Then graph the function.

15. $y = 3x$ 16. $y = -2x + 3$ 17. $y = \frac{3}{5}x + 1$ 18. $y = 4$

● **Lesson 11-6** Do the data in each table represent a linear function? If so, write a rule for the function.

19.

x	0	1	2	3	4
y	8	6	4	2	0

20.

x	-3	-1	1	3	5
y	0	1	2	3	4

21.

x	0	3	6	9	12
y	0	2	4	7	10

● **Lesson 11-7** Make a table and a graph for each quadratic function. Use integers from -4 to 4 for inputs.

22. $y = x^2 + 2$ 23. $y = -2x^2$ 24. $y = 3x^2$ 25. $y = -x^2 + 3$

● **Lesson 11-1**   Tell whether each situation produces an *arithmetic sequence, a geometric sequence,* or *neither.*

26. A tree grows 1 foot each year.

27. The distance a person jogs daily varies between 3 and 5 miles.

● **Lesson 11-2**

28. A library charges 25 cents for each day a book is overdue. After 5 days, the library charges 50 cents per day. Sketch and label a graph that shows the total charge each day a book is overdue.

● **Lesson 11-3**

29. Potatoes cost $.99 per pound. Use function notation to show the relationship between the total cost and the number of pounds you buy. Use the rule to find the cost of 6 pounds of potatoes.

● **Lesson 11-4**

30. Suppose a wheelchair ramp has a slope of $\frac{1}{15}$. If it reaches a doorway that is 2 ft above ground, how far from the doorway does the ramp begin?

● **Lesson 11-5**

31. Agriculture A bamboo plant is 23 cm high and grows 16 cm a day. The plant's height (output) depends on the number of days that have passed (input). Make a table and graph the function.

● **Lesson 11-6**

32. Plumbing A plumber charges $60 for a house call, plus $75 for each hour of work. Write a function rule that shows how the total cost of the plumber's work y depends on the number of hours x the plumber works.

● **Lesson 11-7**

33. Construction Suppose it takes a total of 225 workdays to build a house. With more workers, the number of days to finish the house decreases. The function $y = \frac{225}{x}$ describes the number of days (y) it will take x people to build the house. Make a table and graph the function.

Skills

● **Lesson 12-1**   Simplify each polynomial.

1. $3x - 5 + 23x - 9$

2. $-x^2 + 2x^2 - 6x + 3 - 2$

3. $x^2 - 5x + 3x + 4$

4. $-4 + x - 13x + 10 - 5 + 20x$

5. Write and simplify the polynomial represented by the model below.

● **Lesson 12-2**   Add or subtract.

6. $(2x^2 - x + 1) - (4x^2 - 3)$

7. $(3x + 2) + (2x^2 + 5x - 7)$

8. $(5x^2 + 2x - 10) + (-3x^2 - 2)$

9. $(x^2 + 6x + 4) - (4x - 9)$

● **Lesson 12-3**   Write each expression using a single exponent.

10. $4^8 \cdot 4^{10}$

11. $(-9)^2 \cdot (-9)^4$

12. $3.2^8 \cdot 3.2^3$

13. $7^t \cdot 7^{3t}$

Multiply. Write each product in scientific notation.

14. $(3 \times 10^4)(2 \times 10^{12})$

15. $(5 \times 10^9)(7 \times 10^3)$

16. $(1 \times 10^3)(2.6 \times 10^8)$

17. $(7 \times 10^2)(8 \times 10^{10})$

● **Lesson 12-4**   Simplify each expression.

18. $(-4x^2)(3x^4)$

19. $(6x)(-2x)$

20. $4x^2(2x - 7)$

21. $-6x(x^2 - 5)$

22. Use the area model below to find the product.

$x^2 + 2x$

$3x + 2$

● **Lesson 12-5**   Write each expression using a single exponent.

23. $\dfrac{4^7}{4^5}$

24. $\dfrac{8.1^{15}}{8.1^{12}}$

25. $\dfrac{(-654)^{20}}{(-654)^1}$

26. $\dfrac{2^{3x}}{2^x}$

Simplify each expression.

27. $(-142)^0$ **28.** $(4c)^{-1}$ **29.** 7^{-w} **30.** $(-3)^{-5}$

Word Problems

● **Lesson 12-1**

31. Geometry To find the surface area of the prism shown at the right, you can use the polynomial $x^2 + 2x + 2x + 2x + 2x + x^2$. Simplify the polynomial.

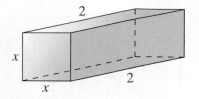

● **Lesson 12-2**

32. City Planning A town is planning the hexagonal park shown below. Write the perimeter of the park as a polynomial and simplify.

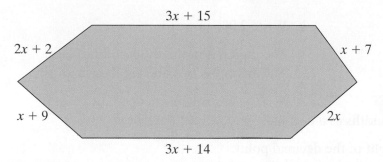

● **Lesson 12-3**

33. Biology There are about 5×10^{10} white blood cells and about 500 times as many red blood cells in a human's bloodstream. Find the number of red blood cells. Write your answer in scientific notation.

34. Sports There are about 2.65×10^{32} possible ways a 30-player football team can form a line to run onto the field. When a thirty-first player is included, there will be about $31 \cdot (2.65 \times 10^{32})$ possible ways. Write this number in scientific notation.

● **Lesson 12-4**

35. A middle school art class is painting a mural on the side of the school building. They plan to use a rectangular area that is $(3x + 5)$ ft long and $8x$ ft wide. Write an expression for the area of the completed mural.

● **Lesson 12-5**

36. Physics The wavelength of red light is 0.0000076 meters. Write this number in scientific notation.

Decimals and Place Value

Each digit in a whole number or a decimal has both a place and a value.
The value of any place is one tenth the value of the place to its left. The
chart below can help you read and write decimals. It shows the place and
value of the number 2,401,262,830.750191.

billions	hundred millions	ten millions	millions	hundred thousands	ten thousands	thousands	hundreds	tens	ones	.	tenths	hundredths	thousandths	ten-thousandths	hundred-thousandths	millionths
2	4	0	1	2	6	2	8	3	0	.	7	5	0	1	9	1

EXAMPLE

a. What is the value of the digit 8 in
the number above?

The digit 8 is in the hundreds place.
So its value is 8 hundreds.

b. Write 2.006 in words.

The digit 6 is in the thousandths place.
The answer is two and six thousandths.

c. Write five and thirty-four ten-thousandths as a decimal.

Ten-thousandths is 4 places to the right of the decimal point.
So the decimal will have 4 places after the decimal point.
The answer is 5.0034.

Exercises

Use the chart above. Write the value of each digit.

1. the digit 9

2. the digit 7

3. the digit 5

4. the digit 6

5. the digit 4

6. the digit 3

Write a decimal for the given words.

7. forty-one ten-thousandths

8. eighteen and five hundred four thousandths

9. eight millionths

10. seven and sixty-three hundred-thousandths

11. twelve thousandths

12. sixty-five and two hundred one thousandths

Write each decimal in words.

13. 0.06

14. 4.7

15. 0.00011

16. 0.9

17. 0.012

18. 0.000059

19. 0.0042

20. 6.029186

Comparing and Ordering Decimals

To compare two decimals, use the symbols < (is less than), > (is greater than), or = (is equal to). When you compare, start at the left and compare the digits.

EXAMPLE

1 Use <, >, or = to compare the decimals.

a. 0.1 ■ 0.06

1 tenth > 0 tenths, so
0.1 > 0.06

b. 2.4583 ■ 2.48

5 hundredths < 8 hundredths,
so 2.4583 < 2.48

c. 0.30026 ■ 0.03026

3 tenths > 0 tenths, so
0.30026 > 0.03026

EXAMPLE

2 Draw number lines to compare the decimals.

a. 0.1 ■ 0.06

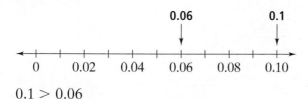

0.1 > 0.06

b. 2.4583 ■ 2.48

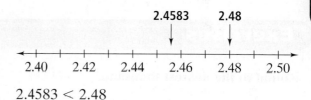

2.4583 < 2.48

Exercises

Use <, >, or = to compare the decimals. Draw number lines if you wish.

1. 0.003 ■ 0.02

2. 84.2 ■ 842

3. 0.162 ■ 0.106

4. 0.0659 ■ 0.6059

5. 2.13 ■ 2.99

6. 3.53 ■ 3.529

7. 2.01 ■ 2.010

8. 0.00072 ■ 0.07002

9. 0.458 ■ 0.4589

10. 8.627 ■ 8.649

11. 0.0019 ■ 0.0002

12. 0.19321 ■ 0.19231

Write the decimals in order from least to greatest.

13. 2.31, 0.231, 23.1, 0.23, 3.21

14. 1.02, 1.002, 1.2, 1.11, 1.021

15. 0.02, 0.002, 0.22, 0.222, 2.22

16. 55.5, 555.5, 55.555, 5.5555

17. 7, 7.3264, 7.3, 7.3246, 7.0324

18. 0.0101, 0.0099, 0.011, 0.00019

19. 0.8, 0.83, 0.08, 0.083, 0.082

20. 4.6, 4.61, 4.601, 4.602, 4.6002, 4.62

Rounding

When you round to a particular place, look at the digit to the right of that place. If it is 5 or more, the digit in the place you are rounding to will increase by 1. If it is less than 5, the digit in the place you are rounding to will stay the same.

EXAMPLE

a. Round 1.627 to the nearest whole number.

The digit to the right of the units place is 6, so 1.627 rounds up to 2.

c. Round 2.7195 to the nearest hundredth.

The digit to the right of the hundredths place is 9, so 2.7195 rounds up to 2.72.

b. Round 12,034 to the nearest thousand.

The digit to the right of the thousands place is 0, so 12,034 rounds down to 12,000.

d. Round 0.060521 to the place of the underlined digit.

The digit to the right of 5 is 2, so 0.060521 rounds down to 0.0605.

Exercises

Round to the nearest thousand.

1. 105,099
2. 10,400
3. 79,527,826
4. 79,932
5. 4,312,349

Round to the nearest whole number.

6. 135.91
7. 3.001095
8. 96.912
9. 101.167
10. 299.9

Round to the nearest tenth.

11. 82.01
12. 4.67522
13. 20.397
14. 399.95
15. 129.98

Round to the nearest hundredth.

16. 13.458
17. 96.4045
18. 0.699
19. 4.234
20. 12.09531

Round to the place of the underlined digit.

21. 7.0615
22. 5.77125
23. 1,522
24. 0.91952
25. 4.243

26. 236.001
27. 352
28. 3.495366
29. 8.07092
30. 0.6008

31. 918
32. 7,735
33. 25.66047
34. 983,240,631
35. 27

Adding and Subtracting Decimals

You add or subtract decimals just as you do whole numbers. You line up the decimal points and then add or subtract. If you wish, you can use zeros to make the columns even.

Skills Handbook

EXAMPLE

Find each sum or difference.

a. $37.6 + 8.431$

$$
\begin{array}{r} 37.6 \\ + 8.431 \\ \hline \end{array} \rightarrow
\begin{array}{r} 37.600 \\ + 8.431 \\ \hline 46.031 \end{array}
$$

b. $8 - 4.593$

$$
\begin{array}{r} 8. \\ - 4.593 \\ \hline \end{array} \rightarrow
\begin{array}{r} 8.000 \\ - 4.593 \\ \hline 3.407 \end{array}
$$

c. $8.3 + 2.99 + 17.5$

$$
\begin{array}{r} 8.3 \\ 2.99 \\ + 17.5 \\ \hline \end{array} \rightarrow
\begin{array}{r} 8.30 \\ 2.99 \\ + 17.50 \\ \hline 28.79 \end{array}
$$

Exercises

Find each sum or difference.

1. $\begin{array}{r}39.7 \\ -36.03 \\ \hline\end{array}$	**2.** $\begin{array}{r}1.08 \\ -0.9 \\ \hline\end{array}$	**3.** $\begin{array}{r}6.784 \\ +0.528 \\ \hline\end{array}$	**4.** $\begin{array}{r}5.01 \\ -0.87 \\ \hline\end{array}$
5. $\begin{array}{r}13.02 \\ +23.107 \\ \hline\end{array}$	**6.** $\begin{array}{r}8.634 \\ +1.409 \\ \hline\end{array}$	**7.** $\begin{array}{r}2.1 \\ -0.5 \\ \hline\end{array}$	**8.** $\begin{array}{r}8.23 \\ -3.1 \\ \hline\end{array}$
9. $\begin{array}{r}1.05 \\ +12.9 \\ \hline\end{array}$	**10.** $\begin{array}{r}2.60 \\ +23.107 \\ \hline\end{array}$	**11.** $\begin{array}{r}0.1 \\ 58.21 \\ +1.9 \\ \hline\end{array}$	**12.** $\begin{array}{r}12.2 \\ 3.06 \\ +0.5 \\ \hline\end{array}$
13. $\begin{array}{r}9.42 \\ 3.6 \\ +21.003 \\ \hline\end{array}$	**14.** $\begin{array}{r}15.22 \\ 7.4 \\ +8.125 \\ \hline\end{array}$	**15.** $\begin{array}{r}3.7 \\ 20.06 \\ +16.19 \\ \hline\end{array}$	**16.** $\begin{array}{r}12.22 \\ 9.8 \\ +2.375 \\ \hline\end{array}$

17. $76.39 - 8.47$

18. $8.7 + 17.03$

19. $32.403 + 12.06$

20. $20.5 + 11.45$

21. $8.9 - 4.45$

22. $1.245 + 5.8$

23. $3.9 + 6.57$

24. $14.81 - 8.6$

25. $11.9 - 2.06$

26. $3.45 + 4.061$

27. $8.29 + 4.3$

28. $7.06 - 4.235$

29. $5.002 - 3.45$

30. $6.8 + 3.57$

31. $0.23 + 0.091$

32. $0.5 - 0.18$

33. $8.3 + 2.99 + 17.52$

34. $9.5 + 12.32 + 6.4$

35. $4.521 + 1.8 + 3.07$

36. $57 + 0.6327 + 189.007$

37. $741 + 6.08 + 0.0309$

38. $0.045 + 16.32 + 8.6$

39. $4.27 + 6.18 + 0.91$

40. $3.856 + 14.01 + 1.72$

41. $11.45 + 3.79 + 23.861$

Multiplying Decimals

Multiply decimals as you would whole numbers. Then place the decimal point in the product. To do this, add the number of decimal places in the factors.

EXAMPLE

1 Multiply 0.068×2.3.

Step 1 Multiply decimals without the decimal point.

$$
\begin{array}{r}
0.068 \\
\times\, 2.3 \\
\end{array}
\qquad
\begin{array}{r}
68 \\
\times\, 23 \\
\hline
204 \\
+\ 1360 \\
\hline
1564 \\
\end{array}
$$

Step 2 Place the decimal point.

$$
\begin{array}{r}
0.068 \\
\times\ 2.3 \\
\hline
204 \\
+\ 1360 \\
\hline
0.1564 \\
\end{array}
$$
← three decimal places
← one decimal place

← four decimal places

EXAMPLE

2 Find each product.

a. 3.12×0.9

$$
\begin{array}{r}
3.12 \\
\times\ 0.9 \\
\hline
2.808 \\
\end{array}
$$

b. 5.75×42

$$
\begin{array}{r}
5.75 \\
\times\ 42 \\
\hline
1150 \\
+\ 23000 \\
\hline
241.50 \\
\end{array}
$$

c. 0.964×0.28

$$
\begin{array}{r}
0.964 \\
\times\ 0.28 \\
\hline
7712 \\
+\ 19280 \\
\hline
0.26992 \\
\end{array}
$$

Exercises

Multiply.

1. $\begin{array}{r} 1.48 \\ \times\ 3.6 \end{array}$

2. $\begin{array}{r} 191.1 \\ \times\ 3.4 \end{array}$

3. $\begin{array}{r} 0.05 \\ \times\ 43 \end{array}$

4. $\begin{array}{r} 0.27 \\ \times\ 5 \end{array}$

5. $\begin{array}{r} 1.36 \\ \times\ 3.8 \end{array}$

6. $\begin{array}{r} 6.23 \\ \times\ 0.21 \end{array}$

7. $\begin{array}{r} 0.512 \\ \times\ 0.76 \end{array}$

8. $\begin{array}{r} 0.04 \\ \times\ 7 \end{array}$

9. $\begin{array}{r} 0.136 \\ \times\ 8.4 \end{array}$

10. $\begin{array}{r} 3 \\ \times\ 0.05 \end{array}$

11. 2.07×1.004

12. 0.12×61

13. 3.2×0.15

14. 0.74×0.23

15. 0.42×98

16. 6.3×85

17. 45×0.028

18. 76×3.3

19. 8.003×0.6

20. 42.2×0.9

21. 0.6×30.02

22. 0.05×11.8

Zeros in a Product

When you multiply with decimals, you may have to write one or more zeros to the left of a product before you can place the decimal point.

EXAMPLE

① Multiply 0.06×0.015.

Step 1 Multiply.

$$
\begin{array}{r}
0.015 \\
\times\, 0.06 \\
\hline
90
\end{array}
$$

Step 2 Place the decimal point.

$$
\begin{array}{rl}
0.015 & \leftarrow \text{three decimal places} \\
\times\, 0.06 & \leftarrow \text{two decimal places} \\
\hline
0.00090 & \leftarrow \text{The product should have five decimal places,} \\
& \quad\ \text{so you must write three zeros before placing} \\
& \quad\ \text{the decimal point.}
\end{array}
$$

EXAMPLE

② **a.** 0.02×1.3

$$
\begin{array}{r}
1.3 \\
\times\, 0.02 \\
\hline
0.026
\end{array}
$$

b. 0.012×2.4

$$
\begin{array}{r}
2.4 \\
\times\, 0.012 \\
\hline
48 \\
+\ 240 \\
\hline
0.0288
\end{array}
$$

c. 0.022×0.051

$$
\begin{array}{r}
0.051 \\
\times\ 0.022 \\
\hline
102 \\
+\ 1020 \\
\hline
0.001122
\end{array}
$$

Exercises

Multiply.

1. $\begin{array}{r} 0.03 \\ \times\, 0.9 \end{array}$

2. $\begin{array}{r} 0.06 \\ \times\, 0.5 \end{array}$

3. $\begin{array}{r} 2.4 \\ \times\, 0.03 \end{array}$

4. $\begin{array}{r} 7 \\ \times\, 0.01 \end{array}$

5. $\begin{array}{r} 0.05 \\ \times\, 0.05 \end{array}$

6. $\begin{array}{r} 0.016 \\ \times\, 0.12 \end{array}$

7. $\begin{array}{r} 0.031 \\ \times\, 0.08 \end{array}$

8. $\begin{array}{r} 0.03 \\ \times\, 0.2 \end{array}$

9. $\begin{array}{r} 0.27 \\ \times\, 0.033 \end{array}$

10. $\begin{array}{r} 0.014 \\ \times\, 0.25 \end{array}$

11. 0.003×0.55

12. 0.01×0.74

13. 0.47×0.08

14. 0.76×0.1

15. 0.3×0.27

16. 0.19×0.05

17. 0.018×0.04

18. 0.43×0.2

19. 0.03×0.03

20. 4.003×0.02

21. 0.5×0.08

22. 0.06×0.7

23. 0.3×0.24

24. 0.67×0.09

25. 3.02×0.006

26. 0.31×0.08

27. 0.14×0.05

28. 0.07×0.85

Dividing Decimals by Whole Numbers

When you divide a decimal by a whole number, the decimal point in the quotient goes directly above the decimal point in the dividend. You may need extra zeros to place the decimal point.

EXAMPLE

1 Divide $2.432 \div 32$.

Step 1 Divide.

$$
\begin{array}{r}
76 \\
32 \overline{)2.432} \\
-2\,24 \\
\hline
192 \\
-192 \\
\hline
0
\end{array}
$$

Step 2 Place the decimal point.

$$
\begin{array}{r}
0.076 \\
32 \overline{)2.432} \\
-2\,24 \\
\hline
192 \\
-192 \\
\hline
0
\end{array}
$$

← You need two extra zeros to get the decimal point in the correct place.

EXAMPLE

2 **a.** $37.6 \div 8$

$$
\begin{array}{r}
4.7 \\
8 \overline{)37.6} \\
-32 \\
\hline
5\,6 \\
-5\,6 \\
\hline
0
\end{array}
$$

b. $39.33 \div 69$

$$
\begin{array}{r}
0.57 \\
69 \overline{)39.33} \\
-34\,5 \\
\hline
4\,83 \\
-4\,83 \\
\hline
0
\end{array}
$$

c. $4.482 \div 54$

$$
\begin{array}{r}
0.083 \\
54 \overline{)4.482} \\
-4\,32 \\
\hline
162 \\
-162 \\
\hline
0
\end{array}
$$

Exercises

Divide.

1. $17.92 \div 7$

2. $16.5 \div 5$

3. $6.984 \div 9$

4. $91.44 \div 6$

5. $35.16 \div 4$

6. $8.848 \div 56$

7. $2.42 \div 22$

8. $1{,}723.8 \div 26$

9. $17.52 \div 2$

10. $37.14 \div 6$

11. $0.1352 \div 8$

12. $0.0324 \div 9$

13. $0.0882 \div 6$

14. $0.8682 \div 6$

15. $12.342 \div 22$

16. $29.792 \div 32$

17. $22.568 \div 26$

18. $11.340 \div 36$

19. $45.918 \div 18$

20. $79.599 \div 13$

21. $0.0672 \div 48$

22. $171.031 \div 53$

23. $79.53 \div 11$

24. $3.2 \div 8$

25. $0.378 \div 5$

26. $9.76 \div 32$

27. $0.133 \div 7$

28. $61.915 \div 35$

Multiplying and Dividing by Powers of Ten

You can use shortcuts to multiply or divide by powers of ten.

When you multiply by...	Move the decimal point ...	When you divide by...	Move the decimal point ...
10,000	4 places to the right.	10,000	4 places to the left.
1,000	3 places to the right.	1,000	3 places to the left.
100	2 places to the right.	100	2 places to the left.
10	1 place to the right.	10	1 place to the left.
0.1	1 place to the left.	0.1	1 place to the right.
0.01	2 places to the left.	0.01	2 places to the right.
0.001	3 places to the left.	0.001	3 places to the right.

EXAMPLE

1 Multiply.

a. 0.7×0.001

Move the decimal point three places to the left.   0.000.7

$0.7 \times 0.001 = 0.0007$

b. 0.934×100

Move the decimal point two places to the right.   0.93.4

$0.934 \times 100 = 93.4$

EXAMPLE

2 Divide.

a. $0.605 \div 100$

Move the decimal point two places to the left.   0.00.605

$0.605 \div 100 = 0.00605$

b. $0.38 \div 0.001$

Move the decimal point three places to the right.   0.380.

$0.38 \div 0.001 = 380$

Exercises

Multiply or divide.

1. $10,000 \times 0.056$

2. 0.001×0.09

3. 5.2×10

4. $0.03 \times 1,000$

5. $236.7 \div 0.1$

6. $45.28 \div 10$

7. $0.9 \div 1,000$

8. $1.07 \div 0.01$

9. 100×0.08

10. $1.03 \times 10,000$

11. 1.803×0.001

12. 4.1×100

13. $13.7 \div 0.001$

14. $203.05 \div 0.01$

15. $4.7 \div 10$

16. $0.05 \div 100$

Dividing Decimals by Decimals

To divide by a decimal divisor, multiply it by the smallest power of ten that will make the divisor a whole number. Then multiply the dividend by that same power of ten.

EXAMPLE

Find each quotient.

a. $3.348 \div 6.2$

Multiply by 10.

```
        0.54
6.2,)3.3,48
     -3 1 0
       2 48
      -2 48
          0
```

b. $2.4885 \div 0.35$

Multiply by 100.

```
         7.11
0.35,)2.48,85
      -2 45
         3 8
        -3 5
          35
         -35
           0
```

c. $0.0576 \div 0.012$

Multiply by 1000.

```
          4.8
0.012,)0.057,6
       -48
         9 6
        -9 6
           0
```

Exercises

Divide.

1. $268.8 \div 3.2$ **2.** $123.5 \div 1.9$ **3.** $135.6 \div 0.3$

4. $170.2 \div 2.3$ **5.** $252.8 \div 7.9$ **6.** $10.26 \div 5.7$

7. $71.53 \div 2.3$ **8.** $16.12 \div 3.1$ **9.** $24.18 \div 7.8$

10. $14.49 \div 6.3$ **11.** $134.42 \div 5.17$ **12.** $89.96 \div 3.46$

13. $160.58 \div 5.18$ **14.** $106.59 \div 6.27$ **15.** $62.4 \div 3.9$

16. $260.4 \div 8.4$ **17.** $316.8 \div 7.2$ **18.** $162.4 \div 2.9$

19. $1.512 \div 0.54$ **20.** $3.225 \div 0.43$ **21.** $2.484 \div 0.69$

22. $511.5 \div 5.5$ **23.** $0.992 \div 0.8$ **24.** $4.53 \div 0.05$

25. $3.498 \div 0.06$ **26.** $59.2 \div 0.8$ **27.** $2.198 \div 0.07$

28. $14.28 \div 0.7$ **29.** $1.98 \div 0.5$ **30.** $26.36 \div 0.04$

31. $3.922 \div 7.4$ **32.** $23.52 \div 0.98$ **33.** $71.25 \div 7.5$

34. $114.7 \div 3.7$ **35.** $0.832 \div 0.52$ **36.** $1.125 \div 0.09$

37. $9.666 \div 2.7$ **38.** $1.456 \div 9.1$ **39.** $0.4374 \div 1.8$

Zeros in Decimal Division

When you are dividing by a decimal, sometimes you need to use extra zeros in the dividend or the quotient, or both.

EXAMPLE

1 Divide $0.045 \div 3.6$.

Step 1 Multiply by 10.

$$3.\underset{\curvearrowright}{6.}\overline{)0.0\underset{\curvearrowright}{45}}$$

Step 2 Divide.

$$\begin{array}{r} 125 \\ 36\overline{)0.4500} \\ -36 \\ \hline 90 \\ -72 \\ \hline 180 \\ -180 \\ \hline 0 \end{array}$$

Step 3 Place the decimal point.

$$\begin{array}{r} 0.0125 \\ 36\overline{)0.4500} \\ -36 \\ \hline 90 \\ -72 \\ \hline 180 \\ -180 \\ \hline 0 \end{array}$$

EXAMPLE

2 Find each quotient.

a. $0.4428 \div 8.2$

Multiply by 10.

$$\begin{array}{r} 0.054 \\ 8.\underset{\curvearrowright}{2.}\overline{)0.4\underset{\curvearrowright}{4}28} \end{array}$$

b. $0.00434 \div 0.07$

Multiply by 100.

$$\begin{array}{r} 0.062 \\ 0.\underset{\curvearrowright}{07.}\overline{)0.00.\underset{\curvearrowright}{434}} \end{array}$$

c. $0.00306 \div 0.072$

Multiply by 1,000.

$$\begin{array}{r} 0.0425 \\ 0.\underset{\curvearrowright}{072.}\overline{)0.003.\underset{\curvearrowright}{0600}} \end{array}$$

Exercises

Divide.

1. $0.0023 \div 0.05$

2. $0.000162 \div 0.02$

3. $0.009 \div 0.12$

4. $0.021 \div 2.5$

5. $0.0019 \div 0.2$

6. $0.9 \div 0.8$

7. $0.000175 \div 0.07$

8. $0.142 \div 0.04$

9. $0.0017 \div 0.02$

10. $0.003 \div 0.6$

11. $0.0105 \div 0.7$

12. $0.034 \div 0.05$

13. $0.00056 \div 0.16$

14. $0.0612 \div 7.2$

15. $0.217 \div 3.1$

16. $0.052 \div 0.8$

17. $0.000924 \div 0.44$

18. $0.05796 \div 0.63$

19. $0.00123 \div 8.2$

20. $0.0954 \div 0.09$

21. $0.0084 \div 1.4$

22. $0.259 \div 3.5$

23. $0.00468 \div 0.52$

24. $0.104 \div 0.05$

25. $0.00063 \div 0.18$

26. $0.011 \div 0.25$

27. $0.3069 \div 9.3$

28. $0.00045 \div 0.3$

Mixed Numbers and Improper Fractions

A fraction such as $\frac{10}{7}$, in which the numerator is greater than or equal to the denominator, is an improper fraction. You can write an improper fraction as a mixed number that shows the sum of a whole number and a fraction.

Sometimes it is necessary to do the opposite and write a mixed number as an improper fraction.

EXAMPLE

a. Write $\frac{11}{5}$ as a mixed number.

$$\frac{11}{5} \rightarrow \begin{array}{r} 2 \quad \leftarrow \text{whole number} \\ 5\overline{)11} \\ -10 \\ \hline 1 \quad \leftarrow \text{remainder} \end{array}$$

$\frac{11}{5} = 2\frac{1}{5}$ ← whole number + $\frac{\text{remainder}}{\text{denominator}}$

b. Write $2\frac{5}{6}$ as an improper fraction.

$2\frac{5}{6} = 2 + \frac{5}{6}$

$= \frac{12}{6} + \frac{5}{6}$ ← Write 2 as $\frac{12}{6}$.

$= \frac{12 + 5}{6}$ ← Add the numerators.

$= \frac{17}{6}$

$2\frac{5}{6} = \frac{17}{6}$ ← Simplify.

Exercises

Write each improper fraction as a mixed number.

1. $\frac{7}{5}$ 2. $\frac{9}{2}$ 3. $\frac{13}{4}$ 4. $\frac{21}{5}$ 5. $\frac{13}{10}$

6. $\frac{49}{5}$ 7. $\frac{21}{8}$ 8. $\frac{13}{7}$ 9. $\frac{17}{5}$ 10. $\frac{49}{6}$

11. $\frac{17}{4}$ 12. $\frac{5}{2}$ 13. $\frac{27}{5}$ 14. $\frac{12}{9}$ 15. $\frac{30}{8}$

16. $\frac{37}{12}$ 17. $\frac{8}{6}$ 18. $\frac{19}{12}$ 19. $\frac{45}{10}$ 20. $\frac{15}{12}$

21. $\frac{11}{2}$ 22. $\frac{20}{6}$ 23. $\frac{34}{8}$ 24. $\frac{21}{9}$ 25. $\frac{42}{4}$

Write each mixed number as an improper fraction.

26. $1\frac{1}{2}$ 27. $2\frac{2}{3}$ 28. $1\frac{1}{12}$ 29. $3\frac{1}{5}$ 30. $2\frac{2}{7}$

31. $4\frac{1}{2}$ 32. $2\frac{7}{8}$ 33. $1\frac{2}{9}$ 34. $5\frac{1}{5}$ 35. $4\frac{7}{9}$

36. $9\frac{1}{4}$ 37. $2\frac{3}{8}$ 38. $7\frac{7}{8}$ 39. $1\frac{5}{12}$ 40. $3\frac{3}{7}$

41. $6\frac{1}{2}$ 42. $3\frac{1}{10}$ 43. $4\frac{6}{7}$ 44. $8\frac{1}{8}$ 45. $6\frac{1}{3}$

Adding and Subtracting Fractions With Like Denominators

When you add or subtract fractions with the same denominator, add or subtract the numerators and then write the answer over the denominator.

EXAMPLE

1 Add or subtract. Write the answers in simplest form.

a. $\frac{5}{8} + \frac{7}{8}$

$$\frac{5}{8} + \frac{7}{8} = \frac{5+7}{8} = \frac{12}{8} = 1\frac{4}{8} = 1\frac{1}{2}$$

b. $\frac{11}{12} - \frac{2}{12}$

$$\frac{11}{12} - \frac{2}{12} = \frac{11-2}{12} = \frac{9}{12} = \frac{3}{4}$$

To add or subtract mixed numbers, add or subtract the fractions first. Then add or subtract the whole numbers.

EXAMPLE

2 Add or subtract. Write the answers in simplest form.

a. $3\frac{4}{6} + 2\frac{5}{6}$

$$\begin{array}{r} 3\frac{4}{6} \\ + 2\frac{5}{6} \\ \hline 5\frac{9}{6} = 5 + 1 + \frac{3}{6} = 6\frac{1}{2} \end{array}$$

b. $6\frac{1}{4} - 1\frac{3}{4}$ ← Rewrite 6 as $5\frac{4}{4}$ and add it to $\frac{1}{4}$.

$$\begin{array}{rcl} 6\frac{1}{4} & & 5\frac{5}{4} \\ -1\frac{3}{4} & \rightarrow & -1\frac{3}{4} \\ \hline & & 4\frac{2}{4} = 4\frac{1}{2} \end{array}$$

Exercises

Add or subtract. Write the answers in simplest form.

1. $\frac{4}{5} + \frac{3}{5}$

2. $\frac{2}{6} - \frac{1}{6}$

3. $\frac{2}{7} + \frac{2}{7}$

4. $\frac{7}{8} + \frac{2}{8}$

5. $1\frac{2}{5} - \frac{1}{5}$

6. $\frac{3}{6} - \frac{1}{6}$

7. $\frac{6}{8} - \frac{3}{8}$

8. $\frac{2}{9} + \frac{1}{9}$

9. $\frac{4}{5} - \frac{1}{5}$

10. $\frac{5}{9} + \frac{7}{9}$

11. $9\frac{1}{3} - 8\frac{1}{3}$

12. $8\frac{6}{7} - 4\frac{2}{7}$

13. $3\frac{1}{10} + 1\frac{3}{10}$

14. $2\frac{2}{9} + 3\frac{4}{9}$

15. $4\frac{5}{12} - 3\frac{1}{12}$

16. $9\frac{5}{9} + 6\frac{7}{9}$

17. $5\frac{7}{8} + 2\frac{3}{8}$

18. $4\frac{4}{7} - 2\frac{1}{7}$

19. $9\frac{3}{4} + 1\frac{3}{4}$

20. $8\frac{2}{3} - 4\frac{1}{3}$

21. $8\frac{7}{10} + 2\frac{3}{10}$

22. $1\frac{4}{5} + 3\frac{3}{5}$

23. $7\frac{1}{5} - 2\frac{3}{5}$

24. $4\frac{1}{3} - 1\frac{2}{3}$

25. $4\frac{3}{8} - 3\frac{5}{8}$

26. $5\frac{1}{12} - 2\frac{7}{12}$

Classifying and Measuring Angles

Recall that an angle is a geometric figure formed by two rays with a common endpoint. The rays are sides of the angle and the endpoint is the vertex of the angle. You can name the angle at the right in three different ways: $\angle A$, $\angle BAC$, or $\angle CAB$.

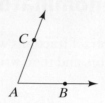

Classify angles by their measures.

Acute angle	Right angle	Obtuse angle	Straight angle
less than 90°	90°	greater than 90° but less than 180°	180°

EXAMPLE

Measure the angle. Classify it as *acute, right, obtuse,* or *straight.*

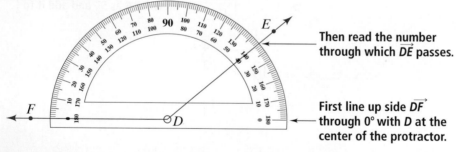

Then read the number through which $\overrightarrow{DE}$ passes.

First line up side $\overrightarrow{DF}$ through 0° with D at the center of the protractor.

The measure of the angle is 140°. The angle is obtuse.

Exercises

Measure each angle. Classify it as *acute, right, obtuse,* or *straight.*

1. A

2. B

3. C

4. D

Classify each angle as *acute, right, obtuse,* or *straight.*

5. 30°   6. 45°   7. 95°   8. 180°   9. 140°   10. 170°

Bar Graphs

Use bar graphs to compare amounts. The horizontal axis shows the categories and the vertical axis shows the amounts. A multiple bar graph includes a key.

EXAMPLE

Draw a bar graph for the data in the table at the right.

Place the categories (in the first column) on the horizontal scale. Place the amounts (in the second and third columns) on the vertical scale. Include a key to the two price categories.

List and Sale Prices

Item	List	Sale
Pocket PC	$450	$400
Digital Camera	$500	$350
Minidisc Player/Recorder	$230	$180

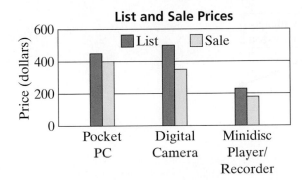

Exercises

Draw a bar graph for each set of data.

1. **Meat Consumption (pounds per person per year)**

Beef	Chicken	Pork	Turkey
62.9	53.9	46.7	13.7

SOURCE: U.S. Department of Agriculture. Go to **PHSchool.com** for a data update.
Web Code: asg-9041

2. **Pets in Students' Homes**

Number of Pets	0	1	2	3	more than 3
Number of Students	11	16	9	11	6

Draw a multiple bar graph for the set of data.

3. **Weekly Leisure Time (hours)**

Activity	Sports	Reading	Working
Anna	12	8	12
Tobi	6	12	10

4. **Average SAT Math and Verbal Scores**

Year	1	2	3
Math	514	514	516
Verbal	505	506	504

SOURCE: U.S. Dept. of Education. Go to **PHSchool.com** for a data update.
Web Code: asg-9041

Line Graphs

Use line graphs to show changes over time. A multiple line graph shows more than one category changing over time.

EXAMPLE

Display the data in the table below in a line graph.

Monthly Average Temperatures (°F)

Month	J	F	M	A	M	J	J	A	S	O	N	D
Houston, Texas	50	54	61	68	75	80	83	82	78	70	61	54
Chicago, Illinois	21	25	37	49	59	69	73	72	64	53	40	27

SOURCE: National Climatic Data Center. Go to **PHSchool.com** for a data update. Web Code: asg-9041

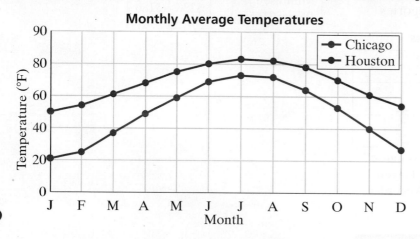

Exercises

Draw multiple line graphs for the data below.

1. Average Baseball and Hockey Salaries
(millions of dollars)

Year	1998	1999	2000	2001
Baseball	1.4	1.6	1.9	2.1
Hockey	1.3	1.4	1.4	1.6

SOURCE: Major League Baseball Players Association and National Hockey League

2. U.S. Newspaper Circulation (millions)

Year	2000	2001	2002	2003
Morning	46.8	46.8	46.6	46.9
Evening	9.0	8.8	8.6	8.3

SOURCE: U.S. Census Bureau. Go to **PHSchool.com** for a data update. Web Code: asg-9041

3. Movies Rented per Household

Year	1	2	3	4	5
Videos	40.8	40.1	38.9	35.2	33.8
DVDs	3.1	8.5	10.9	25.4	29.9

4. Space Launches

Year	1	2	3	4	5
United States	38	36	33	31	24
Russia	29	25	28	36	23

Table 1 Measures

Metric	Customary
Length	**Length**
10 millimeters (mm) = 1 centimeter (cm)	12 inches (in.) = 1 foot (ft)
100 cm = 1 meter (m)	36 in. = 1 yard (yd)
1,000 m = 1 kilometer (km)	3 ft = 1 yd
	5,280 ft = 1 mile (mi)
	1,760 yd = 1 mi
Area	**Area**
100 square millimeters (mm^2) = 1 square centimeter (cm^2)	144 square inches ($in.^2$) = 1 square foot (ft^2)
10,000 cm^2 = 1 square meter (m^2)	9 ft^2 = 1 square yard (yd^2)
	4,840 yd^2 = 1 acre
Volume	**Volume**
1,000 cubic millimeters (mm^3) = 1 cubic centimeter (cm^3)	1,728 cubic inches ($in.^3$) = 1 cubic foot (ft^3)
1,000,000 cm^3 = 1 cubic meter (m^3)	27 ft^3 = 1 cubic yard (yd^3)
Mass	**Mass**
1,000 milligrams (mg) = 1 gram (g)	16 ounces (oz) = 1 pound (lb)
1,000 g = 1 kilogram (kg)	2,000 lb = 1 ton (t)
Capacity	**Capacity**
1,000 milliliters (mL) = 1 liter (L)	8 fluid ounces (fl oz) = 1 cup (c)
	2 c = 1 pint (pt)
	2 pt = 1 quart (qt)
	4 qt = 1 gallon (gal)

Time

1 minute (min) = 60 seconds (s)
1 hour(h) = 60 min
1 day(d) = 24 h
1 year(yr) = 365 d

Table 2 Math Symbols

Symbol	Meaning	Page
$+$	plus (addition)	p. 4
$-$	minus (subtraction)	p. 4
$\times, \cdot$	times (multiplication)	p. 4
$\div, \overline{)}$	divide (division)	p. 4
$=$	is equal to	p. 5
$(\ )$	parentheses for grouping	p. 6
$[\ ]$	brackets for grouping	p. 6
$-a$	opposite of a	p. 10
$\dots$	and so on	p. 10
$^\circ$	degrees	p. 10
$|a|$	absolute value of a	p. 10
$\stackrel{?}{=}$	Is the statement true?	p. 34
$\approx$	is approximately equal to	p. 63
$\frac{b}{a}$	reciprocal of $\frac{a}{b}$	p. 73
A	area	p. 81
ℓ	length	p. 81
w	width	p. 81
h	height	p. 81
b_1, b_2	base lengths of a trapezoid	p. 81
d	distance	p. 82
r	rate	p. 82
t	time	p. 82
P	perimeter	p. 82
a^n	nth power of a	p. 86
$\sqrt{x}$	nonnegative square root of x	p. 106
π	pi, an irrational number approximately equal to 3.14	p. 108
(a, b)	ordered pair with x-coordinate a and y-coordinate b	p. 124
$\overline{AB}$	segment AB	p. 128
A'	image of A, A prime	p. 136
$\triangle ABC$	triangle with vertices A, B, and C	p. 136
$\rightarrow$	arrow notation	p. 137
$a:b, \frac{a}{b}$	ratio of a to b	p. 160
$\cong$	is congruent to	p. 181
$\sim$	is similar to	p. 181
$\angle A$	angle with vertex A	p. 181
AB	length of segment $\overline{AB}$	p. 181
$\overrightarrow{AB}$	ray AB	p. 186
$\%$	percent	p. 210
$P(\text{event})$	probability of an event	p. 246
$<$	is less than	p. 281
$>$	is greater than	p. 281
$\leq$	is less than or equal to	p. 281
$\geq$	is greater than or equal to	p. 281
$\neq$	is not equal to	p. 282
$\angle ABC$	angle with sides $\overrightarrow{BA}$ and $\overrightarrow{BC}$	p. 303
$m\angle ABC$	measure of angle ABC	p. 303
$\perp$	is perpendicular to	p. 304
$\overleftrightarrow{AB}$	line AB	p. 308
$\parallel$	is parallel to	p. 308
b	base length	p. 328
C	circumference	p. 336
d	diameter	p. 336
r	radius	p. 336
S.A.	surface area	p. 368
B	area of base	p. 369
L.A.	lateral area	p. 369
ℓ	slant height	p. 374
V	volume	p. 380
$n!$	n factorial	p. 492
$_nP_r$	permutations of n things taken r at a time	p. 493
$_nC_r$	combinations of n things taken r at a time	p. 497
$f(n)$	the function value at n, f of n	p. 524
b	y-intercept	p. 535
m	slope of a line	p. 535
$\sin A$	sine of $\angle A$	p. 646
$\cos A$	cosine of $\angle A$	p. 646
$\tan A$	tangent of $\angle A$	p. 646

Table 3 Squares and Square Roots

Number n	Square n^2	Positive Square Root $\sqrt{n}$	Number n	Square n^2	Positive Square Root $\sqrt{n}$
1	1	1.000	51	2,601	7.141
2	4	1.414	52	2,704	7.211
3	9	1.732	53	2,809	7.280
4	16	2.000	54	2,916	7.348
5	25	2.236	55	3,025	7.416
6	36	2.449	56	3,136	7.483
7	49	2.646	57	3,249	7.550
8	64	2.828	58	3,364	7.616
9	81	3.000	59	3,481	7.681
10	100	3.162	60	3,600	7.746
11	121	3.317	61	3,721	7.810
12	144	3.464	62	3,844	7.874
13	169	3.606	63	3,969	7.937
14	196	3.742	64	4,096	8.000
15	225	3.873	65	4,225	8.062
16	256	4.000	66	4,356	8.124
17	289	4.123	67	4,489	8.185
18	324	4.243	68	4,624	8.246
19	361	4.359	69	4,761	8.307
20	400	4.472	70	4,900	8.367
21	441	4.583	71	5,041	8.426
22	484	4.690	72	5,184	8.485
23	529	4.796	73	5,329	8.544
24	576	4.899	74	5,476	8.602
25	625	5.000	75	5,625	8.660
26	676	5.099	76	5,776	8.718
27	729	5.196	77	5,929	8.775
28	784	5.292	78	6,084	8.832
29	841	5.385	79	6,241	8.888
30	900	5.477	80	6,400	8.944
31	961	5.568	81	6,561	9.000
32	1,024	5.657	82	6,724	9.055
33	1,089	5.745	83	6,889	9.110
34	1,156	5.831	84	7,056	9.165
35	1,225	5.916	85	7,225	9.220
36	1,296	6.000	86	7,396	9.274
37	1,369	6.083	87	7,569	9.327
38	1,444	6.164	88	7,744	9.381
39	1,521	6.245	89	7,921	9.434
40	1,600	6.325	90	8,100	9.487
41	1,681	6.403	91	8,281	9.539
42	1,764	6.481	92	8,464	9.592
43	1,849	6.557	93	8,649	9.644
44	1,936	6.633	94	8,836	9.695
45	2,025	6.708	95	9,025	9.747
46	2,116	6.782	96	9,216	9.798
47	2,209	6.856	97	9,409	9.849
48	2,304	6.928	98	9,604	9.899
49	2,401	7.000	99	9,801	9.950
50	2,500	7.071	100	10,000	10.000

Table 4 Trigonometric Ratios

Angle	Sine	Cosine	Tangent
1°	0.0175	0.9998	0.0175
2°	0.0349	0.9994	0.0349
3°	0.0523	0.9986	0.0524
4°	0.0698	0.9976	0.0699
5°	0.0872	0.9962	0.0875
6°	0.1045	0.9945	0.1051
7°	0.1219	0.9925	0.1228
8°	0.1392	0.9903	0.1405
9°	0.1564	0.9877	0.1584
10°	0.1736	0.9848	0.1763
11°	0.1908	0.9816	0.1944
12°	0.2079	0.9781	0.2126
13°	0.2250	0.9744	0.2309
14°	0.2419	0.9703	0.2493
15°	0.2588	0.9659	0.2679
16°	0.2756	0.9613	0.2867
17°	0.2924	0.9563	0.3057
18°	0.3090	0.9511	0.3249
19°	0.3256	0.9455	0.3443
20°	0.3420	0.9397	0.3640
21°	0.3584	0.9336	0.3839
22°	0.3746	0.9272	0.4040
23°	0.3907	0.9205	0.4245
24°	0.4067	0.9135	0.4452
25°	0.4226	0.9063	0.4663
26°	0.4384	0.8988	0.4877
27°	0.4540	0.8910	0.5095
28°	0.4695	0.8829	0.5317
29°	0.4848	0.8746	0.5543
30°	0.5000	0.8660	0.5774
31°	0.5150	0.8572	0.6009
32°	0.5299	0.8480	0.6249
33°	0.5446	0.8387	0.6494
34°	0.5592	0.8290	0.6745
35°	0.5736	0.8192	0.7002
36°	0.5878	0.8090	0.7265
37°	0.6018	0.7986	0.7536
38°	0.6157	0.7880	0.7813
39°	0.6293	0.7771	0.8098
40°	0.6428	0.7660	0.8391
41°	0.6561	0.7547	0.8693
42°	0.6691	0.7431	0.9004
43°	0.6820	0.7314	0.9325
44°	0.6947	0.7193	0.9657
45°	0.7071	0.7071	1.0000

Angle	Sine	Cosine	Tangent
46°	0.7193	0.6947	1.0355
47°	0.7314	0.6820	1.0724
48°	0.7431	0.6691	1.1106
49°	0.7547	0.6561	1.1504
50°	0.7660	0.6428	1.1918
51°	0.7771	0.6293	1.2349
52°	0.7880	0.6157	1.2799
53°	0.7986	0.6018	1.3270
54°	0.8090	0.5878	1.3764
55°	0.8192	0.5736	1.4281
56°	0.8290	0.5592	1.4826
57°	0.8387	0.5446	1.5399
58°	0.8480	0.5299	1.6003
59°	0.8572	0.5150	1.6643
60°	0.8660	0.5000	1.7321
61°	0.8746	0.4848	1.8040
62°	0.8829	0.4695	1.8807
63°	0.8910	0.4540	1.9626
64°	0.8988	0.4384	2.0503
65°	0.9063	0.4226	2.1445
66°	0.9135	0.4067	2.2460
67°	0.9205	0.3907	2.3559
68°	0.9272	0.3746	2.4751
69°	0.9336	0.3584	2.6051
70°	0.9397	0.3420	2.7475
71°	0.9455	0.3256	2.9042
72°	0.9511	0.3090	3.0777
73°	0.9563	0.2924	3.2709
74°	0.9613	0.2756	3.4874
75°	0.9659	0.2588	3.7321
76°	0.9703	0.2419	4.0108
77°	0.9744	0.2250	4.3315
78°	0.9781	0.2079	4.7046
79°	0.9816	0.1908	5.1446
80°	0.9848	0.1736	5.6713
81°	0.9877	0.1564	6.3138
82°	0.9903	0.1392	7.1154
83°	0.9925	0.1219	8.1443
84°	0.9945	0.1045	9.5144
85°	0.9962	0.0872	11.4301
86°	0.9976	0.0698	14.3007
87°	0.9986	0.0523	19.0811
88°	0.9994	0.0349	28.6363
89°	0.9998	0.0175	57.2900
90°	1.0000	0.0000	

Table 5 For Use With Problem Solving Applications

Chapter 4
Animated Movies

Movie	Year Released	Budget (millions of dollars)	Run Time (minutes)
Snow White and the Seven Dwarfs	1937	1.5	83
Fantasia	1940	2.3	120
The Lion King	1994	79.3	89
Hercules	1997	70.0	92
A Bug's Life	1998	45.0	96
Toy Story 2	1999	90.0	92
Chicken Run	2000	42.0	84
Lilo & Stitch	2002	80.0	85

SOURCE: The Internet Movie Database

Chapter 8
Typical Measurements of Bird Species and Nest Sizes

Species	Typical Wingspan (in.)	Typical Length (in.)	Typical Nest Diameter (in.)
Bald Eagle	84	38.5	60
Red-Tailed Hawk	52	22	29
Scarlet Ibis	38	25	10
American Crow	36.5	17.5	24
Blue Jay	16	11	7.5
Ruby-Throated Hummingbird	4.25	3.5	1.5

SOURCES: *A Field Guide to the Birds' Nests: United States East of the Mississippi River*
Birds of North America

Formulas and Properties

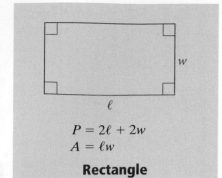

$$P = 2\ell + 2w$$
$$A = \ell w$$

Rectangle

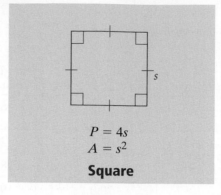

$$P = 4s$$
$$A = s^2$$

Square

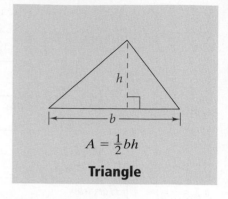

$$A = \tfrac{1}{2}bh$$

Triangle

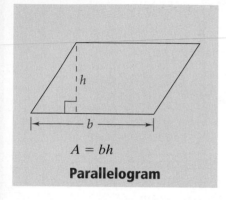

$$A = bh$$

Parallelogram

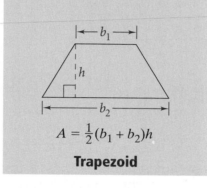

$$A = \tfrac{1}{2}(b_1 + b_2)h$$

Trapezoid

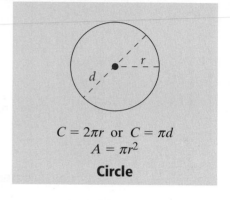

$$C = 2\pi r \ \text{ or } \ C = \pi d$$
$$A = \pi r^2$$

Circle

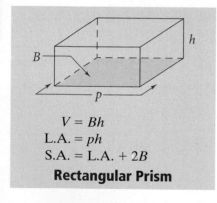

$$V = Bh$$
$$\text{L.A.} = ph$$
$$\text{S.A.} = \text{L.A.} + 2B$$

Rectangular Prism

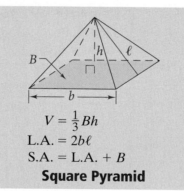

$$V = \tfrac{1}{3}Bh$$
$$\text{L.A.} = 2b\ell$$
$$\text{S.A.} = \text{L.A.} + B$$

Square Pyramid

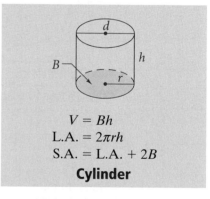

$$V = Bh$$
$$\text{L.A.} = 2\pi rh$$
$$\text{S.A.} = \text{L.A.} + 2B$$

Cylinder

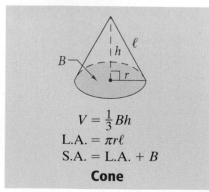

$$V = \tfrac{1}{3}Bh$$
$$\text{L.A.} = \pi r\ell$$
$$\text{S.A.} = \text{L.A.} + B$$

Cone

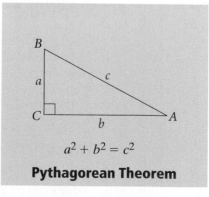

$$a^2 + b^2 = c^2$$

Pythagorean Theorem

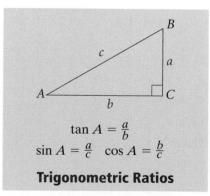

$$\tan A = \frac{a}{b}$$
$$\sin A = \frac{a}{c} \quad \cos A = \frac{b}{c}$$

Trigonometric Ratios

Properties of Real Numbers

Unless otherwise stated, the variables a, b, c, and d used in these properties can be replaced with any number represented on a number line.

Identity Properties

Addition	$a + 0 = a$ and $0 + a = a$
Multiplication	$a \cdot 1 = a$ and $1 \cdot a = a$

Commutative Properties

Addition	$a + b = b + a$
Multiplication	$a \cdot b = b \cdot a$

Associative Properties

Addition	$(a + b) + c = a + (b + c)$
Multiplication	$(a \cdot b) \cdot c = a \cdot (b \cdot c)$

Inverse Properties

Addition

$a + (-a) = 0$ and $-a + a = 0$

Multiplication

$a \cdot \frac{1}{a} = 1$ and $\frac{1}{a} \cdot a = 1 \ (a \neq 0)$

Distributive Properties

$a(b + c) = ab + ac \quad (b + c)a = ba + ca$
$a(b - c) = ab - ac \quad (b - c)a = ba - ca$

Properties of Equality

Addition	If $a = b$, then $a + c = b + c$.
Subtraction	If $a = b$, then $a - c = b - c$.
Multiplication	If $a = b$, then $a \cdot c = b \cdot c$.
Division	If $a = b$, and $c \neq 0$, then $\frac{a}{c} = \frac{b}{c}$.
Substitution	If $a = b$, then b can replace a in any expression.
Reflexive	$a = a$
Symmetric	If $a = b$, then $b = a$.
Transitive	If $a = b$ and $b = c$, then $a = c$.

Cross Products Property

$\frac{a}{c} = \frac{b}{d}$ is equivalent to $ad = bc$.

Zero-Product Property

If $ab = 0$, then $a = 0$ or $b = 0$.

Closure Property

$a + b$ is a unique real number.
ab is a unique real number.

Density Property

Between any two rational numbers, there is at least one other rational number.

Properties of Inequality

Addition	If $a > b$, then $a + c > b + c$.
	If $a < b$, then $a + c < b + c$.
Subtraction	If $a > b$, then $a - c > b - c$.
	If $a < b$, then $a - c < b - c$.

Multiplication

If $a > b$ and $c > 0$, then $ac > bc$.
If $a < b$ and $c > 0$, then $ac < bc$.
If $a > b$ and $c < 0$, then $ac < bc$.
If $a < b$ and $c < 0$, then $ac > bc$.

Division

If $a > b$ and $c > 0$, then $\frac{a}{c} > \frac{b}{c}$.
If $a < b$ and $c > 0$, then $\frac{a}{c} < \frac{b}{c}$.
If $a > b$ and $c < 0$, then $\frac{a}{c} < \frac{b}{c}$.
If $a < b$ and $c < 0$, then $\frac{a}{c} > \frac{b}{c}$.

Transitive

If $a > b$ and $b > c$, then $a > c$.

Comparative

If $a = b + c$ and $c > 0$, then $a > b$.

Properties of Exponents

For any nonzero number a and any integers m and n:

Zero Exponent	$a^0 = 1$
Negative Exponent	$a^{-n} = \frac{1}{a^n}$
Product of Powers	$a^m \cdot a^n = a^{m + n}$
Quotient of Powers	$\frac{a^m}{a^n} = a^{m - n}$

EXAMPLES

A

Absolute value (p. 10) The absolute value of a number is its distance from 0 on a number line.

-7 is 7 units from 0, so $|-7| = 7$.

Valor absoluto (p. 10) El valor absoluto de un número es su distancia del 0 en una recta numérica.

Acute angle (p. 640) An acute angle is an angle with a measure between 0° and 90°.

Ángulo agudo (p. 640) Un ángulo agudo es un ángulo que mide entre 0° y 90°.

$0° < m\angle 1 < 90°$

Acute triangle (p. 318) An acute triangle has three acute angles.

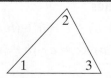

Triángulo acutángulo (p. 318) Un triángulo acutángulo tiene tres ángulos agudos.

$\angle 1$, $\angle 2$, and $\angle 3$ are acute.

Addition Property of Equality (p. 33) The Addition Property of Equality states that if you add the same value to each side of an equation, the results are equal.

If $a = b$, then $a + c = b + c$.
Since $\frac{20}{2} = 10$, $\frac{20}{2} + 3 = 10 + 3$.

Propiedad Aditiva de la Igualdad (p. 33) La Propiedad Aditiva de la Igualdad establece que si se suma el mismo valor a cada lado de una ecuación, los resultados son iguales.

Addition Property of Inequality (p. 282) The Addition Property of Inequality states that if you add the same value to each side of an inequality, the relationship between the two sides does not change.

If $a > b$, then $a + c > b + c$.
Since $4 > 2$, $4 + 11 > 2 + 11$.
If $a < b$, then $a + c < b + c$.

Propiedad Aditiva de la Desigualdad (p. 282) La Propiedad Aditiva de la Desigualdad establece que si sumas el mismo valor a cada lado de una desigualdad, la relación entre los dos lados no cambia.

Since $4 < 9$, $4 + 11 < 9 + 11$.

Additive inverses (p. 16) Two numbers whose sum is 0 are additive inverses.

$-a + a = 0$
$(-5) + 5 = 0$

Inversos aditivos (p. 16) Dos números cuya suma es 0 son inversos aditivos.

Adjacent angles (p. 303)   Adjacent angles share a vertex and a side but have no interior points in common.

Ángulos adyacentes (p. 303)   Los ángulos adyacentes comparten un vértice y un lado, pero no tienen puntos interiores en común.

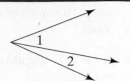

∠1 and ∠2 are adjacent angles.

Algebraic expression (p. 4)   An algebraic expression is a mathematical phrase that contains variables, numbers, and operation symbols.

Expresión algebraica (p. 4)   Una expresión algebraica es un enunciado matemático que contiene variables, números y símbolos de operaciones.

$2x - 5$ is an algebraic expression.

Alternate exterior angles (p. 310)   Alternate exterior angles lie outside a pair of lines and on opposite sides of a transversal.

Ángulos alternos externos (p. 310)   Los ángulos alternos externos se ubican fuera de un par de rectas y a lados opuestos de la secante.

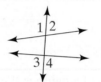

∠2 and ∠3 are alternate exterior angles.
∠1 and ∠4 are also alternate exterior angles.

Alternate interior angles (p. 307)   Alternate interior angles lie within a pair of lines and on opposite sides of a transversal.

Ángulos alternos internos (p. 307)   Los ángulos alternos internos están ubicados entre un par de rectas y a lados opuestos de la secante.

∠2 and ∠3 are alternate interior angles.
∠1 and ∠4 are also alternate interior angles.

Angle (p. 640)   An angle is formed by two rays with a common endpoint called a vertex.

Ángulo (p. 640)   Un ángulo está formado por dos rayos que tienen un punto final común llamado vértice.

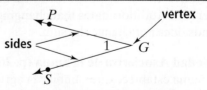

∠1 is made up of $\overrightarrow{GP}$ and $\overrightarrow{GS}$ with the common endpoint G.

Angle bisector (p. 344)   An angle bisector is a ray that divides an angle into angles of equal measure.

Bisectriz de un ángulo (p. 344)   La bisectriz de un ángulo es un rayo que divide un ángulo en ángulos de igual medida.

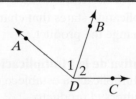

$\overrightarrow{DB}$ bisects ∠ADC, so ∠1 ≅ ∠2.

Angle of rotation (p. 146) The angle of rotation is the number of degrees that a figure rotates.

Ángulo de rotación (p. 146) El ángulo de rotación es el número de grados que se rota una figura.

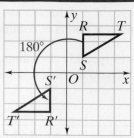

$\triangle RST$ has been rotated $180°$ to $\triangle R'S'T'$.

Arc (p. 340) An arc is part of a circle.

Arco (p. 340) Un arco es parte de un círculo.

$\overset{\frown}{AB}$ is an arc of circle O. $\overset{\frown}{ABC}$ is a semicircle of circle O.

Area (p. 328) The area of a figure is the number of square units it encloses.

Área (p. 328) El área de una figura es el número de unidades cuadradas que contiene.

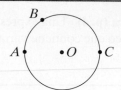

Each square equals $1\ \text{ft}^2$. $\ell = 6$ ft, and $w = 4$ ft, so the area is $6 \cdot 4 = 24\ \text{ft}^2$.

Arithmetic sequence (p. 513) In an arithmetic sequence, each term is the result of adding the same number to the previous term.

Progresión aritmética (p. 513) En una progresión aritmética, cada término es el resultado de sumar el mismo número al término anterior.

The sequence $4, 10, 16, 22, 28, \ldots$ is an arithmetic sequence. You add 6 to each term to find the next term.

Associative Property of Addition (p. 26) The Associative Property of Addition states that changing the grouping of the addends does not change the sum.

Propiedad Asociativa de la Suma (p. 26) La Propiedad Asociativa de la Suma establece que cambiar la agrupación de los sumandos no cambia la suma.

$(a + b) + c = a + (b + c)$
$(2 + 3) + 7 = 2 + (3 + 7)$

Associative Property of Multiplication (p. 26) The Associative Property of Multiplication states that changing the grouping of factors does not change the product.

Propiedad Asociativa de la Multiplicación (p. 26) La Propiedad Asociativa de la Multiplicación establece que cambiar la agrupación de los factores no altera el producto.

$(a \cdot b) \cdot c = a \cdot (b \cdot c)$
$(3 \cdot 4) \cdot 5 = 3 \cdot (4 \cdot 5)$

Balance (p. 243) The balance of an account is the principal plus the interest earned.

You deposit $100 into a bank account and earn $5 interest. Your balance is $105.

Saldo (p. 243) El saldo de una cuenta es el capital más los intereses ganados.

Base (p. 86) When a number is written in exponential form, the number that is used as a factor is the base.

$$5^4 = 5 \times 5 \times 5 \times 5$$
$$\text{base}$$

Base (p. 86) Cuando un número se escribe en forma exponencial, el número que se usa como factor es la base.

Base plan (p. 358) A base plan shows the shape of the base and indicates the height of each part of a solid.

Plano base (p. 358) Un plano base muestra la forma de la base e indica la altura de cada parte de una figura tridimensional.

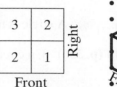

The first drawing is a base plan; the second drawing is an isometric drawing using the base plan.

Biased questions (p. 481) Unfair questions in a survey are biased questions. They can make assumptions that may or may not be true. Biased questions can also make one answer seem better than another.

"Do you prefer good food or junk food?"

Preguntas tendenciosas (p. 481) Las preguntas injustas de una encuesta son preguntas tendenciosas. Pueden hacer suposiciones que pueden o no ser verdaderas. Las preguntas tendenciosas hacen que una respuesta parezca mejor que otra.

Binomial (p. 576) A polynomial that has two terms is called a binomial.

$3x^2 - 1$ is a binomial.

Binomio (p. 576) Se llama binomio a un polinomio que tiene dos términos.

English/Spanish Glossary

Box-and-whisker plot (p. 438) A box-and-whisker plot is a graph that summarizes a data set using five key values. There is a box in the middle and "whiskers" at either side. The quartiles divide the data into four equal parts.

Gráfica de caja y brazos (p. 438) Una gráfica de caja y brazos es un diagrama que resume un conjunto de datos usando cinco valores clave. Hay una caja en el centro y extensiones a cada lado. Los cuartiles se dividen los datos en cuartas partes iguales.

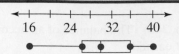

The box-and-whisker plot above uses these data:

16 19 26 26 27 29 30 31 34 34 38 39 40

Center of a circle (p. 336) A circle is named by its center.

Centro de un círculo (p. 336) Un círculo es denominado por su centro.

Circle O

Center of a sphere (p. 393) See *Sphere.*

Centro de una esfera (p. 393) Ver *Sphere.*

Center of rotation (p. 146) The center of rotation is a fixed point about which a figure is rotated.

Centro de rotación (p. 146) El centro de rotación es un punto fijo alrededor del cual se rota una figura.

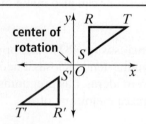

O is the center of rotation.

Central angle (p. 451) A central angle is an angle whose vertex is the center of a circle. The sum of the measures of the central angles is 360°.

Ángulo central (p. 451) Un ángulo central es un ángulo cuyo vértice es el centro de un círculo. La suma de las medidas de los ángulos centrales es 360°.

$\angle AOB$ is a central angle of circle O.

Chord (pp. 336, 340)   A chord is a segment that has both endpoints on the circle.

Cuerda (pp. 336, 340)   Una cuerda es un segmento que tiene ambos extremos sobre un círculo.

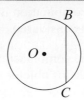

$\overline{CB}$ is a chord of circle O.

Circle (p. 336)   A circle is the set of points in a plane that are all the same distance from a given point called the center.

Círculo (p. 336)   Un círculo es el conjunto de puntos de un plano que están a la misma distancia de un punto dado llamado centro.

Circle graph (p. 450)   A circle graph is a graph of data where the entire circle represents the whole. Each wedge, or sector, in the circle represents part of the whole.

Gráfica circular (p. 450)   Una gráfica circular es una gráfica de datos donde el círculo completo representa el todo. Cada cuña o sector del círculo representa una parte del todo.

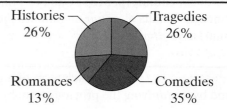

The circle graph represents the types of plays William Shakespeare wrote.

Circumference (p. 336)   Circumference is the distance around a circle. You calculate the circumference of a circle by multiplying the diameter by π.

Circunferencia (p. 336)   La circunferencia es la distancia alrededor de un círculo. La circunferencia de un círculo se calcula multiplicando el diámetro por π.

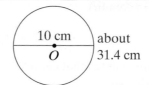

The circumference of a circle with a diameter of 10 cm is approximately 31.4 cm.

Closure Property (p. 109)   A set of numbers is closed under an arithmetic operation if the answer of the operation is unique and in the same set as the original numbers.

Propiedad de Cerradura (p. 109)   Un conjunto de números está cerrado bajo una operación metemática si la respuesta de la operación es única y está en el mismo conjunto de números originales.

Rational numbers are closed under addition because the sum of two rational numbers is a rational number.

Coefficient (p. 566)   A coefficient is the numerical factor in any term of a polynomial.

Coeficiente (p. 566)   Un coeficiente es un factor numérico en cualquier término de un polinómio.

In the expression $2x + 3y - 16$, the coefficient of x is 2 and the coefficient of y is 3.

Combination (p. 496) A combination is a group of items in which the order of the items is not considered.

Combinación (p. 496) Una combinación es una agrupación de objetos en donde el orden de los objetos no tiene importancia.

You choose two vegetables from carrots, peas, and spinach. The possible combinations are: carrots and peas, carrots and spinach, and peas and spinach.

Commission A commission is a percent of sales.

Comisión Una comisión es un porcentaje de las ventas.

A salesperson receives a 6% commission on sales of $200. Her commission is $12.

Common difference (p. 513) Each term of an arithmetic sequence is found by *adding* a fixed number (called the common difference) to the previous term.

Diferencia común (p. 513) Cada término de una progresión aritmética se halla al *sumar* un número fijo (llamado diferencia común) al término anterior.

In the arithmetic sequence $-2, -4, -6, -8, \ldots$, the common difference is -2.

Common ratio (p. 514) Each term of a geometric sequence is found by *multiplying* the previous term by a fixed number (called the common ratio).

Razón común (p. 514) Cada término de una progresión geométrica se halla al *multiplicar* el término anterior por un número fijo (llamado razón común).

In the geometric sequence $3, 18, 108, 648, \ldots$, the common ratio is 6.

Commutative Property of Addition (p. 26) The Commutative Property of Addition states that changing the order of the addends does not change the sum.

Propiedad Conmutativa de la Suma (p. 26) La Propiedad Conmutativa de la Suma establece que al cambiar el orden de los sumandos no se altera la suma.

$a + b = b + a$
$3 + 1 = 1 + 3$

Commutative Property of Multiplication (p. 26) The Commutative Property of Multiplication states that changing the order of the factors does not change the product.

Propiedad Conmutativa de la Multiplicación (p. 26) La Propiedad Conmutativa de la Multiplicación establece que al cambiar el orden de los factores no se altera el producto.

$a \cdot b = b \cdot a$
$6 \cdot 3 = 3 \cdot 6$

Compass (p. 341) A compass is a geometric tool used to draw circles or arcs.

Compás (p. 341) Un compás es una herramienta que se usa en geometría para dibujar círculos o arcos.

Compatible numbers (pp. 168, 214) Compatible numbers are numbers that are easy to compute mentally.

Números compatibles (pp. 168, 214) Los números compatibles son números con los que se puede calcular mentalmente con facilidad.

Estimate $151 \div 14.6$.

$151 \approx 150$, $14.6 \approx 15$
$150 \div 15 = 10$
$151 \div 14.6 \approx 10$

Complement (p. 479) The complement of an event is the collection of outcomes not contained in the event.

Complemento (p. 479) El complemento de un suceso es la colección de resultados que el suceso no incluye.

The event *no rain* is the complement of the event *rain*.

Complementary (p. 304) Two angles are complementary if the sum of their measures is 90°.

Complementario (p. 304) Dos ángulos son complementarios si la suma de sus medidas es 90°.

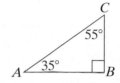

$\angle BCA$ and $\angle CAB$ are complementary angles.

Composite number (p. 52) A composite number is a whole number greater than 1 with more than two factors.

Número compuesto (p. 52) Un número compuesto es un número entero mayor que 1, que tiene más de dos factores.

24 is a composite number that has 1, 2, 3, 4, 6, 8, 12, and 24 as factors.

Compound event (p. 486) A compound event is an event that consists of two or more events. The probability of a compound event can be found by multiplying the probability of one event by the probability of a second event.

Suceso compuesto (p. 486) Un suceso compuesto es un suceso que está formado por dos o más sucesos. La probabilidad de un suceso compuesto se puede hallar al multiplicar la probabilidad de un suceso por la probabilidad de un segundo suceso.

If $P(A) = \frac{1}{3}$ and $P(B) = \frac{1}{2}$, then $P(A \text{ and } B) = \frac{1}{3} \cdot \frac{1}{2} = \frac{1}{6}$, when A and B are independent events.

Compound interest Compound interest is interest paid on the original principal and on any interest that has been left in the account. You can use the formula $B = p(1 + r)^n$ where B is the balance in the account, p is the principal, r is the annual interest rate, and n is the number of years that the account earns interest.

Interés compuesto El interés compuesto es el interés que se paga sobre el principal original y sobre cualquier interés que ha quedado en la cuenta. Se puede usar la fórmula $S = p(1 + i)^t$ donde S es el saldo en la cuenta, p es el principal, i es la tasa de interés anual y t es el tiempo en años en que la cuenta gana interés.

You deposit $500 in an account earning 5% annual interest.

The balance after six years is $500(1 + 0.05)^6$, or $670.05.

Cone (p. 354) A cone has exactly one circular base and one vertex.

Cono (p. 354) Un cono tiene exactamente una base circular y un vértice.

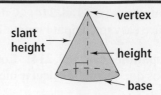

Congruent angles (pp. 181, 313) Congruent angles are angles that have the same measure.

Ángulos congruentes (pp. 181, 313) Los ángulos congruentes son ángulos que tienen la misma medida.

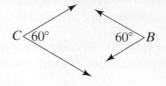

$\angle B \cong \angle C$

Congruent polygons (p. 312) Two polygons are congruent if they have exactly the same shape and size.

Polígonos congruentes (p. 312) Dos polígonos son congruentes si tienen exactamente la misma forma y tamaño.

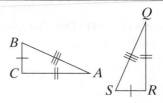

$\triangle ABC \cong \triangle QSR$

Congruent sides (p. 313) Congruent sides have the same length.

Lados congruentes (p. 313) Los lados congruentes tienen la misma longitud.

$\overline{EF} \cong \overline{FG} \cong \overline{GE}$

Conjecture (p. 15) A conjecture is a prediction that suggests what can be expected to happen.

Conjetura (p. 15) Una conjetura es una predicción que sugiere lo que se puede esperar que ocurra.

Every clover has three leaves.

Constant (p. 561) In a polynomial, a term that does not contain a variable is a constant.

Constante (p. 561) En un polinomio, un término que no contiene una variable es una constante.

In the polynomial $4x^3 - 2x + 7$, 7 is a constant.

Continuous data (p. 534) Continuous data are data where numbers between any two data values have meaning. Examples include measurements of temperature, length, or weight. Use a solid line to indicate continuous data.

Datos continuos (p. 534) Los datos continuos son datos donde los números entre dos valores de datos tienen significado. Entre los ejemplos se incluyen medidas de temperatura, longitud o peso. Se usa una recta sólida para indicar los datos continuos.

Data on the average daily temperature in Santa Barbara, California, are continuous data.

Conversion factor (p. 167)   Rates equal to 1.

Factor de conversión (p. 167)   Las razones dan igual a 1.

$\dfrac{3 \text{ ft}}{1 \text{ yd}}$ and $\dfrac{1 \text{ yd}}{3 \text{ ft}}$ are conversion factors.

Coordinate plane (p. 124)   A coordinate plane is formed by the intersection of a horizontal number line called the *x*-axis and a vertical number line called the *y*-axis.

Plano de coordenadas (p. 124)   Un plano de coordenadas está formado por la intersección de una recta numérica horizontal llamada eje de *x* y por una recta numérica vertical llamada eje de *y*.

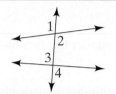

Corresponding angles (p. 307)   Corresponding angles lie on the same side of the transversal and in corresponding positions.

Ángulos correspondientes (p. 307)   Los ángulos correspondientes se ubican al mismo lado de una secante y en posiciones correspondientes.

$\angle 1$ and $\angle 3$ are corresponding angles. $\angle 2$ and $\angle 4$ are also corresponding angles.

Corresponding parts (p. 313)   Corresponding parts of congruent polygons are congruent.

Partes correspondientes (p. 313)   Las partes correspondientes de los polígonos congruentes son congruentes.

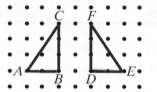

$\overline{AB} \cong \overline{ED}, \ \overline{BC} \cong \overline{DF}, \ \overline{CA} \cong \overline{FE}$
$\angle A \cong \angle E, \ \angle B \cong \angle D, \ \angle C \cong \angle F$
$\triangle ABC \cong \triangle EDF$

Counting principle (p. 492)   Suppose there are *m* ways of making one choice and *n* ways of making a second choice. Then there are *m* · *n* ways to make the first choice followed by the second.

Principio de conteo (p. 492)   Supongamos que hay *m* maneras de hacer una elección y *n* maneras de hacer una otra elección. Entonces hay *m* · *n* maneras de hacer la primera elección seguida por la segunda.

Toss a coin and roll a standard number cube. The total number of possible outcomes is 2 · 6 = 12.

English/Spanish Glossary

Cross products (p. 175) For two ratios, the cross products are found by multiplying the denominator of one ratio by the numerator of the other ratio.

Productos cruzados (p. 175) En dos razones, los productos cruzados se hallan al multiplicar el denominador de una razón por el numerador de la otra razón.

In the proportion $\frac{2}{5} = \frac{10}{25}$, the cross products are $2 \cdot 25$ and $5 \cdot 10$.

Cube (p. 358) A cube is a rectangular prism whose faces are all squares.

Cubo (p. 358) Un cubo es un prisma rectangular cuyas caras son todas cuandras.

Cylinder (p. 354) A cylinder has two bases that are parallel, congruent circles.

Cilindro (p. 354) Un cilindro tiene dos bases congruentes paralelas que son círculos.

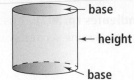

Deductive reasoning (p. 308) A process of reasoning logically from given facts to a conclusion is called deductive reasoning.

Razonamiento deductivo (p. 308) El proceso de razonar lógicamente para llegar a una conclusión a partir de datos dados se llama razonamiento deductivo.

Dependent events (p. 487) When the outcome of one event *does* affect the outcome of a second event, the events are dependent events.

Sucesos dependientes (p. 487) Cuando el resultado de un suceso afecta el resultado de un segundo suceso, los sucesos son dependientes.

Suppose you remove two marbles, one after the other, from a bag. If you do not replace the first marble before removing the second marble, the events are dependent.

Diameter (p. 336) A diameter is a segment that passes through the center of a circle and has both endpoints on the circle.

Diámetro (p. 336) Un diámetro es un segmento que pasa por el centro de un círculo y que tiene ambos extremos sobre el círculo.

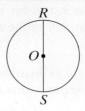

$\overline{RS}$ is a diameter of circle O.

Dilation (p. 187) A dilation is a transformation where the original figure and its image are similar. See also *Enlargement* and *Reduction*.

Dilatación (p. 187) Una dilatación es una transformación donde la figura original y su imagen son semejantes. Ver también *Enlargement* y *Reduction*.

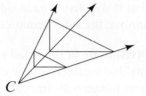

The blue triangle is an enlargement of the red triangle. The red triangle is a reduction of the blue triangle.

Discount (p. 235) The amount the price of an item is reduced is called the discount.

Descuento (p. 235) La cantidad que se reduce el precio de un artículo se llama descuento.

A $20 book is discounted by $2.50 to sell for $17.50.

Discrete data (p. 534) Discrete data are data that involve a count of items, such as numbers of people or numbers of cars. For discrete data, indicate each item with a point but do *not* connect the points with a solid line.

Datos discretos (p. 534) Los datos discretos son los datos que involucran un conteo de elementos, como número de personas o de carros. En los datos discretos cada elemento se indica con un punto, pero los puntos *no* se unen con una recta continua.

Data on the number of people different football stadiums can hold are discrete data.

Distributive Property (p. 28) The Distributive Property shows how multiplication affects an addition or subtraction:
$a(b + c) = ab + ac$.

Propiedad distributiva (p. 28) La Propiedad Distributiva muestra cómo la multiplicatión afecta a una suma o a una resta:
$a(b + c) = ab + ac$.

$$2\left(3 + \tfrac{1}{2}\right) = 2 \cdot 3 + 2 \cdot \tfrac{1}{2}$$
$$8(5 - 3) = 8 \cdot 5 - 8 \cdot 3$$

Divisible (p. 52) A number is divisible by a second whole number if the first number can be divided by the second number with a remainder of 0.

16 is divisible by 1, 2, 4, 8, and 16.

Divisible (p. 52) Un número es divisible por un segundo número entero si el primer número se puede dividir por el segundo número y el residuo es 0.

Division Property of Equality (p. 39) The Division Property of Equality states that if you divide each side of an equation by the same nonzero number, the sides remain equal.

If $a = b$ and $c \neq 0$, then $\frac{a}{c} = \frac{b}{c}$.
Since $3 \cdot 2 = 6$, $\frac{3 \cdot 2}{2} = \frac{6}{2}$.

Propiedad de División de la Igualdad (p. 39) La Propiedad de División de la Igualdad establece que si cada lado de una ecuación se divide por el mismo número distinto de cero, los dos lados se mantienen iguales.

Division Property of Inequality (p. 288) The Division Property of Inequality states that if you divide an inequality by a positive number, the direction of the inequality is unchanged. If you divide an inequality by a negative number, *reverse* the direction of the inequality sign.

If $a > b$ and $c > 0$, then $\frac{a}{c} > \frac{b}{c}$.
Since $2 > 1$ and $3 > 0$, $\frac{2}{3} > \frac{1}{3}$.
If $a < b$ and $c > 0$, then $\frac{a}{c} < \frac{b}{c}$.
Since $2 < 4$ and $3 > 0$, $\frac{2}{3} < \frac{4}{3}$.
If $a > b$ and $c < 0$, then $\frac{a}{c} < \frac{b}{c}$.
Since $2 > 1$ and $-4 < 0$, $\frac{2}{-4} < \frac{1}{-4}$.
If $a < b$ and $c < 0$, then $\frac{a}{c} > \frac{b}{c}$.
Since $2 < 4$ and $-4 < 0$, $\frac{2}{-4} > \frac{4}{-4}$.

Propiedad de División de la Desigualdad (p. 288) La Propiedad de División de la Desigualdad establece que si se divide una desigualdad por un número positivo, la dirección de la desigualdad no cambia. Si se divide una desigualdad por un número negativo, se *invierte* la dirección del signo de desigualdad.

Edge (p. 354) An edge is a segment formed by the intersection of two faces of a three-dimensional figure.

Arista (p. 354) Una arista es un segmento formado por la intersección de dos caras de una figura tridimensional.

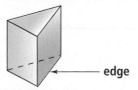

Enlargement (p. 188) A dilation with a scale factor greater than 1 is an enlargement.

See *Dilation*.

Aumento (p. 188) Una dilatación con un factor de escala mayor que 1 es un aumento.

Equation (p. 33) An equation is a mathematical sentence with an equal sign.

$2(3 + 5) = 16$ and $x + 10 = 8$ are examples of equations.

Ecuación (p. 33) Una ecuación es una oración matemática con un signo igual.

Equilateral triangle (p. 318)   An equilateral triangle is a triangle with three congruent sides.

Triángulo equilátero (p. 318)   Un triángulo equilátero es un triángulo que tiene tres lados congruentes.

$\triangle SWL$ is an equilateral triangle.

Evaluating expressions (p. 5)   To evaluate an algebraic expression, replace each variable with a number. Then follow the order of operations to simplify the expression.

Evaluación de una expresiónes (p. 5)   Para evaluar una expresión algebraica, se reemplaza cada variable con un número. Luego se sigue el orden de las operaciones para simplificar la expresión.

To evaluate the expression $3x + 2$ for $x = 4$, substitute 4 for x.
$3x + 2 = 3(4) + 2 = 12 + 2 = 14$

Event (p. 246)   A collection of possible outcomes is an event.

Suceso (p. 246)   Un suceso es un grupo de resultados posibles.

When you toss a coin, "heads" and "tails" are possible events.

Experimental probability (p. 470)   Probability based on experimental data is called experimental probability. You find the experimental probability of an event by repeating an experiment, or a trial, many times, and using the following ratio.

$P(\text{event}) = \frac{\text{number of times event occurs}}{\text{total number of trials}}$

Probabilidad experimental (p. 470)   La probabilidad experimental es la probabilidad que se basa en datos experimentales. La probabilidad experimental de un suceso se halla al repitir un experimento, o prueba, muchas veces y usar la siguiente razón.

$P(\text{suceso}) = \frac{\text{número de veces que ocurre un suceso}}{\text{número total de pruebas}}$

Suppose a basketball player makes 19 baskets in 28 attempts. The experimental probability that the player makes a basket is $\frac{19}{28} \approx 68\%$.

Exponent (p. 86)   An exponent tells how many times a number, or base, is used as a factor.

Exponente (p. 86)   Un exponente dice cuántas veces se usa como factor un número o base.

exponent
$3^4 = 3 \times 3 \times 3 \times 3$

Read 3^4 as "three to the fourth power."

Exterior angle of a polygon (p. 323)   The exterior angle of a polygon is an angle formed by a side and an extension of an adjacent side.

Ángulo exterior de un polígono (p. 323)   El ángulo exterior de un polígono es el ángulo formado por un lado y una extensión del lado adyacente.

Angles 1, 2, 3, 4, and 5 are exterior angles of the polygon.

Faces (p. 354)   The flat surfaces of a solid are called faces.

Caras (p. 354)   Las superficies planas de un sólido se llaman caras.

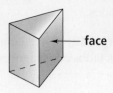

face

Factor (p. 52)   A factor is a whole number that divides another whole number with a remainder of 0.

1, 2, 3, 4, 6, 12, 18, and 36 are factors of 36.

Divisor (p. 52)   Un divisor es un número entero que divide a otro número entero y el residuo es 0.

Factorial (p. 492)   The product of all positive integers less than or equal to a number is a factorial.

$5! = 5 \cdot 4 \cdot 3 \cdot 2 \cdot 1 = 120$

Factorial (p. 492)   Un factorial es el producto de todos los enteros positivos menores o iguales que un número.

Formula (p. 81)   A formula is a rule that shows the relationship between two or more quantities.

The formula $P = 2\ell + 2w$ gives the perimeter of a rectangle in terms of its length and width.

Fórmula (p. 81)   Una fórmula es una regla que muestra la relación entre dos o más cantidades.

Frequency (p. 418)   The number of times a data item occurs is the frequency of the item.

In the data set 2 4 3 2 2 5 10 9 5 2 6, the frequency of 2 is 4.

Frecuencia (p. 418)   El número de veces que un dato ocurre es la frecuencia del dato.

Frequency table (p. 419)   A frequency table lists the frequency of each item in a set of data.

Tabla de frecuencia (p. 419)   Una tabla de frecuencia indica la frecuencia de cada elemento en un conjunto de datos.

Household Telephones

Phones	Tally	Frequency
1	⊮ ///	8
2	⊮ /	6
3	////	4

This frequency table shows the number of household telephones for a class of students.

Function (p. 523)   A function is a relationship that assigns exactly one output value for each input value.

Earned income is a function of the number of hours worked w. If you earn $6/h, then your income can be expressed by the function $f(w) = 6w$.

Función (p. 523)   Una función es una relación que asigna exactamente un valor resultante a cada valor inicial.

Function rule (p. 523)   A function rule is an equation that describes a function.

The function rule that describes the cost c of buying x movie tickets that cost $9 each is $c = 9x$.

Fórmula de una función (p. 523)   Una fórmula de una función es una ecuación que describe una función.

Geometric sequence (p. 514)   In a geometric sequence, each term is the result of multiplying the previous term by the same number.

The sequence $1, 3, 9, 27, 81, \ldots$ is a geometric sequence. You multiply each term by 3 to find the next term.

Progresión geométrica (p. 514)   En una progresión geométrica, cada término es el resultado de la multiplicación del término anterior por el mismo número.

Graph of an equation (p. 131)   The graph of an equation is the graph of all the points whose coordinates are solutions of the equation.

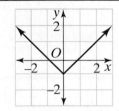

Gráfica de una ecuación (p. 131)   La gráfica de una ecuación es la gráfica de todos los puntos cuyas coordenadas son soluciones a la ecuación.

The coordinates of all the points on the graph satisfy the equation $y = |x| - 1$.

Graph of an inequality (p. 281)   The graph of an inequality containing a variable shows all the solutions that satisfy the inequality.

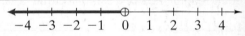

The graph shows the inequality $x < 0$.

Gráfica de una desigualdad (p. 281)   La gráfica de una desigualdad que contiene una variable muestra todas las soluciones que satisfacen la desigualdad.

Greatest common factor (GCF) (p. 53)   The greatest common factor of two or more numbers is the greatest number that is a factor of all of the numbers.

The GCF of 12 and 30 is 6.

Máximo común divisor (MCD) (p. 53)   El máximo común divisor de dos o más números es el mayor número que es divisor de todos los números.

EXAMPLES

Histogram (p. 419) A histogram is a bar graph with no spaces between the bars. The height of each bar shows the frequency of data within that interval.

Histograma (p. 419) Un histograma es una gráfica de barras sin espacio entre las barras. La altura de cada barra muestra la frecuencia de los datos dentro del intervalo.

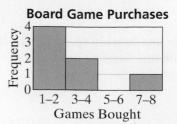

This histogram gives the frequency of board-game purchases at a local toy store.

Hypotenuse (p. 112) In a right triangle, the hypotenuse is the longest side, which is opposite the right angle.

Hipotenusa (p. 112) En un triángulo rectángulo, la hipotenusa es el lado más largo, que es el lado opuesto al ángulo recto.

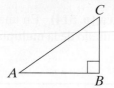

$\overline{AC}$ is the hypotenuse of $\triangle ABC$.

Identity Property of Addition (p. 26) The Identity Property of Addition states that the sum of 0 and *a* is *a*.

Priopiedad de Identidad de la Suma (p. 26) La Propiedad de Identidad de la Suma establece que la suma de 0 y *a* es *a*.

$a + 0 = a$
$7 + 0 = 7$

Identity Property of Multiplication (p. 26) The Identity Property of Multiplication states that the product of 1 and *a* is *a*.

Propiedad de Identidad de la Multiplicación (p. 26) La Propiedad de Identidad de la Multiplicación establece que el producto de 1 y *a* es *a*.

$a \cdot 1 = a$
$7 \cdot 1 = 7$

Image (p. 136) An image is the result of a transformation of a point, line, or figure.

Imagen (p. 136) Una imagen es el resultado de una transformación de un punto, una recta o una figura.

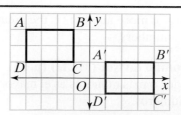

$A'B'C'D'$ is the image of $ABCD$.

Improper fraction (p. 638) An improper fraction has a numerator that is greater than or equal to its denominator.

Fracción impropia (p. 638) Una fracción impropia tiene un numerador mayor o igual que su denominador.

$\frac{24}{15}$ and $\frac{16}{16}$ are improper fractions.

Independent events (p. 486) Two events are independent events if the occurrence of one event does not affect the probability of the occurrence of the other.

Sucesos independientes (p. 486) Dos sucesos son independientes si el acontecimiento de uno no afecta la probabilidad de que el otro suceso ocurra.

Suppose you remove two marbles, one after the other, from a bag. If you replace the first marble before removing the second marble, the events are independent.

Indirect measurement (p. 197) Indirect measurement uses proportions and similar triangles to measure distances that would be difficult to measure directly.

Medición indirecta (p. 197) La medición indirecta usa proporciones y triángulos semejantes para medir las distancias que serían difíciles de medir directamente.

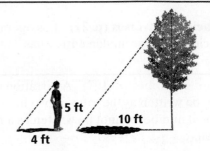

A 5-ft-tall person standing near a tree has a shadow 4 ft long. The tree has a shadow 10 ft long. The height of the tree is 12.5 ft.

Inductive reasoning (p. 512) Making conclusions based on observed patterns is called inductive reasoning.

Razonamiento inductivo (p. 512) Razonamiento inductivo es sacar conclusiones a partir de patrones observados.

Inequality (p. 282) An inequality is a mathematical sentence that contains $<$, $>$, $\leq$, $\geq$, or $\neq$.

Desigualdad (p. 282) Una desigualdad es una oración matemática que contiene los signos $<$, $>$, $\leq$, $\geq$, ó $\neq$.

$x < -5,\ 3 > 8,\ y \leq 1,\ 5 \geq -11$

Integers (p. 10) Integers are the set of positive whole numbers, their opposites, and 0.

Enteros (p. 10) Los enteros son el conjunto de números enteros positivos, sus opuestos y el 0.

$\ldots, -3, -2, -1, 0, 1, 2, 3, \ldots$

Interest (p. 242) Interest is the amount of money paid for the use of borrowed money.

Interés (p. 242) El interés es la cantidad de dinero que se paga por el uso del dinero prestado.

See *Compound interest* and *Simple interest*.

Interest rate (p. 242) The rate, usually expressed as a percent, used to calculate interest.

Tasa de interés (p. 242) La tasa, que generalmente se expresa como porcentaje, se usa para calcular el interés.

English/Spanish Glossary

Interior angle (p. 324) Interior angles are the angles inside a polygon at its vertices.

Ángulo interior (p. 324) Los ángulos interiores son los ángulos que están en la parte interna de los vértices de un polígono.

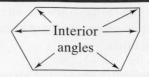

Interior angles

Inverse operations (p. 21) Inverse operations are operations that undo each other.

Operaciones inversas (p. 21) Las operaciones inversas son las operaciones que se anulan entre ellas.

Addition and subtraction are inverse operations.

Irrational number (p. 107) An irrational number is a number that cannot be written as the ratio of two integers. In decimal form, an irrational number cannot be written as a terminating or repeating decimal.

Número irracional (p. 107) Un número irracional es un número que no se puede escribir como una razón de dos enteros. Como decimal, un número irracional no se puede escribir como decimal finito o periódico.

The numbers π and $2.41592653\ldots$ are irrational numbers.

Irregular polygon (p. 327) An irregular polygon is a polygon with sides that are not all congruent and/or angles that are not all congruent.

Polígono irregular (p. 327) Un polígono irregular es un polígono que tiene lados que no son todos congruentes y/o ángulos que no son todos congruentes.

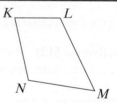

$KLMN$ is an irregular polygon.

Isolate (p. 34) To isolate the variable means to get the variable alone on one side of an equation.

Despejar (p. 34) Despejar la variable quiere decir dejar la variable sola a un lado de la ecuación.

To isolate y on one side of the equation $y - 2x = 4$, add $2x$ to each side. The equation becomes $y = 4 + 2x$.

Isometric view (p. 359) An isometric view is a corner view of a solid. It is usually drawn on isometric dot paper. An isometric view allows you to see the top, front, and side of an object in the same drawing.

Vista isométrica (p. 359) Una vista isométrica es una vista desde una esquina de un sólido. Generalmente se dibuja sobre papel isométrico de puntos. Una vista isométrica permite ver la parte de arriba, del frente y del lado de un objeto en un mismo dibujo.

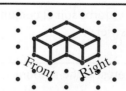

Isosceles triangle (p. 318)   An isosceles triangle is a triangle with at least two congruent sides.

Triángulo isósceles (p. 318)   Un triángulo isósceles es un triángulo que tiene al menos dos lados congruentes.

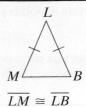

$\overline{LM} \cong \overline{LB}$

Lateral area (p. 369)   Lateral area is the sum of the areas of the lateral surfaces of a solid.

Área lateral (p. 369)   La suma de las áreas de las superficies laterales de un sólido es el área lateral de la figura.

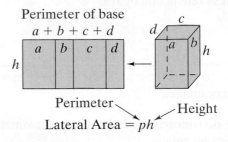

Least common denominator (LCD) (p. 62)   The least common denominator of two or more fractions is the least common multiple (LCM) of their denominators.

Mínimo común denominador (MCD) (p. 62)   El mínimo común denominador de dos o más fracciones es el mínimo común múltiplo (MCD) de sus denominadores.

The LCD of the fractions $\frac{3}{8}$ and $\frac{7}{10}$ is 40.

Least common multiple (LCM) (p. 62)   The least common multiple of two numbers is the smallest number that is a multiple of both numbers.

Mínimo común múltiplo (MCM) (p. 62)   El mínimo común múltiplo de dos números es el menor número que es múltiplo de ambos números.

The LCM of 15 and 6 is 30.

Legs of a right triangle (p. 112)   The legs of a right triangle are the two shorter sides of the triangle.

Catetos de un triángulo rectángulo (p. 112)   Los catetos de un triángulo rectángulo son los dos lados más cortos del triángulo.

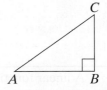

$\overline{AB}$ and $\overline{BC}$ are the legs of $\triangle ABC$.

Like terms (p. 266)   Like terms are terms with exactly the same variable factors.

Términos semejantes (p. 266)   Los términos semejantes tienen exactamente las mismas variables como factores.

$3b$ and $12b$ are like terms. You can combine like terms using the Distributive Property:

$$3b + 12b = 3 \cdot b + 12 \cdot b$$
$$= (3 + 12)b$$
$$= 15b$$

Line (p. 131) A line is a series of points that extends in two opposite directions without end.

Recta (p. 131) Una recta es una serie de puntos que se extiende indefinidamente en dos direcciones opuestas.

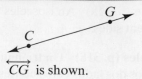

$\overleftrightarrow{CG}$ is shown.

Line of reflection (p. 141) A line of reflection is a line across which a figure is reflected.

Eje de reflexión (p. 141) Un eje de reflexión es una recta sobre la cual se refleja una figura.

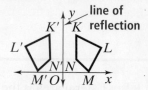

KLMN is reflected over the y-axis.

Line of symmetry (p. 142) A line of symmetry divides a figure into mirror images.

Eje de simetría (p. 142) Un eje de simetría divide una figura en imágenes reflejas.

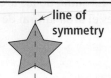

Line plot (p. 418) A line plot is a graph that shows the shape of the data by stacking ✗ marks above each data value on a number line.

Diagrama de puntos (p. 418) Un diagrama de puntos es una gráfica que muestra la forma de un conjunto de datos agrupando ✗ sobre cada valor en una recta numérica.

Pets Owned by Students

```
        X
        X           X
  X     X     X     X
  X     X     X     X     X
  0     1     2     3     4
```

The line plot shows the number of pets owned by each of 12 students.

Linear equation (p. 131) An equation is a linear equation if all of its solutions lie on a line. See also *Slope-intercept form*.

Ecuación lineal (p. 131) Una ecuación es una ecuación lineal si todas sus soluciones se sitúan sobre una recta. Ver también *Slope-intercept form*.

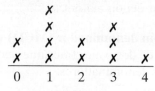

$y = \frac{1}{2}x + 3$ is a linear equation because the graph of its solutions is a line.

Linear function (p. 535) A linear function is a function whose points lie on a line.

Función lineal (p. 535) Una función lineal es una función cuyos puntos están sobre una recta.

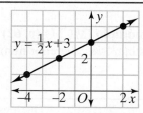

$f(x) = \frac{1}{2}x + 2$ is a linear function.

Markup (p. 234)   The markup is the difference between the selling price and the original cost of an item.

A store buys a shirt for $15 and sells it for $25. The markup is $25 − $15 = $10.

Sobrecosto (p. 234)   El sobrecosto es la diferencia entre el precio de venta y el costo original de un objeto.

Mean (p. 412)   The mean of a set of data values is the sum of the data divided by the number of data items.

The mean temperature (°F) for the set of temperatures 44, 52, 48, 55, 61, and 67 is $\frac{44 + 52 + 48 + 55 + 61 + 67}{6} = 54.5°F.$

Media (p. 412)   La media de un conjunto de valores de datos es la suma de los datos dividida por el número de datos.

Measure of central tendency (p. 412)   A measure of central tendency is a single, central value that summarizes a set of data.

See *Mean, Median,* and *Mode.*

Medida de tendencia central (p. 412)   Una medida de tendencia central es un valor único y central que resume un conjunto de datos.

Median (p. 412)   The median of a data set is the middle value when the data are arranged in numerical order. When there is an even number of data values, the median is the mean of the two middle values.

Temperatures (°F) for one week arranged in order are 44, 48, 52, 55, and 58. The median temperature is 52°F because it is the middle number in the set of data.

Mediana (p. 412)   La mediana de un conjunto de datos es el valor del medio cuando los datos están organizados en orden numérico. Cuando hay un número par de valores de datos, la mediana es la media de los dos valores del medio.

Midpoint (p. 128)   The midpoint of a segment is the point that divides the segment into two segments of equal length.

$X \qquad M \qquad Y$

$\overline{XM} = \overline{YM}$

M is the midpoint of $\overline{XY}$.

Punto medio (p. 128)   El punto medio de un segmento es el punto que divide el segmento en dos segmentos de igual longitud.

Mixed number (p. 638)   A mixed number is the sum of a whole number and a fraction.

$3\frac{11}{16}$ is a mixed number.

$3\frac{11}{16} = 3 + \frac{11}{16}$

Número mixto (p. 638)   Un número mixto es la suma de un número entero y una fracción.

Mode (p. 412)   The mode of a data set is the item that occurs with the greatest frequency.

The mode of the set of prices $2.50, $2.75, $3.60, $2.75, and $3.70 is $2.75.

Moda (p. 412)   La moda de un conjunto de datos es el dato que sucede con mayor frecuencia.

English/Spanish Glossary

Monomial (p. 576) A polynomial that has only one term is called a monomial.

$5x$, -4, and y^3 are all monomials.

Monomio (p. 576) Un polinomio que sólo tiene un término se llama monomio.

Multiplication Property of Equality (p. 38) The Multiplication Property of Equality states that if each side of an equation is multiplied by the same number, the two sides remain equal.

If $a = b$, then $a \cdot c = b \cdot c$.
Since $\frac{12}{2} = 6$, $\frac{12}{2} \cdot 2 = 6 \cdot 2$.

Propiedad Multiplicativa de la Igualdad (p. 38) La Propiedad Multiplicativa de la Igualdad establece que si cada lado de una ecuación se multiplica por el mismo número, los dos lados se mantienen iguales.

Multiplication Property of Inequality (p. 288) The Multiplication Property of Inequality states that if you multiply an inequality by a positive number, the direction of the inequality is unchanged. If you multiply an inequality by a negative number, *reverse* the direction of the inequality sign.

If $a > b$ and $c > 0$, then $ac > bc$.
Since $3 > 2$ and $7 > 0$, $3 \cdot 7 > 2 \cdot 7$.
If $a < b$ and $c > 0$, then $ac < bc$.
Since $3 < 5$ and $7 > 0$, $3 \cdot 7 < 5 \cdot 7$.
If $a > b$ and $c < 0$, then $ac < bc$.
Since $3 > 2$ and $-6 < 0$,
$3 \cdot -6 < 2 \cdot -6$.
If $a < b$ and $c < 0$, then $ac > bc$.
Since $3 < 5$ and $-6 < 0$,
$3 \cdot -6 > 5 \cdot -6$.

Propiedad Multiplicativa de la Desigualdad (p. 288) La Propiedad Multiplicativa de la Desigualdad establece que cuando se multiplica una desigualdad por un número positivo, la dirección de la desigualdad no cambia. Si se multiplica una desigualdad por un número negativo, se *invierte* la dirección del signo de la desigualdad.

Multiplicative inverse (p. 73) The reciprocal of a number is called its multiplicative inverse.

The multiplicative inverse of $\frac{4}{9}$ is $\frac{9}{4}$.

Inverso multiplicativo (p. 73) El recíproco de un número se llama su inverso multiplicativo.

Negative trend (p. 445) There is a negative trend between two sets of data if one set of values tends to increase while the other set tends to decrease.

Tendencia negativa (p. 445) Hay una tendencia negativa entre dos conjuntos de datos si un conjunto de valores tiende a aumentar mientras el otro conjunto tiende a disminuir.

Net (p. 364) A net is a pattern that can be folded to form a solid. A figure's net shows all the faces of that figure in one view.

Plantilla (p. 364) Una plantilla es un patrón bidimensional que se puede doblar para formar un sólido. La plantilla de una figura muestra todas las caras de esa figura en una vista.

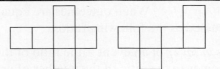

These are nets for a cube.

Nonlinear function (p. 546) The graph of a nonlinear function is not a straight line.

Función no lineal (p. 546) La gráfica de una función no lineal no es una recta.

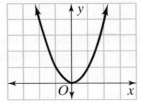

$y = x^2$ is an example of a nonlinear function.

No trend (p. 445) There is no trend between two sets of data if the points show no relationship to each other.

Sin tendencia (p. 445) No hay tendencia entre dos conjuntos de datos si no hay relación alguna entre los puntos.

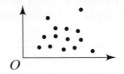

Obtuse angle (p. 640) An obtuse angle is an angle with a measure greater than 90° and less than 180°.

Ángulo obtuso (p. 640) Un ángulo obtuso es un ángulo que mide más de 90° y menos de 180°.

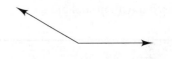

Obtuse triangle (p. 318) An obtuse triangle is a triangle with one obtuse angle.

Triángulo obtusángulo (p. 318) Un triángulo obtusángulo es un triángulo que tiene un ángulo obtuso.

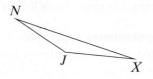

Odds (p. 471) When outcomes are equally likely, odds are expressed as the following ratios:

odds *in favor* of an event = the ratio of the number of favorable outcomes *to* the ratio of the number of unfavorable outcomes

odds *against* an event = the ratio of the number of unfavorable outcomes *to* the ratio of the number of favorable outcomes

Posibilidades (p. 471) Cuando los resultados son igualmente posibles, las posibilidades se expresan como las siguientes razones:

posibilidades *en favor* de un suceso = la razón del número de resultados favorables *al* número de resultados desfavorables

posibilidades *en contra* de un suceso = la razón del número de resultados desfavorables *al* número de resultados favorables

If you roll a standard number cube, the odds in favor of getting a 4 are 1 : 5.

Opposites (p. 10) Opposites are two numbers that are the same distance from 0 on a number line, but in opposite directions.

Opuestos (p. 10) Opuestos son dos números que están a la misma distancia del 0 en una recta numérica, pero en direcciones opuestas.

17 and −17 are opposites.

Ordered pair (p. 124) An ordered pair identifies the location of a point. The *x*-coordinate shows a point's position left or right from the origin. The *y*-coordinate shows a point's position up or down from the *x*-axis.

Par ordenado (p. 124) Un par ordenado identifica la ubicación de un punto. La coordenada *x* muestra la posición de un punto a la izquierda o derecha del origen. La coordenada *y* muestra la posición de un punto arriba o abajo del eje de *x*.

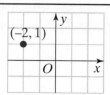

The *x*-coordinate of the point (−2, 1) is −2, and the *y*-coordinate is 1.

Order of operations (pp. 5, 86)
1. Work inside grouping symbols.
2. Simplify the exponents.
3. Multiply and divide in order from left to right.
4. Add and subtract in order from left to right.

Orden de las operaciones (pp. 5, 86)
1. Trabaja dentro de los signos de agrupación.
2. Simplifica los exponentes.
3. Multiplica y divide en orden de izquierda a derecha.
4. Suma y resta en orden de izquierda a derecha.

$$2^3(7 - 4) = 2^3 \cdot 3 = 8 \cdot 3 = 24$$

Origin (p. 124) The origin is the point of intersection of the *x*- and *y*-axes in a coordinate plane.

Origen (p. 124) El origen es el punto de intersección de los ejes de *x* y de *y* en un plano de coordenadas.

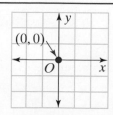

The ordered pair that describes the origin is (0, 0).

Outcome (p. 246) An outcome is any of the possible results that can occur in an experiment.

Resultado (p. 246) Un resultado es cualquiera de los posibles desenlaces que pueden ocurrir en un experimento.

The outcomes of rolling a standard number cube are 1, 2, 3, 4, 5, and 6.

Outlier (p. 413) An outlier is a data item that is much higher or much lower than the other items in a data set.

Valor extremo (p. 413) Un valor extremo es un dato que es mucho más alto o más bajo que los demás datos de un conjunto de datos.

An outlier in the data set 6, 7, 9, 10, 11, 12, 14, and 52 is 52.

P

Parabola (p. 546) The graph of a quadratic function is a U-shaped curve, called a parabola.

Parábola (p. 546) La gráfica de una función cuadrática es una curva en forma de U llamada parábola.

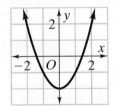

This parabola is the graph of the equation $y = x^2 - 2$.

Parallel lines (p. 308) Parallel lines are lines in the same plane that never intersect.

Rectas paralelas (p. 308) Las rectas paralelas son rectas en el mismo plano que nunca se intersecan.

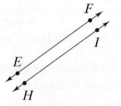

$\overleftrightarrow{EF}$ is parallel to $\overleftrightarrow{HI}$

Parallelogram (p. 319) A parallelogram is a quadrilateral with both pairs of opposite sides parallel.

Paralelogramo (p. 319) Un paralelogramo es un cuadrilátero cuyos pares de lados opuestos son paralelos.

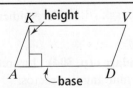

$\overline{KV}$ is parallel to $\overline{AD}$ and $\overline{AK}$ is parallel to $\overline{DV}$, so $KVDA$ is a parallelogram.

Percent (p. 210) A percent is a ratio that compares a number to 100.

Porcentaje (p. 210) Un porcentaje es una razón que compara un número con 100.

$\frac{25}{100} = 25\%$

Percent of change (p. 230) The percent of change is the percent a quantity increases or decreases from its original amount.

Porcentaje de cambio (p. 230) El porcentaje de cambio es el porcentaje que aumenta o disminuye una cantidad a partir de su cantidad original.

The number of employees increases from 14 to 21. The percent of change is $\frac{21 - 14}{14} = 50\%$.

Perfect square (p. 106) A perfect square is a number that is the square of an integer.

Cuadrado perfecto (p. 106) Un cuadrado perfecto es un número que es el cuadrado de un entero.

Since $25 = 5^2$, 25 is a perfect square.

Perimeter (p. 81) The perimeter of a figure is the distance around the figure.

Perímetro (p. 81) El perímetro de una figura es la distancia alrededor de la figura.

The perimeter of rectangle $ABCD$ is 12 ft.

Permutation (p. 491) A permutation is an arrangement of objects in a particular order.

Permutación (p. 491) Una permutación es un arreglo de objetos en un orden particular.

The permutations of the letters W, A, and X, are WAX, WXA, AXW, AWX, XWA, and XAW.

Perpendicular bisector (p. 344) A perpendicular bisector is a segment bisector that is perpendicular to the segment.

Mediatriz (p. 344) Una mediatriz es una bisectriz de un segmento que es perpendicular a ese segmento.

$\overleftrightarrow{MK} \perp \overline{AB}$, $AM = MB$. $\overleftrightarrow{MK}$ is the perpendicular bisector of $\overline{AB}$.

Perpendicular lines (p. 304) Perpendicular lines intersect to form right angles.

Rectas perpendiculares (p. 304) Las rectas perpendiculares se intersecan para formar ángulos rectos.

$\overleftrightarrow{DE} \perp \overleftrightarrow{RS}$

Pi (p. 336) Pi (π) is the ratio of the circumference C of any circle to its diameter d.

Pi (p. 336) Pi (π) es la razón de la circunferencia C de cualquier círculo a su diámetro d.

$\pi = \frac{C}{d}$

Plane (p. 124) A plane is a flat surface that extends indefinitely in all directions.

Plano (p. 124) Un plano es la superficie plana que se extiende indefinidamente en todas las direcciones.

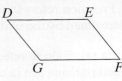

DEFG is a plane.

Point (p. 124) A point is a location that has no size.

Punto (p. 124) Un punto es una ubicación que no tiene tamaño.

• *A*

A is a point.

Polygon (p. 181) A polygon is a closed figure formed by three or more line segments that do not cross.

Polígono (p. 181) Un polígono es una figura cerrada que está formada por tres o más segmentos de recta que no se cruzan.

Polyhedron (p. 354) A polyhedron is a solid with a polygon for each face.

Poliedro (p. 354) Un poliedro es una figura tridimensional cuyas caras son polígonos.

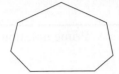

Polynomial (p. 561) A polynomial is one term or the sum or difference of two or more terms.

Polinomio (p. 561) Un polinomio es un término o la suma o diferencia de dos o más términos.

$4x^2 - 3x + 7$ is a polynomial.

Population (p. 480) A population is a group about which information is wanted.

Población (p. 480) Una población es un grupo sobre el que se busca información.

A class of 25 students is a sample of the population of a school.

Positive trend (p. 445) There is a positive trend between two sets of data if one set of values tends to increase while the other set also tends to increase.

Tendencia positiva (p. 445) Existe una tendencia positiva entre dos conjuntos de datos si un conjunto de valores tiende a aumentar mientras el otro conjunto también tiende a aumentar.

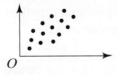

Power (p. 86) A power is a number that can be expressed using a base and an exponent.

Potencia (p. 86) Una potencia es un número que se puede expresar usando una base y un exponente.

$3^4, 5^2,$ and 2^{10} are powers.

Precision (p. 402)   Precision refers to the exactness of a measurement, as determined by the unit of measure.

Precisión (p. 402)   La precisión se refiere a la exactitud de una medida, según está determinada por la unidad de medida.

$\frac{1}{16}$ in. is a smaller unit than $\frac{1}{4}$ in., so $\frac{1}{16}$ in. is more precise than $\frac{1}{4}$ in.

Prime factorization (p. 53)   Writing a composite number as the product of its prime factors is the prime factorization of the number.

Descomposición en factores primos (p. 53)   Escribir un número compuesto como el producto de sus factores primos es la descomposición en factores primos del número.

The prime factorization of 12 is $2 \cdot 2 \cdot 3$, or $2^2 \cdot 3$.

Prime notation (p. 136)   Prime notation is used to identify an image point.

Notación prima (p. 136)   La notación prima se usa para identificar un punto de imagen.

Point $F'(4, 1)$ is the image of point $F(4, 3)$ after a translation.

Prime number (p. 52)   A prime number is a whole number with exactly two factors, 1 and the number itself.

Número primo (p. 52)   Un número primo es un entero que tiene exactamente dos factores, 1 y el mismo número.

13 is a prime number because its only factors are 1 and 13.

Principal (p. 242)   Principal is the original amount deposited or borrowed.

Capital (p. 242)   El capital es el monto original que se deposita o se toma prestado.

You deposit $500 in a savings account. Your principal is $500.

Prism (p. 354)   A prism is a solid with two parallel and congruent polygonal faces called bases. A prism is named for the shape of its base.

Prisma (p. 354)   Un prisma es un sólido que tiene dos caras poligonales paralelas y congruentes llamadas bases. Un prisma recibe su nombre por la forma de su base.

Rectangular Prism   Triangular Prism

Probability of an event (p. 246)   When outcomes are equally likely: $P(E) = \frac{\text{number of favorable outcomes}}{\text{total number of possible outcomes}}$.

Probabilidad de un suceso (p. 246)   Cuando los resultados son igualmente posibles: $P(E) = \frac{\text{número de resultados favorables}}{\text{número total de resultados posibles}}$.

The probability of rolling a 4 on a number cube is $\frac{1}{6}$.

See also *Experimental probability* and *Theoretical probability*.

Proportion (p. 174)   A proportion is an equation stating that two ratios are equal.

$\frac{3}{12} = \frac{9}{36}$ is a proportion.

Proporción (p. 174)   Una proporción es una ecuación que establece que dos razones son iguales.

Pyramid (p. 354)   A pyramid is a solid with triangular faces that meet at a vertex and a base that is a polygon. A pyramid is named for the shape of its base.

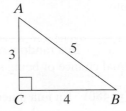

Triangular   Square

Pirámide (p. 354)   Una pirámide es una figura tridimensional que tiene caras triangulares que coinciden en un vértice y una base que es un polígono. Una pirámide recibe su nombre por la forma de su base.

Pythagorean Theorem (p. 112)   In any right triangle, the sum of the squares of the lengths of the legs (a and b) is equal to the square of the length of the hypotenuse (c): $a^2 + b^2 = c^2$.

Teorema de Pitágoras (p. 112)   En cualquier triángulo rectángulo, la suma del cuadrado de la longitud de los catetos (a y b) es igual al cuadrado de la longitud de la hipotenusa (c): $a^2 + b^2 = c^2$.

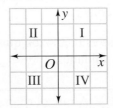

The right triangle has leg lengths 3 and 4 and hypotenuse length 5.
$3^2 + 4^2 = 5^2$

Q

Quadrants (p. 124)   The x- and y-axes divide the coordinate plane into four regions called quadrants.

Cuadrantes (p. 124)   Los ejes de x y de y dividen el plano de coordenadas en cuatro regiones llamadas cuadrantes.

The quadrants are labeled I, II, III, and IV.

Quadratic function (p. 546)   In a quadratic function, the greatest power of the variable is 2.

$y = -\frac{1}{3}x^2 + 7x$

Función cuadrática (p. 546)   En una función cuadrática, la mayor potencia de la variable es 2.

Quadrilateral (p. 319)   A quadrilateral is a polygon with four sides.

Cuadrilátero (p. 319)   Un cuadrilátero es un polígono que tiene cuatro lados.

Quartiles (p. 438) Quartiles are numbers that divide data into four equal parts.

See *Box-and-whisker plot.*

Cuartiles (p. 438) Los cuartiles son números que dividen los datos en cuatro partes iguales.

R

Radius (p. 336) A radius of a circle is a segment that connects the center to the circle.

Radio (p. 336) Un radio de un círculo es un segmento que conecta el centro con el círculo.

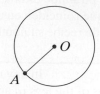

$\overline{OA}$ is a radius of circle O.

Random sample (p. 480) In a random sample, each member in the population has an equal chance of being selected.

Muestra aleatoria (p. 480) En una muestra aleatoria, cada miembro de la población tiene la misma posibilidad de ser elegido.

For the population *customers at a mall*, a random sample would be every 20th customer entering during a 2-hour period.

Range (p. 413) The range of a data set is the difference between the greatest and the least values.

Rango (p. 413) El rango de un conjunto de datos es la diferencia entre los valores mayor y menor.

Data set: 62, 109, 234, 35, 96, 49, 201
Range: $234 - 35 = 199$

Rate (p. 161) A rate is a ratio that compares two quantities measured in different units.

Tasa (p. 161) Una tasa es una razón que compara dos cantidades medidas en diferentes unidades.

You read 116 words in 1 min. Your reading rate is $\frac{116 \text{ words}}{1 \text{ min}}$.

Rate of change (p. 527) A rate of change is a comparison between two quantities that are changing.

$$\text{rate of change} = \frac{\text{change in one quantity}}{\text{change in another quantity}}$$

Tasa de cambio (p. 527) Una tasa de cambio es una comparación entre dos cantidades que cambian. La tasa de cambio se llama también pendiente.

$$\text{tasa de cambio} = \frac{\text{cambio en una cantidad}}{\text{cambio en otra cantidad}}$$

Video rental for 1 day is \$1.99. Video rental for 2 days is \$2.99.

$$\text{rate of change} = \frac{2.99 - 1.99}{2 - 1}$$
$$= \frac{1.00}{1}$$
$$= 1$$

Ratio (p. 160) A ratio is a comparison of two quantities by division.

Razón (p. 160) Una razón es una comparación de dos cantidades mediante la división.

There are three ways to write a ratio: 9 to 10, 9 : 10, and $\frac{9}{10}$.

Rational number (p. 57) A rational number is any number written as a quotient of two integers where the denominator is not 0.

$\frac{1}{3}$, -5, 6.4, 0.666 . . . , $-2\frac{4}{5}$, 0, and $\frac{7}{3}$ are rational numbers.

Número racional (p. 57) Un número racional es cualquier número escrito como cociente de dos enteros, donde el denominador es diferente de 0.

Ray (p. 640) A ray has endpoint and all the points of the line on one side of the point.

Rayo (p. 640) Un rayo tiene un extremo y todos los puntos de la recta a un lado del punto.

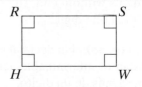

$\overrightarrow{CG}$ represents a ray.

Real numbers (p. 107) Together, rational and irrational numbers form the set of real numbers.

3, -5.25, 3.141592653 . . . , and $\frac{7}{8}$ are real numbers.

Números reales (p. 107) Juntos, los números rationales e irracionales forman el conjunto de los números reales.

Reciprocals (p. 73) Two numbers are reciprocals if their product is 1.

The numbers $\frac{4}{9}$ and $\frac{9}{4}$ are reciprocals.

Recíprocos (p. 73) Dos números son recíprocos si su producto es 1.

Rectangle (p. 319) A rectangle is a parallelogram with four right angles.

Rectángulo (p. 319) Un rectángulo es un paralelogramo que tiene cuatro ángulos rectos.

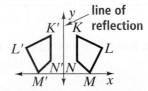

Reduction (p. 188) A dilation with a scale factor less than 1 is a reduction.

See *Dilation*.

Reducción (p. 188) Una dilatación con un factor de escala menor que 1 es una reducción.

Reflection (p. 141) A reflection is a transformation that flips a figure over a line of reflection.

Reflexión (p. 141) Una reflexión es una transformación que voltea una figura sobre un eje de reflexión.

$K'L'M'N'$ is a reflection of $KLMN$ over the y-axis.

English/Spanish Glossary

Reflectional symmetry (p. 142)   If a figure can be reflected over a line so that its image matches the original figure, the figure has reflectional symmetry.

Simetría por reflexión (p. 142)   Si una figura se puede reflejar sobre una recta de modo que su imagen coincida con la figura original, la figura tiene simetría por reflexión.

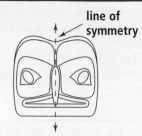

line of symmetry

Regular polygon (p. 325)   A regular polygon is a polygon with all the sides congruent and all the angles congruent.

Polígono regular (p. 325)   Un polígono regular es un polígono que tiene todos los lados y todos los ángulos congruentes.

ABDFEC is a regular hexagon.

Relatively prime (p. 57)   A fraction $\frac{a}{b}$ is in simplest form when a and b are relatively prime, which means they only have 1 as a common factor.

Primos entre sí (p. 57)   Una fracción $\frac{a}{b}$ está en su mínima expresión cuando a y b son primos entre sí, o sea, que sólo tienen el 1 como factor común.

$\frac{9}{10}$, $\frac{1}{4}$, and $\frac{2}{3}$ are relatively prime.

Repeating decimal (p. 58)   A repeating decimal is a decimal that repeats the same digits without end. The repeating block can contain one digit or more than one digit.

Decimal periódico (p. 58)   Un decimal periódico es un decimal que repite los mismos dígitos interminablemente. El bloque que se repite puede ser un dígito o más de un dígito.

$0.888 \ldots = 0.\overline{8}$
$0.272727 \ldots = 0.\overline{27}$

Rhombus (p. 319)   A rhombus is a parallelogram with four congruent sides.

Rombo (p. 319)   Un rombo es un paralelogramo que tiene cuatro lados congruentes.

GHJI is a rhombus.

Right angle (p. 640)   A right angle is an angle with a measure of 90°.

Ángulo recto (p. 640)   Un ángulo recto es un ángulo que mide 90°.

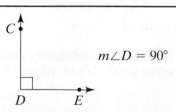

$m\angle D = 90°$

Right triangle (p. 318)   A right triangle is a triangle with one right angle.

Triángulo rectángulo (p. 318)   Un triángulo rectángulo es un triángulo que tiene un ángulo recto.

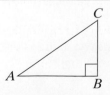

$\triangle ABC$ is a right triangle since $\angle B$ is a right angle.

Rotation (p. 146)   A rotation is a transformation that turns a figure about a fixed point, called the center of rotation.

Rotación (p. 146)   Una rotación es una transformación que gira una figura sobre un punto fijo, llamado centro de rotación.

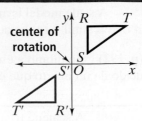

$\triangle RST$ has been rotated about the origin O to $\triangle R'S'T'$.

Rotational symmetry (p. 146)   A figure has rotational symmetry if it can be rotated 180° or less and match the original figure.

Simetría rotacional (p. 146)   Una figura tiene simetría rotacional si se puede rotar 180° o menos y calzar sobre la figura original.

This figure has 60° rotational symmetry.

Sale price (p. 235)   The regular price of an item minus the discount equals the sale price of the item.

Precio rebajado (p. 235)   El precio normal de un artículo menos el descuento es igual al precio rebajado del artículo.

An item that regularly costs $14 and is on sale for $3 off has a sale price of $14 − $3 = $11.

Sample (p. 480)   A sample is a part of the population.

Muestra (p. 480)   Una muestra es una parte de la población.

A class of 25 students is a sample of a school population. The sample size is 25.

Sample space (p. 247)   Sample space is the collection of all possible outcomes in a probability experiment.

Espacio muestral (p. 247)   El espacio muestral es el total de todos los resultados posibles en un experimento de probabilidad.

The sample space for tossing two coins is HH, HT, TH, TT.

Scale (p. 192)   A scale is the ratio that compares a length in a drawing to the corresponding length in the actual object.

Escala (p. 192)   Una escala es la razón que compara la longitud en un dibujo con la longitud correspondiente en el objeto real.

A 25-mi road is 1 in. long on a map. The scale can be written three ways: 1 in. : 25 mi, $\frac{1 \text{ in.}}{25 \text{ mi}}$, 1 in. = 25 mi.

Scale factor (p. 187)   The ratio of the dimensions of the image to the dimensions of the original figure is called a scale factor.

Factor de escala (p. 187)   La razón de las dimensiones de una imagen a las dimensiones de la figura original se llama el factor de escala.

This dilation has center C and scale factor 3.

Scale model (p. 192)   A scale model is an enlarged or reduced model of an object that is similar to the actual object.

Maps and floor plans are scale models.

Dibujo a escala (p. 192)   Un dibujo a escala es un dibujo aumentado o reducido de un objeto que es semejante al objeto real.

Scalene triangle (p. 318)   A scalene triangle is a triangle with no congruent sides.

Triángulo escaleno (p. 318)   Un triángulo escaleno es un triángulo cuyos lados no son congruentes.

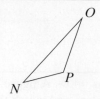

Scatter plot (p. 444)   A scatter plot is a graph that displays two sets of data as ordered pairs.

Diagrama de dispersión (p. 444)   Un diagrama de dispersión es una gráfica que muestra dos conjuntos de datos como pares ordenados.

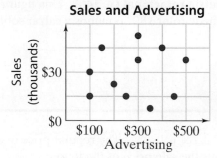

The scatter plot shows amounts spent by several companies on advertising (in dollars) versus product sales (in thousands of dollars).

Scientific notation (p. 92)   A number is in scientific notation if the first factor is greater than or equal to 1 and less than 10, and the second factor is a power of 10.

37,000,000 is written as 3.7×10^7 in scientific notation.

Notatión científica (p. 92)   Un número está en notación científica si el primer factor es mayor que o igual a 1 y menor que 10, y el segundo factor es una potencia de 10.

Segment (p. 128)   A segment has two endpoints and all the points of the line between the endpoints.

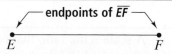

Segmento (p. 128)   Un segmento tiene dos extremos y todos los puntos de la recta entre los puntos extremos.

$\overline{EF}$ represents the segment shown.

Segment bisector (p. 344)   A segment bisector is a line, segment, or ray that goes through the midpoint of a segment.

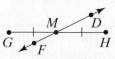

Bisectriz de un segmento (p. 344)   Una bisectriz de un segmento es una recta, segmento o rayo que pasa por el punto medio de un segmento.

$GM = MH.$ $\overleftrightarrow{FD}$ is a bisector of $\overline{GH}$.

Selling price (p. 234) Markup is added to the cost of merchandise to arrive at the selling price.

An item that costs a store $15 and is marked up $7 has a selling price of $15 + $7 = $22.

Precio de venta (p. 234) Se agrega el sobrecosto al costo de la mercadería para llegar al precio de venta.

Semicircle (p. 340) A semicircle is half a circle.

See *Arc*.

Semicírculo (p. 340) Un semicírculo es la mitad de un círculo.

Sequence (p. 512) A sequence is a set of numbers that follows a pattern.

3, 6, 9, 12, 15, . . . is a sequence.

Secuencia (p. 512) Una secuencia es un conjunto de números que sigue un patrón.

Significant digits (p. 402) Use significant digits to determine how precise the answer should be when you multiply or divide measurements. Nonzero digits (1–9) are always significant. Zero digits are only significant in certain places.

0.007500 has four significant digits.

19,200 has three significant digits.

40.290 has five significant digits.

Dígitos significativos (p. 402) Se usan dígitos significativos para determinar cuán precisa debe ser una respuesta cuando se multiplican o dividen medidas. Los dígitos distintos de cero (1–9) siempre son significativos. Los ceros son significativos sólo en ciertos lugares.

Similar figures (p. 181) Similar figures have the same shape, but not necessarily the same size.

Figuras semejantes (p. 181) Las figuras semejantes tienen la misma forma, pero no necesariamente el mismo tamaño.

$\triangle ABC \sim \triangle RTS$

Similar polygons (p. 181) Two polygons are similar if their corresponding angles have the same measure and the lengths of their corresponding sides are proportional.

See *Similar figures*.

Polígonos semejantes (p. 181) Dos polígonos son semejantes si sus ángulos correspondientes tienen la misma medida y las longitudes de sus lados correspondientes son proporcionales.

Similar solids (p. 398) Two solids are similar if they have the same shape and if all corresponding dimensions are proportional.

Sólidos semejantes (p. 398) Dos sólidos son semejantes si tienen la misma forma y si sus correspondientes dimensiones son proporcionales.

Simple interest (p. 242) Simple interest is interest calculated only on the principal. Use the formula $I = p \cdot r \cdot t$ where I is the interest, p is the principal, r is the annual interest rate, and t is time in years.

The simple interest earned on $200 invested at 5% annual interest for three years is $200 \cdot 0.05 \cdot 3 = \$30$.

Interés simple (p. 242) El interés simple se calcula sólo en relación al principal. Se usa la fórmula $I = p \cdot i \cdot t$ donde I es el interés, p es el principal, i es la tasa de interés anual y t es el tiempo en años.

Simplest form (p. 57) A fraction is in simplest form when the numerator and denominator have no common factors other than 1.

The simplest form of $\frac{3}{9}$ is $\frac{1}{3}$.

Mínima expresión (p. 57) Una fracción está en su mínima expresión cuando el numerador y el denominador no tienen otro factor común más que el 1.

Simplify (p. 5) To simplify a numerical expression, replace it with its simplest name.

$8 + 3x - 2$ simplifies to $6 + 3x$.

Simplificar (p. 5) Para simplificar una expresión numérica, se reemplaza con su mínima expresión.

Simulation (p. 484) A simulation is a model of a real-world situation used to find probability.

A baseball team has an equal chance of winning or losing its next game. You can toss a coin to simulate the situation.

Simulación (p. 484) Una simulación es un modelo de una situación real que se usa para hallar la probabilidad.

Skew lines (p. 355) Skew lines lie in different planes. They are neither parallel nor intersecting

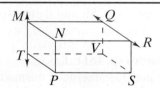

$\overleftrightarrow{MT}$ and $\overleftrightarrow{QR}$ are skew lines.

Rectas cruzadas (p. 355) Las rectas cruzadas están en planos diferentes. No son paralelas ni se intersecan.

Slant height (p. 374) The height of a pyramid's lateral faces is called the slant height and is indicated by the symbol ℓ.

See *Cone, Pyramid*.

Altura inclinada (p. 374) La altura de las caras laterales de una pirámide se llama altura inclinada y se indica con el símbolo ℓ.

Slope (p. 528) Slope is a ratio that describes steepness.

$$\text{Slope} = \frac{\text{vertical change}}{\text{horizontal change}} = \frac{\text{rise}}{\text{run}}$$

Pendiente (p. 528) La pendiente es la razón que describe la inclinación.

$$\text{Pendiente} = \frac{\text{cambio vertical}}{\text{cambio horizontal}} = \frac{\text{elevación}}{\text{desplazamiento}}$$

Slope of a line (p. 528)

$$\text{Slope} = \frac{\text{change in } y \text{ coordinates}}{\text{change in } x \text{ coordinates}} = \frac{\text{rise}}{\text{run}}$$

Pendiente de una recta (p. 528)

$$\text{Pendiente} = \frac{\text{cambio en la coordenada } y}{\text{cambio en la coordenada } x} = \frac{\text{elevación}}{\text{desplazamiento}}$$

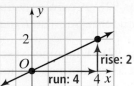

The slope of the given line is $\frac{2}{4} = \frac{1}{2}$.

Slope-intercept form (p. 535) An equation written in the form $y = mx + b$ is in slope-intercept form. The graph is a line with slope m and y-intercept b.

Forma pendiente intercepto (p. 535) Una ecuación escrita en la forma $y = mx + b$ está en la forma pendiente intercepto. La gráfica es una recta en la que m es la pendiente y b es el intercepto y.

The equation $y = 2x + 1$ is written in slope-intercept form with $m = 2$ and $b = 1$.

Solid (p. 354) Solids, or three-dimensional figures, are objects that do not lie in a plane. They have length, width, and height.

Sólido (p. 354) Las figuras tridimensionales, o sólidos, son los objetos que no están en un sólo plano. Tienen longitud, anchura y altura.

A cylinder, a cone, and a rectangular prism are all solids.

Solution (pp. 34, 131) A solution is any value or values that makes an equation or inequality true.

Solución (pp. 34, 131) Una solución es cualquier valor o valores que hacen que una ecuación o una desigualdad sea verdadera.

4 is the solution of $x + 5 = 9$.

7 is a solution of $x < 15$.

Sphere (p. 393) A sphere is the set of all points in space that are the same distance from a center point.

Esfera (p. 393) Una esfera es el conjunto de todos los puntos en el espacio que están a la misma distancia de un punto central.

Square (p. 319) A square is a parallelogram with four right angles and four congruent sides.

Cuadrado (p. 319) Una cuadrado es un paralelogramo que tiene cuatro ángulos rectos y cuatro lados congruentes.

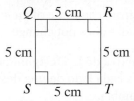

$QRST$ is a square. $\angle Q$, $\angle R$, $\angle T$, and $\angle S$ are right angles, and $\overline{QR} = \overline{RT} = \overline{TS} = \overline{SQ}$.

Square root (p. 106) The square root of a number is a number that when multiplied by itself is equal to the original number.

Raíz cuadrada (p. 106) La raíz cuadrada de un número es un número que cuando se multiplica por sí mismo es igual al número dado.

$\sqrt{9} = 3$ because $3^2 = 9$.

Standard form (p. 92) A number written using digits and place value is in standard form. See also *Expanded form*.

Forma normal (p. 92) Un número escrito usando dígitos y valor posicional está en forma normal. Ver también *Expanded form*.

The standard form of 8.9×10^5 is 890,000.

Stem-and-leaf plot (p. 433) A stem-and-leaf plot is a display that shows numeric data arranged in order. Each data item is broken into a stem (digit or digits on the left) and a leaf (digit on the right).

Diagram a de tallo y hojas (p. 433) Un diagrama de tallo y hojas es una muestra de datos numéricos arreglados en orden. Cada dato se divide en un tallo (dígito o dígitos a la izquierda) y hoja (dígito a la derecha).

stem	leaves
27	7
28	5 6 8
29	6 9
30	8

Key: 27 | 7 means 27.7

This stem-and-leaf plot displays recorded times in a race. The stems represents the whole number of seconds. The leaves represent tenths of a second.

Straight angle (p. 640) A straight angle is an angle with a measure of 180°.

Ángulo llano (p. 640) Un ángulo llano es un ángulo que mide 180°.

180°

T P L

$m\angle TPL = 180°$

Subtraction Property of Equality (p. 33) The Subtraction Property of Equality states that if the same number is subtracted from each side of an equation, the results are equal.

Propiedad Sustractiva de la Igualdad (p. 33) La Propiedad Sustractiva de la Igualdad establece que si se resta el mismo número a cada lado de una ecuación, los resultados son iguales.

If $a = b$, then $a - c = b - c$.
Since $\frac{20}{2} = 10$, $\frac{20}{2} - 3 = 10 - 3$.

Subtraction Property of Inequality (p. 282) When you subtract the same number from each side of an inequality, the relationship between the two sides does not change.

Propiedad Sustractiva de la Desigualdad (p. 282) Cuando se resta el mismo número a cada lado de una desigualdad, la relación entre los dos lados no cambia.

If $a > b$, then $a - c > b - c$.
Since $9 > 6$, $9 - 2 > 6 - 2$.
If $a < b$, then $a - c < b - c$.
Since $9 < 13$, $9 - 2 < 13 - 2$.

Supplementary (p. 304) Supplementary angles are two angles whose measures add to 180°.

Suplementario (p. 304) Los ángulos suplementarios son dos ángulos cuyas medidas suman 180°.

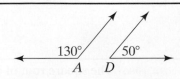

130° 50°
A D

$\angle A$ and $\angle D$ are supplementary angles.

Surface area (p. 368)   The surface area of a solid is the sum of the areas of its surfaces.

Área total (p. 368)   El área total de un sólido es la suma de las áreas de todas sus caras.

Each square = 1 in.²

The surface area of a prism is the sum of the areas of the faces.
$4 \cdot 12 + 2 \cdot 9 = 66 \text{ in.}^2$

Symmetry (p. 142)   A figure has symmetry when one side is the mirror image of the other side.

Simetría (p. 142)   Una figura tiene simetría cuando un lado es la imagen refleja del otro lado.

See *Reflectional symmetry, Rotational symmetry*.

Term (p. 266)   A term is a number, a variable, or the product of a number and a variable.

Término (p. 266)   Un término es un número, una variable o el producto de un número y una variable.

The expression $7x + 12 + (-9y)$ has 3 terms: $7x$, 12, and $-9y$.

Term (p. 512)   Each number in a sequence is called a term.

Término (p. 512)   Cada número de una progresión se llama término.

$1, 3, 9, 27, \ldots$

In this sequence, 1 is the first term, 3 is the second term, 9 is the third term, and 27 is the fourth term.

Terminating decimal (p. 58)   A terminating decimal is a decimal that stops.

Decimal finito (p. 58)   Un decimal finito es un decimal exacto.

Both 0.6 and 0.7265 are terminating decimals.

Tessellation (p. 150)   A tessellation is a repeating pattern of congruent shapes-that completely covers a plane without gaps or overlaps.

Teselación (p. 150)   Una teselación es un patrón repetido de formas congruentes que cubre completamente un plano, sin espacios o sobreposiciones.

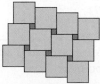

This tessellation consists of small and large squares.

Theoretical probability (p. 471) Theoritical probability describes how likely it is that an event will happen. This probability is based on all the outcomes when the outcomes are equally likely.

Probabilidad teórica (p. 471) La probabilidad teórica describe cuán posible es que ocurra un suceso. Esta probalidad está basada en todos los resultados cuando los resultados son igualmente probables.

Suppose you select a letter from the letters H, A, P, P, and Y. The theoretical probability of selecting a P is $\frac{2}{5}$.

Three-dimensional figure (p. 354) Three-dimensional figures are figures that do not lie in a plane. They are also known as solids.

Figura tridemensional (p. 354) Las figuras tridimensionales son figuras que no están en un solo plano. También se llaman sólidos.

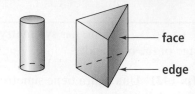

Tip (p. 215) A tip is a percent of a bill given to a person for providing a service.

Propina (p. 215) Una propina es un porcentaje de una cuenta que se le da a una persona por el servicio prestado.

A lunch bill is $18.00. You leave a 20% tip of $3.60.

Transformation (p. 136) A transformation is a change in position, shape, or size of a figure. Three types of transformations that change position only are translations, reflections, and rotations.

Transformación (p. 136) Una transformación es un cambio de posición, forma o tamaño de una figura. Los tres tipos de transformaciones que cambian la posición son las traslaciones, las reflexiones y las rotaciones.

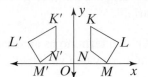

$K'L'M'N'$ is a reflection, or flip, of $KLMN$ across the y-axis.

Translation (p. 136) A translation is a transformation that moves each point of a figure the same distance and in the same direction.

Traslación (p. 136) Una traslación es una transformación que mueve cada punto de una figura la misma distancia y en la misma dirección.

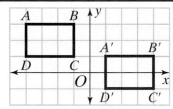

$A'B'C'D'$ is a translation image of $ABCD$.

Transversal (p. 307) A transversal is a line that intersects two or more lines at different points.

Secante (p. 307) Una secante es una recta que corta dos o más rectas en puntos diferentes.

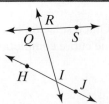

$\overleftrightarrow{RI}$ is a transversal of $\overleftrightarrow{QS}$ and $\overleftrightarrow{HJ}$.

Trapezoid (p. 319)   A trapezoid is a quadrilateral with exactly one pair of parallel sides.

Trapecio (p. 319)   Un trapecio es un cuadrilátero que tiene exactamente un par de lados paralelos.

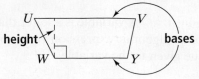

$\overline{UV}$ is parallel to $\overline{WY}$.

Trend (p. 445)   A trend is a relationship between two sets of data.

Tendencia (p. 445)   Una tendencia es una relación entre dos conjuntos de datos.

See *Positive trend*, *Negative trend*, and *No trend*.

Trend line (p. 445)   A trend line is a line you draw on a graph to approximate the data.

Línea de tendencia (p. 445)   Una línea de tendencia es una línea que se dibuja en una gráfica para aproximar los datos.

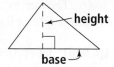

Triangle (p. 313)   A triangle is a polygon with three sides.

Triángulo (p. 313)   Un triángulo es un polígono que tiene tres lados.

Unit cost (p. 161)   A unit cost is a unit rate that gives the *cost per unit*.

Costo unitario (p. 161)   Un costo unitario es una tasa unitaria que da el *costo por unidad*.

$$\frac{\$5.98}{10.2 \text{ fl oz}} = \$.59/\text{fl oz}$$

Unit rate (p. 161)   The rate for one unit of a given quantity is called the unit rate.

Tasa unitaria (p. 161)   La tasa para una unidad de una cantidad dada se llama tasa unitaria.

If you drive 130 mi in 2 h, your unit rate is $\frac{65 \text{ mi}}{1 \text{ h}}$, or 65 mi/h.

Variable (p. 4)   A variable is a letter that stands for a number. The value of an algebraic expression varies, or changes, depending upon the value given to the variable.

x is a variable in the equation $9 + x = 7$.

Variable (p. 4)   Una variable es una letra que representa un número. El valor de una expresión algebraica varía, o cambia, dependiendo del valor que se le dé a la variable.

Venn diagram (p. 424)   A Venn diagram is a diagram that uses regions, usually circles, to show how sets of numbers or objects are related.

Diagrama de Venn (p. 424)   Un diagramna de Venn es un diagrama que usa regiones, generalmente círculos, para mostrar cómo se relacionan conjuntos de números u objetos.

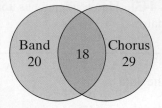

The Venn diagram shows the activities of 67 music students.

Vertex of an angle (p. 640)   The vertex of an angle is the point of intersection of two sides of an angle or figure.

Vértice de un ángulo (p. 640)   El vértice de un ángulo es el punto de intersección de dos lados de un ángulo o figura.

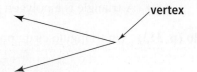

Vertex of a polygon (p. 312)   The vertex of a polygon is any point where two sides of a polygon meet.

Vértice de un polígono (p. 312)   El vértice de un polígono es cualquier punto donde se encuentran dos lados de un polígono.

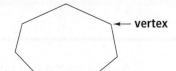

Vertical angles (p. 303)   Vertical angles are formed by two intersecting lines. Vertical angles are opposite each other.

Ángulos verticales (p. 303)   Los ángulos verticales están formados por dos rectas que se intersecan. Los ángulos verticales son opuestos entre sí.

$\angle 1$ and $\angle 2$ are vertical angles, as are $\angle 3$ and $\angle 4$.

Volume (p. 380)   Volume is the number of unit cubes, or cubic units, needed to fill a solid.

Volumen (p. 380)   El volumen es el número de unidades cúbicas que se necesitan para llenar el espacio dentro de un sólido.

The volume of the rectangular prism is 36 in.^{3}.

x-axis (p. 124) The *x*-axis is the horizontal number line that, together with the *y*-axis, forms the coordinate plane.

Eje de *x* (p. 124) El eje de *x* es la recta numérica horizontal que, junto con el eje de *y*, forma el plano de coordenadas.

x-coordinate (p. 124) The *x*-coordinate is the first number in an ordered pair. It tells the number of horizontal units a point is from the origin.

Coordenada *x* (p. 124) La coordenada *x* es el primer número en un par ordenado. Indica el número de unidades horizontales a las que un punto está del origen.

The *x*-coordinate is −2 for the ordered pair (−2, 1). The point is 2 units to the left of the origin.

y-axis (p. 124) The *y*-axis is the vertical number line that, together with the *x*-axis, forms the coordinate plane.

Eje de *y* (p. 124) El eje de *y* es la recta numérica vertical que, junto con el eje de *x*, forma el plano de coordenadas.

y-coordinate (p. 124) The *y*-coordinate is the second number in an ordered pair. It tells the number of vertical units a point is from the origin.

Coordenada *y* (p. 124) La coordenada *y* es el segundo número en un par ordenado. Indica el número de unidades verticales a las que un punto está del origen.

The *y*-coordinate is 1 for the ordered pair (−2, 1). The point is 1 unit up from the *x*-axis.

y-intercept (p. 535) The *y*-intercept of a line is the *y*-coordinate of the point where a line crosses the *y*-axis.

Intercepto *y* (p. 535) El intercepto *y* de una recta es la coordenada *y* del punto donde la recta cruza el eje de *y*.

See *x*-intercept.

English/Spanish Glossary

Zero pair (p. 32) The pairing of one positive tile with one negative tile is called a zero pair.

■ ■ ◀——— a zero pair

Par cero (p. 32) El emparejamiento de una ficha positiva con una ficha negativa se llama par cero.

Zero Product Property (p. 648) The Zero Product Property states that the product of 0 and any number is 0.

$a \cdot 0 = 0$
$6 \cdot 0 = 0$

Propiedad del cero (p. 648) La Propiedad del Cero establece que el producto de 0 y cualquier número es 0.

Chapter 1

Check Your Readiness — p. 2

1. < **2.** = **3.** < **4.** > **5.** 1.234 **6.** 0.96 **7.** 7.29
8. 47.3 **9.** 1.88 **10.** 10.16 **11.** 0.68 **12.** 14.7
13. 15.52 **14.** 0.0138 **15.** 22.53 **16.** 8.512
17. 5.68 **18.** 8.95 **19.** 0.092

Lesson 1-1 — pp. 4–6

Check Skills You'll Need 1. $\frac{3}{4}$ **2.** 96 **3.** 10 **4.** 44.4 **5.** 3

Quick Check 1. $15n$ **2.** 5 **3.** 40 **4.** $100 + 35m$; $520

Lesson 1-2 — pp. 10–11

Check Skills You'll Need 1. An algebraic expression is
a mathematical phrase that uses numbers,
variables, and operation symbols. **2.** 11 **3.** 15
4. 12

Quick Check 1. 7, 7 **2.** −5, 0, 4 **3.** Asia **4.** 15

Checkpoint Quiz 1 p. 14 1. $-3s$ **2.** $v \div 12$ or $\frac{v}{12}$
3. $m \div 10$ or $\frac{m}{10}$ **4.** $4 + f$ **5.** 304 **6.** 15 **7.** 16
8. 3 **9.** 10.5 **10.** 28 **11.** 7.2 **12.** $168 + 35h$; $273

Lesson 1-3 — pp. 16–17

Check Skills You'll Need 1. Answers may vary. Sample:
When you simplify an expression, you write its
simplest name. When you evaluate an expression,
you replace each variable with a number and then
simplify. **2.** 19 **3.** 2 **4.** 38 **5.** 3

Quick Check 1a. 18 **b.** −15 **2a.** 12 **b.** −12 **c.** −200
3. −181 ft, or 181 ft below the surface

Lesson 1-4 — pp. 20–21

Check Skills You'll Need 1. opposites **2.** −6 **3.** −15
4. −6

Quick Check 1. 144 **2.** −18 ft/min **3.** −36

Lesson 1-5 — pp. 26–28

Check Skills You'll Need 1. To simplify an expression
means to replace it with its simplest name. **2.** 99
3. 100 **4.** −21 **5.** 32

Quick Check 1. 48 **2.** −46 **3.** 2,420 **4.** $6m + 18$
5. $162

Checkpoint Quiz 2 p. 31 1. −64 **2.** 37 **3.** −43 **4.** 4
5. 5 **6.** 25 **7.** 119 **8.** 410 **9.** $63.92
10. $-37 - 16.5$ or $-37 + (-16.5)$

Lesson 1-6 — pp. 33–34

Check Skills You'll Need 1. inverses **2.** −11 **3.** 0
4. −7 **5.** −6

Quick Check 1. −3 **2.** $x + 8 = 52$; 44

Lesson 1-7 — pp. 38–39

Check Skills You'll Need 1. undo **2.** 24 **3.** −21 **4.** −2
5. 3

Quick Check 1. −40 **2.** −4

Chapter 2

Check Your Readiness — p. 50

1. 14 **2.** 22 **3.** 2 **4.** 2 **5.** −11, −4, 0, 3
6. −9, −6, 8, 13 **7.** −21, −8, 9, 16
8. −35, −17, −3, 22 **9.** 3 **10.** −13 **11.** −37
12. −25 **13.** −48 **14.** −6 **15.** 42 **16.** 9

Lesson 2-1 — pp. 52–54

Check Skills You'll Need 1. product **2.** −100 **3.** 56
4. 40 **5.** 0

Quick Check 1. composite; divisible by 2
2a. $2 \cdot 2 \cdot 2 \cdot 2 \cdot 2 \cdot 3$ **b.** $2 \cdot 2 \cdot 2 \cdot 2 \cdot 3 \cdot 5$
3a. 9 **b.** 6 **4.** 21 ft

Lesson 2-2 — pp. 57–58

Check Skills You'll Need 1. $2 \cdot 2 \cdot 5 \cdot 5$ **2.** 6 **3.** 4
4. 25 **5.** 4

Quick Check 1. $\frac{12 \div 4}{20 \div 4} = \frac{3}{5}$ **2.** $\frac{3 \cdot 3 \cdot 3}{3 \cdot 3 \cdot 5} = \frac{3}{5}$ **3.** .459
4. $1\frac{21}{50}$

Lesson 2-3 — pp. 62–63

Check Skills You'll Need 1. The numerator represents a
part of the whole. **2.** $\frac{3}{5}$ **3.** $\frac{3}{11}$ **4.** $\frac{1}{4}$ **5.** $\frac{1}{11}$

Quick Check 1. $\frac{3}{18}$, $\frac{2}{18}$; $\frac{1}{6}$ is greater. **2.** dogs; $\frac{12}{17} > \frac{7}{10}$
3. $-\frac{7}{8}$, −0.625, $1\frac{1}{2}$, $\frac{8}{5}$, 1.61

Lesson 2-4 — pp. 66–67

Check Skills You'll Need 1. 2, 0, −6 **2.** −10 **3.** −90
4. 10

Quick Check 1. $\frac{7}{30}$ **2.** $-\frac{3}{20}$ **3.** $6\frac{19}{20}$
4. $17\frac{4}{5} + x = 20\frac{3}{10}$; $x = 2\frac{1}{2}$ in.

Checkpoint Quiz 1 p. 70 1. $2 \cdot 2 \cdot 2 \cdot 3 \cdot 3 \cdot 7$ **2.** 33

3. .296 **4.** $\frac{14}{25}$ **5.** -2.6, $-\frac{15}{7}$, $\frac{8}{25}$, 0.35, 2 **6.** $\frac{7}{9}$
7. $4\frac{3}{5}$ **8.** $-1\frac{23}{24}$ **9.** $-2\frac{9}{20}$ **10.** $1\frac{1}{8}$ cups

Lesson 2-5   pp. 72–73

Check Skills You'll Need 1. $\frac{a}{b}$ **2.** $\frac{1}{3}$ **3.** $\frac{3}{5}$ **4.** $\frac{1}{9}$ **5.** $\frac{6}{11}$

Quick Check 1. $\frac{3}{10}$ **2.** $-2\frac{47}{50}$ **3.** 5 lengths **4.** $8\frac{1}{6}$

Lesson 2-6   pp. 81–82

Check Skills You'll Need 1. add; subtract **2.** 5 **3.** -4
4. -4 **5.** 10

Quick Check 1a. 12.6 cm² **b.** 2 yd² **2.** 1.58 mi/h
3. $w = A + 5$

Lesson 2-7   pp. 86–87

Check Skills You'll Need 1. factor **2.** 4 **3.** 6 **4.** 16
5. 24 **6.** 16

Quick Check 1. $6^2 \cdot 7^6$ **2.** -343 **3.** -343 **4.** 50
5. $5\frac{2}{3}$ m

Checkpoint Quiz 2 p. 91 **1.** $-2\frac{4}{5}$ **2.** $1\frac{7}{9}$ **3.** $\frac{7}{15}$ **4.** $-\frac{2}{57}$
5. -38 **6.** -71 **7.** 100 **8.** 93 **9.** $b = \frac{3T}{a}$
10. $A = 10\frac{1}{72}$ cm² **11.** $h = \frac{4}{\pi}$ cm

Lesson 2-8   pp. 92–93

Check Skills You'll Need 1. power **2.** 20 **3.** 451
4. 1,500 **5.** 18,030 **6.** 2,390,000

Quick Check 1. 7,660,000 km² **2.** 3.476×10^6 m
3. 0.00025 in. **4.** 3.5×10^{-6}

Chapter 3

Check Your Readiness   p. 104

1. -28 **2.** 68 **3.** -9 **4.** 13 **5.** 10 **6.** 0.833 **7.** 0.4
8. 1.615 **9.** 0.864 **10.** $b = c - a$ **11.** $t = \frac{d}{16}$
12. $T = s - 200$ **13.** 25 **14.** 21 **15.** 181

Lesson 3-1   pp. 106–108

Check Skills You'll Need 1. exponent **2.** 4 **3.** 4 **4.** 36
5. 100

Quick Check 1a. 6, -6 **b.** 1, -1 **c.** $\frac{1}{4}$, $-\frac{1}{4}$ **2.** 6
3a. 5.5 s **b.** 6.3 s **4.** Rational; the decimal
repeats.

Lesson 3-2   pp. 112–113

Check Skills You'll Need 1. a number that when
multiplied by itself is equal to the given number
2. 8 **3.** 11 **4.** 9 **5.** 5

Quick Check 1. 20 cm **2.** 33 ft

Lesson 3-3   pp. 118–119

Check Skills You'll Need 1. The Pythagorean Theorem
states that in any right triangle, the sum of the
squares of the lengths of the legs (a and b) is
equal to the square of the length of the
hypotenuse: $a^2 + b^2 = c^2$ **2.** 5 **3.** 8.6

Quick Check 1. 15.8 ft **2.** 17.3 ft

Checkpoint Quiz 1 p. 123 **1.** 9 **2.** Irrational; 13 is not a
perfect square. **3.** Rational; the number is a ratio
of two integers. **4.** Irrational; the decimal does
not terminate or repeat. **5.** 15 cm **6.** 22.5 ft
7. 24 in. **8.** 24.2 m **9.** 8.9 m

Lesson 3-4   pp. 124–125

Check Skills You'll Need 1. They are the same distance
from zero on a number line but on opposite
sides of zero. **2.** $-5, -3, -1, 3$ **3.** $-6, -4, 2, 9$
4. $-10, -8, 0, 6$ **5.** $-5, -2, 4, 7$

Quick Check 1.   **2.** 6 mi

Lesson 3-5   pp. 130–131

Check Skills You'll Need 1. variable **2.** 3 **3.** 21 **4.** 28

Quick Check 1.

Number of CDs	Expression	Total Cost (dollars)
0	15(0)	0
1	15(1)	15
2	15(2)	30
3	15(3)	45
c	15(c)	t

$t = 15c$, where t represents total cost and c
represents number of CDs.

2.

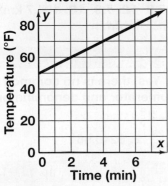

Temperature of a Chemical Solution

7. $(x, y) \rightarrow (x - 3, y + 4)$

8.

Number of Exercises	Expression	Workout Time (min)
0	3(0) + 5	5
1	3(1) + 5	8
2	3(2) + 5	11
3	3(3) + 5	14
x	3(x) + 5	w

$w = 3x + 5$

Lesson 3-6   pp. 136–137

Check Skills You'll Need 1. Quadrant II **2.** (4, 2) **3.** (2, 1)
4. (5, −2) **5.** (1, −1)

Quick Check 1.

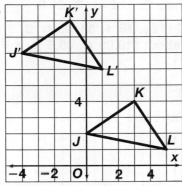

$J'(-4, 7)$ **2.** $(x, y) \rightarrow (x + 6, y + 2)$

Checkpoint Quiz 2 p. 140 1–5.

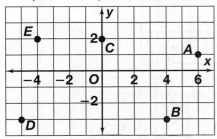

6.

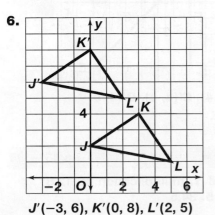

$J'(-3, 6), K'(0, 8), L'(2, 5)$

Lesson 3-7   pp. 141–142

Check Skills You'll Need 1. distance **2.**

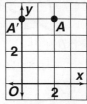

3.   **4.**

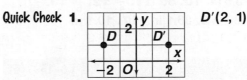

5.

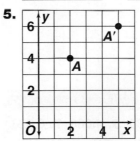

Quick Check 1. $D'(2, 1)$

2. $E'(4, -3), F'(3, -1), G'(1, -2)$

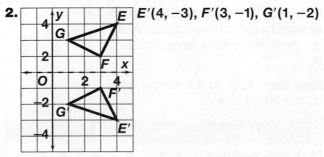

3.

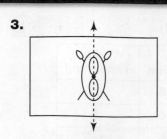

Lesson 3-8   pp. 146–147

Check Skills You'll Need 1. matches **2.** straight
3. obtuse **4.** obtuse **5.** acute **6.** acute **7.** right

Quick Check 1. 72°
2a.

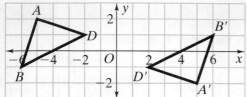

b.

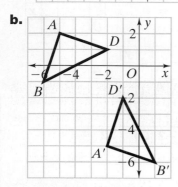

Chapter 4

Check Your Readiness   p. 158

1. $\frac{1}{2}$ **2.** $\frac{2}{7}$ **3.** $\frac{5}{7}$ **4.** $\frac{11}{20}$ **5.** 0.630 **6.** 4.083 **7.** 0.323
8. 2.714 **9.** 0.514 **10.** 56 **11.** $\frac{1}{4}$ **12.** $\frac{5}{6}$ **13.** $\frac{9}{16}$
14. $4\frac{1}{5}$ **15.** 30 **16.** 36.1 in. **17.** 10.1 m
18. 28.8 cm

Lesson 4-1   pp. 160–161

Check Skills You'll Need 1. The least common
denominator is the smallest multiple the
denominators have in common. **2.** $\frac{3}{9}$ **3.** $\frac{4}{5}$ **4.** $\frac{45}{54}$
5. $\frac{7}{12}$

Quick Check 1. $\frac{1}{6}$ **2.** 6.5 deliveries/h
3. the 20-oz box

Lesson 4-2   pp. 166–168

Check Skills You'll Need 1. 1 **2.** $\frac{5}{6}$ **3.** $\frac{5}{9}$ **4.** $\frac{2}{3}$ **5.** $2\frac{2}{7}$

Quick Check 1. 11,880 ft **2.** 13.2 ft/s **3a.** 7 **b.** 5
4. 16.0 qt

Checkpoint Quiz 1 p. 171 1. $\frac{1}{15}$ **2.** $\frac{1}{4}$ **3.** 6 : 1 **4.** $\frac{3}{4}$
5. \$12/book **6.** 12 m/s **7.** 3 gal/min **8.** 8 mi/h
9. 0.20 **10.** 20 **11.** 17.0 **12.** 7.9 **13.** 104.7 km/h
14. \$4.75/page **15.** 12.2 km/min

Lesson 4-3   pp. 174–175

Check Skills You'll Need 1. Yes; there is no common
factor between the numerator and denominator.
2. $\frac{10}{33}$ **3.** $3\frac{1}{2}$ **4.** $\frac{66}{301}$ **5.** $2\frac{4}{5}$

Quick Check 1. no; $\frac{6}{7} \neq \frac{23}{28}$ **2.** \$240.96

Lesson 4-4   pp. 181–182

Check Skills You'll Need 1. $10 \cdot 3 = 15 \cdot 2$ **2.** 39
3. 110 **4.** $506\frac{1}{4}$

Quick Check 1. Yes; the corresponding angles are
equal and the corresponding side lengths are
proportional. **2.** 11.2 in. **3.** 21 ft

Checkpoint Quiz 2 p. 186 1. 38 **2.** 21 **3.** 8 **4.** 52 **5.** 6
6. 2.8 **7.** about \$19.80 **8.** 49.5 **9.** $n = 30$; $y = 12$
10. 51 ft

Lesson 4-5   pp. 187–188

Check Skills You'll Need 1. x **2-5.**

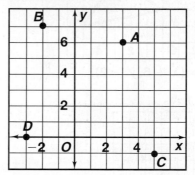

Quick Check 1.

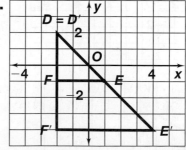

2. $A'(0, 0)$, $B'(0, 4)$, $C'(4, 4)$, $D'(4, 0)$
3. 3; enlargement

Lesson 4-6   pp. 192–193

Check Skills You'll Need 1. multiplication **2.** 12.8
3. 44.84 **4.** 39.6 **5.** 84.5

Quick Check 1. $2\frac{13}{16}$ in. **2.** about 140 mi

Lesson 4-7   pp. 197–198

Check Skills You'll Need 1. shape **2.** $\angle Y$

Quick Check 1. 52.5 ft **2.** about 460.7 m

Chapter 5

Check Your Readiness   p. 208

1. 20 **2.** 15.91 **3.** 237.5 **4.** 1.75 **5.** $\frac{1}{2}$ **6.** $\frac{5}{8}$ **7.** $\frac{1}{12}$
8. $\frac{9}{16}$ **9.** 30 **10.** $8\frac{1}{2}$ **11.** 100 **12.** 36 **13.** 2
14. 32 **15.** 100 **16.** 19 **17.** 85.5

Lesson 5-1   pp. 210–211

Check Skills You'll Need 1. $\frac{a}{b}$, $b \neq 0$ **2.** $\frac{9}{10}$ **3.** $\frac{4}{5}$ **4.** $\frac{7}{20}$
5. $\frac{1}{4}$

Quick Check 1. 55% **2.** 8% **3.** $\frac{3}{2}$ **4.** 0.73, $\frac{3}{4}$, 76%

Lesson 5-2   pp. 214–215

Check Skills You'll Need 1. $\frac{7}{3}$ **2.** 27 **3.** 8 **4.** 54 **5.** 45

Quick Check 1. about 20 **2.** about 8 students
3. about $10.80

Lesson 5-3   pp. 218–220

Check Skills You'll Need 1. proportion **2.** 20 **3.** $66\frac{2}{3}$
4. 100 **5.** 3 **6.** 25

Quick Check 1. 70.3 **2.** 199.75 **3.** 275 students
4. 20%

Lesson 5-4   pp. 224–225

Check Skills You'll Need 1. Equation; it contains an =
sign. **2.** 40 **3.** 1.25 **4.** 15 **5.** 0.03125

Quick Check 1. $11.76 **2.** 90

Checkpoint Quiz 1 p. 229 1. 50% **2.** 9.09% **3.** 37.5%
4. 250% **5.** 40% **6.** about 12 **7.** about 0.24
8. about 11 **9.** about 0.04 **10.** about 1,300,000
people **11.** 50 **12.** 5% **13.** 0.78 **14.** 0.25

Lesson 5-5   pp. 230–231

Check Skills You'll Need 1. percent **2.** 112.5%
3. 27.3% **4.** 26.7% **5.** 366.7%

Quick Check 1. 19.4% **2.** 5.3% **3.** 57.2%

Lesson 5-6   pp. 234–236

Check Skills You'll Need 1. percent **2.** 4 **3.** 200
4. 1,100 **5.** 14,000

Quick Check 1. 90% **2.** $161.80 **3.** $100.51
4. $116.47

Lesson 5-7   pp. 242–243

Check Skills You'll Need 1. formula **2.** $w = \frac{V}{\ell h}$
3. $r = \frac{d}{t}$ **4.** $b = y - x$ **5.** $B = \frac{3v}{h}$

Quick Check 1. $630 **2.** $369

Checkpoint Quiz 2 p. 245 1. 1,000% increase **2.** 1.6%
decrease **3.** 80% decrease **4.** 270.7% increase
5. 3.4% **6.** $23.06 **7.** 15% **8.** $43.75 **9.** $17.10

Lesson 5-8   pp. 246–248

Check Skills You'll Need 1. ratio **2.** 1 : 2 **3.** $\frac{2}{25}$ **4.** $\frac{1}{3}$
5. $\frac{5}{9}$ **6.** 1 : 4

Quick Check 1. $\frac{3}{8}$ **2.** 28% **3.** $\frac{1}{2}$ **4.** $\frac{3}{8}$

Chapter 6

Check Your Readiness   p. 258

1. −2 **2.** −2 **3.** 14 **4.** 123 **5.** −4 **6.** 3 **7.** −3
8. 1 **9.** −1 **10.** 1 **11.** 3 **12.** $5c - 15$
13. $-2w - 16$ **14.** $-54 + 9t$ **15.** $-10 + 2a$
16. $44 - 11b$ **17.** $-x + 2$

Lesson 6-1   pp. 261–262

Check Skills You'll Need 1. to get the variable alone on
one side of the equation **2.** −7 **3.** 6 **4.** 30

Quick Check 1. −8.7 **2.** $0.5 + 0.85c = 3.90$; 4 min

Lesson 6-2   pp. 266–267

Check Skills You'll Need 1. No; 15 can be subtracted
from 5. The simplest form is $3a - 10$.
2. $-8r - 24$ **3.** $-7s + 35$ **4.** $70 - 35t$

Quick Check 1. $-14t$ **2.** Let b = the cost of a board.
Let n = the cost of a box of nails. Let h = the cost
of a hammer. $26b + 3n + h$ **3.** $9 - 6b$

Checkpoint Quiz 1 p. 270 1. 5.5 **2.** 9 **3.** 1 **4.** 3 **5.** 15
6. −28 **7.** $56.\overline{6}$ **8.** −26.65 **9.** −3 **10.** $1.50
11. $-8m + p + 4$ **12.** $8.1g - 13.65$
13. $-2h + 20$ **14.** $10k + 0.11$
15. $-4.81j - 18.27$ **16.** $168 - 3a$ **17.** Let s = the
cost of a sleeping bag. Let f = the cost of a
flashlight. $11s + 7f$

Lesson 6-3   pp. 271–272

Check Skills You'll Need 1. $3x$, $2x$, $-x$ **2.** $12 - 26m$
3. $28 - 12r$ **4.** $8q + 5$

Quick Check 1. −11 **2.** 17 boys

Lesson 6-4 — pp. 276–277

Check Skills You'll Need 1. inverse operations
2. $9t + 47$ **3.** $60 - 12r$ **4.** $-3x - 7$

Quick Check 1. 2 **2.** 61 text messages

Lesson 6-5 — pp. 282–283

Check Skills You'll Need 1. equation **2.** -18 **3.** -13
4. 24

Quick Check 1. $5 \le u$

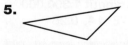

4 5 6

2. At most, 211 more people can attend.

Checkpoint Quiz 2 p. 287 1. $x \ge -2$ **2.** $x < 1$ **3.** -9
4. -1 **5.** -28 **6.** $a \ge -6$ **7.** $g \le 1$ **8.** $y < -23$
9. Let b = the cost of a banana. $4.99 + b = 13b$;
$b = \$.42$ **10.** Let x = the load weight.
$28,500 + x = 64,000$; $x = 35,500$ lb

Lesson 6-6 — pp. 288–290

Check Skills You'll Need 1. No; zero is not a negative
number. **2.** -4 **3.** -101 **4.** 6.2 **5.** -8

Quick Check 1. up to 12 passengers

2. $b \le -4$

$-6\ -4\ -2\ \ 0$

3. $p \le -17$

$-17\qquad -9$

Chapter 7

Check Your Readiness — p. 300

1. 36 **2.** 100.48 **3.** 40 **4.** 8 **5.** 43 **6.** -3 **7.** 32
8. 15 **9.** $1\frac{1}{7}$ **10.** 84 **11.** 35.7 **12.** 216 m^2
13. 28 in.^{2} **14.** 169 ft^2

Lesson 7-1 — pp. 303–304

Check Skills You'll Need 1. subtraction **2.** 18 **3.** 31
4. -41 **5.** -29

Quick Check 1. $\angle DBJ$ and $\angle YBT$; adjacent angles
may vary. Sample: $\angle DBJ$ and $\angle DBY$ **2.** 133°
3. 58°; 90°

Lesson 7-2 — pp. 307–308

Check Skills You'll Need 1. 120° and 60° **2.** 132°
3. 61° **4.** 113° **5.** 49°

Quick Check 1a. alternate interior **b.** corresponding
c. neither **2.** $m\angle 6 = m\angle 7 = 117°$ **3.** The
measure of each angle formed by lines t and ℓ
and lines t and m is 90°. Since pairs of
corresponding angles are congruent, the lines
are parallel.

Lesson 7-3 — pp. 312–314

Check Skills You'll Need 1. equal **2.** Not similar;
corresponding sides are not in proportion.

Quick Check 1. $\triangle TRS \cong \triangle KJL$ **2a.** $\triangle XYZ \cong \triangle RQP$
by SSS **b.** $\triangle KLM \cong \triangle JLM$ by SAS **3a.** 40°
b. 50°

Checkpoint Quiz 1 p. 317 1. vertical **2.** alternate interior
3. corresponding **4.** adjacent **5.** corresponding
6. adjacent **7.** Answers may vary. Sample: SAS,
ASA, or SSS; $\triangle JKD \cong \triangle WTB$. **8.** 23°; 113°
9. 100° **10.** 90° **11.** 120° **12.** 0.9 m **13.** 1.6 m
14. 1.7 m

Lesson 7-4 — pp. 318–319

Check Skills You'll Need 1. 90° **2.** acute **3.** obtuse

Quick Check 1a. isosceles obtuse **b.** equilateral
acute **2a.** Rectangle; the quadrilateral has four
right angles. **b.** Trapezoid; the quadrilateral has
exactly one pair of parallel sides.

Lesson 7-5 — pp. 324–325

Check Skills You'll Need 1. You replace each variable in
the expression with a number and then simplify.
2. 27 **3.** 6 **4.** 36

Quick Check 1. 900° **2.** 151° **3.** 108°

Lesson 7-6 — pp. 328–330

Check Skills You'll Need 1. A formula is a rule that
shows the relationship between two or more
quantities. **2.** 80 cm^2 **3.** 49 ft^2

Quick Check 1. 10.5 cm^2 **2.** 15 yd^2

Checkpoint Quiz 2 p. 335 1. parallelogram; 100.86 cm^2
2. isosceles triangle; 1.7 in.^{2} **3.** trapezoid;
43.35 m^2 **4.** 133° **5–6.** Answers may vary.
Samples are given.

5.   **6.**

Lesson 7-7 — pp. 336–337

Check Skills You'll Need 1. Perimeter is the distance
around a figure. Area is the number of square
units a figure encloses. **2.** 45.5 ft^2

Quick Check 1. 78.5 in.; 490.9 in.^{2} **2.** 193.0 m^2

Lesson 7-8 — pp. 341–342

Check Skills You'll Need 1. Congruent polygons have
the same size and shape.

2. $\angle P \cong \angle T$; $\angle Q \cong \angle U$; $\angle R \cong \angle V$; $\overline{PQ} \cong \overline{TU}$; $\overline{QR} \cong \overline{UV}$; $\overline{RP} \cong \overline{VT}$

3. $\angle A \cong \angle L$; $\angle B \cong \angle M$; $\angle C \cong \angle N$; $\angle D \cong \angle O$; $\overline{AB} \cong \overline{LM}$; $\overline{BC} \cong \overline{MN}$; $\overline{CD} \cong \overline{NO}$; $\overline{DA} \cong \overline{OL}$

Quick Check **1.**

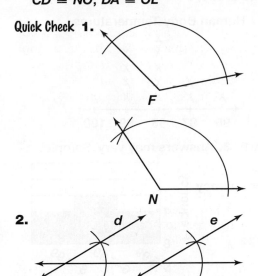

2.

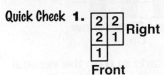

Chapter 8

<table>
<tr><td>Check Your Readiness</td><td>p. 352</td></tr>
</table>

1. 7 ft^2 **2.** 13 m^2 **3.** 96 cm^2 **4.** 54 mm^2
5. 20 in.^{2} **6.** 22 cm^2 **7.** 3 **8.** 7 **9.** 2.5 **10.** 12

<table>
<tr><td>Lesson 8-1</td><td>pp. 354–355</td></tr>
</table>

Check Skills You'll Need 1. Congruent triangles have the same shape and size. **2.** scalene triangle **3.** parallelogram

Quick Check 1. The figure is a pentagonal prism. $\overline{JK}$ is a lateral edge. Points J and K are vertices of the prism. **2.** a trapezoidal prism; a rectangular prism **3.** Answers may vary. Sample: $\overline{AB}$ and $\overline{BC}$ are intersecting line segments; no.

<table>
<tr><td>Lesson 8-2</td><td>pp. 358–359</td></tr>
</table>

Check Skills You'll Need 1. parallelograms **2.** rectangular prisms

Quick Check **1.**

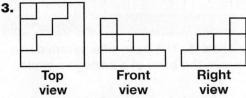

2.

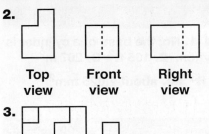

Top view   Front view   Right view

3.

Top view   Front view   Right view

<table>
<tr><td>Lesson 8-3</td><td>pp. 364–365</td></tr>
</table>

Check Skills You'll Need 1. isometric **2.**

Quick Check **1.** six congruent squares
2. pentagonal pyramid

<table>
<tr><td>Lesson 8-4</td><td>pp. 368–370</td></tr>
</table>

Check Skills You'll Need 1. Multiply the length times the width. **2.** 16.5 cm^2 **3.** 12.6 ft^2

Quick Check 1. 936 cm^2 **2.** about 392 in.^{2}
3. 151 m^2

Checkpoint Quiz 1 p. 373 1. triangular prism
2. rectangles **3.**

4.

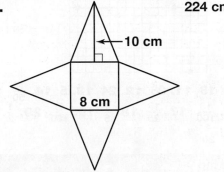

Top view Front view Right view

5. 468 ft^2

<table>
<tr><td>Lesson 8-5</td><td>pp. 374–376</td></tr>
</table>

Check Skills You'll Need 1. hypotenuse **2.** 10 ft^2

Quick Check **1.**   224 cm^2

10 cm

8 cm

2. 922,610 ft^2 **3.** 1,492,635 ft^2 **4.** 113 yd^2

Lesson 8-6
pp. 380–381

Check Skills You'll Need **1.** No; the base of a cylinder is a circle, not a polygon. **2.** 105 ft² **3.** 207 m²

Quick Check **1.** 52.5 ft³ **2a.** about 2,025 mm²
b. 2,120 mm³

Lesson 8-7
pp. 388–389

Check Skills You'll Need **1.** The base of a pyramid is a polygon, whereas the base of a cone is a circle. **2.** 429 in.²

Quick Check **1.** 19,200 in.³ **2.** 113 m³ **3.** $r \approx 6.2$ cm

Checkpoint Quiz 2 p. 392 **1.** 1,155 cm²; 1,911 cm³
2. 1,759 in.²; 4,516 in.³ **3.** 6,552 cm²; 31,164 cm³
4. 126 m³ **5.** 324 in.³ **6.** 40,000 cm³ **7.** about 1 ft
8. about 42 ft³

Lesson 8-8
pp. 393–394

Check Skills You'll Need **1.** The radius is half the diameter. **2.** about 48 cm² **3.** about 108 m²
4. about 27 ft² **5.** about 217 in.²

Quick Check **1.** 616 ft² **2.** 33,510 in.³

Lesson 8-9
pp. 398–399

Check Skills You'll Need **1.** A proportion is an equation stating that two ratios are equal. **2.** 1.75 **3.** 43.2
4. 9

Quick Check **1.** 8.8 m **2.** 486 in.²; 729 in.³

Chapter 9

Check Your Readiness
p. 410

1–9.

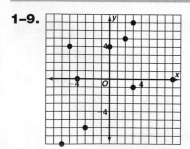

10. 18 **11.** 28 **12.** 24 **13.** 5 **14.** $\frac{13}{50}$ **15.** $\frac{12}{25}$
16. $\frac{13}{100}$ **17.** $\frac{18}{25}$ **18.** $\frac{1}{5}$ **19.** $\frac{47}{100}$ **20.** $\frac{1}{2}$ **21.** $\frac{1}{10}$
22. $\frac{1}{20}$

Lesson 9-1
pp. 412–414

Check Skills You'll Need **1.** subtraction **2.** 18 **3.** 31
4. −41 **5.** −29

Quick Check **1.** 14; 15; 11 **2.** 8.9 **3a.** 1; it lowers the

mean about 1.4. **b.** −18; it lowers the mean about 1.8. **4.** median

Lesson 9-2
pp. 418–419

Check Skills You'll Need **1.** range **2.** 7.9; 8; 7 and 8; 4
3. 0.875; 1; no mode; 9

Quick Check **1.** Human Body Temperatures

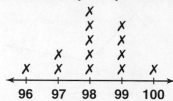

2. 101.5°; 101° **3.** Answers may vary. Sample:

Cost (Dollars)	Frequency
4–5.99	4
6–7.99	6
8–9.99	4

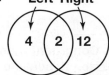

Lesson 9-3
p. 424

Check Skills You'll Need **1.** additive inverses **2.** 16
3. −1 **4.** 7

Quick Check **1.**

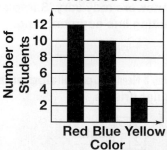

Lesson 9-4
pp. 428–429

Check Skills You'll Need **1.** A bar graph compares amounts. **2.**

Preferred Color

Quick Check **1.** The graph starts at 0 on the vertical axis, so the difference between the airports is portrayed more accurately. **2.** The second graph with the break symbol shows the data more clearly because the scale is more spread out.

Checkpoint Quiz 1 p. *432* **1.** 94.5 **2.** 90 **3.** 88 **4.** 30

5.

Scores	Frequency
61–70	1
71–80	5
81–90	5
91–100	6

6.

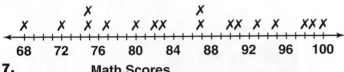

7.

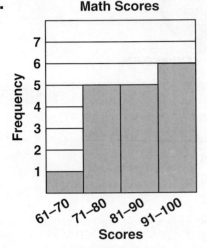

Math Scores

8.

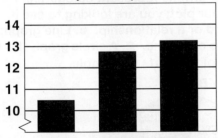

Average Number of Students per Computer

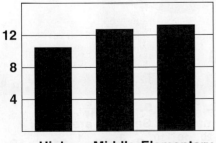

Average Number of Students per Computer

The graph without the break symbol shows more clearly that the numbers of students per computer are similar for all grades.

Lesson 9-5   pp. 433–435

Check Skills You'll Need 1. the frequency of each data value **2.** 29.2 **3.** 30 **4.** 40

Quick Check 1.

Monthly High Temperatures

```
 8 | 6  7
 9 | 1  7
10 | 1
11 | 1  3
12 | 0  0  5  6
13 | 4
```
Key: 13 | 4 means 134

2. The mean and median for the city mileage are 22.6 mi/gal and 22 mi/gal, respectively. The mean and median for the highway mileage are 30 mi/gal and 28 mi/gal, respectively. Both the mean and median give the impression that the highway mileage of the new cars is higher than the city mileage.

Lesson 9-6   pp. 438–439

Check Skills You'll Need 1. median **2.** 24 **3.** 4 **4.** 95

Quick Check 1. Answers may vary. Sample: The range for the girls' heights is greater than the boys'. Overall, the boys tend to be taller than the girls. The girls' upper quartile is equal to the boys' lower quartile.

2.

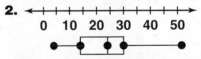

Lesson 9-7   pp. 444–445

Check Skills You'll Need 1. It identifies the location of a point.

2–3.

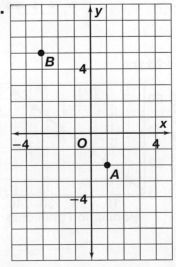

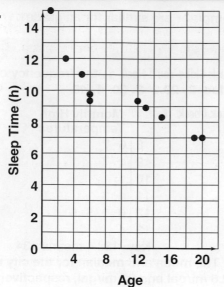

2.

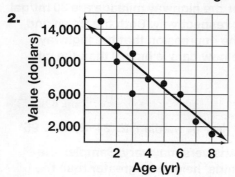

Checkpoint Quiz 2 p. 449 **1.**

```
        Grades
    6 | 8
    7 | 2 5 5 7
    8 | 0 2 3 7 7
    9 | 0 1 3 5 8 9
   10 | 0
   Key: 6 | 8 means 68%
```

2. Ages of WWII Veterans

```
    7 | 3 3 4 5 6 9
    8 | 0 3 6 7 8 9
    9 | 1 1 2 5 5
```

Key: 7 | 3 means 73 yrs.

3.

4. positive trend

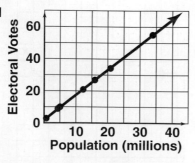

Lesson 9-8   pp. 450–451

Check Skills You'll Need 1. A proportion is an equation stating that two ratios are equal. **2.** 24 **3.** 30 **4.** 28 **5.** $41\frac{2}{3}$

Quick Check 1. about 4,686,000 people

2.   **Fuel Use**

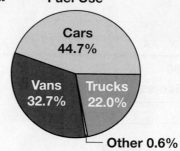

Lesson 9-9   pp. 456–457

Check Skills You'll Need 1. frequency

2.

Hours	Frequency
0–1.9	5
2–3.9	6
4–5.9	2
6–7.9	2
8–9.9	2

Quick Check 1a. Bar graph; scatter plots need to be numerical; bar graphs represent categorical data. **b.** Scatter plot; you are looking to see if there is a trend or a relationship. **c.** Line graph; it shows change over time. **2.** A circle graph shows comparisons of the parts of a whole.

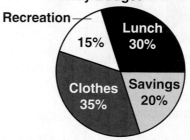

Chapter 10

Check Your Readiness   p. 468

1. $\frac{3}{14}$ **2.** $\frac{4}{25}$ **3.** $\frac{3}{8}$ **4.** $\frac{1}{3}$ **5.** $\frac{9}{17}$ **6.** $\frac{2}{17}$

7–8. Answers may vary. Samples are given.

7. $\frac{2}{4}; \frac{4}{2}; \frac{2}{2}$ **8.** $\frac{20}{30}; \frac{10}{30}; \frac{10}{20}$ **9.** $\frac{3}{8}$ **10.** $\frac{1}{4}$ **11.** $\frac{1}{8}$ **12.** $\frac{1}{2}$

13. $\frac{5}{8}$ **14.** $\frac{3}{8}$

Lesson 10-1 pp. 470–471

Check Skills You'll Need 1. sample space **2.** 1, 2, 3, 4, 5, 6 **3.** $\frac{1}{6}$ **4.** $\frac{1}{2}$ **5.** $\frac{1}{3}$

Quick Check 1. 0.4 **2.** Theoretical; the result is based on the number of possible outcomes. **3.** 5 : 2

Lesson 10-2 pp. 475–476

Check Skills You'll Need 1. cross **2.** 135 **3.** 136 **4.** 4.5

Quick Check 1. about 13 winning caps **2.** 380 votes

Checkpoint Quiz 1 p. 479 1. 0.95 **2.** 0.94 **3.** 0.77 **4.** Experimental; the results are based on a survey. **5.** 10 heads **6.** 9 toys

Lesson 10-3 pp. 480–481

Check Skills You'll Need 1. Experimental probability is based on running numerous trials or experiments, whereas theoretical probability is based on the mathematical likelihood of events. **2.** $\frac{1}{2}$ **3.** $\frac{2}{9}$ **4.** $\frac{5}{18}$

Quick Check 1. Not a random sample; people who are 18–30 years old may not represent all people. **2.** It assumes you either in-line skate or ice skate; answers may vary. Sample: Do you like to In-line skate or ice skate, or neither? **3.** No; she would not get a random sample of all shoppers.

Lesson 10-4 pp. 486–487

Check Skills You'll Need 1. You can set up a proportion to solve, or you can multiply the theoretical probability by the population size. **2.** about 8 **3.** about 8 **4.** 0 **5.** about 25

Quick Check 1. $\frac{21}{400}$ or 0.0525 **2.** $\frac{3}{10}$ **3a.** Independent; the outcome of the first coin flip does not affect the outcome of the second coin flip. **b.** Dependent; since you do not replace the name after you pick it, the outcome of the first pick affects the outcome of the second pick.

Checkpoint Quiz 2 p. 490 1. No; people at the music store are not representative of all the people who read. **2.** Yes; it makes watching a movie seem more appealing than reading a book. **3.** $\frac{1}{50}$ **4.** $\frac{1}{10}$ **5.** $\frac{1}{20}$ **6.** $\frac{9}{100}$ **7.** $\frac{1}{182}$ **8.** $\frac{1}{26}$ **9.** $\frac{3}{91}$ **10.** $\frac{6}{91}$

Lesson 10-5 pp. 491–492

Check Skills You'll Need 1. a collection of all possible outcomes **2.** 12 **3.** 36 **4.** 4

Quick Check 1a. 120 ways **b.** 24 orders **2.** There are 4 times as many ways, or 840 ways. **3a.** 2 **b.** 720 **c.** 24

Lesson 10-6 pp. 496–497

Check Skills You'll Need 1. permutation **2.** 42 **3.** 24 **4.** 90 **5.** 999,900

Quick Check 1. 4 groups **2a.** 21 **b.** 70 **c.** 10

Chapter 11

Check Your Readiness p. 510

1. −5 **2.** −6 **3.** −6 **4.** −8 **5.** 4 **6.** −3

7–9. 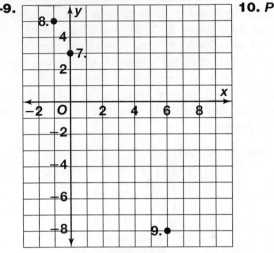 **10.** P

11. (−3, −2) **12.**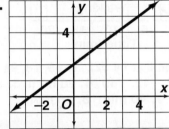

13.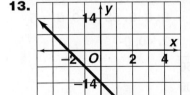

14.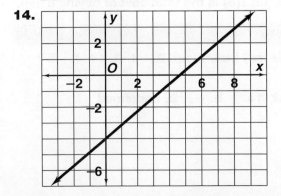

Lesson 11-1   pp. 512–514

Check Skills You'll Need **1.** Replace each variable with a number and then simplify. **2.** $n + 7$ **3.** $5n$ **4.** $12d$

Quick Check **1a.** 33, 40, 47 **b.** 24, 29, 34 **c.** 42, 52, 62 **2.** 0, 3, 6, 9 **3.** $-2n$; -40 **4.** 10; start with 0.1 and multiply by 10 repeatedly; 1,000; 10,000; 100,000.

Lesson 11-2   pp. 518–519

Check Skills You'll Need **1.** Line graphs best display changes over time. **2–3.** Answers may vary. Samples are given. **2.** Line plots best display frequency of data—for example, displaying the number of siblings each class member has. **3.** Bar graphs compare amounts in different categories—for example, the number of students in each grade.

Quick Check **1.** 40 mi/h
2.

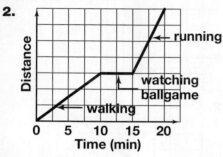

Checkpoint Quiz 1 p. 522 **1.** 65, 78, 91 **2.** $3\frac{3}{4}$, $4\frac{1}{2}$, $5\frac{1}{4}$ **3.** -35, -42, -49 **4.** 20 mi/h **5.** 20 mi **6.** after 1 hour **7.** 40 mi/h **8.** 65 mi/h

Lesson 11-3   pp. 523–524

Check Skills You'll Need **1.** a **2.** 8 **3.** 53 **4.** 9 **5.** -5

Quick Check **1.**

c	d
5	$.50
10	$1.00
15	$1.50

2. 40; 0

3. $f(6) = 12$; $f(6)$ is the total cost of buying 6 fish.

Lesson 11-4   pp. 528–530

Check Skills You'll Need **1.** no **2.** -4 **3.** 14 **4.** -6 **5.** -2

Quick Check **1a.** $\frac{2}{5}$ **b.** $-\frac{1}{2}$ **2.** undefined

3. -2

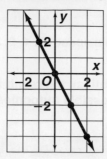

Lesson 11-5   pp. 534–535

Check Skills You'll Need **1.** Divide the change in y by the change in x. **2.** $-\frac{6}{7}$ **3.** 0 **4.** -1

Quick Check **1.**

Tickets	0	1	2	3	4	5	6	7
Cost	0	15	30	45	60	75	90	105

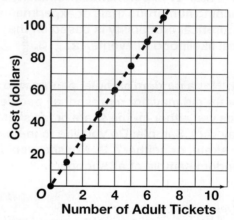

2.

Time	0	1	2	3	4	5	6
Height	4,000	3,400	2,800	2,200	1,600	1,000	400

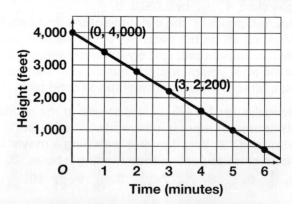

Checkpoint Quiz 2 p. 539 **1.** 1 **2.** -17 **3.** -2 **4.** 28 **5.** 0.99 p **6.** 0 **7.** $\frac{3}{2}$ **8.** -1 **9.** A hill with a rise of 5 and a run of 3 is steeper because it is rising $1\frac{2}{3}$ units for each horizontal unit. The other hill is rising only $\frac{3}{5}$ unit for each horizontal unit.

10.

Hours Worked	Money Earned
0	0
1	7
2	14
3	21
4	28
5	35
6	42
7	49
8	56

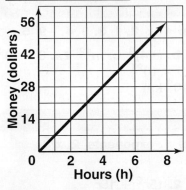

3.

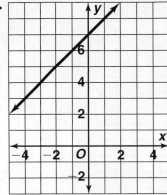

4.

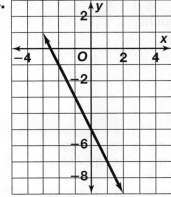

5.

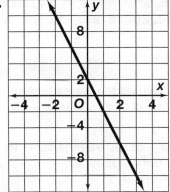

Lesson 11-6   pp. 540–541

Check Skills You'll Need **1.** $y = mx + b$, where m is the slope and b is the y-intercept **2.** 3; −2 **3.** 1; 5 **4.** 8; 0

Quick Check **1.** $y = 298 − 42x$ **2.** no
3. $y − 1 = -\frac{4}{5}(x + 2)$

Lesson 11-7   pp. 546–547

Check Skills You'll Need **1.** The rate of change is constant.

2.

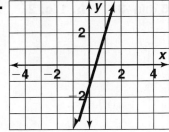

Quick Check **1.**

x	−2	−1	0	1	2
y	3	−3	−5	−3	3

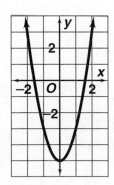

2.

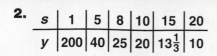

s	1	5	8	10	15	20
y	200	40	25	20	$13\frac{1}{3}$	10

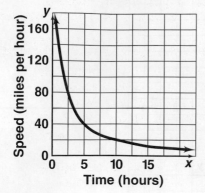

3. $y = x^2 - 2$

Chapter 12

Check Your Readiness   p. 558

1. $22d - 4$ **2.** $-7v + 73$ **3.** $65w - 49$
4. $43f - 23g + 3$ **5.** $36r + 34$ **6.** $-8t + x - 6$
7. $4a - 7$ **8.** $-9b + 21$ **9.** $36f - 88$
10. $-12x - 45$ **11.** $20.44 - 5.7c$ **12.** $5y - 5$
13. 7^5 **14.** $5^2 \cdot c^2$ **15.** a^2b^3 **16.** x^3y^2 **17.** $(3x)^3$
18. $c \cdot d^2 \cdot g^2$ **19.** 16 **20.** 16 **21.** -16 **22.** 32
23. 100 **24.** 1,000

Lesson 12-1   pp. 561–562

Check Skills You'll Need **1.** Yes; all the terms include the same variable, x. **2.** $-2 - t$ **3.** $12w - 10$
4. $35k - 5$

Quick Check **1a.** $x^2 - 2x + 2$ **b.** $-2x^2 + 2x - 3$
2a. $-2x^2 - x + 6$ **b.** $6x^2 - 3x + 2$
3a. $2g^2 + 2g$ **b.** $2y - 5y^2 + 7$

Lesson 12-2   pp. 566–567

Check Skills You'll Need **1.** 1 **2.** $2y^2 - 2y$ **3.** $6x^2 - 1$
4. $8z - 5z^2$

Quick Check **1a.** $5c^2 + 2c + 2$ **b.** $3x^2 + 3x - 7$
2a. $10c + 24$ **b.** $10m - 2$ **3.** $-2y^2 - 2$

Checkpoint Quiz 1 p. 570 **1.** $-x - 2$ **2.** $x^2 + 2x + 2$
3. $x^2 + 2x$ **4.** $5x^2 - 8x + 4$ **5.** $16x^2 - 10x$
6. $2a - 10$ **7.** $26b^2 - b - 7$ **8.** $2c^2 - c + 5$
9. $6d^2 - 29d - 17$ **10.** $16x + 6$ **11.** $22x - 10$

Lesson 12-3   pp. 571–572

Check Skills You'll Need **1.** x **2.** 1 **3.** 9 **4.** -9 **5.** -1

Quick Check **1a.** 6^5 **b.** $(-4)^8$ **c.** m^{12} **2a.** 8×10^9
b. 6×10^{13} **c.** 9.6×10^{21}
3. about 1.08×10^9 km

Lesson 12-4   pp. 576–577

Check Skills You'll Need **1.** exponents **2.** x^{15}
3. $(-a)^{10}$ or a^{10}

Quick Check **1.** $8y^4$ **2.** $15r^2 + 15r$
3a. $2x^2 + 7x + 6$ **b.** $6x^2 + 11x + 4$
c. $2x^2 + 7x + 5$

Checkpoint Quiz 2 p. 580 **1.** 4.7^{21} **2.** $(-4a)^4$ **3.** x^4y^{12}
4. 3.0×10^5 **5.** 1.5×10^{12} **6.** 3.6×10^7 **7.** $28f^8$
8. $15.5g^8$ **9.** $-17.6h^{18}$ **10.** $-5j^3 + 45j^2$
11. $6k^2 - 6k$ **12.** $30m^3 - 40m^2$
13. $8x^2 + 14x + 3$ **14.** $2x^2 + 8x + 6$

Lesson 12-5   pp. 581–583

Check Skills You'll Need **1.** power **2.** 7^4 **3.** 4^3 **4.** 5^2
5. 1^5

Quick Check **1.** w^3 **2.** 8.5 min **3a.** 1 **b.** 1 **c.** 2
4a. $\frac{1}{3}$ **b.** $\frac{1}{w^4}$ **c.** $-\frac{1}{8}$

Selected Answers

Chapter 1

Lesson 1-1
pp. 7–8

EXERCISES **1.** Answers may vary. Sample: An algebraic expression may use variables. A numerical expression does not. **3.** C **5.** A **7.** $7w$ **9.** 3, 5, 8 **13.** 3 **19.** $37b + 205$ **21.** 46.82 **25.** B **31.** 18.89

Lesson 1-2
pp. 12–13

EXERCISES **1.** Answers may vary. Sample: Integers include whole numbers and their opposites. **3.** A **5.** B **7.** 26 **11.** −16, −13, −6, −4, 2, 7, 11 **15.** 48 **21.** $5|-x|$ **23.** Yes; the record in Kansas is −40°C, which is colder than −38°C. **25.** < **27.** < **31.** for all non-positive values of x

Lesson 1-3
pp. 18–19

EXERCISES **1.** 0; 0 + 0 = 0 **3.** negative **5.** 8 **7.** −2 **9.** 1 **11.** −8 **13.** −1 **31.** sometimes; 2 − (−2) = 4 and −2 − 2 = −4 **35.** all integers greater than 1 or less than −3 **39.** <

Lesson 1-4
pp. 22–23

EXERCISES **1.** three **3.** < **5.** > **7.** −35 **9.** 4 **11.** 160 **13.** 36 **23.** −35 **25.** 2 **31.** −25 points **35.** 300 **37.** negative **41a.** −40,230 **b.** Answers may vary. Sample: 8 mi **47.** −6

Lesson 1-5
pp. 29–30

EXERCISES **1.** 1 **3.** Comm. Prop. of Mult. **5.** Comm. Prop. of Add. **7.** Ident. Prop. of Mult. **9.** −17 **11.** $(27 + 73)2$ **13.** 132 **15.** −54 **21.** $5a + 30$ **23.** $-4t - 12$ **35.** Answers may vary. Sample: mental math; $4(5.98) = 4(6 - 0.02) = 24 - 0.08 = 23.92$ **37.** 23,200 **41.** No; 20 lb is 320 oz. Two dozen cans weigh 360 oz. **45.** 36

Lesson 1-6
pp. 35–36

EXERCISES **1.** Answers may vary. Sample: An equation has an equal sign, but an expression does not. **3.** $y - 4 = 8$ **5.** yes **7.** no **9.** yes **11.** 54 **13.** 0 **31.** −3, 3 **35.** 13 lb **37.** 5.55 **45.** −21

Lesson 1-7
pp. 40–41

EXERCISES **1.** A value is a solution if it makes the equation true. **3.** Add. Prop. of Eq. **5.** Subtr.

Prop. of Eq. **7.** yes **9.** yes **11.** no **13.** −5 **15.** 572 **35.** $5.34 **37.** 7 **41.** 360 tickets **47.** 8.4

Chapter Review
pp. 44–45

1. simplify **2.** absolute value **3.** Distributive Property **4.** solution **5.** inverse operations **6.** variable **7.** integers **8.** equation **9.** 6 **10.** −15.5 **11.** −5.6 **12.** $27 + g$ **13.** $\frac{y}{4}$ **14.** $500r$ **15.** < **16.** < **17.** > **18.** = **19.** North America **20.** −12 **21.** −6 **22.** 17 **23.** −40 **24.** −7 **25.** −13 **26.** $263 **27.** −16,800 **28.** 1,094 **29.** −1,800 **30.** $3p - 21$ **31.** $8m + 32$ **32.** $10 + 5k$ **33.** 30 **34.** 3 **35.** 11 **36.** 7 **37.** 48 **38.** 2

Chapter 2

Lesson 2-1
pp. 54–56

EXERCISES **1.** GCF **3.** No; the ones digit is not 0, 2, 4, 6, or 8. **5.** Yes; the sum of the digits is 6, which is divisible by 3. **7.** composite; $2 \cdot 2 \cdot 2 \cdot 2 \cdot 3$ **9.** prime **15.** $2 \cdot 2 \cdot 5$ **17.** $2 \cdot 2 \cdot 2 \cdot 2$ **23.** 6 **25.** 6 **31.** 7 **33.** 15 **45.** 9 **47.** Answers may vary. Samples are given. 7 + 53; 13 + 47; 17 + 43; 19 + 41; 23 + 37; 29 + 31 **49.** It is also divisible by 2. **51.** 7, 17, and 19 are prime. **57.** −210

Lesson 2-2
pp. 59–60

EXERCISES **1.** $\frac{123}{1}$ **3.** D **5.** A **7.** $\frac{3}{4}$ **9.** $-\frac{2}{3}$ **15.** 0.667 **17.** 1.063 **25.** $\frac{33}{100}$ **27.** $4\frac{11}{25}$ **35.** $-\frac{2}{5}$ **43.** 9

Lesson 2-3
pp. 64–65

EXERCISES **1.** The LCM is the smallest number that is a multiple of both numbers. **3.** $\frac{2}{9}$ **5.** $\frac{4}{5}$ **7.** $\frac{4}{25}$ **9.** $-\frac{5}{14}$ **17.** $\frac{19}{11}$ **21.** 0.03, $\frac{3}{10}$, 0.33, $\frac{1}{3}$ **27.** = **31.** your friend **33.** Maria **39.** $48 - 8b$

Lesson 2-4
pp. 68–69

EXERCISES **1.** 10 **3.** 28 **5.** $\frac{1}{2}$ **7.** Positive; $51 > 50$, so $\frac{1}{51} < \frac{1}{50}$, and $\frac{1}{50} - \frac{1}{51}$ is positive. **9.** $1\frac{3}{40}$ **11.** $1\frac{1}{15}$ **21.** $3\frac{1}{6}$ **23.** $-6\frac{3}{8}$ **31.** $2\frac{1}{2}$ **33.** $-\frac{1}{8}$ **37.** $\frac{8}{21}$ **39.** Answers may vary. Sample: $\frac{1}{2} + \frac{1}{3} = \frac{5}{6}$; $\frac{1}{2 + 3} = \frac{1}{5}$ **41.** $a - \frac{2}{3}$ **45.** $\frac{1}{125}$, 0.8, 0.808, $\frac{22}{25}$

Lesson 2-5 — pp. 74–76

EXERCISES 1. multiplicative inverse **3.** 1 **5.** −5
7. $-\frac{3}{5}$ **9.** $-\frac{5}{24}$ **15.** $-\frac{2}{3}$ **17.** 17 **27.** $\frac{3}{5}$ **29.** $-3\frac{3}{4}$
35. 6 **39.** Dividing by a fraction is the same as
multiplying by its reciprocal. The reciprocal of a
number less than 1 is a number greater than 1, so
the answer will be greater. **41.** $10\frac{5}{8}$ yd **47.** 7

Lesson 2-6 — pp. 83–84

EXERCISES 1. ℓ is the length; w is the width.
3. $\frac{7}{8}$ cm² **5.** Area of a trapezoid; h is the height;
b_1 and b_2 are the bases. **7.** Perimeter of a
square; s is the side length. **9.** 24 m² **15.** $t = \frac{d}{r}$
17. $C = K - 273$ **21.** 24 mi/h **23.** $\frac{9}{\pi}$ ft
25a. 2,220 ft **b.** The difference between the dew
point and air temperature will grow larger, and the
height of the base of the cloud will increase.
Examples: H = 222(80 − 70) = 2,220 ft
H = 222(80 − 60) = 4,440 ft **31.** 17

Lesson 2-7 — pp. 88–89

EXERCISES 1. C **3.** B **5.** $9^3 \cdot x$ **7.** z^6 **9.** 64
11. $4^2 \cdot 8^4$ **13.** $5^2 \cdot x^3 \cdot y$ **17.** −32 **19.** −216
33. −360 **37.** 112 ft **41.** yes; when $a = 0$ or
$b = 0$, and when $a = 1$ **47.** $6\frac{9}{25}$

Lesson 2-8 — pp. 94–95

EXERCISES 1. 1 **3.** greater than 0, because the
number remains positive even though the decimal
point moves 5 places to the left **5.** 3,200
11. 1.72×10^4 **15.** 0.0025 **21.** 1.05×10^{-3}
23. 2.7×10^{-5} **27.** 8 **31.** 3.92×10^8
33. 1.5×10^6 km **35a.** 2,750,000 calories
b. 2.75×10^6 calories **37.** 9×10^{28} **41.** −135

Chapter Review — pp. 98–99

1. scientific notation **2.** reciprocals or
multiplicative inverses **3.** LCM **4.** prime
factorization **5.** power **6.** formula **7.** relatively
prime **8.** terminating decimal **9.** GCF
10. exponent; base **11.** $2^2 \cdot 5 \cdot 13$
12. $2^2 \cdot 5^2 \cdot 7$ **13.** $2 \cdot 3^3 \cdot 7$ **14.** $1 \cdot 139$
15. $2^2 \cdot 3^3 \cdot 5 \cdot 13$ **16.** $\frac{4}{25}$ **17.** < **18.** > **19.** =
20. $-\frac{1}{8}$ **21.** $-1\frac{1}{2}$ **22.** $-\frac{2}{3}$ **23.** $\frac{1}{16}$ **24.** $3\frac{1}{4}$
25. $-2\frac{1}{10}$ **26.** 3 **27.** 45 mi/h **28.** $b = \frac{2A}{h}$
29. $b = y - mx$ **30.** $r = \frac{d}{t}$ **31.** 61 **32.** 54 **33.**
24 **34.** 3.5×10^3 **35.** 8.01×10^5 **36.**
2.05×10^{-4} **37.** 8.1×10^{-8} **38.** 380,000,000

Chapter 3

Lesson 3-1 — pp. 108–110

EXERCISES 1. irrational, real **3.** rational, real
5. 2, −2 **7.** 10, −10 **9.** 7, −7 **11.** $\frac{1}{6}$, $-\frac{1}{6}$ **15.** 3 **17.** 9
23. 342 m/s **27.** Irrational; 40 is not a perfect
square. **29.** Rational; 144 is a perfect square.
33. 88 ft **35.** Answers may vary. Sample: $\sqrt{3}$; 3 is
not a perfect square. **37a.** Yes; the sum of even
numbers is an even number. **b.** Yes; the sum of
two irrational numbers is an irrational number.
c. No; the sum of two prime numbers can be a
composite number. **39.** 10 **43.** 4 **47.** 26.1 mi
49. The student took the square root of 4 and
added it to the square root of 9. You must add
4 + 9 first and then take the square root.
55. 6.038×10^6

Lesson 3-2 — pp. 114–115

EXERCISES 1. The hypotenuse is the longest
side. **3.** 17 cm **5.** 7.1 cm **7.** 5 **15a.** 27 in.
b. Answers may vary. Sample: 20 in. by 18 in.
17. 2.8 cm **19.** 17.0 m
23. yes; $3^2 + (3 + 1)^2 \stackrel{?}{=} (3 + 2)^2$ **29.** 102,000
$$3^2 + 4^2 \stackrel{?}{=} 5^2$$
$$9 + 16 \stackrel{?}{=} 25$$
$$25 = 25$$

Lesson 3-3 — pp. 120–121

EXERCISES 1. $\overline{PR}$ and $\overline{RQ}$; $\overline{PQ}$ **3.** 16 in. **5.** 6.7 ft
13. 8.7 ft **15.** 6 **17.** 19.8 **19.** The student added
3^2 to 4^2 instead of subtracting it from 4^2. You must
find $\sqrt{4^2 - 3^2}$. **21.** no; $(a + b)^2 \neq a^2 + b^2$
25. >

Lesson 3-4 — pp. 126–127

EXERCISES 1. B **3.** D **5.** (−4, 3) **7.** (−3, 0)
9. (0, −1) **19.** C
25a.

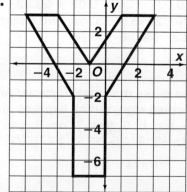

b. the letter Y **27.** 93° W, 45° N; 97° W, 41° N
29. Quadrant I

31.

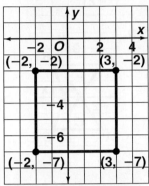

The square is reflected over the *x*-axis. **35.** 7.1

Lesson 3-5   pp. 132–134

EXERCISES 1. C **3.** $g = 0.75t$

11.

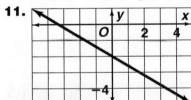

15. 6 letters;

Number of Letters	Expression	Total Cost (dollars)
0	1.50(0) + 10	10.00
1	1.50(1) + 10	11.50
2	1.50(2) + 10	13.00
3	1.50(3) + 10	14.50
ℓ	1.50(ℓ) + 10	c

$c = 1.50\ell + 10$ **17.** Gina; the graph drawn by Gina's father shows the amount owed after Gina gives him $40 each week, not $20. **23.** 25

Lesson 3-6   pp. 137–139

EXERCISES 1. transformation **3.**

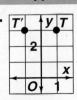

5.

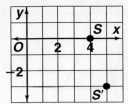

7.

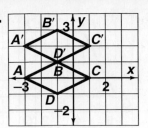

11. $(x, y) \rightarrow (x + 4, y + 3)$ **17.** C
19. Answers may vary. Sample:

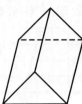

25.

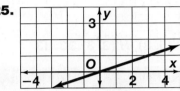

Lesson 3-7   pp. 143–144

EXERCISES 1. Line *a* is a line of symmetry if one half of the figure matches the other half exactly when the figure is reflected over line *a*. **3.** G
5. G **7.** F

15.

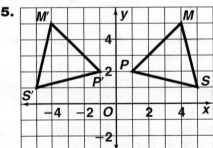

$M'(-4, 5)$, $P'(-1, 2)$, $S'(-5, 1)$

17.

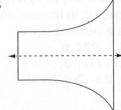

23.

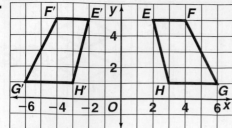

$E'(-2, 5), F'(-4, 5), G'(-6, 1), H'(-3, 1)$

25.

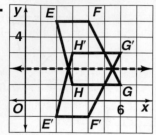

$E'(2, -1), F'(4, -1), G'(6, 3), H'(3, 3)$ **33.** 13

Lesson 3-8   pp. 148–149

EXERCISES 1. 180 **5.** yes; 45°

9.

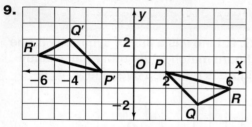

13. A complete rotation has 360°. A square can be rotated 360° ÷ 4 or 90°.

Chapter Review   pp. 152–153

1. *y*-axis; origin; quadrants **2.** translations; reflections; rotations **3.** angle of rotation; rotational symmetry **4.** perfect square
5. hypotenuse **6.** 2.6 ft **7.** 8.9 ft **8.** 13.8 ft
9. Rational; 196 is a perfect square. **10.** Rational; $\frac{25}{36}$ is a perfect square. **11.** Irrational; 57 is not a perfect square. **12.** Irrational; 1.6 is not a perfect square. **13.** Rational; 225 is a perfect square.
14. 10 **15.** 13.4 **16.** 46.6 **17.** 23.2 ft
18. (−3, −2) **19.** (−2, 3) **20.** (1, −3)
21. Quadrant IV **22.** *y*-axis **23.** Quadrant II
24.

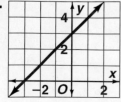

25.

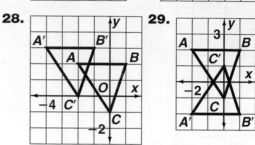

26. **27.**

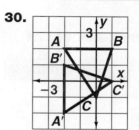

28. **29.**

30.

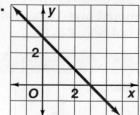

Chapter 4

Lesson 4-1   pp. 162–163

EXERCISES 1. A rate is a ratio that compares quantities measured in different units. The quantities 6 and 23 have the same unit: students.
3. 3 : 4 **5.** $\frac{2}{1}$ **7.** $\frac{2}{3}$ **9.** $\frac{7}{30}$ **11.** $\frac{11}{18}$ **15.** $14/book
17. $1.80/rose **23.** −0.007°C/m **25.** $\frac{21}{83}$
27. 56 mi/h **35.** $\frac{1}{25}$

Lesson 4-2   pp. 169–170

EXERCISES 1. $\frac{12 \text{ in.}}{1 \text{ ft}}$ **3.** A **5.** B **7.** 2.7 **11.** 0.45
15. 12 **19.** 9.8 **21.** 24.8 **27.** 190,080 **29.** 82.4°F
31. 0°C **33.** swimming **35.** dancing **39.** 3 ft 3 in.
43.

Lesson 4-3 — pp. 176–178

EXERCISES 1. cross products **3.** yes; $\frac{6}{27} = \frac{2}{9}$
5. no; $\frac{1}{4} \neq \frac{2}{10}$ **7.** yes; $\frac{7}{6} = \frac{28}{24}$ **13.** 45 **15.** 3
23. 48,387 yen **25.** 22,581 yen **27.** $\frac{x+3}{2} = \frac{5}{4}$;
Write the cross products: $(x + 3)4 = 5 \cdot 2$.
Multiply: $4x + 12 = 10$. Subtract 12 from each
side: $4x = -2$. Divide each side by 4: $\frac{4x}{4} = \frac{-2}{4}$.
Simplify: $x = -\frac{1}{2}$. **29.** h and 25 are reversed.
31. about 3 grams; methods may vary.
33. Answers may vary. Sample: 2 **35.** about $85
37. 15 **45.** −19

Lesson 4-4 — pp. 183–184

EXERCISES 1. No; similar figures must have the
same shape. **3.** D **5.** Yes; the angles are all
congruent and the sides are proportional. **7.** 5
11. 48 **13.** $x = 8, y = 14.4$ **15.** about 19 inches
17. D **19.** They are the same. **23.** =

Lesson 4-5 — pp. 189–190

EXERCISES 1. Reduction; the dilation has a scale
factor less than 1. **3.** 3
5.

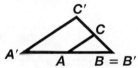

7. $A'(1, 0), B'(1, 1), C'(2.5, 1),$
$D'(2.5, 0)$

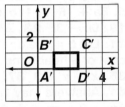

9. $\frac{1}{2}$; reduction
13.

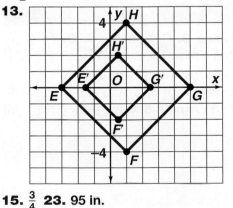

15. $\frac{3}{4}$ **23.** 95 in.

Lesson 4-6 — pp. 193–195

EXERCISES 1. The scale is the ratio of map
distance to actual distance. **3.** 1 : 2; the model is
half as large as the object, compared to a third
as large. **5.** 2.3; 5.75 ft **7.** 15 in.; 3 in. **11.** 25 mi
15. 21.5 in. **19.** 300 mi **23.** 2.5 ft **31.** 21

Lesson 4-7 — pp. 198–200

EXERCISES 1. indirect **3.** indirect **5.** 8 **7.** 8 m
9. 360 m **11.** 1,269.7 m **13.** 27.1 ft **17.** 34 ft
19. about 617 ft **21.** Answers may vary. Sample:
Stand where you can see the basketball hoop in
the mirror. **25.** 0.05

Chapter Review — pp. 202–203

1. unit rate **2.** proportion **3.** scale factor
4. indirect measurement **5.** reduction
6. conversion factor **7.** $\frac{1}{8}$ **8.** $3\frac{1}{3}$ **9.** $\frac{1}{3}$ **10.** $28/h
11. 59 mi/h **12.** 6.25 km/L **13.** Neither, the unit
rate for each container is about $.07.
14. 3,300 cm/h **15.** 256 oz/ft **16.** $16\frac{2}{3}$ mL/s
17. 380,160 ft/day **18.** 50 cm/min **19.** $18/h
20. 16 **21.** 1 **22.** 12 **23.** 72 **24.** 810 euros
25. 10 cm **26.** 7.5 cm **27.** 4.5 cm **28.** 4;
enlargement **29.** 43.4 mi **30.** 66.5 mi **31.** 32.7 mi
32. 57.4 mi **33.** $2\frac{1}{4}$ in. by $1\frac{3}{4}$ in. **34.** 14.4
35. 13.6 **36.** 11 ft 9 in.

Chapter 5

Lesson 5-1 — pp. 212–213

EXERCISES 1. 100 **3.** B **5.** A **7.** 40%
9. 96% **13.** 0.3% **15.** 90% **17.** $\frac{21}{20}$ **19.** $\frac{2}{9}$
23. 0.09%, 0.01, 1.01%, $\frac{1}{99}$ **27.** $\frac{5}{6}$, $0.8\overline{3}$, $83\frac{1}{3}$%
29. $\frac{3}{4}$, $\frac{29}{50}$ **31.** 84% **37.** 3

Lesson 5-2 — pp. 216–217

EXERCISES 1. B **3.** C **5.** Answers may vary.
Sample: $0.25 \times 200 = 50$ **7.** about 36 **9.** about
250 **13.** about 90 **17.** about $1.80 **19.** about
$4.50 **25.** about $23 **27.** about $22.40 **29.** >
31. > **33.** about 121,000,000 Americans
35. about 240 Calories
39. $(x, y) \to (x + 4, y + 5)$

Lesson 5-3 — pp. 220–222

EXERCISES 1.

0   1   1.25   **3.** C

0%   80% 100%

5. 57.6 **7.** 33 **19.** 5 **21.** 950 **25.** 64% **27.** 4%

33. Answers may vary. Sample: A "whole" is an arbitrary number, and you can have a "part" that is more than that arbitrary number. **37.** 76,198.76 **39.** 6 **41.** 1,095.12 **43.** No; for example, if the two numbers are 100 and 200, then (40% of 100) + (30% of 200) = 40 + 60 = 100, but 70% of 300 = 210. **45.** 10,000% **49.** 1 cm : 250 cm

Lesson 5-4　　　　　　　　　　　pp. 226–227

EXERCISES **1.** 24 **3.** 1.4 **5.** 6% **9.** 70 **11.** 445 **17.** $2,650,000 **19.** $946.65 **21.** $943.95 **23.** 15,996,000 people **25.** 0.75(0.8x)(1.065) **29.** $\frac{15}{12}$

Lesson 5-5　　　　　　　　　　　pp. 232–233

EXERCISES **1.** original **3.** 25% increase **5.** 200% increase **7.** 130% **9.** 40% **13.** 3.4% **17.** 33.3% **19.** 26.4% **25.** 75% decrease **27.** 75% decrease **29.** 86.7% decrease **37.** 24

Lesson 5-6　　　　　　　　　　　pp. 237–238

EXERCISES **1.** C **3.** B **5.** 50% **9.** $188.99 **13.** $73.15 **15.** $189.43 **19.** $119.98 **21.** No difference; the final cost is $192.50 either way. **29.** 187.2

Lesson 5-7　　　　　　　　　　　pp. 243–244

EXERCISES **1.** C **3.** A **5.** $82.45 **7.** $1,312.50 **9.** $856 **13.** The account that pays 1.3% simple interest, because 747(1 + 0.013) = $756.71 and 747(1 + 0.02) − 12 = $749.94. **19.** 102.6 ft^2

Lesson 5-8　　　　　　　　　　　pp. 248–250

EXERCISES **1.** Answers may vary. Sample: An outcome is any of the possible results that can occur. An event is the collection of possible outcomes in an experiment. An outcome can be an event if there is only one possible result of the experiment. **3.** $\frac{1}{3}$ **5.** $\frac{1}{6}$ **7.** $\frac{1}{8}$ **9.** $\frac{3}{8}$ **13.** 10% **15.** $\frac{3}{16}$ **17.** $\frac{1}{4}$

21.

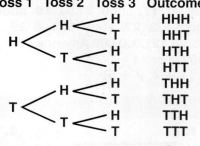

Toss 1	Toss 2	Toss 3	Outcome
		H	HHH
	H	T	HHT
H		H	HTH
	T	T	HTT
		H	THH
	H	T	THT
T		H	TTH
	T	T	TTT

23. $\frac{3}{8}$ **27.** $\frac{1}{5}$ **29.** $\frac{1}{5}$ or 20% **31.** $\frac{2}{9}$ or 22.2% **33.** $\frac{1}{12}$ **37.** 30 lb : 1 lb

Chapter Review　　　　　　　　pp. 252–253

1. markup **2.** principal **3.** outcome **4.** discount **5.** simple interest **6.** 87.5% **7.** 108.33% **8.** 31.25% **9.** 450% **10.** $\frac{9}{25}$ **11.** $\frac{1}{3}$ **12.** $1\frac{6}{25}$ **13.** $\frac{27}{100}$ **14–16.** Answers may vary. Samples are given. **14.** about 25 **15.** about $5.25 **16.** about 63 **17.** about 3 students **18.** 200 **19.** 40% **20.** 18 **21.** 150 **22.** 160 students **23.** 30.8% decrease **24.** 4,300% increase **25.** 0.6% increase **26.** 83.3% decrease **27.** $199.99 **28.** $574.75 **29.** $809.40 **30.** $4,725 **31.** $\frac{5}{9}$

Chapter 6

Lesson 6-1　　　　　　　　　　　pp. 262–264

EXERCISES **1.** 3x − 2 = 7 **3.** Answers may vary. Sample: Add 8 to each side. **5.** Answers may vary. Sample: Add 12 to each side. **7.** about 56 **9.** −4 **11.** 4 **17.** 4x + 5 = 68.96; $15.99 **21.** 11 mg **23.** 7b + 3 = 24; Subtr. Prop. of Eq.: 7b + 3 − 3 = 24 − 3; Div. Prop. of Eq.: $\frac{7b}{7} = \frac{21}{7}$; b = 3 **25.** 12.6 **27.** −6 **31.** x = 7; It is the same. You could avoid working with decimals. **35.** 22.8 m

Lesson 6-2　　　　　　　　　　　pp. 268–269

EXERCISES **1.** No; the variable factors $x^2y^5z^{11}$ and $x^2z^5y^{11}$ are different. **3.** 4x + 7y − 6 **5.** 8a + 15 **7.** 11b **9.** 31x **17.** 5x + 1 **19.** 9n − 3r **23.** 23 − 5a **25.** −27m − 16 **31.** Let b = the cost of a barrette. Let h = the cost of a headband. 5b + 3h **33.** 3x − 2y **35.** x + y + 9 **37.** 31.66y + 8.4 **39.** 12x **41.** Answers may vary. Sample: 2m + m + 8; 4m + 2 − m + 6 **43.** 0.5t − 29v **47.** 20

Lesson 6-3　　　　　　　　　　　pp. 273–275

EXERCISES **1.** like **3.** C **5.** B **7.** −2 **9.** 7 **23.** n + n + 1 = −45; −23 and −22 **25.** n + (n + 1) + (n + 2) = −255; −86, −85, −84 **27.** −1 **29.** 10 **31.** 4m + 5 = 21; m = 4 ft **39.** −75

Lesson 6-4
pp. 277–278

EXERCISES 1. all of them **3.** 11 a and a, $-4.1a^2$ and a^2 **5.** The student added x to the left side but subtracted x from the right side.

$$3x + 4 - x = 7 + x$$
$$2x + 4 = 7 + x$$
$$2x - x + 4 = 7 + x - x$$
$$x + 4 = 7$$
$$x + 4 - 4 = 7 - 4$$
$$x = 3$$

7. -2 **9.** 21 **17.** at about 9:57 A.M. **19.** 0.15 **23.** 3

Lesson 6-5
pp. 284–285

EXERCISES 1. An equation states that two expressions are equal; an inequality compares two expressions that are not usually equal. **3.** $0.6 \le x$ **5.** $y - 4 < 0$ **7.** $x \ge 65$

9. $m < -2$

11. $7 \le n$

25. $x \le 0$ **27.** $>$ **29.** 6 **31.** 5 **37.** $\frac{5}{12}$

Lesson 6-6
pp. 291–292

EXERCISES 1. When you multiply or divide each side of an inequality by a positive number, the relationship between the two sides does not change. When you multiply or divide by a negative number, the direction of the inequality sign reverses. **3.** $d > 12$ **5.** $y > 0$ **7.** $c < 2$ **11.** $4.89s \le 23.50$; 4 specials

13. $r \ge -6$

15. $z \ge 96$

25. a and b must have opposite signs. **27.** a can be positive or negative, but b must be positive. **29.** 4 teachers **31.** No; it is only true if b is positive. If $b = 0$, the problem is undefined. If b is negative, the inequality sign needs to change.

35. $y \le 26$

Chapter Review
pp. 294–295

1. like terms **2.** inequality **3.** term **4.** Mult. Prop. of Ineq. **5.** Add. Prop. of Ineq. **6.** 12 **7.** $-\frac{11}{3}$ **8.** -15 **9.** -9 **10.** $-\frac{5}{6}$ **11.** 40 **12.** 15 cans **13.** 3 shirts **14.** $7 - 3f$ **15.** $3a + 11$ **16.** $11x - 12$ **17.** -4 **18.** 5 **19.** $\frac{16}{5}$ or 3.2

20. -5 **21.** 2.5 lb **22.** $g > 19$

23. $u \le 2$

24. $t \ge -11$

25. $c < 75$ **26.** $x \ge 150$

27. $x < -3$

28. $y \le -2$

29. $a < 7$

30. $w \le 128$

31. $c < -20$

32. $z > 12$

Chapter 7

Lesson 7-1
pp. 305–306

EXERCISES 1. No; they do not share a common side. **3.** No; they do not share a common vertex. **5.** Answers may vary. Sample: $\angle MRQ$ and $\angle NRP$; $\angle NRP$ and $\angle QRP$; 80° **9.** 156° **13.** $m\angle 1 = 152°$; $m\angle 2 = 28°$; $m\angle 3 = 62°$; $m\angle 4 = 90°$ **17.** 58°; 148° **19.** 4.1°; 94.1° **23.** No; they are adjacent. **25.** Answers may vary. Sample: $\angle 5$ and $\angle 7$ **29.** $\angle KBL$ **31.** 76°

Lesson 7-2
pp. 309–310

EXERCISES 1. Answers may vary. Sample: $\angle 2$ and $\angle 4$ **3.** $\overleftrightarrow{UV}$ **5.** False; corresponding angles lie on the same side of a transversal, but alternate interior angles do not. **7.** corresponding **9.** alternate interior **15.** 122° **17.** 122° **21.** Alternate interior angles are congruent. **25.** No parallel lines; alternate interior angles are not congruent.

29. $m\angle 1 = 70°$; $m\angle 2 = 70°$; $m\angle 3 = 110°$; $m\angle 4 = 110°$

31a. $m\angle 1 = 80°$; $m\angle 2 = 40°$; $m\angle 3 = 60°$ **b.** 180° **37.** 31.98

Lesson 7-3   pp. 314–316

EXERCISES 1. size and shape **3.** SAS
5. $\overline{EH} \cong \overline{GF}$; $\angle EHF \cong \angle GFH$; $\overline{FH} \cong \overline{FH}$;
$\angle FEH \cong \angle HGF$; $\overline{EF} \cong \overline{GH}$; $\angle EFH \cong \angle GHF$
7. $PALK \cong PSNK$ **9.** SAS **11.** 104°
13. 0.9 cm **21.** congruent; SAS using vertical
angles **23.** no; $\triangle ABC \ne \triangle DEF$

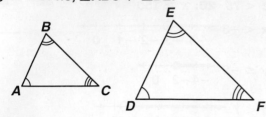

25.

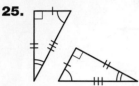

27. 0.09 km **33.** 0.0372

Lesson 7-4   pp. 320–321

EXERCISES 1. C **3.** D **5.** B **9.** isosceles obtuse
11. parallelogram **17.** Answers may vary.
Sample:

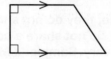

23. If a quadrilateral has two pairs of opposite
sides that are parallel, then it is a parallelogram;
true. **25.** If a triangle is isosceles, then it is
equilateral; not true. **31.** 63.6% increase

Lesson 7-5   pp. 326–327

EXERCISES 1. A regular polygon is a polygon
with all sides congruent and all angles congruent.
3. heptagon **5.** octagon **7.** 540° **9.** 720°
13. 83° **17.** 128.6° **19.** 154.3° **23.** square
25. $a = 105°$; $b = 106°$ **29.** 135° **35.** 132°

Lesson 7-6   pp. 331–332

EXERCISES 1. C **3.** triangle **5.** 50 cm² **7.** 96 m²
9. 84 m² **13.** Each area is 135 ft²; 120 ft².
15. 34 m² **19.** Answers may vary. Sample: about
81,000 km² **21.** 1 : 2 **25.** 1,080°

Lesson 7-7   pp. 338–339

EXERCISES 1. circumference

3. $C = \pi d = \pi(2r) = 2\pi r$
5. 44 km **7.** 88 in. **9.** 15.7 cm; 19.6 cm²

11. 28.9 in.; 66.5 in.² **17.** 22.3 ft² **19.** 1,253.4 ft²
27. 0.27 in.; 0.54 in. **31.** 40.8 in.² **33.** 12 ft
39. $9.60

Lesson 7-8   pp. 342–343

EXERCISES 1. circles and arcs **3.** Place the
compass tip at *A* and draw an arc that intersects
the sides of $\angle A$. Label the points of intersection *C*
and *D*.
5.   **7.**

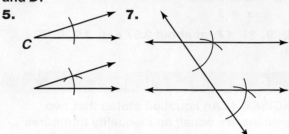

17. $\frac{4}{13}$

Chapter Review   pp. 346–347

1. transversal **2.** scalene **3.** supplementary
4. rhombus **5.** regular polygon **6.** 35°; 55°
7. 48°; 132° **8.** isosceles, acute **9.** scalene,
obtuse **10.** equilateral, acute
11. $\triangle CDE \cong \triangle HGF$; SAS
12. $\triangle JLK \cong \triangle OMN$; SSS **13.** 120° **14.** 135°
15. 150° **16.** 160° **17.** 540 ft² **18.** 24 cm²
19. 124.7 cm²
20.   **21.**

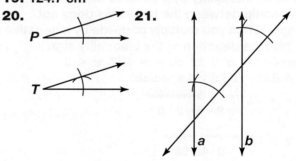

Chapter 8

Lesson 8-1   pp. 356–357

EXERCISES 1. Parallel lines lie in the same plane;
skew lines do not. **3.** triangular **5.** cylinder
7. The base is a square. The figure is a square
pyramid. $\overline{PQ}$ is a lateral edge.
11. $\overline{DE}$ and $\overline{FH}$, $\overline{GD}$ and $\overline{EF}$ **15.** skew
19. triangular prism **25.** 24

Lesson 8-2   pp. 360–361

EXERCISES 1. isometric view **3.** rectangle

5.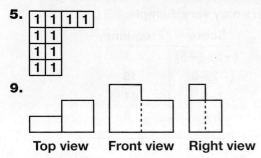

9.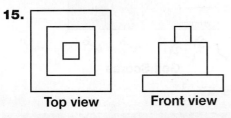

Top view   Front view   Right view

13.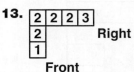

Right

Front

15.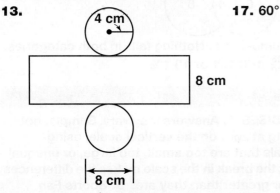

Top view   Front view

17. cone **19.** 6, 8; 6, 8, 10 **23.** 11.9 in.^{2}

Lesson 8-3   pp. 365–366

EXERCISES 1. A net is a two-dimensional pattern, whereas a prism is a three-dimensional solid. **3.** circles **5.** C **7.** cone

13. 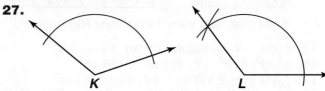   **17.** 60°

4 cm

8 cm

8 cm

Lesson 8-4   pp. 371–372

EXERCISES 1. The lateral area of a prism is the sum of the areas of the lateral faces. The surface area includes the lateral area plus the area of the two bases. **3.** 384 in.^{2} **5.** 2,304 in.^{2} **7.** 96 cm^2 **9.** 600 cm^2 **13.** 275 cm^2 **15.** The 9 cm-by-5.5 cm-by-11.75 cm box will require more cardboard because it has a greater surface area. **17a.** Treat the lighthouse as a cylinder. Multiply 3 × 30 × 150 to estimate the lateral area. L.A. ≈ 13,500 ft^2 **b.** about 20 gallons of black paint and 20 gallons of white paint

19. L.A. = 675 m^2
   S.A. = 1.045 m^2

21. None; the area of the three new surfaces of figure A is exactly the same as the area of three surfaces of cube B. **25.** 118°

Lesson 8-5   pp. 377–378

EXERCISES 1. Lateral area is less than surface area because it does not include the area of the square base. **3.** 14 **5.** S.A. = $56\pi + 16\pi = 72\pi$ **7.** 3.4 yd^2 **9.** L.A. = 3,000 in.^{2}; S.A. = 3,900 in.^{2} **13.** 104 m^2 **17a.** 856 ft **b.** 248,240 ft^2 **19.** 628 cm^2 **21.** yes, because it is equivalent to $\pi r^2 + \pi r \ell$ **23.** Answers may vary. Sample: 270 m^2; 268 m^2.

27.

K   L

Lesson 8-6   pp. 382–384

EXERCISES 1. Answers may vary. Sample: ft^3, in.^{3}, cm^3 **3.** B **5.** C **7.** 3,900 mm^3 **9.** 20 ft^3 **13.** 302 m^3 **17.** 589 ft^3 **19.** doubling the radius, since the radius is squared in calculating the volume **21.** 1,800 m^3 **25.** 539 ft^3 **29.** 35.3%

Lesson 8-7   pp. 390–391

EXERCISES 1. 15 m^3 **3.** B **5.** 72 in.^{3} **9.** 13 ft^3 **13.** 603 cm^3 **15.** no; because the radius is squared in the formula, and the height is not **17.** 1.67 ft

Lesson 8-8   pp. 395–396

EXERCISES 1. C **3.** B **5.** 12.6 m^2 **7.** 1,810 cm^2; 7,238 cm^3 **9.** 95 m^2; 87 m^3 **15.** about 1.5 in.^{2} **17.** She forgot to divide by 3. **19.** 5,027 mm^2; 33,510 mm^3 **21.** 5 cm^2; 1 cm^3 **23.** 83 in.^{2}; 64 in.^{3} **25.** about 3,397 km **29.** 14 in.^{3}

Lesson 8-9   pp. 400–401

EXERCISES 1. Two solids are similar if they have the same shape and all their corresponding lengths are proportional. **3.** 54 cm^2 **5.** 8.4 in. **7.** 1,008 m^2; 2,074 m^3 **11.** 5 m **13.** 1,274 ft^2; 2,382 ft^3 **17.** 10.1 cm **21.** 7.5 × 10^4

Chapter Review   pp. 404–405

1. volume **2.** cone **3.** lateral, surface **4.** cylinder, prism **5.** isometric view **6.** rectangle, parallelograms **7.** square, triangles **8.** circle, curved surface

9.

Base plan Top view Front view Right view

10.

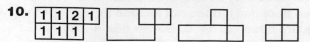

Base plan Top view Front view Right view

11.

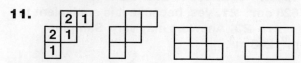

Base plan Top view Front view Right view

12. cone **13.** triangular prism **14.** cube
15. 24 m²; 6 m³ **16.** 196 cm²; 196 cm³
17. 1,014 in.²; 2,197 in.³ **18.** 90 m²; 48 m³
19. 258 cm²; 268 cm³ **20.** 190 ft²; 131 ft³
21. 5.3×10^8 km²; 1.15×10^{12} km³ **22.** 444 yd²;
651 yd³ **23.** 108 in.²; 74 in.³ **24.** 87 m²; 53 m³

Chapter 9

Lesson 9-1   pp. 414–416

EXERCISES 1. No; because none of the data
values are repeated, there is no mode. **3.** 12
5. −9, −8, −3, −2, 0, 1, 2, 6, 7, 11, 11, 15; median:
1.5; mode: 11 **7.** 1; 1; 0; 3 **9.** 8.7̄; 9; 9; 3 **13.** 10;
it raises the mean about 1.05. **19.** 8 **25.** 6, 7, 20
29. −300

Lesson 9-2   pp. 420–422

EXERCISES 1. A histogram is a bar graph
with no spaces between the bars. **3.** 27.4
5.

Hard-Drive Size

```
X     X
X     X     X X
X  X  X  X  X  X  X       X
+--+--+--+--+--+--+--+--+--+
8  10 12 14 16 18 20 22 24
```
Gigabytes

7. 0.7; 1; 0, 1, and 3 **11.** Answers may vary.
Sample: 50–59, 60–69, 70–79, 80–89, 90–99,
100–109
13.

Cars Sold Per Month

```
         X  X  X
   X  X X X X X X    X
+--+--+--+--+--+--+--+
20 22 24 26 28 30
```

26; 26; 24; 26 and 28

17. Answers may vary. Sample:

Score	Frequency
(−5)–(−3)	1
(−2)–0	15
1–3	11
4–6	5

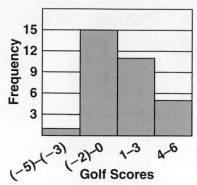

Golf Scores

21. the Bakers **27.** $\frac{1}{3}$

Lesson 9-3   pp. 425–426

EXERCISES 1. objects or people that fall into
both categories **3.** 60 students
5. red shapes triangles

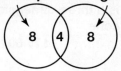

9. 1 number **11.** Nothing falls in both categories.
13. $\frac{105}{580}$ or 0.181 or 18.1%

Lesson 9-4   pp. 429–431

EXERCISES 1. Answers may vary. Sample: not
starting at zero on the vertical scale; using
intervals that are too small, too large, or unequal
3. No; the break in the scale makes the differences
appear greater than they are. **5.** *Sports Fan*
9.

Top Films

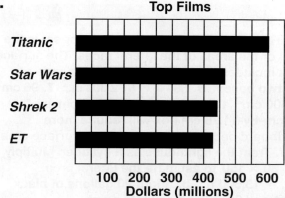

Dollars (millions)

Top Films

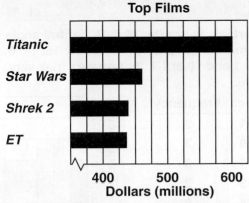

You can approximate the amounts better on the graph with the break, but the differences are exaggerated.

11.

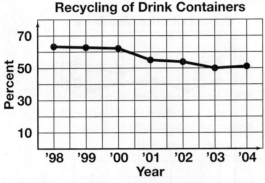

17a. 5; 10; 20; 40 **b.** No; the time differences are not the same, which is misleading. **c.** Yes; each interval is twice the size of the interval before it.
21. 615.8 in.^{2}

Lesson 9-5   **pp. 435–437**

EXERCISES 1. 6 is the stem; 7 is the leaf.
3. 8, 8 **5.** median: 84%, mode: 78%

7.

```
4 | 0  8  9
5 | 0  2  3  4
6 | 1  7  8  9
7 | 3  4  6  8
Key: 4 | 8 means 48
```

11. Both measures of central tendency indicate that the women's blood pressure in the survey was considerably less than the men's blood pressure. **13.** The mean, median, and mode for the men's golf scores are around 278 strokes, while the women's scores were around 280. This indicates that the difference in scores isn't very large. However, the fact that one of the modes for the women's scores was 290 shows that women frequently do have a higher number of strokes.
19. 180.3; 180; 180; 8

Lesson 9-6   **pp. 440–441**

EXERCISES 1. median **3.** E
5. Answers may vary. Sample: the range of percents of on-time arrivals is about the same for Atlanta and Denver. Overall, Denver had a greater percent of on-time arrivals per day in 2004 than Atlanta. The median for Denver is about the same as the upper quartile for Atlanta.

7.

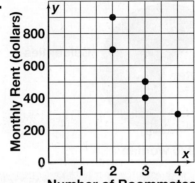

11. 70 **15.** Yes; the upper quartile would move from 162 to 167.5, and the lower quartile would move from 139 to 149.5.

Lesson 9-7   **pp. 446–447**

EXERCISES 1. scatter plot **3.** no trend

5.

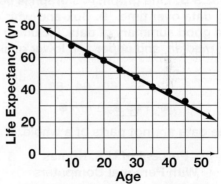

7. negative trend

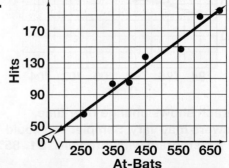

11. Negative trend; as the temperature increases, you wear fewer layers of clothing.
13a–b.

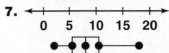

13c. about 140 **d.** about 800

Lesson 9-8   pp. 452–453

EXERCISES 1. 360° **3.** It identifies each sector.
5. football: 60; baseball: 54; soccer: 42;
basketball: 24; swimming: 12; tennis: 8

9.
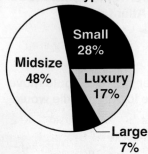

Vehicle Types

Small 28%
Midsize 48%
Luxury 17%
Large 7%

13a.
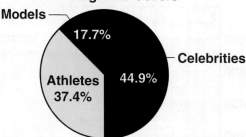

Magazine Covers

Models 17.7%
Celebrities 44.9%
Athletes 37.4%

b. 150 women **c.** 220 women

Lesson 9-9   pp. 457–459

EXERCISES 5. Line graph; this graph is better for
showing data over time. **9.** Box-and-whisker plot;
it gives a good summary of data, including high
and low, median, and upper and lower quartiles.

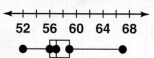

52   56   60   64   68

15a. The data are not parts of a whole.

b.
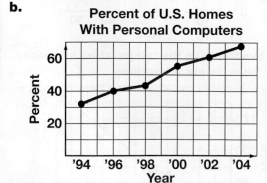

Percent of U.S. Homes
With Personal Computers

'94 '96 '98 '00 '02 '04
Year

A line graph shows change over time.
17. Answers may vary. Sample: You could
choose a histogram with intervals. **21.** 85°

Chapter Review   pp. 462–463

1. quartiles **2.** scatter plot **3.** central angle
4. stem-and-leaf plot **5.** 15.18; 15; 15; 14 **6.** 9.82;
9.85; 9.1 and 10.3; 1.7 **7.** Answers may vary.
Sample:

Number	Frequency
50–54	2
55–59	3
60–64	3
65–69	2
70–74	2
75–79	4
80–84	2

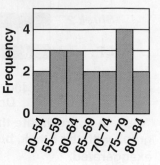

8. 5 artists

9.
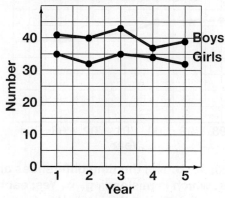

School Chorus Members

Boys
Girls

Year

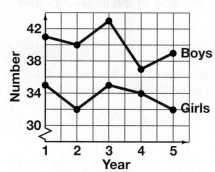

Boys
Girls

Year

The graph with the break symbol tends to
exaggerate the changes.

10.

```
6 | 3 5 7
7 | 2 5 8 8 9 9 9
8 | 5 5 9
9 | 0 9
Key: 9 | 0 means 90
```
79; 79

11.
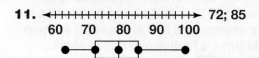
72; 85

60   70   80   90   100

12.

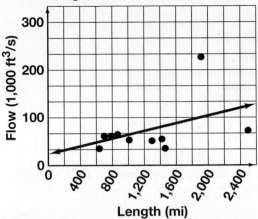

Length and Water Flow of Rivers

13. Scatter plot; it shows the relationship between two sets of data.

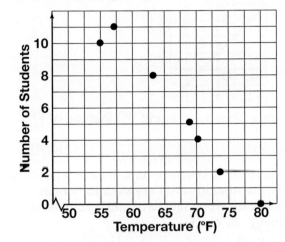

14. Stem-and-leaf plot; it shows numerical data arranged in order.

```
1 | 5 6 7
2 | 0 1 3 9
3 | 0 3
Key: 3 | 0 means 30
```

Chapter 10

Lesson 10-1	pp. 472–473

EXERCISES 1. experimental **3.** $\frac{3}{10}$ **5.** 0.272
9. theoretical **15.** $\frac{38}{171}$ **17.** $\frac{129}{171}$ **19.** $\frac{135}{171}$ **25.** 36°

Lesson 10-2	pp. 476–478

EXERCISES 1. 18 cars **3.** 30 **5.** 300 **7.** 90 **9.** 8
13. 2,400 people **15.** 1,440 people **19.** about
6 bats **21.** 3,000 votes **23.** 3,480 votes
25. 96 students **27.** 288 students
29. 60 students **33.** 14 ft^2

Lesson 10-3	pp. 482–483

EXERCISES 1. Researchers use samples because there are usually too many objects or people in a population to survey. **3.** Answers may vary. Sample: Do you like reality television or homework, or neither? **5.** This is a random sample; the population is the students in the class. **9.** Biased; it makes roses sound more appealing than carnations. **15a.** people who register a car **b.** $\frac{12}{41}$ **17.** Answers may vary. Sample: Do you prefer to swim in a pool or in the ocean, or neither?

Lesson 10-4	pp. 488–489

EXERCISES 1. If the outcome of the first event affects the outcome of the second event, the events are dependent. If the outcome of the first event has no effect on the outcome of the second event, the events are independent.
3. Dependent; after the first card is chosen, the remaining collection of cards has changed.
5. $\frac{1}{36}$ **7.** $\frac{1}{676}$ **11.** $\frac{9}{190}$ **15.** Independent; the first spin does not affect the second spin. **19.** $\frac{5}{32}$
21. 0 **23.** $\frac{1}{36}$ **25.** $\frac{2}{5}$
29.

```
5 | 0 2 5 5 6 7 7
6 | 1 1 4 5 8
7 | 0
Key: 5 | 0 means 5.0
```

Lesson 10-5	pp. 493–495

EXERCISES 1. A permutation is an arrangement of a set of objects in a particular order. **3.** 720
5. 90 **7.** 6 orders **9.** 120 orders **11.** 5,040
13. 3,628,800 **17.** 13,800 **19.** 29,760 **21.** 159,600
23. 30,240 **25.** 3,628,800 **27.** 13,800 arrangements
29. 39,070,080 orders **31.** 504 hours **35.** Circle graph; it shows how the total time using computers is broken into parts.

Lesson 10-6	pp. 498–499

EXERCISES 1. In a permutation, the order matters. In a combination, order does not matter.
3. no; combination **5.** 5 **7.** 36 ways **9.** 4 **11.** 4
21. permutation **23.** 45 games **27.** $\frac{1}{2,184}$
31. 4.5 × 10

Chapter Review

pp. 504–505

1. theoretical probability **2.** random sample
3. permutations **4.** dependent events **5.** 5 : 4
6. 1 : 2 **7.** 1 : 8 **8.** about 15 cases **9.** about
100 students **10.** random **11.** not random
12. Independent; the outcome of the second roll
is not affected by the first roll. **13.** Dependent;
the probability of the second pick is affected by
the first pick. **14.** 66 games **15.** 45 ways

Chapter 11

Lesson 11-1

pp. 514–516

EXERCISES 1. A common ratio involves mult. or
div. A common difference involves add. or subtr.
3. −1 **5.** 2 **7.** 2, 8, 32 **9.** $-\frac{1}{4}$, $-1\frac{1}{4}$, $-2\frac{1}{4}$ **11.** 7, 9,
11, 13 **15.** 3n; 60 **19.** Start with 1 and multiply
by 4 repeatedly; 256; 1,024; 4,096. **21.** Start with
3 and multiply by 2 repeatedly; 48, 96, 192.
25. arithmetic **29.** neither; 26, 37, 50
31. geometric; 162, 486, 1,458 **33.** geometric;
0.125, 0.625, 0.3125 **35.** 12 days **37.** Answers
may vary. Sample: 15.5 − 3n; −44.5 **39a.** 8; 27;
64; 125 **b.** Volume is the length of the side cubed.
c. n^3, where n is length of side **45.** $\frac{10}{171}$

Lesson 11-2

pp. 519–521

EXERCISES 1. Line graphs best display changes
over time. **3.** when the bus stops **5.** Highway;
the bus travels a greater distance over a shorter
period of time on the highway. **7.** 10 weeks
9. −10 km **13.** Al **15.** Carlos

17. **19.**

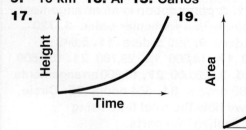

25. 21

Lesson 11-3

pp. 525–526

EXERCISES 1. A function rule is an equation that
describes a function. **3.** Always positive; the
product of two negative numbers is always
positive.

5.

n	t
44	4
132	12
165	15

7. 3 **9.** 7 **15.** no

19.

Input t	Output d
1	50
2	100
3	150
4	200

21a. 96, 92, 88, 84; arithmetic **b.** 3, 4, 3, 0;
neither **25.** −1n; −5, −6, −7

Lesson 11-4

pp. 530–531

EXERCISES 1. run **3.** $-\frac{1}{3}$ **5.** $\frac{3}{5}$

9. −1
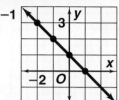

11. Your classmate found $\frac{run}{rise}$ instead of $\frac{rise}{run}$.

Lesson 11-5

pp. 536–538

EXERCISES 1. Discrete data involve a count of
items. Continuous data are data for which
numbers between any two data values have
meaning. **3.** 4; −1

5.

x	−3	−2	−1	0	1	2	3
y	−9	−6	−3	0	3	6	9

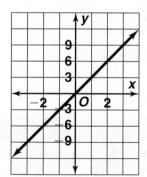

7. continuous

x	p
0	1
10	1.3
20	1.6
30	1.9

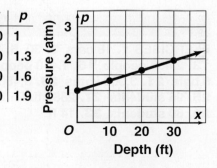

11.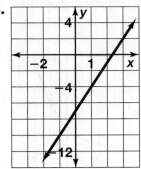

13. 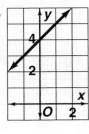 **15.**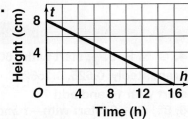

17a.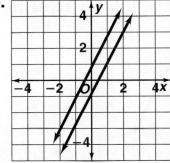

b. 8 cm **c.** 16 h

19.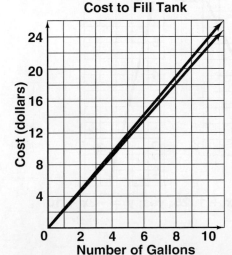

They are parallel but have different *y*-intercepts.
21. $y = 2.3x$; $y = 2.35x$; 6 gallons

Cost to Fill Tank

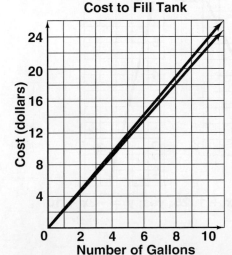

25. 60

Lesson 11-6   pp. 542–543

EXERCISES 1. The slope-intercept form is an example of the linear function rule.
3. $p = 1,200c + 500$ **5.** yes; $y = -3x + 2$
7. $y = -\frac{3}{2}x + 2$ **11a.** $y = 30 + 2x$ **b.** When $x = 12$, $y = 54$; his payment is \$54 for the space and the 12 drawings he sold; $f(12) = 54$.
13. $y + 1 = -\frac{1}{2}(x - 4)$
15. $C = 15 + r$; $C = 30 + 0.50r$;

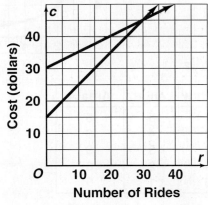

The \$30 plan is cheaper for someone who plans to go on many (more than 30) rides.
19. experimental

Lesson 11-7   pp. 548–549

EXERCISES 1. Graphs of linear functions are straight lines, and graphs of quadratic functions are parabolas.

3.

x	0	1	2	3	4
y	−1	1	7	17	31

5.

x	−3	−2	−1	0	1	2	3
y	18	8	2	0	2	8	18

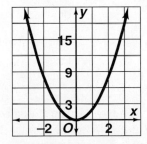

7.

x	−3	−2	−1	0	1	2	3
y	11	6	3	2	3	6	11

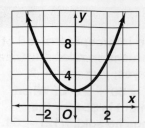

11.

x	1	2	3	4	5
y	8	4	$2\frac{2}{3}$	2	$1\frac{3}{5}$

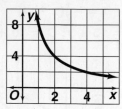

15. $y = -x^2$

19.

Width w	Length	Area A
1	5	5
2	4	8
3	3	9
4	2	8
5	1	5

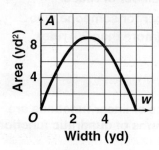

21.

x	-3	-2	-1	0	1	2	3
y	14	6	2	2	6	14	26

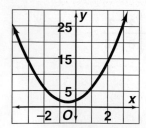

23a. 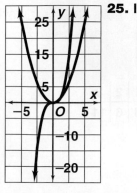   **25.** I

27.

x	$x^2 - 2 = y$
-1	-1
0	-2
1	-1
2	2
3	7

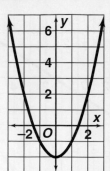

29.

x	$3 \cdot 2^x = y$
1	6
2	12
3	24
4	48

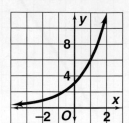

33. 9

Chapter Review   pp. 552–553

1. E **2.** D **3.** A **4.** C **5.** B **6.** $\frac{1}{4}$; start with 160 and multiply by $\frac{1}{4}$ repeatedly; 0.625, 0.15625, 0.0390625. **7.** 7; start with 14 and add 7 repeatedly; 42, 49, 56. **8.** -2; start with -1 and multiply by -2 repeatedly; -16, 32, -64. **9.** 4; start with 13 and add 4 repeatedly; 29, 33, 37. **10.** 3, -8, -19, -30 **11.** $\frac{1}{4}$, $\frac{1}{2}$, $\frac{3}{4}$, 1 **12.** 24, 25, 26, 27

13.

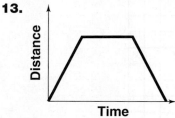

14. 5 **15.** -7 **16.** -27 **17.** -5 **18.** 0 **19.** $\frac{8}{5}$
20. $-\frac{3}{14}$ **21.** -1

22. 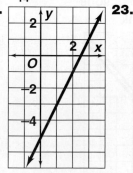 **23.**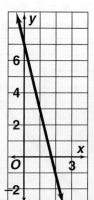

24. yes; $y = \frac{1}{2}x + 1$ **25.** yes; $y = -3x + 10$

26.

x	-2	-1	0	1	2
y	4	-2	-4	-2	4

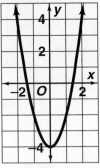

27.

x	-2	-1	0	1	2
y	-2	1	2	1	-2

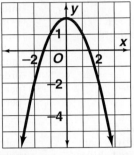

28.

x	1	7	14	21
y	7	1	$\frac{1}{2}$	$\frac{1}{3}$

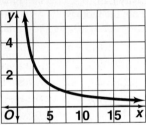

29.

x	1	2	3	4	5
y	7	$\frac{9}{2}$	$\frac{11}{3}$	$\frac{13}{4}$	3

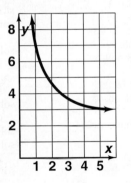

Chapter 12

Lesson 12-1   pp. 563–565

EXERCISES 1. 63, 35 **3.** A **5.** $2x^2 - x + 3$
9. $3x^2 + 2x - 4$ **13.** $2x^2 + x + 1$
17. $x^2 - 2x - 1$ **19.** $7n + 2k$ **21.** 31 **23.** 3
25. 5

Lesson 12-2   pp. 568–569

EXERCISES 1. variable **3.** $-1, -1$ **5.** $5m$
7. $8p^2 + 2p + 1$ **11.** $4x + 6$ **15.** $-x^2 - 2x + 7$
21. $x^3 - 9x + 1$ **23.** $-x^3 - 2x^2 + 2x + 5$
25. $6x^2 + 16x$ **31.** 1,860,480

Lesson 12-3   pp. 573–574

EXERCISES 1. 8 **3.** $(-6)^4$ **5.** 7^{10} **7.** Instead of
just adding the exponents, the student multiplied
the bases and then added the exponents.
9. y^8 **11.** 3.4^{13} **17.** 8×10^9 **19.** 7.2×10^{11}
25. Answers may vary. Sample:
$4 \cdot 4^{11}; 4^2 \cdot 4^{10}; 4^6 \cdot 4^6$ **27.** 6.8×10^{12}
29. 3^{m+n} **31.** $(-4)^{x+y}$ **33.** a^{10} **35.** 3^{6a}
37. $c^3 d^4$ **39.** $3x^8$ **41.** > **43.** > **45.** 2 **49.** about
43 mi/hr

Lesson 12-4   pp. 578–579

EXERCISES 1. A monomial has one term,
whereas a binomial has two terms. **3.** $15a^2$
5. $(x + 4)(2x + 3)$ **7.** $12t^5$ **9.** $-6z^5$ **13.** $a^2 - 3a$
15. $21s^2 + 7$ **21.** $4x^2 + 6x + 2$ **23.** $6x^2 + 4x$
25. $4x^2 + 2x$ **29.** monomial **31.** monomial

Lesson 12-5   pp. 584–585

EXERCISES 1. Positive; any nonzero number to
the power zero is equal to one.
3. $\frac{2 \cdot 2 \cdot 2 \cdot 2 \cdot 2 \cdot 2}{2 \cdot 2 \cdot 2 \cdot 2 \cdot 2} = 2^1$ **5.** $\frac{8 \cdot 8 \cdot 8 \cdot 8 \cdot 8}{8 \cdot 8} = 8^3$ **7.** x^4
9. -1 **15.** 1 **17.** 1 **25.** 12 **27.** 2 **29.** 1 **31.** -8
33. 1.12×10^3 ft/s **35.** False; $8^{-1} = \frac{1}{8}$ and
$(-8)^1 = -8$. **37.** False; $(-2)^{-1} = \frac{1}{-2} = -\frac{1}{2}$ and
$-\frac{1}{2} \neq 2$. **39 a.** $2n^3 - 4$ **b.** $2m^6 + 3m^3 + 1$
43. $58x = 17$; 29.31%

Chapter Review   pp. 590–591

1. polynomial **2.** constant **3.** monomial
4. coefficient **5.** binomial **6.** $2x^2 + 8$
7. $x^2 + 3x + 4$ **8.** $14x^2 + 13x + 6$
9. $13x^2 + 4x - 2$ **10.** $-4x^2 + 2x + 7$
11. $-x^2 + 11x + 7$ **12.** $16x + 5$ **13.** $-3x^2 + 3$
14. $11x^2 - 6x - 2$ **15.** $7x^2 - 3x + 2$
16. $-4x - 7$ **17.** $x^2 + x - 11$
18. $7x^2 - 2x + 13$ **19.** $3x^2 + 6x - 7$ **20.** 8^{19}
21. $(-3)^{13}$ **22.** 2.6^{24} **23.** 11^{11} **24.** 6×10^{18}
25. 7×10^6 **26.** 3×10^{14} **27.** 1.47×10^{20}
28. $-18x^4$ **29.** $14x^2$ **30.** $-30x^2 + 20x$
31. $5x^3 - 15x^2$ **32.** $2x^2 + 9x + 4$
33. $x^2 + 4x + 3$ **34.** 5^3 **35.** $(-8)^{10}$ **36.** 76^6
37. 1.8^1 **38.** 1 **39.** 1 **40.** 1 **41.** 1 **42.** $\frac{1}{625}$
43. $\frac{1}{x^9}$ **44.** $\frac{1}{81}$ **45.** $\frac{1}{h^8}$

Index

C

Calculate, meaning of, 228

Calculator
  changing fractions to decimals, 63
  comparing rational numbers, 63
  computing distance, 107
  converting measurement, 167, 168
  exercises that use, 64
  exponent key, 87
  factorial key, 492
  finding factorials, 492
  finding hypotenuse of right triangle, 113, 125
  finding leg of right triangle, 119
  indirect measurement, 198
  percent, 230
  percent calculations, 450
  pi (π) key, 337
  solving proportions, 175, 218, 225
  surface area, 370
  surface area of cone, 376
  volume of a cone, 389
  volume of a cylinder, 381
  See also Graphing calculator

Calculator Tip, 87, 93, 218, 337, 492

Capacity, units of measurement for, 165, 166. *See also* Volume

Careers
  air-traffic controller, 34
  animal rescue workers, 547
  architects, 87
  child-care workers, 292
  DJs, 215
  farmers, 163
  graphic artists, 453
  mail carriers, 337
  market researchers, 483
  potters, 399
  test pilots, 585
  See also Math at Work

Carry Out the Plan, xxxii–xli, 55, 114, 133, 177, 199, 249, 338, 371, 415, 584

Cartesian plane. *See* Coordinate plane

Cartoons, 19, 60

Celsius temperature, 80

Center of rotation, 146

Central angle, 451, 452

Central tendency. *See* Measures of central tendency

Challenge, 8, 13, 19, 30, 36, 41, 56, 60, 65, 69, 76, 84, 89, 95, 110, 115, 121, 127, 134, 139, 144, 149, 163, 170, 178, 184, 190, 195, 200, 213, 217, 222, 227, 233, 238, 244, 250, 264, 269, 275, 278, 285, 292, 306, 310, 316, 321, 327, 332, 339, 343, 357, 361, 366, 372, 378, 384, 391, 396, 401, 416, 422, 426, 431, 437, 441, 447, 453, 459, 473, 478, 483, 489, 495, 499, 516, 521, 526, 531, 538, 543, 549, 565, 569, 574, 579, 585

Chance. *See* Probability

Change
  constant rate of, 512–513, 514, 515, 516
  describing, 229
  percent of, 230–233, 253
  rate of, 527

Chapter Projects, 598–603
  Balancing Act, 600
  A Better Way, 601
  Great Escape, 601
  How Much Dough?, 603
  Invest in a Winner, 600
  Larger Than Life, 599
  News Flash, 602
  New Year, 598
  One Small Step, 603
  Start With the Stats, 602
  Step Right Up!, 599
  Weather or Not, 598

Chapter Review, 44–45, 98–99, 152–153, 202–203, 252–253, 294–295, 346–347, 404–405, 462–463, 504–505, 552–553, 590–591

Chapter Test, 46, 100, 154, 204, 254, 296, 348, 406, 464, 506, 554, 592

Check for Reasonableness, 24, 34, 35, 68, 73, 80, 82, 116, 161, 167, 175, 179, 198, 220, 224, 230, 272, 279, 289, 370, 381, 385, 394, 454

Checkpoint Quiz, 14, 31, 70, 91, 123, 140, 171, 186, 229, 270, 287, 317, 335, 373, 392, 432, 449, 479, 490, 522, 539, 570, 580

Check Skills You'll Need, 4, 10, 16, 20, 26, 33, 38, 52, 57, 62, 66, 72, 81, 86, 92, 106, 112, 118, 124, 130, 136, 141, 146, 160, 166, 174, 181, 187, 192, 197, 210, 214, 218, 224, 230, 234, 242, 246, 261, 266, 271, 276, 282, 288, 303, 307, 312, 318, 324, 328, 336, 341, 354, 358, 364, 368, 374, 380, 388, 393, 398, 412, 418, 424, 428, 433, 438, 444, 450, 456, 470, 475, 480, 486, 491, 496, 512, 518, 523, 528, 534, 540, 546, 561, 566, 571, 576, 581

Check Your Answer, xxxii–xli, 68, 75, 274, 343

Check Your Readiness, 2, 50, 104, 158, 208, 258, 300, 352, 410, 468, 510, 558

Check Your Understanding, 7, 12, 18, 22, 29, 35, 40, 54, 59, 64, 68, 74, 83, 88, 94, 108, 114, 120, 126, 132, 137, 143, 148, 162, 169, 176, 183, 189, 193, 198, 212, 216, 220, 226, 232, 237, 243, 248, 262, 268, 273, 277, 284, 291, 305, 309, 314, 320, 326, 331, 338, 342, 356, 360, 365, 371, 377, 382, 390, 395, 400, 414, 420, 425, 429, 435, 440, 446, 452, 457, 472, 476, 482, 488, 493, 498, 514, 519, 525, 530, 536, 542, 548, 563, 568, 573, 578, 584

Choose a Method, 30, 39, 41, 74, 75, 132, 134, 176, 177, 202, 204, 225, 227, 273, 275, 330, 331, 382, 383, 434, 476, 493, 494, 536, 563

Chord, 336

Circle
  arc of, 340, 341
  area of, 336–339, 347, 352
  chord of, 336, 340
  circumference of, 336–339
  diameter of, 336, 338, 355
  radius of, 336, 338, 356

Circle graph, 450–454, 463
  defined, 450
  equations and, 454
  exercises that use, 222, 247, 249, 250, 257, 450–453, 454, 455, 456–459, 464, 466, 473, 551, 621
  making, 451, 452, 453
  reading, 450, 452, 551

Circumference
  of a circle, 336–339
  formula for, 336, 337

Clark, Ellery, 231

Classification
  of angles, 640
  of irrational numbers, 108, 109, 152
  of polygons, 324
  of quadrilaterals, 319
  of rational numbers, 108, 109, 152
  of real numbers, 107–108
  of triangles, 318–322, 347

Closed dot on graph of inequality, 290

Closure Property, 109

Coefficient, 566

Combination, 496–499, 505
  defined, 496, 500, 505
  finding using lists, 496, 498
  finding using permutations, 497, 498, 505
  notation, 497, 498, 505

Combine, meaning of, 286

Common difference, 513, 552

Common factor. *See* Factor

Common multiple, 62, 66

Common ratio, 514, 552

Communication. *See* Activity Lab; Error Analysis; Reasoning; Vocabulary Builder; Vocabulary Tip; Writing in Math

Commutative Property
  of Addition, 26, 27, 267, 271
  of Multiplication, 26

Compare, meaning of, 9

Comparing
  data, 438, 440
  decimals, 2, 629
  fractions using LCD, 62, 64
  integers, 11–13, 45, 50
  rational numbers, 62–65, 99
  symbols for, 13
  types of events, 485

Compass, 335, 341, 451

Compatible numbers, 168, 214

Complement, in probability, 479

Complementary angles, 304–306, 346

Composite number, 52–53

Index (vertical tab)

374, 377, 378, 380, 383, 384, 388, 390, 391, 393, 395, 396, 398, 400, 401, 410, 412, 414, 415, 416, 418, 420, 422, 424, 425, 426, 428, 430, 431, 433, 436, 437, 438, 440, 441, 444, 446, 447, 450, 452, 453, 456, 457, 458, 459, 468, 470, 472, 473, 475, 477, 478, 480, 482, 483, 486, 488, 489, 491, 494, 496, 498, 499, 510, 512, 515, 516, 518, 520, 521, 523, 525, 526, 528, 530, 531, 534, 537, 538, 540, 541, 542, 543, 546, 548, 549, 558, 561, 562, 564, 565, 566, 568, 569, 571, 572, 573, 574, 576, 578, 579, 581, 584, 585

Goldbach, Christian, 56

Golden Ratio, 587

GPS. *See* Guided Problem Solving

Graph(s), 418–460
 bar, 223, 641
 box-and-whisker plots, 438–442, 463
 break symbol in, 429, 430, 463
 changing representations, 550
 choosing appropriate, 456–459, 463
 circle graphs, 450–454, 463
 dashed line in, 534
 displaying frequency, 418–423, 462
 finding rate of change from, 527
 histograms, 419, 420, 421, 423, 462
 of inequality, 281, 282, 283, 284, 285
 interpreting and sketching, 518–521, 551
 line, 522, 642
 line plots, 418, 420
 making, as Problem Solving Strategy, xxxiv, 440, 446, 458, 520
 making to tell a story, 432
 matching verbal description, 135
 misleading, 223, 427–432, 463
 modeling with, 518, 519
 percents and, 223
 reading critically, 428–431, 463
 reading displays, 427
 relating to events, 518–521
 scatter plots, 443–448
 stem-and-leaf plots, 433–437, 463
 Venn diagrams, 424–426
 writing equations from, 541, 542
 See also Coordinate plane

Graphical displays, reading, 427–431, 463

Graphical representations. *See* Graph(s); Graphing

Graphing
 in coordinate plane, 124–127, 510
 dilation images, 188–190
 equations with two variables, 131–134, 153, 510
 function rules and tables, 534, 537, 544
 inequalities, 281, 282, 283, 290, 295
 linear equations, 131, 134, 153
 linear functions, 533–538, 544, 553
 nonlinear functions, 546, 547, 548
 points, 124, 125, 126, 153, 410
 quadratic functions, 546, 548, 553
 reflections, 141–142, 143, 144, 153
 rotations, 147, 148, 153
 table of data, 131–134

translations, 136–139, 153
 using slope and *y*-intercept, 535, 536, 537, 553

Graphing calculator
 evaluating expressions, 90
 evaluating formulas, 85
 generating a sequence, 517
 Graph feature of, 423
 graphing equations, 533
 List feature of, 85, 423, 442
 making box-and-whisker plot, 442
 making histograms, 423
 Plot feature of, 423, 442
 Stat feature of, 85
 Table feature of, 90, 517, 533
 Tblset feature of, 517, 533
 Trace feature, 442
 using random numbers, 484
 Zoom feature of, 423, 442, 533
 See also Calculator

Greatest common factor (GCF)
 defined, 53, 98
 finding, 53–54, 55
 simplifying fractions using, 57, 59, 72, 158

Gridded Response example, 43, 54, 113, 167, 242, 277, 308, 394, 445, 476, 524, 582

Gridded Response, 43, 56, 101, 115, 170, 244, 255, 278, 297, 310, 349, 396, 447, 465, 478, 585, 594

Group, working in. *See* Activity Lab

Grouping symbols, 6, 11

Guided Problem Solving, 7, 12, 18, 22, 29, 35, 40, 55, 59, 64, 68, 75, 83, 88, 94, 109, 114, 120, 126, 133, 138, 143, 148, 162, 169, 177, 183, 189, 199, 213, 216, 221, 226, 233, 237, 244, 249, 263, 268, 274, 278, 284, 291, 305, 309, 320, 326, 331, 338, 343, 356, 360, 366, 371, 377, 383, 390, 395, 400, 415, 420, 425, 430, 440, 446, 452, 458, 472, 477, 482, 488, 494, 498, 515, 520, 525, 531, 537, 542, 548, 564, 568, 573, 578, 584
 Equations and Graphs, 454
 Geoboard Area, 333
 Linear Functions, 544
 Practice Solving Problems, 78, 240
 Permutations, Combinations, and Probability, 501
 Solving Equations, 587
 Solving Multi-Step Problems, 24
 Squares and Square Roots, 116
 Using Formulas, 385
 Using Rates and Proportions, 179
 Writing Equations, 279

H _____

Hands On Activity Lab
 Comparing Types of Events, 485
 Estimating Area, 335
 Exploring Pairs of Angles, 302
 Exploring Probability, 245
 Exploring Reflections, 140

Exploring Rotations, 145
 Exploring the Pythagorean Theorem, 111
 Fair Games, 474
 Finding Volume Using Models, 387
 Making Solids From Nets, 363
 Modeling Equations, 32
 Modeling Expressions, 265
 Modeling Fraction Multiplication, 71
 Modeling Multi-Step Equations, 260
 Modeling Surface Area, 367
 Modeling Volume, 379
 Surface Area of a Pyramid, 373
 Using Percents, 239
 Using Similar Figures, 196

Height
 of cone, 376
 of cylinder, 370
 of parallelogram, 328
 of prism, 368, 369
 of pyramid, 374
 slant, 374, 405
 of trapezoid, 81, 329
 of triangle, 328

Heptagon, 324

Hexagon, 324

Histogram
 defined, 419, 462
 exercises that use, 419–422, 423, 426, 428, 432, 456–459, 462, 464, 466, 620, 621
 interval, 419
 making, 419
 making with graphing calculator, 423
 as most appropriate graph, 457

Homework Video Tutor, 8, 13, 19, 23, 30, 36, 41, 56, 60, 65, 68, 75, 84, 89, 95, 109, 115, 121, 127, 133, 139, 144, 148, 162, 170, 177, 184, 190, 195, 200, 213, 216, 221, 226, 233, 244, 249, 263, 269, 274, 278, 285, 291, 306, 309, 316, 321, 327, 332, 339, 343, 357, 361, 366, 372, 378, 383, 391, 395, 401, 416, 421, 425, 431, 436, 441, 447, 453, 458, 473, 478, 482, 489, 494, 498, 515, 520, 525, 531, 537, 542, 549, 564, 569, 574, 579, 584

Horizontal line, 529

Hurlinger, Johann, 82

Hypotenuse, 113–115, 118–121, 153

I _____

Identity Property
 of Addition, 26
 of Multiplication, 26

If-then statements, 321

Image, 136, 153

Improper fraction, 67, 638

Increase, percent of, 230–233, 253

Independent event
 compared to dependent events, 487, 488
 probability of, 485–486, 487, 488, 505

concept maps, 322
concrete, 32, 111, 140, 145, 239, 245, 260, 262, 265, 272, 302, 335, 363, 367, 373, 379, 387, 474, 485. *See also* Hands On Activity Lab
data sets, 438, 439
Distributive Property, 28
events, 518, 519
exercises that use, 8, 15, 35, 46, 49, 54, 156, 178, 180, 194, 199, 200, 226, 256, 262, 275, 285, 305, 306, 310, 320, 331, 356, 357, 360, 361, 365, 366, 371, 372, 377, 378, 383, 384, 390, 391, 395, 396, 400, 401, 404, 405, 406, 407, 408, 409, 468, 564, 569, 570, 578, 579, 580, 590, 591, 592
expressions, 4, 5, 6, 265, 267, 560, 590
formulas, 116
fractions, 71, 72, 73, 214
functions, 524, 540
geometric, 24, 28, 71, 87, 111, 150, 151, 172, 173, 174, 196, 197, 198, 218, 219, 220, 261, 262, 302, 303, 308, 314, 322, 329, 335, 358, 364, 367, 373, 380, 387, 475, 476, 561, 562, 563, 566
with graphs, 518, 519
integers, 10, 11, 15, 17, 20
measurement, 196, 197, 198, 314
midpoint, 128
multiplication, 71
numbers, 10, 11, 15, 17, 20, 24, 53, 54, 63, 71, 128, 172, 173, 174, 214, 218, 219, 220, 239, 247, 281, 282, 283, 288, 289, 438, 439, 474, 475, 476, 484, 485, 512, 513, 514, 518, 519
objects. *See* Modeling, concrete
percent, 214, 218, 219, 220, 239
pictures, 17, 24, 28, 33, 53, 54, 71, 87, 111, 150, 151, 161, 172, 173, 174, 196, 197, 198, 218, 219, 220, 261, 262, 302, 303, 308, 314, 322, 329, 335, 358, 364, 380, 475, 476, 512, 561, 562, 563, 566
polynomials, 561, 562, 563, 566, 576, 577, 578, 591
prime factorization, 53, 54
probability, 247, 474, 475, 476, 484, 485
proportions, 174, 179, 196, 197, 198
Pythagorean Theorem, 111
ratios, 172, 173, 174, 468
reflections, 140
rotations, 145
sequences, 512, 513, 514
simulations, 484
for solving equations, 24, 32, 33, 34, 260, 261, 262, 272, 277
for solving inequalities, 281, 282, 283, 288, 289
surface area, 367, 373
three-dimensional figures, 358, 364
unit rates, 161, 179
using algebra tiles, 32, 260, 262, 265, 272, 561, 562, 563, 566, 576, 577, 578, 590, 591
using number lines, 10, 11, 15, 17, 20, 63, 128, 214, 247, 281, 282, 283, 288, 289, 438, 439

using words, 4, 5, 34, 116, 179, 262, 267, 272, 277, 289, 524, 540, 560
volume, 379, 380, 387
Money
exercises that use, 18, 35, 175, 178, 232, 464
principal and interest, 242–244, 253
sale price, 235–236, 237, 238, 253
selling price, 234, 235, 237, 253
Monomial
defined, 576
multiplying by, 576, 578, 579, 591
More Than One Way, 39, 74, 131–132, 176, 225, 273, 330, 382, 434, 493, 536, 563
Multiple, least common (LCM), 62, 66, 98
Multiple bar graph, 641
Multiple Choice examples, 11, 21, 67, 82, 119, 125, 136, 182, 193, 236, 247, 262, 272, 319, 325, 359, 369, 414, 428, 481, 487, 513, 540, 572, 577
exercises that use, 184, 397, 577
See also Test Prep; Test Prep Cumulative Review; Test-Taking Strategies
Multiple line graph, 642
Multiplication
Associative Property of, 26
Commutative Property of, 26
of decimals, 2, 632
exponents and, 571–573, 591
Identity Property of, 26
of integers, 20–23, 38, 45, 50, 258
of mixed numbers, 72
modeling, 71
of monomials, 576, 578, 579, 591
of more than two integers, 20
of numbers in scientific notation, 572, 573, 591
of polynomials, 576–579, 591
of powers, 571, 573, 574, 635
by powers of ten, 91, 635
of rational numbers, 72–76, 99, 158, 208, 468
for solving equations, 38–41, 45, 73, 75
for solving inequalities, 288–292, 295
for solving two-step equations, 262, 294
using Mental Math, 27
Multiplication Property
of Equality, 38, 41, 175
of Inequality, 288, 290
Multiplicative inverse, 73, 77
Multi-step equation
modeling, 272
solving, 271–275, 295

N

Nanorobots, 581
Negative exponent, 583, 584, 585, 591
Negative numbers
inequalities and, 287, 289–292, 295

powers and, 87
See also Integers
Negative slope, 528, 529
Negative trend, 445, 446
Net, 363–366, 404
for cone, 376
for cylinder, 364, 370, 461
defined, 363, 364, 404
finding surface area using, 368, 371
making solids from, 363
recognizing, 364
for rectangular prism, 364, 368, 371
for square pyramid, 374
New Vocabulary, 4, 10, 16, 20, 26, 33, 38, 52, 57, 62, 72, 81, 86, 92, 106, 112, 124, 130, 136, 141, 146, 160, 166, 174, 181, 187, 192, 197, 210, 230, 234, 242, 246, 266, 282, 288, 303, 307, 312, 318, 324, 328, 341, 354, 358, 364, 368, 374, 380, 393, 398, 412, 418, 424, 433, 438, 444, 450, 470, 480, 486, 491, 496, 512, 523, 528, 534, 546, 561, 566, 576
Nonagon, 324
Nonlinear function, 547, 548
Nonproportional relationships, 172
Notation
arrow, 137
combination, 497, 498
function, 524, 525
permutation, 493, 494
prime ('), 136
scientific. *See* Scientific notation
No trend, 445, 446
Number(s)
absolute value of, 10–13, 45
compatible, 168, 214
composite, 52–53
divisible, 52, 54
irrational, 107–108, 109, 152
modeling, 10, 11, 15, 17, 20, 24, 53, 54, 63, 71, 128, 172, 173, 174, 214, 218, 219, 220, 239, 247, 281, 282, 283, 288, 289, 438, 439, 474, 475, 476, 484, 485, 512, 513, 514, 518, 519
negative. *See* Negative numbers
prime, 52–54
prime factorization of, 53–56, 57, 77, 98
random, 484
real, 107–108
in scientific notation, 92–96, 99
standard form of, 92, 94
See also Integers; Mixed numbers; Rational numbers
Number cubes. *See* Manipulatives
Number line
adding integers on, 17, 18
box-and-whisker plots, 438–442, 463
comparing and ordering numbers on, 11, 63
exercises that use, 8, 12, 15, 46
graphing inequalities on, 281–285, 295
graphing midpoints, 128
graphing points on, 10, 11

division and, 581, 584, 591
multiplication and, 571, 573, 574, 635
negatives and, 87
raising a product to, 586
raising to a power, 586
simplifying, 571, 581, 586
of ten, 91, 92–93, 96, 99, 635
See also Exponent(s)

Power rules, 586

Precision and significant digits, 402

Predictions, 475–479, 505
comparing types of events, 485
exercises that use, 223, 245, 323,
446–447
for fair games, 474
from scatter plots, 443–445, 448
trend lines, 445, 446, 463
using graphs, 427, 444–447, 463
using probability, 475, 477, 478, 505
using surveys, 476, 477, 478, 505

Price
regular, 236, 237
sale, 235–236, 237, 238, 253
selling, 234, 235, 237, 253

Prime factorization
defined, 53, 77
modeling, 53, 54
of numbers, 53–56, 77, 98
for simplifying fractions, 57, 59

Prime notation (′), 136

Prime number, 52–54

Principal, 242

Prism
base of, 354
defined, 354
height of, 368, 369
lateral area of, 367, 375, 377
lateral faces of, 354
naming, 355
pentagonal, 354, 355
rectangular, 355, 362, 364, 369
surface area of, 367–369
trapezoidal, 355
triangular, 355, 365, 380
volume of, 379, 380, 383, 405

Probability, 246–250, 470–501
combinations, 496–499, 501, 505
comparing types of events, 485
complements in, 479
counting outcomes, 492, 494
of dependent events, 485, 487, 488, 505
of an event, 246, 253, 485–489, 505
exercises that use, 248–250, 253, 343,
472–473, 474, 477–479, 482–483, 484,
485, 488–490, 494–495, 498–499,
502–505
experimental, 470, 472, 473, 504
exploring, 245
fair games, 474
finding, 246–247, 468
as fraction, 246, 247, 468
identifying type of, 471, 472, 504
of independent events, 485–486, 487,
488, 505

making predictions, 475–479, 505
modeling, 247, 474, 475, 476, 484, 485
odds, 471, 472, 473, 504
percents and, 247, 249, 250
permutations, 491–495, 497, 498, 501,
505
random numbers, 484
sample space, 247–248, 249, 468
simulations with random numbers, 484
surveys, 480–483, 505
theoretical, 246–247, 253, 471, 504

Problem Solving Application, 46–47,
102–103, 156–157, 206–207, 256–257,
298–299, 350–351, 408–409, 466–467,
508–509, 556–557, 596–597

Problem Solving Handbook, xxxii–xli
practice solving problems, xxxiv–xli

Problem solving model, xxxii–xli
Carry Out, 55, 114, 133, 177, 199, 249,
338, 371, 390, 584
Check, 24, 34, 35, 68, 73, 75, 78, 80,
116, 161, 167, 175, 179, 198, 220, 224,
230, 272, 274, 279, 289, 343, 370, 381,
385, 394, 454
Plan, 55, 114, 133, 143, 177, 183, 189,
199, 244, 249, 274, 284, 291, 309, 338,
343, 390, 415, 584
Understand, 68, 75, 116, 143, 183, 189,
244, 309, 371

Problem Solving Strategies, xxxiii–xli
Act It Out, xxxvii, 361
Choose a Method, 30, 39, 41, 74, 75,
132, 134, 176, 177, 202, 204, 225, 227,
235, 236, 273, 275, 330, 331, 382, 383,
434, 476, 493, 536, 563, 566
Draw a Picture, xxxiv, 24, 25, 55, 78,
79, 180, 268, 345, 356, 383, 520, 587
Estimating the Answer, 216, 251, 390
Guided Problem Solving. *See* Guided
Problem Solving
Look for a Pattern, xxxv, 360
Make a Table, xxxviii, 6, 7, 548
More Than One Way, 39, 74, 131–132,
176, 225, 273, 330, 382, 434, 493, 536,
563
Systematic Guess and Check, xxxvi,
390
Test-Taking Strategies. *See* Test-Taking
Strategies
What You Might Think and What You
Might Write. *See* What You Might
Think and What You Might Write
Word Problem Practice, 25, 79, 117,
180, 241, 280, 334, 386, 455, 502, 545,
588
Work Backward, xl, 589
Work a Simpler Problem, xxxix, 360
Write an Equation, xli, 35, 40, 226, 241,
263, 278, 279, 280, 415, 454, 568, 587

Product
cross product, 175–178, 201, 203
raising to a power, 586
zeros in, 633
See also Multiplication

Projects. *See* Chapter Projects

Properties, 26–30, 648
of Addition, 26
closure, 109
cross products, 175, 176
distributive, 28, 29, 45, 258, 267,
272–273, 274, 277
of equality, 33, 38, 41, 175
identifying and using, 26–30, 45
of inequality, 282
of multiplication, 26, 41
using to simplify polynomials, 562,
563, 590

Proportion
central angles and, 451, 452
corresponding sides, 181–184
cross products of, 175–178, 201, 203
defined, 174
identifying, 172–173, 174–175, 177
for maps, 193–195
modeling, 174, 179, 196, 197, 198
percents and, 218–222, 253
problem solving and, 192
rate, 161, 162, 163
ratios. *See* Ratio
scale models, 192, 193–195
solving, 174–178, 203, 208, 352, 410
using to find part of a whole, 218, 220,
221
using to find a percent, 220, 221
using to find a whole amount, 219, 220,
221

Proportional relationships
changing dimensions, 397
circle graphs, 450–454, 463
compared to non-proportional,
172–173
geometry, 181–185, 192–195, 203
for indirect measurement, 197–200,
203
for maps, 193–195, 203
measurement, 166–170, 192–195, 203
number, 160–163, 174–178, 192–195,
202, 203
probability, 246–247, 253, 470–474, 504
ratios, 160, 162, 163, 202
for scale models, 192–195, 203
for similar figures, 181–185, 203
for similar solids, 397–401, 405
unit rates, 161, 162, 163, 202

Pyramid
base of, 354, 374
defined, 354
height of, 374
lateral area of, 373, 375, 405
lateral faces of, 354, 375
rectangular, 357
similar, 398, 400
slant height of, 374, 405
square, 354, 365, 374, 377, 387, 388
surface area of, 373–375, 377, 405
volume of, 388, 390, 405

Pythagorean Theorem, 111–115, 118–121
converse of, 122

Sales tax, 224, 255

Sample
    conducting surveys, 480–483
    defined, 480, 500, 505
    random, 480, 482, 505

Sample space
    defined, 247, 253
    finding, 247–248, 249

Scale
    defined, 192
    on maps, 193, 194, 195
    selecting, 429

Scale drawing, 195

Scale factor, 187–190, 203
    defined, 187
    of dilations, 187, 188
    finding, 188–190

Scale model, 192–195

Scalene triangle, 318

Scatter plot, 444–447, 463, 464
    exercises that use, 443, 444–447, 448,
        449, 453, 455, 456–459, 463, 565, 597,
        620, 621
    defined, 444
    finding trends with, 445, 446, 447, 463
    making, 444

Scientific notation, 92–96
    defined, 92, 99
    dividing numbers in, 582–583, 584,
        585, 591
    multiplying numbers in, 572, 573, 591
    negative exponents, 93, 94
    numbers less than 1, 93, 94
    using calculators with, 575
    writing measures, 96
    writing numbers in, 93, 94, 99
    writing in standard form, 92, 94

Selling price
    defined, 234, 253
    finding, 235, 237

Semicircle, 340

Sequence, 512–517
    arithmetic, 513, 552
    common difference for arithmetic,
        513, 552
    common ratio for geometric, 514, 552
    defined, 512
    evaluating algebraic expressions for,
        513, 515, 552
    exploring, 517
    geometric, 514, 552
    modeling, 512, 513, 514
    terms of, 512, 515, 552
    using algebraic expressions to write,
        513, 515, 552
    verbal description of geometric, 514,
        515, 517, 552

Shape, graphing reflections of, 142, 143,
    144, 153

Show, meaning of, 228

Side
    congruent, 312
    corresponding, 181, 312

Side-Angle-Side (SAS), 313, 314, 347

Side-Side-Side (SSS), 313, 314, 347

Sign(s)
    for adding and subtracting integers,
        16–17, 45
    different, and adding integers, 16
    different, and multiplying or dividing
        integers, 20
    for multiplying and dividing integers,
        20–21, 45
    negative, and evaluating exponents, 87
    same, and adding integers, 16
    same, and multiplying or dividing
        integers, 20
    for solving inequalities by multiplying
        or dividing, 288–292, 295

Significant digits, 402

Similar figures, 181–184, 203
    proportions and, 181–184, 203
    ratios of, 185
    similarity transformations, 187–190
    using for indirect measurement,
        196–200, 203

Similarity
    enlargements, 188, 201
    indirect measurement and, 196–200,
        203
    reductions, 188
    scale factor and, 188–190
    scale models and, 192–195, 203
    symbol for, 181

Similarity transformations, 187–190, 203

Similar polygons, 181–184
    finding lengths in, 182, 183, 203
    identifying, 181, 183

Similar solids, 398–401, 405
    defined, 398
    finding dimensions using proportions,
        398, 400
    surface area of, 397, 399, 400, 405
    volume of, 397, 399, 400, 405

Similar triangles, 181–184, 203

Simple interest, 242–244, 253
    defined, 242
    formula for, 242, 253

Simplest form
    of fractions, 57, 59, 158, 174, 410
    of mixed numbers, 58, 59
    of ratios, 160, 162, 163, 202

Simplifying
    defined, 5, 44
    equations, 271, 274
    expressions, 5–8, 44, 258, 266–269, 295
    polynomials, 562–563, 564, 590
    powers, 571, 581, 586

Simulations with random numbers, 484

Skew lines, 355, 356

Skills Handbook, 628–642
    adding and subtracting decimals, 631
    adding and subtracting fractions with
        like denominators, 639
    bar graphs, 641
    classifying and measuring angles, 640

comparing and ordering decimals, 629
decimals and place value, 628
dividing decimals by decimals, 636
dividing decimals by whole numbers,
    634
line graphs, 642
mixed numbers and improper
    fractions, 638
multiplying and dividing by powers of
    ten, 635
multiplying decimals, 632
rounding, 630
zeros in a product, 633
zeros in decimal division, 637

Slant height, 374, 405

Slide. *See* Translation

Slope, 527–531, 535
    defined, 528, 553
    finding, 529, 530, 541, 542, 553
    finding from a table, 530, 531
    horizontal line, 529, 530
    negative, 528, 529
    parallel lines, 532
    perpendicular line, 532
    positive, 528, 529
    rate of change, 527
    undefined, 529, 530
    vertical line, 529, 530
    zero, 529, 530

Slope-intercept form of equation, 535,
    536, 537, 553

Software, 191, 344, 460

Solids, 354–357, 404
    defined, 354, 404
    drawing views of, 358–361, 362, 404,
        406
    isometric views of, 359–361, 404, 406
    making from nets, 363
    naming, 354–355, 356
    nets and, 363–366, 368, 404
    prisms. *See* Prism
    recognizing, 355, 356
    similar, 398–401, 405
    sketching using translations, 362
    volume of. *See* Volume
    See also Three-dimensional figures

Solution(s)
    defined, 34, 45
    of equation, 34, 45, 131. *See also*
        Solving equations
    estimating, 80
    finding using equations, tables, and
        graphs, 130–134, 153
    of inequality with two variables. *See*
        also Solving inequalities
    table of, 130–134, 153, 534–535
    of two equations, 544

Solve, meaning of, 286

Solving equations
    by adding, 33–36, 45
    by dividing, 39–41, 45, 261, 272–273,
        274
    by multiplying, 38–41, 45, 73, 75, 262
    by subtracting, 33, 35–36, 45

for angle measures, 311
cover-up method for, 42
linear equations, 131–134, 153
modeling, 24, 32, 33, 34, 260, 261, 262, 272, 277
multi-step equations, 271–275, 295
one-step equations, 33–36, 38–41, 208, 300
simplifying before, 271, 274
two-step equations, 261–264, 294
using Distributive Property, 267–269, 272–273, 274, 277
with variables on both sides, 276–278, 295

Solving inequalities
by adding, 282–285, 295
by dividing, 288–292, 295
by multiplying, 288–292, 295
by subtracting, 282–285, 295
division for,
modeling, 281, 282, 283, 288, 289

Speed of sound, 585

Sphere, 393–396, 405
surface area of, 393, 395, 405
volume of, 394, 395, 405

Spinner, 249, 343, 449, 468, 477, 479, 489, 503

Spreadsheet, graphing data using, 460

Square
area of, 111
defined, 319
perimeter of, 82

Square number, 106–107, 152, 645

Square, perfect, 106, 152

Square pyramid, 354, 365, 374, 387, 388, 390, 405

Square root, 645
defined, 106
estimating value of, 107, 109, 152
finding, 106–110, 152
identifying as irrational number, 108
of perfect square, 106–107, 152
symbol for, 106

Standard form
scientific notation vs., 92, 94
writing numbers in, 92, 94

Standardized Test Prep. *See* Tests, preparing for

Statistics
box-and-whisker plot, 438–442, 463
drawing a scatter plot, 444, 446, 447, 464
frequency, 418–423, 462
histogram, 419, 420, 421, 423, 462
mean. *See* Mean
measures of central tendency, 412–416, 418, 420, 421, 462. *See also* Mean; Median; Mode
median. *See* Median
misleading graphs, 223, 427–432, 463
mode. *See* Mode
outliers, 413, 415
predictions, 443–447

probability, 246–250, 470–501
quartiles, 438, 439
random samples, 480, 482, 505
range, 413, 415, 462
surveys, 480–483, 505
using appropriate graphs, 456–459, 463
See also Data analysis; Data Analysis Activity Lab; Graphing; Survey

Stem-and-leaf plot, 433–437, 463
exercises that use, 433–437, 441, 449, 456–459, 463, 464, 489, 596, 620, 621
back-to-back, 435, 436
defined, 433, 463
finding median and mode using, 434, 435, 436, 437
key, 433
making, 433

Straight angle, 640

Straightedge, 341

Subtraction
of decimals, 2, 631
of fractions, 66, 68, 99, 639
of integers, 17–19, 45, 50, 258
of mixed numbers, 67, 68, 99
of polynomials, 567, 568, 569, 590
precision and, 402
of rational numbers, 66–69, 99
for solving equations, 34–36, 45
for solving inequalities, 282–285, 295
for solving two-step equations, 261–262, 294
using mental math, 27

Subtraction Property
of Equality, 33
of Inequality, 282

Sum, sign of, 16. *See also* Addition

Supplementary angle, 304–306, 346

Surface area, 368–378
of a cone, 376, 377, 405
of a cylinder, 367, 370, 371, 404, 461
defined, 368
estimating, 370, 385
formulas for, 369, 370, 375, 376, 405
modeling, 367, 373
of a prism, 367–369, 405
of a pyramid, 373–375, 405
of similar solids, 397, 399, 400, 405
of a sphere, 393, 395, 405

Survey
conducting, 480–483, 505
exercises that use, 40, 64, 98, 212, 222, 280, 452, 464, 477, 494, 507
identifying bias in questions, 481, 482, 505
judging valid conclusions, 481, 482, 505
predictions using, 476, 477, 478, 505
random samples for, 480, 482, 505
results, 247, 471

Symbols, 644
absolute value, 10
break, 429, 430, 463
for comparing, 13
for congruence, 181
dashed line in a graph, 534

ellipsis, 10
grouping, 6, 11
for inequality, 282
parentheses, 6, 11, 18, 87
for repeating decimal, 58
for similarity, 183
for square root, 106

Symmetry
lines of, 142, 143
reflectional, 142, 143, 144
rotational, 146, 148

***Systematic Guess and Check* Problem Solving Strategy,** xxxvi, 390

T

Table
changing representations, 550
finding rate of change from, 527
finding slope from, 530, 531
frequency, 419, 420, 421, 462
making, and writing equations, 130–134
patterns in, 130
of solutions, 130–134, 153, 534–535
using to graph functions, 534, 537, 544
writing a rule from, 541, 542, 553

Tables, reference, 643–647
For use with Problem Solving Applications, 647
Measures, 643
Reading Math Symbols, 644
Squares and Square Roots, 645
Trigonometric Ratios, 646

Technology. *See* Calculator; Software; Technology Activity Lab

Technology Activity Lab
Evaluating Expressions, 90
Exploring Sequences, 517
Geometry Software and Constructions, 344
Geometry Software and Dilations, 191
Graphing Data Using Spreadsheets, 460
Graphing Equations, 533
Making Box-and-Whisker Plots, 442
Making Histograms, 423
Scientific Notation, 575
Simulations With Random Numbers, 484
Using Formulas, 85

Temperature, 80

Ten, powers of, 91, 92–93, 99, 635

Term(s), 266 295
defined, 266, 512
like, 266–269, 295, 566–569, 590
of sequence, 512, 513, 514

Terminating decimal, 58, 59, 108

Tessellations, 150

Test, Beginning-of-Course Diagnostic, xxx–xxxi

Test Prep, 8, 13, 19, 23, 30, 36, 41, 56, 60, 65, 69, 76, 84, 89, 95, 110, 115, 121, 127, 134, 139, 144, 149, 163, 170, 178,

W

X

Y

Z

Acknowledgments

Staff Credits

The people who make up the **Prentice Hall Math** team—representing design services, editorial, editorial services, educational technology, marketing, market research, photo research and art development, production services, publishing processes, and rights & permissions—are listed below. Bold type denotes core team members.

Dan Anderson, Carolyn Artin, Nick Blake, **Stephanie Bradley,** Kyla Brown, Patrick Culleton, Kathleen J. Dempsey, **Frederick Fellows, Suzanne Finn,** Paul Frisoli, Ellen Granter, **Richard Heater,** Betsy Krieble, Lisa LaVallee, Christine Lee, Kendra Lee, Cheryl Mahan, **Carolyn McGuire,** Eve Melnechuk, Terri Mitchell, Jeffrey Paulhus, Mark Roop-Kharasch, Marcy Rose, Rashid Ross, Irene Rubin, Siri Schwartzman, Vicky Shen, **Dennis Slattery,** Elaine Soares, Dan Tanguay, Tiffany Taylor, Mark Tricca, Paula Vergith, Kristin Winters, Helen Young

Additional Credits

Paul Astwood, Sarah J. Aubry, Jonathan Ashford, Peter Chipman, Patty Fagan, Tom Greene, Kevin Keane, Mary Landry, Jon Kier, Dan Pritchard, Sara Shelton, Jewel Simmons, Ted Smykal, Steve Thomas, Michael Torocsik, Maria Torti

TE Design

Susan Gerould/Perspectives

Illustration Credits

Additional artwork:
Rich McMahon, Ted Smykal

Kenneth Batelman: **11, 246;**
Trevor Johnston: **230;**
Brucie Rosch: **10, 13, 162, 235, 238;**
JB Woolsey: **121, 197, 198, 199, 200, 201, 226;**
XNR Productions: **127, 193, 194, 222**

Photography

Front Cover, Boden/Ledingham/Masterfile
Back Cover, Gary Randall/Getty Images.

Title page: tl, Bob Daemmrich Photography; **tr**, Williamson Edwards/The Image Bank; **bl**, David Muench; **br**, Bob Daemmrich Photography.

Front matter Pages x, Frans Lanting/Minden Pictures; **xi**, Michael Newman/Photo Edit; **xii**, WiteLite/Alamy; **xiii**, Michael Newman/PhotoEdit; **xiv**, Jim West Photography; **xv**, Silver Burdett Ginn; **xvi**, Andrew Laker/AP Wide World; **xvii**, Steve Vidler/Superstock; **xviii**, Joseph Sohm/Chromo Sohm Inc./Corbis; **xix**, Bill Howes; Frank Lane Picture Agency/Corbis; **xx**, Getty Images, Inc; **xxi**, U.S. Navy by Ensign John Gay. **l**, Jack Fields/Corbis; **li**, David Young-Wolff/Getty Images, Inc.; **lii**, Bill Pugliano/Getty Images; **liv**, Phillippe Colombi/Getty Images, Inc.; **lvii**, Kindra Clineff/Index Stock Imagery, Inc.; **xlviii**, Richard Haynes; **xlix**, Richard Haynes

Chapter 1 Pages 3, Miles Ertman/Masterfile; **4**, NASA; **5**, NASA; **6**, Lori Adamski Peek/Getty Images, Inc.; **7**, Ron Behrmann/International Stock/ImageState; **9 t**, Richard Haynes; **11**, Frans Lanting/Minden Pictures; **16**, Tom Hauck/Getty Images, Inc.; **17**, Richard Haynes; **19**, *CALVIN AND HOBBES* ©1990 WATTERSON. Reprinted with permission of Universal Press Syndicate; **20**, Andre Jenny/Alamy; **21**, Photo courtesy Big Bend National Park; **22**, S. Frink/Zefa/Corbis; **26**, Chuck Savage/Corbis; **28**, Michelle Bridwell/PhotoEdit; **30**, Lon C. Diehl/PhotoEdit; **31**, Richard Haynes; **32 t**, Richard Haynes; **34**, Margot Granitsas; **36**, Tony Freeman/PhotoEdit; **38**, Getty Images; **39 ml & br**, Richard Haynes; **49 tl**, Frank Greenaway/Dorling Kindersley; **49 tr**, Dorling Kindersley

Chapter 2 Pages 51, Gary Conner/PhotoEdit; **52**, Tom Carter/Photo Edit; **54**, A. Ramey/PhotoEdit; **55**, Michael Newman/Photo Edit; **58**, David Young-Wolff/Photo Edit; **60**, 1993 King Features Syndicate, Inc. World rights reserved.; **62**, David Young-Wolff/Photo Edit; **65**, Chuck Savage/Corbis; **66**, Don Smetzer/Getty Images; **67**, Tony Freeman/PhotoEdit **69**, Bob Daemmrich/Photo Edit; **70**, Richard Haynes; **73**, Richard Haynes; **74 mr**, Richard Haynes; **76**, David Young-Wolff/Photo Edit; **77**, Richard Haynes; **81**, Paul A. Souders/Corbis; **82**, Frank Flavin/AccentAlaska.com; **83**, George Grall/National Geographic Image Collection/Getty Images; **84**, Dennis Hallinan/FPG International/Getty Images, Inc.; **86**, William Manning/Corbis; **87**, Esbin-Anderson/Photo Network/PictureQuest; **89**, Jeff Greenberg/PhotoEdit; **92**, NASA; **93**, Strauss/Curtis/Corbis; **94**, Omnikron/Photo Researchers, Inc; **95**, NSO/SEL/Roger Ressmeyer/Corbis; **102 tr**, Michael Melford/Getty Images; **102 b**, Dorling Kindersley; **102 ml**, Martin Bough/Fundamental Photographs; **103 r**, Royalty Free/Corbis

Chapter 3 Pages 105, Chris Noble/Getty Images, Inc.; **106**, Spencer Grant/PhotoEdit; **109**, National Postal Museum, Smithsonian Institution; **110**, Walker/Index Stock; **111 t**, Richard Haynes; **112**, Deborah Davis/PhotoEdit; **113**, Richard Haynes; **115**, age fotostock/Superstock; **118**, NASA; **123 bl**, Poulides/ Thatcher/Getty Images, Inc.; **123 br**, Lester Lefkowitz/Corbis; **125**, Vincent Hobbs/SuperStock; **127**, age fotostock/SuperStock; **128**, Douglas Kirkland/Corbis; **130**, WiteLite/Alamy; **131**, Richard Haynes; **132**, Richard Haynes **134**, Bob Daemmrich Photography/Stock Boston; **136**, Koji Sasahara/AP/Wide World Photos; **140 ml, m & br**, Russ Lappa; **140 mr**, Richard Haynes; **141**, Theo Allofs/Corbis; **142**, Russ Lappa; **145**, Richard Haynes; **146 mr**, Runk/Schoenberger/Grant Heilman Photography, Inc.; **146 br**, Andrew J. Martinez/Photo Researchers, Inc.; **148 ml**, Larry Grant/Getty Images, Inc.; **148 mr**, Eric Neurath/Stock Boston; **149**, Russ Lappa; **150**, M. C. Escher's "Symmetry Drawing E25"©1997 Cordon Art-Baarn, Holland. All rights reserved.; **156 t**, Alan Kearney/Getty Images, Inc.; **156 ml**, Jonathan Kannair/Index Stock Imagery, Inc.; **156–157 b**, Michael Orton/Getty Images, Inc.; **157 br**, James Kay/Stock Connection/ PictureQuest

Chapter 4 Pages 159, Michael Geissinger/The Image Works; **161**, Richard Haynes; **163**, Robert Maass/Corbis; **166**, NASA; **167**, Kevin Fleming/Corbis; **168**, Jay Penni; **170**, Comstock Images; **171**, Bob Daemmrich/Stock Boston; **175**, Bob Daemmrich/Photo Edit; **176 mr & ml**, Richard Haynes; **178**, Robin Smith/Getty Images, Inc.; **187**, Francisco Cruz/SuperStock; **192 tr**, Dana Hursey/Masterfile; **192 bl**, Cameramann/The Image Works; **194**, Michael Newman/PhotoEdit; **196 t**, Richard Haynes; **197**, Chrstoph Burkl/Getty Images; **197 ml**, Richard Haynes; **206 tr**, Brian Hagiwara/Foodpix/Getty Images, Inc.; **206 ml**, Paul Taylor/Getty Images, Inc.; **206 bl**, Paul Taylor/Getty Images, Inc.; **207 t & b**, NASA Dryden Flight Research Center

Chapter 5 Pages 209, AP Wide World; **210 mr**, Jim West Photography; **210 ml**, Richard Haynes; **212**, Dana White/ PhotoEdit; **213**, Tom McCarthy/PhotoEdit; **214**, Stewart Cohen/ Getty Images; **215**, Ronnie Kamin/PhotoEdit; **218**, Reuters/ Corbis; **219**, Tony Freeman/PhotoEdit; **219 tl**, Richard Haynes; **221**, Comstock Images/Getty Images; **224**, Spencer Grant/ PhotoEdit; **225 ml**, Richard Haynes; **225 mr**, Richard Haynes; **227**, Rick Bostick/Index Stock; **228**, Richard Haynes; **230**, U.S. Census Bureau; **231**, E.L. Miller/Stock Boston; **232**, Royalty Free/Corbis; **234**, H. Huntley Hersch **242**, Robert Llewllyn/ Imagestate; **245 m**, Richard Haynes; **246**, Courtesy of the U.S. Mint; **248**, Tom Stewart/Corbis; **256 t**, Getty Images; **256–257 b**, Ken Fisher/Getty Images; **257 t**, Getty Images

Chapter 6 Pages 259, Simon Jauncey/Getty Images, Inc.; **260**, Richard Haynes; **261**, Jerry Shulman/SuperStock; **264**, Kathy McLaughlin/The Image Works; **265**, Richard Haynes; **267 tl**, Spencer Grant/PhotoEdit; **267 bl**, Richard Haynes; **270**, Frans Lanting/Minden Pictures; **272**, David Young-Wolff/PhotoEdit; **273**, Richard Haynes; **274**, Silver Burdett Ginn; **276**, Tony Freeman/PhotoEdit Inc.; **283 tl**, Richard Haynes; **284**, NovaStock/Alamy; **286**, Richard Haynes; **288**, Matthias Tunger/ Getty Images; **291**, Ellen Senisi/The Image Works; **298 tr**, Courtesy MGM/RGA; **298 ml & br**, With permission Universal Studios Media Licensing, Matte World Digital and Amblin Entertainment; **299 tr, mr, & br**, Matte World Digital and the National Park Service

Chapter 7 Pages 301, Roger Ressmeyer/Corbis; **302**, Richard Haynes; **303**, David Frazier; **306**, Joy Franklin; **307**, Tony Freeman/PhotoEdit; **308**, Russ Lappa/Prentice Hall; **310**, Richard Bryant/ARCAID; **312**, Tony Freeman/PhotoEdit; **317**, Dorling Kindersley; **318 mr**, Bonnie Kamin/PhotoEdit; **318 br**, Courtesy of Irene Rubin; **323**, Ryan McVay/Getty Images, Inc.; **325**, Sandy Felsenthal/Corbis; **326**, Photo courtesy of Royal Australian Mint; **327**, Dusty Willison/ International Stock/ ImageState; **328**, Bill Aron/PhotoEdit; **329**, Joyce Photographics/ Photo Researchers, Inc.; **330 br & bl**, Richard Haynes; **330 ml**, Stephen Simpson/Getty Images, Inc.; **330 tl**, Richard Haynes; **335 mr**, Richard Haynes; **335 m**, Carol Lee/The Picture Cube; **336**, Richard Haynes; **337**, Andrew Laker/AP/Wide World Photos; **341**, Richard Wood/Index Stock Imagery, Inc.; **350 t & b**, Dorling Kindersley; **351 t**, Ryan McVay/Photodisc/Getty Images; **351 b**, Neil Rabinowitz/Corbis

Chapter 8 Pages 353, Pepe Diaz/The Image Works; **354**, ©Judith Miller/Dorling Kindersley/Freeman's; **355**, Fotopic/Omni-Photo Communications, Inc.; **357**, Ryan McVay/Getty Images, Inc.; **358 ml & br**, Russ Lappa; **360**, Steve Vidler/SuperStock; **363**, Richard Haynes; **364**, Stockbyte; **367**, Richard Haynes; **368**, James D. Wilson/Getty Images, Inc.; **372**, Rob Crandall/The Image Works; **373**, Richard Haynes; **375 br**, Dave G. Houser/ Corbis; **375 mr**, Pictor/ImageState; **378**, Craig Lovell/Corbis; **379**, Richard Haynes; **380 mr**, Russ Lappa; **380 bl**, David J. Sams/ Stock Boston; **381 bl**, Peer Grimm/dpa/Landov; **381 tl**, Richard Haynes; **382 tl & mr**, Richard Haynes; **384**, Stockdisc; **387**, Richard Haynes; **389**, Richard Haynes; **391**, Adam Woolfitt/ Corbis; **392**, Cindy Charles/PhotoEdit; **393**, Courtesy of Drs. Foster & Smith, Rhineland, WI; **394**, A Dressler/Getty Images; **396**, David Stoecklein/Corbis; **397, tl, tr, & mr**, Russ Lappa; **398**, Dorling Kindersley; **399**, Phil Cantor/SuperStock; **401**, Nancy Sheehan/PhotoEdit; **408 tr**, Tim Davis/Getty Images, Inc.; **408 ml**, Simone End/Dorling Kindersley; **408 m**, Dave King/ Dorling Kindersley; **409 tr**, Kenneth Lilly/DK Picture Library; **409 mr**, George Bernard/Photo Researchers, Inc.

Chapter 9 Pages 411, Roland Seitre/Peter Arnold, Inc.; **412**, Corbis; **415**, Tom and Pat Leeson; **418 mr**, G. K. & Vikki Hart/ Getty Images, Inc.; **418 bl**, Richard Haynes; **424**, Dennis MacDonald/Alamy; **428**, David Young-Wolff/PhotoEdit; **430**, Reuters NewMedia Inc./Corbis; **434 ml & mr**, Richard Haynes; **437**, F. Gohier/Photo Researchers, Inc.; **438**, Mark Harmel/Getty Images; **440**, Duomo/Corbis; **441 tm**, Ken O'Donoghue; **444**, Russ Lappa; **450**, Jeff Greenberg/Visuals Unlimited; **451**, Kennan Ward/Corbis; **453**, Stephen Frisch/Stock Boston; **456**, Joseph Sohm/ChromoSohm Inc./Corbis; **457**, Getty Images; **466 tr**, Richard Morrell/Corbis; **467 t**, Royalty Free/Corbis; **467 mr**, Dorling Kindersley; **467 br**, Andy Crawford/Dorling Kindersley

Chapter 10 Pages 469, Doug Dreyer/AP/Wide World Photos; **470**, Ian Shaw/Getty Images, Inc.; **471**, Richard Haynes; **472**, Keren Su/Getty Images, Inc.; **474 mr**, Pearson Education; **474 tl**, Richard Haynes; **475**, Gabe Palmer III/Alamy; **480**, Toshiba America Products Inc. ©2002. All Rights Reserved; **480 Inset**, Corel; **481**, Bob Daemmrich/The Image Works; **483**, Spencer Grant/PhotoEdit; **485 mr**, Russ Lappa **485 tr**, Richard Haynes; **486**, Annebicque Bernard/Corbis SYGMA; **487**, Royalty Free/ Corbis; **489**, Skjold Photographs; **491**, Joseph Sohm, Chromosohm Inc./Corbis; **493 ml**, Richard Haynes; **493 mr**, Richard Haynes; **494**, Ellen Bradley/Brush Hill Boxers; **497 bl**, Bill Howes; Frank Lane Picture Agency/Corbis; **497 tl**, Richard Haynes; **499**, David Young-Wolff/PhotoEdit; **500 t**, Richard Haynes; **508 tr**, Hank Morgan/Photo Researchers; **508 ml**, Flip Nicklin/Minden Pictures; **508–509b**, Joseph Van Os/Getty Images

Chapter 11 Pages 511, Art Wolfe/Photo Researchers, Inc.; **514 ml**, Getty Images, Inc.; **514**, Richard Haynes; **516**, Kobal Collection; **518**, Laima Druskis/Prentice Hall; **523**, Annette Coolidge/PhotoEdit; **524**, G. K. & Vikki Hart/Getty Images; **526**, Tom Stewart/Corbis; **528**, Ryan McVay/Getty Images, Inc.; **535**, Paul Barton/Corbis; **535**, Richard Haynes; **536 mr & tl**, Richard Haynes; **537**, The Art Archive/Dagli Orti; **539 b**, Richard Haynes; **540**, International Stock/ImageState; **543**, Courtesy of Stewart Wood; **546**, Ken O'Donoghue; **547**, AFP/Getty; **548**, Catherine BIBOLLET/TOP/Imagestate; **556 b**, Jon Riley/Getty Images, Inc.; **556 t**, Digital Vision/Getty Images; **557 br**, C Squared Studios/Photodisc/Getty Images

Chapter 12 Pages 559, Hillary Smith Garrison/AP/Wide World Photos; **563 ml & tr**, Richard Haynes; **565**, Tom Dietrich/Getty Images, Inc; **569**, Tony Freeman/PhotoEdit; **571**, Alan Carey/The Image Works; **572**, Richard Haynes; **573**, Albert Einstein™ Licensed by The Hebrew University of Jerusalem, Represented by The Roger Richman Agency, Inc. Photo courtesy of the Archives, California Institute of Technology.; **576**, Holloway/ Getty Images; **577**, Richard Haynes; **580**, Dennis O'Clair/Getty Images Inc.; **581**, Hybrid Medical Animation; **582**, photo by Peter Stättmayer, Bayerische Volkssternwarte München (Bavarian Public Observatory, Munich, Germany); **585**, U.S. Navy by Ensign John Gay; **588**, John Neubauer/PhotoEdit; **596 ml**, Adamsmith/Getty Images; **596 ml(inset)**, Photo Researchers; **596 mr (children)**, Amos Morgan Getty Images; **596 mr (giraffe)**, DK Images/Paignton Zoo